JUN 1 6 2005

THE CAT FANCIERS'
ASSOCIATION
COMPLETE
CAT BOOK

THE CAT FANCIERS' ASSOCIATION COMPLETE CAT BOOK

The Official Publication of the CFA

THE WORLD'S LARGEST REGISTRY OF PEDIGREED CATS

BY CFA AND ITS ASSOCIATES

EDITED BY MORDECAI SIEGAL

CFA CONSULTING EDITOR: ALLENE TARTAGLIA

HarperResource

An Imprint of HarperCollinsPublishers

Photography Credits

Brown: 41 (right), 130 (right), 185 (left). *Cat Fanciers' Association:* 4, 11, 242, 244, 245. *Chanan:* 31, 36 (right), 41 (left), 46, 55, 59, 73 (left), 91, 101, 104, 125, 135, 140, 150, 160, 162 (left), 170, 180, 191, 205, 215, 220. *Childs:* 87. *Dandi:* 73 (right). *Paradox:* 36 (left). *Howard:* 162 (right). *Jackson:* 51, 115 (right), 161 (right), 210. *Johnson:* 155 (right), 196, 201, 225. *McCullough:* 83, 115 (left), 145. *TNT:* 130 (left). *Widmer:* 64, 68, 78, 96, 109, 120, 155 (left), 161 (left), 163, 175.

Chapter 6 artwork by Leslie Falteisek.

Illustration on page 332 by Ande DeGeer.

FIRST EDITION

Designed by Renato Stanisic

Library of Congress Cataloging-in-Publication Data has been applied for.

ISBN 0-06-270233-5

04   05   06   07   08   WBC/QW   10   9   8   7   6   5   4   3   2   1

To the cats no longer with us who touched our hearts,
to the cats with us now who enrich our lives,
and to the cats who will join us in the future and keep us young at heart,
we dedicate this book.

CONTENTS

Part III: The Feline Experience 231

Part IV: Knowing Cats 257

Part V: Feline Nutrition 285

Part VI: The Healthy Cat 329

CONTRIBUTORS

Bob Agresta is a coauthor of the Oriental breed description. He, along with his wife, Joann Kultala, is a Cat Fanciers' Association (CFA) breeder of the Oriental, Siamese, Colorpoint Shorthair, and American Wirehair breeds at Kulta and Kultallac Catteries. He was elected Oriental Breed Secretary for 10 consecutive years.

Kitty Angell, author of Chapter 7, "Feline Behavior and Misbehavior," is an award-winning writer and editor with over 450 articles and columns published nationally and internationally. She wrote the popular "Dear Kitty" column in *CATS* magazine and is currently the feline expert for the Hartz Mountain Corporation Web site, http://www.hartz.com. She established Kitjim Cattery in 1977. Her Scottish Folds and Persians have earned 11 National Wins in the CFA. She is an Allbreed Judge, Past President of the Judges' Association, and Past Executive Secretary of the CFA.

Norman E. Auspitz, Ph.D., is the author of the Abyssinian breed description. He established and maintains the Abizaq Cattery and has been involved in the cat fancy for 33 years. He has been a CFA judge for 11 years and the Secretary of the Abyssinian Breed Council for 5 years. He has bred National Winners in both the Abyssinian and Maine Coon breeds.

Barbara Azan is a coauthor of the Turkish Angora breed description. She is one of the earliest exponents of the breed. Many cats from her Azima Cattery have been National Winners, Regional Winners, and Distinguished Merit Winners and have become foundation stock for the next generation of breeders worldwide.

Nancy J. Bailey is the author of the Somali breed description. She has raised and shown Somali cats for 10 years, under the cattery name Foxbrush. She resides in Michigan with her Somalis, dogs, and Morgan horses.

Donna Bass is the author of the Selkirk Rex breed description. In 1993, she acquired her first Selkirk Rex and established the Woolibaar

Cattery. She started the Selkirk Rex Breed Club and worked with the other members of the club to get the breed advanced into CFA Championship status in 2000. She exhibited the first Selkirk Rex Grand Champion and Breed Winner and bred and exhibited the first Selkirk Grand Premier.

Trish Blees is a coauthor of the Cornish Rex breed description. With her husband, Mike, she is the proud proprietor of AngelWaves Cattery. It is the home of over 31 Cornish Rex Grand Champions, with many Regional and National Winners since 1996.

Paula Boroff is the author of the Birman breed description. Her cattery's name is HenriJean. The late Paula Boroff served as an Approved Allbreed Judge on the CFA's judging panel. She was a certified Master Clerk and enjoyed teaching an annual clerking school for the local cat clubs.

Robert Bradshaw is the author of the American Wirehair breed description. The late Mr. Bradshaw was an International Allbreed Judge, licensed by the CFA in 1975. He bred numerous Regional and National Winners in various breeds from his Fesenbrad Cattery. He served as the American Wirehair Breed Council Secretary.

Dorothea Brocksom is the author of the Egyptian Mau breed description. With her husband, Brock, she has bred and exhibited Egyptian Maus since 1987. Their cattery, Brockhaven, is the home of many Grand Champions and Regional and National Winners. She serves as Egyptian Mau Breed Council Secretary for the CFA.

Daniel P. Carey, D.V.M., is the author of Chapter 10, "Feeding Cats and Aspects of Feline Nutrition." Dr. Carey is a veterinarian serving as Director of Technical Communication in the Research and Development Division of the Iams Company. He earned his D.V.M. from the University of Missouri in 1978. For the past 25 years, he has been involved in clinical nutrition and nutritional research. He is coauthor of *Canine and Feline Nutrition* and coeditor of all three volumes of *Recent Advances in Canine and Feline Nutrition*.

Cheryl Coleman is the author of the Korat breed description. Her cattery's name is Mowl Sima Korats. She has served as the Korat Breed Council Secretary in 1994–1996, 1997–1999, and 2003–2005. She was the first Korat breeder to have two National Winning cats in the same year (2002).

James DeBruhl is the author of the Ocicat breed description. He is a CFA breeder of Ocicats and also Havana Browns, under the cattery name of Timberwild. He served as Ocicat Breed Council secretary for 2 years and on the CFA Board of Directors as Southern Region Director for 2 years. Mr. DeBruhl has bred National and Regional Winners.

Ande DeGeer is the author of the American Shorthair breed description. She and her husband, Gar, have bred and shown American Shorthairs under the name of Hedgewood since 1976. Among their winning cats is the 1984 Cat of the Year with GC, NW Hedgewood's Greatest American Hero, DM. They also enjoy contributing to the cat fancy through their participation in the production of several cat shows each year.

Thomas H. Dent is the author of the Foreword for *The Cat Fanciers' Association Complete Cat Book*. Mr. Dent has been the executive director of the CFA since 1980. He has been a member of the National Council Pet Population Study and Policy since 1993 and served as its first president. He has also been a member of the New Jersey Domestic Companion Animal Council since 1996 and became a board member of the Associated Humane Societies (New Jersey) in 2003. Mr. Dent has served the Winn Feline Foundation as its Treasurer since 1980.

Patti DeWitt is the author of the Bombay breed description. She was the Bombay Breed Council Secretary in 1999 and 2000. Her cattery name is Shadowland, and she has been breeding Bombays since 1993. She has had both National and Regional winning Bombays in the CFA. She is a member of the Frontier Feline Fanciers and Mo-Kan Cat Club.

Lisa Franklin is a coauthor of the Manx breed description. She created and registered Moonsign Cattery in 1992. She is a Breed Council member, has shown Manx to Regional wins, and coedits *Manx Lines* magazine and the related Web site. Additionally, she raises and trains Azteca horses.

Gail Frew is the author of the Maine Coon Cat breed description. She and her husband, Bill, began breeding Maine Coon Cats in 1988 under the name of Mysterymain Cattery. She is serving her fifth term as the Maine Coon Cat Breed Council Secretary.

Ann Gibney is a coauthor of the Devon Rex breed description. In 1977, she became a Devon breeder under her Scattergold prefix. She was instrumental in gaining CFA recognition for Devons, has written extensively on the breed, and was the Devon Rex Breed Council Secretary for many years. Her Devon Rex breeding program is the oldest one still in existence worldwide.

Erika Graf-Webster is the author of the Burmese breed description. She registered her Austriana Cattery in 1973, and she produced numerous Grand Champions, several CFA National Winners, and several Distinguished Merit cats. In 1978 she founded the National Alliance of Burmese Breeders (NABB), the only national CFA breed club, and served numerous terms as President, Secretary, and Director. She also spent a number of years as a CFA Licensed Clerk and 10 years as a member of the CFA Judging panel as a CFA-licensed Allbreed Judge.

Laura Gregory is the author of the RagaMuffin breed description. She first began in the cat fancy showing household pets as a child. After college, she renewed that interest after seeing the RagaMuffin breed. Her cattery is Ragtime Cats. She is proud to have been the founding speaker for the breed's acceptance into the CFA and also to have served as the breed chair.

Jean Grimm is the author of the Scottish Fold breed description. She has managed her Furrytails Cattery since 1976 and has raised Himalayans, British Shorthairs, and Scottish Folds. Her important accomplishments include 20 years as a CFA Judge and having authored articles for various cat magazines and the *CFA Yearbook*. She is the Scottish Fold Breed Council Secretary and the CFA Northwest Regional Director.

Bernard W. Hartman is the author of the Colorpoint Shorthair breed description. He has bred and shown Siamese and Colorpoint Shorthairs in the CFA under the Sanlino Cattery prefix. He is the Colorpoint Shorthair Breed Council Secretary. With his cattery partner, Robert Molino, the Sanlino Cattery has produced several National Winner Colorpoints and four Distinguished Merit mothers.

Pat Jacobberger, R.N., B.A., is the author of Chapter 6, "Identifying Coat Colors and Patterns in the Domestic Cat." Her cattery name is Voyageur. Within the CFA, she is the Chairperson of the Mentor Program, an Allbreed Judge; the former Burmese Breed Council Secretary, Past President of the Twin City Cat Fanciers' Inc., member of the National Alliance of Burmese Breeders, and past member of the CFA Board of Directors. Her articles frequently appear in *Cat Fancy* magazine. In her professional life, Ms. Jacobberger is employed in the Hemodialysis Unit of the Fairview-University Medical Center, Minneapolis, Minnesota. She is the Director of Educational Services, Regional Kidney Disease Program, for which she developed and wrote training programs designed to teach procedures and theories of hemodialysis to patients and families, registered nurses, and dialysis technicians.

Margaret R. Johnson is the author of the Russian Blue breed description. She founded her cattery, Heartbeeps, in 1982 and has bred Russian Blues exclusively for over 20 years. She has held several CFA positions, including CFA Russian Blue Breed Council Secretary and CFA Southern Region Director. Heartbeeps Cattery cats have achieved the titles of National Winner, Regional Winner, Distinguished Merit, and CFA Grand Champion.

Joann Kultala is a coauthor of the Oriental breed description. She has bred numerous CFA Shorthair breeds at her Kulta and Kultallac Catteries with her husband, Bob Agresta, and produced numerous National Winners, Regional Winners, and more Distinguished Merit Orientals than any other cattery. This includes the first Oriental Patched Tabby National Winner, and the first two male Oriental Red Tabby Distinguished Merit Winners.

A.D. Lawrence is the author of the LaPerm breed description. She breeds LaPerm cats under the cattery name Uluru. She has raised several breeds of cats and dogs since 1953 and was an American Kennel Club AKC show judge licensed to handle 48 dog breeds.

Johanna Leibfarth is the author of the Exotic breed description. Her cattery is named Desmin and was registered 1972. The pedigrees of today's Desmin Exotics still include her original outcross in 1973. She has produced 56 Grand Champions, 1 National Winner, several Regional Winners, and 3 Distinguished Merit Winners. She was Secretary of the Exotic Breed Council from 1989 to 1992 and has written numerous articles about the Exotic.

Susan Little, D.V.M., Diplomate ABVP, is the author of Chapter 11, "A Home Veterinary Guide." Dr. Little received her bachelor of science degree from Dalhousie University, Nova Scotia, Canada, in 1983 and her doctorate of veterinary medicine degree in 1988 from the Ontario Veterinary College, University of Guelph, Ontario, Canada. She has been in feline practice since 1990 and achieved specialty board certification (American Board of Veterinary Practitioners) in Feline Practice in 1997. She is part owner of two feline specialty practices in Ottawa, Canada. Her main areas of interest are cattery medicine, feline reproduction, feline genetic diseases, and management of stray and feral cat populations. She has bred and exhibited pedigreed cats in Canada and the United States for 15 years. She currently sits on the Health Committee of the CFA. She is a board member and a writer for the Winn Feline Foundation. In 2002, she joined the Editorial Advisory Committee of *Pets Magazine*. She writes and lectures extensively on cat health issues for the public as well as for veterinarians and breeders.

Gerri Logan is a coauthor of the Devon Rex breed description. She established Loganderry Devon Rex in Seattle, Washington, in 1982. She has served as President of the CFA's Devon Rex Breed Club as well as Editor of its newsletter. Her articles about Devons have appeared in cat-related publications, magazines, and newsletters. She bred three CFA National Winners and four National Breed Winners and is now content to breed only a few litters a year in Gloucester, Massachusetts, where she continues to write.

Ebe McCabe is the author of the European Burmese breed description. He and his wife, Joy, own Sojoy Cattery, where they have bred Burmese since 1984 and European Burmese since 1995. They have bred and shown a National Winner (a Burmese), several Regional Winners, and numerous Grand Champions and Grand Premiers.

Cheryl McGee is a coauthor of the Cornish Rex breed description. Ms. McGee registered her cattery name of Heatwave in 1977; since then, she has produced over 150 CFA Grand Champions or Grand Premiers, including 8 Distinguished Merit cats. She is a freelance writer and an established breeder of Doberman Pinschers.

Cathie McHenry is the author of the Singapura breed description. Her Caj Cattery produced several CFA National Breed Winners, Regional Winners, Distinguished Merit cats, and Grand Champion Singapuras. She was elected Singapura Breed Council Secretary and served as liaison between breeders and the CFA.

Valentine Janet Meriwether, Ph.D., is the author of the Ragdoll breed description. She started in the cat fancy by breeding Balinese and Javanese (Musashi Cattery) and changed to the Ragdoll breed. One of her Javanese graced the cover of an early edition of the *CFA Almanac*. She organized and was a member of the group responsible for writing the original CFA Ragdoll standard.

Joan Miller is the author of Chapter 2, "What Is a Pedigreed Cat?" Ms. Miller emphasizes that she appreciates all cats: pedigreed, random-bred, and feral. She has bred Abyssinians for 20 years. Among her considerable accomplishments in the cat fancy, she is a member of the CFA Board of Directors, CFA Legislative Coordinator, a respected Allbreed Show Judge, and Chairperson of the Center for Companion Animal Health Advisory Board, University of California, Davis. She is Past President of the Winn Feline Foundation. She is a popular public speaker on cat evolution, handling, and other topics for veterinarians and animal shelters. Other speaking engagements include two international genetics conferences and an American Veterinary Medical Association animal welfare forum. She was co-coordinator of the first National Feral Cat Workshop sponsored by the CFA and the American Humane Society.

Mary Mosshammer is the author of the Tonkinese breed description. Her catteries, Sonham (until 1992) and ChateauBrut, produced many Grand Champions, Grand Premiers, Regional and National Breed Winners, and two Tonkinese of Distinguished Merit. She is a member of Tonks West and Seacoast Cat Club. She bred Tonkinese in California from 1981 until retiring to her native New Hampshire in 2001.

Dan Petty and Tracy Petty are coauthors of Chapter 5, "Cat Fanciers' Association Cat Shows." Dan and Tracy Petty, owners of Waveland Cattery, began showing and breeding Cornish Rex cats in 1985. In addition to Cornish Rex, they have shown American Shorthairs, Scottish Fold, Siamese, Oriental Shorthair, Persians, Turkish Vans, and a Norwegian Forest Cat. Both CFA-licensed Master Clerks, Dan and Tracy have been involved in putting on numerous CFA cat shows, small and large, including the prestigious National Capital Cat Show and the CFA International Cat Show, for which Dan served as show manager in 1997. Dan has also held the position of Cornish Rex Breed Council Secretary for several terms, and Tracy entered the CFA Judging Program in 1998.

Colleen Power is the author of the Persian breed description. Her cattery's name is Caliope, and the cattery was established with the CFA in 1969. She is the Editor/Publisher of the *Persian News* and is Secretary of the Inland Empire Cat Club. She is a founding member of the Internet Cat Club and a founding member of the Chico Cat Coalition, involved with capture and placement of feral cats.

Dusty Rainbolt is the author of the Turkish Van breed description. She is a Past President of the Turkish Van breed club, Vantasix. She is the author of *Kittens for Dummies* and a science fiction novel. She writes a monthly cat column and has been on staff at *Whole Cat Journal* and various other local and national publications. Ms. Rainbolt is the recipient of two Muse Medallions from the Cat Writers' Association for her writing.

Jill J. Rasmussen is the author of the Chartreux breed description. For nearly 2 decades, she has bred and shown Chartreux as Jacquelnjil and Carthusian Catteries, winning several National and Regional breed awards. Educating people about this rare breed has been a priority. Now she mentors young exhibitors

in hopes of passing on her knowledge, love of cats, and enthusiasm for the cat fancy.

Anna Sadler is the author of Chapter 4, "Where to Get a Cat and How to Choose the Right One." The late Ms. Sadler bred Persian cats under the cattery name Brannaway since 1976. A freelance writer, she was an author and writer of various articles about cats, cat care, and social issues and legislation involving animals. She served as the CFA's Legislative Information Liaison. Her animal welfare activities included the Cat Behavior Hotline for the SPCA, public liaison for the Dallas–Fort Worth Purebred Cat Rescue program, and Co-Chair of the CFA's Purebred Rescue Committee.

Caroline Scott is the author of the American Curl breed description. She became involved with the American Curl as a result of attending her first cat show at Madison Square Garden in 1986. Two years afterward, she began breeding Curls and began her Procurl Harem Cattery. After producing several CFA National Winners, she served three terms as American Curl Breed Council Secretary.

G. Allen Scruggs, ASID, is the author of the Japanese Bobtail breed description. Together with his partner, J. Douglas Myers, he owns Nekomo Cattery, established in 1985. They have garnered no less than 15 National Winners, 8 Distinguished Merit cats, and innumerable Grand Champions. He is Secretary of the Japanese Bobtail Breed Council.

Dawn M. Shiley is the author of the Norwegian Forest Cat breed description. She has been involved with this breed since 1990 when she began showing an altered male. Her first litter was born in 1993, and she continues to show and breed Norwegian Forest Cats under the Skogeier Cattery name. She was a breeder and owner of the CFA's Fourth Best Cat in Premiership in 2001–2002. Ms. Shiley has chaired the CFA Norwegian Forest Cat Breed Council since 1997.

Mordecai Siegal is Editor of *The Cat Fanciers' Association Complete Cat Book*. He is an author, journalist, public speaker, and consultant to the pet industry. He is the author of more than 30 published books relating to cats, dogs, and horses, among which are *The Cornell Book of Cats*, *Davis Book of Dogs*, and *Davis Book of Horses*. His articles and columns have appeared in many leading magazines, on the Internet, and in the *CFA Almanac*. Mr. Siegal is President Emeritus of the Dog Writers' Association of America and a charter member of the Cat Writers' Association.

Terrie Smith is the author of the Balinese breed description. Terrie has been breeding and showing Balinese cats since 1989. In addition, she has also bred Siamese, Colorpoint Shorthairs, Javanese, and Oriental Longhairs and Shorthairs. Her cats have received numerous Regional and National awards. She has served as the Balinese Breed Council Secretary for the past 5 years and enjoys the hobby of breeding and showing cats immensely.

Joanne Stone is a coauthor of the Manx breed description. She registered her Jayess Cattery with the CFA in 1980. In addition to being an active Manx Breed Council member for many years and showing Manx to both National and Regional wins, she is Secretary/Treasurer of the Cymric Cat Club and coeditor of *Manx Lines* magazine.

Kathryn Sylvia is the author of the American Bobtail breed description. Ms. Sylvia and her family received their first Bobtail as a gift in 1952. Soon afterward, they began breeding

them, under the cattery name Catalons. Her unwavering passion for the American Bobtail makes her one who strives for excellence in all that she does.

B. Iris Tanner is a coauthor of the Turkish Angora breed description. She is a Longhair Apprentice in the CFA Judging Program. Her Silverlock Cattery has produced over 20 Turkish Angora Grand Champions, 7 National Breed Winners, 3 Regional Winners, and 2 Distinguished Merit dams. She also breeds Russian Blues and Oriental Longhairs.

Allene Tartaglia is the CFA Consulting Editor of *The Cat Fanciers' Association Complete Cat Book*. Ms. Tartaglia is the Director of Special Projects for the CFA and has worked for the CFA since 1982. She is a charter member of the Cat Writers' Association and the former editor of *The Cat Fanciers' Almanac*.

Judy Thomas is the author of Chapter 1, "The Way We Were: A History of the Cat Fanciers' Association." She has been a cat lover since 1946, a breeder since 1969, and a CFA Judge since 1987. She breeds and shows American Shorthairs and has also bred Orientals, Colorpoint Shorthairs, Siamese, Abyssinians, and Persians. Additionally, she specializes in educating people about pets, cats in particular, through breed showcases at cat shows and animal education programs in elementary schools. Her formal education has been in history and anthropology, but 34 years of cat breeding has taught her more than her 6 years at university. Ms. Thomas also teaches history at a local community college and maintains her own business of technical writing services.

Lynne Thomas is the author of the Sphynx breed description. She has been breeding and showing cats since 1988. Her first breed was the Burmese, but she currently breeds the Devon Rex and Sphynx with the prefix Shaineh Cattery. Through her love of cats, she has developed many friendships, which she considers the greatest benefit of her involvement in the cat fancy. Her proudest achievement was being part of the presentation to the CFA for the acceptance of her remarkable breed, the Sphynx.

Erin Vosburgh is the author of the British Shorthair breed description. She has been breeding and showing British Shorthairs since 1986 under the cattery name of Atocha. Ms. Vosburgh has been involved in CFA clubs, an Allbreed rescue organization, and CFA's clerking program, and she has served as the British Shorthair Breed Council Secretary.

Betty White is the author of Chapter 9, "Breeding Cats," and the Siamese breed description. She registered her Angkor Rose Cattery with the CFA in 1968. In recognition of her breeding accomplishments and service to the Siamese breed, Mrs. White was given a Lifetime Achievement Award in 2002 by the CFA Siamese Breed Council. She was editor of the *Gulf Shore Siamese Fanciers' Quarterly* for 10 years and has authored more than 40 articles in publications both in the United States and abroad. A CFA Allbreed Judge, she also served 4 years on the CFA Board of Directors and is presently a member of the Board of Directors of the Winn Feline Foundation. She graduated summa cum laude from Mary Baldwin College with a bachelor of arts degree in history.

Kris Willison is the author of the Javanese breed description. Her cattery names are Su-Bali and KLM and were established in 1972 from Northern California while working with Balinese and Javanese. She has occasionally produced Siamese and Colorpoint Shorthairs. She transferred to Houston, Texas, in 1988 and added Orientals to her breeds in 1996. She has been the Javanese Breed Council Secretary since 1995 and received a Lifetime Achievement Award from the Balinese Breed Council in 1999.

Brenda Wood is the author of the Havana Brown breed description. In the mid-1970s, Brenda registered her Kitao Cattery and founded the Golden Triangle Cat Fanciers, which continues to be an active, show-producing CFA club. She also belongs to Peace Bridge Aby Fanciers, Mohawk Trail Cat Fanciers, and the International Havana Brown Society. She has served the CFA as both Clerk and Master Clerk for more than 20 years. The Kitao Cattery has worked with Abyssinians, American Shorthairs, Himalayans, Persians, Havana Browns, and Turkish Angoras. Ms. Wood served as Havana Brown Breed Council Secretary for 2 years (1999–2000).

Marsha Zapp Ammons, author of Chapter 8, "New Kitten Basics," is a breeder and exhibitor of Abyssinians and has achieved National and Regional wins in the CFA under the cattery name of Zapzkatz. She has been a journalist for over 30 years. She has written a pet column for the *Fort Worth Star-Telegram* and has also worked as a reporter and as a copy editor since 1972. She is also a CFA Apprentice Shorthair Judge and is active in numerous cat clubs. She is a member of the Society of Professional Journalists as well as the Cat Writers' Association. She is the recipient of several awards from the Texas State Teachers Association and Louisiana Press Women.

ACKNOWLEDGMENTS

The Cat Fanciers' Association Complete Cat Book *represents in one book the collective dreams, untiring efforts, and vast pool of feline knowledge and insight of a great community of passionate cat lovers. Ever since the creation of the Cat Fanciers' Association (CFA) in 1906, 11 years after the first cat show in the United States, a wealth of knowledge about cats has been accumulating and waiting to be presented in one book. Here it is.*

The editors wish to acknowledge those most instrumental in making it possible to begin and complete this undertaking. Without the help and service of those mentioned here, this book would never have come into being.

We are grateful to the late Craig Rothermel, who, as CFA president in 1998, had the vision to want this book and was instrumental in getting it started.

Many thanks go to former CFA President Donald Williams for his wisdom and positive feelings for this project. His enthusiasm along with the Board of Directors inspired the authors and the editors to keep the faith and continue in the face of unavoidable delays and detours.

We recognize Thomas H. Dent, CFA executive director, for his leadership and his enthusiasm, as well as his efforts to make this project a reality.

For their generous guidance, assistance, and important advice, we thank Betty White, CFA Allbreed Judge and Winn Feline Foundation Secretary; Kitty Angell, CFA Allbreed Judge; Joan Miller, CFA Director-at-Large and Allbreed Judge; Mark Hannon, CFA Club Secretary and CFA breeder and exhibitor; Carol A. Krzanowski, CFA Associate Director and CFA breeder and exhibitor; Connie Sellitto, CFA Programmer/Analyst; Eric Won, CFA breeder and exhibitor; and Kent E. Highhouse, as hard-working a friend as the CFA has ever had.

We thank the CFA board of directors (1999–2004) for their continued support of this project.

Much gratitude goes to Michael W. Brim, former CFA Public Relations Director, for his encouragement and his enthusiasm. His guidance and advice and his help with historical dates and factual accuracy were invaluable.

We offer a special note of gratitude to all of the breed council secretaries who so generously helped choose the contributing authors of the breed descriptions, helped with the selection of the breed photos, and were willing to do whatever was needed, within whatever time frame they were asked to do so.

Many thanks to Pam DelaBar, CFA President and Allbreed Judge; Wayne Trevathan, CFA Allbreed Judge; Kim Everett, CFA Allbreed Judge; and the late Bob Bradshaw, CFA Allbreed Judge, for their help with the selection of the breed photos for providing the breed descriptions.

We wish to extend a very special note of appreciation to Susan Little, D.V.M., Diplomate, American Board of Veterinary Practitioners, for her unending patience with all of our requests to review her major contribution, Chapter 11, "A Home Veterinary Guide." We had to go back to her again and again for updates.

We are also very grateful to Daniel P. Carey, D.V.M., clinical nutrition and nutritional research specialist and the author of Chapter 10, "Feeding Cats and Aspects of Feline Nutrition," for his patience and forbearance with our ongoing request for clarifications and modifications of his impressive work in this book.

Many thanks to Leslie Falteisek, CFA Allbreed Judge and Illustrator, as well as to Pat Jacobberger, CFA Allbreed Judge, for providing the color and pattern illustrations used in Chapter 6, "Identifying Coat Colors and Patterns in the Domestic Cat."

We especially thank Ande DeGeer, CFA breeder and exhibitor, for all her sincere hard work on behalf of this book.

Words are inadequate to express our sincere admiration for and gratitude to the photographers whose photographs of cats grace this book. We are also grateful for their ongoing work that showcases all the beautiful CFA pedigreed cats for the entire world to see and enjoy. These talented photographers are Richard Katris (Chanan Photography), Larry Johnson, Mark McCullough, Jim Brown, Carl Widmer, Vickie Jackson, TNT Photography, and Jane Howard.

Many thanks to Marna Fogarty, the late Joe Fogarty, Pat Decker, Diana Rothermel (CFA Allbreed Judge), and Joan Miller (CFA Director-at-Large and Allbreed Judge) for their kind assistance.

We are grateful to Mel Berger, Vice President, Literary Department, of the William Morris Agency, whose patience and great efforts put the idea for this important enterprise into the right hands.

Thank you, Greg Chaput, Senior Editor at HarperResource, for your understanding when it counted most. We give a special nod to the true hero of this book, Kathryn Huck, Senior Editor at HarperResource, for being persistently demanding and knowing precisely when to bend.

PREFACE

BY DONALD WILLIAMS

FORMER PRESIDENT, THE CAT FANCIERS' ASSOCIATION

Expanding from our earliest days some 100 years ago, when but a handful of cats were exhibited for competition, to our present organization with 41 breeds featured in cat shows worldwide and over 650 clubs around the world, the future remains bright for the Cat Fanciers' Association (CFA). It is only through the efforts of the thousands of fanciers—like you—who breed, exhibit, judge, or simply love cats that such success has been possible.

Central to this success has been the stability that the CFA has offered fanciers around the globe, as the world's largest registry of pedigreed cats. We have maintained high standards in the quality of the cats we recognize in competition. We have continued to pour enormous sums of financial support into feline health studies and education. We have promoted and supported expansive programs of public information on pet care, animal rescue, and pet therapy for the homebound and infirm. We are active and effective participants in legislative debates on protecting the welfare of our feline charges.

As with any stalwart organization, change is adopted and promoted judiciously—and only where it is clear that it supports the welfare of our cats and the objectives of our cat fancy. For example, our approach to modifying breed standards is a deliberate and deliberative process that balances the need for stability—an anchor in a sea of change—with the need to be responsive to changes that are occurring throughout society. These changes are generally promulgated only through the initiative and with the support of breeders and exhibitors who are represented by their breed councils. Changes to the CFA's constitution and show rules are proposed by member clubs and then brought before the entire CFA constituency of affiliated clubs, which meets but once each year to address and vote on such far-reaching changes.

The CFA continues to refine and redefine these standards to reflect the best understandings that we have at any one point. The standards that you will find in this volume are the products of nearly a century of effort to describe the "perfect" cat. Perfection is a combination of *subjective* judgments regarding aesthetic appeal and beauty and *objective* judgments involving health and genetics.

As a registry, the CFA places a premium on understanding the science of genetics and good animal husbandry to achieve our breed standards. Genetics explains the building blocks on which we breed to achieve the highest quality in individual cats; animal husbandry ensures that there is uniformity and predictability in that quality. Genetics and husbandry provide road maps by which our standards might best be achieved through thoughtful study of pedigrees and carefully contemplated breeding programs.

With heartfelt optimism, we look to the next century for cat fanciers around the globe. I hope that this book contributes to your understanding of where we, the cat fanciers, have been over the past 100 years, where we are today, and what the future may hold in store for us. For the initiate to the cat fancy, the pages that follow offer a journey of discovery that I hope you will find both enlightening and inviting. For the experienced fancier, I hope that these pages will continue to enliven your passion for the tremendously rewarding cat fancy.

FOREWORD

BY THOMAS H. DENT

EXECUTIVE DIRECTOR, THE CAT FANCIERS' ASSOCIATION

Since its formation in 1906, the Cat Fanciers' Association (CFA) has promoted pedigreed cats in addition to the welfare of all cats, and as a result, more people have been involved in CFA activities over a wider geographic area than any other cat-related organization. On occasion, the authors of books about cats have relied on the input from a few CFA individuals who could draw on their experience. This book, unlike all the others, has relied completely on the combined years of experience and expertise of dozens of individuals involved with the CFA to produce a work that is a pure expression of CFA values, standards, methods, philosophy, and knowledge. All the authors of this work are CFA people. That is why it is the official publication of this organization.

DEFINING CFA

Anyone may well ask what the Cat Fanciers' Association is. The CFA is a nonprofit organization that registers pedigreed cats and kittens that are recognized CFA breeds. It promulgates the rules for the management of cat shows and licenses cat shows held under those rules. However, the CFA is much more than that. The CFA constitution states plainly that the organization's first objective is "the welfare of all cats." In addition, the CFA establishes and disseminates the rules for the management of cat shows and competition within those shows, and the promotion of the interests of the owners, breeders, and exhibitors of pedigreed cats. While pedigreed cats were the catalyst for the birth of the CFA, the organization has grown to embrace all cats through its animal welfare, disaster relief, and health research programs.

The CFA initially came into existence to maintain records for breeders of pedigreed cats. Without a central place for information storage, the ancestry of the pedigreed breeds would quickly have become confused, erroneous, or lost. The purpose of breeding cats is to preserve the various breeds and produce felines that are consistent with the standard for the breed. The measure of success of any breeding program is the achievement of a breeder's line of cats in the show ring.

Beyond being a place to store data, the CFA became the focal point for groups of people who had an interest in staging cat shows, which would allow breeders to display their achievements. The maintenance of records and production of shows are the two anchors around which wide varieties of activities are clustered. These include breed councils, which have responsibility for setting the standards for each breed; the Judging Program, which allows experienced breeders and exhibitors to share their knowledge through the careful and critical evaluation of cats entered in competition; CFA clubs, which stage the shows on which the cat fancy is dependent; the Clerking Program, which provides a vital link between the judging and scoring process; Junior Showmanship, which allows children an opportunity to experience and learn about breeding and showing cats along with good sportsmanship; the Mentor Program, to help newcomers in the world of breeding and showing; and the Winn Feline Foundation, which funds research benefiting the health of cats.

The CFA maintains the Disaster Relief Fund to provide financial and logistical assistance at times of natural or human emergencies, the Purebred Rescue Committee to assist in the finding of homes for displaced animals, and the Animal Welfare program to ensure that those found guilty of animal neglect and/or cruelty are denied registration services, access to CFA shows, and the placement of advertising in CFA publications. Two other branches of the CFA are the Sy Howard Legislative Fund and the CFA Foundation. The legislative fund addresses issues that may impact the CFA and cat fanciers in general, and the foundation preserves the history of pedigreed cats in art and literature.

Throughout most of its early history, the scope of the organization remained small with the maintenance and storage of records being conducted at the home of a person who was designated the recorder. This environment continued into 1963 when Jean Baker Rose, having lost a second room of her home to the activities of the association, decided it was time to rent office space. In 1968, the CFA withdrew from an awards program administered by *CATS* magazine (no longer published) because of the limitations imposed on the location of cat shows for any given weekend. Once released from these restrictions, CFA clubs were free to stage cat shows whenever and wherever they decided, which led to the CFA's emergence as the leading organization for exhibition of pedigreed cats. That dominance continues today, with more CFA shows being available to the spectator or exhibitor than of any other organization. The CFA offices have grown considerably since the first modest office leased. In addition to the maintenance and storage of records regarding the cats themselves, records from all CFA shows and all CFA programs are maintained within this facility.

A board of directors governs the CFA, determining its policies and activities. These include the acceptance and advancement of breeds, the admission of clubs, acceptance of candidates for the judging program, the formulation of the budget, and the promulgation of rules for shows and awards activities. There are 19 members of the board: 4 officers, 7 board members at large, and 8 regional directors. Officers and directors are elected by the CFA's member clubs and serve 2-year terms.

PROGRAMS AND ACTIVITIES
CFA Clubs

While the formal entity of the CFA is housed in a building in Manasquan, New Jersey, its presence is visible throughout the world in the form of its member clubs. Clubs consist of people who share an interest in and love of cats. Club members need not be breeders of pedigreed cats but may simply be owners of pet cats. These independent groups, whether formally or informally organized, have voluntarily joined with the CFA, bringing benefits to both organizations. Clubs admitted to CFA membership become "shareholders" of the CFA inasmuch as they elect the board of directors and officers and amend the CFA's constitution and bylaws. Clubs perform the mission of promoting pedigreed cats and elevating the status of all cats mainly by staging cat shows. Clubs agree to conduct the shows in accordance with CFA show rules and thus gain the right to advertise their events as CFA shows. This encourages the owners, breeders, or exhibitors of CFA-registered cats to participate. Classes for nonpedigreed cats, known as household pets, may be provided at the show. In addition, local shelters may be invited to bring cats to the show in an effort to increase adoption rates. Organizing and managing a show is truly a labor of love requiring a substantial donation of club members' time and other resources. If a show produces a profit, the club may make a donation to the Winn Feline Foundation, the Disaster Relief Fund (donations are tax deductible), local shelters, or other animal causes. Cat shows provide a positive exposure for cats and are one of the few—if not the only—ongoing nationwide, frequent, and convenient forums to promote the idea that cats are to be valued.

Some clubs exist for the purpose of promoting a specific breed. These breed clubs, although affiliated with the CFA, should not be confused with the CFA breed councils (described later in this section), as they operate independently with their own officers and bylaws. Breed clubs will showcase their breed at the shows of other clubs or may stage shows of their own. Breed club shows usually will have classes for all breeds; however, the competition within the highlighted breed can be intense because of the large number of cats entered.

Other activities of breed clubs may include publication of newsletters and directories and the maintenance of Web sites and discussion forums. Some breed clubs also provide breed rescue/placement services and fund-raising to support health research.

Judging Program

The CFA Judging Program embodies the process through which long-term breeders and exhibitors move from one side of the judging table to the other: They become the evaluators of other breeders' and exhibitors' breeding efforts. Candidates for the Judging Program must be seasoned in the activities of the cat fancy, with experience as breeders, club members, exhibitors, and must have a thorough knowledge of the breed standards. Once accepted into the program, a person works as a trainee with an experienced judge, making real-time evaluations at cat shows. A trainee's evaluations do not affect the awards given at a show but become the basis for discussion with the overseeing judge. On successful completion of the trainee stage, an individual works through additional steps to become an approved judge. The CFA divides breeds into two broad show categories—*Longhair* and *Shorthair**—and the pinnacle of judging success is the title *Approved Allbreed Judge*, which allows the person to judge breeds in both categories for all of the breeds allowed into major competition. CFA Allbreed Judges are the organization's traveling ambassadors, welcomed

---

*While breeds within these groups generally have a coat length indicated by the group name, there are short-haired breeds with the Longhair category and vice versa.

throughout the world to judge at both CFA-sanctioned shows and those of other organizations. A judge receives reimbursement of traveling/accommodation expenses and an amount for each cat entered in the show.

Clerking Program

Partnering with judges in the show ring are participants of the CFA Clerking Program. These individuals manage the activities of the ring—calling cats up to be judged, advising owners when the cats may be removed, supervising the stewards who are responsible for disinfecting the cages in the judging ring, and, most important, ensuring that awards as given by the judge are accurately recorded. Anyone may become a clerk by completing the requirements for this program. Some clerks provide other services at a show by checking the logical accuracy of a judge's awards and by compiling the records of the awards given by all of the judges at a show. These individuals are known as Master Clerks; they ascend to their positions through proficiency as a Certified Clerk and on their knowledge of the show rules. Clerks receive compensation on the basis of the number of cats entered in the show.

Breed Councils

Breed councils are breed-specific groups organized by the CFA to provide input to the CFA board of directors. They are part of the structure of the CFA and do not have their own officers or treasuries, and their activities are governed by the CFA. (Breed councils are the CFA's version of international breed clubs.) There is a breed council for each breed that the CFA recognizes. The primary activity of the breed council is the setting of the standard for the breed. The standard describes the "ideal" specimen for the breed. It is the goal to which breeders aspire and is used by show judges when evaluating cats entered in shows.

Other activities of the breed councils are the discussion of health issues, support of medical research, development of registration policy, recognition of breeder/exhibitor achievements, and promotion of the breed. Members of a breed council vote on proposed standard changes and other issues, and the results are considered by the CFA board of directors. Activities of the breed councils are administered jointly by the breed council secretary (who is elected by the membership), the chairperson of the Breeds and Standards Committee (a unit of the board of directors), and the CFA central office administrative staff. Membership is open to any breeder who is actively breeding and exhibiting cats of the breed or who has achieved a level of breeding/exhibiting success in the past.

Junior Showmanship and Mentor Programs

Two programs designed to encourage new participation in the cat fancy are Junior Showmanship and Mentoring. Junior Showmanship is tailored to children (8 through 15 years of age) and allows them to speak to audiences about their favorite topic—pedigreed cats. This program is actually a competition in which the contestants are judged on their presentations, including knowledge of their breed; its standard; general topics including health, care and grooming, and on their handling of their cat. The cat itself is not judged and is not part of the competition. A CFA-licensed judge moderates the Junior Showmanship ring and evaluates the contestants. The Junior Showmanship Program is funded by a grant from the Nestlé Purina PetCare Company.

The Mentor Program provides one-on-one tutoring for those who have a desire to become a breeder and/or exhibitor but don't know how to get started or who may need help along the way. Experienced breeders volunteer to serve as mentors. A student or protégé need only have a "willingness to learn and grow," according to the program's manual. Information on the program can be obtained by visiting the CFA's Web site (http://www.cfa.org/mentor). Funding for this program has been provided by Hartz Mountain Corporation.

Cat Shows

While most of the cat shows sanctioned by the CFA are managed by member clubs, the CFA itself stages two major events, each intended to highlight a different aspect of the cat fancy and pedigreed cats. The CFA International Cat Show, inaugurated in 1988 as the CFA/Purina Invitational Show, provides the setting for exhibitors from throughout the world to congregate and showcase their breeds. The International, as it became known in 1993, has been the largest show held in North America since its inception, peaking at over 1,300 entries in the year 2000. This 3-day event includes a competition not only for pedigreed cats but also for breed council members who design and construct booths to showcase their breed. Junior Showmanship participants compete at this show too. Additionally, there is a Breed Awareness and Orientation School held that can be a starting point for those intending to enter the Judging Program or for anyone who simply wishes to learn more about the various breeds and how the breed standard applies to a cat. The International ends with a presentation of all the breed winners and the selection of Best in Show.

The second event, the CATS! SHOW New York, held at Madison Square Garden in New York City, is intended to raise public awareness of pedigreed cats. Not as large in size or scope as the International, this show is second to none in response from both the public and the media.

Advocacy

The Winn Feline Foundation, the Disaster Relief and Purebred Rescue programs, and the activities of the Animal Welfare Committee provide benefits distinctly for cats. The Winn Feline Foundation (Winn) was founded in 1968 and is named after Robert H. Winn, an attorney who not only provided legal advice but also guided the activities of the CFA for over 35 years. After his death in 1971, the CFA Foundation, as the foundation was first called, was renamed in his honor. The Winn Foundation, a 501(c)(3) charity, accepts donations from groups and individuals and distributes grants to researchers in the field of feline medicine. Each year dozens of applications for funds are received by the foundation board and medical advisors. Unfortunately, only a small percentage of worthy proposals can be funded. Winn, however, takes pride in the successes achieved by those it has funded and the positive effect achieved in the health of cats. Over $2.3 million has been granted by Winn to various schools of veterinary medicine. Visit Winn's Web site http://www.winnfelinehealth.org for further information.

The Disaster Relief Fund came into being when it became recognized that the cat fancy had resources (cages and experience in handling and care) that were extremely useful during disasters. An outpouring of support for the animal victims of Hurricane Andrew in 1992 provided the financial base for this program, which has since been supported by both the CFA's clubs and individuals. Also, CFA personnel have received training in disaster relief efforts and have participated in animal recoveries. Also, funds have been provided to help shelters recover from fires and floods. Donations to the Disaster Relief Fund are tax deductible.

The Purebred Rescue program works to secure homes for cats when the environment in which they are being kept becomes unhealthy or unsafe or when their owner can no longer care for them. The program chairperson, when advised of such a situation, will first attempt to provide temporary housing and then go on to arrange adoptions into permanent homes. If you have an interest in adopting a rescued, pedigreed cat, please visit http://www.cfa.org/ezine/rescue.html.

The Animal Welfare Committee gathers information when there is evidence suggesting that a person is negligent or inhumane in the treatment or care of animals. The committee does not perform on-site inspections but relies on those conducted by local organizations that have the legal authority to investigate animal cruelty cases. When it is warranted, the gathered evidence is provided to the CFA executive board, which may schedule a hearing during which testimony is heard from both the Animal Welfare Committee and the accused. If found guilty of negligent care or inhumane treatment, a person can be fined and denied use of CFA services permanently or for some specific period of time.

The Sy Howard Legislative Fund was established in 1991 to address issues related to legislation of animal rights and animal welfare, cat population dynamics, and other concerns that may impact the organization and/or cat fanciers. Funds are used to encourage meaningful legislation and solutions to animal welfare and animal population problems that do not erode the ability of the CFA, its participants, and pet owners to promote the enjoyment of and the breeding of pedigreed cats.

Publications and Meetings

All organizations have histories. While it might be said that the CFA's history is kept in show records and in the pedigrees of the cats it registers, it maintains a history in other ways. In 1958, the *CFA Yearbook* debuted. Every year since, it has chronicled the cats and people who have become part of its history. The *Cat Fanciers' Almanac*, a bimonthly magazine published since 1984, records current events. And to provide a home for historical artifacts—books, trophies, artwork, and other memorabilia—the CFA Foundation was established in 1990. Still housed in the CFA central office, the foundation's combination library-museum will someday have a home of its own. Donations of any type are gratefully acknowledged and are tax deductible.

Each June, there is a celebration of the preceding year's activities and triumphs—the annual meeting, which marks the end of one CFA year and the beginning of the next. The winners of the past show season are toasted and cheered, new rules are adopted, new board members are seated, and new committees are formed. Hundreds gather for some events, as few as six or eight for others. Delegates, representing as many as 500 of CFA's clubs, debate and vote on proposed changes to the organization's constitution and bylaws. The crowd in a packed ballroom will watch intently, as Willie Nelson's tune "On the Road Again" plays, while slide after slide pictures cat fanciers in various poses at the cat shows, each viewer hoping to be seen and, more important, in a flattering pose. Thunderous applause will erupt as images of the year's Best Cat appear on the giant screens placed at each end of the stage. What could be more appropriate than to have pictures of an exquisite feline bring to a close the activities of an organization whose total existence centers on this wondrous creature? And while it may at times seem that the programs and functions described throughout this section have more to do with people, they are actually a means to an end—the opportunity to watch, hold, care for, and enjoy the fantastic felines you are about to meet.

My love she is a kitten,
And my heart's a ball of string.
—Henry Sambrooke Leigh

INTRODUCTION

BY MORDECAI SIEGAL, EDITOR

I f you are reading this, I believe it is safe to assume that somewhere at some time some cat or kitten has had you wrapped around its little paw and stirred your emotions beyond expectations. I have made a fool of myself many times with more than a couple of cats that have happily come into my life. So when I was invited to be part of this prodigious volume, I leaped for it, not from the floor to the top of the kitchen counter, but from my desk chair to my feet, just like a cat salivating over what's for dinner.

This book has been a great adventure for me, a journey through the incredible world of pedigreed cats, the Cat Fanciers' Association, working side by side with all those who make it a reality. Like you, cats have always been a part of my life. I've not been a breeder, an exhibitor, a show judge, or a veterinarian—simply someone who has always loved the family cat. And like you, despite my fondness for various domestic cats of unknown lineage, I have always admired and been fascinated by the panorama of glamorous show cats, some unusual, all unique, and all quite captivating because of their behavior and exotic beauty. Many times I have gazed in wonder at the cat in my lap, *le chat ordinaire*, and was able to see in him not only the wild and dangerous cats of the jungles and mountains but also the gorgeous creatures competing for colored show ribbons and prestigious titles such as Champion and Grand Champion.

I have made many friends in the cat fancy and with many who simply live with a cat. These are friendships I cherish. Because of this, my participation in this important reference work has added greatly to my fulfillment as an author and lover of all cats.

Some books are difficult to write, while others are as easy as butter on toast and practically write themselves. *The Cat Fanciers' Association Complete Cat Book* was at times a little bit of both. From the very beginning, we knew it was going to be an important contribution to the literature of the cat, but no one could imagine at the beginning of the project the largeness of the work, the incredible effort it would take on the part of so many, and the time needed to finish it. What made this reference work so challenging is exactly what made it so important. Captured within these pages is the unique accumulation of knowledge, experience, and passion for and about cats so generously shared by the men and women involved with the CFA vision of the cat world. Getting their enthusiastic participation for this mammoth project was the easy part. The hard part was translating all of that excitement and energy into a large, all-encompassing work as accurate as it is complex.

Fact had to be separated from opinion; dates and names were checked, rechecked, and checked again more times than you can imagine. Keeping up with rapid changes in breed standards, new medical information and behavior ideas, and, of course, new breeds accepted by the CFA demanded a willingness to delete or rewrite existing pages. This required added work, open minds, and a heads-up view of what is changing or in the process of changing. There was writing and then there was a lot of rewriting. You can be sure that before the ink dries on these pages, there will be further developments that did not make it to the bindery. Such is the drawback of the printed word. However, there is an abundance of benefits to a work in print such as this one, not the least of which is the confidence that comes from respected sources, commitment to specific ideas and convictions, and a standard of excellence with regard to cats and the lives they lead with humans.

Although *The Cat Fanciers' Association Complete Cat Book* makes for a good read, it is first and foremost a highly useful reference book for pet owners, cat fanciers, and professionals with a stake in the well-being of cats in the human environment. Those who show cats, those with sophisticated catteries, show judges, professional groomers, veterinary technicians, and veterinarians can find what they need to know right here. They need only examine the list of contributors to understand the level of expertise and useful information that is accessible with the turning of a page.

The book is divided into 6 parts and 11 chapters. Each chapter pertains to the overall subject in the part in which it appears. For example, Chapter 1, "The Way We Were: A History of the Cat Fanciers' Association" is in Part I, "The Cat Fanciers' Association and Pedigree Cats." Part II, "The Cat Fanciers' Association Breeds," is so large that it contains only one chapter. The same is true of Part V, "Feline Nutrition," and Part VI, "The Healthy Cat." A Home Veterinary Guide. Each section is a storehouse of information, and it is impossible to prioritize any of it by importance. Suffice to say, the important things you need to know are here.

We believe that just about everything you need to know about your cat is here; from medical information by feline veterinary practitioner Susan Little, D.V.M., to feeding your cat, by nutrition specialist Daniel P. Carey, D.V.M., to understanding feline behavior and misbehavior, by CFA show judge and author Kitty Angell, and more.

Of course, the heart of this book beats within Part II, "The Cat Fanciers' Association Breeds." There you will find important descriptions and useful information about each of the 41 CFA breeds currently accepted for registration. You will also be treated with one or more full-color photos of each breed taken by an assemblage of the finest cat portrait photographers currently working at major CFA cat shows. As an added benefit, the actual CFA standard is reproduced at the end of each breed description.

When it was time to select the authors for this most important part of the book, we asked each of the CFA breed councils to select the best person to write about its breed. This was also the process for selecting breed photos. (A breed council is a body of members that is responsible for the maintenance of and recommended changes to the standard for its respective breed. All changes in a breed standard start with its breed council.)

The usefulness of the format used in each description speaks for itself. Each breed description presents an affirmation of the breed's desirability, its physical description, its personality, its special grooming requirements, special handling, especially for the show ring, and a brief history of how the breed came into existence as well as its acceptance for registration and championship competition in the CFA. This is essential reading for those considering a new pedigreed cat. After carefully reviewing the 41 breed descriptions in Part II, potential cat owners will want to turn to Chapter 4, "Where to Get a Cat and How to Choose the Right One," which is in Part III, "The Feline Experience." Also in Part III are Chapter 5, "Cat Fanciers' Association Cat Shows," by Dan and Tracy Petty, which helps you understand the intricacies of a cat show, and Chapter 6, "Identifying Coat Colors and Patterns in the Domestic Cat," by Pat Jacobberger, which clarifies one of the least understood aspects of pedigreed cats. For example, the term *tabby* refers to a coat pattern and not a breed of cat. Tabby coat patterns appear in various forms and in many different breeds.

Many novice cat owners will need to know what is in the three chapters of Part IV, "Knowing Cats." In addition to learning about behavior and misbehavior in Chapter 7, by Kitty Angell, extremely useful guidance can be found in Chapter 8, New "Kitten Basics," by Marsha Zapp Ammons. And in Chapter 9, "Breeding Cats," Betty White offers enlightened information about the complexities of breeding pedigreed cats along with important caveats.

The Cat Fanciers' Association Complete Cat Book is a stunning move to validate the importance and the great value of the cats in our lives as companions, cat show competitors, and members of our families. The primary goal of this useful reference is to help us understand our cats and treasure them.

The Cat Fanciers' Association and Pedigreed Cats

The Way We Were: A History of the Cat Fanciers' Association

BY JUDY THOMAS

magine walking into your first cat show today, never having been to a show before. The number and variety of cats and the complexity of judging would probably overwhelm you. How did today's cat show develop? How long did it take to get where we are now? Even the most senior of current cat fanciers can only claim 50 or 60 years of participating in the wonderful hobby of showing cats. What was it like for the earlier exhibitors?

Cat shows in the United States started a little over 100 years ago. The first major cat show, the National Capital Cat Show, was held May 8, 1895, at Madison Square Garden in New York City. There were 176 cats entered. The categories in which they could be entered were Longhair (not differentiated by breed), Foreign Shorthair (which at that time included Siamese, Manx, and "Russians"), and Domestic Shorthair. No differentiation was made between intact cats and neutered cats, and there is no record of kittens having been entered. Each cat was judged once, and one cat was chosen as the overall best cat. Fortunately, there are photographs of Cosey, listed as a "brown tabby longhair neuter" owned by Mrs. Fred Brown. Today we would classify him as a Maine Coon Cat, but because no

breed distinctions were made among longhairs at that time, he was recorded simply as being a Longhair. (Originally, the terms *Persian* and *Angora* were used interchangeably. Today the Persian and Turkish Angora are very different from each other, and from that first winner.) That scenario is a far cry from today's show. In the Cat Fanciers' Association today, cats are judged by six to eight judges at each show and more than 37 breeds are accepted for championship competition. Each cat is rigorously evaluated for health, grooming, and condition and then compared to the written standard of perfection for that breed. Let us see how some of those changes happened.

When the first major cat show was held, there were no cat clubs and no cat registering associations. Exhibitors declared what breed

Shorthair were added. Longhairs were recognized in *self* (solid) colors and tabby coat patterns only. Manx cats were recognized in many colors, but only if shorthaired, and only the seal point Siamese was accepted. The cat once shown as the Domestic Shorthair was what we today call the American Shorthair.

The paucity of breeds did not deter cat enthusiasts. Cat shows continued to be held, growing in numbers.

Cosey, a brown tabby longhair neuter. Best In Show at one of the earliest cat shows in the United States, held at Madison Square Garden, May 8, 1895. A photo of this cat is kept at the CFA central office in Manasquan, New Jersey, along with a silver medal marked "National Cat Show, 1895," with a cat face in the middle in addition to a silver cat collar inscribed with "National Cat Show, 1895, Won By Cosey." The photo, the medal, and the collar are significant historical artifacts of the cat fancy.

they were showing on the basis of their cat's looks. In 1899, the first cat club on record, the Beresford Cat Club, was founded in Chicago. By 1901, the members of this club realized that they needed a governing body to set rules for the growing cat fancy. Such an organization, they concluded, should also have the responsibility for registering and recording the pedigrees of cats according to breed. This first cat association was chartered, registered, and named the American Cat Association. Five years later, in 1906, because of a sharp difference of opinion over registration policies, some members split away and formed their own organization, which became the Cat Fanciers' Association (CFA).

When the CFA was founded, the Russian cat disappeared from the list of recognized breeds, and the Abyssinian and the Australian

A cover of one of the leading publications of its time, The Cat Courier. *Although faded into dusty oblivion, it continues to provide a historical perspective. It was a widely read magazine among cat lovers and brought to light how at one time beautiful cats and cat shows were an elite involvement as well as a sporting competition.*

20c per copy $2.00 per year

THE CAT COURIER

FOR MARCH, 1929

THE WHITE HOUSE PET
A Kitten from Friendship Stock
Presented to
MRS. HOOVER
by the
Columbian Cat Fanciers, C. F. A.
Washington, D. C.

of the cat fancy, cats did not necessarily need to have registered parents to be recognized as "apparent purebreds." Up until the 1960s, if a cat appeared to be of a recognized breed, it could be entered in a cat show, and if three judges agreed that it met the standards for the breed, it could then be registered as an example of that breed. In other words, if a cat walked up to your back door and met the criteria put forth at that time to be shown as one of the recognized breeds, it could be shown. If three judges certified that it was "apparently" a member of a specific recognized breed, then it could be registered as that breed. If bred, its offspring would be registerable in the stud book.

The CFA grew quietly, but not radically, for the next 50 years. More cat clubs began to appear around the country. Other breeds and colors joined the aristocracy of show cats

NUMBER OF CFA CAT SHOWS BY SHOW SEASON

May 1–April 30

1949–1950	81
1959–1960	96
1969–1970	92
1979–1980	237
1989–1990	363
1999–2000	404
2002–2003	394
2003–2004	386

At that time, and into the 1950s, showing cats was mainly a hobby for the leisure class. Shows were held on weekdays, and most of the exhibitors were women. A registrar kept records of the pedigrees of cats in volumes called stud books. However, in the early days

20c per copy $2.00 per year

THE CAT COURIER

FOR SEPTEMBER, 1929

MRS. MARGUERITE SAXBY MABIE, SHARON, MASS., and her two fine show cats, Double Champion Saxby Silver Miss Floss, and Champion Saxby Blue Fenwick Mist. "Mist" was Best Female, Boston 1928 Show, and "Floss" has been Best Female under five different judges, and Best Champion four times.

(blue point Siamese in 1927, the Burmese in 1936), and the titles of Champion and Grand Champion were created to honor cats that were excellent examples of their breeds. The breeders and judges compiled written standards describing the desired physical attributes and recognized colors and coat patterns of perfect examples of each breed. By the early 1940s, the cat fancy had changed very little from the quiet, genteel hobby instituted at the turn of the nineteenth century. Shows were still social events. Most clubs had many activities in addition to shows, including dinners, parties, and unscored kitten competitions called kitten matches. Quality cats would be shown for several years in a row, and it was not uncommon to see 7- and 8-year-old unaltered cats competing in shows. In 1959, the titles of Premier and Grand Premier were introduced for cats achieving a certain level of excellence as neuters and spays.

World War II greatly curtailed cat show activity and breeding both in the United States and abroad throughout the decade. In Europe, the rigors of war and the challenge of food rationing meant that many cats perished, and certainly few pedigreed cats were bred. Immediately after the war, especially in England, in an attempt to preserve the remaining gene pool, pedigreed cats of different breeds were bred together if two examples of the same breed were not readily available. Some of the new breeds that were recognized in the 1950s and 1970s may have been the result of these crosses. The peace and prosperity of the 1950s signaled the beginning of a time of change and growth for the breeders of pedigreed cats. Only one new breed was recognized in the 1940s—the Russian Blue in 1949—and only one in the next decade—the Himalayan in 1957—but the cat fancy was undergoing other changes.

In 1954, a major disagreement within the CFA reached a climax and a resolution. The CFA has always made its organizational changes through the votes of member clubs, but there was a vocal minority that believed that rather than "one club, one vote," the rule for the CFA should be "one member, one vote." In 1955, this clash caused some members to leave the CFA and form a new cat association, the American Cat Fanciers' Association (ACFA), which is an individual-membership organization. The CFA began a long period of expansion and innovation despite this breach.

The 1960s heralded the beginning of many new breeds, new show formats, and new frontiers for the CFA. After 70 years of breeding and showing pedigreed cats, some distinct changes had taken place in breeds' looks and definitions and in breeders' objectives. Persians (as the predominant type of longhaired cat was by then called) had been selectively bred to emphasize long coats, short bodies, and short

20¢ per copy — THE CAT COURIER — $2.00 per year

AUGUST, 1931

(Bunnell Photo) Taken Sept., 1930.
MRS. O. B. PALMER, SAN DIEGO, CALIFORNIA
With her Famous Triple Champion The Prince of Silver Gate.
(Chinchilla.)

faces. By then, Siamese included four permitted point colors: seal, blue, chocolate (1952), and lilac (1955). The decision had been made to emphasize the long, streamlined, elegant "royal" Siamese structure, rather than the chunkier, rounder-headed Siamese first imported to this country.

The introduction of Siamese as a pet also produced a major change in our random-bred cat population. Until the 1970s, cats were often allowed to roam freely and pets were rarely neutered or spayed. Consequently, the Siamese freely added their genes to the general cat population, with the result that in urban areas mostly, where pedigreed cats were more common, random-bred cats became more graceful, with longer, more slender bodies and wedge-shaped heads. Breeders of the so-called Domestic Shorthairs wanted to differentiate their sturdy, round-headed cats from the American random-breds that now had a different look, so they changed the name of the descendants of America's original working breed to American Shorthair in 1966.

The desperate efforts of British cat breeders to save their cat breeds and the deliberate hybridizing of existing breeds both in the United States and abroad helped trigger the growth of "new" breeds of cats. There are only three ways of "creating" a breed of cat: by *selective breeding*, to enhance a regional or national variety (natural breeds); by *hybridization*, either purposely by breeders or randomly in feral populations (hybrid breeds); or by *mutation*, which produces cats different in structure, coat, or color from existing recognized cats. All of the original breeds were "natural breeds," although the Manx, which is tailless, is also a mutation, which occurred more than 1,000 years before the cat fancy came into being.

The first international hybrid breed remains one of the great successes of feline selective breeding. In the late 1920s, several cat breeders thought it would be wonderful to produce a cat that combined the most striking attributes of the two most popular breeds of pedigreed cat, the Persian and the Siamese. The intention was to breed a cat that had the structure and the long hair of the Persian but the striking point markings of the Siamese. The result was called the Himalayan. (This color pattern also exists in domestic rodents, where it is called the Himalayan pattern, which is probably why the name of the new breed was chosen.) This aim was much more easily conceived than achieved.

The first cross, between a silver Persian and a seal point Siamese, produced silver Shorthairs and black Shorthairs only. Because very little was known about feline genetics at that time, it took seven generations to produce the first longhaired, pointed cat. And because the structures of the Siamese and the Persian are so dramatically opposite, it took much

longer for the hybrids to begin to resemble Persians in type. It was over 30 years before these cats first took their place on the show bench, and at first, they were much less extreme than the Persians. With dedication to more selective breeding to standard-colored Persians, the Himalayan truly became a "Persian in a Siamese suit," and in 1984, the CFA reclassified it from a separate breed to a color division within the Persian breed.

In the 1960s, cat shows had progressed from one judging to two for each cat. During this period, more breeds were recognized for championship competition. Joining the ranks of elite show cat breeds and colors were the red point and seal tortie point Colorpoint Shorthair, the Cornish Rex and the Havana Brown (1964), the Birman, the Exotic, and the Korat (1967). At cat shows, the final competition consisted of Best and Best Opposite Sex of each competitive category (Grand Champions, Champions, Opens, and Novices). It took four winner's ribbons to become a champion, and the best Novice and Open of each sex competed for the winner's ribbons. One hundred points, one earned for each Champion defeated, were needed to become a Grand Champion. In addition to these titles, points were totaled toward annual national and regional awards.

Over the years, the CFA's view of national awards shifted several times. The first CFA national awards provided cash ($10.00 to $25.00) to the exhibitor winning Best Cat, Best Kitten, or Best Novice the greatest number of times during a show season. Subsequent names for the awards were the CFA Challenge Awards and the Hydon-Goodwin Awards, for which only cats exhibited in the CFA were eligible. In the 1940s, CATS magazine instituted the All-American Awards, and for two periods in the CFA's history (1946–1967 and 1974–1976), CFA cats competed for these with those from other associations. In the late 1970s, the CFA withdrew from the All-American Awards and presented their own prestigious regional and national awards.

The format of CFA cat shows changed once again in the late 1960s and early 1970s. First, the two-ring show disappeared, to be replaced by the four-ring show. A formal program was established to ensure that trained clerks were available to check paperwork for the judges. Top Five ring awards were added to the Grand Champion, Champion, Open, and Novice awards. More people became attracted to the cat fancy, and the number and size of cat shows increased. Show formats varied. Some were one-day shows; some larger shows offered one day for Longhairs and one day for Shorthairs; others became allbreed shows. But judging each cat four times became universally accepted. With the advent of four-ring shows, the winner's ribbon requirement increased to six, the thought being that it should take at least two shows to become a Champion. In the early 1970s, the concept of Best Opposite Sex (that is, if the best Grand Champion is a female, the judge must then choose a best male Grand Champion, and vice versa) became outdated and was changed to Best and Second Best, regardless of gender. In the 1970s, finals awards changed to top 10 overall cats, plus the two best Champions, finally allowing the judges to showcase the best cats entered in the show regardless of title.

An innovation not directly connected to breeding or showing cats but significant nonetheless was the publishing of the first CFA Yearbook in 1958. That first yearbook, printed in black and white, in 5" × 8" format, with a soft cover and spiral-bound, was the beginning of the documentation of CFA cats in one centralized place. Nowhere else can a researcher, prospective breeder, or prospective pet owner trace the development and growth of our hobby so well as by browsing through *CFA Yearbook*s. The first softcover yearbook was a mere shadow of today's hardcover beauty, enhanced with photographs of top cats, judges, exhibitors, and the CFA annual meeting and bursting with lush color ads for catteries and relevant articles about the cat fancy.

During the late 1960s, the CFA established a foundation, now known as the Winn Feline Foundation, as a source of funding for medical studies to improve the health and well-being of cats. In the 1970s, the growth of the foundation leaped forward. Since its inception in 1968, it has awarded more than $2 million for scientific studies, encouraging veterinarians to focus attention on the needs of cats.

In the 1970s, the CFA grew even faster in terms of new breeds. In 1970, the Balinese (long-haired Siamese) was accepted for championship competition. In 1971, the lynx point Colorpoint Shorthairs were accepted (originally listed as blue, brown, and silver lynx point, they were changed in 1973 to the four recognized Siamese colors plus red lynx).

In the 1960s, Americans living in Turkey discovered that the Ankara Zoo had a colony of Angora cats that were very different from Persians. Naturally, cat lovers negotiated to get some of these cats, the descendants of which appeared at cat shows in 1973. Originally, only white Turkish Angoras were allowed to be shown. In the 1980s, colored Turkish Angoras were recognized. In 1976, the Bombay, the Japanese Bobtail, and the Maine Coon Cat joined the ranks of CFA show cats, followed the next year by the Egyptian Mau and the Oriental Shorthair. The American Wirehair and the Scottish Fold were accepted in 1978; the Somali rounded out the decade in 1979.

Longtime Recorder and Executive Director (until 1980) Jean B. Rose had taken the CFA operation from her kitchen table to a rented office space in Red Bank, New Jersey, in 1965. After stud books were discontinued in 1963, individual cat registrations were kept on 3" × 5" index cards, but a better method of keeping records was needed as the cat fancy grew in complexity and numbers of catteries, breeders, and breeds. In 1968, the CFA hired a young man named Thomas H. Dent to look into the possibility of computerizing the registration system. The CFA had by then become the largest registry of pedigreed cats in the world. In 1980, Dent was appointed executive director by the CFA board. The CFA purchased its own building in Ocean, New Jersey; expanded its computer system; and computerized its entire operation, including its registrations, pedigree records, and show results. The CFA had officially entered the computer age.

In the 1980s, seven new cat breeds and several new colors were recognized for championship competition. The British Shorthair arrived in 1980, the Devon Rex in 1983, the Tonkinese in 1984, the Javanese in 1986, the Chartreux and the Ocicat in 1987, and the Singapura in 1988. The blue Abyssinian was recognized in 1984, and the fawn followed shortly after.

Sometimes it is harder to get a new color variety of an established breed recognized than a whole new breed. Often, established breeders are vociferously opposed to new varieties of their breed. In the early 1970s, some Persian breeders fought against the acceptance of bicolor Persians, stating that they were mongrel hybrids—even though calico Persians had been accepted for years, and calico Persians are always females. Therefore, they cannot have calico sons, and instead have black-and-white or red-and-white sons. Many Abyssinian breeders were sure that the acceptance of blue and fawn Abyssinians would ruin the color of the ruddies and reds—of course, the breeders of ruddies had said the same about the reds when they were accepted some 20 years before. Some American Shorthair breeders were convinced that tabby-and-white American Shorthairs would look like household pets even though bicolor American Shorthairs had been shown for years. All of these fears proved groundless.

New breeds were not the only innovations in the CFA in the 1980s. As more became understood about feline genetics, a screening program was added to the registration system to check for "impossible" breeding—for example, the two colors of the parents could not produce the color of the kitten(s).

The CFA central office increased its capabilities by including a separate staff for CFA's beautiful *Cat Fanciers' Almanac*, first published in 1984. Until that time, the minutes of CFA board meetings had been published four times a year in the *CFA Quarterly*, a thin black-and-white booklet with no pictures. The *Almanac* superseded the *Quarterly*—and instantly surpassed it, with regular columns, news articles, and features, as well as a compendium of CFA business.

CFA cat shows also changed in the 1980s. Two "experimental format" six-ring shows were staged in 1980, one in California and one in Maryland, to see if exhibitors would like more judging. The response was overwhelmingly positive. After the first shows were evaluated, the CFA board gave clubs the option of holding a four-ring show or a six-ring show. Within 2 years, almost all shows consisted of six rings. The next innovation was to allow eight-ring shows but on the condition that no cat could be judged more than four times in one day. Most recently was the introduction of the six-ring, one-day show. This show format has become quite popular,

as exhibitors do not have to dedicate an entire weekend to a show. Other associations have as many as 10 judgings per day in some of their shows, but CFA delegates and the board have consistently ruled that more than six judgings are stressful for the cats as well as the exhibitors and judges.

The CFA moved onto the national scene in a big way in the 1980s with the establishment of the Purina/CFA Invitational Cat Show. The first five shows, held 1988–1992, were sponsored jointly by the CFA and the Ralston Purina Company and were by invitation only. To be invited, cats and kittens had to have been shown in their regional qualifier shows and to have been among the highest-scoring cats, either by defeating other cats in breed or by placing in finals. The only exception was that kittens too young to enter in the qualifier could still be entered in the Invitational Show. The response to the Invitational Show was overwhelming, with an average of 762 cats entered at each of the five shows. After the Purina sponsorship ended, the title of the show was changed to the CFA International Cat Show. The International continues to be the largest pedigreed cat show held in the Western Hemisphere, showcasing the world's finest pedigreed felines. The 2000 International holds the record for any cat show ever held in the Western Hemisphere: 1,306 entries, judged by 12 judges over the weekend of November 17–19 in Kansas City, Missouri. During the 1960s, CFA activities moved from North America to Japan with the formation and acceptance by the CFA of the American Siamese Cat Club of Japan in 1962. The first CFA championship cat show in Japan was held on March 16–17, 1963. Since then, Japanese breeders and exhibitors have been strong supporters of the CFA.

The CFA's next big move in the 1980s

Overview of the show hall at a typical CFA International Cat Show. In the forefront is the very busy CFA booth, where informative pamphlets are given away and significant cat books are for sale.

Junior Showmanship provides the opportunity for young people (ages 8–15) to be involved in an educational and meaningful competition focusing on the pedigreed cat. The program is designed to foster knowledge of CFA pedigreed cats and their written standard, general feline health considerations, and grooming and care of cats, as well as to develop qualities such as self-confidence and sportsmanship.

The biggest change for the Central Office, one that was transparent to most exhibitors, was the design and building of a permanent home for the Cat Fanciers' Association. On February 1, 1991, the new Central Office building in Manasquan, New Jersey, was completed and the staff moved in. A formal dedication and tour of the new building

was to become more international in scope and participation, beyond Japan. Late in the decade, the CFA delegation approved a constitutional amendment forming the CFA International Division on June 24, 1988. The CFA currently has member clubs in Austria, Belgium, Brazil, China, Germany, Hong Kong, Italy, Israel, South Korea, Malaysia, Malta, Mexico, the Netherlands, Norway, the Philippines, Taiwan, Thailand, Russia, Singapore, Slovenia, and Ukraine. The CFA sanctions an average of 22 shows a year outside the United States, Canada, and Japan.

During the 1990s, the CFA consolidated its growth. Three new breeds were recognized for championship competition: the American Curl and the Norwegian Forest Cat in 1993 and the Turkish Van in 1994. The Junior Showmanship program was launched in 1999.

Another view of a CFA International Cat Show show hall. To the left are several show rings where CFA-licensed judges evaluate competing cats. Chairs are provided for exhibitors and spectators. To the right are hundreds of benched cages where competing cats stay throughout the show and may be viewed by the public.

20c per copy

THE CAT COURIER

$2.00 per year

FOR JANUARY, 1929

Mrs. Marion F. Hobbs of the Pequossette Cattery, Cochituate, Mass., and her lovely pale Chinchilla Champion, Phay-Ray-Oh.

was held on June 19, 1991, in conjunction with the CFA annual meeting in Philadelphia.

On June 22, 1990, the CFA board of directors approved the formation of the Cat Fanciers' Association Foundation. The new nonprofit organization was established to collect, preserve, and exhibit works of art and literature related to cats. The new office building houses an extensive library of feline-related publications, including all of the *CFA Yearbooks* and *Almanacs*, most issues of different cat-related magazines, and many books about cats. There is also a growing museum of cat-related items, including the collar and medal won by Cosey, the Best Cat at that very first Madison Square Garden Cat Show in 1895, which was donated to the foundation by the committee members of National Capital Cat Show. The owners of that cat would be surprised to see where their trophy resides, and how far the cat fancy has come in its first hundred years. The CFA now has 659 clubs (in 24 countries and on 4 continents), sanctioned 386 shows in the 2003–2004 show season, has 52,000 registered cattery names, and has registered over 2,000,000 cats. What would Peter, the first cat registered by the CFA, an orange-and-white Longhair male, born on May 2, 1906, or the billionth cat registered by the CFA, Grand Champion Tosa Mahogany, think of that?

What's on deck for this millennium? Four new breeds have achieved championship status thus far, the Ragdoll and Selkirk Rex in 2000 and the European Burmese and Sphynx in 2002. Four other breeds, the American Bobtail, the LaPerm, the Siberian, and the RagaMuffin, are just beginning their quest to join the other breeds now registrable for show competition. If this millennium is as exciting and innovative as the last one, the future should prove to be as fascinating as the past.

CFA PRESIDENTS

Mrs. W. A. Hofstra	1906–1912	(6 years)
Mrs. J. C. Michelson	1912–1914	(2 years)
Mrs. G. C. Gillespie	1914–1915	(1 year)
Mrs. J. Edward Davis	1915–1917	(2 years)
Mrs. F. Y. Mathis	1917–1918	(1 year)
Mrs. Ida J. Ketchen	1918–1925	(7 years)
Mr. Arch E. Horne	1925–1928	(3 years)
Mrs. Gertrude Taylor	1928–1933	(5 years)
Miss Elsie G. Hydon	1933–1950	(17 years)
Mrs. Myrtle Shipe	1950–1952	(2 years)
Mrs. Marguerite Saxby-Mabie	1953–1955	(2 years)
Mr. Robert Bruce	1955–1956	(1 year)
Mrs. Lillian Bloem	1957–1966	(9 years)
Mrs. Louise D. Sample	1966–1968	(2 years)
Mr. Richard Gebhardt	1968–1980	(12 years)
Mr. Walter F. Friend	1980–1986	(6 years)
Mr. Donald J. Williams	1986–1994	(8 years)
Mr. Craig Rothermel	1994–1998	(4 years)
Mr. Donald J. Williams	1998–2004	(6 years)
Ms. Pam DelaBar	2004–	

Chapter 2

What Is a Pedigreed Cat?

BY JOAN MILLER

*A*ll cats are beautiful. Those who truly delight in sharing their lives with cats will consider every one to be a splendid creature with inherent grace and dignity. Such a complete appreciation of cats goes beyond the ancestry, appearance, or nature of any particular animal. Feral domestic cats, those who have reverted to a wild-cat existence, may not be touchable, but they are nevertheless admired for their ability to fend for themselves in sometimes harsh conditions.

Many cat lovers commit considerable time and personal funds to trapping, sterilizing, and providing lifetime care for these cats, knowing they may never be social enough to live as indoor pets. Generally cats have a good-natured adaptability to human households, making them ideal companion animals. However, even pampered cats living in secure homes will not fully sacrifice their connection to an instinctive, more primitive heritage. This animalistic character lies below the surface of even the most "well-bred" cat and is part of the mystique that makes these animals so attractive. Pedigreed cats, with their long recorded lineage, provide valuable ties to the historical roots of the domestic cat.

Almost all cats in the United States and elsewhere are random-bred, meaning their background represents a multiplicity of gene-

tic components resulting from centuries of unplanned haphazard matings. There are currently approximately 70 million owned pet cats in the United States, and over 90% of the cats living in households are random-bred. In addition, it is estimated that there may be at least 25 million to 40 million cats,[1] depending on location and time of year, who are un-owned, free-roaming, or feral. Very few individuals have ever had the experience of living with or knowing the small segment of cats who belong to a recognized breed. Pedigreed cats are rare and cherished by less than 5% of the cat-owning households in the United States. Much of the attention given to cats today is generated by the large animal welfare organizations that focus entirely on random-bred cats and/or the plight of homeless cats. U.S. small-animal veterinarians see mainly random-bred household pet cats, and few have knowledge of the physical and personality characteristics of pedigreed cats. The mission of the Cat Fanciers' Association (CFA) is to "preserve and promote the pedigreed cats and to enhance the well-being of all cats." The CFA stands today as the only prominent organization in the world dedicated to raising awareness of pedigreed cats and improving the lives of random-bred and unowned/feral cats. The hundreds of cat fanciers and breeders who belong to CFA member clubs and breed councils form an enthusiastic network devoted to protecting and improving their chosen breeds. As the general public becomes aware of the rich history, predictable personalities, good health, and other advantages of pedigreed cats, purposely bred with care, there is an increased understanding of why the breeds deserve to thrive.

THE ORIGIN OF DOMESTIC CATS

The concept of recognized cat varieties or breeds is not a modern phenomenon. Breed development, as it exists today, is closely tied to the natural evolution of domestic cats as well as influences and gradual changes brought about by their cohabitation with humans over the centuries. Nature is practical—without any human intervention, the cat's appearance will entirely depend on environmental necessity and its temperament will remain essentially cautious and solitary. All domestic cats, *Felis sylvestris catus*, are presumed to have evolved from the African wildcat, *Felis sylvestris lybica*. This cat, small to moderate in size, lean, fast, and agile, still exists in Africa and several other parts of the world. With a short, tawny brown and harelike ticked coat, the African wildcat is well suited to warm climates and wide-open grassy plains. The species will also intermate with domestic cats and, unlike other small wildcats, will tolerate some human association. Feline "domestication" is thought to have begun around 4,000 years ago in North Africa. Compared with the domestication of other animal species, this is a short time. The process is by no means totally complete and possibly never will be. It is believed that the cats themselves initiated the first steps toward a symbiotic relationship with humans as they began to gravitate to the Egyptian granaries, where it was easier to hunt rodents. Gradually the cats let go of their natural defensive and self-sufficient behavior and began to prefer the protection and other advantages offered by humans.[2] It has been speculated that later, when Phoenician traders exported cats to Europe for rodent control, matings with the European wildcat, *Felis sylvestris sylvestris*, most likely introduced the more pronounced tabby striping that provided camouflage for better protection in a wooded landscape. The moderate-size European wildcat, with its stocky body and massive bones, smaller ears, and longer, thick, full coat, added new traits to the genetic formula of the domestic cat.

From about 500 BCE, cats were well established in Europe and were desired everywhere for rodent control. The Romans brought them to Great Britain, and traders took them to and from India and the Far East aboard ships. For centuries, cats were closely tied to shipping not only for vermin control but also because sailors thought they were able to foresee storms and bring good luck. This provided a unique opportunity for cats, and their genes for coat color and pattern, to migrate around the world. Eventually the cats found their way to the Americas with the Spanish in the fifteenth century and later with the French and British settlers in the New England colonies in the 1600s.

CAT BREED DEVELOPMENT

The documented appearance of the domestic cats as they evolved from the small wildcat species indicates that their original physical traits were gradually modified to favor survival in whatever natural environment existed. Eventually, as a result of several well-known ancient genetic mutations, new characteristics came about, such as long hair and solid coat color in place of tabby markings. The "dilute factor" introduced blue and other pleasing lighter coat colors. The white spotting factor created calicoes and other bold bicolor patterns. Cats who originated in different parts of the world began to vary in physical traits, including coat length and texture, pattern, and even color predominance. In some cases extreme geographical isolation led to concentrated intermating that would fix certain genetic characteristics, making all the offspring look similar. The stage was then set for the development of several of the earliest varieties called the natural cat breeds, which are still admired and preserved today.

The Egyptian Mau is one of the oldest known natural breeds. These graceful short-haired cats with spotted coat patterns were pictured in Egyptian paintings dating as far back as 1400 BCE, showing that they were revered as skilled hunters as well as household pets. The Abyssinian breed of today still closely resembles the ancient cats of Egypt portrayed in paintings and sculpture and is the most similar in appearance to the African wildcat. Several original cat breeds developed in isolated remote areas. Examples are the Persian and the Turkish Angora, which are considered to be the earliest known long-haired cats. The gene for long-hair logically occurred in the colder parts of the Middle East and most likely Russia. Long-haired, slender, Turkish cats were discovered in the mountainous plateau area of Kurdistan in eastern Turkey, while long-haired Persian cats with more stocky bodies were first brought into Europe from Iran in the late sixteenth century. Primitive nomadic people who inhabited these areas were unlikely to have imported cats from elsewhere, lending credence to the notion that spontaneous genetic mutation was responsible for these long-haired breeds. Another unusual example of historic mutated genes seemingly occurred on the Isle of Man in the Irish Sea, where tailless cats existed for several centuries in natural isolation, providing the pure heritage for the Manx breed we know today.

Many of the breeds got their start simply because they were valued for their hunting skills. Cats are extraordinary predators, and their specialty is small mammals. With the innate characteristics of agile bodies, extrasensitive eyesight, quick reactions, and the ability to pounce, along with endless patience and the use of stalking strategy, cats can hunt rodents with extraordinary efficiency. Over many centuries, this ability was admired and encouraged, resulting in a proficiency that generally has not diminished in today's cats. It was common throughout Asia for ancient Buddhist temples to house cats to protect the sacred manuscripts from rodents. Cats were bred in the monasteries and therefore isolated, keeping their lineage pure. One of the oldest of these Far Eastern breeds is the Korat, a powerful, short-coated, silvery blue muscular cat from Thailand. For hundreds of years, the Thais have considered these cats to be symbols of good fortune; at one time, they were possessed solely by those in the Thai government or nobility. They were not found on the streets and were only rarely given as gifts to esteemed individuals. Even today all Korat cats in the United States trace their pedigrees to Thailand, where Korats are still bred. This is one of several treasured breeds for which fewer than 100 cats are registered with the CFA each year.

Some breeds came about primarily because of high regard for their remarkable beauty. Domestic cats came into Japan from China and Korea in the early sixth century. Japanese artwork and folklore is rich with portrayals of cats, indicating a special appreciation for the beauty of these creatures beyond their skill as hunters. Many cats are shown with dramatic bicolor markings and unusual short pom-pom twisted tails. Painted screens and woodcuts indicate that Japanese Bobtail cats were pampered and admired as indoor pets. Recognition of differing varieties of Far Eastern cats was documented in the ancient Thai manuscripts *The Cat-Book Poems*, preserved from the city of Ayudha (1350–1767). The scrolls, housed in the Bangkok National Library, include illustrations and descriptions of breeds such as the Copper cats (now known as Burmese) and the Korats. Also described and pictured are Siamese cats with "point-restricted" pattern. These striking, elegant cats with light-colored bodies, long tails, dark seal extremities, and deep blue eyes were especially valued by royalty, and because they were isolated behind high palace walls, their perpetuation was ensured. They are the ancestors of today's popular Siamese breed. The earliest known pointed Siamese cats introduced to the Western world came from the Far East and were recorded in the late 1800s in England.

There were indications that Europeans began to recognize separate cat varieties. French writer George-Louis Leclerc, Comte de Buffon, in *Histoire naturelle* in 1756, clearly distinguished cats known at that time by their appearance. By the mid-1800s in England, people were starting to notice the different cats brought home by British traders and colonists from all over the world. Compared with the familiar stocky British farm cats, the lean, exotic-looking, Far Eastern cats were especially striking. It was the British who created a revolution in public attitude about domestic cats when they began to value cats as delightful household pets rather than merely taking them for granted as working animals. The first cat exhibition was held in the Crystal Palace in London in 1871, and the National Cat Club was founded in England in 1884. Domestic cats acquired special status as the British further refined many of the varieties that provided the foundation for breeds eventually imported and further developed in the United States.

The earliest known cats in the United States with recorded pedigrees were the homegrown Maine Coon Cats. New Englanders were proud of their large long-haired cats with huge raccoonlike tails, who were able to survive the severe northeastern climate, and began to exhibit them at local shows. At the first large cat show in the United States, held in 1895 in New York City, a Maine Coon was Best Cat In Show. When the CFA was founded in 1906, the keeping of ancestry records, the promotion of cat shows as a way to display the best examples of breeds, and the development of an American cat fancy all fostered a heightened respect for pedigreed cats.

MUTATIONS AND HYBRIDS

In more recent years, many interesting breeds have been added to those with a long-established natural history. Cats born in random-bred litters occasionally have unusual physical features that individuals want to perpetuate. These flukes of nature reflect spontaneous genetic mutation, and the unusual cats would most likely disappear in one generation unless individuals intrigued by the newly appearing trait choose to perpetuate the cats. Examples are the racy, high-style Cornish Rex cats, with their short, soft, wavy coat, which were first seen in England in the 1950s, and the Scottish Fold cats, with ears that bend forward against their heads, which appeared in the early 1960s.

Other breeds were established initially as hybrids, achieved through purposeful crossing of two or more existing breeds. The Ocicat is a large spotted cat with a wildcat appearance but developed through initial hybridization of two domestic breeds, the Siamese and Abyssinian. Ocicats have their own distinct appearance and personality without resemblance to either of these two foundation breeds. The Oriental breed, on the other hand, came about through matings of Siamese to various short-haired cats to purposely create a breed with a sleek physical conformation almost identical to that of the Siamese yet distinguished by over 400 full-body colors and patterns.

WHAT CONSTITUTES A BREED?

Considerable debate has been devoted to what would seem to be a simple question. After several years of discussion and input from individual breed councils, the CFA in 2000 established a formal policy designed to define a breed and to protect the integrity of the existing breed identities. This policy allows for a plan if a breed must expand its gene pool for reasons of health and vitality. The policy aims to prevent infringement by cats within one breed who closely resemble the defining features of the cats in another breed. The basic definition states that "a breed is a group of domestic cats (subspecies *Felis catus*) that the governing body of CFA has agreed to recognize as such. A breed must have distinguishing features that set it apart from all other breeds." Not every pedigreed breed recognized by other registries finds a place in the CFA registry, which is acknowledged to be conservative and rigorous in its evaluation of newly proposed breeds. Among the criteria for registration acceptance is evidence that there are at least 10 breeders already working with the breed and that it is not just the whim of one person. There must be genetic information and historical background presented as well as an assurance that the health, temperament, and appearance of the cats will make the new breed an asset to the cat fancy. Once a breed is accepted for registration, it takes many years of show exhibition, judges' reports, and written breed standard modifications for the breed to move through "Miscellaneous," "Provisional," and finally full "Championship" status.

GENETICS AND PURITY IN BREEDING PEDIGREED CATS

Dog breeds come in a huge range of sizes, from the Chihuahua to the Great Dane, and have body forms derived from many different functions. Cat size and conformation extends from the smaller breeds, such as the fine-boned Cornish Rex and muscular, moderately stocky Singapura, to the large, rectangular-shaped Maine Coons. By comparison with dog breeds, most pedigreed cats are essentially similar in size and conformation. The distinguishing features of the cat breeds therefore rely primarily on a combination of subtle nuances such as coat color, patterns or texture, head type, the contour of the eyes or ears, length and shape of the torso, size of leg boning, and general proportion. In planned breeding programs, understanding the essence of the breed and skillfully selecting cats are critical to ensure that the look of one breed continues to be set apart. Several breeds have almost identical genetic makeup, yet because of historical divergence, they have developed entirely different appearances. The science of genetics and the art of breeding cats are not the same things. Though there is genetic basis for all decisions in breeding cats, the qualities that make up the distinction of pedigreed cat breeds are determined primarily by the written standards established and protected by breeders through their CFA breed councils. The methods for achieving these set qualities will be different in each breed. For some, the preservation of historical appearance of the cats is a critical factor. American Shorthairs, for example, are bred to maintain the strong, hardy, working-cat structure that domestic barn cats displayed at the turn of the nineteenth century before the influence of the more lithe imported cats. However, in other breeds, the gradual enhancement of inherent qualities is an important goal that may be undertaken solely for the sake of spectacular beauty. Through continuous breeding selection over more than a century, the long, flowing coats of Persian cats have been exaggerated, resulting in a glorious animal that would not have occurred through natural evolution.

There are several breeds with characteristics that some may believe diminish the cats' capabilities to a certain degree. Examples might be the extraordinary coat length and texture of the Persians or the bareness of the Sphynx hairless cats. Breeders of pedigreed cats have for many years taken the lead in educating pet owners concerning the need for their cats to be kept indoors only or safely confined when outdoors. These protected cats are not required to hunt or survive in cold weather or wander where their coats would become tangled in brush. The need for cats to function today is in the context of a protected home environment, not the wilderness, and physical traits that might hamper free-roaming cats are not a hindrance in the lives of these pedigreed animals.

PEDIGREED VERSUS PUREBRED

The term *pedigreed* is preferred in the cat fancy over *purebred* to describe cats that are registered, or eligible for registration, as a member of a breed. For a cat to be considered pedigreed, documentation of its lineage must exist, which can be certified by a recognized registry like the CFA, and it must belong to a breed accepted for registration by the association. In the opinion of some fanciers, this does not adequately reflect the years of unmixed descent that embodies the concept of purity so important in achieving the goals of predictability and quality in cat breeds. However, "purity" is a tool of relative importance when breeding cats. It is used with other methods to attain the goals of consistency in conformation, personality, and good health. Gene pool expansion, including outcrossing to another breed when necessary for health, is an equally important tool in many breeds. The priority of pureness in breeding depends on the breed. There is also no definition of *pure* as applied to cat breeding. Dictionaries refer to "generations of unmixed descent" in defining *purebred*, but they do not specify how many generations it would take to be considered "pure." Only a few of the natural breeds have more than 100 years of completely uninterrupted pureness, and some of the breeds, such as the Japanese Bobtail, have in more recent years incorporated import policies to allow street cats from their country of origin to be reintroduced. In the mid-1980s, the Persian breed incorporated into the breed the Himalayans, which are pointed cats developed through the introduction of Siamese 50 years before for the purpose of producing a Persian-type cat with point-restricted coloring. Except for the borrowed color pattern, there are probably no other Siamese genetic influences remaining in the Persian breed, but this cannot be known for certain. For some breeds, pure breeding is of lesser importance because they may always need to rely on a parent breed to maintain body type or on an outcrossed breed to avoid heritable disorders. For these breeds, "unmixed descent" is neither possible nor desirable. Though pure breeding is a sound objective in any breed, *purebred* does not signify a special status in the cat fancy.

PRESERVING THE PEDIGREED CAT BREEDS

Over the years many cat breeds have faced threats to their existence. Certainly after World War II, when breeding programs were discontinued in Europe, many of the breeds were almost extinct, and those devoted to raising them had to introduce either random-bred cats or cats of other breeds to build the gene pools again. Pedigreed cat breeders rely on careful selection of the healthiest cats to develop a quality bloodline, but occasionally heritable diseases and disorders have been recognized in various breeds, and these can make preserving the breeds a challenge. Today, with the advent of DNA testing technology, scientific tests are being developed for cats to detect detrimental diseases and disorders early so that the individual cats or affected bloodlines can be spayed or neutered and eliminated from breeding before an entire breed is affected. The CFA's Health Committee and cooperative breeders and veterinary specialists have helped develop strategies to maintain feline stamina and good health. The Winn Feline Foundation, affiliated with the CFA, is one of the few sources of funding for studies to determine the inheritance of detrimental conditions. Several breeds have such small numbers throughout the world that there is always a struggle to find sources for bloodlines to maintain sufficient genetic diversity. With growing Internet communication and broader worldwide contact through the CFA's International Division, the exchange of breeding cats has improved since the 1990s.

Since the early 1990s, some animal interest groups have brought pressure to stop all breeding of cats and dogs. Their stated rationale began with the idea that while animals are being killed in shelters, none should be purposely bred, since these take a limited number of available homes. This position discounts the fact that less than 1% of cats in shelters can be identified as belonging to a breed, and many shelters report that the number is actually negligible. This stance also does not advance the goals of reducing the numbers of homeless cats in shelters or of stopping reproduction of unowned or feral cats. Positive community collaborative programs that include all interested groups working together to find solutions have had greater impact.

Recently, some animal activists have gone even further, opposing any buying and selling of companion animals, on the basis that it is morally wrong to regard animals as "property." Carried to an extreme, this philosophy considers the keeping of animals as pets in a home, whether pedigreed or not, to be exploitation. The substitution of the term *guardian* for *owner* now symbolizes the desire of some activists for the ownership of dogs and cats as pets to eventually be phased out. There are many reasons why these theories are not practical or legally desirable for the protection and well-being of the animals. It has taken years to overcome the general public's perception of cats as "free spirits," only loosely owned in many cases, and to instead promote acceptance of these animals as fully owned and cherished household pets. The close association of cats and humans has been shown to be beneficial to the animals as well as people. The CFA strongly supports efforts to reduce the numbers of surplus homeless cats but believes this can be done without anti-pet ownership actions or actions leading to the extinction of the breeds.

ADVANTAGES OF PEDIGREED CATS

With so many attractive and loving cats waiting for good homes in shelters, it is reasonable, however, to ask why one should consider a pedigreed cat as a pet. In actuality, most people obtain their cats with little to no advance decision making, including whether the cats will be random-bred or pedigreed. According to the latest available data from the National Pet Owners Survey,[3] cats arrive as strays at the doorsteps of approximately one third of those households owning cats. Even more individuals obtain their cats from a friend or relative or keep a kitten from their own cat's litter. Of those who make a choice to actively search for a cat, 18% now obtain their cats from a shelter, 11% through a newspaper ad, and 5% from a pet store. Only 4% go to a breeder for a cat. Even though this percentage is low, it has grown over the last several years, while the number of cats obtained as strays has dramatically gone down. Thanks to the tireless efforts of animal welfare organizations, veterinarians, cat magazines, and other animal advocates, including the CFA, to educate the public concerning the importance of neutering and spaying, several surveys show that an average of 87% of all owned cats are altered. Another 7% are not altered because their owners consider the kittens too young. Because of cooperation among community groups and veterinarians in providing low-cost spaying and neutering services and trap-neuter-return (TNR) programs to stop the reproduction of feral cats, the number of homeless cats in many parts of the United States is beginning to decrease. In the years to come, as there are fewer neighborhood stray cats available, owning a cat will necessitate making a choice and will result in raising the value of all cats.

Certainly for most families, a cat adopted from a shelter is a fine pet. It also brings satisfaction to rehome a cat who otherwise might be euthanized because of a surplus of animals. Of overriding importance, however, is that the addition of one or more cats to one's home is a major life decision, and the commitment to these animals should be for their lifetime, which can easily be 15 years or more with good care and an indoor lifestyle. For some people, being able to count on certain qualities in their pet has significant importance. Many cats waiting for homes in shelters were once wanted kittens who for various reasons were later relinquished to the shelter by their owners. Studies sponsored by the National Council for Pet Population Study & Policy have identified risk factors leading to relinquishment of dogs and cats. One of these factors for cats is when the owner had specific expectations about the cat's role in the family.[4] For those who hope for special characteristics in their pets, a pedigreed cat may be a good choice. In these situations, it's worth doing the research necessary on the breeds and taking the time to find a breeder, because most breeders have far more requests than available kittens.

Predictable Personality

Even though pedigreed cats are relatively rare, they are greatly admired by those who want to bond with a cat with a predictable personality. For some people, certain breeds are compatible with their personal expectations of the ideal cat. If they have children or other animals, a breed known to be highly social, bold, and active may suit their household. Many want a cat who is a vocal communicator with high energy and delightful intelligence. For others, a cat who can be counted on to be quiet or more sedate and likes to sit on laps will be far more desirable. Cats belonging to certain breeds can fill basic expectations, even though the personalities of individual cats will vary. Breeders of pedigreed cats keep their breeding animals indoors or in a secure outdoor area. Because kittens born to these cats do not have an opportunity to learn hunting skills at an early age, most do not have the same strong predatory desires of the typical random-bred cat. Over decades of breeding, this instinct has diminished in many of the breeds to such an extent that the cats have a greater tendency to turn their attention toward their owners and seem totally satisfied with substitute toys and an indoor-only lifestyle. The negative aspect of this tendency in pedigreed cats is that many of the breeds have lost some natural sense of caution, making them especially naïve about car traffic and vulnerable to other dangers of being unprotected outside.

Kittens go through very important development stages that have bearing on their ultimate personality as adult cats, and these can be enhanced when conscientious breeders help guide the process. People generally prefer friendly cats. Because kittens' social interactions begin appearing between 2 and 7 weeks of age,[5] regular handling, started early on, can affect cats' later response to people. Almost all cats' habits, both good and bad, have their origin in kittens' experiences as they emerge from the "kitten box" at around 4–5 weeks of age. At this time, use of the claws for pulling and scratching is a new, interesting sensation, so the litter box is introduced. Kittens' reactions to sounds, commotion, and other animals are greatly influenced by watching and feeling their mother's responses. If she takes things in stride, kittens quickly learn and will most likely not be timid or nervous when grown. Removing any desirable scratching surfaces, such as carpet or sisal, between the important habit-forming ages of 4–8 weeks can reduce or entirely eliminate the tendency for furniture scratching at a later age. Kittens begin to turn away from humans at about 8 weeks and focus mostly on wrestling with their littermates. This becomes a critical time for them to learn what it is like to be cats and to gain self-assurance as competent animals. Most breeders will not consider transferring kittens to a new home earlier than age 12

weeks. The time spent with their mother and littermates adds a great deal to cats' self-confidence later. The influence of kittens' paternal and maternal genes is extremely powerful. The mother will have both direct and inherited effects, but breeders are well aware of personality traits in kittens that mimic those of their father even though they may never have had any contact with him.

Appearance

It is human nature to enjoy distinctive animals. The love of cats associated with their innate beauty goes back to the Egyptians, who embellished their cats with earrings and necklaces and showed their admiration in sculptures and paintings. Shelters report that of the factors important to potential adopters, the appearance of a cat, its unusual markings, eyes, or coat color, will often be the deciding factor in selection. The uniqueness of pedigreed cats can enter the realm of breathtaking. The pleasure of sharing one's life with a creature of sensational refinement cannot be underestimated. Unusual body conformation, coat textures, and some coat colors, such as chinchilla with a pure white coat barely sprinkled with black tipping, are not seen in the random-bred population. Each of the pedigreed breeds has striking features that are unique, and the appearance of all the breeds is highly predictable. The differences between cats kept by breeders for show exhibition and those sold as pets are very often indiscernible except to cat show judges and experts on the breed.

Health

Raising litters of kittens takes considerable skill, along with time and dedication. There is no question that a good home environment is the optimum for kitten rearing. Responsible breeders of pedigreed cats take pride in their knowledge of feline husbandry, genetics, and the veterinary needs of their cats and kittens.[6]

Because of the susceptibility of all cats to infectious diseases, breeders work in collaboration with veterinarians to raise cats with meticulous care and to avoid disease and parasites. Home-raised kittens also have minimal exposure to some of the harmful viruses that are more likely seen in free-roaming cats. It is common for breeders to test all cats, and especially any newcomers, for feline leukemia virus (FeLV). This disease, along with feline immunodeficiency virus (FIV), is virtually unknown in breeding catteries today.[7]

The robustness of kittens born in a responsible breeder's home is a result of good prenatal as well as neonatal care. This means special attention to the highest-quality nutrition for the mother while she is pregnant and, after delivery, for her and the litter. Breeders strive to select cats for breeding that easily reproduce and will deliver kittens free from congenital or heritable disorders. Ideally, by the time kittens are ready to go to their new homes, they will have all their necessary vaccinations and be strong and ready to take the stress of transfer.

Considering the years of planning, probable show career for the mother prior to mating, careful selection of the proper male with good genetic background and the special attention given to raising the litter, the joy and sadness of seeing a kitten go to its new owner is a very emotional time for cat breeders. However, realizing the enrichment their cats contribute to the lives of other people makes breeding pedigreed cats one of the most rewarding experiences for cat fanciers.

Part

II

The Cat Fanciers'
Association Breeds

Introduction to the Breeds: 41 Breed Descriptions and Their Cat Fanciers' Association Show Standards

I n this section, it is with great pride that we share with you written descriptions of each breed currently registered by the Cat Fanciers' Association (CFA). The official CFA breed standard appears at the end of each written description, which will enhance your knowledge of pedigreed cats and help you understand the goals of breeders and exhibitors. In addition, we also present portraits depicting each breed's unique charm, grace, and attractiveness. (Full-color photographs can be found in the color insert following page 194.)

In our opinion, they are the most beautiful cats in the world and among the most pleasing creatures living in the human environment. They represent the very heart of the CFA and its reason for being. They are listed here in alphabetical order:

Abyssinian
American Bobtail
American Curl
American Shorthair
American Wirehair
Balinese
Birman
Bombay
British Shorthair
Burmese
Chartreux

Colorpoint
  Shorthair
Cornish Rex
Devon Rex
Egyptian Mau
European Burmese
Exotic
Havana Brown
Japanese Bobtail
Javanese
Korat

LaPerm
Maine Coon Cat
Manx
Norwegian Forest
  Cat
Ocicat
Oriental
Persian
RagaMuffin
Ragdoll
Russian Blue

Scottish Fold
Selkirk Rex
Siamese
Siberian
Singapura
Somali
Sphynx
Tonkinese
Turkish Angora
Turkish Van

For those considering acquiring a pedigreed cat, this portion of the book will be most useful. It is important to understand that such cats are the result of unimaginable knowledge, skill, expense, time, and very hard work on the part of those engaged in creating them. Pricing on pedigreed cats usually depends on the breed, type, applicable markings, and bloodlines. It is also influenced by the titles earned in the process of breeding and showing, such as Grand Champion (GC); National, National Breed, or Regional winning parentage (NW, BW, and RW); and Distinguished Merit parentage (DM). The DM title is achieved by the dam's (mother) having produced 5 CFA Grand Champions or Grand Premiers (altered) or DM offspring or the sire's (father) having produced 15 CFA Grand Champion or Grand Premier or DM offspring.

Usually, breeders make available kittens between 12 and 16 weeks of age. After 12 weeks, kittens have had their basic inoculations and developed the physical and social stability needed for a new environment, showing, or being transported by air.

Keeping such a rare treasure indoors, neutering or spaying, and providing acceptable surfaces (such as scratching posts) for the natural behavior of scratching are essential elements for maintaining a healthy, long, and joyful feline life. The CFA disapproves of declawing and tendonectomy.

It is worth mentioning that throughout the world, cats that are not pedigreed, that are of unknown lineage, or that are representative of mixed breeds or no breed at all live with many people as house pets and are equally loved and cherished as any pedigreed cat. They are as sweet, as endearing, and as intriguing as all other cats and deserve good homes and loving families. The CFA has gone to great lengths to acknowledge the desirability of *all* cats by allowing household pets to compete for ribbons and prizes in CFA-sanctioned cat shows. To qualify for entry, household pets must be neutered (except for kittens), must have all of their physical properties (ears, limbs, paws, teeth, eyes), and may not be declawed. Unlike pedigreed cat breeds, they are not judged according to a written standard but on the basis of physical condition, cleanliness, presentation, temperament, and attractive or unusual appearance.

INTRODUCTION TO THE SHOW STANDARDS

By Jeanne Singer
(Excerpted from the Cat Fanciers' Association publication "CFA Show Standards.")

What is a standard? It is not a cat. A standard is an abstract aesthetic ideal. The realization of a good standard would result in a work of art or, at the very least, an object possessing artistic unity. Artistic unity requires that individual parts be in harmony with one another; that they possess balance and proportion; that together they enhance one another and strengthen the whole. A good work of art has its own inner logic; there is a feeling of inevitability and rightness about each detail. With a standard, we aim at some satisfying visual shape that possesses a certain style. Style, too, implies an inner harmony and consistency between the parts. In the realm of aesthetics, the whole is really greater than the sum of its parts, but each part enhances or detracts from the whole. Its realization should possess aesthetic and artistic validity.

The standard does not describe a living cat. It is an artistic ideal that is never completely attained in one specimen. We merely try to approach the ideal, always aware that perfection lies beyond our grasp. This is what keeps us inspired, much as an artist is inspired.

No standard can or should set down to

the last millimeter of a whisker or a scientifically exact diagram of a cat. Nature never produces exact replicas anyway. The standard is an objective and artistic guide to a judge's own good taste and educated sense of proportion. In like manner, a composer sets down his notes, tempo, dynamics, and phrasing as a guide to the interpretive musician, but he must rely on the musician's own sensitivity and knowledge of style to make the music live. A cat is a living, breathing, moving being that must be observed as such.

Certain things a good musician never does, such as interpret *slow* for *fast* or *loud* for *soft*. Likewise, a good judge could never interpret *coarse* for *fine* or *short* for *long*, though these terms are merely relative and not absolute. For example, how long is long and how tall is tall? This is the area in which the art of interpretation operates.

Standards are a yardstick by which the breeder may measure his advances toward a perfect feline, by which a judge may compare animals developed according to these guidelines. The ideal cat is a perfectly proportioned animal, of pleasing appearance and superb refinement, a sophisticated version of a domesticated feline. Its whole presentation is pleasant to the eye; it is well groomed, friendly, and manageable, ready for the competition of that day of showing when the judge goes through the mechanical, the ethical, the artistic, and the comparable selection of Bests and Best in Show.

If the various parts of a cat are harmoniously balanced and complement each other well, the whole will be greater than the sum of its parts. The total will be a beautiful cat.

FELINE STRUCTURE

To embody the aesthetic qualities of beauty, grace, and agility that epitomize the cat, the ideal show cat reflects excellent health and sound structure. Variations in structure help differentiate and distinguish the pedigreed cat breeds. Though individual breed standards sometimes describe unusual physical traits, the ideal show cat is free of any characteristics, exaggerated or otherwise, that cause discomfort or jeopardize health and well-being.

Head

The mature skull, regardless of head shape—long, medium, or short—is smooth without undesirable depressions or protuberances. The eyes are clear and bright, with coordinated movement. Breathing is effortless. The mouth closes with proper occlusion. The face and jaw are symmetrical and aligned.

Skeletal Frame

The skeletal frame, regardless of size—small, medium, or large—functions with symmetry and balance. The vertebrae are aligned without fixation or deviation. The spine is supple and the joints are flexible. The legs are parallel and fully support weight and movement.

Body Substance

The body shape, regardless of style—short or long, round or tubular—is smoothly contoured from the gentle outward curve of the chest to the softer continuous line of the abdomen. The muscular development of the shoulders, midsection, and hindquarters reflects strength and compatibility with the body style.

Conclusion

It must never be forgotten that the cat is a living, breathing, moving being. Sound structure and function are integral to the pursuit of the aesthetic.

CONDITION

What does *condition* mean in relation to cats? It refers to the total cat. Diet, care, environment, and heredity all play vital roles in producing a well-conditioned cat; every facet of the cat reflects the results of these important factors.

Physical Condition
The show cat should be in prime physical condition.

Cleanliness and Presentation
The show cat should be faultlessly clean. Grooming should enhance the beauty of the cat, emphasizing the nature of the breed.

Temperament
Well-balanced temperamentally, the show cat should be receptive to the judging procedure.

A calm, stable disposition is an enhancement and allows the judge to evaluate and display the cat to its best advantage.

Appearance
Clear eyes, shining coat, and alert appearance reflect general health and vigor. In movement, the cat will exhibit the grace and beauty characteristic of its breed.

Feel
As the judge handles an exhibit, her hands record the size and shape of the bone structure, the muscle tone, and the basic conformation of the cat. The total cat is equal to the sum of its parts.

ABYSSINIAN

By Norman E. Auspitz, Ph.D.

Abyssinian

Although the Abyssinian is one of the oldest known breeds, there continues to be speculation and controversy concerning its history. In appearance, Abyssinians resemble the paintings and sculptures of ancient Egyptian cats, which portray an elegant feline with a muscular body, beautiful arched neck, large ears, and almond-shaped eyes. Abys today still retain the jungle look of *Felis sylvestris lybica*, the African wildcat ancestor of all domestic cats. The breed is so named not because Ethiopia, formerly Abyssinia, is thought to be the original home of these cats but because the first "Abyssinians" exhibited in shows in England were reported to have been imported from that country.

Physical Description

The Abyssinian of today bears a remarkable resemblance to the noble cats depicted in statues of ancient Egypt. Its singular defining feature is its ticked, richly colored tabby coat free of markings on its legs, tail, and neck but with dramatic facial markings. Each hair is ticked with four to six bands of color: dark at the tip, lighter at the roots, with bands alternating dark and light. The ideal Abyssinian has a bright color at the hair root that matches the color on its underside and on the inside of its legs.

The breed is permitted four coat colors by the CFA. The original or wild color is known as *ruddy*. Its darker bands of color are sepia to black, and its lighter bands are bright orange, giving the impression of an iridescent cat of burnt sienna. Another allowed coat color is the *red*, with darker bands of color that are chocolate brown, creating the impression of a red, iridescent cat. The *blue* coat has slate blue or gray dark bands of color with alternating bands of warm beige, giving the impression of a warm, dark blue cat with a very subtle look. The fourth color is *fawn*, which has darker bands of cocoa brown and lighter bands of rose-beige ticking, giving the impression of a warm, antique rose–colored cat.

The body type of this breed strikes an attractive balance between the extremes of compact, broad-chested cats (cobby type) and svelte, lengthy types (foreign). Because of their long legs, they appear to be standing on the tips of their toes. The typical Abyssinian likes to arch its back when it becomes alert and stands. The head shape is a modified wedge, and the eyes are curved like almonds. The Abyssinian has large, slightly pointed ears. The head, eyes, and ears all fit together in a complementary fashion, favoring neither extreme length nor extreme shortness.

These striking cats appear to have walked out of the forest with a look reminiscent of their wild ancestors, tempered by the reverence bestowed on them by the ancient Egyptians.

Personality

The personality of the Abyssinian is best described by one word: *busy*. These are incredibly intelligent cats, good problem solvers with an insatiable curiosity. Abyssinians want to do everything on their own terms. Unless you understand their unique personality, these fascinating cats can be a great challenge as pets.

Typical Abyssinians are constantly on the move unless they are eating or sleeping. They continually patrol their territory unless something catches their interest. When their interest is aroused, they become intensely focused on whatever is happening, until the next event occurs or they simply lose interest and move on. Looking out at birds or squirrels through a window can be a captivating pastime until they find something else of greater interest, such as the sound of a can opener or a sudden desire for your attention.

They are incredibly playful even into adulthood. Everything they do seems larger than life. When they play, they seem to have no concern for life or limb and commit all of their energy and concentration. They will amuse themselves with one particular toy for months and then suddenly decide not to play with it anymore. Wind-up toys can be a problem because you have to keep winding them up as soon as they run down, or Abys will just ignore them. They can amuse themselves with a crumpled sheet of paper or a plastic bottle cap just as well as with elaborate cat toys. They are very good at training humans to play fetch. You throw the toy, and these cats bring it back just out of reach so that you have to fetch the toy and throw it again.

When they decide they want attention, they know how to get it. Even though they do not like to be restrained, they will cuddle up when they want to be loved. It is not easy to restrain an Abyssinian who does not want to be restrained, given the loose skin under their coats. Should you decide you want to hold them, they will wriggle out of your grasp. When they do, however, they almost never extend their claws. If these cats want attention but their humans are busy, they will find ways to get it. If you are busy reading or typing, for example, the cat will follow your eyes and know exactly what word you are going to read or what key you are going to strike next. He will then place a paw on that spot so you will look at him and not at the unimportant thing you might have been doing. It is amazing how persistent these cats can be. Should you decide to put the cat off the bed, the table, or your lap, the removal process becomes a game in which he immediately returns again and again. It seems that Abys can, with singular concentration, get your attention no matter what you may be doing.

In general, females tend to be more graceful than males, but at times all Abyssinians defy gravity. Add to this their natural athleticism, which comes with their muscular bodies, and you have a potent combination. There are few high perches in the house to which they cannot climb, no matter how impossible access may seem. Living in all three dimensions, these cats make full use of vertical space. They have no fear of heights. Most of the time, they are careful when walking on the upper shelves of a tall bookcase or on top of a kitchen cupboard. However, when they are feeling mischievous, they like to see what will happen when they push some trinket over an edge. If the crash is loud enough, they might even scare themselves. Given their fondness for high places, they should be provided with the means to live vertically as well as horizontally. They appreciate tall, vertical scratching posts or tall, carpeted cat trees and perches, the taller the better.

As a rule, they get along well with older, more considerate children. Toddlers, who are by nature unpredictable, will not be a problem, because these cats know to jump away and avoid them. Once the family children are a little older (and more predictable), an Abyssinian will dote on them.

If you introduce Abyssinians into a household with other pets, they will do well, if introduced slowly and properly. They will get along with dogs, ferrets, large caged birds—just about any pet, including other cats. It cannot be stressed enough, however, that the proper introduction of any new pet to another is vital to their being able to get along.

Abyssinians make wonderful companions if there are other pets or people to keep them company throughout the day. When left alone with no one to play with, they will become bored and find many new and interesting ways to get into trouble. It is best, especially for a kitten, to have a playmate in its new house. (Someone once referred to Abyssinians as Velcro kitties because they seem to stick to everything.)

Many breeders will place or sell an older Aby for a nominal fee. If a kitten is going to a new home but will be by itself, some breeders will encourage the prospective owner to also take an older Abyssinian as a companion. An interesting fact about older Abys (even up to 10 years of age) is that they will still bond with new people. Older Abyssinians learn the rules of a new household more quickly than kittens and may even keep the kittens in line.

Grooming Requirements

For the most part, Abyssinians are low-maintenance cats, although they do enjoy it if you rub them affectionately. They require a bath at least once during the shedding season. Washing them with a good cat shampoo, quick toweling, and drip-drying is all that is needed.

Bathing should be started when they are young, and so should clipping their claws regularly and before each bath.

There are probably as many formulas for bathing and grooming an Abyssinian in preparation for a cat show as there are people who show them. This is understandable because there are many subtle variations on coat length and textures, each of which requires slightly different methods. Before entering a show ring with an Aby, grooming consists of a quick polish by hand and lots of play to make it all seem like fun.

Origin and History

The origin of the Abyssinian is shrouded in mystery. Early cat books do not shed much light on the history of this breed because there were little or no records kept. The name *Abyssinian* may have originated when the first such cat was brought to England after the English army had fought in Abyssinia (Ethiopia). A colored lithograph of a cat with a ticked coat and an absence of tabby markings on its paws, face, and neck first appeared in the book *Cats, Their Points, Etc.*, by Gordon Staples, published in Great Britain in 1874. The caption reads: "Zula, the property of Mrs. Captain Barrett-Lennard. This cat was brought from Abyssinia at the conclusion of the war . . ."

The Abyssinian's beginnings may be deduced from genetic studies showing that it more than likely originated from the coastal areas of the Indian Ocean as well as from Southeast Asia. A ruddy, ticked feline taxidermy exhibit in the Leiden Zoological Museum in Holland was purchased in the mid-1830s and labeled as "Patrie, domestica India." From this one may conclude that colonists or merchants who frequently traveled between England and the Indian subcontinent may have introduced the breed into England from India.

Records of early pedigrees going back to

1904 do exist, few of which show the sire or dam (parents) but do indicate some crosses with cats that were clearly not Abyssinians as we know them. Some of these crosses possibly explain contemporary coat colors and the origin of the long-haired variety known as the Somali.

Although a few of these cats were brought to the United States at the beginning of 1900, it was not until the 1930s that show-quality Abyssinians were imported from England. These were the cats that formed the basis of modern American Abyssinian breeding programs.

Miscellanea

All cats must be able to accept the handling that is involved in an appearance in the show ring. However, cats of this breed respond best to less handling, rather than more, especially if they get to play with toys on the judging table. An Abyssinian experienced with the show ring usually knows where the judges keep their toy cache, which is near the judging table, and find a way to get to them. The only thing that may get its attention faster than a toy is someone eating lunch nearby.

If your cat is uneasy about being shown, gentle coaxing, rather than forcing the issue, is more likely to achieve the desired result—by relaxing the cat. Sometimes appealing to its natural playfulness might bring it out of its shell. For those showing an Abyssinian kitten for the first time, be sure it is familiar with feathers, sparkly toys, and other teasing devices used by judges to get a cat's attention. A kitten being prepared for its first show needs to be given some introduction to what it will encounter. It helps to start showing kittens at an early age so that they can make an easy adjustment to the dynamics of a cat show. At the same time, the show experience should be a happy time, so that kittens associate cat shows with many treats and lots of attention.

Abyssinians often become even more magnificent as they mature. This is evident as you watch an older one in premiership. (Premiership is a category of show competition for neutered or spayed cats that are 8 months of age or older.) Once they are fully mature, their coat, color, and muscle tone become fully developed and they cut a dashing figure on the show bench.

For those who want a portion of the wild kingdom, who want an active, independent, loving cat, this very ancient breed may be just right. These mischievous, highly animated short-haired cats, with their iridescent, colorful coats, can provide years of pleasure for any household. It is not a mystery to see why those who have had an Aby usually have no other breed as a pet. It has become one of the most popular cat breeds of modern times.

POINT SCORE

HEAD (25)

Muzzle	6
Skull	6
Ears	7
Eye shape	6

BODY (30)

Torso	15
Legs and feet	10
Tail	5

COAT (10)

Texture	10

COLOR (35)

Color	15
Ticking	15
Eye color	5

GENERAL: The overall impression of the ideal Abyssinian would be a colorful cat with a distinctly ticked coat, medium in size and regal in appearance. The Abyssinian is lithe, hard, and muscular, showing eager activity and a lively interest in all surroundings. Well balanced temperamentally and physically, with all elements of the cat in proportion.

HEAD: A modified, slightly rounded wedge without flat planes; the brow, cheek, and profile lines all show a gentle contour. A slight rise from the bridge of the nose to the forehead, which should be of good size, with width between the ears and flowing into the arched neck without a break.

MUZZLE: Not sharply pointed or square. The chin should be neither receding nor protruding. Allowance should be made for jowls in adult males.

EARS: Alert, large, and moderately pointed; broad, and cupped at base and set as though listening. Hair on ears very short and close lying, preferably tipped with black or dark brown on a ruddy Abyssinian, chocolate brown on a red Abyssinian, slate blue on the blue Abyssinian, or light cocoa brown on a fawn Abyssinian.

EYES: Almond-shaped, large, brilliant, and expressive. Neither round nor oriental. Eyes accentuated by fine dark line, encircled by light colored area.

BODY: Medium long, lithe, and graceful but showing well-developed muscular strength without coarseness. Abyssinian conformation strikes a medium between the extremes of the cobby and the svelte lengthy type. Proportion and general balance more to be desired than mere size.

LEGS AND FEET: Proportionately slim, fine-boned. The Abyssinian stands well off the ground, giving the impression of being on tiptoe. Paws small, oval, and compact. Toes: five in front and four behind.

TAIL: Thick at base, fairly long and tapering.

COAT: Soft, silky, fine in texture but dense and resilient to the touch, with a lustrous sheen. Medium in length but long enough to accommodate two or three dark bands of ticking.

PENALIZE: Off-color pads. Long, narrow head; short, round head. Barring on legs, dark broken-necklace markings, rings on tail. Coldness or grey tones in the coat. White undercoat on blue or fawn Abyssinians.

DISQUALIFY: White locket, or white anywhere other than nostril, chin, and upper throat area. Kinked or abnormal tail. Dark unbroken necklace. Grey undercoat close to the skin extending throughout a major portion of the body. Any black hair on red Abyssinian. Incorrect number of toes. Any color other than the four accepted colors.

COAT COLOR: Warm and glowing. *Ticking:* Distinct and even, with dark-colored bands contrasting with lighter-colored bands on the hair shafts. Undercoat color clear and bright to the skin. Deeper color shades desired; however, intensity of ticking not to be sacrificed for depth of color. Darker shading along spine allowed if fully ticked.

Preference given to cats *unmarked* on the undersides, chest, and legs; tail without rings. *Facial markings:* Dark lines extending from eyes and brows, cheekbone shading, dots and shading on whisker pads are all desirable enhancements. Eyes accentuated by fine dark line, encircled by light-colored area. *Eye color:* Gold or green, the more richness and depth of color the better.

COLORS: Ruddy, red, blue, fawn.

ALLOWABLE BREEDING OUTCROSSES: none.

AMERICAN BOBTAIL
By Kathryn Sylvia

American Bobtail Longhair

American Bobtail Shorthair

At first glance, you are sure that you have just seen a bobcat. You slowly turn and your gaze falls on this magnificent and untamed-looking creature. It captivates you. Your eyes meet the cat's, and you are drawn to a faraway place where creatures run wild and free. The cat cleans its luxurious fur, blinks its eyes at you, and begins to purr. You long to stroke his soft, thick fur and hold him in your arms, but do you dare? Tentatively, you reach for the amazing animal. He stands up and stretches, allowing you to marvel at his substantial body and his natural short tail. He appears to be a thing of the wild. The cat saunters over to you, demanding attention. You cautiously pick him up and are amazed by his gentle personality. An American Bobtail has stolen your heart.

Physical Description

This breed, with its above-average intelligence, developed naturally so that it could survive primitive environments. It is a medium to large cat with a naturally occurring bobtail; it is a noticeably athletic animal, well muscled, with the appearance of power. The body is moderately long and substantial, with a rectangular stance. The tail is clearly visible above the back when the cat is alert and does not exceed the hock in length. The optimum tail is articulate and nearly straight with the slightest of curves.

The American Bobtail gene is a *dominant* gene (a characteristic that expresses itself wholly or largely to the exclusion of the alternate *recessive* characteristic). It must be a naturally short-tailed cat to produce short-tailed kittens. In addition to short-tailed kittens, it is not unusual for full-tailed kittens to be born in a litter. Unlike the Manx, however, these cats rarely produce kittens with no tail at all, which is referred to as a *rumpy*. With this breed, no two tails are exactly the same. The average length of the tail is 1 to 4 inches; however, some tails may be shorter or longer. The American Bobtail possesses a strong, broad, modified wedge-shaped head, with a distinctive brow above large, almost almond-shaped eyes, giving it a natural hunting gaze. The expression is one of intelligence and alertness. Ear furnishings and Lynx ear tipping are highly desirable features in this breed. Its unique coat comes in a shorthair variety with medium semidense hair and in a longhair variety with shaggy semilong hair. The coat is resilient and resistant to water. The topcoat is hard, with a downy undercoat that insulates the cat from extreme weather.

When the cat is in motion, it should exhibit a natural rolling gate, adding to the cat's look of a wild bobcat. This wild look, though, contrasts with the cat's gentle disposition and adaptability. This is a slow-maturing breed that takes 2–3 years to reach full adult type.

Personality

American Bobtails are loving, kind, and incredibly intelligent cats. They easily adapt to both a busy and a quiet environment. American Bobtails bond with their families the way Golden Retrievers do, and they resemble those dogs in personality and devotion. They get along well with most dogs and welcome newcomers, whether two-legged or four-legged. Long-haul truck drivers have purchased them as cabin companions because they are known to be good travelers if introduced to trips at a young age. Psychotherapists have also used them in their treatment programs because they have been found to be very well behaved and sensitive to people in distress, offering a warm, soft shoulder to cry on when needed.

They are excellent companions for children and do not mind being carried around like a sack of potatoes. With their clownlike personalities, they also serve a great purpose in the home: a source of entertainment. They are known for their love of games and can play fetch or hide-and-seek for hours. They will often try to initiate a game and become persistent until you play with them. They are vocally quiet cats; however, they will trill and chirp, and make clicking sounds when delighted. They are easily leash-trained and love to go for walks. Though technically they are not thieves, their love of shiny objects makes it necessary to keep jewelry boxes closed and even locked. Many of them can open doors by standing on their back legs and turning the doorknob with their paws. These are strong and fit cats with no known genetic predisposition to health problems.

American Bobtails are extremely skillful hunters because their ancestry is from feral domestic stock. However, because it is unwise to allow cats to roam freely, their hunting instincts are satisfied in the home by catching flying insects in midair that make the fatal mistake of entering their domain. They also stalk their toys and carry them in their mouths as they would a freshly caught mouse.

Grooming Requirements

In addition to their engaging personalities, they have coats that need little or no brushing, even in the long-haired variety. An occasional bath and light brushing are all that is needed to keep their coats clean and beautiful.

Origin and History

The arrival of a domestic breed of cat carrying a short-tailed gene into the Americas cannot be disputed. Prior to the arrival of European explorers, no known domestic cats existed on the North American continent. However, there have been colonies of bobtailed cats for centuries on islands belonging to Spain and Portugal. In light of these facts, it is quite likely that the first bobtailed cats introduced in North America came from those Spanish and Portuguese islands and were brought here by ships exploring the New World.

Cats were highly valued on ships because of their ability to control the ever-present rodents. It is unfortunate that the captains did not consider the future and our desire to know the type of cats they had on board that were destined to populate the New World. The manifests of some old ships mention cats on board, and some even mention how many cats, but that is the extent of the information. It is clear that cats were introduced into the Americas by ships from other continents. As for the American Bobtail tail mutation, many researchers believe such cats came from those early voyages. Although we will never know exactly *when* they arrived, we at least know *how* they did.

The American Bobtail is an excellent example of breed development through natural selection. It is a completely domestic cat with no wild strains in its background. No other pedigreed breeds have been introduced into the Bobtail's breeding programs. The foundation stock for this breed was feral, domestic cats possessing a natural bobtail.

Although the Bobtail has been in existence in North America for many generations, the breed began its development as we know it today in the late 1960s. A young couple discovered a bobtail brown tabby male kitten on an Indian reservation in southern Arizona. They fell in love with this unique cat and subsequently bred him to a long-tail female; the resulting offspring were born with bobtails.

Since that time, breeders have used feral cats with natural bobtails as their foundation stock. The most conscientious breeders have used only cats that have sufficiently met the American Bobtail standard in type. Many American Bobtails now have a multigeneration pedigree with no feral cats in several generations.

Miscellanea

American Bobtails make excellent parents, and they nurture and share their offspring with their human families. Mothers of newborns happily trill to their kittens while nursing and are eager to show them to their human companions by rolling on their backs to display their new achievements. Many breeders have clients return for one or two more additions to their American Bobtail family, saying, "They are just like potato chips—one is just not enough." These are happy cats but are not overly demanding, despite their high intelligence. Their breeders hear from many new owners who marvel at their incredible intellect and how they understand everything that is said to them.

★   ★   ★

The breed has been in the making since the 1960s and has become very popular. It was accepted for registration in February 2000 by the CFA, confirming what breeders have known for many years—the American Bobtail has earned its place in the world of pedigreed cats. It is one of America's own, a breed to be proud of. Its wildcat look, full domesticity, and pleasing personality make it a credit to all the breeders who have devoted plenty of time, effort, and energy into shaping this remarkable breed.

CFA SHOW STANDARD FOR THE AMERICAN BOBTAIL (MISCELLANEOUS STATUS)

POINT SCORE

HEAD (40)

Shape	10
Brow	10
Muzzle	10
Ears	5
Eyes	5

BODY (40)

Shape	15
Neck	5
Legs and feet	5
Tail	15

COAT AND COLOR (20)

Texture	10
Color	5
Pattern	5

GENERAL: The American Bobtail is a medium to large naturally occurring bobtailed cat. It is a noticeably athletic animal, well muscled, with the appearance of power. The body is moderately long and substantial, with a rectangular stance and prominent shoulder blades. The tail is short and is to be clearly visible above the back when the cat is alert, not to exceed the hock in length. It possesses a strong, broad, modified wedge-shaped head, with a distinctive brow above large, almost almond-shaped eyes. The expression is one of intelligence and alertness. Females are generally proportionately smaller than males, with type a more important aspect of the breed than size. The American Bobtail, with all of its combined characteristics, possesses a distinctive wild appearance and an exceptionally amiable disposition.

HEAD: Broad, modified wedge without noticeable flat planes or doming, in proportion to the body. Observable muzzle break above a well-defined broad, medium-length muzzle. Fleshy whisker pads. Cheekbones are apparent. Slightly concave curve between nose and brow with good length between brow and ears. Distinctive brow is evident by a slightly rounded forehead to eye ridge; brow border is fleshy, creating an almost hooded appearance to the eye. Nose wide, nose leather large. Chin strong and wide in line with the nose. Widening of the head and stud jowls apparent in adult males.

EARS: Medium. Wide at base with slightly rounded tips, as much on the top of the head as on the side. Ear tipping and furnishings highly desirable. Lighter-colored thumbprints on the back of the ears desirable on all tabbies, including lynx points.

EYES: Large. Almost almond in shape. Deep-set. Outside corner angled slightly upward toward the ears. Medium-wide apart. Distinctive brow above the eye gives the cat a natural hunting gaze.

BODY: Moderately long and substantial, with a rectangular stance. Chest full and broad. Slightly higher in hips, with prominent shoulder blades. Hips substantial, almost as wide as chest. Deep flank. Muscular and athletic in appearance. Allowance should be made for slow maturation.

LEGS AND FEET: In proportion to the body, of good length and substantial boning. Paws large and round. Toe tufts desirable in long-haired varieties. Five toes in front, four in back.

NECK: Medium in length; may appear short due to musculature.

TAIL: Short; may be straight, slightly curved, or slightly kinked or have bumps along the length of the tail. Tail set in line with the top line of the hip. Tail to be broad at base, strong and substantial to the touch, never fragile. Must be flexible, expressive and not kinked to the point it impairs the natural movement of the tail, straighter tails being preferred over kinked tails. Straight tails should exhibit a fat pad at the end of the tail. Length: must be long enough to be clearly visible above the back when alert, not to extend past the hock in length.

COAT: *Shorthair Division:* Length—medium, semidense. Texture—nonmatting, resilient with slight loft. Density—double coat, hard topcoat with a soft, downy undercoat. Miscellaneous—seasonal variations of coat should be recognized. Coat may be softer in texture in dilute colors, lynx points, and silvers. Undercoat may be mouse grey in tabbies. *Longhair Division:* Length—medium-long hair, slightly shaggy. Tapering to slightly longer hair on ruff, britches, belly, and tail. Ruff—slight, muttonchops desirable. Texture—nonmatting, resilient. Density—double coat. Undercoat present, not extremely dense. Miscellaneous—seasonal variations of coat should be recognized. Coat may be softer in texture in dilute colors, lynx points, and silvers. Undercoat may be mouse grey in tabbies.

PENALIZE: Tail too long or too short, affecting the balance and appearance of the cat. Tail kinked or knotted out of shape. Tail rigid, fragile, or set low. Straight tail not exhibiting a fat pad. Round eyes. Weak chin. Extremely short muzzle or nose break. Cottony coat.

COLORS AND PATTERNS: All colors and patterns allowed. High rufousing desirable in all tabbies. Ghost patterns highly desirable in lynx points.

EYE COLORS: All eye colors acceptable except odd eyes. No correlation between eye and coat color.

DEVELOPMENTAL CHANGES: Allowances should be made for slower development in achieving adult body type, as this breed gradually matures over a period of 3 years. **DISQUALIFY:** Total lack of tail or full-length tail. Odd eyes. Delicate bone structure. Incorrect number of toes.

ALLOWABLE BREEDING OUTCROSSES: none.

AMERICAN CURL
By Caroline Scott

American Curl Longhair

American Curl Shorthair

The discovery of a novel cat that eventually leads to a new breed is an event of great importance to feline fanciers. The advent of American Curl was no exception.

Physical Description
Unique ears that curl back in a graceful arc, creating an alert, perky, happily surprised expression, are what distinguish this unusual breed. Most people break into a big smile when seeing the Curl for the first time. Those unusual ears first appeared naturally (or, in CFA terms, they were a *spontaneous mutation*) and are comparable to those of a Lynx, with long tufts accentuating

the swept-back look, which complement its overall elegance and dynamic presence.

Boasting head adornments that could have easily been fashioned by a hat designer, along with a plumed tail that resembles a feather boa, the American Curl has developed a worldwide audience that is often in awe of the breed.

When Curls are born, their ears are straight. In 3–5 days, the ears start to curl back, staying for a while in a tight rosebud position, then unfurling gradually until permanently set at around 16 weeks. This is the time breeders determine if the kittens' ears make them pet or show quality cats. The degree of ear curl can vary greatly, ranging from almost straight (pet quality) to an arc of 90–180 degrees that resembles the graceful curvature of a seashell (show quality). Although the distinctive feature of the American Curl is its uniquely curled ears, the medium-size rectangular body, silky flat-lying coat, and expressive walnut-shaped eyes are equally important aspects of the breed. Curls are available in long- and shorthair coats, which are seen in a variety of colors and patterns.

Personality

The Curl personality is truly enjoyable. Not only are these cats attracted to water, television, and sleeping in salad bowls, but they are also people-oriented, faithful, affectionate soul mates who adjust remarkably fast to other pets, children, and new situations. People say they are very doglike in their attentiveness to their owners, following their humans around so that they do not miss anything. When introduced into a new home, American Curls seem to have an inherent respect for the pets that were there first, giving them room to adjust to the new kid on the block. They are astute and become easily engrossed in assisting their owner in whatever project is at hand, such as helping to fix dinner, rather than just watching. Not overly talkative, the Curl's curiosity and intelligence is expressed through little chirping sounds when it wants to comment or would like an opinion from you on something that is momentarily puzzling. Because they retain their kittenlike personality throughout adulthood, it is not surprising to see a 12-year-old Curl frolicking and jumping effortlessly for a favorite toy, keeping up with the 12-week-olds.

Grooming Requirements

When grooming the American Curl for cat shows, mentor support can be extremely important. The breed's semilong, silky body coat has to be in peak condition and extremely clean when these cats are shown in competition. The show bath and preparation for it is extremely important, as is using the correct grooming tools.

Take precautions with the cat's ears prior to bathing. Gently place a cotton swab soaked with a commercially manufactured nonoily ear cleaner (no alcohol) into the outer furrows of each ear, working up and away from the canal opening. Avoid pulling on the delicate cartilage or getting water inside the ears. Never use an oily cleaner such as mineral oil, and never pour any liquids into the ears.

Start the bath with a cleaner called GOOP (available at grocery and hardware stores), working it well into a wet coat and rinsing it out thoroughly. You may then wash the cat with Dawn dishwashing liquid, again rinsing it very well. Next, shampoo the cat with a quality cat shampoo that is recommended by Curl breeders and proven to be effective. Keep in mind that you can never overrinse—rinsing is probably the most important "part of the entire bath."

Squeeze out the water from the coat with a clean towel and then blow-dry the cat with a hand-held dryer. A professional metal comb, half fine-tooth and half medium-tooth, is an important tool for separating the fur while drying it. Cream rinses are not necessary and can weigh the coat down, but they may be used sparingly in the winter to control static. Working with an experienced grooming mentor is the best way to learn how to bathe a show cat.

Origin and History

Shulamith was the name of the original American Curl from which all authentic pedigreed Curls trace their origin. The story began on a summer day in June 1981 on the doorstep of the unsuspecting Joe and Grace Ruga (Curlniques Cattery).

Grace, 7 months pregnant with their first child, remembers "trying hard not to do anything" on that day. Joe returned home from work that evening and spotted two kittens outside their home that looked to be approximately 6 months old. When Joe went in to change clothes, Grace fed the kittens and immediately noticed that they had "ears that curled back from their heads in a funny way."

The kittens, who appeared to be sisters, had fine, silky coats. Grace named the black one Shulamith, and the other, a black-and-white kitten, she named Panda. Although Shulamith was very protective of her sister, Panda disappeared 2 weeks later, and Shu became the foundation cat for the American Curl breed and Joe's constant companion.

In December 1981 after the birth of Shu's first litter, the Rugas, who described themselves as casual pet owners, realized that her unique ears could well indicate an entirely new cat breed. They contacted two noted geneticists to look into this unusual mutation. Both experts determined that the curled ears were a genetic trait, inherited in every case, meaning that the trait was labeled a dominant gene with no apparent defects. They referred to the cat as a spontaneous mutation; the gene that causes the ear to curl appeared to be following a single dominant pattern. Diligent research and test breeding began, with Shulamith never suspecting that her legacy was to produce several more litters before her untimely death.

A respected CFA judge and breeder of Scottish Folds was contacted and asked to determine if these cats were candidates for recognition by the CFA as a separate breed. The CFA had then, as it does now, the most stringent and thorough registration procedure of all cat associations and is recognized as the most prestigious cat registry in the world. After closely examining Shulamith and her offspring, it was determined that Curls are indeed a potential new breed. All parties involved were warned that the road to breed recogni-

tion and championship status was a very long and hard one. But the Curl's fans were ardent and forged ahead. The first public presentation of the American Curl was at a CFA cat show in Palm Springs, California, on October 23, 1983.

After careful study of CFA breed standards and illustrations from various feline reference works, the first American Curl breed standard was drafted. Although the Abyssinian, Egyptian Mau, and Ocicat standards were used as structure references, the Curl does not resemble these breeds. Because the breed originated as a domestic cat with an unusual mutation, the standard was formulated around Shulamith's characteristics to preserve their unique identity and distinguish the Curl from all other breeds. Significantly, the standard dictated that the only allowable outcross for the Curl would be non-pedigreed domestic cats that closely matched the Curl standard. Not only would this vast domestic gene pool diversity ensure optimum health, vigor, and longevity but it also apparently made Curl litters less susceptible to the usual kitten illnesses and shot reactions seen in their own breeds, according to breeders who worked with other breeds in addition to the Curls. The first Curl-to-Curl breeding occurred in January 1984; the resulting kittens were born in March. Playit By Ear, a black-and-white male kitten from this litter, became the first known homozygous American Curl, meaning that all of his offspring would have curled ears, regardless of his pairing with curled or straight-eared females.

American Curls were first accepted for CFA registration in 1986, achieved Provisional status in 1991, and advanced to Championship status in 1993—a rate of acceptance unprecedented in the CFA for a new breed, owing mainly to an impressive presentation before the executive board. Also unprecedented was that the American Curl was the first breed to be admitted to the Championship Class as one breed with two coat lengths. This was done because Shulamith delivered the first short-haired Curl (with later offspring following suit), producing both long-haired and short-haired kittens. Because of their diverse domestic ancestry, Curls are available in both coat lengths and can be any color or coat pattern, including the rare colorpoint, which initially appeared in Shulamith's first litter. Both coat lengths are presented in the Longhair Division. Because in 1999 more shorthairs started entering the show rings, they also started turning up in the longhair finals—longhairs and shorthairs are judged together.

Miscellanea

Because new Curl owners are so taken by how personable these cats are and how Curls are "unlike any cat" they've ever had, owners usually come back for one or two more. Breeders usually make their new kittens available between the ages of 12 and 16 weeks. Pricing on American Curls usually depends on ear degree, body type, specialized colors such as the blue-eyed colorpoint, and bloodlines.

The American Curl experience is like no other—so it is no wonder that one just never seems to be enough.

CFA SHOW STANDARD FOR THE AMERICAN CURL

POINT SCORE

HEAD (20)	
Shape and size	8
Profile	6
Muzzle	4
Chin	2

EARS (30)	
Degree of curl	10
Shape and size	10
Placement	8
Furnishings	2

EYES (10)	
Shape and size	6
Placement	3
Color	1

BODY (25)	
Torso and neck	9
Size and boning	6
Legs and feet	5
Tail length	5

COAT AND COLOR (15)	
Silky texture	6
Minimal undercoat	4
Body coat length	2
Tail coat length	2
Color	1

GENERAL: The distinctive feature of American Curls is their attractive, uniquely curled ears. The original American Curl, a long-haired female named Shulamith, was first noted in Southern California in 1981. Selective breeding began in 1983. Curls are well balanced, moderately muscled, slender rather than massive in build. Females weigh 5–8 pounds; males weigh 7–10 pounds. Proper proportion and balance are more important than size. Allowance is to be made for normal male characteristics. They are alert and active, with gentle, even dispositions.

HEAD: *Shape:* modified wedge without flat planes, moderately longer than wide, smooth transitions. *Profile:* nose moderate in length and straight, slight rise from bottom of eyes to forehead, gentle curve to top of head, flowing into neck without a break. *Size:* medium in proportion to body. *Muzzle:* rounded with gentle transition, no pronounced whisker break. *Chin:* firm, in line with nose and upper lip.

EARS: *Degree:* minimum 90 degree arc of curl, not to exceed 180 degrees. Firm cartilage from ear base to at least one third of height. *Shape:* wide at base and open, curving back in smooth arc when viewed from front and rear. Tips rounded and flexible. *Size:* moderately large. *Placement:* erect, set equally on top and side of head. *Furnishings:* desirable. *Note:* when Curls are alert with ears swiveled toward front, lines following curve of ear through tips should point to center of base of skull. (Lines following curve of ear through tips beyond 90 and up to 180 degrees may intersect at a point farther up on skull, but not beyond top of skull.)

EYES: *Shape:* walnut; oval on top and round on bottom. *Placement:* set on slight angle between base of ear and tip of nose, one eye-width apart. *Size:* moderately large. *Color:* clear, brilliant, no relation to coat color except blue eyes required in colorpoint class.

BODY: *Torso shape:* semiforeign rectangle, length 1.5 times height at shoulder, medium depth of chest and flank. *Size:* intermediate, with allowances for larger males. *Musculature:* moderate strength and tone, flexible. *Tail:* flexible, wide at base, tapering; equal to body length. *Legs:* length medium in proportion to body, set straight when viewed from front or rear. Medium boning, neither fine nor heavy. *Neck:* medium. *Feet:* medium and rounded.

COAT AND COLOR: *Longhair Division:* Texture—fine, silky, laying flat. Undercoat—minimal. Coat length—semilong. Tail coat—full and plumed. Color—all colors accepted as listed. *Shorthair Division:* Texture—soft, silky, laying flat, resilient without a plush, dense feel. Undercoat—minimal. Coat length—short. Tail coat—same length as body coat. Color—all colors accepted.

PENALIZE: *Ears:* Low-set; abrupt change of direction without smooth curve; pinch, horizontal or vertical crimp; interior surface that appears corrugated. *Body:* Tubular or cobby; excessive size. *Nose:* Deep nose break. *Coat:* Longhair Division—heavy undercoat, heavy ruff, coarse or cottony texture. Shorthair Division—heavy undercoat, coarse texture, dense or plush coats.

DISQUALIFY: Extreme curl in adult where tip of ear touches back of ear or head. Ears that are straight, severely mismatched, or thick or that have inflexible tips. Lack of firm cartilage in base of ear. Tail faults.

COLORS: A wide array of colors in the solid, shaded, smoke, tabby, bicolor, particolor, and pointed patterns.

ALLOWABLE BREEDING OUTCROSSES: domestic longhair or shorthair for litters born before January 1, 2010.

AMERICAN SHORTHAIR

By Ande DeGeer

American Shorthair

If you close your eyes and visualize the beautiful short-haired cat that slept on your bed and comforted you when you were a child, you are very likely picturing a cat that closely resembles the American Shorthair. The perfect family cat, the American Shorthair is known for its intelligence, quiet disposition, beauty, and hardy build.

Physical Description

Every part of the American Shorthair's structure allows it to move with power, endurance, and agility. There is nothing about its appearance that is exaggerated. The general effect is that of a strongly built, well-balanced, symmetrical cat. The cat is surprisingly heavy. Even the female, which may be slightly smaller than the male, has a well-padded and muscular body. The breed usually achieves full growth at approximately 3–4 years of age, with the mature males weighing 11–15 pounds and the mature females weighing 8–12 pounds.

An American Shorthair has a large head with a full-cheeked face, giving the impression of an oval just slightly longer than it is wide. Its eyes have an upper lid shaped like half an almond (cut lengthwise), while the lower lid is a rounded curve. That unique shape that helps protect the eyes from injury produces a sweet, wide-open expression. The American's medium-length nose curves gently from the bridge to the forehead. It has a firm chin, wide muzzle, and powerful jaw that enables it to kill its prey with ease.

The glistening coat is short, thick, and hard in texture. It is dense enough to protect the cat from moisture, cold, and brambles if it were to run through the woods. Everything about an American Shorthair gives the impression that it could take care of itself in the wild if that became necessary.

Known as a cat of many colors, the American Shorthair has more than 80 different colors and patterns. Ranging from handsome brown tabby to glistening blue-eyed white, shimmering shaded cameo to flashy calico, striking tabby and white to subtle dilute, and many colors in between, the American has made its mark in the cat fancy. The most widely recognized American Shorthair color and pattern is the silver classic tabby with dense black markings on a sparkling silver background.

Personality

Although the breed is very affectionate, these cats do not require constant attention. They are very adept at entertaining themselves. American Shorthairs frequently find imaginary friends with whom to play; maybe they are refreshing mouse-hunting skills from bygone days. Whatever it is, they can play happily for a long time with something that is not visible to the human eye. They also love to be part of a communal game, chasing a toy on a string or attacking a waving feather.

While they enjoy high places, like the top shelf of a climbing tree, they are easily trained not to jump onto a counter or bookcase. They also quickly learn to use a scratching post instead of the furniture for claw sharpening.

Generally, an American Shorthair is a sedate cat. However, once in a while, a single cat can make itself sound like a herd of elephants running down the hall. This usually occurs when a cat is playing with her invisible toys; it is difficult to determine if the cat is chasing, being chased, or just running for the sake of running. Most of the time, these cats simply exhibit a quiet patience. They will sit for many minutes waiting for a special treat. It is very easy to understand why they are successful mousers. The need for quiet during hunting may explain one of the most comical attributes of American Shorthairs. Although they are very talkative, they rarely *speak*. The breed is well known for its silent meow. American Shorthairs frequently walk up to their humans, opens its mouth, but makes no sound. Yet, by their facial expression, it is easy to understand what is said because they train us very well.

Part of the human training provides us with little glimpses of their subtle humor. If it is time for attention but the attention is not forthcoming, these cats often use humor to get it: She might decide that a bite on the human's bare toe is in order. From that day forward, she will use a little love bite, accompanied by a grin and wag of her expressive tail, as a reminder of what could occur.

Grooming Requirements

The only requirements for grooming these cats are clipping the claws and keeping the coat tidy. If you start the grooming procedures when the cat is young and make it part of the daily routine, your American Shorthair will enjoy being groomed.

Cats shed. The American Shorthair is no exception. However, shedding can be kept to a minimum by weekly combing (or more frequently, if desired). Use a metal comb or rubber brush, because plastic combs and brushes tend to break the coat. Another tool used by breeders is a chamois, the same type as the one you might use to wash your car. However, when purchasing one for your cat, be certain it has not been treated with soap or any other chemicals. Wiping the coat with the chamois pulls out loose hair, cleans the coat, and adds luster.

An American Shorthair does not normally require a bath unless it is going to be shown or has become exceptionally dirty. A show bath should be given as early in the week prior to the show as possible to allow some oils to return to the coat. If you intend to show your American Shorthair, it would be a good idea to talk to the cat's breeder prior to giving the first bath, because every breeder has preferences for certain shampoos, conditioners, and treatments.

If you are bathing the cat because it has gotten dirty, there are some general guidelines: Use only a shampoo recommended for cats. After shampooing, rinse thoroughly. Squeeze out as much water as possible. Towel to a damp dryness and allow the cat to finish the process. Comb through the coat when it has almost dried, to smooth it and remove loosened hair. Always keep the cat in a warm area until it has completely dried.

Origin and History

Records indicate several short-haired cats arrived in North America on the *Mayflower* and various other ships. Although they probably sneaked aboard, they were soon revered for controlling the rodent population on the ships and, later, on the settlers' farms. Those barn cats were selected more for ruggedness and natural hunting talent than for their beauty. However, as the U.S. cat population grew, farmers began to keep the kittens that appealed to them because of flashy colors, bold patterns, general conformation, and disposition.

The first formal cat show in the United States was held at Madison Square Garden in 1895. The American cat, simply named Shorthair, provided 46 adult and 25 kitten entries in the show. Many were listed for sale for higher prices than the imported Siamese and Persians. The CFA chose to recognize this lovely breed of cat as one of its first five pedigreed breeds. The first Shorthair registered by the CFA was born in 1900. He was an orange (red) tabby named CH Belle of Bradford.

The success of the Shorthair in the show ring grew through the years. At the same time, cat shows grew in popularity, and many more breeds were created and imported. By 1930, breeders of the Shorthairs came to believe their breed needed a more distinctive name. The name Domestic Shorthair was selected to represent the strain of cat developed in the United States. But the name change proved to be a serious mistake. A name that was intended to distinguish U.S.-bred cats from the imported or intentionally-bred varieties came to be equated with domestic (household) servants. The name led such cats from riches to rags. For the next 30 years, the breed struggled in popularity.

In the 1960s, fanciers of the breed realized another name change was needed, so the breed became the American Shorthair in 1966. The name is now consistent with the idea that our native North American breed of short-haired cat is distinctly different from cats found in the neighborhoods and barnyards today. By chance, a nonpedigreed short-haired cat might resemble an American Shorthair, just as any given domestic cat might look like a Siamese or a Persian. The test, however, is in whether that animal can consistently produce kittens of the same conformation, coat quality, and temperament in the same manner as a pedigreed cat. Years of selective breeding and the recording of many generations of cats are what enable today's breeders to be certain that each litter of kittens will have specific qualities. Each litter is planned in order to produce the finest representatives of the breed.

The breed returned from rags to riches throughout the world. In 1965, an American Shorthair (then Domestic Shorthair) gained the coveted title of Cat of the Year. Many American Shorthairs have earned national and regional titles since, including Cat of the Year wins in 1984 and 1996. For the breed to have produced three such cats is quite a record. In fact, the American Shorthair is the only short-haired breed to earn the title since the 1970s. Consistently in the top 10 most popular breeds of cat, the American Shorthair has truly come into its own.

Miscellanea

The American Shorthair is a very social cat. It enjoys people and other animals. Naptime usually finds it curled in someone's lap or snuggled next to another cat. Even though it loves to be held, the American Shorthair typically wants to have at least its back feet on a solid surface. This could be your hand supporting the hindquarters while you carry the cat or, in the case of a show ring, the judge's table. The fact that the cat likes to have its rear legs supported is probably due to the distribution of its body weight. It may also be why a 7-pound female can manage to feel like she carries 50 pounds on one foot when she steps onto your lap to get attention.

Because of its stamina and early ancestry, the American Shorthair is considered to be a true working breed of cat. However, most modern-day cats are on strike. They prefer to stay in the house and allow their humans to do all the work. When necessary, they will rise to the occasion. For example, a large snake found its way into this author's house, but an 8-pound female made quick work of it. For weeks afterward, one of her kittens carried a stick through the house, growling and shaking it in imitation of its mother.

The breed is very adaptable. They travel well and seem to thrive on visiting new, interesting places. It is best to start the cat's travel experiences at an early age. When possible, introduce a kitten to travel in the company of an older, experienced cat. To let the kitten know it is going to return home unharmed, try to take it on several short trips in advance of its first long trip to a show or to the veterinarian. It is especially important not to allow the cat's only travel experience be trips to the veterinarian's office.

A healthy American Shorthair is a low-maintenance cat. As long as it is kept indoors, this cat will live, on average, 15–20 years, with only annual veterinary checkups. If it is not to be part of a breeding program, it is recommended that the cat be neutered or spayed.

When it is time to add an American Shorthair to your family, remember that this breed has worked very hard to earn its well-deserved place in the world of pedigreed cats. Plan to keep your cat indoors and let it remain on strike, so that it can spend many years sleeping on the foot of your bed.

CFA SHOW STANDARD FOR THE AMERICAN SHORTHAIR

POINT SCORE

HEAD (INCLUDING SIZE AND SHAPE OF EYES, EAR SHAPE, AND SET AND STRUCTURE OF NOSE)	**30**
BODY (INCLUDING SHAPE, SIZE, BONE, AND LENGTH OF TAIL)	**30**
COAT	**15**
COLOR (20)	
Tabby pattern	10
Color	10
EYE COLOR	**5**

GENERAL: The American Shorthair is a true breed of working cat. The conformation should be adapted for this, with no part of the anatomy so exaggerated as to foster weakness. The general effect should be that of a strongly built, well-balanced, symmetrical cat with conformation indicating power, endurance, and agility.

SIZE: Medium to large. No sacrifice of quality for the sake of size. Females may be less massive in all respects than males and should be rewarded equally if overall balance is correct.

PROPORTIONS: Slightly longer than tall. (Height is profile measure from top of shoulder blades to ground. Length is profile measure from tip of breastbone to rear tip of buttocks.) Viewed from side, body can be divided into three equal parts: from tip of breastbone to elbow, from elbow to front of hindleg, and from front of hindleg to rear tip of buttocks. Length of tail is equal to distance from shoulder blades to base of tail.

HEAD: Large, with full-cheeked face giving the impression of an oblong just slightly longer than wide. Sweet, open expression. Viewed from front, head can be divided in two equal parts: from base of ears to middle of eyes and from middle of eyes to chin tip.

EARS: Medium size, slightly rounded at tips, and not unduly open at base. Distance between ears, measured from lower inner corners, twice distance between eyes.

FOREHEAD: Viewed in profile, forehead forms smooth, moderately convex continuous curve flowing over top of head into neck. Viewed from front, there is no dome between ears.

EYES: Large and wide, with upper lid shaped like half an almond (cut lengthwise) and lower lid shaped in a fully rounded curve. At least width of one eye between the eyes. Outer corners set very slightly higher than inner corners. Bright, clear, and alert.

NOSE: Medium length, same width for entire length. Viewed in profile, gentle concavely curved rise from bridge of nose to forehead.

MUZZLE: Squared. Definite jowls in mature males.

JAWS: Strong and long enough to successfully grasp prey. Both level and scissors bites considered equally correct. (In level bite, top and bottom front teeth meet evenly. In scissors bite, inside edge of top front teeth touch outside edge of lower front teeth.)

CHIN: Firm and well developed, forming perpendicular line with upper lip.

NECK: Medium in length, muscular, and strong.

BODY: Solidly built, powerful, and muscular with well-developed shoulders, chest, and hindquarters. Back broad, straight, and level. Viewed in profile, slight slope down from hip bone to base of tail. Viewed from above, outer lines of body parallel.

LEGS: Medium in length and bone, heavily muscled. Viewed from rear, all four legs straight and parallel with paws facing forward.

PAWS: Firm, full, and rounded, with heavy pads. Toes: five in front, four behind.

TAIL: Medium long, heavy at base, tapering to abrupt blunt end in appearance but with normal tapering final vertebrae.

COAT: Short, thick, even, and hard in texture. Regional and seasonal variation in coat thickness allowed. Coat dense enough to protect from moisture, cold, and superficial skin injuries.

PENALIZE: Excessive cobbiness or ranginess. Very short tail.

DISQUALIFY: Cats showing evidence of hybridization resulting in the colors chocolate, sable, lavender, lilac, or point-restricted (i.e., Siamese-type markings). Any appearance of hybridization with any other breed—including long or fluffy fur, deep nose break, bulging eye set, brow ridge. Kinked or abnormal tail. Locket or button (white spots on colors not specifying same). Incorrect number of toes. Undershot or overshot bite. Tongue persistently protruding. Obesity or emaciation. Any feature so exaggerated as to foster weakness.

COLORS: A wide array of colors in the solid, shaded, smoke, tabby, parti-color and bicolor patterns.

ALLOWABLE BREEDING OUTCROSSES: none.

AMERICAN WIREHAIR

By Robert Bradshaw

American Wirehair

The American Wirehair breed is a newcomer to the sport of pedigreed cat exhibiting, in the sense that it has been in existence only since 1964. This breed has the distinction of being among the first American spontaneous genetic mutations recognized for registration and championship exhibition in the CFA. Most breeds, before exhibited, registered what would be considered by most normal attributes such as straight (not curly or wiry) hair or straight (not curled or folded) ears. Its first year of championship status in the CFA was 1978, and that same year it had the honor of attaining a national championship award. The parent breed from which the American Wirehair mutated is our own familiar resident breed, the American Shorthair.

Physical Description

At first glance, the American Wirehair looks like any other ordinary feline, but as you gaze closer, you realize that the coat looks and feels different. As a matter of fact, the coat is quite unconventional. At first appearance, it seems coarse, somewhat like steel wool. However, the strange feel of it is softer, creating a very pleasant sensation. It is a mutation of the usual feline coat. Each hair is hooked or crimped, which gives the cat a woolly appearance. The Wirehair coat comes in different degrees of wiriness, from soft wooliness like that of a new bath towel to harsh, sparse, and spare. It has a varied range of textures and densities. The optimum coat has all three types of hairs: *awn, awn down,* and *guard hairs* bent or kinked and present over the entire body of the cat. There is no other breed of cat that has a coat even similar to that of this breed. You cannot help but notice the difference in the coat even from a distance.

Personality

The Wirehair personality can be described as warm happiness. There has never been a Wirehair that does not like to rub its head or leg against its significant human. It is a calm yet alert breed. Socialization is an important aspect for the American Wirehair. Although each will have a favorite member of the family, it is important to them to make time for all family members. This is most obvious at bedtime. American Wirehairs will tuck everyone in before retiring to their favorite pillow. However, everyone must pet them, hug them, and tell them how wonderful they are. They will usually respond with boisterous purring and rub their heads against you as a reward for your efforts. Wherever you are in the house, your Wire companion will be present, supervising or observing.

It is amazing how often you may find this cat napping among your soft clothes whenever you open a dresser drawer. They love the sun, and you can often find them basking in a single ray of sunlight streaming into a room. They also enjoy lying on the kitchen stove when the oven is on. The opening of the refrigerator door is an invitation to check out the larder.

The Wirehair interacts freely with children, dogs, cats, and most other animals. These clever cats sometimes master the skill of opening cabinet doors and full-size doors. They may team up with other cats to open difficult cabinet doors that contain cat food—and then the party is on.

Grooming Requirements

Maintenance of the Wirehair coat for show ring presentation is relatively simple; during the bath, they require only a shampoo that is devoid of conditioner or additives. Texturizing shampoos or cleaners can add to the overall feel of the finished coat. The key to any of these texturizers is that they must be rinsed thoroughly off the cat. Hair sprays and mousses should not be used to enhance the coat. These products can be harmful to cats as well as to humans, and they can leave the coat feeling sticky or gummy. An experienced handler or judge will notice this.

Coat care for pet American Wirehairs is even simpler. An occasional bath is desirable to reduce the effect of shedding. No blow-drying is ever necessary. The cat should be placed in a draft-free area until dry. An American Wirehair will stay as clean as the environment in which he lives.

Origin and History

The first American Wirehairs were born in a barn on the Council Rock Farm in upstate New York, where four wire-coated kittens appeared in a litter as a spontaneous, natural mutation. The litter's parents were named Fluffy and Bootsie and were ordinary barn cats.

The owners of the cats made a call to Mrs. Joan O'Shea of the HI-FI Cattery, in Vernon, New York, a breeder of German Rex and Havana Browns. Mrs. O'Shea was known as "the cat person" in her hometown. She was told that some unusual kittens were born in a barn. Mrs. O'Shea drove to Council Rock Farm and looked at the litter, finding not one but four unusually coated kittens, and she offered to buy all of them. She was turned down. Three days later, the owner of the farm called her and said she could come and take what was left of the litter. Sadly, a weasel had gotten in the barn and attacked the kittens. There was only one kitten left, a red tabby and white that she named Adam. She also took his dam and sire. Mrs. O'Shea bred the two adult cats several times but, alas, lightning did not strike twice. The original sire and dam of the first known kitten with the wirehair mutation never produced any more.

Little did anyone realize that Adam would be the forefather of all Wirehairs. Adam was an orange tabby domestic barn cat. His head was narrow and his ears were large, but he was not a small cat. He was rather a long and lean male. Although Adam was typical of most farm cats, his unusual wire coat was one of a kind. It was kinky from the tip of his nose to the tip of his tail—it stuck straight out from his body. At that time, it was the most different thing anyone had ever seen on a cat. His personality was also even and well balanced. He was living in a large, walk-in cage with two male Havana Browns—three males in one area and no spraying.

Colors produced by Foreign Shorthairs are not allowed; nor are any point colors, such as those on the Siamese. The show standard for this breed has the most point allotment given to any breed for coat: 45 of a total of 100. The American Wirehair is a recognized breed in all cat-registering associations in North America. The CFA was the first to accept the breed for registration in 1967, and it granted the breed championship status in 1978. Since then, the breed has garnered many national and regional honors.

Miscellanea

Wirehair mothers do not require much help when delivering their own kittens. They take excellent care of their kittens, treating all littermates alike, even those with normal coats. There are currently few wire-coated kittens placed in pet homes, but because of the efforts of breeders throughout the world, many will eventually share the joy of living with this special companion animal.

The wire-coated kittens in each litter are often more extroverted than their normal-coated littermates. It has been noted that the wire-coated kittens are usually the first ones to climb out of the birthing box. Too, they are the first ones to venture to the food bowl during the weaning process, which means sitting in the middle of the food dish. These subtle differences are present from a very early stage of development. It is rare to see a shy or temperamental American Wirehair kitten; on the contrary, kittens of this breed usually crave attention and handling.

American Wirehair breeding is not complex, but to breed a cat that comes up to the written standard is difficult. The wirehair mutation is a dominant, semipenetrating gene. This means that only half of any litter will receive the wire gene for coat, when an American Wirehair is bred to an American Shorthair. When breeding is Wirehair to Wirehair, 90% of the litter will be wired. The breed is allowed the same colors that are present in the American Shorthair; color is not the principal objective in American Wirehair breeding.

The American Wirehair is still considered a minority or specialty area in mainstream cat breeding. This is mainly due to the fact that in the outcross litters, half the kittens are unqualified for showing because of their coats, which will be like the American Shorthair coat. Such cats can be sold only as pets. American Wirehairs are hearty and hale in general; there are no known genetic faults. Even with close line breeding, no documented problems concerning health have occurred to date.

Breeders find American Wirehairs easy to care for, resistant to disease, and good producers. Pet owners are delighted with their reserved yet loving ways. From the barn to the show arena—and ultimately to pet homes around the world—these rough-coated treasures will be sure to win your heart.

CFA SHOW STANDARD FOR THE AMERICAN WIREHAIR

POINT SCORE

HEAD (INCLUDING SIZE AND SHAPE OF EYES, EAR SHAPE AND SET)	25
TYPE (INCLUDING SHAPE, SIZE, BONE AND LENGTH OF TAIL)	20
COAT	45
COLOR AND EYE	10

GENERAL: The American Wirehair is a spontaneous mutation. The coat, which is not only springy, dense, and resilient but also coarse and hard to the touch, distinguishes the American Wirehair from all other breeds. Characteristic is activity, agility, and keen interest in its surroundings.

HEAD: In proportion to the body. Underlying bone structure is round with prominent cheekbones and well-developed muzzle and chin. There is a slight whisker break.

NOSE: In profile, the nose shows a gentle concave curve.

MUZZLE: Well developed. Allowance for jowls in adult males.

CHIN: Firm and well developed with no malocclusion.

EARS: Medium, slightly rounded at tips, set wide and not unduly open at the base.

EYES: Large, round, bright, and clear. Set well apart. Aperture has slight upward tilt.

BODY: Medium to large. Back level; shoulders and hips same width; torso well-rounded and in proportion. Males larger than females.

LEGS: Medium in length and bone, well-muscled, and proportionate to body.

PAWS: Firm, full, and rounded, with heavy pads. Toes: five in front and four behind.

TAIL: In proportion to body, tapering from the well-rounded rump to a rounded tip, neither blunt nor pointed.

COAT: Springy, tight, medium in length. Individual hairs are crimped, hooked, or bent, including hair within the ears. The overall appearance of wiring and the coarseness and resilience of the coat are more important than the crimping of each hair. The density of the wired coat leads to ringlet formation rather than waves. That coat, which is very dense, resilient, crimped, and coarse, is most desirable, as are curly whiskers.

PENALIZE: Deep nose break.

DISQUALIFY: Incorrect coat. Kinked or abnormal tail. Long or fluffy fur. Incorrect number of toes. Evidence of hybridization resulting in the colors chocolate or lavender, the Himalayan pattern, or these combinations with white.

COLORS: A wide array of colors in the solid, shaded, smoke, tabby, bicolor, and parti-color patterns.

ALLOWABLE BREEDING OUTCROSSES: American Shorthair.

BALINESE

By Terrie Smith

Balinese

At first glance, the Balinese brings to mind a Siamese cat, except for the length of its coat. Under that long, silky ermine coat he wears so proudly, this beautiful cat is all Siamese, and that includes his personality.

Physical Description

The Balinese has a long, fine, silky coat, covering its long, hard, tubular body. The ideal coat of this breed lies close to the body and ends in a plume at the tail. There is never the appearance of a ruff around the neck, and the coat must not be thick or double. Balinese cats come in four colors: seal point (dark brown), chocolate point (a warmer, milk-chocolate brown), blue point (slate grey), and lilac point (rosy grey). These colors are restricted to the *points* of the cat, which are the tail, the feet, the mask (entire face), and the ears.

The head follows a long, tapering wedge, which starts at the nose and flares out in straight lines to the tips of the ears, forming a triangle. The ears must be large and flared following the wedge, and there should be no breaks at the whiskers. Balinese cats have striking deep blue eyes. They also have svelte bodies with long, tapering lines and are lithe yet muscular. These are medium-size cats, with males ranging from 6 to 8 pounds and females ranging from 5 to 7 pounds. The most distinctive feature of the Balinese is its luxurious tail plume.

Personality

Balinese cats are active, intelligent, social, and vocal. They want to be an everyday part of the lives of their human family. This includes "helping" you with your everyday chores, sleeping under the covers at night, and enjoying energetic play. These beautiful cats will play fetch and return a ball or toy over and over again. They are capable of jumping quite high—from the floor to the top of the refrigerator in one graceful movement, for example. Balinese are very intelligent, so simply hiding a toy in a drawer may not suffice, for they can quickly learn to open doors or drawers if they feel there is something they want in there. At times, they may just prefer to sit on your lap as you watch TV. Balinese get along well with children and other pets and seem to be especially fond of dogs, enjoying their company.

In short, Balinese cats believe they are the same as people and will try to become involved in everything that people do. This includes trying to share the food you are eating, as you eat it. They are quite vocal and have a wide range of vocal capabilities, from purring and quietly carrying on a conversation to loudly demanding attention if they do not believe you are responding quickly enough to one of their demands.

Grooming Requirements

Because the long, fine, silky coat of Balinese does not have an undercoat, they shed very little hair. This also means that the coat will not mat, and consequently, little grooming is required for the pet Balinese except for occasional brushing and a bath when it appears to be necessary.

Grooming the Balinese for competition in a cat show involves bathing the cat as close to the show as possible, preferably the night before. The cat's nails should be trimmed before the bath. The type of shampoo will vary according to what works best for a given cat. Many breeders use the same shampoo and conditioner that they use on their own hair.

The cat should be bathed thoroughly and rinsed until there is no shampoo remaining in the coat. If the cat has a dry coat, you may use a conditioner, but this depends on the requirements of the individual cat. If there are greasy spots that persist—at the base of the tail or behind the ears, for example—you may use a small quantity of Dawn dish soap, dabbing it on before the shampoo. Balinese do not need to be blown dry. Their coats will air-dry; just do a little hand-grooming as they are drying. Most breeders prefer to trim excess hairs just inside the base of the ears, just to give the cat a cleaner look, using round-tipped scissors for safety. It is not preferred practice to trim out the entire ear.

That is all that is needed to prepare Balinese for the show ring, along with maintaining a high-quality diet and allowing them to exercise freely. They are very energetic and need to run, jump, and play with other cats.

Origin and History

Very little is known about when or how the first Balinese appeared, although it is generally accepted that the breed originated as a spontaneous mutation of the Siamese cat. Siamese kittens with longer hair began appearing in Siamese litters in the early 1900s. Because their longer coats were not acceptable for cat shows or desirable for breeding show cats, breeders would place them in homes as pets. It was not until the 1940s that serious efforts were made to promote them as a recognized breed.

Helen Smith of Merry Mews Cattery on Long Island, New York, was one of the first Siamese breeders to fall in love with the "long-haired" Siamese. With the help of a CFA allbreed judge, Smith decided on the name Balinese for the breed because it reminded the two of the graceful movements and svelte lines of Balinese dancers. Sylvia Holland, another Siamese fancier, saw her first Balinese kitten and bought him immediately. That kitten was Rai-Mar's Sputnik of Holland's Farm, and he became the foundation of Holland's cattery, fathering a number of today's Balinese.

Championship status was granted to the Balinese in 1970, and in 1975, the very first Balinese achieved Grand Champion status.

As the 1970s came to an end, the Balinese became less popular. This may have been in part due to the emergence of many new short-haired breeds and to the fact that the Balinese must be bred back to the Siamese for type. Those from such a litter will be short-haired kittens carrying the longhair gene. These short-haired kittens cannot be shown as Balinese but are an integral part of the Balinese breeding program. This might have discouraged some breeders. In addition, during this same period, there was disparity in the type of the Balinese being shown, which was confusing and frustrating for breeders as well as judges.

Despite these drawbacks, some breeders persevered, believing that the journey is worth the effort. Currently, the Balinese is enjoying a resurgence of popularity. Its beauty and intelligence captivate people, and although it is not easy to breed a top show-quality Balinese, the reward is great.

★　★　★

Balinese are very people-oriented and in fact think of themselves as people. If you are looking for an addition to your family, one who will be a true member of the family, the Balinese is the right cat for you. They are happiest when they are with you, doing whatever it is you are doing, whether that is sleeping in your bed, playing catch, or just sitting in your lap watching TV.

The Balinese will be an active, vocal, intelligent and loving addition to your family, giving you unconditional love. The beautiful Balinese is a challenge to breed but a delightful cat that will enrich anyone's life.

CFA SHOW STANDARD FOR THE BALINESE

POINT SCORE

HEAD (20)

Long, flat profile	6
Wedge, fine muzzle, size	5
Ears	4
Chin	3
Width between eyes	2

EYES (5)

Shape, size, slant, and placement	5

BODY (30)

Structure and size, including neck	12
Muscle tone	10
Legs and feet	5
Tail	3

COAT (20)

Length	10
Texture	10

COLOR (25)

Body color	10
Point color (matching points of dense color, proper foot pads and nose leather)	10
Eye color	5

GENERAL: The ideal Balinese is a svelte cat with long, tapering lines, very lithe but strong and muscular. Excellent physical condition. Neither flabby nor bony. Not fat. Eyes clear. Because of the longer coat, the Balinese appears to have softer lines and less extreme type than other breeds of cats with similar type.

HEAD: Long, tapering wedge. Medium size in good proportion to body. The total wedge starts at the nose and flares out in straight lines to the tips of the ears, forming a triangle, with no break at the whiskers. No less than the width of an eye between the eyes. When the whiskers and face hair are smoothed back, the underlying bone structure is apparent. Allowance must be made for jowls in the stud cat.

SKULL: Flat. In profile, a long, straight line should be felt from the top of the head to the tip of the nose. No bulge over the eyes. No dip in nose.

EARS: Strikingly large, pointed, wide at base, continuing the lines of the wedge.

EYES: Almond-shaped. Medium size. Neither protruding nor recessed. Slanted toward the nose in harmony with lines of wedge and ears. Uncrossed.

NOSE: Long and straight. A continuation of the forehead with no break.

MUZZLE: Fine, wedge-shaped.

CHIN AND JAW: Medium size. Tip of chin lines up with tip of nose in the same vertical plane. Neither receding nor excessively massive.

BODY: Medium size. Graceful, long, and svelte. A distinctive combination of fine bones and firm muscles. Shoulders and hips continue same sleek lines of tubular body. Hips never wider than shoulders. Abdomen tight. The male may be somewhat larger than the female.

NECK: Long and slender.

LEGS: Bone structure long and slim. Hind legs higher than front. In good proportion to body.

PAWS: Dainty, small, and oval. Toes: five in front and four behind.

TAIL: Bone structure long, thin, tapering to a fine point. Tail hair spreads out like a plume.

COAT: Medium length, fine, silky; without downy undercoat lying close to the body, the coat may appear shorter than it is. Hair is longest on the tail.

COLOR: *Body:* Even, with subtle shading when allowed. Allowance should be made for darker color in older cats, as Balinese generally darken with age, but there must be definite contrast between body color and points. *Points:* Mask, ears, legs, feet, tail dense and clearly defined. All of the same shade. Mask covers entire face, including whisker pads, and is connected to ears by tracings. Mask should not extend over top of head. No ticking or white hairs in points.

PENALIZE: Lack of pigment in the nose leather and/or paw pads in part or in total. Crossed eyes. Visible protrusion of the cartilage at the end of the sternum under normal handling. *Soft or mushy* body.

DISQUALIFY: Any evidence of illness or poor health. Weak hind legs. Mouth breathing due to nasal obstruction or poor occlusion. Malocclusion resulting in either undershot or overshot chin. Emaciation. Visible kink in tail. Eyes other than blue. White toes and/or feet. Incorrect number of toes. Definite double coat (i.e., downy undercoat).

COLORS: Seal point, chocolate point, blue point, lilac point.

ALLOWABLE BREEDING OUTCROSSES: Siamese.

BIRMAN

By Paula Boroff

Birman

A Birman can strike a pose that would entice the finest portrait artist, hypnotizing his audience with his beautiful blue eyes, luxurious coat, and color combinations—and abruptly taking a romp down the hall, chasing an invisible mouse.

Physical Description

Birmans are colorpointed cats, which means they have a darker color on their tail, legs, ears, and face, like the Siamese or the Himalayan Division of the Persian. Like other colorpointed breeds, they are born with a creamy white coat. When they are just a few days old, their color will begin to appear if they are going to be seal points. Other colors take a few days more to come into view. At the start, Birmans were permitted only four point colors to be eligible for CFA championship competition: seal point, chocolate point, blue point, and lilac point. Currently, Birmans are accepted in many more point colors: the original four and a variety of lynx point, parti-color point, and red factor solid-color point. The unique white color of the feet and up the back of the hind legs is probably what draws the most at-

tention from spectators at cat shows. They are referred to as gloves and laces. The white color begins to appear on the feet of the darker colors within a few days after Birmans are born.

Although the Birman body is white at birth, a lighter shade of its point color develops on its coat as it matures and is called golden mist. When a Birman lies in the sunlight, the golden mist is reminiscent of a morning mist hovering near the ground. Beneath the mist lies a lighter shade at the roots.

These cats' distinctive heads ideally include a strong, broad, rounded skull with a medium-length Roman nose, full cheeks, heavy jaw, and a well-developed chin. Their eyes are almost round and blue, are set well apart, and the outer corners are tilted slightly upward. Birmans can steal your heart. The body should be long and stocky with medium-length heavy legs; large, round paws; and a medium-length tail. Females are generally more petite than males, but they too have substantial boning in proportion to their size. The standard calls for penalizing of delicate bone structure.

The long, silky hair of the Birman is not comparable to the thicker coat of the Persian, and it does not mat because of its finer texture. The coat envelops a thick, long body in a silky profusion of luxurious fur. The color should be light and warm, with a shimmering of gold, as if applied with a fine mist. The traditional points should be dark, as for the Siamese and colorpointed Persian. The very distinctive white feet are ideally symmetrical. The gloves on the front feet, if perfect, go across in an even line, and the laces on the hind feet end in a point up the back of the leg. It is very difficult to breed a cat with four perfect white gloves.

Personality

Birmans are often referred to as "middle of the road" cats. Of course, individual cats vary, but Birmans do not tend to be as active as short-haired breeds such as Abyssinians or as laid back as other long-haired cats such as Persians.

Birmans are loving animals who may prefer to sit beside their human, lay on their human's lap, or sit on their human's head at 4:00 in the morning. Generally a soft-spoken cat, a Birman will let you know when attention is needed *now*! After a brief scratch behind the ears or a major hug, they are ready to go their way until the next time attention is required. It could be in a few minutes, a few hours, or a day or two, but they will let you know if they think you are paying insufficient attention.

Birmans have been known to be "helpful" when reading the newspaper: they lie in the middle of your paper until you pick them up. It is typical of Birmans not to like being the only animal in a home. They are not very fussy about whether their companion is another Birman, a cat of mixed parentage, or even a dog. They are social animals by nature, and if their human companions are gone most of the time, they become very lonely. Several people have adopted a Birman only to find that they need to add another kitten to their household within a few months.

Grooming Requirements

Birmans have semilong, silky hair that is not inclined to mat because of its texture. Consequently, frequent grooming is not necessary. However, it is a good idea to comb out the coat a few minutes a day as part of the attention your cat receives on a regular basis. An occasional bath will keep a Birman looking great. How frequent you bathe a cat depends on how dirty it gets. A general rule of thumb is once a month.

Any quality brand of *cat* shampoo can be used to bathe a Birman. Human shampoos are not recommended because the pH factors (the measure of acidity and alkalinity) of human and feline hair are different. For this reason, human shampoos will not get the ideal result. Products formulated for cats work best.

Place your cat in the sink; wet her down with lukewarm water and work shampoo through the coat. It is important to rinse a Birman's coat thoroughly. Leftover soap can cause the hair to stick together, and she may look worse than she did before you bathed her. A cream rinse is generally not necessary when grooming this breed, but if your cat's coat has a lot of static electricity, one may be used. Birmans usually tolerate an electric hair dryer well, and your cat's coat will look its best if it is blown dry rather than air-dried. Air-drying can also result in the formation of mats, which can be painful to remove later. A Birman who is shown on a regular basis may be bathed each week without causing harm to the coat's naturally silky texture.

If your cat has an upper respiratory infection or has a fever, it is not uncommon for white hairs to appear in the mask, especially in darker point colored cats. This is known as ticking and will probably disappear the next time your cat sheds her coat.

Origins and History

Unlike the case of some of the breeds that are recognized for championship competition by the CFA, there is no clear record behind the origin of Birmans. Other CFA-recognized breeds can trace their origins to a spontaneous mutation (such as the American Wirehair or the Scottish Fold) or to an intentional cross of other breeds to create a new breed or color (such as the Bombay, Colorpoint Shorthair, or Ocicat). Birmans cannot.

The Birman cat is believed to have originated in Burma, where it was considered sacred, the companion cat of the Kittah priests. There is a legend as to how the Birmans developed the colors they are today: Originally, the guardians of the Temple of Lao Tsun were yellow-eyed white cats with long hair. The golden goddess of the temple, Tsun-Kyan-Kse, had deep blue eyes. The head priest, Mun-Ha, had as his companion a beautiful cat named Sinh. One day the temple was attacked and Mun-Ha was killed. At the moment of his death, Sinh placed his feet on his master and faced the goddess. The cat's white fur took on a golden cast, his eyes turned as blue as the eyes of the goddess, and his face, legs, and tail became the color of earth. However, his paws, where they touched the priest, remained white as a symbol of purity. All the other temple cats became similarly colored. Seven days later, Sinh died, taking the soul of Mun-Ha to paradise.

The modern history of the Birman is almost as shrouded in mystery as its legendary origin. What is known for certain is that probably around 1919, a pair of Birman cats was clandestinely shipped from Burma to France. The male cat did not survive the arduous conditions of the long voyage, but the female, Sita, did survive and, happily, was pregnant.

From this small foundation, the Birman was established in the Western world. The French cat registry recognized the Birman as a separate breed in 1925. By the end of World War II, only two Birmans were left alive in Europe, and a program of outcrossing was necessary to reestablish the breed. Most cat registries require at least five generations of pure breeding after outcrossings to fully accredit a breed for championship competition. Birmans were recognized by England in 1966 and by the CFA in 1967.

It took 5 years from their initial acceptance into championship competition in the CFA for the first Birman to earn the title of Grand Champion. This may have been largely because initially there were not many Birmans being shown. Although they may have gotten off to a slow start, Birmans are now well represented in the show ring. The first Birman to earn a national win achieved the feat in 1989.

Miscellanea

Birmans mature slowly and may not reach their full growth until the age of 3 years. They are notoriously clumsy. Occasionally one will walk across the back of the sofa or along a ledge, only to fall off for no apparent reason. When you go to check if she is all right, she will look at you as if to say, "I did that on purpose," and continue on her way. If you own more than one Birman, "chaser/chasee" is a popular game. The rules are that one cat chases the other down the hall and through the rooms and then on the return trip, the former chaser becomes the cat being chased.

They are not usually fussy eaters, although they can be in some circumstances. It is common practice to leave various types of dry food in different places around the house, a practice known as free feeding. Kittens are almost always fed canned food as they are weaned from their mothers, until they are able to eat cereal-type food. Canned food may also be given on a regular basis if you choose to do so. It can also serve as comfort food when a kitten does not feel well or has just returned from a visit to the veterinarian for an examination, vaccination, or medical procedure such as neutering. A kitten requires plenty of fresh drinking water made available at all time.

Birmans are healthy cats and live relatively long lives. A Birman of 15 years or more is not unusual, and sometimes they just pass peacefully in their sleep at 20 years of age and older.

No story about Birmans would be complete without a few words regarding the convention for naming them. Most Birman breeders in the United States follow the French tradition of naming kittens with the same letter of the alphabet throughout the same year: 2001 was a *Y* year; in 2002 Birman kittens were given names beginning with *Z*; and 2003 starts all over again with the letter *A*. No letters of the alphabet are skipped, recycling back to *A* every 26 years. This can be a great challenge. In a *Q* year, one owner named a cat Qsmakemecrazy.

Whether playing with a feather in a judge's ring or sitting quietly beside its owner, Birmans are wonderful cats. They are at their best as companion animals for children, senior citizens, or those anywhere between the age groups. One Grand Champion who sired several litters of kittens before he was altered now spends his days accompanying his owner to her job at a senior citizen care center. Whether the residents are inclined to play with him or hold him on their laps, he is content spending his retirement with his adopted human retirees.

It has been said that Birmans house the souls of the priests from the legend. Perhaps this is true.

CFA SHOW STANDARD FOR THE BIRMAN

POINT SCORE

HEAD, BODY TYPE, AND COAT (65)

Head (including boning, nose, jaw, chin profile, ear and eye shape and set)	30
Body type (including boning, stockiness, elongation, legs, tail)	25
Coat (including length, texture, ruff)	10

COLOR, INCLUDING EYE COLOR (35)

Color except gloves (including body color, point color, eye color)	15
Gloves (including front and rear gloves, laces, and symmetry)	20

GENERAL: A cat of mystery and legend, the Birman is a colorpointed cat with long, silky hair and four pure-white feet. It is strongly built, elongated, and stocky, neither svelte nor cobby. The distinctive head has strong jaws, firm chin, and medium-length Roman nose. There should be good width between the ears, which are medium in size. The blue, almost round eyes are set well apart, giving a sweet expression to the face.

HEAD: Skull strong, broad, and rounded. There is a slight flat spot just in front of the ears.

NOSE: Medium in length and width, in proportion to size of head. Roman shape in profile. Nostrils set low on the nose leather.

PROFILE: The forehead slopes back and is slightly convex. The medium-length nose starts just below the eyes and is Roman in shape (which is slightly convex). The chin is strong, with the lower jaw forming a perpendicular line with the upper lip.

CHEEKS: Full with somewhat rounded muzzle. The fur is short in appearance about the face, but to the extreme outer area of the cheek, the fur is longer.

JAWS: Heavy.

CHIN: Strong and well developed.

EARS: Medium in length. Almost as wide at the base as tall. Modified to a rounded point at the tip; set as much to the side as into the top of the head.

EYES: Almost round, with a sweet expression. Set well apart, with the outer corner tilted *very* slightly upward. Blue in color—the deeper and more vivid the blue, the better.

BODY: Long and stocky. Females may be proportionately smaller than males.

LEGS: Medium in length and heavy.

PAWS: Large, round, and firm. Five toes in front, four behind.

TAIL: Medium in length, in pleasing proportion to the body.

COAT: Medium long to long, silken in texture, with heavy ruff around the neck, slightly curly on stomach. This fur is of such a texture that it does not mat.

COLOR EXCEPT GLOVES: *Body:* Even, with subtle shading when allowed. Strong contrast between body color and points. *Points except gloves:* Mask, ears, legs, and tail dense and clearly defined, all of the same shade. Mask covers entire face, including whisker pads, and is connected to ears by tracings. No ticking or white hair in points. *Golden mist:* Desirable in all point colors is the golden mist, a faint golden beige cast on the back and sides. This is somewhat deeper in the seal points, and may be absent in kittens.

GLOVES: *Front paws:* Front paws have white gloves ending in an even line across the paw at or between the second and third joints. (The third joint is where the paw bends when the cat is standing.) The upper limit of white should be the metacarpal (dew) pad. (The metacarpal pad is the highest-up little paw pad, located in the middle of the back of the front paw, above the third joint and just below the wrist bones.) Symmetry of the front gloves is desirable. *Back paws:* white glove covers all the toes, and may extend up somewhat higher than front gloves. Symme-

try of the rear gloves is desirable. *Laces:* The gloves on the back paws must extend up the back of the hock and are called laces in this area. Ideally, the laces end in a point or inverted V and extend one half to three quarters of the way up the hock. Lower or higher laces are acceptable but should not go beyond the hock. Symmetry of the two laces is desirable. *Paw pads:* Pink preferred, but dark spot(s) on paw pad(s) acceptable because of the two colors in pattern. *Note:* ideally, the front gloves match, the back gloves match, and the two laces match. Faultlessly gloved cats are a rare exception, and the Birman is to be judged in all its parts, as well as the gloves.

PENALIZE: White that does not run across the front paws in an even line. Persian- or Siamese-type head. Delicate bone structure. White shading on stomach and chest. Lack of laces on one or both back gloves. White beyond the metacarpal (dew) pad.

DISQUALIFY: Lack of white gloves on any paw. Kinked or abnormal tail. Crossed eyes. Incorrect number of toes. Areas of pure white in the points, if not connected to the gloves and part of or an extension of the gloves. Paw pads are part of the gloves. Areas of white connected to other areas of white by paw pads (of any color) are not cause for disqualification. Discrete areas of point color in the gloves, if not connected to point color of legs (exception, paw pads). White on back legs beyond the hock.

COLORS: A variety of colors in solid point, lynx point, and parti-color point.

ALLOWABLE BREEDING OUTCROSSES: none.

BOMBAY

By Patti DeWitt

Bombay

Imagine being in a jungle, when out of the corner of your eye you spot a beautiful black panther slinking into the underbrush. This, in miniature, could be the Bombay.

Physical Description

The Bombay's body is so solid and dense that you can see the muscles rippling as it grabs for a toy or runs across a room to retrieve a sparkle ball. The Bombay coat is like jet-black patent leather, so gleaming and shiny you can almost see your reflection. The eyes are gold to copper, the deeper the intensity of color the better, like a copper penny. This is why Bombays are called "the patent leather kids with the new-penny eyes."

These are medium-size, well-balanced cats, with males weighing an average of 8–10 pounds and females averaging 7–8 pounds, a surprising weight for their size. Although the Bombay is similar to the Burmese, its profile should not present a pugged or a snubbed look. The ideal Bombay should have a sweet facial expression and an unmistakable look of its own.

Personality

Bombays are wonderful companions and will sit on your lap hour after hour; they love to be around people. They will follow you wherever you go, changing rooms whenever you move. They want to be the center of attention and in the middle of everything. Forget trying to wrap presents with Bombays in the room; they will offer all the help you will ever need—and then some.

They are highly intelligent cats that love to play and are easy to train. All Bombays love sparkle balls and will fetch them for hours. They can be taught to fetch the ball, come back with it, drop it at your feet, and then sit in front of you. Your throwing the ball again is a reward for a job well done. They get along very well with dogs, children, and other cats, usually in that order. These are very personable cats, not at all shy. When the doorbell rings, they will usually be the first one at the door. Of course, they are convinced that everyone who visits is there for them alone.

This is neither an overly active breed nor an inactive breed. It is somewhere in the middle. Some Bombays can be quite talkative, while others are quiet. They love to sleep with their humans, some under the covers and others on top of them. Obviously, they are very affectionate cats. They enjoy rubbing their heads and faces on humans, and offering kisses as well. When you return home, your Bombay will be waiting for you at the door.

Bombays are inquisitive cats. Typically, they think everything hidden behind a kitchen or bathroom cabinet door is theirs for the taking. They may slip a paw underneath the door to open and remove whatever they feel is worthy of play. This usually includes toilet tissue, paper towels, and potatoes—yes, potatoes. What could be more fun to roll around the kitchen floor? A reflection of their great intelligence is their love of investigating everything and anything. You will not need to spend a fortune on toys, because a grocery sack or a soda box can entertain them for hours. Other sources of playful enjoyment are toys that are furry and feathery. They will protect their newfound "prey" by growling at those who try to take it away and then move it to a quieter spot, not wanting to share. Even kittens can be possessive and territorial.

They also adapt their schedules according to yours. If you work outside of the home, you will find that they will adjust their sleeping habits. By the time you get home from work, they will be wide awake and ready to entertain. If you want a breed that is affectionate, requires a lot of attention, and is smart and clever, then the Bombay is the cat for you.

Grooming Requirements

The Bombay is one of the easiest breeds to groom and bathe. Because these cats' coats are so short and satiny, there is very little shedding. If they are given a monthly bath, shedding is almost nonexistent. They have what is called a wash-and-wear coat. Use a quality cat shampoo and conditioner. After bathing, simply dry the cat with a towel that has been warmed up in the clothes dryer. If you are bathing the cat in the winter months, it is a good idea to place the cat in a carrier located in a warm room until its coat is dry. This avoids the cat's getting chilled. A rubber curry brush can be used to remove unwanted hair from the coat. Apply pressure with the brush as you run it through the coat. The hair will attach to the brush for easy removal. A curry brush is an important grooming tool for this breed. It can be purchased at cat shows or pet supply stores and through catalogs.

If you have acquired a cat you plan to show, you may need to do a common grooming procedure called *stripping the coat*. Not all Bombays require this, but it is helpful when the coat is heavier or thicker than usual. Stripping the coat pulls the heavier undercoat out and helps the coat to lay flat, giving it a sleeker appearance. To accomplish this, you will need a grooming tool called a stripping comb. This comb has the appearance of a small knife with a handle. The actual comb part has very small, razor-sharp teeth. There are several styles available; all should do a good job. Stripping is not a simple grooming technique. Before you strip the coat for the first time, get help from another Bombay owner or breeder.

Start clipping your kitten's nails at an early age. He can become quite resistant if you do not make this part of a weekly procedure.

Even more important than grooming is your cat's diet. Provide high-quality food for your pet. This is certain to enhance his health and coat. During the winter months, an oil supplement will help with any dander or dry-skin problems. You may also purchase a multi-vitamin and mineral supplement to add to the food or give orally.

The Bombay cat is very slow to mature into full development. Most breeders will keep their kittens until they are 16 weeks of age. Even at that age, it is difficult to know if that kitten will blossom into a show-quality cat. A ruffled coat can transform itself into a sleek and close-lying coat and weak eye color can develop into the beautiful copper eye color expected of the breed.

Origins and History

Nikki Horner, a serious breeder, created the Bombay as a breed in 1966 in Louisville, Kentucky, by mating a black American Shorthair with a sable Burmese. After many years of selective breeding, she developed a cat that was totally black with large copper eyes. The result of this process is a hybrid cat breed. Because of the Burmese muscularity and the coat's patent-leather sheen, Horner named these minipanthers Bombay, for the black leopard of India and the city of Bombay. The Bombays were accepted for registration by the CFA in 1970. The requirements for moving to Provisional status were met in May 1974. By May 1976, Bombays became eligible to compete in the Championship classes. The first Bombay to win at the national level did so in 1982.

Miscellanea

If you have purchased or plan on purchasing a Bombay that has not been spayed or neutered, you will need to know that these cats can be quite precocious when it comes to breeding and can reach sexual maturity as early as 6 months of age. Because of their early sexual maturity, it is suggested that you get your Bombay spayed or neutered between 6 and 8 months of age. Unneutered males and unspayed females can develop habits of marking (spraying) their territories with scented urine at an early age. Neutering and spaying at an early age should help eliminate this behavior. This does not apply to show cats or those that are part of a serious breeding program.

If you are planning to show your Bombay at cat shows, there are several things you can do to promote their show attitude. Go to cat shows and examine the toys being used by the judges. While your kitten is still young, use the same type of toys to play with him. Leave them around the house in order to make playing with them an enjoyable experience.

Handle your kitten in many different positions. Some kittens even enjoy being carried upside down. If you do not have children, bring children in from your neighborhood to handle the kittens. Create different noises in your house. Bear in mind that the sounds a cat hears at cat shows will be loud and very different from the sounds heard at home.

It can be helpful to work with your kitten on a small table or counter. This will simulate a judging table and may make your kitten or cat more at ease when being judged at a cat show. The kitten will need to get used to having his profile, bite, and head examined. It is important when the kitten is young to work with his head, eyes, and mouth. It is difficult to analyze the head if the cat will not allow the judge to touch his head. When carrying a Bombay to the show ring, carry it close to your side or out in front of your body. You want the cat to feel confident being carried in front, not to feel vulnerable. Judges will usually take the Bombay out of the judging cage and just place it on the table. Bombays do not like being held in a restrictive position or pinned to the judging table. They do a wonderful job of showing off their muscularity when going after a toy on the judge's table.

Bombays are also good travelers. If you are going to show your Bombay, which requires a great deal of traveling, it is a good idea to get him used to it at a young age. When traveling by car, make sure he is always kept in his carrier. It is much safer for the cat and for you if he is confined when the car is in motion. A number of accidents have occurred where the cat has been thrown outside of the vehicle and lost because it was not in a carrier inside the car.

The Bombay is a wonderfully intelligent, humorous, beautiful, and entertaining cat. Even though there are not many Bombay breeders and you find yourself on a waiting list for such a kitten, it will be worth the wait. These cats are lovable companions and make fine additions to any household.

POINT SCORE

HEAD AND EARS (25)

Roundness of head	7
Full face and proper profile	7
Ears	7
Chin	4

EYES (5)

Placement and shape	5

BODY (20)

Body	15
Tail	5

COAT (20)

Shortness	10
Texture	5
Close-lying	5

COLOR (30)

Body color	20
Eye color	10

GENERAL: The Bombay originated as a hybrid between the Burmese and the American Shorthair. With its je gleaming coat, gold-to-copper eyes facial expression, the an unmistakable look of its own. It natural breed but a genetic hybrid, with distinctive features that separate it from its foundation (parent) breeds. The Bombay is a medium-size cat, well balanced, friendly, alert, outgoing, and muscular, and has a surprising weight for its size. The body and tail should be of medium length. The head should be rounded, with medium-size, wide-set ears; a moderate nose "stop" that is visible (not a break); large, rounded, wide-set eyes; and an overall look of excellent proportions and carriage.

HEAD: The head should be pleasingly rounded with no sharp angles. The face should be full with considerable breadth between the eyes, blending gently into a broad, well-developed, moderately rounded muzzle that maintains the rounded contours of the head. In profile, there should be a moderate visible stop; however, it should not present a "pugged" or "snubbed" look. Moderate stop is to be considered not a break, but a slight indentation at the bridge of the nose between the eyes, thus providing a change of direction from the rounded head to the medium, rounded muzzle. The end of the nose is slightly rounded down, thus completing the roundness of the head.

EARS: The ears should be medium in size and set well apart on a rounded skull, alert, tilting slightly forward, and broad at the base and have slightly rounded tips.

CHIN: The chin should be firm, neither receding nor protruding, reflecting a proper bite.

EYES: Set far apart, with rounded aperture.

BODY: Medium in size, muscular in development, neither compact nor rangy. Allowance is to be made for larger size in males.

LEGS: In proportion to the body and tail.

PAWS: Round. Toes: five in front, four in back.

TAIL: Straight, medium in length; neither short nor "whippy."

COAT: Fine, short, satinlike texture; close-lying with a shimmering patent-leather sheen.

PENALIZE: Excessive cobbiness or ranginess.

DISQUALIFY: Kinked or abnormal tail. Lockets or spots. Incorrect number of toes. Nose leather or paw pads other than black. Green eyes. Improper bite. Extreme break that interferes with normal breathing and tearing of eyes.

COLOR: The mature specimen should be black to the roots. Kitten coats should darken and become more sleek with age. *Nose leather and paw pads:* Black. *Eye color:* Ranging from gold to copper; the greater the depth and brilliance, the better.

ALLOWABLE BREEDING OUTCROSSES: black American Shorthair, sable Burmese.

BRITISH SHORTHAIR
By Erin Vosburgh

British Shorthair

The British Shorthair, probably the oldest English breed of cat, traces its ancestry back to the domestic cat of Rome. Although it continues to gain in popularity, it is a comparatively rare cat in the United States. Although first known as the British Blue, owing to the breed's original color, its native country incorporated a wide variety of colors under the term British Shorthair in the 1950s. The CFA also recognizes the British Shorthair in many different colors and patterns.

Physical Description

The British Shorthair is a medium to large cat of compact build, powerful and well balanced. Taking years to mature, British Shorthairs often do not reach full size and development until the age of 3. Once having reached full maturity, British Shorthairs are a sight to see. With a full, broad chest, medium to short strong legs, rounded paws, and modified tail, these cats present a football-player physique. The British Shorthair has a massive round head that sits almost immediately on broad shoulders. Females are smaller than males but retain the overall roundness and bulk associated with the breed. Their ears are set far apart. Even though their ears do not appear to react, there is no doubt they catch every sound. The eyes are round and wide open, as befits a true predator.

Unfortunately there are many outdoor hazards and dangers for cats, creating the need for them to be diligently cared for indoors. Still, it is easy to see how a cat of this shape and form could withstand the rigors of the English countryside. Today's breeders zealously sustain the cats' overall health and stamina. One of the most appealing features is the Brit's built-in smile, which is caused by its round, prominent whisker pads. This smile was best displayed on the Cheshire Cat in Lewis Carroll's *Alice in Wonderland*, which was a tabby British Shorthair in the original illustration.

The British Shorthair coat is like no other—short and as dense as deep pile carpet. That coat is another factor that serves these cats well in English gardens during the winter. No other breed of cat has as dense a coat, with more hairs per square inch, as the British Shorthair does. Running your fingers through the coat is so pleasurable that breeders often extend this courtesy to onlookers, when politely asked. Inevitably, the eyes of those not familiar with the breed light up at the first touch. Though the short coat is luxurious to pet, it needs minimal care.

Personality

Living with British Shorthairs is relaxing. They are not overly active cats, which is why they are comfortable in apartments as well as houses. With true British reserve, they will wait for an invitation to join you at your side on a couch or chair. These cats are content to be with you and stare at you as you read, watch TV, or sew. Occasionally they will put a single paw onto your work to make sure you know they are still watching. British Shorthairs are the great supervisors. They watch everything and even follow you from room to room to make sure you adhere to your daily routine; they do not need to be underfoot to do this. Often British Shorthairs will be seen on a chair or ledge simply observing what is going on with the people in their world. Quiet cats, British Shorthairs do meow, but only now and then.

They are confident cats and do well with other pets. However, do not expect them to ignore small rodents and birds, even if you do have such animals as pets. They can adjust well to dogs and other cats, and it is not unusual for British Shorthairs to rise as leaders of the family hierarchy. Brits are great family pets because they are more than willing to spread their love and attention to everyone. They possess the gift of great patience and are excellent with children, belying their rugged looks. With a little adult cultivation, the relationship between a British Shorthair and a child is deep and long lasting. When too overwhelmed to continue participating in a child's activities, British Shorthairs will simply move away to a quiet, out-of-reach place where they can resume their role as household supervisor.

Grooming Requirements

Caring for British Shorthairs is not difficult. The coat requires only weekly brushing to catch any shedding. Of course, more extensive grooming is required for British Shorthairs presented at a cat show. A bath several days ahead of the exhibition ensures that a proper amount of oil returns to the coat, giving it a healthy body. Toenails are always clipped on exhibition cats, and most British Shorthairs accept this procedure with good grace. Nail clipping is a simple procedure every pet owner can learn from his or her cat's breeder, from a veterinarian, or from a professional groomer. These cats' ears are kept free of dirt and wax. A warm, damp, soft cloth can clean the easily reached areas; a veterinarian must clean within the deeper portion of the ears.

Origins and History

In 1871, the first properly organized cat show was held in London's Crystal Palace. Among the cats exhibited were the luxuriously coated Persians and the British Blues (early name for British Shorthairs), with their wonderfully dense coats, designed by nature as a defense against the cool, damp British climate. Also at this show, the Western world got its first glimpse of a rare Siamese. Harrison Weir, who organized this first modern cat show, was a great admirer of the British Shorthair. "The ordinary garden cat," he wrote, "has survived every kind of hardship. That he exists at all is a tribute to his strength of character and endurance." Mr. Jung, who was to become one of the first cat show judges, shared Mr. Weir's devotion to the short-haired British cats. He believed if these beautiful cats were thoughtfully bred, a race of cats with aristocratic pedigrees and the same inherent goodness and quality would be developed.

By 1910, no cat had done as well as the British Shorthair silver tabby male and his silver tabby sister. Their success as well as others like them caused quite a stir among fanciers. This created a great demand for cats of this color, many of which were exported to the United States. World War I was very tough for all species of pedigreed animals, and crossbreeding became necessary to reestablish populations and characteristics eliminated through wartime stress.

At this time, Persian cats were introduced to enhance the appearance of the British Shorthair, including Blue Persians with 60 years of color breeding behind them. This addition gave them a somewhat different look from other shorthair breeds. However, the breeders' goal was always to enhance the British Shorthair, and so attention was spent on the short-haired kittens of these matings. Through the war years, the introduction of Persians plus random-bred moggies (British English vernacular for nonpedigreed cats) was instrumental in reestablishing the British Shorthair as the wonderful specimen it is today. In this century, the British Shorthair is recognized and registered in various colors and patterns and is popular in every country that has pedigreed cat registration.

As previously mentioned, silver tabbies were imported in large numbers in the early twentieth century. Registrations of imported British Shorthairs continued in the United States as Domestic Shorthairs until the 1950s. At that time, U.S. cat associations began to recognize the British Blue as a distinct breed.

While Brits were just hitting the U.S. show bench, a British Shorthair from the United Kingdom was about to make history.

It was a British Shorthair, a blue male named Brynbuboo Little Monarch, that was the first adult of any breed to gain the title Grand Champion under the rules of the Governing Council of the Cat Fancy (GCCF, the pedigreed cat registrar in the United Kingdom). Virtually every British Shorthair today can track its ancestry back to this cat because of his use as stud and to the selling of his progeny.

Other imported colors of British Shorthairs continued to be registered as Domestic/American Shorthairs in the United States until a black female British, Manana Charmaine, was imported. She was registered and shown in another association as an American Shorthair. When she did substantial winning, other breeders complained that this was not an American Shorthair but rather a British Shorthair. This opened the eyes of other American fanciers to realize British Shorthairs came in many other colors besides blue. In the 1970s, CFA British Shorthair breeders concentrated on achieving Championship status for the breed. Breeders attended the CFA board meeting in Texas and were allowed to enter the process to gain championship status.

In 1980, over a century since the first cat show, the CFA granted the British Shorthair Championship status and a white female earned the first Grand Champion title. Since those early years, the number of National Winners (NWs) have grown, as have the number of Distinguished Merit (DM) cats. The DM title is the CFA's award given for producing cats that have contributed to their breed by producing Grand Champions. British Shorthair breeders are proud that their cats are basically the same worldwide. Cats of this breed, imported from as far afield as Great Britain, Australia, New Zealand, and the Netherlands, as well as those bred in the United States, have enjoyed great success at CFA shows. This includes the full range of solid, parti-color, and tabby British Shorthairs.

Miscellanea

The British kittens are large and vigorous at birth. Litters averaging four to five newborns are common, with the mothers giving birth easily. British Shorthair lines contain the two blood types identified in cats: A and B. A third very rare blood type, AB, has also been documented. It is important for new breeders to work closely with a mentor to help them understand the ramifications of differing blood types. By testing, being informed, and planning a breeding accordingly, breeders experience few problems with these blood types.

Although British Shorthair mothers are loving and attentive, they are still willing to spend time with their humans even while their kittens are young. The eyes of newborn kittens usually open in less than a week; the kittens show interest in solid foods as early as 3 weeks of age. At this stage, the kittens are very attached to their mother and will continue to seek her out for love and food as long as she allows it.

British Shorthair kittens put on weight fast, staying round but not fat through kittenhood. Their adolescent stage can be frustrating for the breeder/exhibitor because of their erratic growth spurts. They are at their worst as they enter the CFA Adult Classes at 8 months of age and require patience. Just like human teenagers, Brits must naturally progress during this gangly period. They mature slowly, not reaching their peak until about 5 years of age. Because the breed matures late, British Shorthairs tend to look good for many years and are long lived.

A mature British Shorthair in good health will have a well-padded, muscular body. However, care must be taken that this padding does not turn from muscle to excess fat. The British Shorthair must not be allowed to overeat; food intake of an adult Brit should be restricted to a sensible level. Exercise is encouraged. A fat British Shorthair is not a healthy British Shorthair. For your cat's sake, do not allow him to turn into a British Doorstop. Because Brits are more sturdy and massive, they are uncomfortable with their legs off the ground. Most British Shorthairs do not favor being picked up and carried around.

From the times of the Romans, British Shorthairs have populated the British Isles. These cats most likely developed from those early domestic cats, and perhaps crossed with the native wildcats. Though initially prized for their strength and hunting ability, they became the undisputed heirs to the fireside hearths and pleasant additions to the home as their personality, grace, and confidence were discovered. Today British Shorthairs reign supreme in their homeland and are gaining great popularity in the United States. Their patience, adaptability, confidence, ease of care, and strength make them highly valued as family companions today.

CFA SHOW STANDARD FOR THE BRITISH SHORTHAIR

POINT SCORE

HEAD (25)

Muzzle and chin	5
Skull	5
Ears	5
Neck	5
Eye shape	5

BODY (35)

Torso	20
Legs and paws	10
Tail	5

COAT (20)

Texture, length, and density	20

COLOR (20)

Eye color	5
Coat color	15

GENERAL: The British Shorthair is compact, well-balanced, and powerful, showing good depth of body; a full, broad chest; short to medium-length strong legs; rounded paws; and a tail thick at the base with a rounded tip. The head is round with good width between the ears; round cheeks; firm chin; medium ears; large, round, and well-opened eyes; and a medium broad nose. The coat is short and very dense. Females are less massive in all respects, with males having larger jowls. This breed is slow to mature.

HEAD: Round and massive. Round face with round underlying bone structure well set on a short, thick neck. The forehead should be rounded, with a slight flat plane on the top of the head. The forehead should not slope.

NOSE: Medium, broad. In profile there is a gentle dip.

CHIN: Firm, well developed in line with the nose and upper lip.

MUZZLE: Distinctive, well developed, with a definite stop beyond large, round whisker pads.

EARS: Ear set is important. Medium in size, broad at the base, rounded at the tips. Set far apart, fitting into (without distorting) the rounded contour of the head.

EYES: Large, round, well opened. Set wide apart and level.

BODY: Medium to large, well knit, and powerful. Level back and a deep, broad chest.

LEGS: Short to medium, well boned, and strong. In proportion to the body. Forelegs are straight.

PAWS: Round and firm. Toes: five in front and four behind.

TAIL: Medium length in proportion to the body, thicker at base, tapering slightly to a rounded tip.

COAT: Short, very dense, well bodied, resilient, and firm to the touch. Not double-coated or woolly.

COLOR: For cats with special markings: 5 points for coat color and 10 points for markings. Shadow tabby markings in solid color, smoke, shaded, shaded golden, bicolor, or calico kittens are not a fault.

PENALIZE: Definite nose stop. Overlong or light undercoat. Soft coat. Rangy body. Weak chin.

DISQUALIFY: Incorrect eye color, green rims in adults. Tail defects. Long or fluffy coat. Incorrect number of toes. Locket or button. Improper color or pigment in nose leather and/or paw pads in part or total. Any evidence of illness or poor health. Any evidence of wryness of jaw, poor dentition (arrangement of teeth), or malocclusion. Evidence of hybridization resulting in the colors chocolate, lavender, the Himalayan pattern, or these combinations with white.

COLORS: A wide array of colors in the solid, shaded, smoke, tabby, parti-color and bicolor patterns.

ALLOWABLE BREEDING OUTCROSSES: none.

BURMESE
By Erika Graf-Webster

Burmese (sable)

Burmese (dilute)

Bring a Burmese into your house, and you have brought an extra dollop of joy and love into your life. While a rich, glossy brown coat and big gold eyes might be the first things that attract you to the breed, it is the Burmese personality that gets you hooked for life. Simply put, Burmese have hearts brimming with love, which they are more than willing to lavish on their human family.

Physical Description

The word that comes to mind when looking at the Burmese is *round*. Picture a small to medium-size cat with large, round gold eyes on a round head, sitting on a compact, rounded body. The facial expression of a Burmese is sweet and innocent. It has been said that when the Burmese looks at you, you feel as if it is looking into your soul.

The body of the Burmese is akin to that of a little bulldog. There is nothing dainty about a Burmese; it is strong and muscular, with a broad chest. The body feels hard like that of an athlete. What consistently surprises people is how heavy Burmese are, given their relatively small size. There is a lot of muscle and power packed into that small frame.

This little bundle is clothed in a shiny, close-lying coat that feels like satin. The Burmese coat comes in four colors: sable, champagne, blue, and platinum. Sable is the most common of the four and is a deep chocolate brown color. Burmese compete in CFA cat shows in two official divisions, the Sable Division and the Dilute Division, the latter of which includes the remaining three colors, champagne, blue, and platinum.

Personality

Burmese are the ultimate companion cats. They love being with people, playing with them, and keeping them entertained. They crave close physical contact and are referred to by some breeders as Velcro cats. They abhor an empty lap, follow their humans from room to room, and sleep in bed with them, preferably under the covers and cuddled as close as possible. At play, they will turn around to see if their humans are watching and being entertained by their crazy antics.

The love of a Burmese is not based on blind devotion, however. These are very intelligent cats, and they have strong personalities, often showing considerable stubbornness. Sometimes situations turn into battles of wills between humans and their cats. You can tell them 20 times that they must get off the counter, but they will try it for the twenty-first time just to see if they can get away with it. Burmese will, however, become well-behaved members of the household once they fully understand the rules. At times, though, it is hard to tell who has trained whom, especially when the cat manages to get its human to retrieve its toys and to bring it food. A

scratching post should always be available so that these cats can express the stretching and scratching behavior common to all cats.

Both males and females are wonderfully affectionate pets, but there is an interesting difference between them. Males generally do not show a preference for any one member of the family, but females often form a strong bond with a specific person. Males may act as though they are your best buddy, while females tend to be take-charge individuals. It is a true delight to have one of each in the same house to enjoy these charming differences.

Burmese love to be handled. They like being carried around, either in the crook of their human's arm or on their human's shoulder. Some Burmese are definitely shoulder cats, so it is important to warn unsuspecting visitors that a Burmese can easily jump up to someone's shoulder from the floor.

Grooming Requirements

Burmese are low-maintenance cats that do not require combing or bathing or any unusual handling. The coat is kept in condition by simply stroking it with your hand and occasionally with a rubber brush, just to remove dead hairs. The rubber brush is recommended in late spring, when all cats shed their winter coats.

Origins and History

The Burmese breed as we know it today was developed in the United States from a single cat, Wong Mau, who in 1930 was brought from Asia to New Orleans by a sailor and given to a doctor in San Francisco. Wong Mau was described as "a rather small cat, fine boned, but with a more compact body than that of a Siamese, with shorter tail, a rounded, short-muzzled head, with greater width between rounded eyes." Her color was described as walnut brown, with darker brown points. Selective breeding later demonstrated that Wong Mau herself was a hybrid—that is a Burmese–Siamese cross (just like today's Tonkinese breed). Her dark brown kittens bred true, however, producing only dark brown kittens and thus established the Burmese breed.

Early Burmese in the late 1930s and early 1940s caused quite a stir in the show circuit and gained considerable popularity. A great demand for Burmese kittens developed. Breeders continued to use Siamese to increase the very limited breeding stock, thereby producing a large number of hybrids. Eventually, the CFA put a stop to this practice and suspended registration of Burmese in 1947. The CFA ruled that there had to be three generations of pure Burmese (not hybrids) in the pedigreed for it to be registered as Burmese. This was quite disheartening to the breeders because of the great difficulty in maintaining breeding stock. However, serious breeders stopped using the hybrids and concentrated on breeding the type of cat that made the Burmese unique. Achieving the three-generation "pure" pedigreed was slow, but finally accomplished for three cats in 1956. By late 1957, there were sufficient numbers and the CFA resumed registration of the Burmese.

In 1958, the newly formed United Burmese Cat Fanciers set a goal of developing a single standard for Burmese that would be accepted by all the cat fancy organizations. The standard was adopted by the CFA in 1959, and, except for some refinement of wording and an addition to the "Penalize" section, has stood unchanged since then, maintaining the vision of the Burmese as a "round" cat throughout the years.

Burmese were highly successful in the show ring from the outset, reaching the peak of their popularity in the 1970s, when they were the third most popular breed behind Persians and Siamese. For a breed that had started in the United States with one cat in 1930, the Burmese have come a long way. They have become solidly established as a highly popular and successful member of the cat fancy.

Miscellanea

New owners of Burmese need to be aware of one aspect of their personality: They resist strong restraint. A Burmese will resent being held with force in order to do something possibly unpleasant, such as a trip to the veterinary clinic. The least amount of restraint necessary is always the best approach with this breed. It is also a good idea to get a Burmese used to such events as getting nails clipped or being transported in a cat carrier. These and other activities possibly not to their liking should be introduced in short spurts as soon as possible, even if the cat is still a kitten.

Because Burmese often form a strong attachment to their environment as well as to their human family, moving to a new house may require a period of adjustment, until they feel as comfortable in their new environment as they were in the previous home. This usually takes 1–3 weeks.

Burmese should not be confined and separated from human contact for more than a few hours at a time. They crave human contact, and if they are denied it for long periods, they will become withdrawn and may even lose their affectionate personality. Breeders recommend that people who work full time and are away from the house for several hours every day get a pair of kittens or start with an adult Burmese. It is easier and more fun to have two Burmese than one. They will not only keep each other company but will also provide endless entertainment for their humans through their play.

The most striking aspect of these cats is how much they love their human family. Burmese are generally acknowledged as the most affectionate of all the cat breeds. Their personality is maintained by offering close human contact in a loving home.

When selecting a pet kitten, bear in mind that Burmese are slow to mature, which makes them look smaller for their age than most other breeds. A Burmese should be between 3 and 4 months old before going to a new home as a pet and should weigh approximately 3 pounds. Because of their slow maturation, kittens younger than 3 months are simply not physically and socially mature enough to leave their mothers.

Do not be concerned if a Burmese kitten has a slight discharge from its eyes. Because Burmese eyes are very large and somewhat protruding, blinking generates a clear discharge as a mechanism for clearing the large surface. Sometimes the discharge hardens into a small bit of brown matter at the inner corner of the eye. Although this is normal and not harmful, it is best to gently remove it with a tissue. A small, clear discharge is normal, but a white or yellow discharge is not and should be looked at by a veterinarian.

Burmese kittens do not reach their full adult color until they are approximately 1 year old. Sable brown kittens, for example, are medium beige when they are born. They will darken to a light to medium brown by 3 or 4 months of age but are still a long way from the rich, dark chocolate adult color. The dilute colors follow a similar darkening process.

Finding an adult Burmese for your home is usually easy because many breeders retire their breeding and show cats. A beautiful adult makes a great pet, is usually less expensive than a kitten, and has many years ahead to be a happy member of a new household.

Burmese live long lives and age gracefully. It is almost impossible to tell whether an adult is 4 or 12 years old, because these cats appear to be in their prime for a long time. Most Burmese develop white whiskers in the later years, but this is often the only indication of their advancing age. Some of the most famous show winners and prolific studs have lived to be 18 and 19 years old. They usually enjoy good health until the end of their lives, spending just a few months at the end with reduced physical capabilities. Older Burmese are usually very sweet and very needy of their people and engender great dedication and affection from their owners.

What one receives from a Burmese is love—lots of it—but without submissiveness. Living with a Burmese is like living with a small person who has a mind of her own but whose love for you is boundless. Burmese are cats to be cherished, and they give joy to all who share their lives with these captivating creatures.

CFA SHOW STANDARD FOR THE BURMESE

POINT SCORE

HEAD, EARS, AND EYES (30)

Roundness of head	7
Breadth between eyes and full face	6
Proper profile (includes chin)	6
Ear set, placement, and size	6
Eye placement and shape	5

BODY, LEGS, FEET, AND TAIL (30)

Torso	15
Muscle tone	5
Legs and feet	5
Tail	5

COAT (10)	
Short	4
Texture	4
Close-lying	2

COLOR (30)	
Body color	25
Eye color	5

GENERAL: The overall impression of the ideal Burmese would be a cat of medium size with substantial bone structure, good muscular development, and a surprising weight for its size. This, together with a rounded head, expressive eyes, and a sweet expression, presents a totally distinctive cat that is comparable to no other breed. Perfect physical condition, with excellent muscle tone. There should be no evidence of obesity, paunchiness, weakness, or apathy.

HEAD, EARS, AND EYES: Head pleasingly rounded without flat planes, whether viewed from the front or side. The face is full, with considerable breadth between the eyes, and blends gently into a broad, well-developed, short muzzle that maintains the rounded contours of the head. In profile, there is a visible nose break. The chin is firmly rounded, reflecting a proper bite. The head sits on a well-developed neck. The ears are medium in size, set well apart, broad at the base, and rounded at the tips. Tilting slightly forward, the ears contribute to an alert appearance. The eyes are large, set far apart, with rounded aperture.

BODY: Medium in size, muscular in development, and presenting a compact appearance. Allowance to be made for larger size in males. An ample, rounded chest, with back level from shoulder to tail.

LEGS: Well proportioned to body.

PAWS: Round. Toes: five in front and four behind.

TAIL: Straight, medium in length.

COAT: Fine, glossy, satinlike texture; short and very close-lying.

PENALIZE: Distinct barring on either the front or rear outer legs. Trace (faint) barring permitted in kittens and young adults. Elongated muzzle with severe narrowing, resulting in a wedge-shaped head that detracts from the rounded contours of the head. Green eyes.

DISQUALIFY: Kinked or abnormal tail, lockets or spots. Blue eyes. Crossed eyes. Incorrect nose leather or paw pad color. Malocclusion of the jaw that results in a severe underbite or overbite that visually prohibits the described profile and/or malformation that results in protruding teeth or a wry face or jaw. Distinct barring on the torso. Any color other than the four accepted colors of sable, champagne, blue, and platinum.

COLORS: Sable, blue, champagne, platinum.

ALLOWABLE BREEDING OUTCROSSES: none.

CHARTREUX

By Jill J. Rasmussen

Chartreux

Old as antiquity, the robust and muscular French Chartreux (pronounced "Shar-*trew*") is built for survival. Its physical appearance still reflects its ancient origin in the harsh arid cold of mountainous Asia Minor.

Physical Description

Its large body mass conserves heat, aided by a dense woolly coat that repels dew and seasonal weather. Small, fur-covered appendages—ears, legs, and tail—prevent heat loss and resist frostbite. Its large belly promotes efficient food consumption and easy storage as body fat. Broad chest, a bull neck, and powerful shoulders propelled by narrow hips with long, well-muscled hind legs allow the Chartreux to be an expert climber, capable of bounding effortlessly after prey through rugged, rocky terrain. This powerhouse can walk quite silently. Medium-size ears set upright, close together, and high on the head easily pinpoint prey. Large, heavily muscled jaws grip prey with precision. Its large size, hunting prowess, and fearlessness make the Chartreux a superb predator.

Personality

The Chartreux remains a master at adaptation. Now pampered and kept strictly indoors as a beloved pet, the Chartreux is well behaved, self-sufficient, and quiet, rarely meowing. The modern-day Chartreux, still very much aware of its own strength, is a gentle giant.

In the absence of prey, the Chartreux expends its great energy and power in hearty play and retains its joie de vivre into old age. Kittens and adolescents, even at 2–3 years of age, are highly active; mature adults have short bursts of energy lasting 15-30 minutes, when they gallop about madly. They love to play; favorite games include Fetch, Chase, and Tag. They are highly inventive and truly effective in subtly training their owners.

Despite their taciturn nature, Chartreux are highly communicative. Very active tails, ear movements, ever-changing facial expressions, and a vast repertoire of trills, chirps, and coos speak volumes to the observant owner.

Males can be twice the size of females. However, females will not be bullied; while he would not think of throwing his weight around, she might. Both sexes, when neutered and spayed, make excellent companions for the individual or the family. They adapt well to being single pets as well as to being part of a multipet household. They are also remarkably friendly toward other creatures—particularly dogs.

Chartreux pick a favorite person within the household but are not possessive. The Chartreux makes the choice and shows special devotion toward its favorite. The cat may prefer this person's company, sleep on his or her bed, follow him or her throughout the house, or play its most favorite games only with the chosen one. While others in the household are treated with affection and politeness, favoritism will be evident to all. For this reason, families should not get a Chartreux for a specific child; the cat might just choose a sibling or parent instead.

This loyalty is also noticeable in its protective, nonaggressive attitude toward the favored person and cautiousness toward strangers. A Chartreux may prefer to observe strangers while safely hidden beneath furniture or peering out from the doorway of the next room. With familiarity and maturity, however, the cat may change from seeming shy to becoming an official greeter.

Most Chartreux do not like to be carried around, preferring to have at least their back legs firmly on the ground. Instead, Chartreux tag along everywhere, attentively watching whatever is going on and occasionally asking for an invitation to participate.

Individual personalities vary to a degree. Some Chartreux are more sociable and outgoing than others by nature. Some Chartreux insist on sitting in your lap, while others may prefer to sit nearby. When selecting a Chartreux, discuss your expectations and household situations with breeders, who can then help to match these with an individual Chartreux kitten, adolescent, or adult whose personality is best suited.

An amusing legend has evolved: It is said that like monks, Chartreux cats took a vow of silence. However, when these cats do choose to vocalize, it is often with soft, breathy whispers or musical trills, chirps, and coos. Some Chartreux pose as if praying, sitting with front paws raised together, gazing heavenward.

Grooming Requirements

Chartreux are easy to care for and have few grooming requirements. Combing during spring and fall sheds is highly recommended, as a mature Chartreux develops an extraordinarily thick undercoat that can mat on the flanks. Use a metal medium- or coarse-toothed comb or a shedding comb. Brushes tend to pull out too much undercoat, leaving the coat with a spiky look. Combing helps prevent hairballs and reduces the amount of downy hair floating throughout the house.

Bathing a Chartreux is not usually necessary for the pet. But show cats need to be bathed a couple of days before a show to allow the natural oils to redistribute and to allow the coat to have a woolly texture. Use a pH-balanced shampoo for cats that is tearless and hypoallergenic. Try texturizing shampoo for double-coated breeds and shampoo with whiteners or brighteners. Experiment with different brands to find the right ones for your cat. Avoid conditioners, as they tend to flatten the coat, which is naturally oily.

The most critical step in bathing a Chartreux is getting it wet down to the skin; the coat is highly water repellent. Hold a spray nozzle close to the skin and aim it against the lie of the hair; then move the spray nozzle slowly over the entire cat. Shampoo twice, with a good rinse in between. After the final shampoo, rinse extremely well to make sure all soap is removed from the thick undercoat. Blow-drying is desirable because it adds loft to the coat and hastens drying.

Origins and History

The history of the Chartreux is somewhat cloudy. How the breed came to France is uncertain, although historical documents offer several explanations. One story is that returning crusaders might have brought back these blue-gray cats as gifts to monks of the Carthusians or Chartreux contemplative order founded in France, whose metallurgical expertise had provided swords for the conquests. According to legend, Chartreux cats kept by such monks on the Mediterranean islands, such as Cyprus and

Malta, would venture out of the monasteries in the morning and into the countryside to kill poisonous serpents but not consume them. In the evening, when the monks rang the bells, the cats would return to the monasteries for their evening dinner. Monasteries on the continent might have valued the Chartreux for its ability to control large, aggressive, and plague-carrying rats. Medieval institutions also might have valued them for ridding archives and libraries of gnawing rodents.

The Chartreux has survived into modern times largely because of the efforts of two sisters whose family moved in 1926 to Belle Ile off the stormy French coast. They noticed a colony of blue cats on the island that matched the Chartreux cats described by the eighteenth-century French naturalist, Buffon, whose works they had studied in horticulture school. The sisters began the first recorded selective breeding of Chartreux in 1928 and continued breeding Chartreux for 60 years.

Other Chartreux breeders had parallel breeding programs under way in Paris and in the French interior (Massif Central), using "natural Chartreux," or blue-gray cats living in the countryside.

World War II left registries of pedigreed animals in shambles. Certain breeders began crossing the few surviving Chartreux with the more numerous and readily available British Blues (the old term for what is now a British Shorthair with a blue coat). Without a concentrated effort to select against undesirable influences from the British Blues, the Chartreux began losing its distinctiveness.

In 1970, most European cat registries assimilated the Chartreux with the British Blue, and both were registered as the same breed, causing great confusion. Fortunately, some Chartreux breeders were fiercely committed to preserving the original Chartreux type and coat.

Thanks to their efforts, most registries separated the Chartreux from the British Blue in 1977 and reinstated the original Chartreux standard.

About the same time Chartreux and British Blues were being assimilated in Europe, a woman from California, having read about these legendary cats and being unable to locate any in North America, began her quest to bring Chartreux to the United States and to interest other breeders in them. Between 1970 and 1976, a total of 12 Chartreux were imported from France and Belgium. About half of these imports formed the foundation of the North American Chartreux population. Much to the credit of the early breeders and to the inherent good health of the Chartreux, the breed continues to be remarkably sound and robust.

Aware of European hybrids, North American breeders vowed to preserve the Chartreux: Theirs would be a breeding population geographically removed and carefully protected from the hybridization pressures in Europe. Breeders set up rules governing importation, registration, and breeding of Chartreux and adopted a breed standard based on the French one.

The CFA accepted the Chartreux for registration as a natural breed in October 1979. Provisional status was granted in 1986. Advancement to full championship status became effective May 1, 1987. While there are relatively few Chartreux, the breed has steadily increased in popularity both as a pet and for show. In little more than a decade, many Chartreux had achieved the ranks of National and Regional Winners, and several sires and dams had earned coveted Distinguished Merit titles.

Miscellanea

Diet management is an important aspect of the look as well as the health of the cat. Because this breed becomes obese very easily, it is best to measure food rather than to feed freely. Using a "light" cat food may be a good option for maintaining an appropriate weight. Taking weight off a Chartreux takes patience, time, and a special diet designed for weight reduction. Fasting is very dangerous for cats and should never be used for weight control.

Chartreux are named according to the French convention of using the letter of the alphabet assigned to a given year. For example, kittens born during calendar year 2005 have names beginning with the letter *A*; in 2006, *B*; in 2007, *C*; and so on. The letters *K*, *Q*, *W*, *X*, *Y*, *Z* are not used, so letters repeat every 20 years. As a result, fanciers can tell the age of a Chartreux simply by knowing its name.

★ ★ ★

The French Chartreux is one of the oldest natural breeds in the world and is by far the most primitive of the Old World "Blues." Its woolly blue coat with iridescent sheen and a strikingly unbalanced appearance are unique to the breed. Its personality is equally distinct, giving the overall impression of great dignity, patience, discretion, and stability. As an early U.S. breeder observed, "It is only in play that the Chartreux appears the clown, having perhaps the best humor in the cat world." The Chartreux, a master at survival, has finally secured its place in our homes and won over our hearts with its general good nature and politeness. It is truly a treasure, a living legend.

CFA SHOW STANDARD FOR THE CHARTREUX

POINT SCORE

HEAD (35)

Shape and size	6
Profile/nose	5
Muzzle	5
Ear shape and size	5
Ear placement	5
Eye shape and size	5
Neck	4

BODY (30)

Shape and size	8
Legs and feet	8
Boning	5
Musculature	5
Tail	4

COAT (20)

Texture	15
Length	5

COLOR (15)

Coat color	10
Eye color	5

GENERAL: The Chartreux is a sturdy, short-haired French breed coveted since antiquity for its hunting prowess and its dense, water-repellent fur. Its husky, robust type is sometimes termed primitive, neither cobby nor classic. Though amply built, Chartreux are extremely supple and agile cats; they are refined, never coarse or clumsy. Males are much larger than females and slower to mature. Coat texture, coat color, and eye color are affected by sex, age, and natural factors and should not be penalized. The qualities of strength, intelligence and amenability, which have enabled the Chartreux to survive the centuries unaided, should be evident in all exhibition animals and preserved through careful selection.

HEAD AND NECK: Rounded and broad but not a sphere. Powerful jaw; full cheeks, with mature males having larger jowls. High, softly contoured forehead; nose straight and of medium length/width, with a slight stop at eye level. Muzzle comparatively small, narrow, and tapered, with slight pads. Sweet, smiling expression. Neck short and heavyset.

EARS: Medium in height and width; set high on the head; very erect posture.

EYES: Rounded and open; alert and expressive. Color range is copper to gold; a clear, deep, brilliant orange is preferred.

BODY AND TAIL: Robust physique; medium-long, with broad shoulders and deep chest. Strong boning; muscle mass is solid and dense. Females are medium; males are large. Tail of moderate length; heavy at base, tapering to oval tip. Lively and flexible.

LEGS AND FEET: Legs comparatively short and fine-boned, straight, and sturdy. Feet are round and medium in size (may appear almost dainty compared to body mass).

COAT: Medium-short and slightly woolly in texture (should break like a sheepskin at neck and flanks). Resilient undercoat; longer, protective topcoat. *Note:* Degree of woolliness depends on age, sex, and habitat, with mature males exhibiting the heaviest coats. Silkier, thinner coat permitted on females and cats under 2 years of age.

PENALIZE: Severe nose break; snubbed or upturned nose; broad, heavy muzzle; palpable tail defect; eyes too close together, giving angry look.

DISQUALIFY: White locket, visible tail kink, green eyes; any signs of lameness in the hindquarters.

COLOR: Any shade of blue-gray from ash to slate; tips lightly brushed with silver. Emphasis on color clarity and uniformity rather than shade. Preferred tone is a bright, unblemished blue with an overall iridescent sheen. Nose leather is slate gray; lips are blue; paw pads are rose-taupe. Allowance made for ghost barring in kittens and for tail rings in juveniles under 2 years of age.

ALLOWABLE BREEDING OUTCROSSES: none.

COLORPOINT SHORTHAIR

By Bernard W. Hartman

Colorpoint Shorthair

Picture an active, elegant breed with basically two speeds—fast and off. Extremely inquisitive, Colorpoint Shorthairs will get into almost anything at least once at any level, a testament to their athleticism and highly developed intelligence. They are loyal to their human companions, and have in fact been called the most doglike cats. These cats are vocal, insistent, and totally endearing in their ability to communicate. Sound familiar? With very good reason, Colorpoint Shorthairs evoke qualities, both visual and temperamental, of their closest relatives, the Siamese.

Physical Description

After World War II, breeders on both sides of the Atlantic considered the possibilities of an expanded color palette to the accepted four Siamese colors: seal point, chocolate point, blue point, and lilac point. A color gene responsible for the color red (the O gene) not found in the Siamese in its native land was readily available in both England and the United States, and experimental breeding with this color commenced. What resulted was a thoroughly modern incarnation of a Siamese-type cat, a new breed with tortie point girls (points with red and black) and their typical joie de vivre and vibrant red point boys spicing the show scene in both countries. First accepted for CFA registration in the late 1950s, Colorpoint Shorthairs did not take part in CFA championship competition until the 1964 show season.

Reverently known to many as the color-pointed Siamese, today's Colorpoint Shorthairs are identical in structure to their Siamese first cousins, yet they've dressed to kill in 16 colors. Breeders did not stop with that red (O) gene, either. The impetus to stripe the points in assorted colors came from England. Called tabby point in that country, the pattern immigrated via breeders to the United States, where it was called lynx point. What grew from one color in 1964 is today a variety of 16 colors in three major classes: solid points (red and cream points), lynx points (red, cream, seal, chocolate, blue, and lilac lynx points and their parti-color derivatives), and the parti-colors (seal tortoiseshell, chocolate tortoiseshell, blue-cream, and lilac-cream points). For a real understanding of how color genetics operates in the feline, consult Chapter 6, "Identifying Coat Colors and Patterns in the Domestic Cat."

From the basic description of the ideal Colorpoint Shorthair, we build on a medium-size cat with the musculature of an athlete. *Svelte* is a word surviving the years to describe this beautiful cat that has fine bones and long limbs and stands tall to reach for any and all of the many items that pique their curiosity. Like the Siamese, the Colorpoint should have a long, smooth head resembling a fine wedge, and large, wide-placed ears that flow into the top of the wedge created by the head. From the side, the profile should be straight from the tip of the nose to the forehead. The graceful body starts with a long, slender neck connected to a tubular, muscled body. Not skinny, the body should be the same width and depth from the shoulders to the hips when viewed from any angle. Completing this elegant body is a long, whippy tail that when viewed overall, is the single element with the most point color on the body of the Colorpoint Shorthair.

Endlessly deep blue eyes are part of this breed's allure. Almond-shaped and flowing into the wedge-shaped head, the eyes simply dazzle onlookers and add to the regal air of elegance. Some of the colors in the Colorpoint Shorthair even make the expressive eyes appear to be set off by eyeliner. The eyes provide one of the most significant displays of emotion. When open wide, they express playfulness and curiosity; when closed, they demonstrate the affection and trust this cat has for the attention it demands at all levels.

The ideal coat is short and silky and lies close to the body, although on the red and cream points, their white coats tend to be slightly longer in length but should still lie close. Most kittens have very clear coats, meaning that the color of the points will not show through, but as the kitten ages some shading does come through on the main coats. The key is that this shading is much lighter in younger cats, with darker color in the points on the head, feet, and tail. Maturity will normally bring darker shading, as in the Siamese, throughout the entire body in the color and pattern of the points. Point color is found on the extremities, or those areas that are colder than the rest of the body of the cat, so the degree of color on the points is a function not only of genetics but also can be environmental.

Personality

The active and busy Colorpoint Shorthair is an exceptionally athletic and agile cat and not for those who want a docile couch potato. Of course, toys are always good—at least for the first 5 minutes, until this cat has figured out all the workings. Put an empty, open box down on the floor and it becomes an unexplored cave beckoning the spelunker within every curious Colorpoint. A crumpled piece of paper becomes a soccer ball to be played with incessantly until it joins all the others under the refrigerator. Teaching a Colorpoint to fetch is not uncommon, but people have even been able to train their Colorpoints to shake paws with or high-five their human companions. An adoptee of Colorpoint Shorthair kittens told a breeder how he and his wife spent a small fortune in toys and scratching posts, yet their kitten would dash across the house to retrieve a piece of paper in the process of being crumpled. He confided that he wished his kids had as much natural talent at soccer as his kitten. A joy to watch and an even greater joy to have in one's life, the graceful and playful Colorpoint Shorthair is an endearing variation of the renowned Siamese.

This cat expects to have the run of your house or apartment and will hang out wherever you happen to be, in whatever position gives him the best view. A floor-to-ceiling cat tree adds immeasurably to your cat's pleasure and your own entertainment watching him. Of course, the best gift you can give a Colorpoint Shorthair is your time and attention, to be repaid to you with 100% devotion.

Grooming Requirements

Grooming for either pet or show-quality Colorpoint Shorthairs is minimal. At home, baths are infrequent, as most of these cats continually groom themselves. (If a bath before a show seems desirable, be sure to use a gentle shampoo and give the bath a few days prior to the show so that natural oils can return to the coat.) An occasional brushing with a rubber brush to remove dead hair and a nice pedicure are all that is required. At the show, grooming is still not a huge chore. A good brushing with a quality product to help the hair lay down at the beginning of the day, combined with the use of a chamois and a product to give the hair a silky feel before showtime will do just fine. Most Colorpoint exhibitor do take the time to trim the cats' ear hair with blunt scissors to give the ears a cleaner, larger appearance, and cleaning the cats' eyes is a must before putting in an appearance in the ring.

Origins and History

For the first 30-plus years, Colorpoint Shorthairs were often ignored in favor of their Siamese cousins. A more recent concentration on the breed has resulted in the garnering of awards in record-setting numbers. During the first 30 years, Colorpoints achieved only two National Wins and two Distinguished Merit awards. The combined number of awards in these categories has more than doubled since 1994.

Some of the world's best Siamese catteries maintain Colorpoint Shorthairs in their programs. The CFA still allows the use of Siamese in Colorpoint breeding programs because the gene pool is still relatively small in the Colorpoint Shorthair programs, and because they closely resemble their Siamese cousins except in color. All felines born with a Colorpoint Shorthair parent are considered Colorpoints in the CFA registry, including some kittens that are Siamese colors. This is because the CFA's registry rules require that cats registered as Siamese have only Siamese in the cat's pedigreed (background).

Miscellanea

One of the interesting aspects of watching Colorpoint Shorthairs in a cat show is how well behaved they are while being carried to a judging ring and while being handled by the judge in the ring. Many choose to ride on their handler's shoulder, watching the crowd as they pass. They can range from shy to playful in outlook, and they often get more outgoing as time in the ring passes.

Colorpoint Shorthairs are wonderful for both the pet owner and the cat-show enthusiast. They show intelligence, love, and devotion, and their activity always has a purpose. And as members of a breed with a growing number of fans, more and more of these cats will enjoy not only greater popularity in the show ring but also the heightened visibility that winning multiple awards brings.

POINT SCORE

HEAD (20)

Long, flat profile	6
Wedge, fine muzzle, size	5
Ears	4
Chin	3
Width between eyes	2

EYES (10)

Shape, size, slant, and placement	10

BODY (30)

Structure and size, including neck	12
Muscle tone	10
Legs and feet	5
Tail	3

COAT

COAT	10

COLOR (30)

Body color	10
Point color (matching points of dense color, proper foot pads and nose leather)	10
Eye color	10

GENERAL: The Colorpoint Shorthair is a medium-size, svelte, refined cat with long, tapering lines, very lithe but muscular. Males may be proportionately larger. The ideal is a cat with type identical to that of the Siamese, but with its own distinct colors. While the color differences set it apart as a unique breed, the purpose of the hybridization was to establish cats identical in type to the Siamese but with separate colors. The Colorpoint Shorthair standard reflects this objective and preserves it's unique colors.

HEAD: Long, tapering wedge. Medium in size, in good proportion to body. The total wedge starts at the nose and flares out in straight lines to the tips of the ears, forming a triangle, with no break at the whiskers. No less than the width of an eye between the eyes. When the whiskers are smoothed back, the underlying bone structure is apparent. Allowance must be made for jowls in the stud cat.

SKULL: Flat. In profile, a long, straight line is seen from the top of the head to the tip of the nose. No bulge over eyes. No dip in nose.

NECK: Long and slender.

NOSE: Long and straight. A continuation of the forehead with no break.

MUZZLE: Fine, wedge-shaped.

EARS: Strikingly large, pointed, wide at base, continuing the lines of the wedge.

EYES: Vivid blue; no other shades or colors allowed. Almond-shaped. Medium size. Neither protruding nor recessed. Slanted toward the nose in harmony with lines of wedge and ears. Uncrossed.

CHIN AND JAW: Medium in size. Tip of chin lines up with tip of nose in the same vertical plane. Neither receding nor excessively massive.

BODY: Medium size. Graceful, long, and svelte. A distinctive combination of fine bones and firm muscles. Shoulders and hips continue same sleek lines of tubular body. Hips never wider than shoulders. Abdomen tight.

LEGS: Long and slim. Hind legs higher than front. In good proportion to body.

PAWS: Dainty, small, and oval. Toes: five in front and four behind.

TAIL: Long, thin, tapering to a fine point.

COAT: Short, fine textured, glossy. Lying close to body.

CONDITION: Excellent physical condition. Eyes clear. Muscular, strong, and lithe. Neither flabby nor bony. Not fat.

COLOR: *Body:* Subtle shading is permissible, but clear color is preferable. Allowance should be made for darker color in older cats, as Colorpoint Shorthairs generally darken with age, but there must be definite contrast between body color and points. *Points:* Mask, ears, feet, legs, and tail dense and clearly defined. All of the same shade. Mask covers entire face, including whisker pads, and is connected to ears by tracings. Mask should not extend over the top of the head. No white hairs in points.

PENALIZE: Pigmentation of nose leather and/or paw pads that is not consistent with the cat's particular color description. Palpable and/or visible protrusion of the cartilage at the end of the sternum.

DISQUALIFY: Any evidence of illness or poor health. Weak hind legs. Mouth breathing due to nasal obstruction or poor occlusion. Emaciation. Visible kink. Eyes other than blue. White toes and/or feet. Incorrect number of toes. Malocclusion resulting in either undershot or overshot chin.

COLORS: A variety of colors in solid and lynx points.

ALLOWABLE BREEDING OUTCROSSES: Siamese for litters born before January 1, 2019.

CORNISH REX
By Cheryl McGee and Trish Blees

Cornish Rex

If you were to enter a room with a dozen Cornish Rex, it would probably take several hours to disengage yourself from them. If you never had the pleasure of meeting the breed before, it could throw you into a state of panic or euphoria. It is easy to get hooked on such cats. Discussions with potential owners about the breed often begin with: "You know, they leap from high places such as door casings, refrigerators, antique pieces too tall to dust, and much more, with a single bound." Some prospective owners are looking for a cat of convenience that does not shed. (Shedding is not really a valid reason to reject a kitten.) However, there are those whose main consideration is that the cat becomes a part of the family. They will not mind a cat that licks the drops of water off their feet after they come out of the shower, that helps eat the last peppers and anchovies off their pizza, or that sleeps across their face and complains if their eyes have not opened by 6:00 in the morning. The Rex is just the cat for people like that. It will be a true member of the family, and, by the way, it adores dogs.

Physical Description

Words inadequately describe the first sight of a Cornish Rex, a breed meant for those who appreciate living art. These cats move, stretch, and arch their elegant bodies, looking like living works of living art.

If you are a novice cat person, you might think that Cornish Rex look nothing like the cats you're used to. Take your time to get to know them—their graceful manner and constant expressions of affection will soon work their charms on you. They are built for speed and endurance, not for lap-sitting. These cats have unusual coats of wavy, downlike hair that you may suspect also contains Velcro, because they are always stuck to you wherever you go. They come in every imaginable color, including colorpoints, lavender, chocolate, and all the basic colors plus white.

Color has never been more than a personal preference for Cornish breeders, as it carries only 5 points of the total 100 when the Cornish Rex are judged. What makes them sparkle is their wonderful attitude: They stand tall on their powerful legs, announcing to all that they are the king of cats.

Do not let the *Rex* part of the breed name fool you. These cats are small to medium in size, with the males being proportionately larger. The word *Rex* is a shortening of the genetic term *astrex*, meaning the absence of guard hairs, which are the coarse topcoat hairs that provide insulation. The result is that these cats can get chilled very easily. The coat is crimped. As they mature, it becomes incredibly soft and velvety to the touch and marcelled, from the top of their heads to the sides of their legs and to the tip of their long and slender tail. They

even have crinkling whiskers. The little bit of shedding or molting they do usually goes unnoticed with regular hand stroking.

A Cornish Rex with a good body type can leave you breathless. Their bodies resemble those of Greyhounds, with a naturally arched back and large thigh muscles that enable them to launch themselves at a moment's notice. Their heads are smallish and egg-shaped with a "skully" appearance. They possess huge, luminous eyes. No cat has ears like the Cornish Rex—the bigger, the better, as long as the ears are set high on the head.

Personality

These are thinking cats with great appetites, so do not allow food to lie around on open counters if you consider it valuable. Whether you have set out a steak to thaw or a fresh loaf of bread, a head of lettuce, carrots, or even cantaloupe, any food will become a target for these feline omnivores. Nothing is safe from their appetite, so you had better put food away or get it into a container.

They love to play, but in their exuberance, they may break things made of glass or crockery. If they do, then as far as they are concerned, the broken pieces just increase the amount of toys to play with. They may suddenly have a burst of energy and race through the house, run up and down the stairs, dash from the scratching post back up the stairway again, and run from room to room. Then, just as suddenly, as if their manic racing had never happened, they come to a halt and become all love and kisses. Their antics are what make them well known as cats in clown suits. Although their activity level is high, however, it is not any more than that of an Abyssinian or Siamese.

Whether they are vocal or not becomes a matter of what you will allow. For some cats, only a human is permitted to talk loudly.

Grooming Requirements

The Cornish are among the easiest cats to groom and maintain. They require little effort to retain their good looks. However, the earlier you start bathing them, the better, because they can be stubborn.

To keep a cat in top show condition, you must bathe it a few days prior to showing it in competition. This will allow enough time for its natural oils to return to the coat and maintain its close-lying appearance. Otherwise, you will have a fluffy-coated cat without much wave in its fur. When bathing your cat, use a high-quality shampoo formulated for cats, pay close attention to the toes and ears and under-belly, and be sure to rinse the coat thoroughly. Do not use a cream rinse for this breed. It is essential that you towel-dry the cat and not use a blow dryer. The ears on the Cornish also must be cleaned often. They tend to develop a wax buildup that accumulates faster than on most breeds, but it is a problem that a Q-Tip can cure.

Origins and History

The golden moment began in Cornwall, England, in about 1950 when a barn cat gave birth to a litter of five that included an odd curly-coated kitten. As the kitten matured, its huge batlike ears and long, slender tail and body fascinated its owner. When the curls in its coat became more pronounced, the cat was named Kallibunker. Genetically, the cat was understood to be a natural mutation. Its owner decided to strengthen the line by mating the cat back to its mother. A new litter was born with two curly-coated kittens, and they were referred to as Rex because of the owner's previous experience with breeding curly-coated Rex rabbits.

A new gene for this cat breed was discovered in 1960; the word *Cornish* was then added to the breed's name. The Cornish Rex type is caused by a recessive gene, meaning that two Cornish have to be bred together to have curly coated kittens. When Kallibunker was bred to Siamese, Burmese, and British Shorthair cats, the resulting kittens had only normal coats. However, those normal-coated kittens carried the recessive gene, so that when they were bred back to a Cornish Rex or to each other, curly-coated kittens were likely to be born. These breedings increased the gene pool and shaped the Cornish into the breed that exists today.

A group of very dedicated American breeders were responsible for bringing this breed to the United States. The Cornish Rex was accepted for registration by the CFA in 1962 and quickly advanced to Championship status in May 1964.

Miscellanea

The Cornish Rex has a very healthy appetite and will eat as much as you put in the bowl. If your Cornish is overweight, she may not be getting enough exercise. Cut back on how much you feed her.

This is a long-living breed. Many of these cats continue into their twenties, with the life span average in the range of 12–18 years.

Today the Cornish Rex is one of the most popular breeds exhibited in cat shows; these cats are natural show cats and love the attention. Most are born travelers and have a great sense of adventure, whether they go by car, boat, or plane. One sentence in the standard says it all: "The Cornish Rex stands high on its legs." So if a highly intelligent, loving, unusual cat is what you want, then the Cornish Rex might well be the breed for you.

POINT SCORE

HEAD (25)

Size and shape	5
Muzzle and nose	5
Eyes	5
Ears	5
Profile	5

BODY (30)

Size	3
Torso	10
Legs and paws	5
Tail	5
Bone	5
Neck	2

COAT (40)

Texture	10
Length	5
Wave, extent of wave	20
Close-lying	5

COLOR	5

GENERAL: The Cornish Rex is distinguished from all other breeds by its extremely soft, wavy coat and racy type. It is surprisingly heavy and warm to the touch. All contours of the Cornish Rex are gently curved. By nature, the Cornish Rex is intelligent and alert, and it generally likes to be handled.

PROFILE: A curve comprised of two convex arcs. The forehead is rounded, the nose break smooth and mild, and the Roman nose has a high, prominent bridge.

HEAD: Comparatively small and egg-shaped. Length about one third greater than the width. A definite whisker break, oval with gently curving outline in front and in profile.

MUZZLE: Narrowing slightly to a rounded end.

EARS: Large and full from the base; erect and alert; set high on the head.

EYES: Medium to large in size, oval in shape, and slanting slightly upward. A full eye's width apart. Color should be clear, intense, and appropriate to coat color.

NOSE: Roman. Length is one-third length of head. In profile, a straight line from end of nose to chin with considerable depth and squarish effect.

CHEEKS: Cheekbones high and prominent, well chiseled.

CHIN: Strong, well developed.

BODY: Very distinctive, small to medium in size, males proportionately larger but never coarse. Torso long and slender, not tubular, showing a deep but not broad chest. The general outline is composed of graceful arches and curves without any sign of flatness. The back is naturally arched and evident when the cat is standing naturally. The underline gently curves upward from the rib cage to form a smallish (tucked up in appearance) waistline. Hips and thighs are muscular and feel somewhat heavy in proportion to the rest of the body.

SHOULDERS: Well knit.

RUMP: Rounded, well muscled.

LEGS: Very long and slender. Thighs well muscled, somewhat heavy in proportion to the rest of the body. The Cornish Rex stands high on its legs.

PAWS: Dainty, slightly oval. Toes: five in front and four behind.

TAIL: Long and slender, tapering toward the end and extremely flexible.

NECK: Long and slender.

BONE: Fine and delicate.

COAT: Short, extremely soft, silky, and completely free of guard hairs. Relatively dense. A tight, uniform marcel wave, lying close to the body and extending from the top of the head across the back, sides, and hips, continuing to the tip of the tail. Size and depth of wave may vary. The fur on the underside of the chin and on chest and abdomen is short and noticeably wavy.

CONDITION: Firm and muscular.

PENALIZE: Sparse coat or bare spots.

DISQUALIFY: Kinked or abnormal tail. Incorrect number of toes. Any coarse or guard hairs. Any signs of lameness in the hindquarters. Signs of poor health.

COLORS: A wide array of colors in the solid, shaded, smoke, tabby, bicolor, particolor, and pointed patterns.

ALLOWABLE BREEDING OUTCROSSES: none.

DEVON REX
By Gerri Logan and Ann Gibney

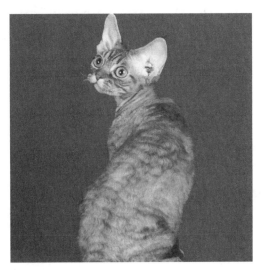

Devon Rex

The appearance of the Devon Rex makes one rethink the concept of "cat." Its distinctive head catches and holds the eye. With an elfin face featuring large, intensely expressive eyes, an upturned nose, and chipmunk cheeks, the Devon nicely fits the definition of *cute*. Add huge batwing ears that suggest a creature capable of flight, and one suddenly thinks of E.T., the extraterrestrial, pedaling a bicycle across the night sky, silhouetted against a full moon, or playfully tucked between teddy bears and dolls in a child's closet. But this "E.T." has a short coat of curls, swirls, and waves.

Physical Description
The almost unchanging Devon remains strikingly close in appearance to Kirlee, the cat with the genetic mutation on which the breed was established. While outcrossing to other breeds continues, it is to the type of the founding cat that the Devon always returns.

The *rexed* coat is the original reason for the perpetuation of the Devon Rex as a breed and is produced by a unique mutation. Guard hairs are present but in very weakened form and reduced numbers. They vary in diameter throughout their length, making them lumpy and giving the coat a fuller feeling and a more open and uneven wave, completely unlike the marcel wave of the Cornish Rex coat, which lacks guard hairs entirely. Eyebrows and whiskers are also curly, but Devons that have only bent stubs for whiskers are not uncommon.

Like baby birds, Devon Rex molt out their birth coats in favor of more substantial coats at about 8 weeks of age. The speed with which new coats grow varies widely, from a few days to a year or more. The typical kitten in molt is covered in a fine down that has the soft, slightly resistant feel of suede. This suede-like down frequently remains the only covering on the stomach area even in heavily coated adults. It is the lack of an insulating coat that permits the higher body temperature common to all felines to be felt more readily in Devons. Selective breeding is gradually producing Devons that effect coat exchanges in such a seamless manner that kittens appear not to molt at all.

The Devon body has a heft and a muscularity that surprise when you first lift and feel the cat. The chest is unexpectedly broad, given the slender neck that arises from it, and the front legs, though not bowed, come off the chest in a bulldog stance. The Devon is a small- to medium-size cat whose long legs add a rakish appearance.

Personality

The Devon Rex is as friendly and comical as its charming appearance suggests. Devons attempt to be all things to all people who love them: companion, court jester, soul mate. They are consummate people-pleasers that respond eagerly to their names, follow their people about the house, and sleep snuggled next to them in bed.

They delight in shared body warmth; curling themselves into your lap or draping across your shoulder without invitation. They enjoy basking in rays of warm sunlight and follow them from door to window as the day moves closer to one of its highlights, dinnertime.

Devons have a robust appetite, and eating is a passion for most of them—asparagus, cantaloupe, and chicken being just a few favored treats. They rarely overeat and generally maintain good weight throughout their lives when fed a well-balanced diet designed specifically for cats.

Devon conversation is blissfully soft-voiced, with plenty of chirps, peeps, and trills. Visitors are greeted at the front door by the Devon of the house with much friendly chatter, purring, and happy doglike tail wagging. Friendly, curious, and ever seeking approval, these cats have a need for people that has resulted in their plunging into bathtubs or joining someone in the shower. Banishing a Devon from a room accomplishes little besides eliciting plaintive mewing from beyond the closed door. Aloofness is quite unknown in the Devon Rex.

A Devon makes a good playmate for a gentle, cat-savvy child. A bonneted Devon being pushed in a doll carriage is a common sight when little children are around; "baby" is only one of countless games to be arranged between child and cat. These cats are themselves perpetual children, remaining playful into their senior years. Many live long lives, with some attaining 20 years or more. They readily accept most dogs as roommates or as pillows. Do not expect a Devon to be a mouser, as he is far more likely to make friends with a mouse rather than do it harm.

Grooming Requirements

Most Devons require little to no bathing, but people with allergies may wish to give weekly baths. A good moisturizing shampoo and conditioner will not overdry the coat. The primary grooming tool, a dampened washcloth, is used to wipe down the coat daily to remove surface dirt and to stimulate a deeper wave.

Origins and History

As for the history of the breed, it began in 1959, in a deserted tin mine near Buckfastleigh, in Devon, England, where a feral tomcat had sought shelter. Local people noted ringlets of curly fur all over his body. This feral cat is credited with siring the kitten on which the breed was founded, by way of a normal-coated, tortie-and-white female stray. It is further surmised she was also his daughter, because the gene necessary to reproduce his curly coat was later shown to be a simple recessive gene, which requires both parents to carry the gene or display it in the form of a curly (rex) coat.

The stray female produced a litter of kittens, of which only one, a male, had the same curly coat as that tin-mine tom. In a stroke of good fortune, the litter was born and raised in the garden of Beryl Cox, who took a liking to the curly-haired kitten's looks, amusing antics, and loving nature. She took him into her home, naming him Kirlee.

He was a charming character, agilely walking a tightrope, fetching toys, and wagging his tail to express happiness just like a dog. He also proved irresistible to English breeders working with a curly mutation that had occurred 10 years earlier in the neighboring county of Cornwall. Miss Cox thought he would contribute to this new breed, so she agreed, in 1960, to sell Kirlee because it appeared that he was of that same mutation. This later proved not the case at all.

Kirlee was mated to a variety of females displaying or carrying the previously mutated rex gene. Although many kittens resulted, not one had a curly coat. The bad news was that Kirlee could not help, as he was not one of them. The good news was that another entirely new kind of rex gene had been discovered. It was dubbed gene II, with the original known as gene I. No further crossing of the two strains was attempted, and they proceeded to develop as two independent breeds. However, this did not extend to the removal of those cats already carrying the opposite rex gene from either breed, a shortcut that unfortunately caused double rex to occur. Such anomalies still arise today, although very rarely, in both the Devon and Cornish breeds.

Kirlee was bred with several breeds and curious breed mixtures, with some resulting females being bred back to him. He sired only 10 recorded gene II litters before being neutered, after which he lived in a pet home until his accidental death in 1970.

Kirlee's progeny were bred to Siamese, British Burmese, Persians, and British Shorthairs in the process of perpetuating the gene II rex mutation. The gene pool was further expanded when descendants were later outcrossed to the Abyssinian, Korat, Russian Blue, and Oriental Shorthair. Today's Devon Rex carries and displays a gamut of colors and patterns transferred to them in the breed's infancy.

The British breeders applied for recognition by the cat registry in the United Kingdom, which was granted in 1967, with the condition that cats bearing gene I be called Cornish Rex and those bearing gene II be called Devon Rex. The Devon Rex was accepted for registration by the CFA many years later, in 1979, and the breed was granted Championship status at CFA shows beginning with the May 1983 show season.

The original standard of perfection was based on Kirlee. Today the standards of perfection in cat associations the world over, with few exceptions, remain faithful to the original standard.

Miscellanea

Devons enjoy being carried, and many are comfortable perching on a shoulder, much like a parrot. Most travel easily and accept new surroundings with confidence.

Training to stay off counters may be achieved with a spray bottle. Repetition may be necessary despite the fact that these cats are quite clever, because they often display a deep and abiding stubbornness. Many Devons can be trained to walk on a lead, retrieve, and even bring the proverbial pipe and slippers, except that it's usually just one slipper, and not always yours. Nevertheless, they are intelligent, eager to please, and willing to learn. Praise and hugs are essential for success.

In the show ring, you may note that experienced judges permit Devons to stand on the table without visible restraint. Devons, unlikely to bolt from the table, rebel at attempts to restrain them physically. They intensely dislike hands placed under their bellies as a means of control and will persistently attempt to step away from this type of handling. Home practice sessions before the first show will familiarize them with standing, playing, and remaining on a small judging table.

You may see a judge pulling back a male cat's jowls or pressing a fingertip into the nose area between the cat's eyes. This is done to reveal the boning and ear shape being hidden by the jowls, and to ensure that the nose stop (a change in direction, seen in profile, at the top of the nose) is not just an illusion. Playing games at home that involve facial manipulation will condition the cat to accept this activity in the show ring with good grace.

Many who have cat-related allergies can experience the joy of a cat by owning a Devon, possibly because these cats don't shed much. Other factors may contribute to this phenomenon but are not yet understood. Many people attest to living with Devons without their allergies being triggered.

The Devon Rex has enjoyed an ever-increasing population growth and show presence as more and more people discover the joy of life with these unusual cats. The Devon Rex is indeed laying claim to the hearts of cat lovers everywhere. Although it remains a relatively rare breed, it has proven itself a stylish, humorous, and worthy competitor in CFA show halls, as well as a loving, loyal companion bringing joy and laughter into the homes of the people who love them.

CFA SHOW STANDARD FOR THE DEVON REX

POINT SCORE		
HEAD (35)		
Size and shape		10
Muzzle and chin		5
Profile		5
Eyes		5
Ears		10
BODY (30)		
Torso		10
Legs and paws		10
Tail		5
Neck		5
COAT (30)		
Density		10
Texture and length		10
Waviness		10
COLOR		5

GENERAL: The Devon Rex is a breed of unique appearance. Its large eyes, short muzzle, prominent cheekbones, and huge, low-set ears create a characteristic elfin look. A cat of medium-fine frame, the Devon is well covered with soft, wavy fur; the fur is of a distinctive texture, as the mutation that causes its wavy coat is cultivated in no other breed. The Devon is alert and active and shows a lively interest in its surroundings.

HEAD: Modified wedge. In the front view, the wedge is delineated by a narrowing series of three distinct convex curves: outer edge of ear lobes, cheekbones, and whisker pads. Head to be broad but slightly longer than it is broad. Face to be full-cheeked, with pronounced cheekbones and a whisker break. In profile, nose with a strongly marked stop; forehead curving back to a flat skull. Allowance to be made for stud jowls in the adult male.

MUZZLE: Short, well developed. Prominent whisker pads.

CHIN: Strong, well developed. In profile, chin shall line up vertically with nose, being neither undershot nor overshot.

EYES: Large and wide-set, oval in shape, and sloping toward outer edges of ears. Any eye color is acceptable, as no points are assigned to eye color (although colorpoints generally will have blue and minks generally will have aqua eyes).

EARS: Strikingly large and set very low, very wide at the base, so that the outside base of ear extends beyond the line of the wedge. Tapering to rounded tops and well covered with fine fur. With or without ear-muffs and/or ear-tip tufts.

BODY: Hard and muscular, slender, and of medium length. Broad in chest and medium fine in boning, with medium fine but sturdy legs. Carried high on the legs with the hind legs somewhat longer than the front. Allowance to be made for larger size in males, as long as good proportions are maintained.

LEGS AND PAWS: Legs long and slim. Paws small and oval, with five toes in front and four behind.

TAIL: Long, fine, and tapering, well covered with short fur.

NECK: Medium long and slender.

COAT: *Density:* The cat is well covered with fur, with the greatest density occurring on the back, sides, tail, legs, face, and ears. Slightly less density is permitted on the top of head, neck, chest, and abdomen. Bare patches are a fault in kittens and a serious fault in adults; however, the existence of down on the underparts of the body should not be misinterpreted as bareness. Sparse hair on the temples (forehead in front of the ears) is not a fault. *Texture:* The coat is soft, fine, full-bodied, and rexed (i.e., appearing to be without guard hairs). *Length:* The coat is short on the back, sides, upper legs, and tail. It is very short on the head, ears, neck, paws, chest, and abdomen. Kittens may have very short fur all over; even if not long enough to wave, it must cover the kitten evenly, so that no bare patches are evident. *Waviness:* A rippled wave effect should be apparent when the coat is smoothed with one's hand. The wave is most evident where the coat is the longest, on the body and tail.

PENALIZE: Narrow, long, round, or domestic-type head; extremely short muzzle; misaligned bite; small or high-set ears; short, bare, or bushy tail; straight or shaggy coat; bare patches.

DISQUALIFY: Extensive baldness, kinked or abnormal tail, incorrect number of toes, crossed eyes, weak hind legs. Any evidence of illness or poor health.

COLORS: A wide array of colors in the solid, shaded, smoke, tabby, bicolor, parti-color, pointed, and mink patterns.

EGYPTIAN MAU
By Dorothea Brocksom

Egyptian Mau

History suggests that our domestic cats are the descendents of the cats of ancient Egypt. This is most apparent in the Egyptian Mau. *Mau* is the Egyptian word for cat. The ancestors of these cats are highly visible in the artwork of the ancient Egyptians, which depicts many heavily spotted felines bearing the distinctive mascara marking and barring of the Egyptian Mau of today.

Physical Description

The Egyptian Mau's spots, which might be considered more characteristic of wildcats than of domestic breeds, are the first thing about this cat to catch the eye, but the beauty of the Mau goes far beyond its coat and beguiling gooseberry green eyes. One immediately senses a spirit, a mysteriousness that reflects the deity it once was in ancient Egypt.

The Egyptian Mau is sleek and muscular, with a flap of skin extending from the posterior end of the rib cage to the hind legs that gives the Mau an uncanny leaping ability, a long stride, and the capability of great bursts of speed. The shoulder blades are high and the legs are long; the longer hind legs give the cat a cheetahlike gait and the appearance of being on tiptoe. A Mau can be sitting serenely one moment, grooming itself, and the next moment it will leap and move completely across the room without hesitation.

The head is fine-boned, with a brow line and eyes beautified by mascara lines, giving the Mau a rather concerned or worried expression. A scarab marking (a beetle held sacred by the ancient Egyptians) on the forehead and large ears that are often tufted at the tips complete the look.

Personality

The Egyptian Mau possesses extraordinary senses of smell, hearing, and sight. They are incredibly intelligent cats, always aware of everything in their surroundings. In spirit, Maus are especially sensitive to the needs and feelings of their families, both human and feline. They are quiet cats with low, melodious voices and enjoy engaging their people in subdued conversations. Often, you will find them chirping with each other or sitting at a window "chattering" at the birds flying outside.

They are wonderful pets, patient and gentle with children, and get along well with other animals in the house. The Egyptian Mau is affectionate within the family but can be reserved with strangers. Given a bit of time, you will find them next to your houseguests, inspecting the newcomers for new wonderful smells. They are marvelous parents, attentive to their kittens and taking great pleasure in teaching them proper household manners.

Egyptian Maus are dauntless, fun-seeking souls. They love games and toys, the latter of which they will take exclusive possession with lightning speed. Some Maus love to fetch, and you will soon find that you will tire of the game before they do. Maus have excellent dexterity with their paws, meaning that you will need to put small items out of sight if you don't want them to become cat toys you might never see again. You will watch in wonder as a Mau picks up a pen or other small item in its paws and then transfers it to his mouth and runs away with his newest toy.

The Egyptian Mau has often been thought of as aloof and shy. To a certain extent this is true, but cats of this breed have a special affinity with people, developing close cat–human bonds that are different from those formed by other breeds. A typical Mau will command your attention. He will not allow you to push him away, as he craves the touch of special people that are his and his alone. These cats become the center of your world, and they know it. They take over your life with incredi-

ble but gentle persistence and insist on being the sole reason for your existence. They are intensely loyal and yet happy to go about the business of being a cat. But when they are ready for you, there is no stopping the love, attention, and adoration Maus bestow on you.

Grooming Requirements

Grooming should be established as a routine for your cat or kitten as soon as possible. Because cats love to be stroked, it is convenient to use petting as an opportunity to remove dead and loose hairs from the coat. Check their ears to make sure they are clean. You can use a tissue to clean them. As with all healthy cats, eyes should be bright and shining. Nails should be trimmed at least once every 2 weeks. When handling your Mau, make sure you touch his feet, so he will get used to the idea of having his nails trimmed.

Bathing a Mau is seldom required, unless, of course, you plan to show the cat. This is a relatively simple procedure that you can learn from your breeder or mentor. The fine points of grooming come with time and experience. You will find that your fellow exhibitors and breeders are always happy to share their grooming secrets with you.

Origins and History

Many experts believe that the Egyptian Mau is the cat fancy's oldest breed, domesticated more than 4,000 years ago from a spotted subspecies of the African wildcat, *Felis libyca ocreata*. Of all the domestic cats of today, the Mau has the distinction of being the only naturally spotted breed.

Ancient Egyptians had an intense reverence for their cats. They were worshipped as deities, cherished as household pets, and protected by law. Deliberately harming a cat was punishable by death. One historian recorded the mob killing of a Roman who had caused the death of a cat. When a beloved pet died, members of the household shaved their eyebrows to express their grief. On their demise, cats were taken to the city of Bubastis, mummified, and buried in sacred repositories.

In recent times, the aristocracy and diplomatic corps of Egypt throughout the Middle East kept the descendants of these cats as treasured pets. While living in Rome, exiled Russian princess Nathalie Troubetskoy was given a spotted silver female Egyptian Mau kitten by a young boy with whom she was acquainted. He had obtained the kitten from a member of a Middle Eastern embassy. The princess was fascinated by the breed and was particularly taken by the unique beauty of this kitten, which she named Baba. Using her contacts among foreign ambassadors, she was able to secure additional Egyptian Maus through the Syrian embassy, which she used to help establish her breeding lines.

In December 1956, after years of red tape, Princess Troubetskoy immigrated to the United States. She carried with her in a wicker basket the silver female Baba, a bronze male called JoJo, and a younger silver kitten named Liza. Once settled, she began breeding Maus, firmly establishing them in North America. They are now bred extensively in Japan and Europe and have achieved a definite place in modern feline history.

The ultimate goal of any new breed, which is CFA Championship status, was achieved in 1977. That same year also brought the first CFA grand title to a silver male within the breed. In 1993, a silver female became the first Egyptian

Mau national winner, finishing the year with two National Wins (one in the Championship category and one in the Kitten category), giving all Mau breeders and fanciers cause to celebrate.

Miscellanea

Cats of this breed love to eat and if allowed unlimited food will quickly become overweight. A controlled feeding environment is essential for the well-being of these cats. Fresh water must be available at all times, but you will find that for some cats, the water dish is as much a place to play as it is to drink.

Egyptian Mau kittens require handling from birth, with special attention paid to exposure to new people and places as well as to acclimation to new, loud, or strange sounds. Leaving the television or radio on will help accustom them to different noises. They do not like to be "dangled," so using both hands when carrying them is essential: Place one hand gently under the chest and the other just forward of the back legs. They prefer to have all four feet on the floor or on the table.

People are entranced by the call of the wild evident in these most exotic-looking cats with the phenomenal spots and facial highlights. Egyptian Maus never fail to amaze with their loyalty and gentle, playful nature. With their great beauty of body and spirit, it is not surprising that they were worshipped in ancient Egypt, traveled with royalty to the United States, and now endear themselves to cat fanciers throughout the world.

CFA SHOW STANDARD FOR THE EGYPTIAN MAU

POINT SCORE

HEAD (20)

Muzzle	5
Skull	5
Ears	5
Eye shape	5

BODY (25)

Torso	10
Legs and feet	10
Tail	5

COAT (5)

Texture and length	5

PATTERN (25)

	25

COLOR (25)

Eye color	10
Coat color	15

GENERAL: The Egyptian Mau is the only natural domesticated breed of spotted cat. The Egyptian's impression should be one of an active, colorful cat of medium size with well-developed muscles. Perfect physical condition with an alert appearance. Well balanced physically and temperamentally. Males tend to be larger than females.

HEAD: A slightly rounded wedge without flat planes, medium in length. Not full-cheeked. Profile showing a gentle contour with slight rise from the bridge of the nose to the forehead. Entire length of nose is even in width when viewed from the front. Allowance must be made for jowls in adult males.

MUZZLE: Should flow into existing wedge of the head. It should be neither short nor pointed. The chin should be firm, not receding or protruding.

EARS: Medium to large, alert and moderately pointed, continuing the planes of the head. Broad at base. Slightly flared, with ample width between the ears. Hair on ears short and close-lying. Inner ear a delicate, almost transparent, shell pink. May be tufted.

EYES: Large and alert, almond-shaped, with a slight slant toward the ears. Skull apertures neither round nor oriental.

BODY: Medium long and graceful, showing well-developed muscular strength. Loose skin flap extending from flank to hind-leg knee. General balance is more to be desired than size alone. Allowance to be made for muscular necks and shoulders in adult males.

LEGS AND FEET: In proportion to body. Hind legs proportionately longer, giving the appearance of being on tiptoe when standing upright. Feet small and dainty, slightly oval, almost round in shape. Toes: five in front and four behind.

TAIL: Medium long, thick at base, with slight taper.

COAT: Hair is medium in length, with a lustrous sheen. In the smoke color, the hair is silky and fine in texture. In the silver and bronze colors, the hair is dense and resilient in texture and accommodates two or more bands of ticking separated by lighter bands.

PENALIZE: Short or round head. Pointed muzzle. Small, round, or oriental eyes. Cobby or oriental body. Short or whip tail. If no broken necklaces. Pencilings in spotting pattern on torso. Solid stripes on underside of body instead of "vest button" spots. Poor condition. Amber cast in eye color in cats over the age of 1½ years.

DISQUALIFY: Lack of spots. Blue eyes. Kinked or abnormal tail. Incorrect number of toes. White locket or button distinctive from other acceptable white-colored areas in color sections of standard.

MAU PATTERN (COMMON TO ALL COLORS): Markings on torso are to be randomly spotted, with variance in size and shape. The spots can be small or large, round, oblong, or irregular-shaped. Any of these are of equal merit, but the spots, however shaped or whatever size, shall be distinct. Good contrast between pale ground color and deeper markings. Forehead barred with characteristic M and frown marks, forming lines between the ears that continue down the back of the neck, ideally breaking into elongated spots along the spine. As the spinal lines reach the rear haunches, they meld together to form a dorsal stripe that continues along the top of the tail to its tip. The tail is heavily banded and has a dark tip. The cheeks are barred with "mascara" lines; the first starts at the outer corner of the eye and continues along the contour of the cheek, with a second line, which starts at the center of the cheek and curves upward, almost meeting below the base of the ear. On the upper chest, there are one or more broken necklaces. The shoulder markings are a transition between stripes and spots. The upper front legs are heavily barred but do not necessarily match. Spotting pattern on each side of the torso need not match. Haunches and upper hind legs to be a transition between stripes and spots, breaking into bars on the lower leg. Underside of body to have "vest button," spots, dark in color against the correspondingly pale ground color.

EYE COLOR: Light green—"gooseberry green." Amber cast is acceptable only in young adults up to 1½ years of age.

COLORS: Silver, bronze, smoke.

ALLOWABLE BREEDING OUTCROSSES: none.

EUROPEAN BURMESE

By Ebe McCabe

European Burmese

European Burmese is the CFA name for the 10-color Burmese breed developed outside North America. The name reflects the breed's origin and marks it as a different CFA breed from the round, compact, 4-color Burmese breed. Besides having 6 more colors, the European Burmese are moderate, gently rounded cats with a longer body and head.

Physical Description

With their luminous eyes and striking colors, the European Burmese are exceptionally beautiful. Up close, their silky, close-lying coat and harmonious conformation become more evident. These cats are medium in size and length, with a solid, hefty body and remarkable yellow to amber eyes. Because the European Burmese are highly intelligent, affectionate, and extremely loyal, they make outstanding pets.

Initially, the European Burmese were shaped like the original Burmese breed developed in California in the early 1930s. Some cat fanciers even considered them to be a dark, amber-eyed version of the Siamese. As time passed, the Siamese became longer and more svelte and the CFA Burmese became round and compact. But the European Burmese conformation has basically stayed the same.

When Burmese were first imported into England, the only accepted Burmese color was sable brown. However, the English breeders endorsed color variety. Long before any color but brown was accepted in the CFA Burmese, the European Burmese had become a 10-color breed (brown, blue, chocolate, lilac, red, and cream and the brown, blue, chocolate, and lilac tortie colors).

Personality

European Burmese have exceptional aplomb, calmness, and friendliness in the home or show ring. These cats have a delightfully inquisitive and playful nature that lasts all their lives. Often, European Burmese follow their owners around the home, and park themselves in the same room (or bed) as their human families. Snuggling, with the cats seeming to melt into their companions' body, is a favorite pastime.

European Burmese are very adept at getting what they want, including toys to play with and retrieve. Many purr constantly when held. Often veterinarians have remarked about being unable to hear anything else in their stethoscopes. One European Burmese attention-getter is sitting on the floor, staring at a person's face, and purring very loudly. Another is fearlessly casting its body at someone's feet, rolling and purring, completely confident of being rewarded with attention and affection. They love to scuffle, but their very trusting nature makes it important to treat them gently during play.

Many European Burmese adore children,

although a few do not. Therefore, it is good to bring the family along when selecting a cat or kitten. The animals that enjoy children will gravitate toward them, while those who do not will quietly make themselves scarce.

European Burmese need companionship. When their human family is out, other cats and friendly dogs make good companions. For homes without suitable companionship for much of the day, a more independent cat breed should be chosen.

The European Burmese are also known for their intelligence. Some even learn to open doors. Most European Burmese quickly make willing servants of their human families, and their owners consider the breed's engaging and laid-back temperament equaled only by that of the Burmese.

Grooming Requirements

European Burmese require very little grooming because of their short, close-lying coats and natural cleanliness. Regular face-washing with a warm, damp washcloth (unsoaped) is proper. Weekly nail-clipping and ear-cleaning (with a cotton swab) are also needed. Occasional brushing can reduce the already minimal shedding from the short coat, but that is more a matter of owner preference than need. Most European Burmese keep themselves very clean and do not have to be bathed (except before being shown). If bathing is needed for hygiene, a gentle cat shampoo should be used.

Before you enter a European Burmese in a cat show, getting detailed grooming advice from the cat's breeder or an experienced exhibitor is a good idea. Grooming a short-haired cat is less involved than grooming a long-haired one. Still, a preshow bath plus careful brushing and combing is required in addition to nail-clipping. Doing grooming well takes practice and is best learned from someone who grooms well.

Origins and History

The history of the European Burmese is an interesting study of genetics and cat breeding. Dark chocolate brown, amber-eyed Siamese were reported in England in 1889, which indicates the Burmese gene has been in the Siamese gene pool for a long time. However, the Burmese did not become a unique breed until 1930, when Dr. Joseph Thompson began to develop the original sable Burmese breed in California. It was from California that the first two Burmese were imported into England in 1949.

A mere six brown Burmese from the United States were initially used to establish the breed in England. Later, several imports from the United States and a Burmese–Siamese hybrid from the Far East were used to expand the gene pool.

In 1952, the brown European Burmese were recognized for Championship competition in England. Three years later, one of the original brown imports sired a blue kitten in a mating to one of his daughters. Producing more cats with the new color was avidly pursued, and blue was recognized as the second European Burmese color in 1960.

In 1964, red was introduced into the European Burmese in England by an unplanned mating between a blue Burmese and a short-haired ginger tabby tomcat. A black-and-red tortie from that breeding was selected for further breeding. Two deliberate matings of European Burmese to red cats came next. One of these was to an English red-point Siamese. The other was to an unregistered tortie carrying the Siamese gene. Selected offspring from those matings were bred back to other European Burmese. A difficult but highly effective breeding program to minimize tabby markings in the red and cream colors followed.

In 1969, several Burmese imports from

the United States brought the chocolate color to England. Their offspring included the first chocolate and lilac European Burmese.

Cream European Burmese were accepted for Championship competition in England in 1973. When the chocolate, lilac, red, and all four tortoiseshell colors were then accepted for Championship status in 1974, the breed achieved its 10-color status.

The European Burmese breed spread throughout Europe and then to Africa, Australia, and New Zealand. It is now one of the world's most popular short-haired cat breeds. It was recognized for registration by the CFA in 1993 and achieved Championship status in CFA shows in May 2002.

Today, the CFA European Burmese consist of imports into North America from overseas countries and descendants of these imports. No interbreeding is permitted between the European Burmese and any other breed (including the CFA Burmese). Moreover, only European Burmese with no North American Burmese on their certified pedigrees for at least five generations qualify for registration as CFA European Burmese. This measure protects the genetic and conformation distinctiveness of both the Burmese and European Burmese.

Miscellanea

At cat shows, judges usually find the European Burmese easy to handle. Because these cats are so friendly and easygoing, other people usually have no problem handling them either.

A European Burmese can be comfortably held close to your body by supporting the animal's chest with one hand or arm and supporting the cat's rear legs with the other hand. Many European Burmese prefer to be carried with their chest against their holder's chest, with their front paws resting on their holder's shoulder.

European Burmese are strikingly lovely cats that interact very well with people. Their marvelous temperament and loving nature are, by far, their most endearing traits. This is a very special breed best suited to homes where the cats become treasured family members. Once people own and are owned by a European Burmese, they typically decide to never again be without one.

CFA SHOW STANDARD FOR THE EUROPEAN BURMESE

POINT SCORE

HEAD, EARS AND MUZZLE	25
EYES AND EYE COLOR	25
BODY, LEGS, FEET AND TAIL	20
COAT AND COAT COLOR	30

GENERAL: The European Burmese is an elegant cat breed of Far Eastern origin, of moderate type with gently rounded contours. Any oriental elongation or excessive cobbiness is incorrect and should be regarded as a fault.

HEAD: Top slightly rounded. Good breadth between the ears. Wide cheekbones, tapering to a short, blunt wedge.

EARS: Medium in size. Set well apart. Slight forward tilt. Broad at the base. Slightly rounded tips. The outer line continues the shape of the upper face, except as that may not be possible in mature, full-cheeked males.
MUZZLE: Visible nose break. Jaw wide at the base. Strong lower jaw. Strong chin.
EYES: Large. Alert. Set well apart. Top line slightly curved, with an oriental slant toward the nose. Lower line rounded.
EYE COLOR: Yellow to amber. The deeper the color, the better. Lustrous and bright.
BODY: Medium length and size. Hard and muscular. Heavier than it looks. Chest strong and rounded in profile. Back straight from the shoulder to the rump.
LEGS AND FEET: Legs rather slender, but in proportion to the body. Hind legs slightly longer. Feet small and oval.

TAIL: Medium length. Not thick at the base. Tapering slightly to a rounded tip.
COAT: Short, fine close-lying. Very glossy. Satinlike in texture. Almost without undercoat.
PENALIZE: Pronounced muzzle pinch (top view). Oriental eye shape. Round eyes. Green eyes. Pigmentation spots (freckling) on nose leather, lips, or paw pads.
DISQUALIFY: White patches. Noticeable numbers of white hairs. Visible tail kink. Excessive tabby markings.
COLORS: Brown, blue, chocolate, lilac, red, cream, brown tortie, blue tortie, chocolate tortie, lilac tortie.

ALLOWABLE BREEDING OUTCROSSES: none.

EXOTIC
By Johanna Leibfarth

Exotic

Exotics are a delightful shorthair version of the Persian cat. Often referred to as "teddy bear cats," they have the charming appearance, and the mild, gentle disposition of their full-coated cousins, without the demanding requirements for daily grooming.

Physical Description
Exotics are identical to Persians in every respect, except for coat length. Their luxurious coats are shorter than Persians' are, being medium in length, and do not resemble the coats of any other short-haired cat. There is no ruff around the neck and no feathery hair on the tail. The fur is a little shorter on the face and on the legs, but otherwise it is even all over. Its texture should not be silky or wiry; it should be medium soft. Most importantly, the coat has to be very dense, like the winter coat of a bear or a mountain goat. This coat does

not exist in any other breed; it is strictly the result of combining Persians and Shorthairs.

All cats are affected by seasonal cycles. In spite of thousands of years of domestication, of centuries of indoor living with fireplaces or potbellied stoves, cats still have thicker coats in the winter than in the summer. By summer, the Exotic's coat is at its worst. Even though an Exotic's coat does not tangle, in late spring and early summer when the heavy undercoat is being shed, the hair can become almost felt-like. At that point, only a thorough bathing can remedy the situation. The Exotic begins to rebuild its dense winter coat in September; the coat reaches its peak quality during the coldest, darkest months of the year.

Virtually any coat color that occurs naturally in the cat can also be found in the Exotic, and almost all of them can be registered and shown. Exotics seem to follow the popularity trends of the Persians. For example, since the 1990s, bicolor and calico Persians have become quite fashionable and numerous. Predictably, Exotics are following suit. White combined with black and red, or brown tabby, or blue makes for a stunning cat. Therefore, it is no surprise that more and more bicolor and calico Exotics are being bred. But all Exotics, regardless of color, compete as one breed. Colors range from solid black to lynx point, from copper-eyed white to spotted chocolate tabby, from brown classic tabby to lilac smoke.

In spite of the enormous spectrum available, most Exotics are of the more familiar colors such as blue, black, cream or red, tortoiseshell, and tabby. There are only a few Exotics shown with the Himalayan color pattern, and rarely will there be smokes. The first Exotic to become a Grand Champion was a shaded silver. Regrettably, silvers are extremely rare today.

It happens at every cat show: A visitor will walk by the cage and say, "What kind of cat is this? It looks like a Persian, but it doesn't have long hair!" To the owner, that is a much-appreciated compliment.

Yes, Exotics should resemble a good-quality Persian in every aspect except for coat length. A well-built Exotic should be "round" from every angle. The head of a good Exotic should resemble a softball with small, rounded ears. The nose should be small, snub, and placed between the large, round eyes. The lips should gently curve upward to accentuate the roundness of the muzzle and the cheeks. Overall, an Exotic should have a sweet, open, wide-eyed, intelligent, and alert expression. The body should be relatively short and cobby, with stocky legs, tidy round feet, and a "bottlebrush" tail that is not too long.

Personality

Most everyone is familiar with the quiet nature of Persians. Because Exotics have been bred with Persians for so many years, their personality has become much like that of a Persian, no longer resembling their ancient shorthair ancestors.

In general, Exotics are quiet, docile, and affectionate. When introduced as kittens to an environment with dogs or children, they adjust with ease and quickly become loving playmates. Exotic kittens are not destructive. They do not climb curtains or chew blankets, and they rarely use their claws. They can easily be trained not to jump on the kitchen counter or dining-room table. Having just the right dose of independence, Exotics respect your privacy and do not constantly demand attention. Yet they want to be close to you at all times and quietly follow you from room to room. They are content to sit in a window and watch the world go by and meditate, or doze while you are away from home. Even though Exotics are outgoing and friendly, they generally do not approach strangers without caution. Once they decide that you are "safe," they will unobtrusively mold themselves into the couch, right next to you and purr contentedly.

Although they sleep during most of the day, even Exotics are prompted by their biological clocks. They are nocturnal animals by nature, most active in the evening and in the early morning. During these hours, they are very playful and extremely busy. It is always a surprise to discover what amuses them. One of the most pleasant attributes of Exotics is that they have the ability to entertain themselves for hours with a simple toy like a paper ball. Yet as soon as they hear or smell a can of food being opened, they sit on the kitchen floor, their feet neatly tucked under, patiently waiting.

Grooming Requirements

Like most cats, the Exotic relishes being combed. A quality steel comb is all that is needed. How often an Exotic should be combed depends largely on the time of year. Even though an Exotic's coat does not mat or tangle, a brief but thorough combing once or twice a week will be sufficient most of the year. During shedding time, however, even daily combing may not be enough. This is the time when an Exotic will need a bath now and then. For a routine, general-maintenance bath, any good, cat-safe, tearless pet shampoo will work. It is certainly easier for the animal when this routine has been maintained throughout the year, but most Exotics endure a bath with patience, even if it is only a once-a-year event.

After the cat has been shampooed, rinsed well, and towel-dried, it will have to be dried with either a professional or hand-held dryer. If a professional stand dryer is not available, it is easier if two people are available to do the drying.

Bathing an Exotic for show is just as time-consuming and involved as it is for a Persian. In preparation for a show weekend, an Exotic should be bathed as close to showtime as possible. The technique is much the same as it is for Persians. If you have a Persian breeder friend who shows his cats in impeccable condition, ask him for his secret. It should work equally well for your Exotic. The principal difference between preparing an Exotic and preparing a Persian for show is that an Exotic cannot be dried in a cage. It must be totally blow-dried while it is being diligently combed. It is important not to forget the tail and the legs, because any area that is left to dry on its own will lay flat and become wavy. The properly prepared coat should look beautifully "sifted" on every part of the cat.

Origins and History

The history of the breed goes back to the late 1950s, when several breeders on the U.S. West Coast crossed Persians with short-haired cats. These breedings were not officially sanctioned, and their intention was not to create a new breed.

The kittens resulting from these cross-breedings, however, were adorable beyond expectation. They had a little bit of the Persian's features, but they did not have long hair. Their heads were too round, their hair was too fine and too thick, their coat was too plush, and their bodies were too cobby (stocky) to match any existing breed. Nonetheless, they were so cute that it was hard to resist showing them. At that time, the American Shorthair breed had an open registry, and because early Exotics resembled American Shorthairs, they were registered as American Shorthairs. In spite of their darling appearance, many of their characteristics did not fit the standard of the American Shorthair. However, some judges overlooked their obviously hybrid features and honored them with high placements in the show ring.

Soon the existence of these hybrid cats became a very controversial subject in the cat fancy, and in 1966 the CFA board of directors decided to establish a legitimate place for them. At first, they were to be called Sterlings, because most of these hybrid shorthair cats were shaded silvers or chinchillas. However, the CFA soon realized that other colors (such as black, blue, tortoiseshell, or smoke) were sure to follow. It was agreed to call them Exotic Shorthairs because silver and chinchilla did not naturally exist as colors in shorthair breeds. To many people, exotic means anything but round, chubby, and placid. For many years, Exotic breeders have tried to find a more appropriate name for this unique breed, but the only change occurred when the *Shorthair* part was dropped.

A standard for this new breed was written and based on the standard for the Persian, and everyone working with cats originating from Persian–American Shorthair crosses was given the opportunity to register their animals as Exotic Shorthairs. With the beginning of the 1967–1968 show season, Exotic Shorthairs were granted full Championship status at all CFA shows. The Exotic is one of the few breeds of cats that can honestly claim to be "made in America."

In spite of its odd name, the Exotic has become a very popular little cat, and people all over the world are working with this breed. Thanks to a tremendous jump start by U.S. breeders, some wonderful animals are being produced in other countries as well as in the United States. The progress the Exotic has made in a few short decades is truly remarkable. The first time an Exotic placed among the top-winning cats in the CFA was in 1973. Since then, they have been found among the National Winners almost every year.

Because the standard for the Exotic was, from the very beginning, the same as a Per-

sian's, it was a logical goal for breeders to produce a Persian-type cat with a shorter coat. Once the original cross had been made and the shorthair gene had been introduced, Exotics were consistently bred back to Persians and not to their shorthair ancestors. In 1987, the Exotic Shorthair Breed Council decided it was no longer necessary to use original crosses with American Shorthairs to obtain genetic diversity. Since then, only Exotics and Persians have been allowed as parent animals; American Shorthairs can no longer appear on an application for a litter registration.

Because the Exotic is a hybrid breed, some kittens are born with long hair. These kittens have to be registered as AOV (Any Other Variety). They may be used in Exotic breeding programs. They also can be entered and judged at a show, but they are not eligible to receive an award or gain a title. These longhair Exotics are in every respect Persian cats, in appearance as well as in their genetic makeup. But, because at least one of their parents is an Exotic, they are still simply considered by-products of an Exotic breeding program. Most of these beautiful longhair Exotics find their way into pet homes.

In the show ring, Exotics compete as longhair cats in the "Longhair Specialty" with other longhair breeds, including Persians. It is somewhat confusing when an Exotic is referred to as a longhair cat, because its coat is certainly not long, but it is not short either. However, because of its overall appearance, its bone structure, and its body conformation, it is a Persian-type cat and belongs in this group.

Miscellanea
Well padded and sufficiently insulated, Exotics prefer to sleep in the coolest place in the house. The designer cat bed just purchased at the local pet store and the cozy down comforter are usually shunned. Instead, these cats

prefer a porcelain basin or the tiles on the bathroom floor.

Exotics, like Persians, mature slower than most other breeds. Therefore, it is not necessary to have a male neutered when he is 6 months old. Neither males nor females spray. Occasionally an intact male (or stud male) will spray during mating season, but in general, they are fastidiously clean and tidy. The males are exceptionally gentle and loving. When neutered, they make the most desirable pets. Not only are the females loyal to their owner but they are also attentive and protective mothers. They raise their babies with ease, care, and total devotion.

Males and females are very quiet, with soft, mellow voices. When a female is in heat, she will alert her owner more through her gestures than through a "mating call"; at most, there will be a gentle chirp.

It seems that this hybrid cat called Exotic has inherited the best of both worlds, not only in appearance and ease of care but also in disposition. This breed is truly an ideal blend—quiet, loyal and peaceful, intelligent, and forever playful in a nondestructive way. And yet it requires only a minimal amount of care.

CFA SHOW STANDARD FOR THE EXOTIC

POINT SCORE

HEAD (INCLUDING SIZE AND SHAPE OF EYES AND EAR SHAPE AND SET)	30
BODY TYPE (INCLUDING SHAPE, SIZE, BONE, AND LENGTH OF TAIL)	20
COAT	10
BALANCE	5
REFINEMENT	5
COLOR	20*
EYE COLOR	10

GENERAL: The ideal Exotic should present an impression of a heavily boned, well-balanced cat with a sweet expression and soft, round lines. The large, round eyes set wide apart in a large round head contribute to the overall look and expression. The thick, plush coat softens the lines of the cat and accentuates the roundness in appearance.

HEAD: Round and massive, with great breadth of skull. Round face with round underlying bone structure. Well set on a short, thick neck.

NOSE: Short, snub, and broad, with break centered between the eyes.

CHEEKS: Full.

JAWS: Broad and powerful.

CHIN: Full, well developed, and firmly rounded, reflecting a proper bite.

EARS: Small, round-tipped, tilted forward, and not unduly open at the base. Set far apart and low on the head, fitting into (without distorting) the rounded contour of the head.

EYES: Brilliant in color, large, round, and full. Set level and far apart, giving a sweet expression to the face.

*For cats in the tabby division, the 20 points for color are to be divided: 10 for markings and 10 for color. For cats in the bicolor division, the 20 points for color are to be divided: 10 for "with white" pattern and 10 for color.

BODY: Of cobby type, low on the legs, broad and deep through the chest, equally massive across the shoulders and rump, with a well-rounded midsection and level back. Good muscle tone, with no evidence of obesity. Large or medium in size. Quality the determining consideration rather than size.

LEGS: Short, thick, and strong. Forelegs straight. Hind legs are straight when viewed from behind.

PAWS: Large, round, and firm. Toes carried close, five in front and four behind.

TAIL: Short, but in proportion to body length. Carried without a curve and at an angle lower than the back.

COAT: Dense, plush, soft, and full of life. Standing out from the body because of a rich, thick undercoat. Medium in length.

Acceptable length depends on proper undercoat. Cats with a ruff or tail-feathers (long hair on the tail) shall be transferred to the AOV class.

DISQUALIFY: Locket or button. Kinked or abnormal tail. Incorrect number of toes. Any apparent weakness in the hindquarters. Any apparent deformity of the spine. Deformity of the skull resulting in an asymmetrical face and/or head. Crossed eyes. For pointed cats, disqualify for white toes, eye color other than blue.

COLORS: A wide array of colors in the solid, shaded, smoke, tabby, parti-color, bi-color, and pointed patterns.

ALLOWABLE BREEDING OUTCROSSES: Persian.

HAVANA BROWN
By Brenda Wood

Havana Brown

Chocolate delights is one phrase that Havana Brown enthusiasts use to describe this beautiful chocolate brown cat with mesmerizing green eyes. The North American Havana Brown bears very little resemblance to the Havana, or Oriental Chocolate, found in Europe and Britain, where it originated in the early 1950s.

Physical Description

The Havana Brown is best described as a cat of medium size and structure. It should be neither long nor slinky like its Siamese ancestors or Oriental cousins, nor should it be short and cobby like the Persian or Burmese breeds. In all aspects, it is a medium cat.

The well-toned, muscular body conveys a sense of power. When picked up, these cats should always feel heavier than they look. Males naturally tend to be proportionally larger and more heavily boned than females. A fully developed adult weighs 6–10 pounds.

There is nothing medium about its deep, rich, glistening, mahogany brown color. The soft, silky coat of the Havana Brown is short to medium in length. Lying close to the body, it should be smooth and lustrous in appearance. It feels like a luxurious mink or the finest of pure silks. A rich, evenly colored shade of warm chocolate brown tending more to red-brown (mahogany) is the most desirable color characteristic of the breed. Too little or no red-dish tone in the coat results in a flat look and is undesirable; likewise, too much red or black-brown shades similar to the sable color found in Burmese are also unacceptable. Kittens and young adults may show ghost tabby markings that should disappear as they mature. It may take up to 2 years for the coat to reach full ma-turity. Lighter shades of rich, warm brown are preferred but are also more likely to display ghost tabby markings. The best coats exhibit little or no ghosting on the body.

One of the most distinguishing features of the Havana Brown is the magnificent head, which is slightly longer than it is wide. The profile should neither be straight like that of the Siamese or Oriental, nor should it have a definite break like that of the Persian. There should be an obvious change in angle or stop at eye level where the skull meets the muzzle when the head is viewed in profile.

The unique combination of roundness and square shape in the overall appearance of the Havana Brown head and muzzle has re-sulted in many descriptive comparisons. It looks like a lightbulb, like a corncob stuck on an orange; like the head has been stuck in a softdrink bottle, like a teddy bear.

The nose is wide with rosy-toned brown leather. The whiskers must be brown to com-plement the coat. The Havana Brown is the only breed of cat whose standard specifies a required whisker color.

The enticing oval-shaped green eyes are one of the most captivating features of the Havana Brown. According to the standard, the eye color must be green. Any uniform shade of green is acceptable, with deeper shades be-ing preferred. Beautiful brilliant green eyes and large, forward-pricked ears contribute to the characteristic sweet expression on the face of the Havana Brown.

Elegant and graceful in appearance, the Havana Brown stands tall on its legs. Its paws are dainty and oval in shape. Characteristic of all chocolate-colored cats, the paw pads must be rosy in color.

The medium-length tail tapers gently to a slightly pointed tip. Most Havana Browns carry their tails high above their backs. How-ever, some like to carry their tails with a for-ward curl, not unlike a coat hanger . . . or a monkey. When these cats are sitting in repose, their tails are usually wrapped around the body.

Personality

These cats possess alert, intelligent, affection-ate, and occasionally mischievous personalities, so it is no surprise that those most familiar with this delightful breed often refer to them as Brownies. There is something magical about Havana Browns.

Living with Havana Browns is both a privilege and a pleasure. Generally, they are somewhat shy and soft-spoken and prefer to devote themselves to only one owner and to enjoy a quiet, comfortable home environ-ment. However, each cat has its own distinc-tive character. Individual personalities may vary from shy and aloof to extremely outgo-ing and talkative with a delightful coquettish manner. These little brown characters will in-sist on having the very last word on absolutely everything.

Havana Browns living comfortably in a household together or in the company of other cats tend to be gregarious. They habitually greet other feline companions with a friendly head butt. A favorite amusement is hiding around corners or behind furniture waiting for an opportunity to slap a passerby on the derriere before dashing off. Havana Browns like nothing better than sleeping in tangled piles. Sleeping partners may be other felines or their favorite human companions.

They are moderately active cats when compared with some other shorthair breeds. Occasionally, they will engage in a sprint around the house or a wild game of tag if there are other cats to join in, but generally, they confine themselves to less active occupations, such as batting their toys about, bathing themselves, napping, or grand theft. Some Havana Browns are pack rats and will carry off treasures such as jewelry and pens to special secret hiding places that only they know about.

For the most part, Havana Browns can be described as well behaved. They tend to use scratching posts without much effort to train them. The hemp-covered scratching post is probably the most effective for any indoor cat. Heights and open cupboard doors do not always invite investigation from demure Havana Browns. Although quite capable of feats of agility, they have also been described as somewhat clumsy at times. Not making the attempted jump successfully usually results in an embarrassed self-bathing session and a look that says, "I really meant to do that, you know!"

No matter how the personality is expressed, most Havana Browns are people-oriented and make delightful and unforgettable additions to almost any household. It has been said that once a Havana Brown owns you, you will never want to live without one.

Grooming Requirements

The Havana Brown is a short-haired breed and requires a minimum of routine grooming and maintenance. A weekly grooming routine includes cleaning the ears with a moistened cotton swab and trimming the nails, both front and back. Good-quality stainless-steel nail clippers for cats can be purchased at a pet supply store.

The first step in grooming is to trim the toenails on a regular weekly or biweekly schedule. Start by placing the cat on your lap, preferably lying on its back or sitting on your lap. Gently squeeze each paw pad until the claw appears, and then clip off the clear tip. Do not forget to trim the dewclaws, which are higher up the inside of the front paws. Front paws should be done regularly, but back paws might need to be trimmed only every other session. The tip of the nail is made up of clear protein and has no feeling. If you trim a nail too close to the quick (where a thick vein of blood appears), use a styptic stick or styptic powder to stop the bleeding.

One of the positives about this breed is the minimal amount of hair loss or shedding. To ensure that this remains the case, establish a regular bathing routine. Most Havana Browns love attention and will happily submit to a full-body combing with a fine-toothed steel comb once or twice a week. To bring up the gloss and flatten the coat, buff it with a silk scarf or a soft, damp chamois on a regular basis. Do not underestimate the value of a petting with loving hands as the most satisfying of grooming aids. Stroke the cat firmly from the head to the tip of the tail with your bare hands.

To prevent daily grooming becoming a battle, start handling kittens from an early age. Havana Brown kittens should be started on a grooming and bathing routine at 8–12 weeks of age to prepare them for future handling.

Show bathing a Havana Brown or any shorthair breed requires almost as much time and effort as for a longhair breed, but the drying process takes less time. Most Havana

Brown exhibitors like to give the show bath 2 or 3 days before the show to allow time for the natural oils to return to the coat and restore the close-lying, not fluffy, look. Havana Brown coats should have a soft, silky touch, with the coat lying tight and shimmering a rich, reddish mahogany brown tone.

Origins and History

The Havana Brown is a hybrid or intentionally created breed. Some refer to it as one of the designer breeds. It is the result of carefully planned breeding for a specific genetic design. The story began long before the appearance of the Havana Brown as we know it today. Documentation indicates that all-brown Siamese-type cats existed in the United Kingdom and Europe in the late 1800s. The eleventh edition of the *Encyclopaedia Britannica* mentions a "wholly chocolate-coloured strain of Siamese."

Swiss Mountain Cat was one of the names given these early chocolate brown cats. However, these cats disappeared, probably because the Siamese Cat Club of Britain published a statement circa 1920 that "the club much regrets it is unable to encourage the breeding of any but blue-eyed Siamese." As a result, all solid-chocolate brown cats with nonblue eyes were rejected from Siamese classes at shows until interest was renewed after World War II.

By the time the breed had acquired recognition in English cat registries, the name had been modified to *Chestnut Brown*. In North America, not only the name Havana Brown but also the distinctive look of the cat has been retained. In England, breeding to Siamese has continued; therefore, the original type of the cat has been lost. A Chestnut Brown of today resembles the North American Chestnut Oriental Shorthair in appearance. North American breeders have endeavored to maintain the original look of the 1950s-style Siamese. The

Havana Brown is a moderate cat with a distinctive head, an exquisite coat, and a captivating personality.

The Havana Brown was accepted by the CFA for registration in 1959 and gained Championship status in 1964. Records and old pedigrees indicate that some North American breeders emulated some of the English breeding practices by introducing Russian Blues and Siamese into their early breeding programs. However, this practice came to an end when the breed was closed to outcross breeding in 1974.

In 1998, the CFA again approved opening the breed to outcross breeding in an effort to increase the gene pool for these magnificent cats. As a result, Havana Brown breeders can choose to breed Havana Browns to Havana Browns; to solid-color Orientals, Shorthair Division (chestnut preferred); or to solid-color domestic shorthairs (black or blue only). In 1999, CFA also approved the use of chocolate point or seal point Siamese with full Havana Browns.

First generation (F1) cats may not be shown in Havana Brown classes at CFA shows. However, they can be extremely useful in breeding programs, and those that are not deemed to be suitable candidates for breeding provide beautiful pets when neutered or spayed and placed in pet homes. Second (F2) and following generations (F3, F4, and so on) are recognized for competition in Havana Brown classes at CFA-sanctioned shows.

Miscellanea

Havana Brown kittens should be handled and fussed over from an early age to give them confidence and prepare them for new homes and experiences later in life. Likewise, early show hall and ring experience conditions the show-quality kitten for the potential show career ahead.

In the show ring, show-quality specimens of the breed must be relaxed and responsive to handling. Breeders and owners who intend to exhibit Havana Browns must work with kittens to prepare them for handling in the judging ring. One key area to focus on is the head because so much emphasis is placed on the unique head structure of this breed.

Indeed, true show cats rarely need much handling on the judging table, as they thoroughly enjoy taking advantage of the limelight if allowed the freedom to do so. Judges who take the time to stroke gently and offer interesting toys will likely be rewarded with a playful response. Again, breeders and owners of prospective show kittens spend time using a variety of teasers and toys to prepare for the possibilities of the show ring. Because the Havana Brown is a descendant of the Siamese, it is appropriate to stretch this breed to show off its rich, mahogany color and elegant style.

Undoubtedly a credit to their mixed ancestry, Havana Browns come equipped with a hodgepodge of traits to enchant those with whom they share their lives. They are naturally inquisitive and characteristically reach out with a paw to touch and feel when investigating curiosities in their environment. Other breeds are more inclined to use their noses and sense of smell first to investigate anything that intrigues them. Nevertheless, Havanas do not reserve the use of their paws for snooping. Being truly sensitive by nature, they frequently reach out to gently touch their human companions, as though extending a paw in genuine understanding and friendship. One of the traditional poses most often caught on film by photographers presents the Havana Brown with one of its elegant forepaws raised and slightly curled.

Although not a particularly vocal breed, Havana Browns are extremely attentive parents. Some females may talk constantly to their kittens. Litter size may range from one to six kittens or more, with two to four being the average.

One of the surprising aspects of Havana Browns is their apparent lack of interest in "people food." Most seem content with their favorite canned or dry cat food and rarely show much interest in snatching foods over which other cats insist on making nuisances of themselves. Young kittens are the exception. They can be quite insistent about having a taste of whatever their human may be sampling. Beware; tiny needlelike teeth and sharp claws can be hazardous to fingers and lips.

With continued dedication, judicious encouragement and mentoring of new breeders, and constructive cooperation amongst existing breeders and enthusiasts, this extraordinary breed, created so meticulously through the cooperative efforts and vision of a small group of English breeders, will continue to win hearts.

POINT SCORE

HEAD (33)

Shape	8
Profile/stop	8
Muzzle	8
Chin	4
Ear	5

EYES (10)

Shape and size	5
Color	5

COLOR (22)

Coat color	20
Paw pads, nose leather, and whiskers	2

COAT	**10**
BODY AND NECK	**15**
LEGS AND FEET	**5**
TAIL	**5**

GENERAL: The overall impression of the ideal Havana Brown is a cat of medium size with a rich, solid color coat and good muscle tone. Because of its distinctive muzzle shape, coat color, brilliant and expressive eyes, and large, forward-tilted ears, it is comparable to no other breed.

HEAD: When viewed from above, the head is longer than it is wide, narrowing to a rounded muzzle with a pronounced break on both sides behind the whisker pads. The somewhat narrow muzzle and the whisker break are distinctive characteristics of the breed and must be evident in the typical specimen. When viewed in profile, there is a distinct stop at the eyes; the end of the muzzle appears almost square; this illusion is heightened by a well-developed chin, the profile outline of which is more square than round. Ideally, the tip of the nose and the chin form an almost perpendicular line. Allowance to be made for somewhat broader heads and stud jowls in the adult male. Allow for sparse hair on chin, directly below lower lip.

EARS: Large, round-tipped, cupped at the base, wide-set but not flaring; tilted forward, giving the cat an alert appearance. Little hair inside or outside.

EYES: *Shape:* Aperture oval in shape. Medium-size; set wide apart; brilliant, alert, and expressive. *Color:* Any vivid and level shade of green; the deeper the color, the better.

BODY AND NECK: Torso medium in length, firm and muscular. Adult males tend to be larger than their female counterparts. Overall balance and proportion rather than size to be determining factor. The neck is medium in length and in proportion to the body. The general conformation is midrange between the short-coupled, thickset, and svelte breeds.

LEGS AND FEET: The ideal specimen stands relatively high on its legs for a cat of medium proportions in trunk and tail. Legs are straight. The legs of females are slim and dainty; slenderness and length of leg will be less evident in the more powerfully muscled, mature males. Hind legs slightly longer than front. Paws are oval and compact. Toes: five in front and four behind.

TAIL: Medium in length and in proportion to the body; slender, neither whiplike nor blunt; tapering at the end. Not too broad at the base.

COAT: Short to medium in length; smooth and lustrous.

DISQUALIFY: Kinked tail; locket or button; incorrect number of toes; any eye color other than green; incorrect color of whiskers, nose leather, or paw pads.

COLOR: A rich and even shade of warm brown throughout; color tends toward red-brown (mahogany) rather than black-brown.

ALLOWABLE BREEDING OUTCROSSES: solid color Orientals, shorthair division (Chestnut preferred); solid-color domestic shorthairs (black or blue only); chocolate point or seal point Siamese with full Havana Browns.

JAPANESE BOBTAIL

By G. Allen Scruggs, ASID

Japanese Bobtail Longhair

Japanese Bobtail Shorthair

The Japanese Bobtail is hardy, sound, and athletic, yet elegant, sophisticated, and reminiscent of refined Japanese porcelain. The Bobtail is a delightful, loving pet. One could even say that it is one of Asia's most intriguing secrets.

Physical Description

The Japanese Bobtail is a medium-size cat with long, clean lines. Its body is long, lean, strong, and level from hip to shoulder, with the hind legs much longer than the forelegs. The level back is achieved by the deep angulation of the back legs. The leg conformation clearly accounts for the unique gait exhibited by these beautiful cats. Many think that the lack of a full tail obstructs balance, but nothing could be further from the truth. This cat's exuberant antics can, however, result in occasional household accidents. The CFA Japanese Bobtail foundation breeders wrote the standard to fit the look of the ancient Japanese Bobtail. These cats were depicted in sixteenth- and seventeenth-century silk screens and wood-block prints, usually with elegant ladies. The Bobtails of antiquity were flashy, refined cats, mostly white with spots. The Japanese Bobtail of today is a living piece of preserved ancient Japanese art. It was only after Japanese Bobtails were released onto the streets of Japan, by an imperial order toward the end of the seventeenth century, that they became heavier, larger cats. This was the result of random breeding with street cats for survival.

The ideal Japanese Bobtail is Japanese in look, which is to say that it has large oval, slanted eyes, high cheekbones, and a noticeable whisker break. Among the important things to note, when learning correct type, is that the whisker break creates a pom-pom not unlike the one at the other end of the cat. The pom-poms at both ends create a nice balance.

The Bobtail's head should form an equilateral triangle that does not include the ears. More simply said, the head is as wide as it is long. The ears should be large, upright, and tilted forward even when relaxed. For show purposes, both the longhair and the shorthair Japanese Bobtail are grouped in the shorthair division in CFA. The coat of the breed's shorthair division is medium in length and single. It is flat-lying, smooth, and silky, requiring minimal grooming. The coats of longhair division cats require more work, similar to the coats of other longhair breeds.

Japanese Bobtails are accepted in a variety of colors and patterns—solids, bicolors, and tabbies—however, the preferred cats of today are, as in ancient Japanese art, the flashy spotted bicolors and van bicolors (predominantly white cats with color found only on the head and tail, with occasional spots on the legs). The Mi-Ke (pronounced "mee-KAY") or calico was once the most prized color. Today all colors compete equally. Recently, more tabbies (mackerel) and a few dilute colors have found their way to the show ring. Any eye color is acceptable, from gold to green to blue to odd eyes (both eyes not being the same color). No one eye color is preferred over another.

The tail, the very thing that first identifies the breed, is as unique to the cat as its CFA registration number. There are no known abnormalities identified with the genes that produce its unusual tail. Sophisticated breeders believe that the genes that produce the foreshortened tail are dominant. Though there are variations of this breed's tail, such as the shaving brush, corkscrew, clown's pom-pom, fan, and hook, no one type is preferred. The only requirement is that the tail be clearly visible and less than 3 inches long away from the body. These cats' tails, which are kinked, sometimes fused, and definitely sensitive, should be gently handled. Do not try to manipulate the tails at all; just run your hand over them lightly. Be especially careful when combing and bathing these cats not to hurt their tails. Otherwise, Bobtails should be handled like all cats—with love and respect. It is delightful to see that most Bobtails will wiggle, and perhaps even wag their little bunny tails, a trick that always elicits a smile.

Their Asian appearance, which even includes slanted eyes and erect ears, complete the stylized Japanese look, much like a feline version of Kabuki or Noh theater players. In fact, most Bobtails seen at cat shows in the United States are parti-colored, which is to say mostly or largely white, making them appear even more to be in Japanese theatrical makeup, pure white accented by strong color (red, black, and so on). These cats' rich, complicated history, delightful personality, exotic looks, and general good health make them excellent pets and show choices. They are sound, usually long lived, and as easily housed as most breeds. Plenty of interaction with humans is integral to their reaching full potential on or off the show bench.

Personality

The Japanese Bobtail is among the liveliest breeds. Its ability to quickly assess a situation, its short attention span, and its mischievous responses put it in a league of its own. It appeals to those who prefer spirited cats over laid-back felines. These cats had to be bright to survive for centuries in Japan. They learned to catch and consume vermin, cross streams (some love water), and avoid fastidious gardeners. Inquisitive by nature, Bobtails love to open cabinet doors; hide under covers; and sleep in shopping bags, in big bowls and baskets, and on top of kitchen cabinets. They are playful, enjoy exercising when teased with feathers, toys, tassels, and even wadded-up paper.

Grooming Requirements

The shorthair Bobtail is easy to groom. Frequent combing with a flea comb removes dead coat, encourages new coat growth, and is greatly enjoyed by the cat. Kittens should be introduced to grooming at a young age by getting an occasional bath and having their claws clipped and eyes cleaned. The longhair Bobtail requires more careful grooming. It should be blown dry after its bath (not so for the shorthair) and should undergo more extensive brushing to maintain the good-looking longer coat.

Origins and History

Historical Japanese religions and fine art incorporated superb illustrations of the Bobtail. Tokyo's Gotokuji Temple (constructed in 1697) was dedicated to the Japanese Bobtail, which is represented by the Maneki Neko, the beckoning good-luck cat. Numerous silk and handmade paper scroll paintings, wood-block prints, and netsuke (small decorative carved objects used as toggles to fasten a pouch or purse to the kimono sash) attest to this cat's popularity in fine art. Internationally acclaimed artists such as Chi Kanoliu (1874), Toyokune (1786–1864), the great Hiroshige, (1797–1858), Shosan, and Hiromi used the Bobtail in their work.

Exactly when or where the mutation that created the bobbed tail occurred will probably never be known. Bobbed-tailed cats are seen in most of Asia, indicating that the event probably happened in prehistoric times. Bobtails were possibly brought to Japan from Korea in the sixth century or later during the reign of Emperor Idi-Jo (986–1011) to protect manuscripts from mice. Bobtails were owned only by members of the court. They later became street cats when, in 1602, Japan's silk industry was threatened with total devastation because of an overabundance of vermin and an imperial order was passed that all cats were to be set free. It was forbidden to house, feed, buy, sell, or exchange cats as gifts. The diminutive bob-tailed cats of Japan took to the task of dealing with the rodents with exuberance, and the silkworms soon thrived again. Only the smartest and strongest cats survived their sudden abandonment to the streets of Japan. From that time, the Bobtails of Japan have been the street and farm cats. They are noted for their cunning, intelligence, and vigor. It was only after the Japanese Bobtail was released out onto the streets by imperial order that they became a heavier and larger cat. This was the result of random breeding with street cats for survival.

The shorthair Bobtail was accepted for CFA registration in 1969, achieved Provisional status in 1971, and full Championship recognition in 1976. The Japanese Bobtail first gained American attention in the 1960s, principally from American military families living in Japan. The first kittens imported in 1968 were carefully bred and selected by an American in Japan to display the look of the ancient Japanese Bobtail depicted in Japanese art of the sixteenth and seventeenth centuries. Recognizing the need for the Japanese Bobtail to be clearly distinguishable from the tailless Manx, the CFA board of directors granted acceptance to the leaner, longer, more porcelain-like cat. The cobbier, heavier-boned look was to remain favored by Manx fanciers.

The Japanese Bobtail almost lost its Championship status with the CFA in the 1970s because there were very few cats being shown that met the standard. Most of the earlier Bobtails shown were more like the street cats of Japan, a larger, coarser, and more heavily colored cat. Thankfully, a few dedicated breeders insisted on breeding to the standard for a refined, flashy little cat, which is what we see today in the cat fancy.

In the United States, Bobtails have enjoyed increasing recognition both regionally and nationally. They are quite competitive, with many on a long list of distinguished National, Regional, and Distinguished Merit winners.

Longhair Bobtails were seen for years in the fine art of Japan's northern island of Hokkaido. In the United States, they sometimes appeared in shorthair litters and were "petted out." Because of its longer hair, Longhair Japanese Bobtails have ruffs, "britches," and bigger and fluffier tails. Their body coats are also longer and not considered as plentiful. Like Shorthairs, however, they are single-coated, smooth, and silky. They were accepted to AOV (Any Other Variety) status in February 1991. From that date until they became eligible for full Championship competition, in May 1993, a number of enthusiasts showed them far and wide. The enthusiasm of breeders, exhibitors, judges, and pet buyers proved strong.

Miscellanea

It's been said for years that the Japanese have not prized the Japanese Bobtail as Americans have. Many Bobtails were shown; some still are, as household pets in Japan. Now, however, there are a growing number of Japanese cat fanciers focusing on their native breed. American-bred Japanese Bobtails are even making their way back to Japan, rather like taking coals to Newcastle.

Japanese Bobtails have learned to adapt quickly. They can delight people of all ages with their exquisite appearance and charming skirmishes. They talk (presumably in Japanese), though not as much as Siamese. Occasionally they retrieve, and they are often cliquish when kept in numbers.

The Japanese aesthetic is a fascinating one, symbolized by such cultural icons as kimonos, raku pottery, haiku, sushi and sashimi and green tea and sake, and even by its distinctive flora and fauna. Centuries of isolation on the Japanese islands account for such exotic refinement. The feline expression of that aesthetic, the Japanese Bobtail, is delightful, charming, and intensely beautiful. Its beguiling personality and flashy appearance surely enhances its popularity, both in the show hall and in the homes of people fortunate enough to be sharing their lives with this wondrous breed.

POINT SCORE

HEAD	20
TYPE	30
TAIL	20
COLOR AND MARKINGS	20
COAT	10

GENERAL: The Japanese Bobtail should present the overall impression of a medium-size cat with clean lines and bone structure, well muscled but straight and slender rather than massive in build. The unique set of its eyes, combined with high cheekbones and a long parallel nose, lends a distinctive Japanese cast to the face, especially in profile, quite different from the other oriental breeds. Its short tail should resemble a bunny tail, with the hair fanning out to create a pom-pom appearance that effectively camouflages the tail's underlying bone structure.

HEAD: Although the head appears long and finely chiseled, it forms almost a perfect equilateral triangle (the triangle does not include the ears) with gentle curving lines, high cheekbones, and a noticeable whisker break; the nose is long and well defined by two parallel lines from tip to brow with a gentle dip at, or just below, eye level. Allowance must be made for jowls in the stud cat.

EARS: Large, upright, and expressive, set wide apart but at right angles to the head rather than flaring outward, and giving the impression of being tilted forward in repose.

MUZZLE: Fairly broad and rounding into the whisker break; neither pointed nor blunt. Chin: Should be full, neither undershot nor overshot.

EYES: Large, oval rather than round, but wide and alert; set into the skull at a rather pronounced slant when viewed in profile. The eyeball shows a shallow curvature and should not bulge out beyond the cheekbone or the forehead.

BODY: Medium in size, males proportionately larger than females. Torso long, lean, and elegant, not tubular, showing well-developed muscular strength without coarseness. No inclination toward flabbiness or cobbiness. General balance of utmost importance.

NECK: Neither too long nor too short, in proportion to the length of the body.

LEGS: In keeping with the body, long, slender, and high, but not dainty or fragile in appearance. The hind legs noticeably longer than the forelegs, but deeply angulated to bend when the cat is standing relaxed, so that the torso remains nearly level rather than rising toward the rear. When standing, the cat's forelegs and shoulders form two continuous straight lines, close together.

PAWS: Oval. Toes: five in front and four behind.

COAT (SHORTHAIR): Medium length, soft and silky, but without a noticeable undercoat.

COAT (LONGHAIR): Length medium-long to long, texture soft and silky, with no noticeable undercoat in the mature adult. Frontal ruff desirable. Coat may be shorter and close-lying over the shoulders, gradually lengthening toward the rump, with noticeable longer hair on the tail and rear britches.

Ear and toe tufts desirable. Coat should lie so as to accent the lines of the body.

TAIL: The tail is unique not only to the breed but also to each individual cat. This is to be used as a guideline, rather than promoting one specific type of tail out of the many that occur within the breed. The tail must be clearly visible and is composed of one or more curves, angles, or kinks or any combination thereof. The furthest extension of the tailbone from the body should be no longer than 3 inches. The direction in which the tail is carried is not important. The tail may be flexible or rigid and should be of a size and shape that harmonizes with the rest of the cat.

COLOR: In the bicolors and tricolors (Mi-Ke), any color may predominate, with preference given to bold, dramatic markings and vividly contrasting colors. In the solid-color cat, the coat color should be of uniform density and color from the tip to the root of each hair and from the nose of the cat to the tail. Nose leather, paw pads, and eye color should harmonize generally with coat color. Blue eyes and odd eyes are allowed.

PENALIZE: Short, round head; cobby build.

DISQUALIFY: Tailbone absent or extending too far beyond body. Tail lacking in pom-pom or fluffy appearance. Delayed bobtail effect (i.e., the pom-pom being preceded by 1 or 2 inches of normal tail with close-lying hair rather than appearing to commence at the base of the spine).

COLORS: A wide array of colors in the solid, tabby, parti-color and bicolor patterns and also some colors with the addition of white.

ALLOWABLE BREEDING OUTCROSSES: none.

JAVANESE
By Kris Willison

Javanese

Take one Balinese, dip it in the colors of the rainbow, and you have a Javanese. The Javanese is everything that is Balinese, and then some . . . the intelligence, grace, and refinement of the Siamese; the luxurious silk of the Balinese coat; and the designer colors of the Colorpoint Shorthair. The Javanese was named for the island of Java, near Bali, and has been around for as long as the Balinese has.

Physical Description
Some Javanese first appeared spontaneously in litters of Colorpoint Shorthair, but most are the result of Balinese breeders' using the Colorpoint Shorthair to introduce lynx and tortie point colors and patterns into the Balinese breed. The Javanese standard is identical to that of the Balinese, which is to say a cat of Siamese type with long, flowing coat; the only differ-

ence is in the colors accepted for championship.

Javanese are seen in a variety of colors in solid point, lynx point, and parti-color point. Javanese may also come in seal, blue, chocolate, and lilac point colors, similar to the Siamese and Balinese. However, these colors in the Javanese are not eligible for championship competition in the CFA. Javanese breeders use Siamese and Colorpoint Shorthairs in their breeding programs, producing variants that might look like Siamese or Colorpoint Shorthairs. The coats have a richer feel than that of a true shorthair. Because of the number of genetic variables, the kittens that are marked like Siamese are almost always sold as pets, while those that are marked like Colorpoint Shorthairs are used within breeding programs.

Coat development varies from kitten to kitten, even within the same litter. Some will have a respectable coat and plume (tail) by age 4 months. Still others might appear to be shorthairs (from a distance) until they get closer to 8 months or even older. Frills on the belly and pantaloons do not always mean that the kitten will be Longhair. Longhair kittens will have a much softer, silkier texture to their coats, and combing against the grain will reveal the actual length. The most desirable coat drapes softly, softening but not concealing the sleek lines of the body. Hair is shortest on the legs and around the face, and longest on the tail, to form a regal plume.

Javanese are a study of contradictions: elegantly refined, sometimes fragile in appearance, but in reality hard and muscular, with surprising strength. Their slender lines and flowing coat hide a rock-hard body capable of amazing acrobatic feats.

Personality

The Javanese is a breed for folks who want a little spice in their lives. Highly intelligent, these cats become familiar with their human's routine. They will talk, gently reminding when you are late with meals or playtime, joyously greeting you whenever you have been away. As a rule, the Javanese voice is softer and gentler than that of the Siamese. They use their paws like little hands to open cabinets and drawers in search of a favorite toy they saw you hide. Many fetch, but do not fool yourself that you taught them this game. In reality, they have cleverly taught you how to throw.

Javanese have specific personalities linked to each color. Tortie points (points are the differing colors on the face, legs, ears, and tail) are an acquired taste; you like them or you do not. Their markings can vary from a soft sprinkling of red and cream on a background of seal, blue, chocolate, or lilac to bold splashes of color, sometimes creating a clownlike appearance. Tortie points, with their splashes of red and cream mixed with the background color, can't seem to make up their minds how they are supposed to behave. They speak their minds freely and entertain you with their antics.

Red and cream points must get their color from Cupid's arrow; this has to be the most laid-back and easygoing personality of all colors. They seem to exist only to love you. While they thoroughly enjoy playing and doing the same things that so-called normal cats do, they take frequent breaks to reassure you of their devotion. They need to feel a part of your life and happy to "help," offering suggestions from a short distance before moving in to assist you with the project in question.

Lynx points seem to be the most popular pattern. There is nothing quite as dramatic as silvery stripes on a seal point background. Lynx points also come in blue, chocolate, lilac, red, and cream point colors, along with all possible tortie point colors. Lynx point personalities seem to vary from being very regal and dignified to seemingly being part monkey or squirrel—creative and always entertaining with tricks and toys.

Grooming Requirements

Cats of this breed are very easy to care for. The Javanese coat never mats and tends to need less grooming than the Siamese or Colorpoint Shorthair coat, making these cats a "lazy person's Longhair." The average pet Javanese will require only occasional combing and nail-clipping. Most will have had at least one bath during their early training, because a periodic bath freshens the coat and promotes healthy skin.

Some breeders use the same hair products on their cats as they do on their own hair; others swear by products discovered at shows or a combination of products arrived at by lengthy experimentation. There is simply no one right or wrong way to groom a Javanese other than to keep it simple. Everything about showing a Javanese should be fun. The minute that grooming and show preparation start to feel like work, you are probably doing something wrong.

The show bath should be as close to the date of the show as possible; the Javanese coat is most glorious and silky when squeaky-clean. The cat should be protected from drafts and chills, but blow-drying is not necessary. Nails must be clipped prior to the first judging; eyes and ears should be checked and then cleaned if necessary. Some exhibitors also trim the hair slightly around the ears although this is not absolutely necessary. Trimming should not be attempted without detailed instructions and a demonstration from an experienced breeder/exhibitor.

Origins and History

The Javanese became a separate breed from the Balinese because of their added coat colors. Most registries around the world group the Colorpoint Shorthair with the Siamese and initially accepted Balinese in all the same colors and patterns. During the mid-1970s, there was increased interest in these different-colored Balinese by breeders all over the United States and Canada. A controversy grew between various Balinese breed clubs when these colors and patterns were added. Some clubs refused the new colors and patterns, while others embraced them. Eventually most Balinese breeders agreed to accept the new colors and patterns, but only as a separate breed. In spite of the controversy, there was no stopping the enthusiasm for the additional colors and getting them accepted by the CFA.

In October 1979, a group of breeders met with the CFA board of directors in Chicago to petition for acceptance of these colors and patterns as new colors of the Balinese. The board examined the cats and discussed the issues. Because the CFA recognized the Balinese as a mutation of the Siamese and the Colorpoint Shorthair (same colors as the Javanese) as a hybrid, the cats in question could not be accepted as Balinese because they had been crossed with Colorpoint Shorthairs. For a similar reason, they could not be accepted as Colorpoint Shorthairs, because they had been crossed to Balinese. The board's final decision was that the new colors would have to be brought in as a separate breed, which would require a new name prior to registration. Anticipating such a decision, those with the cats in question met and discussed several possible names. At this meeting, the breeders sat down with some Asian maps and guidebooks and noticed the island of Java, next to Bali, on the maps. The two islands share a common language, culture, and religion, but Java is the larger, richer, and more fertile island, a twist they rather enjoyed. *Javanese* was one of the names that had been suggested, and new research confirmed it as appropriate. And so the breed was named.

We are fortunate that a few key breeders involved in promoting the Javanese breed, working toward its advancement in the CFA, are still actively breeding. Although the roots of the Javanese breed spread wide, pedigreed research indicates that the majority of noteworthy Javanese can be traced back to two "foundation" females: Alonale's Willo-the-Wisp (Canada, 1978) and Mishna M'Lady of Su-Bali (California, 1972).

In May 1986, the Javanese were advanced to Championship status, and on November 1 of that year, the race for the first CFA Grand Champion was won. Not just one but three Javanese earned their grands that month. Since that time, many Javanese have achieved prestigious titles, including National and Regional Winners and Distinguished Merit awards.

A review of the statistics year after year shows that a fairly steady number of Javanese cats are being shown. The drawback of a progressive breeding program is that an entire litter might be composed of all AOVs (Any Other Variety, which means, for this breed, the wrong color and/or wrong hair length). For this reason, any breeder at any given time might end up on the bench for an entire show season or even longer.

Miscellanea

Show preparation actually starts before the kittens are weaned. While taking time to kiss and tickle furry bellies, the experienced breeder and exhibitor will be unable to resist "playing show" with each baby. Supporting the tiny body at waist and chest, the kitten is stretched and taught to fly. *Flying* is a term used for carrying the cat in a stretched position, much like Superman, with all legs extended. The kitten is then stood on its hind legs (chest still supported) and the body and legs are stroked to check the refinement of boning and development of muscle tone. Last, the breeder will check the smoothness of the profile and wedge by smoothing back the facial hair with their fingers. It is this special handling that helps to mold a polished show cat and/or loving pet. Some kittens are so taken with the idea of flying that they decide their owner's shoulder is their favorite vantage point. As grown cats, they might be observed calmly sitting on or draped around their owner's neck as they are taken to a show ring for judging.

These long-haired, colorful beauties are a magnificent gift to the world combining the best qualities from some of the best cats of two continents.

POINT SCORE

HEAD (20)

Long flat profile	6
Wedge, fine muzzle, size	5
Ears	4
Chin	3
Width between eyes	2

EYES (5)

Shape, size, slant, and placement	5

BODY (30)

Structure and size, including neck	12
Muscle tone	10
Legs and feet	5
Tail	3

COAT (20)

Length	10
Texture	10

COLOR (25)

Body color	10
Point color (matching points of dense color, proper foot pads and nose leather)	10
Eye color	5

GENERAL: The ideal Javanese is a svelte cat with long, tapering lines, very lithe but strong and muscular. Excellent physical condition. Neither flabby nor bony. Not fat. Eyes clear. Because of the longer coat, the Javanese appears to have softer lines and less extreme type than other breeds of cats with similar type.

HEAD: Long, tapering wedge. Medium size in good proportion to body. The total wedge starts at the nose and flares out in straight lines to the tips of the ears, forming a triangle, with no break at the whiskers. No less than the width of an eye between the eyes. When the whiskers and face hair are smoothed back, the underlying bone structure is apparent. Allowance must be made for jowls in the stud cat.

SKULL: Flat. In profile, a long, straight line should be felt from the top of the head to the tip of the nose. No bulge over the eyes. No dip in nose.

EARS: Strikingly large, pointed, wide at base, continuing the lines of the wedge.

EYES: Almond-shaped. Medium size. Neither protruding nor recessed. Slanted toward the nose in harmony with lines of wedge and ears. Uncrossed.

NOSE: Long and straight. A continuation of the forehead with no break.

MUZZLE: Fine, wedge-shaped.

CHIN AND JAW: Medium size. Tip of chin lines up with tip of nose in the same vertical plane. Neither receding nor excessively massive.

BODY: Medium size. Graceful, long, and svelte. A distinctive combination of fine bones and firm muscles. Shoulders and hips continue same sleek lines of tubular body. Hips never wider than shoulders. Abdomen tight. The male may be somewhat larger than the female.

NECK: Long and slender.

LEGS: Bone structure long and slim. Hind legs higher than front. In good proportion to body.

PAWS: Dainty, small, and oval. Toes: five in front and four behind.

TAIL: Bone structure long, thin, tapering to a fine point. Tail hair spreads out like a plume.

COAT: Medium length, fine, silky; without downy undercoat, and lying close to the body, the coat may appear shorter than it is. Hair is longest on the tail.

COLOR: *Body:* Even, with subtle shading when allowed. Allowance should be made for darker color in older cats, as Javanese generally darken with age, but there must be definite contrast between body color and points. *Points:* Mask, ears, legs, feet, tail dense and clearly defined. All of the same shade. Mask covers entire face, including whisker pads, and is connected to ears by tracings. Mask should not extend over top of head. No ticking or white hairs in points.

PENALIZE: Lack of pigment in the nose leather and/or paw pads in part or in total, except as allowed in the color definitions for lynx and tortie points. Crossed eyes. Visible protrusion of the cartilage at the end of the sternum under normal handling. Soft or mushy body.

DISQUALIFY: Any evidence of illness or poor health. Weak hind legs. Malocclusion resulting in either undershot or overshot chin. Mouth breathing due to nasal obstruction or poor occlusion. Emaciation. Visible kink in tail. Eyes other than blue. White toes and/or feet. Incorrect number of toes. Definite double coat (i.e., downy undercoat).

COLORS: A variety of colors in solid point, lynx point, and parti-color point.

ALLOWABLE BREEDING OUTCROSSES: Balinese, Colorpoint Shorthair, Siamese.

KORAT
By Cheryl Coleman

Korat

The Korat shimmers, its coat a silver-tipped blue. In Thailand, its country of origin, people describe this color as "rain-cloud grey," and the silvering effect as "sea foam." The color appears to absorb light, creating the appearance of a halo.

Physical Description
The breed has a single coat, short and close-lying. The roots are a light silvery blue, a color that increases in shade up the shaft to a deeper blue, until it reaches the tips, which are silver; silver tipping is more prevalent on the muzzle and toes. The Korat comes in only one color, silver-tipped blue; no other color is accepted. As the cat moves, the coat appears to break, or separate, making the silver shimmer more prominently.

Another feature unique to the Korat that gives it a captivating mystique is the head structure. It is the cat with five hearts, three of which are on the head. Looking at the Korat straight on, you see the Valentine-shape heart of the head that can be gently traced around the head. The second heart is found by looking down over the top of the head, and the third heart is the nose. The other two hearts, which are not part of the head, are the muscular area of the chest when the cat is sitting and—most commonly forgotten—the heart inside the cat. As the cat matures, the heart shapes on the head become more pronounced.

The remaining features of the head complete the overall beauty of the Korat. The eyes are large, wide open, luminous, alert, and always observant. Eye color is peridot green (a yellowish green) in mature cats (2–4 years of age), but kittens have an amber to golden-green eye color that gradually changes as they mature. The ear set is a continuation of the heart-shaped face. The ears have rounded tips, with a large flare at the base. They give the Korat a very alert expression, complementing the heart shape, and do not sit too low or too high on the head. The eyebrow ridge across the top of the eyes further accentuates and clarifies the heart-shaped face. The Korat, when viewed from the side, has a lionlike downward curve to the nose.

The body of the Korat is semicobby, not long and lean like a Siamese or short like a Manx, but with a tapered waist. It is heavier than it appears. When you lift the Korat, you will be surprised to find that it has an unexpected heft, the way lifting a stone can be surprising. It is easy to compare the cat to a body builder; it feels like a firm steel spring. The bulk of the weight is carried toward the front, through rounded, well-developed muscular shoulders. The neck is fairly short and heavy, connecting to a broad chest, making the shoulders somewhat wider than the chest. In movement, the back of the Korat forms a slight arch, looking as though the cat is in a defensive mode. This body was designed by nature to create a survivor, one that is graceful, even though it has the look of great strength, and agile enough to move quickly. The Korat is possibly the only breed of cat that most closely resembles its original look. In comparing Korats today with photos of their earliest ancestors, you will see little difference over time.

Personality

Korats are extremely expressive. You can look at them and almost know what they are thinking; the scary part is, they *do* know what *you* are thinking. Theirs is almost a human expression that wins you over completely. Once you meet and live with a Korat, you will understand this.

Korats are very observant; they watch everything you do and then try to imitate you. They learn on their own how to open doors, turn on water faucets, and open lidded containers. You may think these things are cute, but once a Korat has learned tricks like those, you will never break them of the habits.

These cats are extremely loyal, giving you their total love and respect. They will greet you at the door when you come home, and then follow you to wherever you go. They will race you up a flight of stairs, and then wait for you if you have gone behind a closed door. They will trust you completely, knowing that you know what is best for them. One Korat, while getting a bath, was told to stay in the sink while the owner answered the phone. When the owner came back a few minutes later, there the Korat sat, all but saying, "Mom, I thought you'd never get back." How many cats do you know who would be that patient?

Korats are either going 100 miles per hour around the house or are in "Velcro kitty" mode. They want to be with you, near you, and helping you all the time. Although they are not in your face, they like to be involved in your activities. When in this mode, Korats will sit next to you while you are watching TV or reading a book. They have to be touching you, even if they have to lie on top of another Korat, who has already staked his claim to your lap, to be with you.

Playtime is a very serious activity for these cats. They have the mentality of "get the toy at all costs." Sometimes, they forget to land on their feet. When playing with feather toys, Korats make believe it's the real thing, stalking, chirping, and finally attacking the prey. Be forewarned: Never leave a feather toy out or there will be nothing left of it when you come back.

Many Korats enjoy a game of fetch. They will run after a toy, bring it back to you, and will not stop even though they are panting and you are both exhausted. There was a Korat at a show in which the judge had lost a grip on the feather toy she was holding. It fell to the floor in front of the judging table, and the Korat jumped after it. A spectator picked up the toy and put it back on the table, and the Korat hopped right up after it, back onto the table. It was her game, and she was not going to let the toy get away.

Korats are not very vocal, unless they have something serious to say, such as "My food dish is empty" or "I know you didn't mean to lock me out of the room." They sometimes make a chirping sound when playing but will keep their opinions to themselves.

These are homebody cats. They would much rather be at home than in a car, at the veterinarian's office, or visiting a relative. They are most comfortable in their own environment; however, they adapt quickly and quite well to new places.

Grooming Requirements

Korats require very little grooming. Because they have a single, close-lying coat that does not shed, a soft cloth or a rubber brush used lightly does the job. Bathing is not necessary unless you plan on showing your Korat. Bathing is usually done 2 or 3 days before a show. This allows the natural oils to return through the hair shaft.

Bathe the Korat using a shampoo for white cats—usually a blue shampoo. Unless the coat is greasy, one lathering is sufficient. A light conditioner is sometimes used to make the coat smooth and shiny. You can let the Korat air-dry. After it has completely dried, brush the coat lightly with a rubber brush to smooth it out, allowing it to lay flat against the body. Do not brush too hard, to avoid creating bald spots. At the show, the only grooming you will need is to smooth the coat down with a chamois cloth or silk scarf.

Origins and History

The Korat was discovered in Ampur Pimai of the Korat province in Thailand. The earliest known recording of the Korat is represented in the ancient book of paintings and verses known as *The Cat-Book Poems*, or *Smud Khoi of Cats*, in Bangkok's National Library. It was produced sometime during the Ayudhya period of Siamese history (1350–1767). The book presents 17 "good luck" cats of Thailand, which include the Korat, and is presently located at Bangkok's National Library. King Rama V named the breed when he remarked, "What a pretty cat. Where is it from?" and was told, "Korat." There is much tradition and folklore behind the Korat. One belief is that Korats with kinks in their tails increase your luck in Thailand.

The Thai people refer to the Korat as Si-Sawat cat ("see-sa-what") and say it is the "real" Siamese cat.

The first Korats were imported into the United States in June 1959. They were a brother and sister named Nara and Darra. These cats were from the Mahajaya Cattery of

Thailand. In 1967, the CFA accepted the Korat into Championship status. The first Korat Grand Champion in the CFA was chosen in the mid 1960s, and the first Korat to receive a National Win in the CFA did so in 1981.

Miscellanea

Korats do not need special handling unless they are being shown. As with cats that are destined for the show ring, they are exposed to a lot of handling and noise as kittens. However, Korats have an extraordinary sense of hearing and smell. They can hear sounds far off in the distance, such as a female in season across the show hall, or a male calling. They can also smell things that you cannot, such as another male or female cat. Even perfumes can sometimes get their hormones going. This sometimes adds to the challenge of showing a Korat, because they are aware of everything.

Korats always voice their opinion in the show ring. Although they are not very talkative at home, in the show ring they tell you how they feel about the situation. "Don't lift me high in the air." "Keep my feet on the ground." "Give me a toy." "Put me back in the cage." "Take me home." A show judge once referred to them as the "mother-in-law" cat—they are just very opinionated.

Show judges who have seen Korats frequently enjoy handling and recognizing them when they see their quality. In the show ring, Korats do not tolerate being held up in the air; they like to keep their hind legs on the table or have a secure feeling when being held. Their heftiness makes them uncomfortable when they are lifted in the air by judges. They should not be stretched, because their bodies are semi-cobby, not long and lean, and there is no need to overhandle the head. A show judge can see the heart shape of their heads quite easily by looking straight at them and over their top. An outline of the heart can be gently traced around the face, but if Korats feel that their head is being restrained, they may panic. They are extremely responsive to a gentle touch.

The Korat is a treasure that is waiting to be discovered by the general cat-loving public. Who would not want a cat that loves, respects, and trusts you unconditionally? Both the early breeders who gave them their start in the United States and the breeders of today are to be thanked for their efforts toward maintaining the integrity of these one-of-a-kind, silver-tipped blue cats of Thailand—cats with a lot of heart.

CFA SHOW STANDARD FOR THE KORAT

POINT SCORE

HEAD (25)		EYES (15)	
Broad head	5	Size	5
Profile	4	Shape	5
Breadth between eyes	4	Placement	5
Ear set and placement	4	**BODY (25)**	
Heart shape	5	Body	15
Chin and jaw	3	Legs and feet	5
		Tail	5

COAT (10)	
Short	4
Texture	3
Close-lying	3

COLOR (25)	
Body color	20
Eye color	5

GENERAL: The Korat ("Koh-raht") is a rare cat even in Thailand, its country of origin, and because of its unusually fine disposition is greatly loved by the Thai people, who regard it as a "good luck" cat. Its general appearance is of a silver blue cat with a heavy silver sheen, medium-size, hard-bodied, and muscular. All smooth curves with huge eyes that are luminous, alert, and expressive. Perfect physical condition, alert appearance.

HEAD: When viewed from the front, or looking down from just back of the head, the head is heart-shaped with breadth between and across the eyes. The eyebrow ridges form the upper curves of the heart, and the sides of the face gently curve down to the chin to complete the heart shape. Undesirable: any pinch or narrowness, especially between or across the eyes.

PROFILE: Well defined, with a slight stop between forehead and nose, which has a lionlike downward curve just above the leather. Undesirable: nose that appears either long or short in proportion.

CHIN AND JAW: Strong and well developed, making a balancing line for the profile and properly completing the heart shape. Neither overly squared nor sharply pointed, nor a weak chin that gives the head a pointed look.

EARS: Large, with a rounded tip and large flare at base, set high on head, giving an alert expression. Inside ears sparsely furnished. Hairs on outside of ears extremely short and close.

BODY: Semicobby, neither compact nor svelte. The torso is distinctive. Broad-chested with good space between forelegs. Muscular, supple, with a feeling of hard, coiled-spring power and unexpected weight. Back is carried in a curve. The males tend to be larger than females.

LEGS: Well proportioned to body. Distance along back from nape of neck to base of tail appears to be equal to distance from base of tail to floor. Front legs slightly shorter than back legs.

PAWS: Oval. Toes: five in front and four behind.

TAIL: Medium in length, heavier at the base, tapering to a rounded tip. Nonvisible kink permitted.

EYES: Large and luminous. Particularly prominent, with an extraordinary depth and brilliance. Wide open and oversized for the face. Eye aperture, which shows as well rounded when fully open, has an Asian slant when closed or partially closed. Undesirable: small or dull-looking eyes.

COAT: Single. Hair is short, glossy and fine, lying close to the body. The coat over the spine is inclined to break as the cat moves.

DISQUALIFY: Visible kink. Incorrect number of toes. White spot or locket. Any color but silver-tipped blue.

COLOR: Silver-tipped blue all over; the silver should be sufficient to produce a silver halo effect. The hair is usually lighter at the roots, with a gradient of blue that is deepest just before the tips, which are silver. Adults should be without shading or tabby markings. Allow for ghost tabby markings in kittens. Where the coat is short, the sheen of the silver is intensified. Undesirable: coats with silver tipping on only the head, legs, and feet. *Nose leather and lips:* Dark blue or lavender. *Paw pads:* Dark blue ranging to lavender with a pinkish tinge. *Eye color:* Luminous green preferred; amber cast acceptable. Kittens and adolescents have yellow or amber to amber-green eyes. Color is not usually true until the cat is mature, usually at 2–4 years of age.

ALLOWABLE BREEDING OUTCROSSES: none.

LAPERM
By A. D. Lawrence

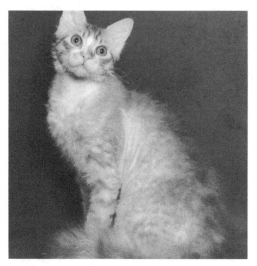

LaPerm Longhair

LaPerm Shorthair

The LaPerm is a curly-haired bundle of affection. It's hard to know which is more tenacious—the love that emanates from these cats or the wave of their unusual coat.

Physical Description
The LaPerm, as its name indicates, is set apart from other breeds by its undulating fur. It can sport anything from waves to ringlets, the latter of which can appear in any form from small, tight ringlets to long corkscrew curls.

The tightest curls occur on the underside of the cat, on the throat, and at the base of the ears.

The long-haired variety is generally blessed with a curly plumed tail and often with a full, curly ruff (similar to the mane on a lion). The coat has a moderately soft texture, yet each cat's coat is unique. The short-haired variety has more texture to the coat. It has a "bottle brush"-type tail and the coat generally stands away from the body, parting down the middle, but it does not have a ruff. The LaPerm is accepted by the CFA in any color or pattern.

Some kittens are born hairless, but most have short, wavy hair at birth. Often they will go practically bald, beginning with a spot on the top of their heads. This process generally starts when the kittens are about 2 weeks old, and they can be in varying stages of baldness during the first 4 months or so. The coat will generally come back, but the cat can lose it again and again. Although it is not common, they can also be born with straight hair and then lose that, with the hair growing back curly. For the first 6 months, it is a guessing game as to what you might have.

The coat on both long- and short-haired varieties may vary in length and fullness, depending on the season and the maturity of the cat. Both males and females of the long-haired variety may have a full ruff on the neck at maturity. Both varieties will have a saddle of shorter hair over their shoulders, although this is much more apparent on the Longhair.

The face and head of the LaPerm is somewhat triangular in shape, with fairly wide-set ears that continue the shape of the wedge, relatively full whisker pads, and large, expressive eyes. They boast a splendid set of curly whiskers and eyebrows.

In adulthood, males tend to weigh between 9 and 12 pounds and females weigh between 6 and 9 pounds. The breed is seen in both long and short hair.

Personality

LaPerms are very gentle and affectionate cats, although they are also very active. They seek human contact and purr as soon as they become aware of your presence. These cats are face-lovers; they will reach for your face with their paws and rub their face against yours but will settle for your head or neck. They love being kissed and will kiss back. LaPerms beg to be held, draped over a shoulder or cradled in your arms while resting on their backs.

Though these cats are extremely active, they are content to be lap cats, a paradox not found in most other active breeds. They are often content to follow your lead. Even if your cat is busy playing and you want to sit and relax, you can pick him up and sit down with him and he will stay on your lap, accepting all the attention you give him. These cats are inquisitive by nature, always wanting to know what is going on around them. Kittens have been known to stop nursing and seek out the source of a human voice before their eyes have opened.

LaPerms have quiet voices but may become vocal when they want attention. Being working farm cats by nature; they are excellent hunters as well as gentle companions. They adapt well to apartment life, too, because of their strong bonding instincts.

Grooming Requirements

The breed is a low-maintenance one, requiring a minimum of grooming because the coat does not easily mat. LaPerms' curls hold the hair, much like that of a Poodle; therefore, shedding is minimal. Grooming for cat shows takes a bit more effort but is still relatively easy. Confer with your cat's breeder or a fellow exhibitor for helpful hints regarding products and bathing technique.

A bath is necessary only once a month, at the most, unless you have a male with *stud tail* (a medical condition involving excessive oil production along the tail). Frequent baths will dry out the coat and cause it to become brittle. When to bathe depends on how oily your cat's coat becomes. For some cats with not much coat, the Thursday before a show is fine. For others with a denser coat, you may have to bathe on the Monday before a show. (Cat shows are held on Saturdays and Sundays.)

Trial and error will tell you when to bathe your cat. If you bathe too late, the cat will not have enough time for the replacement of natural oils and the coat will not show its curl.

Regular maintenance for nonshow cats is very easy and much like between-show maintenance for show cats. The best product for keeping the coat in shape is a metal comb with rolling teeth—a comb with teeth that are not stationary but instead roll when grooming. (This type of comb can be found at PETsMART and is sold by some cat show vendors.) A comb of this nature will not pull hair out that is not ready to come out. It removes only dead hair. Use it for that purpose two or three times a week. It will only take a minute or two and will keep the cat's coat in excellent condition. Your cat will begin to look forward to being groomed with the comb, purring all the while you are working on him. This will be pleasure time for you and the cat. Do not comb your cat or use a dryer immediately after the bath, as doing so may damage the hair. A simple towel-drying before letting your LaPerm air-dry is the best method to protect the coat. For the first 3 or 4 days after a bath, your cat will shed much more than usual, so it is important to use the comb during that time. Combing also stimulates the circulation and helps bring back the natural oils for coat texture. Combing out dead hair also helps prevent hairballs and matting.

Origins and History
The breed first made its appearance in Oregon's Columbia River Gorge, one of the most beautiful areas in the world. The area abounds with ancient Indian hunting and fishing grounds. In the midst of these grounds, near the town The Dalles, in Oregon, the LaPerm came into existence in the spring of 1982.

The first LaPerm was the result of a natural mutation, and sprang from strong, healthy, domestic "barn cat" stock. The original cat was remarkable in a number of ways, other than just the lack of hair at birth. The body type and temperament are as much a part of the breed as the "Rex" gene, which is responsible for its unusual coat.

A barn cat gave birth to a litter of six kittens, one of which was born completely bald, looking nothing like her mother or littermates. It was, without a doubt, an ugly kitten, having no hair; large, wide-spaced ears, and a blueprint on her skin that mimicked a classic tabby pattern.

Within 8 weeks, the kitten began to grow very soft, curly hair. By 3–4 months of age, the kitten had a full coat of curly hair. She was named Curly. Not being very knowledgeable about cats, owner Linda Koehl accepted the kitten as just different and thought nothing more of the matter.

Curly's soft fur was so inviting to the touch that Linda found herself constantly picking her up. Curly's temperament was different too; she was affectionate but not demanding, patiently and quietly waiting for her turn. She was gentle and trusting.

Curly was taken by surprise at the onset of labor, and instead of seeking shelter in a barn, she gave birth to five kittens under a tree during a rainstorm, all male and all as bald as Curly had been at birth. Linda realized this was some sort of "Rex" mutation. She thought of it as novel, not something unprecedented. Future litters provided only occasional hairless kittens of both sexes. Curly's insistence on being an outdoors cat eventually led to her disappearance. Linda never found out what had become of her. She just stopped showing up for her morning visits, leaving behind a number of kittens who had all inherited her soft, curly coat and marvelous disposition.

During the next 10 years, Linda made no attempt to breed the cats selectively, but as the frequency of bald kittens increased, she began to seek additional information about unusual cats. She had no knowledge of genetics or breeding, and thus she allowed the cats to roam free through the barns and orchard for several years. They were excellent mousers and kept the property rodent free.

As Linda became more aware of how unusual the cats were, she started to confine and control the breeding and decided on the breed name of LaPerm, which means "wavy" or "rippled" in several languages. It appeared that the curly gene was dominant and carried by both males and females. An occasional breeding accident led to a slight enlargement of the gene pool but maintained the same physical and personality characteristics.

To paraphrase the Beatles, "there is a long and winding road" for the recognition of a new breed. No truer phrase could be applied to the emergence of the LaPerm, which started with the birth of "a very ugly kitten."

The CFA accepted the breed for the Miscellaneous Class in February 2000.

Miscellanea

The LaPerm is generally accepting of new situations such as traveling or being handled by strangers. Bear in mind, however, that each cat, regardless of breed, may differ slightly from the ideal, so use caution until you learn what your cat prefers. Generally speaking, this is a breed that knows no strangers and readily adapts to being handled by humans.

A LaPerm cradled in your arms can melt your heart as you listen to the purr of a cat with unmatched love and respect for humans. This cat's delightful-to-touch fur and people-oriented personality makes a powerful combination that captivates nearly everyone who sees a LaPerm.

CFA SHOW STANDARD FOR THE LAPERM (MISCELLANEOUS STATUS)

POINT SCORE

HEAD (40)

Size and shape	10
Muzzle and chin	10
Profile	10
Ears	5
Eyes	5

BODY (32)

Torso	17
Neck	5
Legs and feet	5
Tail	5

COLOR AND PATTERN (28)

Coat	3
Texture and length	10
Curl or waviness	15

GENERAL: The LaPerm is a naturally occurring mutation producing both long- and short-haired cats. It is medium-size, is curly-coated, and has a semiforeign type. All colors are acceptable. All parts of the body are in harmony with the size of the cat. There is evidence of surprising weight for size. The cat is alert and seems to be walking tall on his feet. Coat texture will be distinctly different than that of any other Rex mutation and will vary within the breed. Males will generally have a curlier coat, but not always.

HEAD: The skull is a modified wedge with rounded contours. There is a gentle convex curve rising from the bridge of the nose to the brow.

MUZZLE: Slightly broad in proportion to the wedge. Chin strong and firm, presenting a perpendicular line down from the tip of the nose. Slight whisker pinch. Allow for jowls on mature males.

EARS: Placed to continue the modified wedge of the head, slightly flared and cupped, medium to large, with full furnishings and earmuffs. Lynx tipping preferred.

EYES: Medium large and expressive, almond in shape at rest, and rounder when alert. Set moderately far apart and slightly slanted toward base of ear. Eye color has no relation to coat color.

BODY: Medium in size, semiforeign, medium-fine boning, with back slightly higher in rear.

NECK: Carried erect, medium long in length in proportion to body.

LEGS AND FEET: Medium long to match body length. Forelegs may be slightly shorter than hind legs. As with body, medium-fine boning, with rounded feet.

TAIL: In proportion to body, with tapering shape.

COAT: The perfect cat will have a moderately soft, springy coat texture, with hair standing away from the body in ringlet-type curls or waves over most of the cat. The longest curls are on the underside of the neck and at the base of the ears. Both males and females can have a full neck ruff. The curlier, the better. There are very few guard hairs; however, the thicker and heavier the coat, the better. Short-haired LaPerms do not have the ruff or a plumed tail.

PENALIZE: Lack of ear furnishings. On Longhair LaPerms, crossed eyes. Nonvisible tail faults.

DISQUALIFY: Cobby body. Short legs. Incorrect number of toes. Visible tail faults. Straight hair.

COLORS: All colors and patterns.

ALLOWABLE BREEDING OUTCROSSES: domestic longhair and domestic shorthair. Kittens born on or after January 2010 may have only LaPerm parents.

MAINE COON CAT

By Gail Frew

Maine Coon Cat

Maine Coon Cats are the first pedigreed cats native to the United States. Despite their size and ruggedness, they are often called the gentle giants of the cat fancy because of their loving nature.

Physical Description

The Maine Coon is a massive cat with a broad chest and a long, rectangular body covered with a long, flowing coat. Its outstanding coat is a distinctive feature of the cat. The fur is short at the shoulders, long on the stomach, and longer on the back legs. The coat is heavy and shaggy, an overall uneven-looking coat that is nonetheless silky to the touch. The tail is so long and full that when a Maine Coon takes a nap, she wraps herself up with it.

The Maine Coon has five color classes: solid, tabby, tabby with white, parti-color, and "all other colors." Patterns include the classic tabby (marked in circles), the mackerel tabby (marked with stripes), and the patched tabby (splashes of red on the coat). Only females are patched tabbies.

Males average between 16 and 19 pounds, although some can weigh 20 pounds or more. Females are smaller, averaging between 8 and 12 pounds. The head is medium in width and length with a square-looking muzzle. The cheekbones are high, and the chin is firm, in line with the nose and upper lip. The nose is medium long, with a slight concavity in the profile.

Personality

As a breed, Maine Coon Cats are gentle and loyal. They are strong, tranquil, and a pleasure to see and touch. They have easygoing temperaments that make them ideal family pets. They get along well with children and dogs. Depending on the breed of dog in a household, the Maine Coon can be bigger than Fido. Maine Coon Cats are very sociable and enjoy helping their owners when they read by lying across the book or newspaper, batting at the pen when they are working a crossword puzzle, or chasing the thread while they are doing needlepoint or knitting. These cats happily join the family in such pursuits as watching TV, preparing dinner, or even taking a shower. The Maine Coon can be content with his own company and will pursue a variety of activities that he considers entertaining, including playing with toys, watching birds outside through the window, splashing in his water bowl, and, of course, sleeping, usually on your head.

These large cats have an interesting vocabulary, which includes not only the meow but also a variety of cheeps, trills, and purrs. A truly affectionate Maine Coon will leap onto your lap to be petted, then stand up, place her paws on your shoulders, and butt her head against yours. Being a politically wise feline, she will do this with all family members. This intelligent, easygoing companion has become a great favorite with men, who find these actions very appealing.

Grooming Requirements

Grooming the Maine Coon Cat is relatively easy. The coat is simple to maintain with uncomplicated combing and brushing, several times a week. This will keep it looking silky and flowing. These 5- to 10-minute sessions will help prevent dreaded hairballs. Claws on all four feet should be clipped every 10–14 days (for show and nonshow cats alike). The Maine Coon will use a scratching post when one is provided. Show grooming for the Maine Coon also includes shampooing and conditioning the coat weekly, drying with a hair dryer, brushing, and combing the coat out for its final presentation.

Origins and History

The Maine Coon's origins are shrouded in the mists of time and the legends told by their owners. Many people once believed the Maine Coon originated by interbreeding the American bobcat with the domestic cats brought to North America on the various sailing ships that came to the New England shores. Probably the tufted ears and feet of the Maine Coon, which are similar to the bobcat, gave some credence to this legend. The tufts curl outward from the inside of the ears; tufts of fur are also found between the toes. Taking fantasy one step further is the belief that the domestic cats of New England mated with raccoons. The early Maine Coons may simply have looked like raccoons to the natives, because the brown tabby, with its bushy ringed tail, occurs most commonly in nature. Adding to the fantasy is the fact that the Maine Coon also converses with an endearing trill or chirp, somewhat like the cry of a young raccoon. However, it is genetically impossible for domestic cats to breed with either raccoons or bobcats; these are separate species and cannot crossbreed.

There are various other romantic versions of the Maine Coon's development that have been handed down over the years. The first involves Captain Samuel Clough and Marie-Antoinette. Captain Clough was one of the principals (or so the legend goes) in a plot designed to smuggle the French queen consort out of France and bring her to Wiscasset, Maine. The scheme was cut short, but not before Clough had loaded his ship, the *Sally*, with the queen's luxurious furnishings and accoutrements plus six of her favorite long-haired cats. Sadly, Marie-Antoinette was seized and eventually beheaded. Captain Clough sailed with all haste to escape repercussions for his part in the attempted rescue, and with him went the queen's possessions and the cats still in his care. It is assumed that the queen's cats bred with the American cats and voilà—the origin of the Maine Coon.

Still another legend concerns an English sea captain, improbably named Coon, who was excessively fond of cats. He sailed up and down the New England coast with his army of predominantly long-haired cats. When the captain went ashore, so did his cats. When long-haired kittens began appearing in local litters, the owner's comment would be: "One of Coon's cats."

A more logical conclusion is that the Maine Coon developed from the domestic short-haired cats of settlers who came to America with all their worldly goods and the family pet. Later, as the country became more civilized and the trading ships returned from their travels, the sailors returned with long-haired cats. The new long-haired cats in turn bred with the local short-haired cats and began populating the Eastern Seaboard. Those cats that survived the harsh New England winters produced the next generation of kittens.

It was to be expected that these intelligent cats would find their way into the settlers' homes and become beloved pets as well as good working mousers. By the 1860s, farmers were telling stories and bragging about the powers and intelligence of their Maine Coons. During that decade, those same farmers began having their own cat show at the Skowhegan Fair, where Maine Coons from all over the territory competed for the title of Maine State Champion Coon Cat.

The earliest writer to describe Maine Coon Cats was F. R. Pierce. Mrs. Pierce, an American from the state of Maine, wrote the chapter titled "Maine Cats" for *The Book of the Cat*. This classic cat book published in England in 1903 was primarily written by British author Frances Simpson. Mrs. Pierce wrote the chapter on the Maine Coon Cats from her extensive personal knowledge and experience. Co-owner of a black-and-white Maine Coon Cat named Captain Jenks of the Horse Marines, she documented the early history of domestic cats in the United States and of the Maine Coon Cat in particular. Mrs. Pierce gave not only names and dates of cat shows along the Eastern Seaboard but also names of the cats who won them. She stated emphatically that large shows were held in all the populous eastern cities, with some held as far west as Chicago in the 1870s.

The most famous and largest of the early shows was held at New York's Madison Square Garden in May 1895. A brown tabby male Maine Coon named Cosey, owned by Mrs. Fred Brown, won that show. Cosey was awarded a silver medallion marked "National Cat Show, 1895" and bearing a cat face in the middle and a silver cat collar engraved "National Cat Show, 1895, won by Cosey," and he had his picture taken while wearing his collar ribbon, which was marked "National Cat Show."

The silver collar, an important piece of cat fancy history, was purchased and donated to the CFA Foundation for its Jean Baker Rose Memorial Library housed at the CFA central office.

In the twentieth century, "show fever" hit the fancy, and cat shows began to spread from the Northeast to the Midwest and finally to the West Coast. At about the same time, the CFA, founded in 1906, was keeping the only breed record books we have of this period, *The CFA Stud Book and Registry*. In Book I, 28 Maine Cats, as they were still known, were listed under a special proviso that depended on a sworn statement that the sire and dam were the "same breed, long hair and that neither is a shorthaired." It is noteworthy that CFA Registration #5 was a tortoiseshell female Maine Cat named Molly Bond.

Soon after this, the Maine Coon Cat decreased in popularity as other long-haired cats with pedigrees came into greater favor. The Maine Coon had its last recorded victory for over 40 years when a "longhaired blue Maine Cat" took first place in his class and Best of Show in 1911. After that, Maine Coons slipped into the background and were shown occasionally under the Any Other Variety (AOV) category. Remaining in the background during the next four decades, the Maine Coon Cat was declared extinct in the late 1950s. The Maine Coon's extinction, like Mark Twain's death, was an exaggeration.

In the early 1950s, the Central Maine Cat Club began an effort to end the Maine Coon's slide into a status as a regional oddity and to give impetus to record keeping and showcasing for the breed. The club sponsored shows and kept records as a means to call attention to all cats and the Maine Coon Cat in particular. Before the club's demise in 1963, its achievements included creating one of the first written standards for the breed, keeping breeding records for the Maine

Coon, and making people aware that the Maine Coons existed and had credentials. People in other parts of the country were starting to breed and show Maine Coons as well as keep them as pets. The cats were beginning to reappear in the show halls from which they had disappeared.

In the 1960s, a group of Maine Coon Cat breeders created a club whose purpose was to preserve and protect the breed. This dedicated group of people had the will and determination to see the project through. These early movers and shakers were completely dedicated to Maine Coons.

During the early 1970s, Maine Coon breeders began the quest for CFA provisional status. After two unsuccessful attempts to gain that status, the breeders were advised to form a breed club. The Maine Coon Cat Club was formed in 1973. In the spring of 1974, the breeders met all the requirements for recognition of the Maine Coon Cat as a provisional breed: They had a standard, a breed club, and 133 cats registered. The Maine Coon Cat was accepted for CFA provisional status May 1975. Championship status was achieved in May 1976. America's native longhair was back on the show bench.

Since 1976 the Maine Coon Cat has been a rising star both in show competition and as a companion in the home. Though this popular breed of the nineteenth century once drifted into obscurity, it is the second most popular breed in the CFA registry today.

Maine Coons are well known for their loving nature and great intelligence. They are sturdy, skilled working cats (with regard to their mousing talents). Maine Coon Cats are especially good with children and dogs and are now a popular, highly sought after companion, much admired for their beauty.

CFA SHOW STANDARD FOR THE MAINE COON CAT

POINT SCORE

HEAD (30)

Shape	15
Ears	10
Eyes	5

BODY (30)

Shape	15
Neck	5
Legs and feet	5
Tail	5

COAT	**20**

COLOR (15)

Body color	10
Eye color	5

BALANCE	**5**

GENERAL: Originally a working cat, the Maine Coon is solid and rugged and can endure a harsh climate. A distinctive characteristic is its smooth, shaggy coat. A well-proportioned and balanced appearance, with no part of the cat being exaggerated. Quality should never be sacrificed for size. With an essentially amiable disposition, it has adapted to varied environments.

HEAD SHAPE: Medium in width and slightly longer in length than width, with a squareness to the muzzle. Allowance should be made for broadening in older studs. Cheekbones high.

MUZZLE/CHIN: Is visibly square, medium in length, and blunt-ended when viewed in profile. It may give the appearance of being a rectangle but should not appear to be tapering or pointed. Length and width of the muzzle should be proportionate to the rest of the head and present a pleasant, balanced appearance. The chin should be strong, firm, and in line with the upper lip and nose. When viewed in profile, the chin depth should be observable and give the impression of a square, 90-degree angle. A chin lacking in depth (i.e., one that tapers from the jawline to the lip) is not considered strong, firm, or desirable.

PROFILE: Should be proportionate to the overall length of the head and should exhibit a slight concavity when viewed in profile. The profile should be relatively smooth and free of pronounced bumps and/or humps. A profile that is straight from the brow line to the tip of the nose is not acceptable. The profile should not show signs of having a break or stop.

EARS: *Shape:* Large, well-tufted, wide at base, tapering to appear pointed. *Set:* Approximately one ear's width apart at the base; not flared.

EYES: Large, expressive, wide-set. Slightly oblique setting with slant toward outer base of ear.

NECK: Medium long.

BODY SHAPE: Muscular, broad-chested. Size medium to large. Females generally are smaller than males. The body should be long, with all parts in proportion, to create a well-balanced rectangular appearance, with no part of the anatomy being so exaggerated as to foster weakness. Allowance should be made for slow maturation.

LEGS AND FEET: Legs substantial, wide-set, of medium length, and in proportion to the body. Forelegs are straight. Back legs are straight when viewed from behind. Paws large, round, well-tufted. Five toes in front; four in back.

TAIL: Long, wide at base, and tapering. Fur long and flowing.

COAT: Heavy and shaggy; shorter on the shoulders and longer on the stomach and britches. Frontal ruff desirable. Texture silky, with coat falling smoothly.

PENALIZE: A coat that is short or overall even.

DISQUALIFY: Delicate bone structure. Undershot chin (i.e., the front teeth—incisors—of the lower jaw overlapping or projecting beyond the front teeth of the upper jaw when the mouth is closed). Crossed eyes. Kinked tail. Incorrect number of toes. White buttons, white lockets, or white spots. Cats showing evidence of hybridization resulting in the colors chocolate, lavender, the Himalayan pattern or unpatterned agouti on the body (i.e., Abyssinian-type ticked tabby).

COLORS: A wide array of colors in the solid, shaded, smoke, tabby, bicolor, and parti-color patterns.

ALLOWABLE BREEDING OUTCROSSES: none.

MANX

By Joanne Stone and Lisa Franklin

Manx Longhair

Manx Shorthair

The courage of a lion, strength of a bear, wisdom of the ages, heart of a child, and *a bowling ball on legs*—these are all phrases commonly used to describe one of the more unusual breeds of cat, the Manx.

Physical Description

CFA-registered Manx are bred to be medium-size cats, males averaging between 10 and 12 pounds, females between 8 and 10. When viewed from any angle, the Manx should appear round. The body will be shorter than that of the average cat, the hind legs will be a bit longer than many cats', and the back will form a natural arch when standing.

Their legs are thick and stocky, rather than long and thin like the legs of a Siamese. Manx should weigh more than they might appear to. This makes it easy to understand the bowling-ball description. Despite the impression of strength, power, and independence they create, this breed is a true pussycat in every sense of the word.

The Manx has a thick, plush, double coat. On close examination, it is apparent that the coat of the short-haired Manx consists of somewhat hard guard or top hairs and a dense, soft undercoat. This gives the cat a well-padded feel and provides superior protection against the elements in the feral state. The long-haired Manx has a softer, flowing coat, which includes britches and a ruff around the neck. Most longhairs have ear tufts.

Any color is acceptable except those that show evidence of hybridization, such as chocolate brown or colorpoints like those found on the Siamese. These colors do not naturally occur in the Manx gene pool. Like many other cat breeds, the Manx can sport one of two tabby coat patterns—classic (round, circular markings) and mackerel (vertical stripes on the body)—as well as solids and patterns such as calico or tortoiseshell.

The lack of tail is perhaps the most recognized characteristic of a Manx, but not all Manx are completely tailless—that is, not all Manx are without tail vertebrae and do not have a slight hollow where the tail might otherwise start (rumpy). They may be born with one or two tail vertebrae (riser); three or more vertebrae (stubby), where movement is back and forth as well as up and down; or regular long tails. Even if full-tailed, these cats are every bit as much a Manx as their rumpy counterparts, having the Manx body, coat characteristics, personality, and heritage. The perfect show Manx, however, must be born without a tail, and the showing of a docked-tailed Manx is against CFA show rules. It is interesting to note that although you will find an occasional *kink* in the stub or the tail of a Manx, you seldom find the curls and twists that occur in some other breeds.

Personality

Manx are fun-loving creatures. They like to retrieve (you will tire of the game long before they will), play in water, and carry things around in their mouths. They will bring you a toy when you are in bed, reading, or doing something where you would rather not be bothered and will try in every manner they can think of to get you to join in their games. That failing, they will go off to finish the game alone, seemingly forgetting that the original intent had been play for two. These are rather doglike characteristics, and as a matter of fact, Manx tend to get along well with dogs and are often compared to them. It is not unusual to find them napping close together or actually chasing each other about the house in a friendly game of tag. It is quite a sight to see a Manx scurry from a room with a dog in hot pursuit, only to return a few moments later hot on the heels of its canine playmate.

These cats attach themselves to their human family with uncanny devotion, often claiming one individual over the others as their special friend. The bonds that Manx form with their human families can be so strong that it is not uncommon to find them somewhat wary of strangers who come to the home. Manx may well sit back and take stock of these newcomers before deciding that all is well.

The personality of Manx also makes them a perfect choice for families who have children. They are very patient and seem to know that the young human who is perhaps tugging a bit too hard at an ear or holding a bit too tight around the middle must be tolerated. Rather than scratching or biting, a Manx will usually just squirm to get away and, once free, return to the child as if to give him another chance. By the same token, a Manx will know to stay clear of a child who is constantly overaggressive toward it. This would be a clue to the parents that their child may need a little more schooling in the proper way to handle pets.

Generally not loud cats, Manx prefer to communicate with quiet chirps, trills or purrs, and gentle head bumps. They are not in-your-face cats and usually conduct themselves with dignity, preferring a warm lap to perching on your head or the top of the curtain rod. This is not to say, however, that Manx do not have their momentary lapses. Many owners tell stories of Manx who are calmly walking across a room at one moment, only to jump straight up and race about the house the next moment—for no apparent reason. The hour of 10:00 P.M. also seems to hold some special significance for the Manx cat. It is at this time that many Manx will revert to kittenhood for a few minutes, casting aside all semblance of adulthood, running, chasing, and acting like clowns. Why this hour? No one knows. Some speculate that it is a final release of energy before bedding down for the night. Others believe the behavior stems back to the Isle of Man, fairies, and all that made a Manx a Manx. We may never know—the Manx are not telling.

Grooming Requirements

Although Manx do shed, grooming is not a problem. All cats benefit from grooming, with particular attention paid to their ears and their nails. The long-haired Manx, by the very nature of its coat, requires more upkeep than the short-haired variety, but the texture of this coat makes it much less likely to mat than the coat of most other long-haired breeds.

For the long-haired Manx, a wide-tooth comb works best for the grooming sessions. Pay particular attention to the areas under the legs and to the sides of the face, as this is the first place mats form. A thorough combing every few days will keep this coat in top shape. For the Shorthair Manx, either a brush or a comb will do. Your cat will come to look forward to regular grooming sessions.

With few exceptions, bathing Manx is not a problem. This could be a result of their natural affinity for water. The frequency of baths depends on the individual cat's needs. Show cats should be bathed weekly, whereas a family pet may need a bath once a year or less. Be sure to use the type of shampoo to best suit the specific needs of your Manx—and only products formulated for use on cats. The use of dog products on your Manx could prove disastrous. Many people allergic to cats can tolerate a Manx in the home. If you suffer from such allergies, a Manx may very well be the cat for you.

Origins and History

As mentioned before, the Manx cat is an old, natural breed. The earlier *CFA Stud Book* shows that the Manx was recognized as a CFA breed as far back as the 1920s. At first, the CFA recognized only short-haired Manx. The first CFA Manx Grand Champion was an Isle of Man import that was shown in the 1950s and became a Grand Champion in 1958. It was not until 1989 that the CFA officially recognized the long-haired Manx, then called a Cymric (pronounced "Kim-ric"). Several years later, the Manx Breed Council and the Cymric Breed Council asked the CFA for long-haired Manx status, which was approved in May 1994.

The tail mutation was first recorded on the Isle of Man in the sixteenth century, where sailing ships from many countries docked over a course of several hundred years. The lack of tail makes the Manx a breed steeped in folklore. One story tells how, in the old days, the warriors on the Isle trimmed their helmets with the long tails of cats. Over time, the mama cats, fearing for the safety of their kittens, began gently chewing off the tails of their newborns, until all that remained on the Isle of Man were tailless cats.

Another tells of how a tailless cat swam to shore from a ship belonging to the Spanish Armada that was wrecked on a rock near the Isle of Man. On reaching the Isle, he became the ancestor of all tailless cats there and also the reason that most Manx like water to this day.

Perhaps the most endearing of these legends is the one in which the tail of the late-arriving cat gets caught in the door of the Ark as Noah is closing it for the final time. It is most likely that the original mutated cat stemmed from British Shorthairs, because cats were so commonly kept on ships for rodent control and companionship.

In any case, the Manx is historically regarded as a product of the Isle of Man, an almond-shaped island measuring about 10 by 30 miles and laying in the Irish Sea between Ireland and England. Because they lived on an island of limited size, eventually all free-roaming cats carried the gene that limited the length of tail. Today's Manx are direct descendants of those Isle of Man cats. Careful breeding over the years has preserved and enhanced this breed's unique characteristics.

★ ★ ★

t is a joy to be owned by a Manx. A well-loved, well-cared for Manx will become an important part of any family for many years (often fifteen or more). Once they have entered your heart, you will find it hard to ever be without a Manx. These are truly cats for everyone.

CFA SHOW STANDARD FOR THE MANX

POINT SCORE

HEAD AND EARS	25
EYES	5
BODY	25
TAILLESSNESS	5
LEGS AND FEET	15
COAT	
Length	10
Texture	10
COLOR AND MARKINGS	5

GENERAL: The overall impression of the Manx cat is that of roundness; round head with firm, round muzzle and prominent cheeks; broad chest; substantial short front legs; short back, which arches from shoulders to a round rump; great depth of flank and rounded, muscular thighs. Manx should be alert, clear of eye, with a glistening, clean, well-groomed coat. They should be surprisingly heavy when lifted. Manx may be slow to mature, and allowances should be made in young cats.

HEAD AND EARS: Round head with prominent cheeks and a jowly appearance (more evident in adult males) that enhances the round appearance of the breed. In profile, head is medium in length, with a gentle dip from forehead to nose. Well-developed muzzle, very slightly longer than it is broad, with a strong chin. Definite whisker break, with large, round whisker pads. Short, thick neck. Ears wide at the base, tapering gradually to a rounded tip. Medium in size in proportion to the head, widely spaced and set slightly outward. When viewed from behind, the ear set resembles the rocker on a cradle. The furnishings of the ears are sparse in Shorthair Manx and full furnishings for Longhair Manx.

EYES: Large, round, and full. Set at a slight angle toward the nose (outer corners slightly higher than inner corners). Ideal eye color conforms to requirements of coat color.

BODY: Solidly muscled, compact and well-balanced, medium in size, with sturdy bone structure. The Manx is stout in appearance, with broad chest and well-sprung ribs. The constant repetition of curves and circles give the Manx the appearance of great substance and durability, a cat that is powerful without the slightest hint of coarseness. Males may be slightly larger than females. Flank (fleshy area of the side between the ribs and hip) has greater depth than in other breeds, causing considerable depth to the body when viewed from the side. The short back forms a smooth, continuous arch from shoulders to rump, curving at the rump to form the desirable round look. Length of back is in proportion to the entire cat; height of hindquarters equal to length of body. Males may be somewhat longer. Because the Longhair Manx has longer coat over the rump area and breeches, the body may appear longer.

TAILLESSNESS: Appearing to be absolute in the perfect specimen. A rise of bone at the end of the spine is allowed and should not be penalized unless it is such that it stops the judge's hand, thereby spoiling the tailless appearance of the cat. The rump is extremely broad and round.

LEGS AND FEET: Heavily boned, forelegs short and set well apart to emphasize the broad, deep chest. Hind legs much longer than forelegs, with heavy, muscular thighs and substantial lower legs. Longer hind legs cause the rump to be considerably higher than the shoulders. Hind legs are straight when viewed from behind. Paws are neat and round, with five toes in front and four behind.

COAT LENGTH, SHORTHAIR: Double coat is short and dense, with a well-padded quality due to the longer, open outer coat and the close cottony undercoat. Coat may be thinner during the summer months.

COAT TEXTURE, SHORTHAIR: Texture of outer guard hairs is somewhat hard; appearance is glossy. A softer coat may occur in whites and dilutes because of color–texture gene link but should not be confused with the silky texture found in the Longhair Manx.

COAT LENGTH, LONGHAIR: The double coat is of medium length, dense, and well padded over the main body, gradually lengthening from the shoulders to the rump. Coat of breeches, abdomen, and neck ruff is usually longer than the coat on the main body. Cheek coat is thick and full. The collarlike neck ruff extends from the shoulders, being biblike around the chest. Breeches should be full and thick to the hocks in the mature cat. Lower leg and head coat (except for cheeks) should be shorter than on the main body and neck ruff, but dense and full in appearance. Toe tufts and ear tufts are desirable. All things being equal in type, preference should be given to the cat showing full coating.

COAT TEXTURE, LONGHAIR: Coat is soft and silky, falling smoothly on the body yet being full and plush because of the double coat. Coat should have a healthy, glossy appearance. Allowance to be made for seasonal and age variations.

COLOR AND MARKINGS: Manx colors and tabby patterns are recognized as described below under Colors. Colors and patterns showing evidence of hybridization (chocolate/lavender/ticked tabby/pointed or these combinations with white) are not allowed. Cats with no more white than a locket and/or button(s) do not qualify for the bicolor or OMC (Other Manx Colors) Class. Such cats shall be judged in the color class of their basic color with no penalty for such locket or button(s).

TRANSFER TO AOV (ANY OTHER VARIETY): Definite, visible tail joint.

PENALIZE: On the Longhair Manx, coat that lacks density, has a cottony texture, or is of one overall length.

DISQUALIFY: Evidence of poor physical condition; incorrect number of toes; evidence of hybridization; evidence of weakness in the hindquarters; in profile, pronounced stop or nose break.

COLORS: A wide array of colors in the solid, shaded, smoke, tabby, bicolor, and parti-color patterns.

ALLOWABLE BREEDING OUTCROSSES: none.

NORWEGIAN FOREST CAT

By Dawn M. Shiley

Norwegian Forest Cat

From its heavily tufted ears to its magnificently plumed tail, the Norwegian Forest Cat (Norsk Skogkatt) is the gift of the Norse gods to the cat kingdom. Celebrated in Norse mythology and nineteenth-century Nordic fables, this cat has an air of enchantment. It awed Thor and pulled Freya's chariot. Asbjomsen and Moe embellished their Norwegian fairy tales with descriptions of these "huge and furry Troll cats." Today, the Norwegian Forest Cat, lovingly called the Wegie, with its bright eyes, robust body, flowing hair, and sweet expression, continues to endear itself to its human companions.

Physical Description

The Norwegian Forest Cat possesses a strong body and a profuse coat, the product of survival in the harsh wilds and icy winters of its native land. The coat is the most striking quality of this breed. It is endowed with a warm and water-repellent fur combination: a woolly undercoat topped with silky, flowing guard hairs of varying lengths. The coat also is seasonal, differing greatly in look from summer to winter. In autumn, the thick woolly undercoat develops. As the shorter days of winter approach, the full frontal ruff and britches covering the back legs flourish. Sometime in the spring, as the days lengthen and warm, the Wegie begins to shed the woolly undercoat. The mane will appear smaller, and the guard hairs lie close to the body. From a distance, the bushy tail may be the only indication that the Wegie is a long-haired cat.

Many other features of the Norwegian Forest Cat's coat set it apart from other breeds. Its ears are tufted with long, wispy hairs—sometimes as long as 4 inches—designed to deflect wind and snow. The cat's large round paws have heavy tufting between the toes, which provides snowshoes, a protective layer of fur between the feet and the cold ground. Because Mother Nature designed these cats, their coats come in a wide array of colors, from solid white and black to parti-color and tabby. The darker cats may have slightly less fur because they more easily can soak up the warmth from the sun.

Beneath the fur, the Norwegian Forest Cat has many qualities that make it a distinctive breed. It matures slowly and may take 4 or 5 years to reach its full potential. It is a strongly built cat of medium to large size. Average females may weigh between 8 and 12 pounds, while average males will be between 10 and 16 pounds. The Forest Cat's hind legs are longer than its front legs, a characteristic that enabled its ancestors to climb trees easily as well as traverse the rocky Scandinavian landscape. Its body is muscular, and a mature cat has well-developed, heavy thighs. There are stories and pictures of the Wegie using its powerful legs to descend from trees by climbing down the tree trunk headfirst.

The Norwegian's alert and intelligent expression is a product of a well-proportioned head. The refinement of the head is written in the science of geometry. When seen from the front, the head shape is a triangle that is formed by lines of equal distance from the base of its well-tufted ears to the tip of its strong chin. The muzzle line from the tip of the nose to the base of the ear is smooth and straight. The Forest Cat has a strong nose that, in profile, is straight. In profile, the chin is firm and is in a straight line with the front of the nose. The ears are medium to large and follow the lines from the side of the head down to the muzzle. The look is finished with large, expressive, almond-shaped eyes that tilt upward to the outside corner of the ear, creating a sweet and expressive face.

Personality

Norwegian Forest Cats generally are friendly, highly intelligent, and alert. As all cat lovers know, cat personalities vary from cat to cat as much as human personalities vary from person to person. Forest Cats usually are adaptable and can be inquisitive and courageous. They tend to get along well in new environments and with other cat breeds, dogs, and children. Many Forest Cats will be extremely loyal to one family member. They are not unfriendly with others in the household but will give more attention to one person than to the others.

Many people claim that Norwegian Forest Cats are not lap cats. Some of them are, and some of them are not. Not being lap cats does not mean they do not interact. They will demand petting, head bumps, and chin scratches. Most will follow their special people around the house as they move from room to room. The Forest Cat is people-oriented and likes to be where the action is.

Normally a calm and composed breed, the Norwegian Forest Cat easily can be stirred into action when its owner produces a favorite toy. Though the Forest Cat will start to play with reckless abandon, its hunter instincts will turn the game into a contest of wills between the cat and its illusive adversary. Coiling the body and swishing the tail, the Forest Cat signals its intention to attack. With its eyes locked on its "enemy," the Forest Cat leaps fiercely in pursuit. Grabbing the toy and throwing it in the air, the Wegie brings its foe to life. This pitched battle can last anywhere from a few seconds to several minutes before the enemy is vanquished and the Forest Cat pauses for a quick bath or well-deserved nap.

An obsession with toys is a normal trait of theirs. Spots of light hold a special fascination for them: Whether light comes from a laser light or is an errant sunbeam casting a spot on the wall, the Forest Cat simply does not understand that some prey cannot be captured. If anything interrupts the Wegie's game, its attention is not easily diverted. It is not unusual to find a Forest Cat patiently waiting for a spot of light to reappear more than an hour after the game is finished.

One of the most engaging Norwegian Forest Cat traits is its variety of birdlike songs. This is no one-note cat. While not extremely vocal, the Wegie can run through a chorus of sounds to express its moods. From its soft purr to its excited chirps, this cat's songs will tug on its owner's heart. Without question, the Norwegian Forest Cat makes an affectionate companion and an entertaining pet.

Grooming Requirements

While a profuse woolly undercoat may sound like it could be difficult to groom, just the opposite is true. For most Wegies, the coat is easier to care for than that of most other long-haired cats. As one breeder is fond of saying, "Mother Nature does not have hairdressers in the deep woods, so she did not design the cat to require the daily attention necessary for some other longhair breeds." Comb or brush the nonshow cat once a week. During the shedding period, usually a sign of spring, it is recommended to increase the grooming to three or four times a week. This helps avoid knots that could develop when the loose hairs tangle in the coat.

Preparing the Norwegian Forest Cat for the show ring is another story. The cat's natural coat is designed to be waterproof and is somewhat oily. For a beautiful cat competing in the show ring, the coat should be free of oil and every hair should stand apart. The first challenge is to wet the "waterproof" cat. Most breeders recommend that a degreasing shampoo be applied to and worked through the dry coat. It is very important to work the shampoo into the coat behind the ears and through the frontal rough. Adding a bit of water allows the groomer to move the suds down to the cat's skin and finally get the cat completely wet. After the degreasing, the coat should be rinsed and then washed again with a shampoo formulated for cats.

Every cat will have different requirements. Trial and error eventually will determine the proper technique to use for an individual cat. Some cats will have softer coats and need texturizing shampoo. Some cats (particularly intact males) are oilier than others and require additional degreasing steps. Some cats with a lot of white will need brighteners to enhance these areas. Others will look best with color shampoos that bring out the natural brown and red hues. Because of the oiliness of the coats, Wegies generally do not require conditioners. A good rule to follow is to make sure that the cat is well rinsed. Generally, when groomers think their cats are rinsed, they should continue rinsing for 2–5 more minutes, because the coat is so thick and dense that shampoos are easily retained.

The Wegie is as hard to dry as it is to get wet. The dense coat retains the water for a long time. It usually is best to let the cat partially dry by itself. This can be done by putting the cat in a carrier placed in front of a heater that is blowing warm air or by using a cage dryer. The heat of a dryer can be dangerous. Therefore, caution must be used when employing this method of drying. Maintain a safe distance and constantly check on the cat to ensure that it does not overheat. Finish up with a blow dryer. The Forest Cat should be blow-dried until every hair is dry and separated. Final blow-drying time will vary from cat to cat but averages between 45 minutes to 1 hour. Particular attention must be paid to the hair on the belly and the britches because it tends to curl. Avoid this problem by gently combing the coat while blow-drying.

A well-groomed Forest Cat will require little preparation in the show hall prior to showing in the ring. If grooming is done properly, the owner should be able to quickly comb the cat and take it to a ring. In fact, overcombing and overhandling will stimulate oils to form, which is to be avoided. In the wintertime, or in show halls where the air is particularly dry, static can be a problem. Applying a small amount of antistatic spray to the groomer's hands and lightly working it into the coat with upward motions can avoid this problem.

Origins and History

The Norwegian Forest Cat emerged from the forest some 4,000 years ago. Most likely, the ancestors of the Skogkatt were southern European short-haired cats that migrated to Norway in prehistoric times. Through natural selection, those cats survived that adapted to meet the challenges posed by the difficult climate. Eventually, the Forest Cat became a working farm cat, useful for rodent control.

The cat fancy in Norway started in the 1930s, and out of it grew a movement to preserve the Forest Cat as the Norwegian national breed. The movement was interrupted by World War II and was not resurrected until the 1970s when changes in Norway had improved the chances of the short-haired housecats' survival. Crossbreeding between the Forest Cats and the short-haired housecat and other breeds was bringing the Skogkatt close to extinction. In December 1975, a dedicated group of breeders in Norway formed the first Norwegian Forest Cat breed club, Norsk Skogkattring, to save the breed by developing a breeding program. The next year, a European cat registry recognized the breed with Provisional status. Then, in 1977, it officially accepted the Norwegian Forest Cat for competition. From then until 1990, the breeders worked diligently to find appropriate nonpedigreed examples of the breed and have them certified for registration by a panel of judges. The goal was to develop a gene pool large enough to ensure that the breed would not have to rely on inbreeding and the risks that can be involved.

In 1979, the first breeding pair of Norwegian Forest Cats was imported into the United States. Two years later, the first surviving litter of kittens was born. CFA acceptance of the "new" breed was a major goal of Norwegian Forest Cat breeders in the United States. The Norwegian Forest Cat secured CFA Championship status in 1993.

Miscellanea

As for most breeds, there is little special show handling required for the Norwegian Forest Cat. Some novices think they should be held in the stretched position, the way judges in the ring stretch Maine Coons. The Forest Cat's almost square body and its depth of flank can make this an awkward position. Some cats even will tell you that they do not like it by tensing or hissing. It is better to support the heavily muscled hindquarters with your hands and keep the cat in a pseudositting position when carrying it. Some cats will let you know that in addition to that position, they like being cradled in your arms like a baby.

Like most cats, the Norwegian Forest Cat likes to have its feet on the ground. During examination, some show judges will hold the cat up in the air at eye level to get a special look. Some cats will wiggle excessively in this position but will settle down the minute that all four feet touch the ground. It is assumed that the cats feel safer and more in control in this position.

This robust breed, which emerged from the dark forests and colorful Norwegian legends, has taken its rightful place in the cat kingdom. The Norwegian Forest Cat owes its destiny to its enduring relationship with people who recognized the value of preserving this gentle-spirited national treasure. From the Viking ships to the modern show hall, the Norwegian Forest Cat continues to inspire wonder and entice the imagination.

POINT SCORE

HEAD (50)

Nose profile	10
Muzzle	10
Ears	10
Eye shape	5
Eye set	5
Neck	5
Chin	5

BODY (30)

Torso	10
Legs/feet	10
Boning	5
Tail	5

COAT LENGTH/TEXTURE	10
COLOR/PATTERN	5
BALANCE	5

GENERAL: The Norwegian Forest Cat is a sturdy cat with a distinguishing double coat and easily recognizable body shape. It is a slow-maturing breed, attaining full growth at approximately 5 years of age.

HEAD: Equilateral triangle, where all sides are of equal length as measured from the outside of the base of the ear to the point of the chin. The neck is short and heavily muscled.

NOSE PROFILE: Straight from the brow ridge to the tip of the nose without a break in the line. The flat forehead continues into a gentle curved skull and neck.

CHIN: The chin is firm and should be in line with the front of the nose. It is gently rounded in profile.

MUZZLE: Part of the straight line extending toward the base of ear without pronounced whisker pads and without pinch.

EARS: Medium to large, rounded at the tip, broad at base, set as much on the side of the head as on top of the head, alert, with the cup of the ear pointing a bit sideways. The outsides of the ears follow the lines from the side of the head down to the chin. The ears are heavily furnished. Lynx tips are desirable but not required.

EYES: Large, almond-shaped, well opened and expressive, set at a slight angle, with the outer corner higher than the inner corner.

BODY: Solidly muscled and well balanced, moderate in length, substantial bone structure, with powerful appearance showing a broad chest and considerable girth without being fat. Flank has great depth. Males should be large and imposing; females may be more refined and may be smaller.

LEGS: Medium, with hind legs longer than front legs, making the rump higher than the shoulders. Thighs are heavily muscled; lower legs are substantial. When viewed from the rear, back legs are straight. When viewed from the front, the paws appear to be "toe out." Large, round, firm paws with heavy tufting between toes.

TAIL: Long and bushy. Broader at the base. Desirable length is equal to the body from the base of tail to the base of neck. Guard hairs desirable.

COAT: Distinguishing double coat, consisting of a dense undercoat, covered by long, glossy, and smooth, water-resistant guard hairs hanging down the sides. The bib consists of three separate sections: short collar at neck, side muttonchops, and frontal ruff. Britches are full on the hind legs. The coat may be fuller in the winter than the summer because the dense undercoat has its full development in the winter. Softer coats are permitted in shaded, solid, and bicolor cats. Type and quality of coat is of primary importance; color and pattern are secondary.

PATTERNS: Every color and pattern is allowable with the exception of those showing hybridization resulting in the colors chocolate, sable, lavender, lilac, cinnamon, fawn, point-restricted (*Himalayan*-type *markings*), or these colors with white.

COLORS AND PATTERN: The color and pattern should be clear and distinct. In the case of the classic, mackerel, and spotted tabbies, the pattern should be well marked and even.

DISQUALIFY: Severe break in nose, square muzzle, whisker pinch, long rectangular body, cobby body, incorrect number of toes, crossed eyes, kinked or abnormal tail, delicate bone structure, malocclusion resulting in either undershot or overshot chin, cats showing evidence of hybridization resulting in the colors chocolate, sable, lavender, lilac, cinnamon, fawn, or point-restricted (Himalayan-type markings) or these colors with white.

EYE COLOR: Eye color should be shades of green, gold, or green-gold. White cats and cats with white may have blue or odd eyes.

COLORS: A wide array of colors in the solid, shaded, smoke, parti-color and bicolor patterns.

ALLOWABLE BREEDING OUTCROSSES: none.

OCICAT
by James DeBruhl

Ocicat

"Oh look—spots! Is it tame? What kind of cat is this? It must be something special." These are comments frequently heard by Ocicat enthusiasts. And indeed they are special. This magnificent spotted cat never fails to steal the show, not to mention the hearts of those fortunate enough to live with them. Wildcats, whether large or small, have captured the imagination of humans since the beginning of time. The Ocicat, while wild in appearance, is a lovable companion that manages to evoke the excitement of a wild jungle cat while striking the right balance of playfulness, independence, and devotion to its human. What first attracts you to this breed is its striking spots and feral appearance. What holds your fascination is its outgoing and loving nature.

Physical Description

No "wild blood" or genes from feral cats, referred to colloquially as wildcats, were ever introduced to the all-domestic breed known as the Ocicat. This breed is wild in appearance only and has been bred to mimic its cousins appearing in nature. Briefly, an Oci is a well-spotted, short-haired, feral-looking domestic feline with a pleasing personality and temperament.

A healthy Ocicat, regardless of its gender, will feel heavy for its size because of its musculature and the fact that this breed is supposed to be a medium to large cat of considerable strength. This heavy feel is partially the result of this cat's athletic prowess and overall muscle tone. People who meet an Ocicat for the first time are surprised at how dense it feels for its size.

A good Ocicat coat pattern consists of large, separate, thumbprint-shaped spots on the sides of the torso suggestive of the classic tabby pattern, where a spot is circled by other spots, appearing somewhat similar to a bull's-eye. Other large spots should be scattered across the shoulders, on the hindquarters, and down the legs at least to the knee, and the belly should always be well spotted. Except for hair on the tip of the tail, every hair in the coat of an Ocicat has bands of color, and a spot is formed where the tipped, or agouti, hairs fall together. It is the striking contrast between these spots and the background color that adds tremendously to the overall attractiveness and appeal of the Ocicat to cat fanciers in general.

Imagine all these spots with dynamic contrast produced in 12 colors. The primary colors are tawny, chocolate, and cinnamon, the diluted corresponding colors are blue, lavender, and fawn. As if that were not enough variety, there is also a silver version of each primary and diluted color: ebony silver (tawny), chocolate silver, cinnamon silver, blue silver, lavender silver, and fawn silver.

Personality

While the Ocicat looks wild, its temperament is anything but ferocious. It is a lot like a dog in that it is absolutely devoted to its people. The Ocicat is not a demanding, clinging-vine type but is confident as well as dedicated to its owners. Most Ocicats are also quite extroverted around strangers, not at all bashful about checking out the possibilities for a few playmates or a lap to curl up on when visitors come to call.

Ocicats are quite bright and easily trained. Many will fetch, walk on a leash, respond to voice commands, and readily adapt to household rules. Because of their adaptability, they are a joy to work with and easily get used to traveling. Their sociable nature may make them less suited than some other breeds to being left alone for long periods of time, but it does make them a good choice for a household already blessed with other cats or dogs.

Ocicat kittens are generally very playful but can be rather possessive of their cat toys. Litter size has remained constant at approximately three kittens per litter, with slightly more males than females. Ocicat females are generally easy to breed and experience few problems when delivering kittens. Many breeders believe that kittens should be handled at a very young age so that they are conditioned to human contact early in life and develop a pleasing and friendly personality as full-grown Ocicats.

These cats love human interaction so much that they will follow you from room to room, watching as you perform even the dullest activities. Many will fetch the way our canine friends will, others are agreeable to being leash-trained, and most will respond to a rather wide range of verbal commands.

They possess an athletic constitution and a playful inclination, and although not continually underfoot or annoying, they are active and curious. However, on occasion they will demand attention. Their playfulness and curiosity often result in comical antics. In general, Ocicats adapt well to life in groups or with individuals of other breeds as long as their personalities and energies do not conflict. They are more rambunctious than most long-haired breeds but jump about less than their Oriental cousins.

Grooming Requirements

Ocicats do not require excessive grooming. A show-quality Ocicat is bathed on Wednesday or Thursday in preparation for an upcoming weekend cat show. A bronze-tone shampoo is recommended if your cat has a tawny, cinnamon, or chocolate coat color; pearl-tone shampoo is recommended for the lavender, blue, and fawn; and whitening shampoo is suggested for the silvers. Many exhibitors highly praise chamois cloth for its ability to shine the Ocicat coat, and it can be used as often as needed in the show hall and at home.

Origins and History

The first Ocicat (when the breed had not yet been named) occurred by accident. The year was 1964, and on a cold and blustery morning in Berkley, Michigan, Virginia Daly and her daughter Virginia watched with great excitement their soon-to-be-momma cat with the odd-sounding name of Dalai She. This ruddy Aby-coated hybrid female was about to deliver the offspring of Champion Whitehead Elegante Sun, called Sunny. He was a large, well-muscled, dark-colored chocolate point Siamese. Together, Sunny and She produced a litter of kittens, one of which was not the Aby-pointed Siamese Ms. Daly was attempting to get.

This "ugly duckling" was a golden spotted male kitten. On first sight, Virginia, the daughter, remarked, "He looks like a baby ocelot," and in the next breath asked, "Can we call him an Ocicat?" Very shortly after his

birth the kitten was named Tonga. Little did he know that he had a place in feline history. From his birth, this little hybrid spotted fellow would be the first of his kind and carry the banner of a new breed of domestic cat. The only complication was that this new breed was not the goal Ms. Daly had in mind. Therefore, Tonga was neutered and sold as a pet.

When the Detroit newspaper publicized the lovely spotted cat and when noted geneticist Dr. Clyde Keeler expressed his desire to see a domestic cat that would mimic some of the vanishing wild species, the breeding was repeated to produce more Ocicats. In an effort to develop other Ocicat lines, breeders followed Mrs. Daly's recipe and added an ingredient of their own by introducing the American Shorthair, thus ensuring a broad genetic base. The addition of this third breed into the Ocicat gene pool gave the new offspring more substance to the body and contributed the beautiful silver gene.

Tonga's story did not end here. He was the first public relations ambassador for the Ocicat breed. Tonga, as the first Ocicat, was shown along with 16 other cats labeled "Special Exhibits" February 20–21, 1965, at a CFA show in Detroit. The show catalog presented them as "Breeds of the Future." How right that catalog was.

Feline enthusiasts have always been awed by the spotted cats of the wild: ocelots, margays, leopards, and others. Never before was there such an effort to breed an entirely domestic cat that could offer the spotted beauty of the wildcats while maintaining the lovely, predictable disposition of the domestic cat.

The Ocicat was recognized for CFA registration in 1966, but it took another 20 years to develop the breed and gain the support for Provisional status, which was granted in 1986. The advancement to Championship status followed quickly thereafter in May 1987. The

Ocicat registry was closed to Siamese and American Shorthair outcrosses in 1986, but the Abyssinian breed remains an allowable outcross until 2015.

Miscellanea

Because of the arrangement of the Ocicat's specific muscle groups, plus its overall musculature, judges or anyone else handling an Ocicat need to keep the rear feet of the cat on the table or floor at all times. A fully grown Ocicat is simply uncomfortable being placed in what is referred to as the Persian Stretch and usually will not tolerate this form of handling. Generally, the show-quality Ocicat has a good time while on the judging table and if treated with respect will help the judge who is attempting to present each cat to its full potential.

The Ocicat's agreeable temperament, coupled with its environmental adaptability, makes the cat a truly enjoyable and loving companion. The Ocicat is an undeniably wild-looking cat whose friendly, outgoing nature belies its feral appearance.

CFA SHOW STANDARD FOR THE OCICAT

POINT SCORE

HEAD (25)

Skull	5
Muzzle	10
Ears	5
Eyes	5

BODY (25)

Torso	15
Legs and feet	5
Tail	5

COAT AND COLOR (25)

Texture	5
Coat color	5
Contrast	10
Eye color	5

PATTERN	**25**

GENERAL: The Ocicat is a medium to large well-spotted agouti cat of moderate type. It displays the look of an athletic animal: well muscled and solid, graceful and lithe, yet with a fullness of body and chest. It is alert to its surroundings and shows great vitality. There are 12 accepted Ocicat colors divided into 8 color classes, with all specimens possessing darker spots that appear in deep contrast to a lighter background. The determining factor in answering any and all questions as to the correct color of an Ocicat will be the color of the tail tip without any comparison to the color of other body markings (see Colors below). Each hair (except on the tip of tail) has several bands of color. It is where these bands fall together that a thumbprint-shaped spot is formed. This powerful, athletic, yet graceful spotted cat is particularly noted for its wild appearance.

HEAD: The skull is a modified wedge showing a slight curve from muzzle to cheek, with a visible but gentle, rise from the bridge of the nose to the brow. The muzzle is broad and well defined, with a suggestion of squareness, and in profile shows good length. The chin is strong and the jaw firm, with a proper bite. The moderate whisker pinch is not too severe. The head is carried gracefully on an arching neck. An allowance is made for jowls on mature males.

EARS: Alert, moderately large, and set so as to corner the upper outside dimensions of the head. If an imaginary horizontal line is drawn across the brow, the ears should be set at a 45-degree angle (i.e., neither too high nor too low). When they occur, ear tufts extending vertically from the tips of the ears are a bonus.

EYES: Large, almond-shaped, and angling slightly upward toward the ears, with more than the length of an eye between the eyes.

TORSO: Solid, hard, rather long-bodied, with depth and fullness, but never coarse. The Ocicat is a medium to large cat with substantial bone and muscle development, yet with an athletic appearance, and should have surprising weight for its size. There should be some depth of chest, with ribs slightly sprung; the back is level to slightly higher in the rear, and the flank is reasonably level. Preference is given to the athletic, powerful, and lithe, and objection taken to the bulky or coarse. Females are generally smaller than males. The overall structure and quality of this cat should be of greater consideration than mere size alone.

LEGS AND FEET: Legs should be of good substance and well muscled, medium-long, powerful, and in good proportion to the body. Feet should be oval and compact with five toes in front and four in back, with size in proportion to legs.

TAIL: Fairly long; medium-slim with only a slight taper and with a dark tip.

COAT TEXTURE: Short, smooth, and satiny in texture with a lustrous sheen. Tight, close-lying, and sleek, yet long enough to accommodate the necessary bands of color. There should be no suggestion of woolliness.

TICKING: All hairs except the tip of the tail are banded. Within the markings, hairs are tipped with a darker color, while hairs in the ground color are tipped with a lighter color.

COAT COLOR: All colors should be clear and pleasing. The lightest color is usually found on the face around the eyes, and on the chin and lower jaw. The darkest color is found on the tip of the tail. Contrast is scored separately.

CONTRAST: Distinctive markings should be clearly seen from any orientation. Those on the face, legs, and tail may be darker than those on the torso. Ground color may be darker on the saddle and lighter on the underside, chin, and lower jaw. Penalties should be given if spotting is faint or blurred, though it must be remembered that pale colors will show less contrast than darker ones.

EYE COLOR: All eye colors except blue are allowed. There is no correspondence between eye color and coat color. Depth of color is preferred.

PATTERN: There is an intricate tabby M on the forehead, with markings extending up over the head between the ears and breaking into small spots on the lower neck and shoulders. Mascara markings are found around the eyes and on cheeks. Rows of round spots run along the spine from shoulder blades to tail. The tail has horizontal brushstrokes down the top, ideally alternating with spots, and a dark tip. Spots are scattered across the shoulders and hindquarters, extending as far as possible down the legs. There are broken bracelets on the lower legs and broken necklaces at the throat—the more broken, the better.

Large, well-scattered, thumbprint-shaped spots appear on the sides of the torso, with a subtle suggestion of a classic tabby pattern—a spot circled by spots in place of the bull's-eye. The belly is also well spotted. The eyes are rimmed with the darkest coat color and surrounded by the lightest color. Penalties should be given for elongated spots following a mackerel pattern.

DISQUALIFY: White locket or spotting, or white anywhere other than around eyes, nostrils, chin, and upper throat (except white agouti ground in silvered colors). Kinked or otherwise deformed tail. Blue eyes. Incorrect number of toes. Long hair. Because the spotted patched tabby (torbie) cats result from the sex-linked O gene, no reds, creams, or torties are allowed. Very rufous cinnamons and fawns may resemble red or cream but never produce female torbies.

COLORS (ALL SPOTTED): Tawny, cinnamon, chocolate, blue, fawn, lavender, ebony silver, cinnamon silver, chocolate silver, blue silver, fawn silver, lavender silver.

ALLOWABLE BREEDING OUTCROSSES: Abyssinian for litters born before January 1, 2015.

ORIENTAL
By Bob Agresta and Joann Kultala

Oriental Longhair

Oriental Shorthair

The Oriental is a magical breed of variety and color. It starts with the essence of a Siamese and adds the sprinkled flavorings of the rainbow. Orientals are referred to by many cat lovers as the Rainbow Cat and are often portrayed as having an infinite number of color and pattern combinations. Perhaps the quaintest descriptive phrase is "a Siamese in designer genes."

Physical Description

In all of the fanciful descriptions, there lies an element of truth. The Oriental has all the physical characteristics of a Siamese cat; long, elegant legs, a long tubular body; a wedge-shaped head; and almond-shaped eyes. It is the picture of elegance. It is, and will continue to be, a replica of its parent breed. Where it parts company is in the variety of colors and patterns with which it is adorned.

In choosing an Oriental, most people find themselves captivated by a specific color or pattern. Imagine, for a moment, a Siamese wearing a coat of a single color. These "solids" come in white, red, cream, ebony, blue, chestnut, lavender, cinnamon, and fawn. The nine basic colors lay the foundation for the rest of the patterns. For a sparkling undercoat, stir in the silver gene (to all but the white), and voilà: the smoke Oriental. Restrict the color to the tips of the hair, with distinctive mascara marks around the eyes: the shaded Oriental. Paint splashes of red or cream on any of these coats and you have a parti-color.

Want stripes? Then look to the tabbies. They come in 4 basic patterns: classic, mackerel, spotted, and ticked. Cross the 4 patterns with the 8 available colors and 32 combinations emerge. Add patches of red or cream and you have the popular "patched tabby" and another 24 combinations. Finally, layer in the sparkle of the silver gene, and count 56 more. That is 112 tabby combinations in total.

The bicolor pattern, one of the latest additions to the accepted CFA colors, essentially puts a tuxedo pattern on the cat. With the clear white underside, legs, chest, and inverted white V on the face, these distinctly marked members of the breed have already developed a following of devoted fans. Bicolor Orientals come combined with any of the above colors and patterns, and recently added the pointed-and-white pattern to their wardrobe. This unique look demonstrates the Oriental's genetic diversity.

Finally, one can choose a coat length. Short-haired and longh-aired Orientals parallel their paired counterparts; the Siamese and the Balinese, and the Colorpoint Shorthair and the Javanese. For the short-haired Oriental, the coat appears painted on and is soft and satinlike to the touch. Its narrow, long, whippy tail seems to go on forever. The long-haired Orientals carry the same graceful bodies with the addition of a long, silky coat, goatee, and beautifully plumed tail.

Personality

What makes an Oriental interesting? It is that forever-popular combination of personality and good looks. The antics of the Oriental are well documented. These cats are always to be found near the people they claim as their own. At your busiest moments, they'll find a way to interrupt your activities: a little nudge while you eat, a close examination of your toothbrush prior to use, or some help tying your shoes before you leave in the morning. It is understood that you will need help deciding which items to select from the refrigerator. In the calmest of times, they will share the warmth of your lap, provide a comforting purr, and nuzzle your chin when you need it the most. They eagerly greet you at the door and tell you all about their day. If you are late, they will scold you and tell you how worried they were that you did not call. Did you hide or mislay their favorite toy? They'll find it. Their curiosity and intelligence provide them a means of finding anything and everything. They have been known to open a drawer or empty a purse to discover a pen or a crumpled-up piece of paper that they can chase around the kitchen. Give them the attention and affection they so desperately need, and they will do anything to please you. Ignore them, and they will droop with despair.

Grooming Requirements

Grooming needs for the Oriental are based on their coat length, but the basics of grooming these cats for either pet life or the show ring are as follows:

Clip all claws on the front and back feet. The mechanics here are simpler than one might imagine. Tuck the cat between your body and your arm. Hold each paw separately and press it between your thumb and finger. This will extend the claws from their sheath. Using a standard nail clipper designed for cats, clip off the sharp tip.

Clean their ears with a moist cotton swab. As with humans, concentrate on the external parts of the ear.

Brush your cat well. The preferred type of brush for an Oriental with a short coat is the solid rubber curry type available from vendors at shows and in most pet supply stores. Lay the brush in the palm of your hand, curved side out, and use it to pet your cat firmly in long, sweeping strokes in the direction the hair grows. The curved side of the brush is designed to remove loose, dead, or extra plush hair and has the added benefit of giving your cat the massage of his life.

For Longhairs, a quality steel comb can provide the same effect as the brush, because the longer hairs are more easily split or broken. Sometimes just a damp cloth run over the body is an effective way of gathering the loose hairs. Brushing or combing is a wonderful way to bond with your pet, and most cats look forward to a serious grooming session.

Finally, wipe the cat down either with your hands or a natural chamois to remove the hairs loosened by brushing. Again, do this in the direction the hairs grow so that you have laid them down smoothly. The result, if done properly, is a cat with the high-gloss glow of fine satin.

Origins and History

Literary references to the "Self Colored" (solid color) Oriental date back to the late 1800s in the writings of the *Cats of Siam*. The development and recognition of the Oriental breed began in earnest in the 1950s in Europe but did not generate much interest at the time. It took a full decade for chestnut solid, lavender solid, and white solid Orientals to be accepted by the Governing Council of the Cat Fancy, a European registry.

In the late 1960s and early 1970s, some breeders in the United States attempted to repeat the earlier efforts in England, but their efforts were fragmented across the continent. The breed needed an organized group to bring it to full CFA recognition. Carrying the breed's original name, the Oriental Shorthair International club (OSI) can claim credit for putting the Oriental on the map. OSI, formed in 1973, became the motivation behind the plan and by 1974 had achieved CFA registration status for the breed. They progressed to Provisional status in 1976 and full Championship status in 1977.

This highly focused team of people had achieved the impossible: recognition of the Oriental with 50 different color and pattern combinations in 2 years. No other breed had advanced through the steps so quickly, and that was only the beginning. Throughout the 1980s and 1990s, the Oriental breeders have increased the number of recognized colors from seven to nine, adding the cinnamon and fawn. All the colors have been expanded into each of the pattern groups of solids, smokes, parti-colors, tabbies, shadeds, and bicolors. In 1995, the Oriental added the long-haired variety into its range of alternatives. All of these activities have helped to sustain the Oriental as one of the CFA's more popular breeds.

Miscellanea

For Orientals, any form of handling is special. They are hands-on cats that crave attention. In the show halls, they are judged for their long, tubular bodies, so it is not unusual to see them stretched out between a judge's hands or reaching up the entire length of a pole or scratching post. Orientals are equally at home curled up on the couch, in your lap, or by any source of heat. Talk to them, and they will talk back. These cats are low-maintenance, high-involvement members of the family.

★ ★ ★

Orientals represent the best of the best for grace, beauty, variety, and affection. They offer a high degree of loyalty to their owners and return the attention they receive fivefold. If you are looking for an active participant in your daily life, a graceful, visual attraction in your home, or a warm friend to share the comfort of your lap at the end of a long day, then you need look no further. The Oriental is the custom-made cat for you.

CFA SHOW STANDARD FOR THE ORIENTAL

POINT SCORE

HEAD (20)	
Long, flat profile	6
Wedge, fine muzzle, size	5
Ears	4
Chin	3
Width between eyes	2

EYES (10)	
Shape, size, slant, and placement	10

BODY (30)	
Structure and size, including neck	12
Muscle tone	10
Legs and feet	5
Tail	3

COAT	10

COLOR (30)	
Coat color (color, 10; pattern, 10)	20
Eye color	10

GENERAL: The ideal Oriental is a svelte cat with long, tapering lines, very lithe but muscular. Excellent physical condition. Eyes clear. Strong and lithe, neither bony nor flabby. Not fat. Because of the longer coat, cats in the Longhair Division appear to have softer lines and less extreme type than those in the Shorthair Division.

HEAD: Long, tapering wedge, in good proportion to body. The total wedge starts at the nose and flares out in straight lines to the tips of the ears, forming a triangle, with no break at the whiskers. No less than the width of an eye between the eyes. When the whiskers (and face hair for the Longhair Division) are smoothed back, the underlying bone structure is apparent. Allowance must be made for jowls in the stud cat.

SKULL: Flat. In profile, a long, straight line is seen from the top of the head to the tip of the nose. No bulge over eyes. No dip in nose.

NOSE: Long and straight. A continuation of the forehead with no break.

MUZZLE: Fine, wedge-shaped.

CHIN AND JAW: Medium size. Tip of chin lines up with tip of nose in the same vertical plane. Neither receding nor excessively massive.

EARS: Strikingly large, pointed, wide at the base, continuing the lines of the wedge.

EYES: Almond-shaped, medium size. Neither protruding nor recessed. Slanted toward the nose in harmony with lines of wedge and ears. Uncrossed.

BODY: Long and svelte. A distinctive combination of fine bones and firm muscles. Shoulders and hips continue the same sleek lines of tubular body. Hips never wider than shoulders. Abdomen tight. Males may be somewhat larger than females.

NECK: Long and slender.

LEGS: Long and slim. Hind legs higher than front. In good proportion to body.

PAWS: Dainty, small, and oval. Toes: five in front and four behind.

TAIL: Long, thin at the base, and tapered to a fine point. *Longhair Division:* tail hair spreads out like a plume.

COAT SHORTHAIR DIVISION: Short, fine-textured, glossy or satinlike, lying close to body.

COAT LONGHAIR DIVISION: Medium length, fine, silky, without downy undercoat; lying close to the body, the coat may appear shorter than it is. Hair is longest on the tail.

COAT COLOR: The Oriental's reason for being is the coat color, whether solid, shaded, smoke, parti-color, bicolor, or tabby patterned. *Solid:* In the solid-color cat, the coat color should be of uniform density and color from the tip to the root of each hair and from the nose to the tail. The full coat color score (20) should be used to as-sess the quality and the correctness of the color. *Shaded:* The shaded cat has a white undercoat, with a mantle of colored tipping shading down from the sides, face, and tail from dark on the ridge to white on the chin, chest underside, and under the tail. *Smoke:* Cat in repose appears solid in color. In motion, the color is clearly apparent. Extremities are solid in color and have a narrow band of white at the base of hairs next to the skin, which may be seen only when the fur is parted. *Parti-color:* A solid cat with patches of red or softly intermingled areas of red on both body and extremities. (Presence of several shades of red acceptable; dilute colors exhibit cream instead of red.) *Bicolor:* Bicolors should conform to the established standard for their coexisting pattern, with the addition of white feet, legs, underside, chest, and muzzle, including an inverted V blaze on the face. *Tabby:* In the tabby-patterned cat, the quality of the pattern is an essential part of the cat. The pattern should match the description for the particular pattern and be well defined. The pattern should be viewed while the cat is in a natural standing position. The remaining 10 points are allotted to the correctness of the color; it matches the color description.

EYE COLOR: Green. White Orientals and bicolor Orientals may have blue, green, or odd-eyed eye color.

PENALIZE: Crossed eyes. Palpable and/or visible protrusion of the cartilage at the end of the sternum.

DISQUALIFY: Any evidence of illness or poor health. Weak hind legs. Mouth breathing due to nasal obstruction or poor occlusion. Emaciation. Visible kink in tail. Miniaturiza-

PERSIAN
By Colleen Power

Persian (bicolor and calico)

Persian (Himalayan)

The judge lifts a black Persian from its cage and drops it dramatically on the table. The audience gasps as the judge turns the coat and the dramatic contrasting white undercoat shimmers in the light, slipping through the fingers like the rarest of silks.

Physical Description

Despite the general notion of the Persian as a long-haired white cat, the principle characteristic of the Persian should be the remarkable conformation possible by 100 years of selected breeding. Most incredible are the eyes, huge and mesmerizing, and the nose, shortened, tilted, and even with the eyes. There is a sense of soft roundness to this breed, an impression not shared by Turkish Angoras, the breed most often confused by the general public with Persians.

Round head, round body, round eyes, round muzzle—the observer should see circles when looking at a Persian. Even the 8-inch-long tail fur creates the illusion of a rounded tail, as wide as it is deep and long. The ears should be small and rounded and set to the side of the head, and the eyes should be widely

Persian (parti-color)

Persian (shaded and smoke)

set straight. The body is broad in the chest and broad in the hips, giving the appearance of a sturdy and solid-standing cat. The paws are large and well rounded and set straight ahead, without toeing out. The tail sweeps downward, with no sign of curl or kink tail faults.

There are now more than 100 coat colors and patterns; a tremendous variation in coloring is recognized in the Persians. In fact, there are so many colors of Persians in the CFA that for purposes of show, the breed is now separated into several divisions based on these color patterns: solid, tabbies, silver/golden, shaded/smoke, parti-colors, bicolors/calicos, and Himalayan.

There are three types of hair on the cat: guard hairs, down (wool), and awn (bristle). The guard hairs are straight and usually rather stiff. The awn is thinner and tapers to the tip. The down is usually somewhat shorter, is very fine, and sheds readily. The Persian has all three types of coat classifications, and in the very finest specimens, the three elements are of the same length. The guard hairs do tend to become darker with age, stiff, and most noticeable. These are frequently "tipped" off in

the solid-color show cats. However, the down is very fine and often crimps; it is what gives the Persian cat's coat lift and is the type of hair most often damaged by faulty combing techniques.

The density of the Persian coat is a variable selected through more than a century of breeding, resulting in very dense coats under which the skin often cannot be seen. Cats with this very woolly texture, which is highly desirable for the show ring, are usually kept shaved once their show careers are completed. The density of the coat will affect the appearance of the various patterns, creating blurred tabbies, without strong markings, and greyed ruffs on blacks.

Personality

The Persian looks like a kitten all of its life, with its very round head and large eyes. The cat's placid personality and implicit trust of its human means it needs a human who does not release the cat to wander—such a cat is very likely to be scooped up by strangers and carted away if it is allowed to roam. Preferring cuddling and having people around, the Persian

Persian (silver and golden)

Persian (solid)

seems to blossom when given the attention its coat demands. But the Persian must be trained early on—starting at age 6–8 weeks—so that it will accept the grooming needed in later life.

The short legs and heavy body of the typical Persian are not made to climb the drapes, sit on the top shelf of the bookcase, or walk the curtain rods. However, it will often try to mimic its more svelte cousins, the oriental breeds, in these pursuits.

The desire for human attention makes Persians very responsive to positive reenforcement. They may spend hours following their humans from room to room, watching for the opportunity to jump into the next available lap. Despite the teasing of the judges about "nobody home" when the Persian is sitting on the judging stand, Persians are readily bored with most toys. Most are bright, are extremely tractable, and will learn their names quickly. They are often notorious for teaching their owners the game of fetch, and they perhaps understand and obey the "no" command most readily of any cat breed.

Grooming Requirements

Two tools are essential for living with Persians: a very good vacuum cleaner and a steel comb with very fine, long teeth. Imported long-tooth steel combs, of the Belgian or Greyhound brands, are highly effective in separating and preventing the thick Persian coat from tangling and rapidly matting. Additional useful items are a small wire rake, often referred to as a slicker brush, which is useful for picking up stray tufts of hair, and cotton balls for cleaning up eyes and ears.

Changes in diet may result in intestinal upsets and messy "pantaloons." Bottom baths are recommended when this occurs. If this messiness is a regular occurrence, consider clipping the bottom fur very closely. It is also recommended to keep Persians on the same food, not switch quickly from one food to another. This will reduce the frequency of bottom baths.

Some Persians are notorious for water-soaked ruffs. If your cat is not being shown, consider keeping the ruff clipped short about the face and chin. Beyond regular grooming is the magnificent show grooming made famous

Persian (tabby)

by all the pictures. Typically, the show groom consists of twice-weekly bathing, as a minimum, with at least three to five separate shampoos and conditioners, and even hot oil treatments. The coat is trimmed about the face to round the face as much as possible. Cheek fur is evened up with thinning shears, and the "horns," spikes of hair extending up from the top of the forehead, between the ears, are trimmed to accentuate the well-rounded dome. Hair on the tips of the ears is trimmed to round off the ears, as is hair that falls over the eyes, blocking a clear view of them.

The coat is then hand-dried with professional grooming dryers for 2–4 hours to obtain the maximum volume and minimize coat curling. Some of the messier cats are hand-fed to keep from dirtying the ruffs, or they wear small bibs. At the shows, a variety of protective devices are used to minimize self-licking, including bibs, coffee filters, and paper plates cut to fit about the face. The cat may be bathed again each day of the show. This is not for the fainthearted.

The cats seem to endure this grooming with a great deal of aplomb. Exhibitors are constantly sharing recipes for more successful coat volume, information on the best dryers to use, or details on the latest rinse to give just the desired feel to the coat. Judges do not look on the use of powder favorably, because unless it is blown out in the grooming process, its use might be regarded as an intention to deceive, by lightening the coat's color or changing its hue.

Origins and History

As for the Persian history, one must ask, "Where did this remarkable cat originate?" No one knows for certain. The most romantic tale is that the first long-haired cats came from the Middle East with the Crusaders and their ladies, carrying the name Angora, after the city of Ankara in Turkey. More likely they did come from Turkey or Persia, but probably in wicker baskets with traders eager to fill the demands of European nobility for unusual specimens in their menageries.

Theories that postulate a wildcat origin, such as Pallas's cat (*Felis manul*), the sand cat (*Felis margarita*), or the European wildcat (*Felis sylvestris sylvestris*) are highly improbable from two perspectives. Biologically, most wildcat domestic crosses result in sterile progeny, and behaviorally, the most docile of domestic cats is the Persian, suggesting a very long period of domestication.

In 1626, Italian trader and explorer Pietro della Valle returned from his trips to Persia and India, bringing with him an impressive, heavily coated cat breed from Persia. This cat became very fashionable and was rivaled in popularity only by an equally elegant long-haired cat, the Angora, from Turkey. Another explorer, Frenchman Nicole de Pereise, brought long-haired cats from Turkey to France a century later, only to see them be crossed with the earlier Persians originating with della Valle. Long-nosed, long-tailed, and long-coated, these dainty cats were white. Bred with local cats to create a sturdier cat with thicker coats and shorter noses and ears, the crossbreds were more enduring of the European winters. Colors other than white began to appear as a result of these matings.

Regardless of the Persian's origin, by the turn of the eighteenth century, illustrations and paintings began to reveal a pampered new pet of the wealthy and the royals: A cat with hauntingly large eyes, a full, long coat, and unusual coloring is seen luxuriating in the lap of many a lady portrait. These are suspected to be the earliest Persians, although no registry was developed for pedigreed cats until the 1870s. The chubby, thick-coated cats of Persian origins gradually replaced the longer, leaner Angoras in popularity during the early twentieth century.

The first known Persian imports into the United States arrived in the late 1880s. Several sources note that a Mrs. Locke showed a beautiful imported blue Longhair by the name of The Beadle, who was awarded first prize in an 1896 Chicago cat show. By 1906, cat clubs had formed on the West Coast. Persians had reached California. One can only imagine these pampered Persian cats traveling across the country by train or around Cape Horn by ship.

An examination of the CFA studbooks indicates that in the early twentieth century, *Longhair* was the term used in all the registries for the Persians and Angora breeds. There was no distinction made between the two breeds in the registration numbers. The first listed Grand Champion in CFA competition was a red tabby imported Longhair male born in 1929. Additional U.S.-bred Longhairs were issued Grand Champion certificates soon after, in 1931. The breed designation *Longhair* was replaced officially in the studbooks with the heading *Persians or Angora* in the year 1958.

Angora cats were recognized as a separate breed, with a distinctively different, longer,

more svelte appearance. The heavyset, round-faced Persians continued to grow in numbers and popularity. Today, more than 60% of the cats registered by the CFA are of the Persian patterns and colors, each with particular eye color requirements.

Miscellanea

One of the most important rules of breeding and judging Persians is that the house must be built properly before painting it. This means that the structure of the Persian must be regarded first and foremost in judging and in breeding, before color. As the judge lifts the cat from the cage, the observer will note that the cat rests firmly on the judge's hands or in his or her arms, is not stretched out, and is set on the table with all four legs squarely planted. Often the judge will stand back to observe the overall square stance, and examine the proper structure underneath, and then the grooming.

Then the judge moves to the head; nearly 50% of the total point count is on the structure of the head, eyes, and ears. The judge will check that the forehead is smooth and rounded, called doming. The forehead should be on an even line with the nose and rounded chin when seen in profile. The standard calls for the eyes to be even with the nose break. Disqualification at this point includes asymmetrical skull or face or incorrect eye color.

Most Persians remain standing or sitting on the table, often ignoring the toys flicked in front of them. Persians are noted for their sensitivity to the humans about them and are eager to please. Their calm stance on the judging table usually results from hours of grooming by the breeder with kittens as young as 4 weeks of age to get them used to the necessary hours of coat care for show. These hours of training, combined with a long history of breeding for personality, make the Persian one of the favorites for advertising campaigns and show campaigns alike.

The well-bred show Persian is a sturdy, gentle cat with a generally long life. A recent survey showed that stud cats may sire even after the age of 15 years, and breeding queens, until 12 years of age. Maturing slowly, with a show life extending up to 12 years and an expected lifespan of 18–20 years, the Persian is an ideal playful and affectionate companion at any age.

CFA SHOW STANDARD FOR THE PERSIAN

POINT SCORE

HEAD (INCLUDING SIZE AND SHAPE OF EYES, EAR SHAPE AND SET)	30
BODY TYPE (INCLUDING SHAPE, SIZE, BONE, AND LENGTH OF TAIL)	20
COAT	10
BALANCE	5
REFINEMENT	5
COLOR*	20
EYE COLOR	10

GENERAL: The ideal Persian should present an impression of a heavily boned, well-balanced cat with a sweet expression and soft, round lines. The large, round eyes, set wide apart in a large, round head, contribute to the overall look and expression. The long, thick coat softens the lines of the cat and accentuates the roundness in appearance.

HEAD: Round and massive, with great breadth of skull. Round face with round underlying bone structure. Well set on a short, thick neck.

NOSE: Short, snub, and broad, with break centered between the eyes.

CHEEKS: Full.

JAWS: Broad and powerful.

CHIN: Full, well developed, and firmly rounded, reflecting a proper bite.

EARS: Small, round-tipped, tilted forward, and not unduly open at the base. Set far apart and low on the head, fitting into (without distorting) the rounded contour of the head.

EYES: Brilliant in color, large, round, and full. Set level and far apart, giving a sweet expression to the face.

BODY: Of cobby type, low on the legs, broad and deep through the chest, equally massive across the shoulders and rump, with a well-rounded midsection and level back. Good muscle tone, with no evidence of obesity. Large or medium in size. Quality is the determining consideration rather than size.

LEGS: Short, thick, and strong. Forelegs straight. Hind legs are straight when viewed from behind.

PAWS: Large, round, and firm. Toes carried close, five in front and four behind.

TAIL: Short but in proportion to body length. Carried without a curve and at an angle lower than the back.

*For cats in the tabby division, the 20 points for color are to be divided as follows: 10 for markings and 10 for color. For cats in the bicolor division, the 20 points for color are to be divided as follows: 10 for "with white" pattern and 10 for color.

COAT: Long and thick, standing off from the body. Of fine texture, glossy, and full of life. Long all over the body, including the shoulders. The ruff is immense and continues in a deep frill between the front legs. Ear and toe tufts long. Brush very full.

DISQUALIFY: Locket or button. Kinked or abnormal tail. Incorrect number of toes. Any apparent weakness in the hindquarters. Any apparent deformity of the spine.

Deformity of the skull resulting in an asymmetrical face and/or head. Crossed eyes. For pointed cats, also disqualify for white toes, eye color other than blue.

COLORS: A wide array of colors in the solid, shaded, smoke, tabby, bicolor, particolor, and pointed patterns.

ALLOWABLE OUTCROSS BREEDINGS: none.

RAGAMUFFIN
By Laura Gregory

RagaMuffin

When you first see a RagaMuffin from a distance, you will find yourself in awe. There lies a gorgeous, massive cat with large, expressive eyes that are just begging you to come closer. You will not believe its sumptuous color, its soft coat, or the substantial size of its body. At the moment you touch its luxurious coat, you will think you are in heaven.

Physical Description

RagaMuffins come in all coat colors and patterns. These are striking cats whether their coats are solid color, tabby, colorpoint, tortoiseshell, or mink, with or without some white on the body (colorpoints are not showable, only registerable). Their coat patterns and symmetry are not considered terribly important, but all RagaMuffin breeders love the unique patterns and varieties that occur naturally within the breed.

These cats' coats are medium-long and fully furred—similar to that of a rabbit. Their overall softness makes you want to continually pet them, and when you do, these massive cats love every minute of your attention and just keep purring.

RagaMuffins are classically large cats, with females averaging between 10 and 15 pounds and males averaging between 15 and 20 pounds. Some of them get much larger. Each is heavy-boned and muscular, with a tendency toward a fatty pad on the lower abdomen. They are completely mature at 4 years of age and enjoy a long life expectancy. As a general rule, RagaMuffins are strong and healthy, and there are no known genetic health problems within the breed.

Personality

A RagaMuffin's personality is one of extreme sweetness. This is hard to describe and is best understood when one of these cats owns you. Over time, you begin to understand their exceptional personality and how it differs from that of most other cats. RagaMuffins form a strong bond with their families, and once your home has been blessed with one, you will be forever taken with the breed. Because they are addictive, you may soon discover that one of these large, cuddly teddy bears is just not enough.

RagaMuffins are wonderful with children. Their calm and patient temperament lends itself to the boisterous, robust play of youngsters, and they at times can be found participating in tea parties and riding in baby strollers. RagaMuffins want to please, and some pet owners even report they can be taught tricks, such as fetching. They also make wonderful companions for those who live alone, because they provide much-needed company and support. They listen to you and offer their love as a response.

They are quite likely to go limp in your arms, as the *rag* part of their name implies. As for their disposition, they tend to be calm and are likely to be found curled in your lap as you read a book or watch TV. Yet these are not lazy cats. Just pull out their toys and you will find them ready for action. Because they are very trusting animals, they must be kept indoors. There are far too many dangers for them beyond the front door.

Grooming Requirements

RagaMuffins are low-maintenance cats. Although their coats are thick and plush, surprisingly they do not tend to mat or clump and are easy to maintain.

Origins and History

The RagaMuffin was developed in 1994 from Ann Baker's "Cherubim" breed, which began in Riverside, California, in the early 1960s. The exact development of the breed is clouded. The full story will likely stay a mystery, but the end result is that owning a Raga-Muffin is as rewarding as it is pleasurable.

The name *RagaMuffin* was chosen because the original gene pool was developed from the street cats of Riverside, California. They were truly ragamuffins, endearing street urchins living on their own. The breeders worked very diligently to develop these cats with the unique appearance, while preserving their original characteristics, which were prized within the breed. The CFA granted RagaMuffins registration status in 2003, making them the newest breed in the organization at this writing.

Miscellanea

As a breed, RagaMuffins travel well. Their easygoing personality allows them to adapt to almost any environment or situation, as long as they have their humans' attention and interest.

RagaMuffins are people-lovers, with personality traits of those similar to an endearing lapdog. These cats thrive on attention, and it is not unusual for them to greet you at the door, follow you from room to room, and become your faithful companion. They make wonderful family pets. With so much affection to give, they have much to share with everyone in the family, including your other pets.

CFA SHOW STANDARD FOR THE RAGAMUFFIN (MISCELLANEOUS STATUS)

POINT SCORE

HEAD (35)

Shape	20
Sweet expression	5
Ears	5
Eyes	5

BODY AND TAIL (30)

Body	20
Legs and feet	5
Tail	5

COAT	**20**
COLOR	**5**
CONDITION	**10**

GENERAL: The overall impression of the RagaMuffin should be one of sweetness and robust health. RagaMuffin females are generally considerably smaller than males, both being muscular and heavy, with a tendency toward a fatty pad (greater omentum) on the lower abdomen. RagaMuffins attain full maturity at approximately 4 years of age. The cat is striking whether it is a dramatically marked tabby or a breathtaking calico. The only extremes in this cat are large size, large expressive eyes, and docile nature. A RagaMuffin is people-loving and affectionate—a large, cuddly, feline teddy bear.

HEAD: The head is a broad modified wedge with a rounded appearance. The forehead should be moderately rounded. Muzzle is round, slightly shorter than moderate in length, tending to broadness. The chin is firmly rounded, reflecting a proper bite.

There is puffiness to the whisker pad, which results in the characteristic sweet look of the RagaMuffin. Cheeks are full. In profile, there is an obvious nose dip, giving the impression of a scoop rather than a break. Neck is short, heavy, and strong, particularly in older males. An allowance is made for jowliness in mature adult males.

EARS: Medium in size, set to the side of the head, with slight flaring, tilted slightly forward, rounded, with moderate furnishings, in pleasing proportion to the head. The ears should be set as much on the side of the head as on top of the head.

EYES: Large, walnut-shaped, expressive, and moderately wide set, the eyes contribute to the characteristic sweet look. A slight oriental tip to the eye is acceptable. The more intense the eye color, the better. Lighter eye color in dilutes is allowed. Eye color requirements: minks—green, blue-green, turquoise, blue, odd-eyed; solids—all colors, including odd-eyed.

BODY: Rectangular, broad chest and broad shoulders, and moderately heavy muscling in the hindquarters, with the hindquarters being equally as broad as the shoulders. There should be a fatty pad (greater omentum) in the lower abdomen. Fitness should be determined by the muscle tone in the hind legs. These cats are fully fleshed. The backbone and ribs should not be visible to the eye and on palpation should feel well covered with flesh.

TAIL: Long, in proportion to the body. It is fully furred, similar in look to a plume or soft bottlebrush, medium at the base with a slight taper.

LEGS AND PAWS: Legs should be heavily boned, medium in length, with the back legs slightly longer than the front legs, yet in proportion to the body. The paws should be large and round, able to support the weight of the cat without splaying, and with tufts beneath and between the paws. Allowance is made for finer boning in females.

COAT: The fur is to be medium to medium-long. Texture is to be dense and silky, similar to a heavily furred rabbit. Texture will vary slightly with color. Fur length is to be slightly longer around neck and outer edges of face, resulting in the appearance of a ruff, and increasing in length from top of head down through shoulder blades and back, with the coat on the sides and stomach being medium to medium-long. The fur on the front legs is thick and short to medium in length. The fur on the hind legs is medium to medium-long and thick, with the appearance of a wispy frill on the hindquarters.

COLOR: Every color and pattern is allowable with or without white, except pointed colors. Any amount of white is allowed (e.g., white spots on paws, back, chest or belly; a blaze, a locket, etc). The degree of symmetry, whether in the pattern or the white spotting, is of no importance. Nose leather and paw pads are accepted in all colors and in any color combination, not necessarily related to coat color. Cats with white on feet may have pink paw pads, or they may be bicolored or multicolored. Body darkening in older cats and lighter or incomplete markings in kittens and young cats is allowed.

CONDITION: Cat must exhibit excellent health and good care. It is to be clean and well groomed, with bright eyes and clean ears, and have no sign of parasites.

ALLOWANCES: Lighter eye color in dilutes. Shorter fur on the legs for cats with medium-length coat. Seasonal changes in coat length and texture. Smaller size in females and cats under 4 years of age. Short ruff on whole cats. Body darkening in older cats and lighter incomplete markings in kittens and young cats.

PREFERENCES: Affectionate nature, white tip on the tail, and deep, bright eye color.

PENALIZE: Extreme cranial doming, nose break, Roman nose, small ears, pointed ears. Cobby body, short tail, cottony undercoat.

DISQUALIFY: Poor health or condition, crossed eyes, visible tail kink, or polydactyl, pointed colors.

ALLOWABLE BREEDING OUTCROSSES: Ragdoll and Persian. Kittens born after July 15, 2006, may have only RagaMuffin parents.

RAGDOLL

By Valentine Janet Meriwether, Ph.D.

Ragdoll

Ragdolls are large, spectacular-looking cats with sumptuous coats that are moderately long, flowing with the lines of the body. The first impression is that of a beautiful toy for grown-ups. They are irresistible to look at or to touch.

Physical Description

Ragdolls are quite large with beautiful blue eyes and soft, plumed tails. They are moderate-type cats, with no extreme features. Altered males may reach 20 pounds or more, with an average range of 10–16 pounds. Females may reach 15 pounds, with an average range of 8–12 pounds. Ragdolls have good longevity. They typically live for 12–15 years or more and remain healthy and vigorous. They naturally have a fat pad on their abdomen even when they are underweight.

Their light-colored bodies have darker Siamese-type points on the face, legs, tail, and ears. In three of their four coat patterns, white markings partly cover the dark points. Their soft coats feel more like cashmere than cat fur.

Ragdolls have four coat patterns: pointed, mitted, bicolor, and van. Each pattern comes in six colors: seal, blue, chocolate, lilac, red, and cream. Points may be solid, lynx (tiger-striped points), or tortie (tortoiseshell points).

Pointed Ragdolls have the classic, Siamese-type markings: dark masks, ears, legs, and tails, with a pale, creamy, or misty-colored body.

Mitteds look like pointeds that went wading in whipped cream and sneaked a taste. Their mittens and boots are soft, fluffy white, and so are their chins.

Bicolors look like they lay down in whipped cream and dunked their faces in for a deep drink. All four legs, their underbodies, chest, and an upside-down V marking on their faces are white, and they may have a splash or two of pure white on their backs. Only the tail, ears, and the outer part of their masks show the darker markings.

Vans look like they went swimming in whipped cream. Their crystal white bodies contrast dramatically with their point markings and blue eyes. Only the top of the mask, ears, and tail, and perhaps a few spots on the body, show darker markings.

Ragdolls are slow to mature; they may take 4 years to reach full size, weight, and coat. Kittens are born pure white. Their colored point markings develop gradually, with full point color coming in at 2 years. The CFA accepts bicolors and vans for showing. Mitteds and pointeds are registered.

Personality

These are gentle cats, careful not to scratch people, and they are good with children, older people, and dogs. They tend to be floor cats, rather than jumpers. They understand that humans prefer purrs to yowls and so keep their voices soft and musical. Ragdolls are loving companions, well behaved, and eager to please.

These laid-back cats are people-oriented.

They greet you at the door when you come home, follow you from room to room, sleep with you, and will not let you go to the bathroom in peace. They never really grow up, and like eternal kittens, continue to be playful into old age. They are extremely gentle and rarely bite or scratch, even when frightened or in pain.

On top of this, they have the moderate energy level of domestic Longhairs. They are floppy and relaxed. You will not find them dangling from the curtain rod or banking off the wall during a game of chase. They prefer to lie on the floor, preferably on your foot, or on the sofa beside you. They will lie in your lap and purr while you drink your coffee, rather than knock the cup out of your hand to express their devotion.

Ragdolls love attention and human contact. They each have their own preferences. Some enjoy being held like a baby, some are foot floppers, some are lap layers, some prefer perching on shoulders, and some are attached hip and thigh whenever their humans sit down.

As a rule, they do not talk much, but when they do, they say a word or two in soft, musical voices. They are intelligent cats who like to play fetch, and they can be trained to walk with a leash. Their gentle manner makes them a good choice for families with children as well as elderly people, and their devotion makes them wonderful companions for those who live alone. They are called "puppycats" for good reason.

Grooming Requirements

Ragdolls are considerate of their humans' busy schedules, so they bathe and groom their moderately long, silky coats by themselves. Their coats, which have abundant guard hairs, and flow with the body rather than stand away from it, are not thick or dense and have a minimal undercoat. As a result, they shed very little, rarely develop a mat, seldom have hairballs, and rarely need grooming unless they are show cats. They are almost maintenance free. If they do get an occasional knot, it will usually be in the mane or "armpit." However, Ragdolls enjoy a daily combing, and if they are used to it, they will not be upset if actual grooming is needed. Bathing is optional for pets.

Kittens should be groomed with a steel comb as a part of cuddling (one hand stroke, one comb stroke; one hand stroke, one comb stroke . . .). Use a very fine toothed steel comb to remove any loose hair, and a coarse-toothed steel comb to remove any knots. Never use a slicker brush—or anything else you would not want to scrape across your own cheek—on a Ragdoll.

Grooming Ragdolls for cat shows is easy in comparison to what is necessary for other breeds. Just use a shampoo formulated for white cats and bathe them until they are immaculate. With adults, especially whole males, it is best to use a degreaser first, bathe them several times the weekend before the show, and then rebathe them. Use the degreaser and then lather and rinse again at least three times the night before the show.

Because of their weight, Ragdolls normally should be lifted and carried with two hands, rather than dangled from one hand.

Origins and History

The Ragdoll was developed in California in 1963 from a combination of sturdy, free-roaming domestic Longhairs of unknown ancestry. The foundation cat, Josephine, was a white domestic Longhair with a loving, gentle personality. She carried Siamese-type markings known as the Himalayan pattern. Josephine's white fur masked either a seal mitted or a black tuxedo pattern. All Ragdolls are descended from Josephine or unknown domestic Longhair males, or from Josephine and her seal-mitted son, Daddy Warbucks.

The originator of the Ragdoll was a gifted breeder, Ann Baker. She had a fine eye and a clear sense of purpose, understood the potential of the cats she found, and was determined to create a wonderful new breed. By selecting individuals with the look she wanted for her breeding program, she created the classic type standard for the Ragdoll.

In 1998, the CFA voted to accept the van-patterned Ragdoll, in addition to the original three patterns: pointed, mitted, and bicolor. Vans occur in about one quarter of the kittens from bicolor-to-bicolor matings. Point-restricted vans are a natural part of the Ragdoll breed. The pattern genetics were not as well understood in earlier years, and the vans that were produced by bicolor-to-bicolor matings were considered to be bicolors "with a lot of white on them."

Initially, most breeders were primarily interested in developing and establishing the breed, rather than showing it. Over time, breeders worked together to have their cats recognized and registered in various associations. The CFA began registering them in 1993, and they were advanced to Championship status at the CFA show in 2000. Today, Ragdolls are bred and shown all over the world.

CFA-registered Ragdolls are bred from two Ragdoll parents and must have at least three generations of Ragdolls in their immediate ancestry. No outcrossing is permitted.

Miscellanea

Ragdoll growth patterns are completely unpredictable. Some kittens grow slowly and steadily into adulthood, taper off gradually, and stop. (This is rare; Ragdolls usually have at least one explosive growth spurt.) Most kittens have several bursts of rapid growth and take rests in between. Some kittens grow explosively, reach their full size at age 10 months, and stop. Some stop for a year or two and then start growing again! This can happen anytime within the first 4 years of life. Because of their rapid but unpredictable growth patterns, Ragdolls have special feeding requirements. Most wet and dry cat foods provide lists of recommended daily feedings based on the weight of the kittens. For Ragdoll kittens, limiting food to these amounts can be a disaster.

Ragdoll kittens are capable of gaining up to 2 pounds in a single month when they are having a major growth spurt. What was plenty last week may be a starvation diet this week. And of course, when kittens are in a growth spurt, they need far more food than kittens of the same size and weight who are growing moderately. Furthermore, their fat little tummies can deceive owners (and veterinarians) into thinking the kittens are well fed. The Ragdoll stomach pad of fat is genetic, not nutritional. A Ragdoll kitten may be down to skin and bones, yet still have a fat pad on its belly. A healthy Ragdoll should be meaty and solid—built like a wrestler, not like a marathon runner. Therefore, to avoid unrecognized malnutrition and stunted growth, give Ragdoll kittens unlimited access to dry kitten food in a very large bowl or a self-feeder. Wet food should be given in amounts slightly greater than they are able to finish. A polished plate is a sure sign of a still-hungry kitten. Put down a few more spoonfuls, until the kitten stops eating.

Will free-feeding make the kitten obese? No. Kittens that are *always* given unlimited access to food will snack when the urge arises but aren't very interested in food—because they know it is always there. No deprivation means no bingeing. Free-fed Ragdolls are a bit meaty but not obese. Remember, they always have a genetic stomach fat pad. Once they reach adulthood, continue free-feeding with adult food, as Ragdolls may continue growing, off and on, up to 4 years of age.

Families with young or very active children should consider choosing male Ragdolls, because they are often much bigger, sturdier, and meatier than females and thus can handle minor mishaps more easily. Larger, older kittens are also a good choice. Also, breeders occasionally retire adults to good homes. These are less expensive and make wonderful family pets.

Ragdolls are extremely affectionate and love to lie on their humans. Therefore, petite, physically limited, or elderly people may prefer female kittens because of their smaller size and weight.

★ ★ ★

Ragdolls have no breed-specific genetic or health problems. Kitten mortality is low. Ragdoll fertility is fair to very good. Mothers take excellent care of their nursing kittens.

It is not unusual for new Ragdoll owners to contact a breeder for a second companion kitten. Over the years, Ragdolls have developed a consistent reputation as wonderful cats with easy-to-live-with personalities.

CFA SHOW STANDARD FOR THE RAGDOLL

POINT SCORE

HEAD (40)

Large, broad equilateral triangle	20
Eyes large; vivid blue ovals	10
Ears medium, wide set, moderately flared	5
Profile slightly curving; nose straight, chin strong	5

BODY (30)

Medium to large size and heavy boning	15
Long, rectangular body	10
Legs moderately long; tail long	5

COAT (30)

Moderately long length, with abundant guard hairs, but minimal woolly undercoat	20
Color of body and points*	10

GENERAL: The ideal Ragdoll is a medium to large, moderately long-haired, blue-eyed, pointed cat. The point markings may be covered by a range of white overlay patterns. The head forms a broad, equilateral triangle, modified by a gently rounded muzzle. The eyes are large, vivid blue ovals. The rectangular body is large, long, broad, and solid, with heavy boning. It has moderately long legs and a long plumed tail. The naturally non-matting, moderately long coat has abundant guard hairs, with minimal woolly undercoat, and flows with the body. The Ragdoll is bred to conform as perfectly as possible to the moderate type of the foundation cats.

HEAD: Proportionately large and broad. Triangular shaped, where all sides are of equal length as measured from the outside of the base of the ear to the end of the gently rounded muzzle. Appearance of a flat plane between ears. Cheeks in line with wedge. Allow for jowls in adult males. When whiskers and fur are smoothed back, the underlying bone structure is apparent.
EYES: Large, vivid blue ovals. Wide set and moderately slanted, complementing wedge.

*The 10 points for color are to be divided as follows: 5 for white markings and symmetry and 5 for body and point color.

EARS: Medium size. Wide set and moderately flared, continuing the line of wedge. Wide at base, with rounded tips, and tilted forward.

PROFILE: Slightly curving, ending in straight, medium-length nose. Chin well developed, strong, in line with nose and upper lip.

NECK: Heavy and strong.

BODY: Large and long, broad and solid, with heavy boning. Rectangular in shape, with a full chest and equal width across shoulders and hindquarters. Body firm and muscular, not fat. Moderate stomach pad on lower abdomen acceptable. Females may be substantially smaller than males. Allow for slow maturation in young adults.

LEGS: Heavily boned, moderately long. Hind legs longer than front. Shorter fur on front legs, longer fur on hind legs, with full, feathery britches.

PAWS: Proportionately large, round, and feather-tufted.

TAIL: Long, with full plume.

COAT: The naturally nonmatting, moderately long fur is characterized by abundant guard hairs and minimal woolly undercoat. It flows with the body. Ruff preferred. Short on face, longer on ruff, shorter on shoulder blades, lengthening toward tail. Allow shorter coats in unaltered adults, and seasonal variations.

PENALIZE: *Coat:* Thick undercoat, standing off from the body. *Eyes:* Small or round. *Eye color:* Very pale blue or blue so dark as to appear black. *Nose:* Roman nose. *Body:* Cobby body low on legs. *Short tail;* nondirectional lump on tail.

DISQUALIFY: *Nose:* any break. *Color:* Body and point color other than those listed; eyes other than blue. *Various:* Directional kink in tail. Crossed eyes. Extra toes.

(The above penalties and disqualifications apply to all Ragdolls. Additional penalties and disqualifications are listed under each pattern description.)

BICOLOR PATTERN: *Mask:* White inverted V remains within outer edge of eyes. Symmetry preferred. *Nose leather:* Pink. *Body:* Chin, chest, and underside are white. Upper body may show white spotting. *Legs and feet:* All white preferred. May have minor dark spots. *Paw pads:* Pink preferred, but mixture of colors on paw pads and fur acceptable because of two colors in pattern. (When determining color, point color of ears is the deciding factor.) *Penalize:* V extending beyond outer edges of eyes, or excessively asymmetrical. White marking on ears. *Disqualify:* V absent *or* has dark spotting. Extensive dark area on any leg.

VAN PATTERN: *Points:* Point color restricted to ears, tail, and upper part of mask. Ear and tail color dense and clearly defined, with minor white spotting allowed. Upper part of mask may show gradual fading of color. *Body, legs, and feet:* Pure, glistening white; minor spotting allowed. *Nose leather and paw pads:* Pink. *Penalize:* More than 20% color on body. *Disqualify:* Total absence of point color on head or tail.

COLORS (ALL PATTERNS): The six point colors are seal, blue, chocolate, lilac, red, and cream. Point colors may be solid, shaded, or smoke; lynx (including tortie-lynx); and parti-colored (or tortie). All Ragdolls are pointed, but points are partially overlaid with white in the bicolor and van patterns. *Body:* Even, subtle shading is permissible, but clear color is preferable. Allowance should be made for darker color in older cats, as Ragdolls generally darken with age, but there must be definite contrast between body color and points. *Points (except for white overlay):* Mask, ears, legs, feet, tail dense and clearly defined. All of the same shade. Mask covers entire face, including whisker pads, and is connected to ears by tracings. Mask should not extend over the top of the head. No ticking in points. Stomach pad may have darker shading.

ALLOWABLE BREEDING OUTCROSSES: none.

RUSSIAN BLUE

By Margaret R. Johnson

Russian Blue

With its plush, silvery coat, vivid green eyes, and sweet smile, a Russian Blue is unlike any other blue cat. Many people are first attracted to the elegance and beauty of Russian Blues, but these cats' loving and playful disposition is the major reason this breed has so many devoted followers. Conservative by nature, Russian Blues are thoughtful, intelligent cats who are very affectionate once they get to know you. When introduced properly, they get along well with children and other pets. The Russian Blue is a good choice for anyone looking for a feline companion to become a good friend and an important member of their family.

Physical Description

The most distinctive feature of the Russian Blue is its beautiful fur, which seems to be frosted with powdered sugar. The Russian Blue coat is soft, silky, and so plush that your fingers leave marks in it until you smooth them away. This thick double coat is often compared to the fur of a seal or beaver. The coat is water resistant and dense because its original purpose was to protect this demure cat from the harsh climate of northern Russia. The coat is blue with silver tipping that gives the cat a luminous appearance. The lighter shades of blue are preferred as long as the silver tipping remains distinct.

After marveling at the coat, you get to those mesmerizing emerald green eyes reminiscent of the forests of Russia. A Russian Blue's eyes are large, rounded, and set wide apart. A shy cat, the Russian Blue prefers not to look you directly in the eye. When she chooses to grace you with a thoughtful gaze, it is hard not to fall under her spell. At first she avoids looking at you, and then she catches you unaware as she stares directly at you as if she could read into your soul.

The Russian Blue head is a study of planes and angles framed by large ears set rakishly toward the sides of the head. The muzzle and upturned mouth form a sweet, smiling expression, as if the cat is enjoying some secret thought or joke. The Russian Blue's broad, wedge-shaped head is often compared to the flared head of a cobra. The seven flat planes of the Russian Blue head differentiate it from the head of any other breed. The profile has four flat planes, one from the nose to the brow, one from the brow to the back of the head, one from the nose to the chin, and one from the chin to the neck. From the front, the Russian Blue has three more flat planes: One is from ear to ear, and the others are on each side of the face, from the muzzle to the base of the ear. The muzzle is smooth without a prominent nosepad or whisker break.

The Russian Blue is the dancer of the cat fancy, with a lithe, muscular body; fine-boned long legs; and a long tail proportionate to the length of the body. Dainty, rounded paws make this cat appear to be walking on tiptoes. Like a dancer, the Russian Blue is very graceful and often strikes a regal pose to let you know how truly elegant she really is.

Russian Blue males tend to be a bit larger than the females, though all are medium-size cats. The Russian Blue's plush fur often makes it appear larger than it is. Russian Blue females run between 5 and 8 pounds, while males run between 7 to 10 pounds. They love their food, so it is up to their owners to help them maintain their svelte figures.

Personality

The breed is normally shy. Nevertheless, as for all breeds, personalities vary from cat to cat. The Blue's keen senses and cautious nature may be a throwback to a time when the cat had to fend for itself and fight for survival. While most Russian Blues are wary around strangers, some are very outgoing and friendly and do not seem to know what the word stranger means. As is the case for humans when making new friends, winning the Blue's trust and love usually takes a little effort and time. Once you win this cat over, you have a loyal and very affectionate friend. Blues become very attached to their owners. They like a small circle of close friends, so they are not inclined to bond with everyone who enters your house. Even so, some Russian Blues seem able to sense those who do not like cats and can become quite a pest in trying to win them over.

Once a Russian Blue settles in, you soon discover what a charming, entertaining creature you have invited into your home. Your Russian Blue will follow you from room to room just to be with you. These cats' favorite place is on your lap or shoulder. They show their love for you by rubbing against your head and licking your face. Thoughtful creatures, these cats are sensitive to their surroundings. They will clown around in an attempt to lighten your mood or quiet a crying child. They sit with you when you are sick, help you read your paper, and are always ready to play.

Although Russians are careful when trying something for the first time, they become quite stubborn when they decide they want to do something. Intelligent creatures, Russians never forget. They remember where you put the feather or the food and will often open the cupboard or drawer to get the object of their desire. They love to play and will train you to throw toys that they can retrieve. Russians are great jumpers and go crazy for feathers and other toys.

Grooming Requirements

These are clean cats who require little grooming. At home, your Russian Blue will require few baths. Grooming will consist primarily of combing to prevent shedding, clipping nails, and keeping ears and eyes clean.

The show ring demands more effort to present your Russian Blue at its best. Basic home grooming for nails, ears, and eyes are mandatory for showing. In addition, a bath will help your Russian Blue be more competitive. Russian Blue coats vary just as human hair does, so it may take a few experiments to determine the best shampoo and conditioner. Shampoos for blue or white cats, texturizing shampoos, and body shampoos are among those to try to enhance the fullness and color of your Russian Blue's coat. A light conditioner or vinegar rinse is a good finish to a Russian Blue bath. Bathing should be part of your Russian Blue's show training. The bath should consist of thoroughly wetting the coat, lathering once or twice, rinsing thoroughly, using a conditioner, and doing a final rinse. If your Russian Blue will tolerate blow-drying, blow the hair against the fur to enhance the fullness of the coat. At the show, various coat-conditioning sprays and combing can help put the final touches on your cat's coat.

Origins and History

The Russian Blue is a natural breed believed to have originated from the Archangel Isles in northern Russia. While little written history on this breed is available, many stories and legends surround it. Some legends about these dainty cats have them living in the wild, riding with the Cossacks, and sleeping with royalty. Other stories say they were hunted for their luxurious fur for the lining of hats and muffs. Another has these reserved cats riding the shoulders of their Cossack masters into battle. Russian Blues are also rumored to have been favorite cats of royalty, at court with several Russian czars and two English queens. In Russian folklore, Russian Blues were also thought to have a healing influence and even to bring good luck.

Sailors were believed to have brought the first Russian Blues to England and northern Europe in the mid–nineteenth century. In 1875 at a cat show at the Crystal Palace in England, a Russian Blue was shown as an Archangel Cat. Early Russian Blues were often called the Archangel Cat, Maltese, or Foreign Blue and competed in a class with all other blue cats. The diary of Mrs. Carew-Cox of England describes her work breeding several blue cats that were imported from Russia in the 1890s. It even indicates that she bought one of her first Russian Blues with a leg of mutton. It was not until 1912 that the Russian Blue was given a class of its own. From the early twentieth century through World War II, English and Scandinavian breeders worked to develop the bloodlines from which our modern Russian Blues are descended.

Although the first Russian Blues were imported to the United States in the early 1900s, little is known about them. The real story of the Russian Blue in the United States begins after World War II when U.S. breeders began importing Russian Blues from Europe. CFA registration of the Russian Blue began in 1949. For several years, two distinctive types of Russian Blues were being shown: one based on the pale, plush coats of the English bloodlines and the other based on the green eyes and stylish heads of the Scandinavian bloodlines. During the 1960s, U.S. breeders began to combine the English and Scandinavian bloodlines to produce the Russian Blues we know today. As breeders combined these bloodlines and worked to improve the temperament of this breed, the Russian Blue became more popular, and it is now a favorite at home and at shows.

Miscellanea

Patience should be the rule when introducing a new Russian Blue to your household. The Russian likes to take things slowly. A good start is to select a single room or area of your home to house your new Russian Blue for the first few days or weeks. This will allow you and your new cat to get used to each other before he gets too busy exploring his new home. A bedroom is a good choice for several reasons. First, your bedroom is full of your signature smell. Cats use their sense of smell to recognize everything around them. Second, being with sleeping people is an easy, nonthreatening way for a new cat to get to know you. Your new Russian Blue can tiptoe around the bed and check you out while you are asleep. Third, the Russian loves to sleep with her people. After thoroughly investigating her new human, your Russian will likely find a good spot on your bed and cuddle up for a catnap. If a bedroom is not a good choice for you, any room where you can spend some quality time with your new cat will do. The Russian loves to play, so sitting on the floor with a toy is a good ice-breaker. Spend as much time with your new Russian as possible, even if it is just reading or watching TV. Russian Blues truly enjoy being combed, so combing your cat during TV time is a great way to bond.

The time it takes a Russian Blue to become acclimated to a new environment will vary from cat to cat. A good rule is that once the cat responds to your call, she is probably ready to begin her investigation of the rest of your home. Short, supervised visits to new areas of your home are the best approach. She will want to explore every nook and cranny of the house. Russian Blues love high, small places, so do not be surprised when you find them in the most unlikely spots. They have been known to jump up on a doorjamb or to the top of a cupboard to find the perfect vantage point to keep an eye on everything. Russians also can fit themselves into the smallest places, so don't rule out looking under the dresser or behind the stereo when your cat is playing hide-and-seek with you.

Russian Blue females make very good mothers. Even young females who have never had kittens often take to babysitting and grooming their companions. Normally quiet, Russian Blue females are often very noisy when they are in season. Males can also be quite talkative when they are feeling amorous.

The average size of a Russian Blue litter is three kittens. Kittens usually weigh between 2 and 3 ounces when born. Like most kittens, their eyes open at 10–15 days. Kittens start out with blue eyes that often change to khaki or gold before finally turning to green. The speed of eye color development varies, but the eyes should be showing some green by 4 months of age, with the adult eye color usually setting in prior to 1 year. Kittens often display faint tabby markings in their fur that usually disappear when they get their adult coat. Russian Blue kittens start being very mobile around 3 weeks of age. They start eating on their own between 3 and 4 weeks of age. They can be quite enthusiastic when they first start eating and are sometimes found standing in the middle of the food dish, acting as if it is their last meal.

Kittens are usually weaned between 4 to 6 weeks of age. About the time of weaning, they become quite interested in exploring their world. This discovery period can last until they are 3–4 months old. During this phase, they are more interested in their surroundings than in their human friends. Around 4 months of age, Russian Blue kittens start associating their human companions with some of the finer things in life such as food, fun, and love.

Because of their shy disposition, it is imperative to start show training for Russian Blues as early as possible, if that is where your interests lie. As soon as the kitten starts moving around, show handling should begin. Show handling consists of kitten games such as Show Stretch, Helicopter, and Airplane. Show Stretch includes getting the kitten used to being handled and stretched, as she would be in a judging ring. Helicopter is an up-and-down movement to get kittens used to being off the floor. Airplane is a more energetic version of Helicopter, to be used as the kitten gets a little older. In addition to show handling, Russian Blue kittens should be exposed to as much noise and activity as possible to get them used to the type of atmosphere you find at a show hall. Playing a radio on a rock station is a good way to help them get acclimated to noises.

At cat shows, Russian Blues prefer gentle, firm handling. They never forget, so make sure you make their show experience as enjoyable as possible. A special food treat, extra playtime, and extra attention are often all it takes for Russian Blues to take pleasure in showing. It is also very important to remain calm. Russian Blues are very aware of your feelings, so they will pick up on any nervousness or fear. They may also prefer a cage of their own. Russian Blues who are great friends at home often become quite indignant and blame one another for being away at the show. Once home, they act like they missed each other.

Whether it is their luxurious coat, flashing green eyes, sweet smile, or affectionate disposition, Russian Blues continue to attract many dedicated breeders as well as cat owners. They provide their owners with a unique combination of elegance, intelligence, playfulness, and friendship. They are always in charge of the relationship but are very kind and gentle about having the upper hand. Once a Russian Blue has owned you, no other breed of cat will do.

CFA SHOW STANDARD FOR THE RUSSIAN BLUE

POINT SCORE

HEAD AND NECK	20
BODY TYPE	20
EYE SHAPE	5
EARS	5
COAT	20
COLOR	20
EYE COLOR	10

GENERAL: The good show specimen has good physical condition, is firm in muscle tone, and is alert.

HEAD: Smooth, medium wedge, neither long and tapering nor short and massive. Muzzle is blunt, and part of the total wedge, without exaggerated pinch or whisker break. Top of skull long and flat in profile, gently descending to slightly above the eyes, and continuing at a slight downward angle in a straight line to the tip of the nose. No nose break or stop. Length of top-head should be greater than length of nose. The face is broad across the eyes because of wide eye-set and thick fur.

MUZZLE: Smooth, flowing wedge without prominent whisker pads or whisker pinches.

EARS: Rather large and wide at the base. Tips more pointed than rounded. The skin of the ears is thin and translucent, with little inside furnishing. The outside of the ear is scantily covered with short, very fine hair, with leather showing through. Set far apart, as much on the side as on the top of the head.

EYES: Set wide apart. Aperture rounded in shape.

NECK: Long and slender, but appearing short because of thick fur and high placement of shoulder blades.

NOSE: Medium in length.

CHIN: Perpendicular to the end of the nose and to the level under chin. Neither receding nor excessively massive.

BODY: Fine boned, long, firm, and muscular; lithe and graceful in outline and carriage without being tubular in appearance.

LEGS: Long and fine boned.

PAWS: Small, slightly rounded. Toes: five in front and four behind.

TAIL: Long, but in proportion to the body. Tapering from a moderately thick base.

COAT: Short, dense, fine, and plush. Double coat stands out from body because of density. It has a distinct soft and silky feel.

DISQUALIFY: Kinked or abnormal tail. Locket or button. Incorrect number of toes. Any color other than blue. Long coat.

COLOR: Even bright blue throughout. Lighter shades of blue preferred. Guard hairs distinctly silver-tipped, giving the cat a silvery sheen or lustrous appearance. A definite contrast should be noted between ground color and tipping. Free from tabby markings. *Nose leather:* Slate gray. *Paw pads:* Lavender pink or mauve. *Eye color:* Vivid green.

ALLOWABLE BREEDING OUTCROSSES: none.

SCOTTISH FOLD
By Jean Grimm

Scottish Fold Longhair

Scottish Fold Shorthair

No one can forget his or her first encounter with a Scottish Fold. It is such an unusual-looking cat with its tiny folded ears and large, round eyes that people often have to look a second time to make sure this beautiful cat is actually real and not a stuffed toy or some sort of exotic creature. It truly is an actual cat, with very humble origins as a Scottish farm cat.

Physical Description

All aspects of the Scottish Fold are round, with the head appearing even rounder because of the caplike fit of the forward-folding ears. Even the tips of the ear are gently rounded. The neck is short and blends into a round, well-padded body. The cat stands firmly on strong legs with a wide stance that reflects the wide breadth of the body. The chest is deep; the body is the same width from shoulder to hips. The legs are straight and strong, and the rounded paws have five toes in the front and four in the back. The back legs are slightly angled at the hock and appear straight when seen from the back. The tail, in proportion to the body, is also rounded, with a moderate taper. It is important that the tail be flexible and without kinks or anomalies. Whether kitten or adult, the Scottish Fold is always a solid, well-balanced cat.

The sweet, open expression on the Fold's face is found in both males and females. The eyes, especially appealing, are large and round. Without the distraction of upright ears, the eyes almost seem to overwhelm the face. Even in the straight-eared Folds, the eyes are unusual and dominating, which is why these cats are sometimes compared to owls. The kittens especially are often described as "all eyes."

The folded ears are, of course, the reason these cats exist as a breed, but not all kittens will grow up with folded ears. These will be the straight-eared variety. Straight-eared cats are also wonderful pets and are also used for breeding, as one parent must be straight-eared and the other parent fold-eared. Even with straight ears, these kittens are easily identified as coming from a Scottish Fold litter. They have the same endearing features and the same chubby bodies. Both varieties of kitten are often acquired together, making an interesting and attractive pair.

The ears are the Scottish Fold's most arresting feature. They fold forward and downward over the top of the head in a rounded caplike shape that follows closely the contour of the head. They are small and rounded at the tip. There are variations in the degree of individual folding, but those with the greatest degree of folding are chosen as show cats. More important than the actual degree of folding is the way the ears fit the curve of the head. The ears should fit like a cap, enhancing the rounded structure of the head. They should not be too close together but rather should blend around the natural curve of the head. These ears are very soft and feel exactly like any nonfolded cat's ears. They are not clamped tightly against the head, and their shape or position do not affect hearing.

The overall appearance of the Scottish Fold is based on the European type, as found in the British Shorthair. The domestic cat of England is a heavy, well-padded cat with a coat heavy enough to protect against inclement weather. The first Scottish Fold breeders often used whatever they had available to perpetuate the ear mutation. The first crosses included the local domestic and the most obvious choice, the British Shorthair. An Exotic, a Burmese, and Persians were recorded in the first generations. Breeding goals were established in 1976, and outcrosses were then restricted to the British Shorthair and the American Shorthair.

Many options can be found in the combinations of Scottish Fold coats. First, there is the choice between long-haired and short-haired; second, there is a choice of a wonderful array of colors. The early influence of the British Shorthair and the Persian helped determine that the cats would have heavy, thick coats. In the long-haired version, the length and distribution is modified to produce a coat that is fullest and longest around the ruff and britches, with the coat draping softly without the long, heavy bluntness of a Persian cat's coat. The long-haired cat will also sport toe tufts and ear tufts. If there is anything more enchanting in appearance than the short-haired Scottish Fold, the same cat wearing long hair would be it. Colors from many sources were combined and allowed in the development of the Scottish Fold. Only the colors lilac or chocolate and the evidence of the colorpoint gene, as seen in the Siamese, are not permitted. Colors include the usual solid colors and tabby patterns available with or without the combination of white. Gold and green or blue-green eyes are found in the solid-color and tabby-marked cats; blue, copper, and odd eyes are found in the whites, vans, and bicolors.

Personality

If you choose to include a Scottish Fold in your life, do not expect either a curtain-climbing daredevil or a constantly clinging sort of cat. You can expect a playful, friendly companion who will thrive on attention and love. A Scottish Fold is never haughty or standoffish but is sometimes reserved and careful how it shares its love. It enjoys the company of people and will bond with all family members but will not take to rough handling or rude remarks about its unusual ears. They can adapt well to other family pets, though other cats are sometimes surprised by their first view of a cat with folded ears, that being an accepted sign of anger among cats.

Scottish Fold kittens are as adventurous and as playful as kittens of other breeds. If you want a cozy lap cuddler, try instilling the interest at an early age. One kitten shopper listed these desired qualities: a kitten that did not shed, did not scratch the rugs, did not deposit hairballs on the rugs, would come when called, and would sit endlessly on her lap. A stuffed toy was suggested instead of a live kitten.

Grooming Requirements

Grooming is basically the same for the long-haired and the short-haired varieties of Scottish Fold. The Longhair will naturally require more combing and a longer drying time than the Shorthair. All cats should be conditioned at an early age to tolerate bathing, nail clipping, and ear cleaning. Cleaning the Scottish Fold's ear is simple, especially if the cat has been accustomed to having its ears handled at an early age. The tip of the ear is held between two fingers and gently drawn upward to reveal the ear opening underneath. The inside of the ear should be wiped out carefully with a cotton swab or a damp cloth. Clean only the outer visible surfaces.

Bathing should start when the cat is still a kitten. A deep sink with a good rubber mat on the bottom can be filled with warm water before the cat is placed in it. Wet the cat and lather it up with a gentle cat shampoo. Rinsing can be done in another sink of water or with a spray attachment. Towel the cat thoroughly and finish with an electric dryer and a comb until the coat is completely dry. Here is a very important hint: Clip the nails before the bath. You will find that the upkeep for the Scottish Fold is easy.

Origins and History

The appearance of a domestic cat with folded ears in Scotland in 1961 introduced a new breed to the cat fancy. The first known Scottish Fold was a copper-eyed white female named Susie. She was discovered on a farm in Coupar Angus in the Tayside region of Perthshire in Scotland. There was a second folded-ear kitten in the litter, a male, but he had already vanished when Susie was noticed by William Ross, a shepherd and neighbor of Susie's owners, the McRaes.

William and Molly Ross were very intrigued by the interesting mutation. Wishing to preserve this mutation, they requested a folded-ear kitten from Susie. Since both straight-eared and folded-ear kittens may appear in the same litter, the wait was two years long. Three months after Susie produced her first and only litter, Susie (living the outdoor life of a domestic farm cat) was killed in a road accident. In 1968, from this single litter, the Rosses received Snooks, a copper-eyed white daughter of Susie's. Further breedings, including a domestic male and then a British Shorthair, resulted in folded-ear kittens and the foundation cats for the Scottish Fold breed.

The Scottish Fold was granted CFA registration status in 1974. On October 16, 1976, the breed was accepted for CFA Provisional status. CFA Championship status was conferred in October 1977, thereby allowing the Scottish Fold to begin competition in the new show year, which started in May 1978. The short-haired version of the Scottish Fold was the first accepted division, even though the long-haired version had been present in the early generations. The long-haired version gained acceptance first as a breed called the Highland Fold in 1991. In the following year, Highland Fold designation was dropped in favor of creating two divisions in which the Scottish Fold now compete, the Longhair Division and the Shorthair Division. The first national win achieved by a Scottish Fold was in 1979.

Miscellanea

Scottish Folds are not finicky eaters. In fact, care must be taken to help them not overeat, in view of their docile and not-too-active lifestyle.

These cats, as with all pedigreed cats, should never be left outdoors. They traded their street smarts for life by the fireside many generations ago. Their feline instincts remain very strong, so they will actively admire every bird that comes near the window and will be delighted if a mouse finds its way inside to play with them. They have been observed to be fully capable of performing the same rodent control for which their British relations are so prized.

You may expect a long life from your Scottish Fold. Many are known to have reached the age of 18 years.

When handling Scottish Folds, always carry them with both hands or tucked against one hip with an arm around them. These are heavy, compact cats, and they will not appreciate casual handling. Setting them down rather than dropping them is the considerate thing to do for all cats.

The show Scottish Fold must approximate the CFA standard as closely as possible. As with all competition cats, it must be presented in excellent health. There is no tolerance in the ring for a cat presented with less than perfect grooming or with any evidence of illness or parasites. Judges will withhold awards or disqualify a cat when presented with any of these situations. A cat's disposition is of great importance. If a cat is hostile or frightened, it cannot present itself well to a show judge. There are show rules that deal with aggressive, hostile behavior; judges will dismiss cats behaving in such fashion.

A cat competing in show should be carried to the ring using a two-handed hold. A judge will not stretch the cat, as is the method for an Oriental, but will allow the cat to stand by itself to show off its sturdy confirmation. The judge may lift the show cat by placing a hand under the front legs to check for soundness of the back legs and to gauge the chest width. Show cats should be accustomed to responding to the movements of toys or feathers, which the judge may use when doing further examination of mobility and expression.

The Scottish Fold has become an important and popular addition to the ranks of show cats as well as a beautiful, delightful companion in the home. They are as undemanding and loving as they are beautiful. It was a special day when a little white Scottish farm cat introduced a new breed into our homes and hearts. If you decide the Scottish Fold is the right cat for you, you will have chosen well.

CFA SHOW STANDARD FOR THE SCOTTISH FOLD

POINT SCORE

HEAD (55)	
Ears	25
Head shape, muzzle, neck, chin, profile	15
Eyes	15
BODY (40)	
Body structure of torso, legs, and paws	10
Tail	20
Coat	10
COLOR (5)	
Color of coat and eyes	5

GENERAL: The Scottish Fold cat occurred as a spontaneous mutation in farm cats in Scotland. The breed has been established by crosses to British Shorthairs and domestic cats in Scotland and England. In the United States, allowed outcrosses are the American Shorthair and the British Shorthair. All bona fide Scottish Fold cats trace their pedigreed to Susie, the first fold-ear cat discovered by the founders of the breed, William and Mary Ross.

HEAD: Well rounded, with a firm chin and jaw. Muzzle to have well-rounded whisker pads. Head should blend into a short neck. Prominent cheeks, with a jowly appearance in males.

EYES: Wide open, with a sweet expression. Large, well rounded, and separated by a broad nose. Eye color to correspond with coat color. Blue-eyed and odd-eyed are allowed for all white and bicolor and van patterns.

NOSE: Nose to be short with a gentle curve. A brief stop is permitted. Profile is moderate in appearance.

EARS: Fold forward and downward. Small. The smaller, tightly folded ear preferred over a loose fold and large ear. The ears should be set in a caplike fashion to expose a rounded cranium. Ear tips to be rounded.

BODY: Medium, rounded, and even from shoulder to pelvic girdle. The cat should stand firm with a well-padded body. There must be no hint of thickness or lack of mobility in the cat due to short, coarse legs. Toes to be neat and well rounded, with five in front and four behind. Overall appearance is that of a well-rounded cat with medium bone; fault cats obviously lacking in type. Females may be slightly smaller.

TAIL: Tail should be medium to long but in proportion to the body. Tail should be flexible and tapering, may end in a round tip. Longer, tapering tail preferred.

COAT—SHORTHAIR: Dense, plush, even. Short to medium-short in length. Soft in texture. Full of life. Standing away from body because of density, not flat or close-lying. Coat texture may vary because of color and/or regional/seasonal changes.

COAT-LONGHAIR: Medium-long to long hair length. Full coat on face and body desirable, but short hair permissible on face and legs. Britches, tail plume, toe tufts, and ear furnishings should be clearly visible, with a ruff being desirable. Seriously penalize cottony coat, except in kittens.

PENALIZE: Brow ridge.

DISQUALIFY: Kinked tail. Tail that is foreshortened. Tail that is lacking in flexibility because of abnormally thick vertebrae. Splayed toes, incorrect number of toes. Any evidence of illness or poor health. Palpable nose break. Any color or pattern showing evidence of hybridization resulting in the colors chocolate or lavender or in the pointed pattern, or combinations of these colors with white, and so on.

COLORS: A wide array of colors in the solid, shaded, tabby, parti-color, and bicolor patterns.

ALLOWABLE BREEDING OUTCROSSES: British Shorthair, American Shorthair.

SELKIRK REX
By Donna Bass

Selkirk Rex Shorthair

Selkirk Rex Longhair

A strange-looking kitten found in the Big Sky Country of Montana has provided the cat fancy with a new breed: the cat in sheep's clothing, or the Selkirk Rex. These cats have a following with their lambs' wool coat and clownish personality.

Physical Description

The Selkirk Rex kitten is covered with a downy, curly coat, with every little hair arranged in little ringlets that lie close to its body. Even the hair on the tiny little tail is curly. If the whiskers are curly, the breeder knows she has a kitten that may grow up to be a top show cat. Straight whiskers indicate a straight-haired kitten that will never see a show hall.

The amount of curl in the coat at birth seems to be an indicator of how curly the mature cat will be. As the kitten grows and develops, the coat can fluctuate in curliness. When the cat is about 1 year old, the coat settles down, the breeder can breathe a sigh of relief if the kitten has developed the wonderful curls that are treasured, or sigh in frustration if the coat lacks the spectacular curl. Even during the teenage gangly stage, the coat should exhibit some curl around the neck and on the tummy.

Mature males, neutered or not, and spayed females will have the best coats. In the best examples of the breed, the curling is strongest on the flanks, on the tummy, and around the neck, with some curl on the back. The harder hair on the back seems to be the most difficult to keep in curl, regardless of the softness of the rest of the coat, especially on the short-haired variety. The long-haired variety has long enough hair that curling becomes more obvious.

The hair of a mature whole (unspayed) female, however, can at times appear either curly or nearly straight, depending on the state of her hormones. Her whiskers will continue to be curly, regardless of her hormonal state. In estrus (heat), pregnancy, and lactation, a female's coat looks nearly straight. Between cycles, the coat *can* curl back to its normal state, but it may not. At no time, however, is the coat entirely straight. It is just not as curly as it was before hormones started raging.

Think of your favorite teddy bear when it was new. The body was covered with a thick, plush fur that encouraged you to cuddle, stroke, and pat it. The Selkirk Rex coat feels and looks the same: thick, full, and plush, with no thin patches, whether the coat is long or short.

The second thing people notice about the Selkirks (after the coat, of course) is the whis-kers. Every Selkirk Rex exhibitor hears "Did you clip its whiskers?" "What's wrong with its whiskers?" "Doesn't it need the whiskers to find its way around?" and on and on. Because Selkirks grow up with short curly whiskers, they are used to finding their way around just fine.

The newborn's fine little whiskers can be difficult to see late at night, which is when the mothers almost always want to have their babies with them. However, the morning light allows for proper classification as either a straighthair or a curly. A magnifying glass would be helpful as would strong light. The kittens should be kept out of the light as much as possible, however.

The whiskers on a Selkirk can be described as short, curly, and sparse. Because the whiskers are curly and brittle, they break off when they get too long. Occasionally, long ones will be visible, but they do not last long. The whiskers do not change as the cat gets older. If they are curly at birth, they are curly in adulthood. At any age, few Selkirks show more than a few whiskers—certainly not a full set—at any one time.

This breed is called the cat in sheep's clothing because the coat (especially in Short-hairs) can feel like lambs' wool, but without the oily lanolin feel. Younger cats can look like Persian lambs with little spit curls all over. This is a coat that begs to be played with, enjoyed and treated like your favorite teddy bear. Though it is difficult to keep from stroking and playing with the curls, too much handling (as in a show ring) can relax the curls too much. But a spritz of water (between ring times) brings the coat back to its original plush, curly condition.

The Selkirk Rex is a medium to large cat, with males weighing between 12 and 15 pounds and females weighing between 10 and 12 pounds. The should be solid, with boning in proportion to the size of body and neither too refined nor too coarse, to match the body and head length.

A Selkirk Rex's head is round, as are its eyes, which are set well apart—at least one eye's diameter apart. The cat should have a sweet open expression to match its personality. This is a breed that has a definite muzzle—and a nose for getting into everything.

Personality

Imagine a clown covered with lambs' wool who will steal your heart . . . or a toy. Or a big, plush teddy bear that will trip you up by opening doors or sucking on your toes or that will climb on your back when you bend over to clean the litter box. The combination of intelligence and a silly streak makes these plush little charmers hard to resist. Even whole males love to have their people cuddle them, almost enough to make them forget female cats.

The original Selkirk Rex, Miss DePesto, got her name because she was a pest for attention and she has passed that trait on to her descendants. These are friendly cats that can be in your face expecting attention and love when you are around, but will accept a lick and a promise if time is short. They have quiet little voices and will not demand immediate attention at all hours of the day or night, but they will not accept being ignored for long periods.

The combination of quiet voice, curly coat, big round eyes, and loud purrs can convince even the most hard-hearted that the Selkirk is the perfect lap cat. Although these cats prefer to have all four feet on the floor, a warm lap is even better. If you like to talk to your cats, these kitties will answer back. If you need entertaining, they are more than happy to oblige with a quick chase or a little peek-a-boo. If you have a teaser toy such as a feather or a laser pen (even a flashlight), your Selkirk

will be in cat heaven. These plush clowns are quite capable of doing a forward roll, swiveling their hips in midair, and making a graceful leap to the top of a cat tree. Children and Selkirks can get along as long as the cats are not handled roughly.

Rarely does a Selkirk Rex turn down food. But although these cats do like to eat, they are not gluttons and can have food in front of them all day without overeating.

Grooming Requirements

The Selkirk Rex rarely needs a bath. If you are a pet owner, you will need no fancy grooming tools for this breed. The best tools are attached to the end of your arms—they are your hands. Use your fingers in a gentle scratching motion to help your kitty's curls look their best. When your pet is on your lap, an excellent way to spend quality time together is by gently running your fingers or a comb through the coat. This removes the dead hair and keeps hairballs to a minimum. Because the Selkirk is a full-coated cat, it sheds just like any other full-coated cat. The Selkirk Rex coat does not mat easily, even in the longhairs, but combing will make sure no mats form.

If a bath is required, a moisturizing shampoo is usually all that is needed. Coat conditioner is rarely necessary. Blow-drying a Selkirk can give it a poodle look. Rewetting the coat will bring the curl back. The coat will air-dry in a few hours.

Show grooming for the Selkirk is a little more involved. The process and the products chosen depend on the length and feel of your cat's coat. A short-haired cat with a stiff, oily coat requires different grooming than a cat with a soft, floaty, long-haired coat. No matter what kind of coat your cat has, always err on the side of cleanliness. Proper grooming for show is a trial-and-error process until you discover what works best for your cat. What works for you may not work for someone else. Show grooming begins with combing out the complete coat to remove loose hairs so that they will not be licked up by the cat during the drying process and cause hairballs.

If the coat has greasy areas, especially at the base of the tail or behind the ears, use a degreasing soap. For heavy greasiness, GOOP hand cleaner is recommended. For lighter greasiness, Dawn dishwashing liquid works well. If no signs of greasy coat are obvious, (by feel or look) you can avoid the degreasing stage to keep from drying out the coat too much. Rinse the cat well.

Next, shampoo the cat with a good oily-hair shampoo for people, or use an antimicrobial shampoo. Rinse the cat well. Shampoo the cat for a final time with a shampoo appropriate to your cat's color. (Ask your breeder or someone at a pet supply outlet for shampoo recommendations.) Rinse the cat well, then rinse some more. Remember that you cannot rinse too much.

Experience will teach you whether your cat's coat requires a conditioner and what kind. As with the shampooings, rinse until you are sure your kitty is clean, then rinse some more. Never allow your cat's coat to be greasy or too dry.

Gently blot the cat as dry as possible with a clean towel. Then gently comb the coat (using a medium comb, rather than a fine or large comb) to remove additional loose hair and to check for mats that may have formed during the shampooing. After combing the coat through, leave the cat in a warm room to dry. During the drying process, squeeze the coat to help it loosen up and curl. For long-haired cats, separate any large clumps with a hair pick. (This is an invaluable tool, especially for longhairs, and can be found at beauty supply shops). Allow your cat to air-dry thoroughly.

Just before taking your cat to the show ring, spritz it lightly with a leave-in conditioning spray or rehydrating spray. A light spritz is all you need. Do not put on more than will dry before the cat is handled. Do not use too much during the day. Squeeze the cat's coat lightly against the grain to accentuate the curl. If the curls look too clumpy, separate them with a hair pick.

Check the ears, eyes, nose, and under the tail for cleanliness. These areas are easy to overlook but can get dirty on even the cleanest cat.

Unlike the coat of a Devon or Cornish Rex, the Selkirk coat should not be smoothed down, especially on the back, which is the one place where the curl is apt to be least noticeable. To enjoy the Selkirk coat, rake your fingers through the hair to lift the curls and allow them to fall free, so that you can feel the density of the thick, plush coat.

Origins and History

The Selkirk Rex began the same way that many breeds did—with a spontaneous mutation producing an unusual-looking kitten. But the Selkirk Rex almost did not come to be. A woman who ran a shelter out of her home in Sheridan, Montana, rescued a dilute calico in 1986 that was missing a foot after being caught in a trap.

The cat had a litter of kittens shortly after being rescued. A female from the litter of six kittens was born with an unusual coat. The unusual kitten was placed with someone when she was very young, but she came back because the new owner could not stand her crying. When she was 7 months old, a Persian breeder in Livingston, Montana, took her in and named her Miss DePesto of NoFace. Her whiskers were curly, her ears were full of steel-wool hair, and her coat looked as if she had had a body wave.

At 14 months of age, Miss DePesto was

bred to a black Persian male. She gave birth on July 4, 1988, to six babies (four short-haired, two long-haired), three of which had definite curly coats. The breeder discovered that no one had seen a curly-coated male in the vicinity, and no other curly-coated kittens had been produced. Thus, it was believed that Miss De-Pesto was the start of a new mutation, a dominant coat modification gene.

Unlike many new breeds, Selkirk Rex were not named for the country or area of origination; otherwise, they would have been American Rex or Montana Rex, just as the Cornish and Devon were named for the parts of England from which they came. Instead, the breeder decided to honor her stepfather by incorporating his family name—Selkirk—into the breed's name. The word *rex* historically was used to mean a coat that was not a standard coat (that is, one that is sraight). Thus, it was that *Rex* was added to this new breed's name.

At the February 1992 board meeting, the CFA accepted the Selkirk Rex for registration, and in February 2000, the Selkirk Rex achieved Championship status.

Miscellanea

This is a big breed that prefers to have "four on the floor" when being bathed or handled at the show hall. Because of their size, most of these cats do not like to be off the ground for very long, and they show how upset they are by wiggling until they are set down. Holding up the front of these cats to check the tummy for curls is usually acceptable to them, because many of the breeders do the same thing with their cats, to enjoy the curls. Selkirks like to play with toys and despite their size can be quite agile when chasing a teaser or a peacock feather.

The Selkirk Rex is an intelligent, silly, friendly, cuddly, curly-coated, purring, living big teddy bear. What more could you want in a cat?

CFA SHOW STANDARD FOR THE SELKIRK REX

POINT SCORE

HEAD (30)	
Skull	10
Muzzle and chin	10
Ears and eyes	10
BODY (30)	
Torso	15
Legs and feet	10
Tail	5
COAT (texture, curl, and density)	30
COLOR (including eye color)	10

GENERAL: The Selkirk Rex is the result of a dominant spontaneous mutation that causes each hair (guard, down, and awn) to have a gentle curl, giving the coat a soft feel. This is a medium to large cat with heavy boning that gives it surprising weight and an impression of power. Females may be less massive than males, but they are not dainty in appearance. The Selkirk Rex is an active cat with a sweet and endearing personality.

HEAD: *Skull:* Round, broad, and full-cheeked in both males and females. Round underlying bone structure with no flat planes. Muzzle: The muzzle is medium width. The underlying bone structure is rounded with well-padded whisker pads to give the impression of squareness. The length is equal to half the width. Profile shows a muzzle clearly visible beyond the curve of the cheek. The tip of the chin lines up with the tip of the nose and the upper lip in the same vertical plane. Profile reveals a nose stop. The nose has a downward slant with a convex curve and is set below the eye line. *Chin:* Firm and well developed, balanced in proportion to rest of head. *Ears:* Medium in size, broad at the base, tapering, set well apart. Should fit into (without distorting) the rounded contour of the head. Furnishings, if present, are curly. *Eyes:* Large, rounded, set well apart. The eyes should not appear almond- or oval-shaped, and inside and outside corners of eyes are in the same level horizontal plane.

BODY: *Torso:* Medium to large and well balanced. The substantial muscular torso is more rectangular than square, but not long. Back is straight, with a slight rise to the hindquarters. Shoulders and hip should appear to be the same width. *Legs:* Medium to long. Substantial boning. Should be in proportion to the body. *Feet:* Large, round, and firm. *Toes:* Five in front, four behind. *Tail:* Medium length, proportionate to body. Heavy at base, neither blunt nor pointed at tip.

COAT: *Coat length:* Two lengths—short and long. The differences in coat length are most obviously seen on the tail and ruff. On the Shorthairs, the tail hair is the same length as the coat (approximately 1–2") and tail curls are plush and lie compactly around the tail. The ruff is the same length as the coat fur. On the longhairs, the tail curls are plumy and stand out away from the tail.

The ruff hairs are also longer and frame the face. *Shorthair:* Texture—the coat texture is soft, plushy, full, and obviously curly. Density—the coat is dense and full with no bald or thinly covered areas of the body. The coat stands out from the body and should not appear flat or close-lying. Curl—this is a random, unstructured coat, arranged in loose, individual curls. The curls appear to be in clumps rather than an allover wave. Although curl varies by hair length, sex, and age in an individual, the entire coat should show the effect of the Rex gene. Curliness may be evident more around the neck, on the tail, and on the belly. Allowance should be made for less curl on younger adults and kittens. *Longhair:* Texture—the coat texture is soft, full, and obviously curly. It does not feel or appear to be as plush as the shorthair coat; however, it should not appear to be thin. Density—the coat is dense and full, with no bald or thinly covered areas of the body. The coat may stand out from the body but may appear and feel less than plush, but not close-lying. Curl—this is a random, unstructured coat, arranged in loose, individual curls. The curls appear to be in clumps or ringlets rather than an allover wave. Although curl varies by hair length, sex, and age in an individual, entire coat should show the effect of the Rex gene. Curliness may be evident more around the neck, on the tail, and on the belly. Allowance should be made for less curl on younger adults and kittens.

PENALIZE: Excessive cobbiness or sleek oriental appearance.

DISQUALIFY: Extreme nose break, lack of visible muzzle, malocclusion, tail kinks, crossed eyes, obvious physical deformities, including polydactl feet, no evidence of curl.

COLORS: All colors and patterns.

ALLOWABLE BREEDING OUTCROSSES: British Shorthair, Persian, or Exotic.

Kittens born on or after January 1, 2010, may have only Selkirk Rex or British shorthair parents. Kittens born on or after January 1, 2015 may have only Selkirk Rex parents.

SIAMESE
By Betty White

Siamese

To know anything at all about pedigreed cats is to know the Siamese. The captivation of the Western world by the "royal cats of Siam" has been crucial to the history of the cat fancy from its very beginnings, as well as to its subsequent development through the years. It was largely the discovery of this one breed by the English well over 100 years ago that provided the impetus for the world of cats we know today. The striking, contrasting Siamese color pattern on an elegant frame, made all the more dramatic by dark blue eyes, is the stuff of dreams. If imitation is the sincerest form of flattery, then the Siamese has the undisputed claim to the title of most beloved feline breed: The Siamese has been the inspiration, if not the primary genetic source, for many other breeds and has served to maintain and stabilize breeds threatened with extinction. The Siamese is, in short, a feline treasure. It is understandable, then, that cat lovers everywhere have set this ancient breed apart. The universal love affair with the Siamese has been both its glory and its nemesis.

Physical Description

The Siamese breeding tradition began generations ago, but the Siamese of today still have the graceful elegance suggested in the earliest breed standards. Simply put, a Siamese is a living, breathing work of art that shuns a display shelf in favor of a lap. Long head, long body, long tail, long neck, long legs—everything about a Siamese is long, with the exception of its short coat, which accentuates the body lines and lends a porcelain-like quality to the cat's looks. A tubular body, large ears, and fine bones contribute to this exquisite refinement of type. The long, wedge-shaped head, graced by large ears that complete that triangle, straight profile, and lovely almond-shaped eyes contribute to a unique expression of feline beauty. When the color contrast is excellent and correct, the body color is even and clear, and the eyes are a gorgeous deep blue, the resulting Siamese belongs in that "takes your breath away" category of all riveting great art. There are four lovely Siamese colors in the CFA—seal point, chocolate point, blue point, and lilac point.

Personality

An indication of successful, lengthy domestication of any animal can be found in a high level of communication with and affection for human beings. Given the innate independence of the feline species and its territorial nature, any cat that exhibits a marked ability to communicate and that wants to associate with people is testifying to a long period of domestication. No breed surpasses the Siamese in its ability to communicate and in its love for human beings. Whether by vocalizing or by body language, the Siamese is determined to communicate. The degree to which they are talkative depends a good deal on the amount of conversation that is directed their way. In addition, they tend to be vocal in direct proportion to the desired end, always demanding the last word.

Siamese do not tolerate isolation well, or being ignored. They want to be a part of their owners' lives, as they hold firmly to the belief that they are humankind's best friend. They are in your lap, on your newspaper, in your bed, and completely in your heart. They are not simply pleased to take these various positions; Siamese insist on it. Those who live with this breed will laughingly remark about the letters sent to friends and family "with teeth marks." This phenomenon might have something to do with attention being given to the letter being written instead of to the cat on your lap. The same reasoning explains why the Siamese is determined to sit *on* the newspaper (or in front of it, staring at your face), as opposed to quietly allowing it to be read.

There is no better companion cat than the "royal cat of Siam," a feline thoroughly acquainted with the term *togetherness.*

There is also the fact that Siamese are heat-seekers. They are elegant, sleek creatures with short, fine coats. It is no stretch of the truth to say that with regard to temperature, they have a narrow comfort range. To this breed, more is better. (Not only do they love you for your sterling qualities but they also love you because you are warm.) A Siamese can find the warmest spot in your house. Do not be surprised if that place in the summertime is a spot of sunshine on the rug, the pilot light of your water heater, or the refrigerator vent.

Our canine friends are well known for playing fetch, a game that most of them play outdoors. A Siamese loves to play the game just as much, and you, as his owner, do not need to wait for good weather. Not only that, the balled-up paper cup, the ideal missile to throw, will be returned to a lap, and not dropped at your feet.

Grooming Requirements

While rubber brushes, if used sparingly, are fine aids for removing excess hair, grooming by hand is by far the best way to maintain a Siamese coat. Wet hands are used to stroke the coat until they dry, gently removing dead hair in the process. A Siamese that lives in the house with his owner will seldom need a bath, as daily hand grooming will suffice. If a bath is called for, however, it should be given using a gentle no-tears baby shampoo, followed by a conditioner. The best time to bathe a Siamese prior to a show is 2 or 3 days beforehand, to allow the natural oils to return to the coat. Nothing really conditions the Siamese coat better than an excellent diet, although there is much to be said for a bit of cottage cheese added to that diet to produce an added gloss. The inside of the ears should be trimmed for show grooming, but this is best done sparingly and with special ear/nose blunted scissors. The ears should be free of excess hair but should not present a bald appearance reminiscent of shaving, nor should the trimming continue much beyond the ear.

Origins and History

It is interesting that the earliest publications in England consistently refer to the breed as both the royal cat of Siam and Siamese. This has to do with the claim of protection and breeding under royal supervision in Siam by those who chronicled the earliest imports into the West. Was the Siamese a true blueblood, a companion of kings? Possibly, and it certainly makes a wonderful story. That the breed was prized in its native land is thoroughly documented, however. The translation into English in 1998 of the historic *Thai Cat Poems*, or *Tamra Maew* (published in *The Legend of Siamese Cats*, by Martin R. Clutterbuck) clearly describes a white cat with black ears, face, paws, and tail known as Maew Kaew, or Wichien-maas. These poems are between 100 and 200 years old but reflect a literary culture much older. The book itself contains many illustrations from very old manuscripts.

Imported into England in the late nineteenth century and appearing in catalogs of the Crystal Palace Show as early as 1881, the Siamese was recognized in seal point. A description by Harrison Weir in *Our Cats and All About Them* (1889) of the ideal show specimen bears repeating:

The head should be long from ears to eyes, and not over broad, and then rather sharply taper off towards the muzzle, the forehead flat, and receding, the eyes somewhat aslant downwards towards the nose, and the eyes of a pearly, yet bright blue colour, the ears usual size and black with little or no hair on the inside, with black muzzle, and round the eyes black. The form should be slight, graceful and delicately made, body long, tail rather short and thin, and the legs somewhat short, slender, and the feet oval, not so round as the ordinary English cat. The body should be one bright, uniform, even colour, not clouded, either rich fawn, dun or ash. The legs, feet and tail black. The back slightly darker is allowable, if of a rich colour, and the colour softened, not clouded.

Clearly, this was an exotic creature in 1889—and it still is today.

Having conquered the hearts of the mighty British Empire at a time when few four-legged creatures could boast such a thing, the Siamese cat crossed the Atlantic in numbers large enough to suggest that that vast body of water was but a pond. Siamese are found in the Beresford Cat Club Stud Books in 1900, and the first Siamese to be awarded Best Cat in Show was in 1907. With characteristic charm, the breed vanquished North America as thoroughly and decisively as it had captured the hearts of merry old England. Classes became large; color classes expanded to four: seal point, blue point, chocolate point, and lilac point. The CFA recognized the blue point in 1934, the chocolate point in 1952, and the lilac point in 1955, 5 years before the English did so. In the year 2003, the four Siamese colors had been together on the CFA show bench for 48 years.

It was in the years directly preceding and following World War II that the popularity of the Siamese soared, along with the burgeoning of the American cat fancy. Siamese and Persians dominated the show scene, with classes of well over 100 Siamese being commonplace. Having fallen hopelessly in love with the Siamese color pattern, the consequence of a temperature-controlling enzyme that restricts color to the coolest parts of the body, the American public clamored for this glamorous pet. Overall quality suffered in the rush to supply this demand, resulting in a misconception of the breed that still lingers today.

The Siamese cat is so much more than a color pattern; one shared with the Himalayan rabbit, for instance. The exotic structure of the Siamese was overlooked in the fascination with its paint job. Anyone who remembers those frenetic times may also recall the many poor examples of the breed on the show bench, a state of affairs familiar to fanciers of other animal breeds, which is often referred to as being "loved to death."

Cats with heavy boning, round heads, and washed-out blue eyes began to appear in increasing numbers, a sure sign of mixed ancestry and indiscriminate breeding. It has been with a sigh of relief that those who treasure the Siamese nowadays have seen that Siamese to be found in cat shows now are much more representative of the breed and consistent in type, because breeders dedicated to preserving the finest attributes of this ancient cat exhibit them.

The Siamese having set an unequalled example of beauty and temperament for the world, it is hardly surprising that the Siamese gene pool has been used many times over the years to create other visions of beautiful cats. Its most obviously direct descendants are the Balinese, Colorpoint Shorthair, Javanese, Oriental, Himalayan Persian, and Tonkinese. Added to these breeds are the contributions of the Siamese in the development and maintenance of the Burmese, Havana Brown, and Ocicat. Not only is the Siamese a mainstay of the pedigreed cat world for its own distinct, intrinsic beauty but it is also an unsurpassed genetic wellspring to which many breeds owe their existence and, in some cases, continued well-being.

Miscellanea

A Siamese show cat expects to be stretched aloft. Owners do it; the judges do it. This handling method accentuates the cat's length, demonstrates its elegance, and gives the Siamese a chance to stretch its neck to add to the effect. The cat also can be encouraged to pose unaided and stretch that neck, although this will be a test of individual personality and patience.

It is well known that cats of all breeds from areas throughout Asia have traditionally exhibited crossed eyes and kinked tails. Nonetheless, most fanciers of the Siamese always considered both these conditions grievous faults. In *Cats and All About Them*, published in 1902, Frances Simpson categorically states that on the question of kinked tails, "His Majesty the King of Siam is quoted as saying they ought not to be." Crossed eyes, sometimes called a squint, have likewise been forbidden on the show bench. Breeders have selected against these faults for many generations and rarely produce kittens with either defect. That both crossed eyes and kinked tails still occasionally occur is due to their recessive genetic nature.

The refrain from the movie *Lady and the Tramp* that goes "We are Siamese, if you please. We are Siamese if you don't please!" captures the essence of the Siamese cat. This is truly a singing, talking, bent-on-communicating feline. The slanty eyes and slinky bodies painted with points portrayed in caricatures and in pop art do not do justice to the gorgeous Siamese. Loved for many, many years for its endearing ways and heart-stopping beauty, the Siamese is, quite simply, a Siamese.

Abyssinian   *(Chanan)*

American Bobtail Longhair   *(Paradox)*

American Bobtail Shorthair   *(Chanan)*

American Curl Longhair   *(Chanan)*

American Curl Shorthair *(Brown)*

American Shorthair *(Chanan)*

American Wirehair *(Jackson)*

Balinese *(Chanan)*

Colorpoint Shorthair *(McCullough)*

Egyptian Mau *(Widmer)*

Devon Rex *(Chanan)*

Cornish Rex *(Childs)*

European Burmese *(Chanan)*

Exotic *(Chanan)*

Havana Brown *(Widmer)*

Japanese Bobtail Longhair *(McCullough)*

Japanese Bobtail Shorthair *(Jackson)*

Korat *(Chanan)*

Javanese *(Widmer)*

LaPerm Longhair *(TNT)*

LaPerm Shorthair *(Brown)*

Maine Coon Cat *(Chanan)*

Manx Longhair *(Chanan)*

Manx Shorthair *(Chanan)*

Norwegian Forest Cat *(McCullough)*

Ocicat *(Chanan)*

Oriental Longhair *(Widmer)*

Oriental Shorthair *(Johnson)*

Persian (bicolor and calico) *(Chanan)*

Persian (Himalayan) *(Chanan)*

Burmese (sable) *(Chanan)*

Burmese (dilute) *(Dandi)*

Chartreux *(Widmer)*

Birman *(Chanan)*

British Shorthair *(Widmer)*

Bombay *(Widmer)*

Persian (parti-color)   *(Widmer)*

Persian (shaded and smoke)   *(Jackson)*

Persian (silver and golden)   *(Chanan)*

Persian (solid)   *(Howard)*

Persian (tabby) *(Widmer)*

RagaMuffin

Ragdoll *(Chanan)*

Russian Blue *(Widmer)*

Scottish Fold Longhair *(Chanan)*

Scottish Fold Shorthair *(Chanan)*

Selkirk Rex Shorthair *(Brown)*

Selkirk Rex Longhair

Siamese *(Chanan)*

Singapura *(Johnson)*

Siberian *(Johnson)*

Somali *(Chanan)*

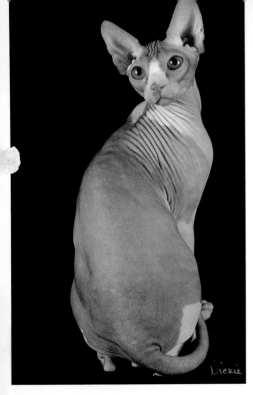

Sphynx *(Jackson)*

Tonkinese *(Chanan)*

Turkish Angora *(Chanan)*

Turkish Van *(Johnson)*

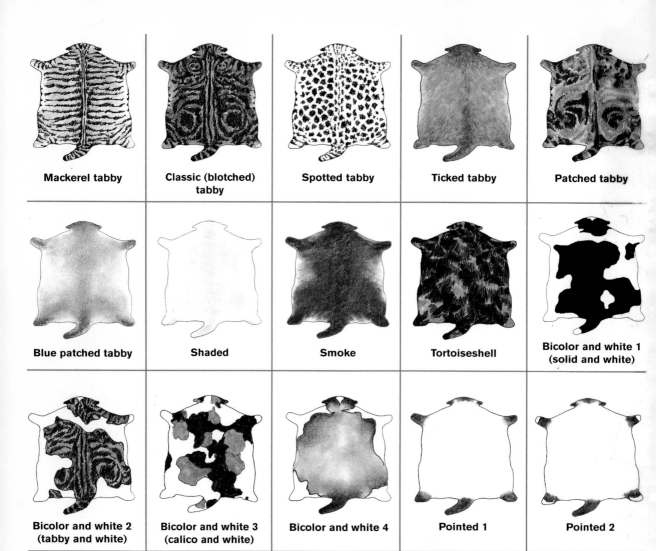

Mackerel tabby

Classic (blotched) tabby

Spotted tabby

Ticked tabby

Patched tabby

Blue patched tabby

Shaded

Smoke

Tortoiseshell

Bicolor and white 1 (solid and white)

Bicolor and white 2 (tabby and white)

Bicolor and white 3 (calico and white)

Bicolor and white 4

Pointed 1

Pointed 2

Solid

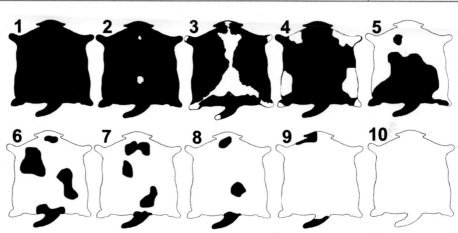

1 2 3 4 5

6 7 8 9 10

10 bicolors

POINT SCORE

HEAD (20)

Long, flat profile	6
Wedge, fine muzzle, size	5
Ears	4
Chin	3
Width between eyes	2

EYES (10)

Shape, size, slant, and placement	10

BODY (30)

Structure and size, including neck	12
Muscle tone	10
Legs and feet	5
Tail	3

COAT | 10

COLOR (30)

Body color	10
Point color (matching points of dense color, proper foot pads, and nose leather)	10
Eye color	10

GENERAL: The ideal Siamese is a medium-size, svelte, refined cat with long, tapering lines, very lithe but muscular. Males may be proportionately larger.

HEAD: Long, tapering wedge. Medium in size, in good proportion to body. The total wedge starts at the nose and flares out in straight lines to the tips of the ears, forming a triangle, with no break at the whiskers. No less than the width of an eye between the eyes. When the whiskers are smoothed back, the underlying bone structure is apparent. Allowance must be made for jowls in the stud cat.

SKULL: Flat. In profile, a long, straight line is seen from the top of the head to the tip of the nose. No bulge over eyes. No dip in nose.

EARS: Strikingly large, pointed, wide at base; continuing the lines of the wedge.

EYES: Almond-shaped. Medium size. Neither protruding nor recessed. Slanted toward the nose in harmony with lines of wedge and ears. Uncrossed.

NOSE: Long and straight. A continuation of the forehead with no break.

MUZZLE: Fine, wedge-shaped.

CHIN AND JAW: Medium size. Tip of chin lines up with tip of nose in the same vertical plane. Neither receding nor excessively massive.

BODY: Medium size. Graceful, long, and svelte. A distinctive combination of fine bones and firm muscles. Shoulders and hips continue same sleek lines of tubular body. Hips never wider than shoulders. Abdomen tight.

NECK: Long and slender.

LEGS: Long and slim. Hind legs higher than front. In good proportion to body.

PAWS: Dainty, small, and oval. Toes: five in front and four behind.

TAIL: Long, thin, tapering to a fine point.

COAT: Short, fine textured, glossy. Lying close to body.

CONDITION: Excellent physical condition. Eyes clear. Muscular, strong, and lithe. Neither flabby nor bony. Not fat.

COLOR: *Body:* Even, with subtle shading when allowed. Allowance should be made for darker color in older cats, as Siamese generally darken with age, but there must be definite contrast between body color and points. *Points:* Mask, ears, legs, feet, tail dense and clearly defined. All of the same shade. Mask covers entire face, including whisker pads, and is connected to ears by tracings. Mask should not extend over the top of the head. No ticking or white hairs in points. **PENALIZE:** Improper (i.e., off-color or spotted) nose leather or paw pads. Soft or mushy body. Visible protrusion of the cartilage at the end of the sternum under normal handling. **DISQUALIFY:** Any evidence of illness or poor health. Weak hind legs. Mouth breathing due to nasal obstruction or poor occlusion. Emaciation. Visible tail kink. Eyes other than blue. White toes and/or feet. Incorrect number of toes. Malocclusion resulting in either undershot or overshot chin. Long hair.

COLORS: Seal point, chocolate point, blue point, lilac point.

ALLOWABLE BREEDING OUTCROSSES: none.

SIBERIAN

By members of the Siberian Cat Club, Cat Fanciers' Association Siberian Breed Committee, and TAIGA (International Siberian Breed Club)

Siberian

Living with a cat can be very pleasurable, but living with a Siberian cat is a very rewarding, life-changing experience. Siberians can be your best friend, confidant, problem-solver, and house clown. They are among the most ancient breeds and began as the Russian forest cat. We have images of them roaming the Siberian *taiga* (forestland) even today, and they can be seen in large numbers in the wild Siberian outlying territories. However, another story unfolds in Russia. Siberian cats are now prized house cats, and many Russian families tell fond tales of their Siberian cats and their amazing personalities and great loyalty. In 1990, when the USSR collapsed and free trade opened up, the importation of Siberian cats to the United States began.

Physical Description

The Siberian is a medium-large cat with the overall appearance of excellent physical condition, massive strength, power, and alertness, modified by a sweet facial expression. The general impression of the body is one of circles and roundness rather than rectangles and triangles indicative of the other forest cat breeds. Females are considerably smaller than males. Eye color varies from gold to green and all shades in between. They also come in colorpoints; these cats have blue eyes. Siberians have a very dense, water-resistant triple coat, which is medium to long in length. They have a full, dense coat in the winter, while the summer coat is somewhat shorter and less dense. The hair is shorter on the shoulders. There is a ruff at the neck, full fluffy britches, and a bushy tail that is carried up with pride. Owners of Siberians often e-mail pictures to each other bragging about "the fluff on that tail!" Ear tipping is desired, and full ear furnishings are required. This means that the tops of the ears can have hair, which makes the ears look pointed when in fact they are rounded, and that the inside of the ear has hair that protects it from the elements.

Siberians are a natural breed, and they come in all colors, including colorpoints: brown, red, blue, silver, white, black, and any combinations of these colors. They come in solid, spotted, ticked, mackerel, and classic patterns. A mackerel-patterned cat has stripes going up and down on its sides; a classic-patterned cat has circles on its sides. The most common color is a brown mackerel tabby with or without white. Colorpoint Siberians have markings similar to those of other pointed cats.

Personality

Siberian cats are very personable and want to be near their owners. They will meet you at the door when you come home and explain their day to you. They are quiet cats and express themselves melodically with sweet mews, trills, chirps, and lots of purring. They love to sit in your lap and be groomed. A favorite pastime of theirs is to find something and bring it back so it can be thrown and fetched. All types of toys intrigue them, and they will play with just about anything. They are fascinated with the moving cursor on the computer screen. You will need to shut the door of your computer room if you want to get any typing done. Some Siberians learn to stay off the keyboard at an early age, but others will insist on adding indecipherable letters to your most crucial correspondence. Others will sit in the cubbyholes of your computer desk and watch,

entranced, as you type, periodically extending a paw of support.

If you share your home with Siberians, you will never be alone. They will watch TV with you, go to the bathroom with you, and then go to bed with you. If you are trying to do something, they will insist on helping. Reading a newspaper, book, or magazine is next to impossible. If they like something, they will take it and play with it, and in the process it will be lost.

Siberians also enjoy the company of dogs, other animals, and children. They are fearless and easygoing. Not much disturbs their natural calm and equanimity. Many parents affirm that their Siberian will always sleep with the children, lying at the foot of their bed as a sentinel. Some Siberians become the nurse in the family, spending time with the sick person who needs the support. Most often, they have a high level of intuition and know when they are needed for psychological and moral support. Almost always they get out of your way when you are tense and too busy to deal with them. However, there are those who are underfoot no matter what. Through all the hard times in life, Siberians give support—even if those hard times are only headaches.

The acrobatic nature of the Siberian is well known among owners. They will play hard, often executing amazing somersaults in pursuit of a feather toy. Some balance on clothing racks and seem to be executing an uneven parallel bar routine rivaled only by Olympic athletes. Others balance carefully on lamp shades as they watch their owners read. Many an overenthusiastic kitten has had to be rescued while attempting to climb the bricks on the fireplace or to jump to the top of a bookshelf that it cannot reach. Nevertheless, Siberians are always happy to be helped. They stay playful throughout their lives and are rarely mistaken for a couch potato.

Grooming Requirements

Siberians tend to be self-grooming, meaning that they remain relatively tangle free, though males can and do get knotty in the springtime if not combed daily. Pet Siberians do not require extensive grooming. For the most part, they do not shed much; instead, they molt twice a year. When a Siberian molts, the hair will start to mat and then shed in large clumps. There are always exceptions—some shed constantly and profusely. The molting period is about 10 days. Daily brushing is required to expedite the molting process and to prevent matting. This process is nothing to be alarmed about; it is normal in some Siberians. Otherwise, occasional grooming is acceptable, unless your cat insists on more.

Show grooming is more extensive. You need to bathe your cat to remove any buildup of dirt and oil in the fur. Be sure to rinse your Siberian completely to remove all traces of soap. Then you must completely dry the fur. At the show, you fluff the coat before taking the cat into a show ring. Most Siberians tolerate their baths, especially if they were introduced to bathing as kittens. Some Siberians even like playing in the water and will try to take showers or baths with you.

Origins and History

Siberians are Russia's native cats, coming from the unforgiving climate of the Siberian forest. They first appeared in recorded history around the year 1000. Russian farmers and tradespeople were their primary caretakers. Siberians were needed to protect grain and other products from rodents, as Russia was then an agricultural country. Shopkeepers in Moscow were known to compete with one another over whose cat was the biggest and thickest. Russians like cats, and most children from the agricultural era grew up with a kitten, the favorite being the Siberian. Siberians even played roles in Russian fairy tales as protectors of children and as magical beings who opened gateways to realms beyond our ordinary senses.

The Siberian cat was one of the three longhairs represented at the first cat shows in England in the 1700s. The first cat show in the city of Leningrad, Russia, was in 1987. Two cat clubs, Kotofei and Kis, organized it. Breeding of Siberians began in Saint Petersburg (Leningrad) at about that time. The Soviet Felinological Association registered the Siberian breed. It included both the traditional colors and the Siberian colorpoint (often referred to as Neva Masquerade in Europe).

An entry about Siberian cats appears in a book originally published in 1900 by Helen M. Winslow, entitled *Concerning Cats*. The entry reads: "Mrs. Frederick Monroe of Riverside Ill. owns a remarkable specimen of a genuine Russian cat, a perfect blue of extraordinary size. The Russian long-haired pet is much less common even than the Persian and Angora."

The first breeding Siberians in the United States were introduced in 1990. Elizabeth Terrell imported the initial kittens as a trade for her Persian-Himalayans. They arrived on June 28, 1990. Their names were Kaliostro Vasenjkovich of Starpoint, Ofelia Romanova of Starpoint, and Naina Romanova of Starpoint.

The Siberian was accepted for registration in the CFA in February 2000 and currently competes in the Miscellaneous Category at CFA shows.

Miscellanea

The Siberian cat is also known to be suitable for some allergy sufferers. Although it has not been proven medically or scientifically, many people adamantly believe that the Siberian is hypoallergenic. They believe this because they are living proof. After living for decades with cat allergies, some adults cry because these loving cats have climbed all over them and they had no allergic reactions.

Siberians seem to have lower-than-usual levels of enzymes in their saliva, and many allergy sufferers have a sensitivity to enzymes. When a cat licks its fur, the saliva dries and falls off as dander, and this is often what causes people to be allergic to cats. This is a cat-by-cat, person-by-person concept. If you are allergic to cats and want to test your allergic response to Siberians, find someone near you with a Siberian or two. Spend a few hours with the cats and find out how you react. Approximately 75% of the people who test themselves with a Siberian this way have little or no reaction. There are no guarantees, but there is hope for allergy sufferers.

Siberians take up to 5 years to fully mature. Males continue to develop muscle and begin to look heftier as they age past 5 years. Some owners have noticed their cats gaining muscle as they approach 10 years of age. Moreover, reports of altered males weighing 25 pounds have been verified. How would you like that teddy bear on your bed? These cats are very healthy, with few if any medical issues and no documented genetic problems.

If you are considering a cat as a lifelong companion, the Siberian, with its loving personality, will give you years of happiness. Some choose Siberians for their doglike loyalty. Others purchase them for their hypoallergenic qualities. Choosing the remarkable Siberian cat as a pet marks the beginning of a loving, adventurous, and sometimes hilarious companionship.

CFA SHOW STANDARD FOR THE SIBERIAN CAT (MISCELLANEOUS STATUS)

POINT SCORE

HEAD (25)

Shape	5
Size	5
Profile	5
Ears	5
Eyes	5

BODY (30)

Shape	5
Size	10
Boning	10
Musculature	5

LEGS AND FEET	5

TAIL	5

COLOR/PATTERN	15
CONDITION/BALANCE	10
COAT	10

GENERAL: The Siberian is a medium to medium-large strong cat that hails from the very unforgiving climate of Siberia. They first appeared in recorded history around the year 1000. According to folklore, these magnificent animals made their homes in Russian monasteries, where they would walk along the high beams as lookouts for intruders. Their agility, speed, and strength made them worthy opponents in the monasteries' shadowy interiors. But the monks who cared for these animals regarded them as loyal and loving companions. One fact is undeniable: The Siberian is Russia's native cat. The overall appearance should be one of strength and force, with an excellent physical condition and alertness and a sweet facial expression. The breed is extremely slow to mature, taking as long as 5 years, and allowances should be made for younger cats. The general impression is one of roundness and circles, rather than rectangles and triangles.

HEAD: The head is a modified wedge of medium size with rounded contours, broader at the skull and narrowing slightly to a full and slightly rounded muzzle with a well-rounded chin. Female muzzles may be more delicate than that of males. The cheekbones are neither high-set nor prominent. There should be a good distance between the ears and eyes. The top of the head is flat, with a slight nose curvature of a gentle slope from the forehead to the nose and a slight concave curvature before the tip. The neck is medium, rounded, substantial, and well muscled. The whiskers are strong and long.

EARS: The ears are medium wide at the base and set as much on the sides of the head as on the top; ideal position is 1 to 1½ ear widths apart. The tips are rounded, and the ear tilts forward. Lynx tipping is desirable. Hair over the back of the ears is short and thin; from the middle of the ear, the furnishings become longer and cover the base completely. The inner ear has an abundance of ear tufts. In juveniles and young kittens only, the ears may appear to be medium-large and closer together, usually no more than one ear width apart.

EYES: Large, round, wide-set. If not held fully open, the eye will appear to have the outer corner slightly angled toward the lower base of the ear. In the traditional colors, there is no relationship between eye color and coat color/pattern. Acceptable eye color may cover the entire green, gold, hazel or copper spectrum. Blue or odd eyes allowed in white cats. The typical adult color is green to green-gold. In the color-point class, the eyes are blue.

BODY: Substantial. The back is medium in length and very slightly curved or arched but appears to be horizontal when in motion. A convex muscular torso and a round, compact belly appear with age.

LEGS AND FEET: Fur on front legs is thick and short to medium in length. Fur on hind legs is medium to long, thick, and featherlike. Legs are thick, dense, and medium in length. The feet are big and round, and toe tufts are desirable.

TAIL: The tail is medium, somewhat shorter than the length of the body, wide at the base, blunt at the tip without thickening or kinks, evenly and thickly furnished.

COAT: Plush, of medium length, with hair on the shoulder blades and lower part of the chest being thick and slightly shorter. There should be a ruff setting off the head, though allowances should be made for juvenile cats. There is a tight undercoat, thicker in cold weather. Allow for warm-climate coats. The hair may thicken to curls on the belly and britches, but a wavy coat is not characteristic. The skin may have a bluish cast. Clear, strong colors and patterns are desirable but are secondary to type. Coat texture may vary with the color.

PENALIZE: Adult cats not having substantial weight. Straight profile, narrow or foxlike muzzle, almond-shaped eyes, very long legs, thin legs, small ears, large ears.

WITHHOLD: Kinked tails, incorrect number of toes, crossed eyes.

COLORS: All colors and patterns.

ALLOWABLE BREEDING OUTCROSSES: none.

SINGAPURA
By Cathie McHenry

Singapura

Enchanting, beguiling, and *endearing* are often the first words people use to describe a Singapura. Initially, it is their deceptively delicate appearance coupled with the angelic face that makes these cats so special. However, the true secret to these little charmers is their captivating personality. Because of their rarity, there can be a wait to obtain a Singapura. Nevertheless, to those lucky enough to live with or work with the breed, there is simply nothing like them.

Physical Description

The Singapura is a small to medium cat. Adult males weigh approximately 6–7 pounds. Adult females weigh between 4 and 5 pounds. Singapuras have a finely ticked (agouti) coat pattern. *Ticking* refers to the presence of bands of different color on each individual hair shaft. In nature, ticking often provides camouflage, allowing the animal to blend into the background. The coat is short, silky, and close-lying. There is some barring on the inner front legs and knees on the hind legs. When viewed from the side, the body and legs should form a square rather than the elongation typical of oriental breeds. The head should be rounded and medium length, with good width at the eye level. The muzzle of the Singapura is of medium length and square. Remnants of the tabby M are visible on the forehead, along with "cheetah" lines extending down from the inner corner of the eyes. Eyes and ears should be noticeably large. Eye color can be hazel, green, or yellow. Singapuras all have the same coloration; only one color is allowed—dark brown ticking on an old ivory ground color. Their undersides are the color of unbleached muslin. This coloration gives the impression of delicacy, but do not be fooled—the Singapura is a muscular, although small, cat.

Personality

These are highly intelligent, active, and curious cats with the bonus of being just as affectionate as they are active. You could even say they are addictive. If you are looking for the stereo-typical aloof couch potato type of cat, the Singapura is definitely not for you. Singapuras are extremely interactive. Whatever you are doing, they want to be there. Singapuras seem to gen-uinely need their people—constantly.

Their attitude is "The world is my oyster. I'm going for the pearl, and you can't stop me. get out of my way . . . please?" They have a low-key way of getting exactly what they want, somewhat like a small child who looks at you with huge imploring eyes that say, "Please, please, please . . ." Before you know it, you have given in.

These beguiling creatures with large eyes and ears do not miss much going on around them. They are lively, curious, and intelligent—some would say too intelligent. Singapuras know they can do anything and everything bet-ter than you. Cooking is a particular favorite ac-tivity. Pens and computer keyboards make great toys, especially when you are trying to write. This playful nature remains well into and fre-quently throughout adulthood, but many do outgrow it. While they are extremely playful, they are also very sensitive to the moods of their family. If you are feeling under the weather, your Singapura may be in the bed under the covers with you (its usual place), but it will probably wait at the foot of the bed to be asked.

Singapuras are not confrontational cats; they rarely squabble among themselves. Some have never met a stranger. Others are more cau-tious and prefer to observe from the sidelines until they size up the visitor. In either case, once they approach the stranger, they will be solicit-ing attention. They do not care for loud noises, so a Singapura may not be the best choice for a family with boisterous children. However, many families enjoy living with a Singapura; it just de-pends on the makeup of the family. Chasing a Singapura is frustrating and a complete waste of time: The cat is too fast to catch and is alarmed by being chased. If you want a Singapura to come to you, it is far better to walk after it call-ing its name. Then it will stop and come to you. The Singapura knows it is in charge at all times.

Singapuras are generally confident in their own environment. They are quick to sense when things are different and, largely be-cause they are intelligent, they may become wary. In a show hall environment, they prefer to keep all four feet on the judging table. Making direct eye contact with a cat in a strange environment is likely to be interpreted by the cat as aggressiveness. If the cat is relaxed and playful, it is because the cat has come to enjoy the show experience over time.

Grooming Requirements

The Singapura is truly a wash-and-wear cat. Their short, close-lying coat makes everyday and show grooming essentially the same; the only variable being timing. Before an upcom-ing weekend show, the bath is normally most effective if performed on a Wednesday or Thursday. It is a simple rinse–lather–rinse pro-cedure; finish up with a flea comb to remove any excess hair. Hair dryers are not advised, as blow-drying has a tendency to fluff the coat, thereby losing the look of a short, tight coat with painted-on coloring.

Singapuras are tactically sensitive. They fre-quently do not like to have their nails trimmed. Therefore, it is particularly important to trim the nails regularly, starting in kittenhood, to de-sensitize these cats to the process. One breeder has reported a system that greatly reduces the stress for both the cat and the owner. She runs the water inside of a double kitchen sink, then places the cat in the other (dry) side. It seems that the cat believes that it is going to get a bath and is then good as gold, sitting very still in the sink for the nail trimming.

Origins and History

Although most of the world may think of the city-state of Singapore as the commercial giant at the tip of the Malay Peninsula, cat lovers have a different view. To them it is the reputed birthplace of the Singapura. In the early 1970s, Hal Meadow and his wife, Tommy, an American couple on their return to the United States after a stay in Singapore, introduced the cat they called the Singapura. The three original foundation cats were Puss'e, a young female, Ticle, a male kitten, and Tes, his female littermate. Then in 1980 a female Singapura, Chiko, was found in the Singapore SPCA and imported to the United States. The fascination with the Singapura had begun.

The first Singapura breeders worked diligently to promote the Singapura to the cat fancy. In 1981, the breed was accepted in CFA. Then in 1986, the CFA accepted the Singapura for Provisional show status. It looked as though the Singapura would make the big time. The cats did well in the show ring, they entranced the public, and the numbers were growing.

Having successfully advanced through the rigorous screening process, the Singapura was granted Championship status beginning May 1988. Shortly thereafter, the first Singapura earned the coveted title of Grand Champion. Despite their small numbers, Singapuras have gone on to earn many titles (Grand Champion, Grand Premier, Distinguished Merit, and national and regional winners).

Miscellanea

The Singapura remains a rare cat. Because it is considered a natural breed, only Singapura-to-Singapura matings are allowed. The average litter size is two to three kittens. Another factor that contributes to its small numbers is that it matures more slowly than other cats. Females may not have their first heat cycle until they are 1 year old; males mature around the same time. But the small numbers do not reflect the Singapura's acceptance with either breeders or the public; many breeders maintain a waiting list for kittens.

Are Singapuras trainable? Certainly. The only problem is that they seem to be better trainers of people than we are of them. It is not unusual for new Singapura exhibitors to become so enchanted with their first Singapuras that the cats end up terribly spoiled. As you can imagine, this has led to many adored cats with unfulfilled show potential.

Largely because they are so intelligent, they are not always easy cats to show. If they do not like the show ring, they can very quickly figure out how to avoid it. Therefore, the successful exhibitor must know the individual Singapura and how to make the show fun for that cat. Singapuras seem to be able to find just the right way to get out of being shown. Some do it by bluffing the judge, and making him or her think they are going to bite them (they have no intention of doing so). They will grumble and complain as you carry them to and from the ring, which is another form of bluffing. However, Singapuras are as sweet as they look.

Whether a veteran show cat or a pet, the intelligent and loving Singapura makes a wonderful and entertaining companion. These are endearing little charmers from Singapore.

POINT SCORE

HEAD (15)

Skull shape	4
Width at eye	4
Muzzle shape	4
Profile	3

EARS (10)

Size	4
Set	4
Openness	2

EYES (10)

Size	6
Shape	3
Color	1

BODY, LEGS AND TAIL (20)

Neck	3
Proportion	10
Legs and feet	5
Tail	2

COAT 15

COLOR AND MARKINGS (30)

Color	10
Ticking	9
Facial markings	6
Leg markings	5

GENERAL: The appearance of an alert, healthy, small to medium-size muscular-bodied cat with noticeably large eyes and ears. Cat to have the illusion of refined delicate coloring.

HEAD: Skull rounded front to back and side to side, with rounded width at the outer eye narrowing to a definite whisker break and a medium-short, broad muzzle with a blunt nose. In profile, a rounded skull with a slight curve well below eye level. Straight line nose to chin. Chin well developed.

EARS: Large, slightly pointed, wide open at the base, and possessing a deep cup. Medium set. Outer lines of the ear to extend upward at an angle slightly wide of parallel. Small ears a serious fault.

EYES: Large, almond-shaped, held wide open but showing slant. Neither protruding nor recessed. Eyes set not less than an eye width apart. Color hazel, green, or yellow, with no other color permitted. Brilliance preferred. Small eyes a serious fault.

BODY: Small to medium overall size. Moderately stocky and muscular body, legs, and floor to form a square. Midsection not tucked but firm.

NECK: Tends toward short and thick.

LEGS AND FEET: Legs heavy and muscled at the body, tapering to small, short, oval feet.

TAIL: Length to be short of the shoulder when laid along the torso. Tending toward slender but not whippy. Blunt tip.

COAT: Fine, very short, silky texture, lying very close to the body. Springy coat a fault.

PENALIZE: Coldness or grey tones in the coat, grey undercoat next to the skin, barring on outer front legs, necklaces, nonvisible tail faults, lack of nose liner.

DISQUALIFY: White spotting, barring on tail, top of the head unticked, unbroken necklaces or leg bracelets. Very small eyes or ears. Visible tail faults. Blue eyes. Any color other than sepia agouti (dark brown ticking on an old ivory undercoat).

COLOR: Sepia agouti only; color to be dark brown ticking on a warm old-ivory ground color. Each hair to have at least two bands of dark ticking separated by light bands. Light next to the skin and a dark tip. Dark tail tip with color extending back toward the body on upper side. Spine line *not* a fault. Muzzle, chin, chest, and underside to be the color of unbleached muslin. Cat to show some barring on inner front legs and back knee only. Allowance to be made for undeveloped ticking in kittens. Hair between toes to be dark brown. *Facial markings:* Dark lines extending from brows and outside corner of eyes, dark lines extending downward alongside nose bridge from inner corner of eyes (cheetah lines), and cheekbone shading are all desirable. Eyeliner, lips, whisker apertures, noseliner to be dark brown. *Nose leather:* Pale to dark salmon. *Paw pads:* Rosy brown. Salmon tones to the ears and nose bridge *not* a fault.

ALLOWABLE BREEDING OUTCROSSES: none.

SOMALI
By Nancy J. Bailey

Somali

With its flash of deep, hot color and signature flourish of a plumy tail, there is no mistaking a Somali. This vivacious creature has a mix of that notorious feline quality, curiosity, with burning athleticism and wicked sense of humor. With this combination of striking beauty and inventiveness, be prepared for a feline companion who demands to be noticed.

Physical Description
This medium-size, long-haired version of the Abyssinian is identical in many ways to that breed. The Somali is leggy and elegant, with a glowing presence and ticked fur. It is muscular, and though it is not an overly large cat, it is solid and surprisingly heavy. Its head is moderate in type, neither too long nor too short or round. It has a full muzzle, with dots on the whisker pads. Its eyes, which can be green or gold, are large, expressive, and almond-shaped. The large, flaring ears and etched facial markings complete the obvious similarities to the Abyssinian. The coat makes the difference. The Somali is adorned with a ruff around the throat, fluffy britches, and a big brush tail that is carried with pride, like a flag. The coat is considered medium length, with shorter hair on the shoulders and body.

The CFA recognizes the Somali in four colors, identical to the Abyssinian colors: ruddy, red, blue, and fawn. All colors are rich, bright, and warm. Ruddy is burnt sienna ticked with black, which lends a beautiful contrast between the top and undercoat. The undercoat of a red is similar to that of a ruddy but is ticked with brown. This leads to a glowing, almost brick red appearance overall. Fawn, which is a dilute of red, has a warm rosy beige undercoat with cocoa brown ticking. A good fawn looks almost pink or has a lovely salmon-colored hue. The most surprising color is blue, the dilute of ruddy. Because it is ticked with slate grey, normally a cold tone, one would expect the overall appearance to be less dramatic than the others. Not so. A good blue has a deep, warm beige undercoat that glows with a richness equivalent to that of the other colors.

The first impression many people express when seeing a Somali is that it looks like a fox. This comment usually alludes to the burning color, large ears, and full tail, but the image is further promoted when the Somali moves. Light and quick, on tiptoe, the Somali is athletic and swift as a fox, and every bit as intelligent.

Personality

The beauty of this cat is second only to its personality. Blessed with a lively sense of humor and brimming with quirky traits, Somalis are active, curious, and bold. They can manipulate latches and knobs, opening cupboards and doors. They adapt quickly to many situations. They play vigorously by themselves but are happiest when they have companionship. They will warm up quickly to other cats, and most will learn to like dogs too. They love interactive games such as fetch, chase, and hide-and-seek. Provided with plenty of toys and activity, they are perfectly happy to live indoors and even do well in apartments.

While all this activity may give the impression that Somalis are difficult to live with, they have a meltingly sweet side to their well-balanced temperament. They are not extremely vocal, and when they do talk, their voices are usually soft. They are a wonderful combination of cuddly and quick. Most Somalis are inordinately affectionate. They are masters of head-butts and feline hugs and are emphatic lap cats. They follow their people from room to room, settling in to purr and knead their paws in quiet hours, and then exploding with energy during busy times. This tendency to match moods with their people, along with their affinity for water (a dripping faucet is a Somali magnet) and love for retrieving toys, has caused them to be compared to dogs on many occasions.

Another doglike quality in Somalis is their appetite. They seem to be practically omnivorous. Many of them love to eat fresh fruits, vegetables, and breads, as well as things not quite so digestible such as broom straws, plants, and rubber bands. Cat-proofing is always a good idea when one lives with a Somali. They are eternally inquisitive, often carry small objects around, and quite often will experimentally ingest things.

Grooming Requirements

Although Somalis have the appearance of full-coated cats, grooming them does not usually require much effort. Most of them have coats that are relatively tangle free. For pets, an occasional brushing will do nicely. Most breeders will bathe a Somali before a show, rinsing extensively to remove any residual soap. The cat is then blown dry, with special attention to blowing the ruff, britches, and tail hair backward, to accentuate the fullness in these areas. If bathed regularly as kittens, most Somalis are not a problem to groom, and many enjoy the attention. Some Somalis have a tendency to accumulate oil around the base of their tail and along their spine. This can cause the hair to stand up in clumps. Many people use a bit of oil-cutting dish soap in the cat's bath. Other breeders use nontoxic hand cleaners touted by mechanics. After using any of these items, it is important to rinse the cat thoroughly. If the cat has an oily coat, it is likely that it will have feline acne, which usually manifests itself on the chin. It is black and highly visible and often seems irritating to the cat. The most effective way to control this is to simply pack cornstarch on the chin each day. Overall, the Somali is a very low maintenance creature, grooming-wise. A good diet, plenty of exercise, and a stress-free life are the keys to good health, and the cat's appearance will reflect that. A well-cared-for Somali is easy to keep looking beautiful.

A quick brush-over to fluff the ruff, tail, and britches is usually all that is needed to prepare the Somali for the show ring.

Origins and History

The Somali was granted registration status in 1976 and has gained popularity since 1979, the first year that the CFA recognized the breed and admitted it to championship competition. This recognition, granted to red and ruddy cats only, opened the doors for early breeders eager to show off the beautiful cats they were producing. Somalis had been around for a long time by then, as the long coats were carried in certain Abyssinian lines.

To this day, many people ask what breeds were combined to create the Somali. However, a Somali is genetically identical to the Abyssinian, only with long hair. The longhair gene is recessive, so both parents must carry the trait. When two Abyssinians carrying long hair are bred, they statistically have a 25% chance of producing a Somali.

Originally, Abyssinian breeders had been startled to find these dark, fuzzy kittens appearing in their litters. Most long-haired kittens in those days were sold for pets. Finally, in the late 1960s, a collective effort began to recognize them. Breeders began working with Abyssinians known to occasionally produce long-haired

kittens. The slow process of pursuing the elusive longhair gene began. The breed was dubbed Somali, after Somalia, for that country's proximity to ancient Abyssinia (now Ethiopia).

In 1979, the breed's first year at CFA shows, a ruddy male Somali achieved his Grand Championship, and went on to attain a National Win in the same season. The breed was off and running. It was 7 years before the blue Somali graced the CFA show circuit. Then in 1986, the blue was recognized, and finally in 1990 the fawn joined the other three colors in the CFA breed standard.

Miscellanea

Its irrepressible nature makes the Somali a natural in the show ring. The CFA show standard actually calls for a good temperament, saying that a Somali should be "showing an alert, lively interest in all surroundings, with an even disposition and easy to handle."

Carrying the cat stretched instead of balled up will display the Somali's beautiful length of body and leg. The best thing a judge can do, in order to show a Somali off to its greatest advantage, is to get out a feather or similar toy. This will bring out the natural spark in most Somalis, and they will stand on their tiptoes, with tail up and back arched, or spin or grab for the toy. Somalis seem to know their job, and most that are experienced hams will not jump off the judging table.

Though it is a "minority" breed, there is plenty of genetic diversity available, because the Abyssinian lines are available for outcrossing. Most Somalis, if cared for properly, will live well into their teens. They remain active and kittenish throughout their lives. Despite the tendency to taste-test everything, they enjoy good overall health. The Somali is a natural breed, moderate in type, so it does not tend toward structural abnormalities.

Today the Somali continues to glean recognition at shows, from judges and spectators alike. The breed has earned its rightful place in the world of pedigreed cats.

★ ★ ★

This is in part because of the efforts of those who recognized the beauty in this long-haired Aby and strove to ensure that it was acknowledged. It is especially because of the charisma of the cats themselves. After all, who can ignore a Somali?

CFA SHOW STANDARD FOR THE SOMALI

POINT SCORE

HEAD (25)

Skull	6
Muzzle	6
Ears	7
Eye shape	6

BODY (25)

Torso	10
Legs and feet	10
Tail	5

COAT (20)

Texture	10
Length	10

COLOR (30)

Color	10
Markings	5
Ticking	10
Eye color	5

GENERAL: The overall impression of the Somali is that of a well-proportioned medium to large cat, with firm muscular development, lithe and showing an alert, lively interest in all surroundings, with an even disposition and easy to handle. The cat is to give the appearance of activity, sound health, and general vigor.

HEAD: A modified, slightly rounded wedge without flat planes; the brow, cheek, and profile lines all show a gentle contour. A slight rise from the bridge of the nose to the forehead, which should be of good size with width between the ears flowing into the arched neck without a break.

MUZZLE: Shall follow gentle contours in conformity with the skull, as viewed from the front profile. Chin shall be full, neither undershot nor overshot, having a rounded appearance. The muzzle shall not be sharply pointed, and there shall be no evidence of snippiness, foxiness, or whisker pinch. Allowance to be made for jowls in adult males.

EARS: Large, alert, moderately pointed, broad, and cupped at the base. Ear set on a line toward the rear of the skull. The inner ear shall have horizontal tufts that reach nearly to the other side of the ear; tufts desirable.

EYES: Almond-shaped, large, brilliant, and expressive. Skull aperture neither round nor oriental. Eyes accented by dark lid skin encircled by light-colored area. Above each, a short, dark, vertical pencil stroke with a dark pencil line continuing from the upper lid toward the ear.

BODY: Torso medium long, lithe, and graceful, showing well-developed muscular strength. Rib cage is rounded; back is slightly arched, giving the appearance of a cat about to spring; flank level, with no tuck-up. Conformation strikes a medium between the extremes of cobby and svelte, lengthy types.

LEGS AND FEET: Legs in proportion to torso; feet oval and compact. When standing, the Somali gives the impression of being nimble and quick. Toes: five in front and four in back.

TAIL: Having a full brush, thick at the base, and slightly tapering. Length in balance with torso.

COAT: Texture very soft to the touch, extremely fine, and double. The more dense the coat, the better. A medium-length coat, except over shoulders, where a slightly shorter length is permitted. Preference is to be given to a cat with ruff and britches, giving a full-coated appearance to the cat.

PENALIZE: Color faults—cold grey or sandy tone to coat color; mottling or speckling on unticked areas. Pattern faults—necklaces, leg bars, tabby stripes, or bars on body; lack of desired markings on head and tail. Black roots on body.

DISQUALIFY: White locket or groin spot or white anywhere on body other than on the upper throat, chin, and nostril area. Any skeletal abnormality. Wrong color paw pads or nose leather. Any other colors than the four accepted colors. Unbroken necklace. Incorrect number of toes. Kinks in tail.

COAT COLOR: Warm and glowing. *Ticking:* Distinct and even, with dark-colored bands contrasting with lighter-colored bands on the hair shafts. Undercoat color clear and bright to the skin. Deeper color shades desired; *however*, intensity of ticking not to be sacrificed for depth of color. Preference given to cats *unmarked* on the undersides, chest, and legs; tail without rings. *Markings:* Darker shading along spine continuing through tip of tail; darker shading up the hocks, shading allowed at the point of the elbow; dark lines extending from eyes and brows, cheekbone shading, dots, and shading on whisker pads are desirable enhancements. Eyes accentuated by fine dark line, encircled by light-colored area. *Colors:* Ruddy, red, blue, fawn.

EYE COLOR: Gold or green, the more richness and depth of color the better.

ALLOWABLE BREEDING OUTCROSSES: Abyssinian.

SPHYNX

By Lynne Thomas

Sphynx

One of the questions most asked about these seemingly hairless cats is, "Don't they get cold?" They do. If it is too cold for you, it will be too cold for a hairless cat. However, they are smart enough to find a warm human, dog, or cat to curl up with or to get under your bed covers. In the winter, many Sphynx breeders put sweaters on their cats when they take them out in their carriers. They also make sure that the carriers are covered. A hot water bottle can come in handy when you have Sphynx cats in a colder environment. However, their hairlessness does not mean they are fragile. These are hearty cats with a strong immune system and no serious inherited breed-related problems, no skin problems, no breeding problems, and a low kitten mortality rate. For some, they are perfect cats.

The oldest cat on record was a Sphynx named Grandpa Rex's Allen. He was estimated to be 32 years old when he passed in 1998. Many Sphynx have lived 18 years or more. Yearly veterinary examinations and vaccines are normally all the medical expenses that a Sphynx pet owner will have for a very long time.

Physical Description

Even though the Sphynx gene is called hairless, these are not totally hairless cats. There is fine down on the body that feels like that on a peach. Some light hair is often present on the nose, tail, and toes. The feel of a Sphynx has been likened to that of a suede hot water bottle, a horse's warm muzzle, and a heated chamois. Sphynx kittens are very wrinkled, but as they get older and the body fills out, some of these wrinkles disappear. It is desirable for an adult Sphynx to have as much wrinkling as possible. They come in every color that a cat can be, and the color is seen in the pigment of the skin and in the few hairs that they have. It can be difficult for Sphynx breeders to determine the correct color of their kittens. Without hair, there are other clues, such as the color of the paw pads and nose leather.

These are substantial cats, medium-size but strong. An adult female will weigh between 6 and 8 pounds, and a male will weigh between 8 and 11. Sphynx have good muscle development and should have a bit of a belly, as if they just finished dinner. They have an open-eyed, intelligent face and a friendly expression. They have a bouncy gait and often use their toes as fingers. Sphynx cats are unique even when asleep: They contort themselves into what seems to be extremely uncomfortable positions, often with a leg up in the air, and they can sleep deeply and soundly like that for a long time.

Personality

The Sphynx personality is also unique. Kittens are precocious from the beginning of their lives. They often open their eyes when they are 2 or 3 days old and walk and climb out of the kittening box by the time they are 3 weeks old. A 3-week-old Sphynx kitten will usually start eating its mother's food and using the litter box. Their adult temperament remains as fun-loving as their kittenhood antics indicate. Sphynx delight in making direct eye contact with people and they flirt outrageously. They literally bend over backward to get human attention. Sphynx will always be ready to get into some mischief.

Sphynx will greet every stranger who comes to visit. In a flash, they will leap onto an unsuspecting person's shoulder, purr, and head-butt. They follow you everywhere and have to help you with all the household chores. This means that they will position themselves in the pile of crumbs and dust when you sweep the kitchen floor. They sit in the litter box when you want to scoop—but the real trick is to make the bed with three Sphynx on the sheets.

You can forget about having fresh cut flowers when you own a Sphynx. It is wise to put child safety locks on all your cupboard doors and to never, ever leave food out where a Sphynx can get it. These cats eat a lot, and they eat almost anything. Stealing people food is a game at which they excel.

Sphynx cats love to be looked at, and they enjoy the attention that they get at cat shows. They are fearless and perform silly antics for your entertainment, and they are sometimes downright clumsy—on purpose, it would seem. These cats prefer the company of people but are great with dogs and other cats. They rarely have a problem fitting in to any situation. Sphynx thrive on human attention and should never be left alone for long periods of time. They need at least one constant companion animal. A dog or cat makes a good friend for Sphynx, but they prefer the company of another Sphynx; two Sphynx interact and play together in their own special way. They love children of all ages, grandparents,

and the delivery person. They are always with you, on you, or showing off for you. Sphynx will be under the covers at night and stay tucked up against you until morning. These amazing cats are very loving.

Grooming Requirements

When grooming Sphynx, it is important to understand that even though they are almost hairless, they are not a no-maintenance breed. Because of the lack of hair that would normally absorb body oils, Sphynx cats need to be bathed periodically. Every cat is different, but generally, a pet Sphynx that is altered should need bathing every 2 weeks. This is not a difficult task with a cat that has been used to bathing from kittenhood, and it takes no time at all to dry a Sphynx. Their ears get dirtier than those of other cats and the fold of skin behind each claw collects oil secretions. These two areas need particular care and cleaning. An intact male gets dirty very quickly and needs bathing every few days. A well-groomed Sphynx at a cat show should be scrupulously clean and needs a bath each morning of the show. Often by the afternoon of a cat show, a Sphynx will need a wipe-down with a washcloth and no-rinse shampoo.

Sphynx can be good pets for people who are allergic to cats. While we know that there is no such thing as a nonallergenic cat, some people who suffer from cat allergies can tolerate Sphynx cats. However, each individual's allergic reactions are different, and there are those who cannot live with this or any other cat breed. If you are allergic to cats, it is best to contact a Sphynx breeder and make an appointment to handle a cat before you buy one, so that you can determine if you have an allergic reaction to it. Most Sphynx breeders have had a lot of experience selling to allergic people and would have a good idea of the type of allergy sufferer who could comfortably live with a Sphynx cat. It has been proven that frequent bathing for pet cats does reduce the amount of the allergens shed by any type of cat.

Origins and History

Where did the Sphynx come from? The answer is Canada. This is the only natural Canadian breed of cat. In 1966, in Toronto, a domestic cat gave birth to a hairless kitten. It was discovered to be the result of a natural or spontaneous mutation, and thus the Sphynx cat. This cat and several others found in other parts of the world have been the foundation for the breed. Cat breeders in Europe and North America have bred the Sphynx to normal-coated cats and then back to hairless for more than 30 years. The purpose of these breedings was to create a genetically sound cat with a large gene pool.

There are differing opinions as to the Sphynx's exact origins. Very little factual documentation is available from the first breeders. We know that the hairless cat was presented to the CFA at a meeting of the board of directors in the early 1970s. David Mare, who was on the board at the time, named the breed Sphynx and became a Sphynx breeder himself.

At the turn of the nineteenth century, there were two hairless cats in Mexico that were known to be the last of their line. No one knows what became of them, but they did not breed or contribute to the genetic makeup of the Sphynx of today. Two natural-mutation Sphynx from Toronto were sent to the Netherlands to Dr. Hugo Hernandes. Punkie and Paloma were sisters, and they were bred primarily to Devon Rex. Many of the Sphynx pedigrees of today go back to these two cats and were extremely influential in the development of the breed. In Europe and in North America, there were Sphynx breeders outcrossing their hairless Sphynx to other pedigreed cats. Most

of the time it was because they were already involved in the cat fancy with the breed they used for Sphynx outcrosses.

In 1975, a Sphynx named Epidermis was born on a farm in Minnesota, and a year later another Sphynx named Dermis was born from the same mother. These two cats were incorporated into the Sphynx gene pool and bred to American Shorthairs and then to Devon Rex. There have been a few other natural-mutation Sphynx to turn up over the years. They were test-mated and then became a part of the gene pool once they had been proven to have the same gene.

The Sphynx is one of the CFA's newer and most unusual breeds. On February 6, 1998, at the CFA board meeting in Houston, the Sphynx breed was accepted for registration. The Sphynx was so popular that the breed advanced to Provisional and then immediately to Championship status at the same CFA board meeting in February 2002.

Miscellanea

Because the Sphynx is a mutation that occurred naturally by the whim of Mother Nature, this is a breed that had its start from the gene pool of ordinary domestic cats. The Sphynx gene for hairlessness is a simple recessive. When a normal-coated cat is bred to a Sphynx, all the kittens will have a normal coat. This first generation of hybrids is called the F-1 generation. When an F-1 hybrid is bred back to a Sphynx, 50% of the resulting kittens will be hairless F-2, or second generation. In the F-2 litter, the kitten that has a normal coat is called a hybrid and the kitten that expresses the gene for hairlessness is called a Sphynx. When a Sphynx is bred to a Sphynx all the kittens will be hairless.

Since the mid-1960s when the Sphynx was in its infancy as a breed, these hairless cats were selectively mated to many different normal-coated cats of both the pedigreed and the nonpedigreed variety. That is how they survived and became the hearty breed they are today. All the outcrossing that has been done is the reason that Sphynx cats can be produced in any possible color or pattern. All eye colors are accepted as well.

The cat fancy today recognizes that the Sphynx gene pool is still extremely limited, which is why there are allowable outcrosses. The CFA allows Sphynx breeders to outcross their cats to American Shorthairs or to Domestic Shorthairs. The Domestic Shorthair of unknown ancestry is registered in the CFA as a Domestic Sphynx Outcross and is given a registration number.

With a concentration on hybrid breeding, not as many top show-quality cats will be produced as when breeding Sphynx to Sphynx, but that is to be expected. Health and temperament are the foremost considerations of breeders who have hybrid programs. In a few more generations, the cats from hybrids will be serious contenders for top honors on the show scene.

Sphynx pet buyers might like to consider adopting a hybrid Sphynx. Breeders frequently have adults and kittens available, and they charge very little for them. Hairless or coated, they all have the special personality traits of the Sphynx breed. The same health guarantee would apply to a hybrid kitten as it does to all of their kittens. These cats and kittens may have normal coats, but they are raised with the same love, care, and attention as the hairless Sphynx. Taking a hybrid would also be making a great contribution to the Sphynx breed. Placing these cats in good homes allows the breeder to move on to the next generation or to take in another outcross breeding cat. Breeders can keep only a limited number of cats.

The Sphynx is demanding, loving, and very mischievous. This is the perfect breed of cat for people who spend a lot of time at home and want a cat who is an interactive member of the family. A Sphynx thrives on attention, needs people and animal companionship, and loves to be on display at cat shows. Availability of Sphynx kittens is very limited, but the pleasures of living with a Sphynx or two make it well worth the wait. Practically all who share their lives with Sphynx cats claim that they are pure enchantment.

CFA SHOW STANDARD FOR THE SPHYNX

POINT SCORE

HEAD (35)

Size/shape	5
Ears	10
Muzzle/chin	5
Profile	5
Cheekbones	5
Eyes	5

BODY (35)

Neck	5
Chest	10
Abdomen and rump	10
Legs and feet	5
Tail	5

COAT/SKIN	**30**

GENERAL: The most distinctive feature of this cat is its appearance of hairlessness. The Sphynx is of medium size and body conformation, with substantial weight for its size. Females are generally smaller than males. The head shape is a modified wedge, with prominent cheekbones and whisker pads, giving a squared appearance to the muzzle. The body is warm and soft to the touch, with a skin texture akin to either a soft peach or a smooth nectarine. The Sphynx is sweet-tempered, lively, intelligent, and amenable to handling.

HEAD: The head is slightly longer than it is wide, with prominent cheekbones and a distinctive whisker break. The skull is slightly rounded, with a flat plane in front of the ears. The nose is straight and there is a slight to moderate palpable stop at the bridge of the nose.

CHEEKS AND CHEEKBONES: Prominent, rounded cheekbones that define the eye and form a curve above the whisker break.

MUZZLE AND CHIN: Whisker break with prominent whisker pads. Strong, well-developed chin forming perpendicular line with upper lip.

EARS: Large to very large. Broad at the base, open, and upright. When viewed from the front, the outer base of the ear should begin at the level of the eye, neither low-set nor on top of the head. The interior of the ears is naturally without furnishing.

EYES: Large, lemon-shaped, with wide-open center while coming to a definite point on each side. Placement should be at a slight upward angle, aligning with the outer base of the ear. Eyes to be wide set apart, with the distance between the eyes being a minimum of one eye width. Eye color immaterial.

BODY: The body is medium length, hard, and muscular, with broad, rounded chest and full, round abdomen. The rump is well rounded and muscular. Back line rises just behind the shoulder blades to accommodate longer back legs when standing. Boning is medium.

NECK: The neck is medium in length, rounded, well muscled, with a slight arch. Allowance to be made for heavy musculature in adult males.

LEGS AND FEET: Legs are medium in proportion to the body. They are sturdy and well muscled, with rear legs being slightly longer than the front. Paws are oval with well-knuckled toes; five in front and four behind. The paw pads are thick, giving the appearance of walking on cushions.

TAIL: Slender, flexible, and long while maintaining proportion to body length. Whiplike, tapering to a fine point.

COAT/SKIN: The appearance of this cat is one of hairlessness. However, short, fine hair may be present on the feet, outer edges of the ears, the tail, and the scrotum. The bridge of the nose should be normally coated. The remainder of the body can range from completely hairless to a covering of soft peachlike fuzz, no longer than $\frac{1}{8}$ inch (2 millimeters) in length. This coat/skin texture creates a feeling of resistance when stroking the cat. Wrinkled skin is desirable, particularly around the muzzle, between the ears, and around the shoulders. There are usually no whiskers but if whiskers are present they are short and sparse.

COLOR: Color and pattern are difficult to distinguish and should not affect the judging of the cat. White lockets, buttons, or belly spots are allowed.

PENALIZE: Hair other than as described

above. Delicate or frail appearance. Thin abdomen, thin rump, or narrow chest. Bowed front legs. Should not resemble the Devon Rex, Cornish Rex, or Oriental body type.

DISQUALIFY: Kinked or abnormal tail. Structural abnormalities. Aggressive behavior endangering the judge.

COLORS: All colors and patterns, in any combination, found in felines is acceptable in the Sphynx, with the exception of any of the colors or patterns that are determined by the placement of color on the single shaft of hair (e.g., shaded, cameo, smoke, chinchilla, ticked, or otherwise tipped hair shaft). Being a cat noted for its lack of hair, these descriptions would not apply to the Sphynx. *Note:* Exposure to sun will intensify all colors.

ALLOWABLE BREEDING OUTCROSSES: American Shorthair, domestic shorthair–domestic Sphynx outcross. Sphynx born on or after December 31, 2010, may have only Sphynx parents.

TONKINESE
By Mary Mosshammer

Tonkinese

The Tonkinese cat blends the best features of its ancestors into one beautiful, medium-size cat that proudly wears three coat patterns, each of which comes in four colors. It can display the densely colored coat of its Burmese predecessor, with sparkling yellow-green eyes setting off the deep brown that Tonkinese breeders call natural, a blue that is reminiscent of slate, champagne that rivals a fine milk chocolate, and platinum that looks for all the world like the precious metal. Its Siamese ancestors have contributed their pointed coat pattern, complete with glittering deep blue eyes. The contrast of richly colored ears, mask, leggings, and tail with the almost white-to-warm ivory of the body is startling. In between, these two extremes of contrast are the "mink" patterned Tonkinese, with incredible aqua eyes that stand out in the world of cats. The natural mink blends the deep brown of the ears, mask, leggings, and tail almost imperceptibly into the corresponding lighter shade of brown of the body color. The blue mink is equally beautiful, with the gentle shading into the body color from deep slate blue points. Milk or darker chocolate combines with the golden color of a fine champagne in the mink of the same name. The platinum mink is a picture of platinum or fine pewter on its points, shading gently into a body color that is a glowing, paler version. Kittens will be lighter in color than adults, as it takes 16–24 months for the full development of color in the Tonkinese.

Physical Description

The Tonkinese is a cat whose body is medium in size, not cobby like the Burmese, nor long and svelte like the Siamese. They are remarkably dense and muscular and are surprisingly heavy. The head is slightly longer than wide, a modified wedge in shape, with gently planed cheekbones. The muzzle is slightly rounded, as long as it is wide, and there is a slight whisker break that is gently curved following the line of the wedge. The ears are oval tipped and broad at the base, and when viewed from the front they appear to be as much on the side of the head as on the top. Viewed from the side, the tip of the chin aligns with the nose, in the same vertical plane. There is a gentle rise from the tip of the nose to a stop (a slight change of direction) at eye level leading to a gently rounded forehead. The eye shape is much like an almond, slightly flatter on top than on the bottom. The size should appear to fit with the size of the head, not too large or too small. The overall appearance of the Tonkinese is one of balance: everything fits together well. The cat is true poetry in motion.

Personality

These cats are intelligent and gregarious. They have a sense of humor. They are firmly convinced that humans were put on earth to love them. This colorful personality makes them ideal companions. They will take possession of your lap and shoulder, and they will supervise your activities. They are warm, loving, and highly intelligent and have an incredible memory and senses as perceptive as radar. They are very strong willed, and their humans are wise to use persistent persuasion in training them. Essential in every home run by a Tonkinese is a collection of spray bottles filled with water, strategically placed. After once making the point, for instance, that rearranging the mantel is not allowed, just picking up the squirt bottle re- inforces the lesson. It is at this point that Tonks treat their humans to the best "Who, me?" face in the cat fancy. They are naturals at inventing and playing games, using favorite toys to play fetch, and delighting in games of tag with each other. Of course, hide-and-seek is a favorite game, played equally well with humans as with other Tonks. They become your door greeter and will happily entertain your guests. They are equally adept at supervising repair people. Enthusiastic owners have described them as part puppy (following their owner around the house), part monkey (their acrobatics and leaping and climbing abilities are legend), and part elephant (running noisily through your house when they choose). Their affectionate ways are impossible to ignore, they quickly take over and run your home and your life, and they endear themselves to family and friends forever.

Owners of Tonkinese find themselves to be imitators of Dr. Doolittle, for these cats carry on conversations with their humans in complete sentences. Awakening from a nap, they will seek the whereabouts of their humans by talking, using an unmistakable "Where are you?" tone. Their voices are very pleasant, and their meanings are unmistakable. No guesswork here.

Grooming Requirements

Caring for Tonkinese is as simple and easy as feeding a well-balanced feline diet, clipping their nails weekly, and using a rubber brush to groom them.

Having the nails clipped is something every kitten or cat can become accustomed to, if clipping is started at a very young age. Providing an interesting scratching post or cat tree and insisting they use it is imperative. Tonks love high places, so a well-placed tall cat tree with scratching surfaces (sisal is a favorite) and interesting platforms and cubbyholes helps to solve problems of boredom and scratching inappropriate surfaces. Placed near a window, perhaps with a bird feeder or bright wind sock within view, a cat tree can occupy a Tonk for hours. Grooming with a rubber brush (the feline equivalent of a curry brush) on a routine basis will help keep seasonal shedding to a minimum, as well as become a bonding exercise between you and your cat. Except in the case of the show cat, bathing is seldom necessary; Tonks are very fastidious and bathe themselves often. The flat side of the rubber brush helps keep the sheen on their coat.

Origins and History

Although relatively new to modern cat show competition, this is the same breed depicted in *The Cat-Book Poems* of Siam during the Ayudha period (1358–1767) and imported to England in the early 1800s as "Chocolate Siamese." In the United States, both Tonkinese and Burmese can trace their beginnings back to Wong Mau, a small walnut-colored cat imported to California by Dr. Joseph Thompson in 1930. There were a few fanciers who bred Tonkinese in the early years, but the first selective breeding program is generally attributed to a New York fancier. In Canada, in the middle 1960s, recognition was achieved, and the Tonkinese was granted Championship status there in 1971. During this time, an American breeder approached several U.S. associations for registration. The Canadian and American breeders worked to publicize the breed, wrote standards for the Tonkinese and corresponded with other fanciers. An American breeder went on a televised game show, which reached a nationwide audience, and the floodgates were opened. Interested fanciers from across the country joined the small group of Tonkinese breeders. This relatively small group of Tonkinese fanciers applied to the CFA for recognition, and registration was granted in 1978.

In 1979, the Tonkinese Breed Association was organized and affiliated with the CFA specifically to work to advance the Tonkinese in CFA. Provisional status for Tonkinese was effective with the beginning of the show year on May 1, 1982. By 1984, they had purred their way through several years and four presentations to the board of directors of the CFA, finally achieving their Championship goal on May 1, 1984. Tonkinese cats know they belong, too. In the beginning, only the mink coat Tonkinese could compete at CFA shows. Beginning with the 2002 show season, all three Tonkinese coat patterns competed in the show ring, showing off the full range of point-to-body contrast. Since 1984 there have been many Grand Champions, Grand Premiers, and the ultimate CFA title for a breeding cat: Distinguished Merit. The Tonkinese in the CFA have produced national and regional winning cats.

Miscellanea

When someone purchases a Tonk kitten or adult, the breeder will inform the new owner what diet is being fed and when a change should be made. For instance, a kitten may be fed a specific growth food (such as a kitten diet) until it reaches a certain age, then make a gradual change to adult food. The nutritional needs of kittens are very different from that of adults.

The Tonkinese is an indoor-only cat, as are all pedigreed breeds. A thorough inspection of your home prior to your Tonk's arrival will help ensure that he remains indoors. Making certain that window screens and doors are secure can help keep him safely inside. Cat-proofing your home, much as you would childproof for a visiting 2-year-old human on the loose, is bound to save you frustration. Knickknacks and breakables put behind glass doors can be enjoyed without the danger of being broken or moved by an intrepid Tonk. Plants, particularly those poisonous to cats, should be moved outside, to another room where your Tonk is not allowed (they really don't have to take over the entire house), or hung up high where they cannot be reached by a Tonk. Rotating different toys every so often helps keep them occupied when you have other things to do besides playing with them. Humans who work outside the home find that two Tonks will keep each other company, particularly in the case of kittens, as well as lessen the mischief one bored Tonk can get into.

A purchaser with children should seek out a Tonkinese breeder whose cats have been raised around children. Tonkinese that have been retired from breeding programs (usually 5 years of age and under), and have been altered can and do lead wonderful lives with their humans. They travel in motor homes, as content to run a home on wheels as one that is stationary. Because human laps are a favorite place for Tonkinese, less physically active or older humans are wonderful owners. This breed is not for people who want a couch potato, however, or who object to a purring fur piece around their neck or on their shoulders.

The Tonkinese wears a rainbow of colors, but no matter which color or coat pattern a purchaser may choose, they may be assured they are joining an enthusiastic Tonkinese fan club. This breed's personality is unbeatable. For those humans who relish an active purring feline friend, Tonkinese are ideal. Humans who are owned by Tonks will happily tell everyone that they embarked on the most joyful experience of their lives the day they took home a Tonkinese.

CFA SHOW STANDARD FOR THE TONKINESE

POINT SCORE

HEAD (25)	
Profile	8
Muzzle and chin	6
Ears	6
Eye shape and set	5

BODY (30)	
Torso	15
Legs and feet	5
Tail	5
Muscle tone	5

COAT	10

COLOR (35)	
Body color (including point color in mink and pointed colors)	25
Eye color	10

GENERAL: The ideal Tonkinese is intermediate in type, neither cobby nor svelte. The Tonkinese should give the overall impression of an alert, active cat with good muscular development. The cat should be surprisingly heavy. While the breed is considered medium in size, balance and proportion are of greater importance.

HEAD AND MUZZLE: The head is a modified, slightly rounded wedge somewhat longer than it is wide, with high, gently planed cheekbones. The muzzle is blunt, as long as it is wide. There is a slight whisker break, gently curved, following the lines of the wedge. There is a slight stop at eye level. In profile the tip of the chin lines with the tip of the nose in the same vertical plane. There is a gentle rise from the tip of the nose to the stop. There is a gentle contour, with a slight rise from the nose stop to the forehead. There is a slight convex curve to the forehead.

EARS: Alert, medium in size. Oval tips, broad at the base. Ears set as much on the sides of the head as on the top. Hair on the ears very short and close-lying. Leather may show through.

EYES: Open almond shape. Slanted along the cheekbones toward the outer edge of the ear. Eyes are proportionate in size to the face.

EYE COLOR: *Mink colors:* Aqua. A definitive characteristic of the mink color pattern, best seen in natural light. *Full-body colors:* Green to yellow-green. *Pointed colors:* Blue. Depth, clarity, and brilliance of color preferred.

BODY: Torso medium in length, demonstrating well-developed muscular strength without coarseness. The Tonkinese conformation strikes a midpoint between the extremes of long, svelte body types and cobby, compact body types. Balance and proportion are more important than size alone. The abdomen should be taut, well-muscled, and firm.

LEGS AND FEET: Fairly slim, proportionate in length and bone to the body. Hind legs slightly longer than front. Paws more oval than round. Trim. Toes: five in front and four behind.

TAIL: Proportionate in length to body. Tapering.

COAT: Medium short in length, close-lying, fine, soft, and silky, with a lustrous sheen.

BODY COLOR: *Mink colors:* The mature specimen should be a rich, even, unmarked color, shading almost imperceptibly to a slightly lighter hue on the underparts. Allowance to be made for lighter body color in young cats. With the dilute colors in particular, development of full-body color may take up to 16 months. Cats do darken with age, but there must be a distinct contrast between body color and points. *Full-body colors:* Body color in the full-body colors may be a slightly lighter shade of the point color, with very little contrast between the points and body color. There will be more contrast between the points and body color for the champagne and platinum than for the natural and blue. *Pointed colors:* Body color in pointed colors should be off-white. Any shading is relative to the point color, and overall body color should be in marked contrast to the points.

POINT COLOR: Mask, ears, feet, and tail all densely marked but merging gently into body color. Except in kittens, mask and ears should be connected by tracings.

PENALIZE: Extreme ranginess or cobbiness. Definite nose break. Round eyes.

DISQUALIFY: Yellow eyes in mink colors. White locket or button. Crossed eyes. Tail faults.

COLORS: Natural, champagne, blue, and platinum in mink, full-body, and pointed patterns.

ALLOWABLE BREEDING OUTCROSSES: none.

TURKISH ANGORA

By B. Iris Tanner and Barbara Azan

Turkish Angora

Graceful, elegant, refined, yet possessed of strength, intelligence, and a will that belies its delicate appearance—this is the study in contradictions that is the Turkish Angora.

Physical Description

No other breed has a coat so sensuously silky or a body that combines the elongated shape of the oriental breeds with the solidity and firmness of a more moderate cat. Their extra-large, erect ears are set high and close together on the head, giving them a "bunny rabbit" look that is enhanced by large, soulful eyes. Another distinctive feature is the tail, which billows out into a glorious plume of fur.

The beauty of these exquisite creatures is best appreciated by seeing them in motion (which tends to be during most of their waking hours). Ornamental though they may be, sitting still to be admired is not one of their favorite pastimes. The hidden treasures that may be con-cealed in an owner's purse or the ray of sunlight that briefly flickers across a room are far more important to them. As a Turkish Angora leaps off in pursuit, it moves with fluid, coordinated grace, its gossamer coat shimmering with the movement of each muscle and its tail carried proudly erect, like a flag. A high activity level, ethereal appearance, and predilection for high-up places make the Turkish Angora appear only loosely anchored to the earth.

Personality

All Turkish Angoras registered with the CFA can still trace their ancestry back to imports from Turkey and, consequently, to original wild stock. As a result, their natural instincts are closer to the surface than those of many other breeds. This may account for their innate intelligence and strong will. They make excellent hunters, stalking a mouse or a feathery toy with equal zeal. Once captured, prey is not willingly relinquished, and breeders quickly learn that the best way to take anything away from a Turkish Angora is to distract it with a toy while quickly withdrawing the first object. Seasoned owners realize that firmness with these cats is an important part of loving them. However, this strength of will is part of the innate intelligence that makes them such fascinating cats to their admirers.

The Turkish Angora personality is as striking as its appearance, surpassing many other breeds when it comes to playfulness and affection. They quickly form devoted attachments to their owners, lavishing adoration unstintingly on them. However, a well-adjusted, properly raised cat will often appear equally friendly to strangers, welcoming them with the level of enthusiasm that you would be more likely to expect from a dog rather than a cat. Their curiosity and interest in their human companions knows no bounds. Few indeed are the household activities that do not benefit from a bit of Turkish

Angora assistance. Their intelligence enables them, among other things, to devise ways of opening doors, cabinets, and drawers that you would never expect of a cat. Consequently, they often conceal themselves in surprising places. It may be a necessity to search your clothes closet before leaving the house in order to extract the cat playing hide-and-seek there.

This is a cat that approaches everything with an intensity that often surprises newcomers to the breed. When a Turkish Angora is happy, a simple purr alone does not suffice; the cat rolls over on its back, with its feet kneading joyfully in the air, and accompanies this exhibition with an extremely loud purr. When this cat is in a playful mood, you can expect to find him walking across curtain rods or door tops and playfully attacking pens, keys, or any other unattended small objects. Pushing interesting objects off tables onto the floor is also one of their favorite games. This has the added side benefit of teaching the owner to put things away. It is a rare Turkish Angora that is able to resist the temptation of a roomful of baubles and knickknacks, which they regard as toys placed in the room for their pleasure. Owners of the breed generally believe that changes in housekeeping habits are worth the effort, because of the devotion, beauty, and entertaining antics of this breed.

Anything involving water holds a particular fascination for Turkish Angoras; in their wild state, they once swam in pursuit of fish, like their Turkish Van cousins.

While both these breeds came from the same ancestral stock, selective breeding over the past 50 years has clearly separated them into two entirely distinct looks. The Turkish Van is larger, stockier, and more muscular, with shorter, thicker fur and lower-set ears. These differences are important to keep in mind when comparing the two, because the characteristic Van markings can also occur in bicolor Turkish Angoras.

Grooming Requirements

Grooming a Turkish Angora is relatively simple in comparison to grooming other longhair breeds. The Turkish Angora's silky, single-coated fur rarely mats. Twice-a-week combing is recommended to keep the coat in its best condition and prevent the ingestion of fur, although heavy-coated older animals may require more frequent attention. It is important to regularly bathe and trim the nails from early kittenhood so that the cat gets used to these procedures and accepts them as a normal part of the routine.

Bathing is recommended every 8–10 weeks for white cats, while colored cats can go a few weeks longer between baths. The difference between regular maintenance bathing and a show bath is simply the number of lathers and the drying method used. Bathing methods vary widely, depending on the equipment available. The two most popular approaches employ either a kitchen sink or laundry sink equipped with a sprayer or a bathtub with a hand-held showerhead.

Maintenance baths should include two lathers, and show baths include three to five lathers, depending on the age of the cat and the length and thickness of coat. Because the silky coat can become oily with time and handling, the first lathering should generally be with a special degreasing shampoo, a clarifying shampoo, or a dilute solution of dishwashing liquid and water. Subsequent lathering should be with a conditioning shampoo best suited to the cat's color. Many good brands of whitening shampoos are available and should be used for bicolors and smoke or cameo cats as well as whites. Be sure to work up a rich lather all over the cat's body, legs, and tail, and do not forget the stomach, paws, and hocks, which usually need special attention in white cats. Use a washcloth around the face, muzzle, and top of the head, and be careful to avoid getting water in the ears, because that may be a cause of ear infections. Cleaning the ears gently with a cotton swab after bathing is a good safety measure.

The rule of thumb when rinsing is to rinse until all the soap seems to be gone, then rinse for at least 2 minutes longer, because insufficient rinsing leaves the coat looking flat and greasy. Creme rinses are not generally recommended for this breed, because they can be too rich and leave the delicate coat with a greasy feel. It is better to stick with a conditioning shampoo and use a light spray-on conditioner or texturizing spray after the bath, if needed.

Drying is most easily accomplished by putting the cat in a carrier and propping up a dryer to blow into it. A coffee can is the perfect support for a regular hand-held dryer. Inexpensive stand-up dryers (a popular brand name is Duck) are available from most pet supply catalogs. When using this approach, it is best to use a medium heat setting and place the dryer 6–8 inches from the carrier. Check on the cat every few minutes to make sure it is not becoming overheated. When preparing a Turkish Angora for a show, many breeders like to hold the cats on their laps and comb out the fur while blow-drying. This adds volume and silky texture to the coat and also helps remove dead hair and prevent tangles. To use this method, comb first in the direction of the hair growth to remove any minor tangles, then gently reverse-comb until the hair is dry.

Origins and History

The survival instincts of a self-sufficient, independent animal live on in even the most playful and loving pet Turkish Angora. Understanding their heritage is essential to understanding the breed today. It is the oldest of all longhair breeds, first documented in the sixteenth century but with a history that undoubtedly goes back several hundred years before that. Although they first came to light in the vicinity of Ankara, Turkey, some sources claim that the cat was brought to Turkey in the twelfth century, that it was originally domesticated by the Tartars, and that its characteristic long, silky coat is a gift from some far-off wild ancestor.

What is known is that the Turkish Angora came to Europe during the Renaissance and entered the pages of history in the writings of sixteenth-century French naturalist Nicholas-Claude Fabri de Peiresc. From France, it was a short trip to England and the beginnings of the cat fancy. However, this was also where the Turkish Angora and the Persian were first interbred. By World War I, the interbreeding had merged the two to such an extent that the Turkish Angora virtually ceased to exist as a separate breed.

The breed still had some of its nine lives left, however. In the 1930s, the Turkish government realized that their country's national breed had become almost extinct. A rescue operation was set up. From all over the country, Angoras (or cats that looked like them) were gathered in the Ankara Zoo. This was not an easy task, for reports tell us that in 1966, there were fewer than 30 Angoras present in the zoo. The Turks concentrated only on white cats, removing any colored cats from the program.

In 1954, the first Turkish import was brought to the United States. Others arrived in subsequent years, and by 1968, the CFA was accepting Turkish Angoras of all colors for registration. However, the white cats still had an edge. Provisional status was granted only to the whites in 1970, and they were approved for Championship competition in 1972. The first Grand Champions were achieved in 1975 and 1976. However, it was not until 1986 that the breed produced its first National Winner.

In 1978, after a long struggle, the colored Turkish Angoras were finally given the same Championship privileges as their white relatives. Some breeders still prefer the pure white cats extolled in the Turkish legends. However, colored cats have achieved considerable recognition in recent years, with a calico female achieving the National Best of Breed award in 1999. She was the first nonwhite Angora to achieve this high honor.

Turkish Angoras, though of dainty structure, are hardy, long-lived cats that become even more beautiful as they mature. They never lose their love of toys and games and can enrich a pet owner's life for 20 or more years. The playful nature and loving disposition of this breed make the Turkish Angora an excellent choice as a pet for children or older people. They get along very well with dogs and other cats. When compatibility with other cats is a consideration, however, some breeders recommend more reserved breeds such as Persians or Russian Blues. Pairing them with these breeds is a wonderful combination. The Turkish Angora's influence makes a sedate cat more outgoing, while the calm demeanor of such a cat offsets the Turkish Angora's intensity. However, it is not uncommon for the Turkish Angora to adapt well to the companionship of another Turkish Angora or of equally active breeds such as Abyssinians or Siamese—or of any other breed, for that matter.

Miscellanea

Females are not prone to birthing problems. They usually produce kittens quickly and efficiently and make excellent mothers. The average litter contains three to five kittens, but larger litters are not uncommon, with seven or eight occurring frequently in some lines.

If you think you'd like to show your Turkish Angora, it's a good idea to attend cat shows and see how judges handle these cats, stretching out the long, lean body, checking the tail length, and feeling the face to check for bumps, breaks, or undesirable curves. Judges also use toys to get the cats' attention and evaluate ear set, shape, and size. Kittens destined for a show career should be handled in the same manner at home, so that they will become accustomed to the routine. Many breeders begin to stretch kittens even before their eyes are open, as part of the daily handling that is so important when raising kittens of any breed.

While the traditional white cats are still the most frequent choice of pet owners, colored cats are fast gaining ground. One reason for the increasing popularity of nonwhite Turkish Angoras is that white cats are subject to deafness because of a defect in the dominant white gene. Blue-eyed white cats are most susceptible; approximately 50% are affected. Because a hearing, blue-eyed white is the most frequently requested choice for a pet and most breeders prefer to retain such cats for their breeding programs, many buyers quickly decide to compromise on the eye or coat color of their desired pets. However, those who do accept a deaf cat quickly learn that there is virtually no difference in terms of daily interaction and personality. In fact, many breeders believe that the deaf cats are even more affectionate and interactive than their hearing siblings.

The other eye colors of whites, gold, green, or odd-eyed (one blue and the other either gold or green), are much less likely to be affected by deafness. Including colored cats in a breeding program is the only way to reduce the incidence of deafness. Today even breeders who focus on white cats usually have a colored cat or two in their breeding programs. Other beautiful and popular color choices now available are the nonwhite solids, black, blue, cream, and an occasional (but very rare) red; tabbies (in brown, blue, red, cream, silver, and cameo); parti-colors (tortoiseshell and blue-cream); bi-colors (any of the previous colors in combination with white); and smoke and shaded colors.

★   ★   ★

In the final analysis, the only thing a Turkish Angora really needs in life is a human companion who will give it the loving attention, affection, and respect it deserves. This will be repaid many times over by the all-encompassing affection given in return.

CFA SHOW STANDARD FOR THE TURKISH ANGORA

POINT SCORE

HEAD (40)	
Head shape and profile	15
Ears (size, 5; placement, 10)	15
Eye size, shape, and placement	10

BODY (35)	
Size and boning	10
Torso, including neck	15
Legs and tail	5
Muscle tone	5

BALANCE	10

COAT	10

COLOR	5

GENERAL: The ideal Turkish Angora is a balanced, graceful cat with a fine, silky coat that shimmers with every movement, in contrast to the firm, long, muscular body beneath it. **HEAD:** *Size:* Small to medium, in balance with the length of the body and extremities. Shape: a medium long, smooth wedge. Allowance is to be made for jowls. *Profile:* Two planes formed by a flat top head and the line of the nose meeting at an angle slightly above the eyes. *No break.* **MUZZLE:** A continuation of the smooth lines of the wedge, with neither pronounced whisker pad nor pinch. **EARS:** Large, wide at base, pointed and tufted. Set closely together, high on the head, vertical and erect. **EYES:** Large, almond-shaped, slanting slightly upward with open expression. **EYE COLOR:** Eye color can be any shade of green, gold, green-gold, copper, blue, or odd-eyed. There is no relationship between eye color and coat color. Uniformity and depth of eye color should be taken into consideration as a part of the overall head score, with deeper, richer color preferred. **NOSE:** Medium in length. **NECK:** Slim, graceful, and rather long. **CHIN:** Firm, gently rounded. Tip in profile to form perpendicular line with nose. **BODY:** Medium size, however, overall balance, grace, and fineness of bone are more important than actual size. Males may be slightly larger than females. Torso long and slender. Shoulders the same width as hips. Rump slightly higher than shoulders. Finely boned with firm muscularity. **LEGS:** Long. Hind legs longer than front. **PAWS:** Small, round and dainty. Tufts between toes preferable.

TAIL: Long and tapering from a wide base to a narrow end, with a full brush.

COAT: Single coated. Length of body coat varies, but tail and ruff should be long, full, and finely textured and have a silklike sheen. Britches should be apparent on the hind legs.

BALANCE: Proportionate in all physical aspects, with a graceful, lithe appearance.

PENALIZE: Obviously oversize, coarse appearance.

DISQUALIFY: Cobby body type. Kinked or abnormal tail. Crossed eyes.

COLORS: A wide array of colors in the solid, shaded, smoke, tabby, bicolor, and parti-color patterns.

ALLOWABLE BREEDING OUTCROSSES: none.

TURKISH VAN
By Dusty Rainbolt

Turkish Van

The dilemma occurs in many families: One parent wants a cat; the kids want a Labrador Retriever. It sounds like a hopeless deadlock, doesn't it? It isn't if you consider adding a Turkish Van to the family. A Turkish Van offers the best of both worlds. In addition to the traits that endear people to cats, Vans also have traits that are almost exclusively associated with some hunting dogs; they are loyal companions, love a good game of fetch, and, under the right circumstances, enjoy a cool dip in the pool. However, they do not retrieve ducks.

Physical Description

The Turkish Van is a natural breed that originated centuries ago around the Lake Van area in what is now part of Turkey. Along with its legendary love of water, Turkish Vans are known for their full, brushlike tail, exquisitely soft cashmere fur, strong muscular body, and high level of intelligence. Of course, what the public knows best about the breed is its distinctive van pattern.

It is thought that the van pattern originated centuries ago with the Turkish Van, and it is now found in a variety of pedigreed as well as mixed-breed cats. A van-patterned cat is an all-white cat with colored markings restricted primarily to the head and tail. The van pattern is due to the degree of expression of the piebald gene. This gene is responsible for the appearance of white on cats in many patterns, such as the tuxedo, bicolor, and harlequin patterns. The different degree of expression of the piebald gene is graded on a scale of 1–10; a tuxedo pattern cat is a 2, a bicolor is a 5, and an all-white cat is a 10. Therefore, a van-patterned cat with color on the head and tail is in the 8–9 range.

The pedigreed Turkish Van is a chalk-white, semilong-haired cat with the color of the van pattern occurring in red, black, brown tabby, patched tabby, or with the dilute versions (e.g., blue, cream) of those colors. A white blaze from the nose to past the ears is most desirable, creating two matched head markings. Very expressive peach pit–shaped eyes, which come in amber, glacial blue, or one blue and one amber (also known as odd-eyed), complete the Van's ensemble. Some Van cats possess a colored marking on their shoulder called "the mark" or "thumbprint of Allah" in its homeland. It is considered a sign that the cat has been blessed.

The tail has become one of the Turkish Van's most distinguished trademarks. Some people say it resembles the tail of a fox. Although Van kittens' tails are almost pencil-like, the mature cat has a tail that remains full and plush year round. Not only is the tail beautiful, but it is also expressive. Like the Van itself, the tail is frequently in action. Although Vans will thrash their tails about when angry or agitated, their tails often flick and sway even when they are completely relaxed and happy.

The Van's fur is also distinctive in that it has no woolly undercoat. The fur feels like cashmere, almost rabbitlike in softness. In the wild, this unique coat repels water during these cats' renowned swims in the shallow waters around Lake Van or, in the case of domesticated cats, in swimming pools or ponds. Turkish Vans are one of the easiest long-haired cats to care for. Most of them have a wash-and-wear, nonmatting coat requiring no special shampoos and no blow-drying. Their fur is generally thicker and longer in the winter and shorter in the summer as a result of climatic extremes in their native land.

But even cats who live indoors are affected by changes in the seasons that influence the thickness and length of their coats.

Vans are wide-bodied, among the largest of all domestic breeds, and just slightly smaller than the Maine Coon, although Vans are more densely muscled. The head is wide and moderately wedge-shaped. Generally, a mature Van's chest is broad enough to fit several fingers between his front legs. The body is long, sturdy, and muscular.

It is not uncommon for the casual observer to assume that the Turkish Van is simply a Turkish Angora with different markings. In reality, these cats are quite distinct from each other in appearance. A side-by-side comparison will illustrate that the Angora is a delicate, finely boned cat, whereas the Van possesses impressive mass. Most other breeds of cat achieve their full size at 2–3 years of age; the Turkish Van can take up to 5 years to reach full maturity. A CFA Allbreed judge once said, "Angoras are the ballerinas of the Turkish cats; Vans are the sumo wrestlers." The Van's well-feathered ears are large, set fairly high and well apart, and are rounded at the tips. The ears of the Angora are more erect. Instead of two triangles sitting straight up on the top of the head, like an Angora's, the Van's ears sit closer to the corners of the head, with the inside edge slightly tilted toward the outside.

Personality

Because Turkish Vans are not graceful cats, they are action-packed comedians on a level with Chevy Chase or Jerry Lewis, occasionally toppling things, then looking at you as if to say, "I meant to do that." Most people fortunate enough to own a Van agree that life is never dull. These cats like interactive games with their owners. They love toys made of natural materials like feathers or fur on a string. A constant supply of new toys should keep Vans entertained for hours. New toys are often required because of the vigorous play they lavish on their favorite old ones.

Another favorite pastime common to most Vans is a vigorous game of fetch. What they fetch is up to the individual Van. Some like balls of paper; others cannot resist milk jug rings. Still others prefer wads of tape and countless other things. The pitcher's arm is likely to tire before the cat does. Still, it is hard to say no when you see him trot up with his favorite toy in his mouth and drop it at your feet or on your keyboard as if to say, "Please?"

These cats have amazing problem-solving abilities and the energy to carry through schemes like climbing into cabinets. Sometimes, this can be a problem in itself, but most of the time, they challenge their humans to keep up with them. Although they aren't big on being held or carried, when playtime is over they do like to curl up next to their owners or crawl in their laps while they read a book or enjoy a good rerun on TV. Turkish Vans seldom argue about which channel to watch. Like dogs, they are immensely loyal to their chosen masters. When times are tough, your cat will let you know he is your friend through it all.

Although they have earned the name Swimming Cat, most Vans do not swim because of a lack of available pool or pond options, but they are fascinated by running water or a dripping faucet. It is not uncommon to see them dip a paw in the water bowl and then lick it or shake the paw to watch the drops fly. Do not be surprised if you have assistance shaving or showering in the mornings. These cats also have voracious appetites because of their high level of activity.

Grooming Requirements

One of the great things about Turkish Vans is that despite their splendid semilong hair and elegant appearance, they are low-maintenance cats. The cashmere quality of their fur and the absence of an undercoat make their coat easy to maintain. Owners of pet-quality Vans need only run an occasional comb through the coat to get rid of the dead hair. Turkish Vans with a heavy winter coat will need more attention than when sporting their summery rabbitlike coat. It is easy to determine if their winter coats are dead by the fur's strawlike texture. Usually, Vans do not need daily grooming and are meticulous in maintaining their appearance. Clipping nails weekly will keep the Van accustomed to the procedure. While you are at it, take a quick peek inside the ears to check for dirt.

Bathing a Turkish Van is a combination of ease and challenge. It has been written that because Vans love water, they also love to take a bath. That is like saying if a 5-year-old boy enjoys playing in the swimming pool, it should be no problem to get him in the bathtub for a good scrubbing. The truth is that Vans feel the same as other breeds about bathing: If it is your idea, he would probably rather not bathe, thank you. However, if you start bathing him when he is young, he will generally become accustomed to it and, ultimately, more accepting.

Vans are extremely clean cats, so regular bathing is not necessary. In the event a bath is needed, a good-quality shampoo made specifically for cats will generally suffice. However, additional bathing steps are required for specific problem areas or if preparing your Van for a cat show. If you have a cat with a lot of oil in his fur or a bad case of stud tail (a medical condition involving excessive oil production along the tail), you can use a degreasing shampoo (several varieties especially for cats are available) or dishwashing detergent (e.g., Dawn) diluted 1:1 with water for an initial bathing, and then follow up with the cat's regular shampoo. Remember to rinse the cat thoroughly after bathing, leaving no residual shampoo. This is particularly important for the Turkish Van, whose thick fur tends to hold the soap.

Because Turkish Vans do not have the undercoat that complicates life for other breeds, they can simply air dry in a warm room. Cat show judges prefer Vans to be squeaky clean, so don't make the mistake of powdering them, except for a light touch to offset some of the problems of stud tail. If the Van's freshly washed coat looks a little clumpy, it could be because there is still soap in the fur. Go back and rinse, rinse, rinse.

Origins and History

These cats go by numerous names: Turkish Vans, Vancats (the *a* being pronounced like the *o* in *Ron*, not *a* as in *ran*) and of course, the Swimming Cat. Whatever you call them, the breed is an ancient, natural breed from the Middle East, still very much in its original form.

Evidence of cats called Turkish Vans goes back to the Bronze Age. The first records of a white, semilong-haired cat with ringed tails appeared as carvings on Hittite jewelry sometime between 1600 and 1200 BCE. The land changed hands several times and was conquered by the Romans (CE 75–387). A cat with a "light self-color and a ringed tail" was adopted by one Roman legion to display on its battle standard and armor. A natural and ancient breed, the Turkish Van originally roamed the Lake Van region of Turkey not far from Mount Ararat. This is where the breed received the name of Swimming Cat by going for a dip in the mountain streams to cool off when the Turkish summers became swelteringly hot.

Jumping ahead 2,000 years, two photographers from England were given a pair of unrelated cats while traveling around Turkey for the Turkish Tourist Board in 1954. When they returned to England with their feline treasures, they discovered that they bred true. The kittens were replicas of their parents.

In 1983, a husband and wife from Florida imported Turkish Vans from France and later from Holland. Other breeders followed suit and imported more cats from England and from their original homeland in eastern Turkey. The CFA began registering the Turkish Van in February 1988. The Van was granted Provisional status in 1993 and was advanced to Championship status in February 1994.

Miscellanea

If you plan on showing your Turkish Van, he should enter kitten classes at age 4 months to enable him to become accustomed to handling by judges and the sights and smells of a crowded show hall. These cannot be replicated at home. In preparing a kitten for its show career, you should practice stretching the kitten and turning its head as part of its play routine, so that the kitten will be well accustomed to these things when a judge does it. Although Vans demand attention from their owner and could easily spend the evening lounging next to you or snoozing in your lap, many do not like being carried around or manhandled. Just as with swimming or taking a bath, it has to be their idea. That is why practicing before a cat show is very important. "Stretching" entails supporting the chest with one hand behind the kitten's front legs and supporting the belly with the other hand in front of their hind legs. Gently separate your hands to stretch the kitten to its length, which displays the full body. After a little practice, your kitten will enjoy being carried like this. The Vans' center of gravity is toward the front of the body, so they simply do not feel comfortable on two feet. They also do not like being held up in the air the way many other breeds do; they prefer to keep all four feet on the judging stand. Nevertheless, they can learn to be stretched and held up like Turkish Angoras and Siamese, provided they get practice at home. Start with short holds before or after the cat receives a treat. Gradually increase the length of time the cat is held and begin moving around the room.

★　★　★

The Turkish Van has a mind of its own but also has fierce loyalty to and love for its owner. If you do not mind stepping over a few toys, building up your pitching arm, and occasionally wearing out a toy, then a Turkish Van might just be the right cat for you.

CFA BREED STANDARD FOR THE TURKISH VAN

POINT SCORE

HEAD (30)

Shape (boning, chin, nose, cheekbones, profile)	18
Ears (shape, placement and size)	7
Eyes (shape, placement and size)	5

BODY (35)

Type (boning, muscle, length, size)	20
Legs and feet	5
Tail	10

COAT	**15**

COLOR AND PATTERN	**20**

GENERAL: The Turkish Van is a natural breed from the rugged, remote, and climatically varied region of the Middle East. The breed is known for its distinctive pattern . . . the term *van* has been adopted by a variety of breeds to describe white cats with colored head and tail markings. The Turkish Van is a solidly built, semilong-haired cat with great breadth to the chest. The strength and power of the cat is evidenced in its substantial body and legs. This breed takes a full 3 to 5 years to reach full maturity and development; therefore, allowances must be made for age and sex. Despite age and sex, as adults, individuals should convey an overall impression of a well-balanced and well-proportioned appearance in which no feature is exaggerated to foster weakness or extremes. Turkish Vans are very intelligent and alert cats, and as such, feel more secure and handle better with all four feet on a solid surface.

HEAD: Substantially broad wedge, with gentle contours and a medium-length nose to harmonize with the large muscular body; ears are not to be included in the wedge. Prominent cheekbones. In profile, the nose has a slight dip below eye level marked by a change in the direction the hair lies. Allowances must be made for jowling in the males. Firm chin in a straight line with the nose and upper lip; rounded muzzle.

EARS: Moderately large, in proportion to the body, set fairly high and well apart; the inside edge of the ear is slightly angled to the outside, with the outside edge fairly straight but not necessarily in line with the side of the face; wide at the base. Tips are slightly rounded. Insides should be well feathered.

EYES: Moderately large, a rounded aperture slightly drawn out at the corners, set at a slant, equidistant from the outside base of the ear to the tip of the nose. Eyes should be clear, alert, and expressive.

BODY: Moderately long, sturdy, broad, muscular, and deep-chested. Mature males should exhibit marked muscular development in the neck and shoulders. The shoulders should be at least as broad as the head and flow into the well-rounded rib cage and then into a muscular hip and pelvic area. Turkish Van males are substantially larger than females and exhibit much greater development.

LEGS AND FEET: Moderately long, muscular legs. They are set wide apart and taper to rounded, moderately large feet. Legs and feet should be in proportion to the body. Toes: five in front, four behind.

TAIL: Long but in proportion to the body, with a brushlike appearance. Tail hair length is in keeping with the semilong coat length.

COAT: Semilong with a cashmerelike texture; soft to the roots with no trace of undercoat. Because of the extremes in climate of this breed's native region, Vans carry two distinctive coat lengths, and allowances must be made for the seasonal coat. The summer coat is short, conveying the appearance of a shorthair; the winter coat is substantially longer and thicker. There is feathering on the ears, legs, feet, and belly. Facial fur is short. A frontal neck ruff and full brush tail become more pronounced with age. The above description is that of an adult; allowances must be made for short coats and tail hair on kittens and young adults.

COLOR AND PATTERN: Van pattern only on glistening chalk-white body, with colored markings confined to the head and tail desirable. One or more random markings, up to color on 20% of the entire body, are permissible. Random markings should not be of a size or number to detract from the van pattern, making a specimen appear bicolor. A symmetrical pattern of head markings, divided by white up to at least the level of the front edge of the ears, is desirable.

PENALIZE: Any evidence toward extremes (i.e., short cobbiness or svelte, fine boning); flat profile.

DISQUALIFY: Total absence of color on the head or tail; definite nose break; genetic/skeletal defects such as flattened rib cage; kinked or abnormal tail; incorrect number of toes; crossed eyes. Color in excess of 20% of the entire body.

COLORS: Solid and white, tabby and white, and parti-colors and white.

ALLOWABLE BREEDING OUTCROSSES: none.

Part

III

The Feline Experience

Chapter 4

Where to Get a Cat and How to Choose the Right One

BY ANNA SADLER

T*he hard work is done. Hours have been devoted to researching the breeds, personality type, care requirements, and the seemingly endless considerations to ensure that the new feline family member will be an exact fit with the family's expectations and desires. Now comes the easy part, the selection of the cat or kitten you will take home. Right?*

Think again. There's more research to do and more decisions to be made. Approaches will vary considerably, depending on whether the cat is intended as a family pet or as a breeding cat in addition to being a pet; whether it is one of the more easily found breeds, one of the rare ones, or perhaps a nonpedigreed cat.

The sources of pedigreed cats and kittens are breeders, pet shops, breed rescue organizations, and occasionally animal shelters. Of course, nonpedigreed cats can be adopted from most of the same sources in addition to veterinary offices, animal hospitals, neighbors, and most frequently from animal shelter organizations.

PET SHOPS

Certainly pet shops are the most convenient source of pedigreed kittens (and some non-

pedigreed kittens) for the majority of shoppers, but more and more pet stores are discontinuing the sale of animals.

Even though "that kitten in the window" of the local pet shop may be the perfect breed and color, may appear healthy, and may be guaranteed, chances are strong that it originated at a commercial breeding facility. Even if commercial breeders have scrupulously clean operations (many do not) with adequate veterinary care and food (maybe), the fact remains that there is more to rearing a healthy, well-socialized, quality cat. Purchasing a kitten from a pet shop denies you the one-on-one relationship with the breeder, the one person most familiar with all the nuances of your cat's breed and a source of advice on cat care for years to come. This is important when purchasing a pet kitten and absolutely vital if you're thinking of breeding or showing your cat.

Most breeders prefer to sell their kittens directly to those who will live with the cat so that they can exercise more discretion about which homes their kittens will go to live. If the trend continues, fewer pet shops will be able to purchase such kittens for resale. Other arrangements may emerge, though, in which pet shops and breeders might work together. For example, pet stores may eventually provide referrals for breeders in return for a percentage of the sale price, or display cat breeds in the shops, with the breeders exercising ultimate sales discretion.

RESCUE ORGANIZATIONS

If cost is a major factor in obtaining a pedigreed cat, an emerging source is breed rescue organizations. Some rescue projects encompass all breeds and are run by local cat clubs. These organizations work with shelters in their areas, rescuing cats of any recognizable breed. The rescued cats are first examined by veterinarians, vaccinated, neutered or spayed if necessary, and placed in new homes. Because almost all cats relinquished at shelters are adults, these rescue programs rarely have kittens available.

There are also a number of rescue efforts operating for specific breeds. Persians represent more than 60% of all pedigreed cat registrations and therefore are numerous enough for some metropolitan areas to have rescue programs just for them. National breed clubs and independent breed-specific rescue groups are developing networks of supporters beyond their own states. These breed rescue groups depend on fostering and locating new adoptive homes with the help of breed clubs by word of mouth and by information put up on the Internet. Because rescued cats must frequently be shipped to different locations, club members locate people who are willing to drive or fly with the newly adopted cat.

If obtaining a cat from a breed rescue organization sounds appealing, it is necessary to understand that according to the American Humane Association, less than 1% of all cats entering shelters are purebred. Therefore, in all likelihood, there will be a waiting list for any chosen breed, and with a rare breed, a cat might never be available through a rescue organization. Anyone who might not be able to afford a kitten of a specific breed but who would like the satisfaction of giving a homeless cat a place to live might want to adopt any cat he or she can.

The CFA's central office maintains a list of contacts for both allbreed and breed-specific rescue organizations that are known to them. They can be contacted for this list by telephone (1-732-528-9797) or by e-mail (cfa@cfa.org).

RESPONSIBLE BREEDERS

Finding a responsible breeder for any particular breed depends on the breed's rarity. Some of the CFA's rarest breeds are available only because of the interest and efforts of a handful of dedicated breeders scattered across the United States. Several of these breeds are hundreds of years old but are so rare that fewer than 100 kittens are born each year. Obtaining such a kitten may necessitate being placed on a waiting list, buying it sight unseen, and paying the airfare to have it shipped to you. By contrast, the search for the more available breeds often creates the problem of too many choices.

A phone call (1-732-528-9797), letter, or e-mail (cfa@cfa.org) to the CFA will produce a list of breeders in any given location within its influence.

If you call the CFA or visit its Web site (http://www.cfa.org/shows.html), you can find lists and dates for cat shows in your area.

Going to cat shows is the best way to look at the breeds in which you are interested and to make contact with some of their breeders. Referrals from satisfied customers or from veterinarians are also an excellent place to start your search.

There are good breeders—those who adhere to the high ethical breed standards set forth by the CFA and bad breeders—those "backyard breeders" who don't. Whether making contact with breeders through the CFA, through cat shows, through referrals from veterinarians, or by responding to an ad, you will need a few rules of thumb by which you can tell the difference. Here are some guidelines:

1. A responsible breeder will take the time to talk with the prospective owner and share information about the breed, the kitten being sold, and the parents of the kitten, both before and after the purchase.
2. A responsible breeder will interview the prospective owner to determine the kind of home the kitten or cat will have.
3. A responsible breeder will not sell a kitten to just anyone. If he or she feels that the new kitten is not going to a good home with kind, responsible people, then the sale will be canceled.
4. A responsible breeder will not sell kittens before they are 12–14 weeks old and have been vaccinated. Some kittens selected as pets will already be neutered or spayed; for others, the owner will be contractually required to have them altered by a certain age.
5. A responsible breeder does not refuse to offer a written guarantee for a kitten's health. When purchasing a kitten, avoid any breeder who will not give you this.

Also, most reference materials advise people to visit the home of the breeder to look at the sire and dam of the kittens, as well as their other cats to determine their state of health and temperament. Another important purpose is to evaluate the kitten's environment for hygienic practices and cleanliness, because it has an influence on the health of the cats. Undoubtedly, in the best of all possible worlds, this is sound advice and many responsible breeders still invite prospective purchasers into their homes. However, when purchasing a kitten from a breeder in another state, or at a cat show, a home visit may not be possible. Moreover, some breeders, especially those who live alone, may be reluctant to allow strangers into their home. This does not necessarily reflect one way or the other on the quality of the kitten's environment and should be considered in such transactions.

When a home visit is not possible, you can look for other ways to determine if a kitten comes from a clean and healthy environment. One such assurance comes from the CFA's Voluntary Cattery Environment Inspection Program. Developed by the CFA Animal Welfare Committee, this program sets specific minimum requirements for all aspects of feline husbandry within a home cattery. An annual inspection by a veterinarian, using the CFA-supplied checklist, will determine whether the cattery is rated either Approved and meets the minimum standards or Cattery of Excellence and exceeds the minimum standards.

You can also ask a breeder for references from people who have previously purchased kittens; or ask for permission to discuss the breeder's cats with his or her veterinarian.

Ultimately, however, you must accept the fact that cats, like all other living creatures, do get sick. This happens despite the efforts of responsible breeders who may use the best genetic screening techniques available and still produce some kittens with inherited medical conditions or problems. Because of this, a responsible breeder will provide a buyer with a contract containing a written health guarantee. There are tremendous variations in these guarantees, but they should at the very least set forth a period of time during which the buyer may take the kitten or cat to his own veterinarian for inspection. It should also specify what recourse the buyer has if that inspection should determine an illness or defect. The desire to own a purring bundle of fur should not overcome the buyer's good sense, and the contract should be acceptable and fair to everyone concerned.

As important as the contract is under ordinary circumstances, it becomes even more so when the kitten is to be shipped as a breeding cat or as a show cat. In addition to the basic health of the kitten, other important considerations must be made absolutely clear in unambiguous terms. For example, which party is responsible for the cost of return shipping if the kitten is unsuitable for its agreed purpose? Which party must pay for the health certificate for the shipping? In the case of breeding cats, what is the buyer's recourse should the cat fail to breed or should it develop a disqualifying fault that could be passed on to the kittens? One must be very thoughtful about most possibilities when entering into a contract.

WHEN BUYING A KITTEN FOR BREEDING OR FOR SHOWING

Because breeding and show-quality cats involve a larger outlay of money than pet cats, numerous other considerations are as important as the advice given in this chapter. You should consider that you are buying the results of generations of selective breeding for your cat's health and appearance as it pertains to the breed's written standard of perfection. The breed's written standard as set forth by the CFA provides the genetic makeup for the next generation, which will then be your responsibility. When you buy such a kitten, ideally an added benefit is having the breeder become your mentor and guide you through the ins and outs of this hobby, assuming you are a novice.

If you are considering breeding and showing cats, review your cat's breed standard and breed profile in this book. These describe what the ideal example of your breed should look like. However, reading a standard without seeing a living example of the breed is like trying to describe the *Mona Lisa* in words without seeing the painting. Merely developing a mental image is an exercise in futility. Therefore, going to as many cat shows as possible is essential to fully appreciating a kitten's potential. In doing so, you will become much more knowledgeable about the next kitten you acquire. To the novice, all cats may be beautiful. The differences between a Best in Show cat and a pet-quality cat can be subtle to the untrained eye. The next step should be to spend time looking at the winning cats in order to better translate the words of the breed's standard into a visual reality.

Why is cat breeding appealing? The response "I want to make some extra income breeding cats" is likely to send experienced breeders into gales of laughter, because when done ethically and responsibly, breeding is more likely an expensive hobby than a business. Few things in life give such pleasure and a sense of accomplishment as seeing one's protégé being recognized as Best in Show, but few things in life require such dedication, devotion, and just plain work.

For that and for other reasons, experienced breeders are reluctant to let their best kittens go to a novice breeder, no matter how much he or she is willing to pay. They want to be sure that the purchase is not just a whim and that their hard work will be appreciated and perpetuated in future generations.

The very best advice is to find a breeder who is willing to sell a cat for showing in the Premiership classification, which is for neutered or spayed pedigreed cats. Breeders who are reluctant to sell a breeding cat to a novice are much more likely to sell him or her a show cat that has been altered and cannot breed. Showing in Premiership for 6 months or a year has the following benefits:

1. There is normally much less an investment for an altered show cat than for one to be shown in Championship competition and subsequently bred.
2. The novice can learn the ropes of the chosen breed from the inside and can learn the fine points of grooming and care for a show cat. The novice will also learn more about the breed and might have a change of mind about which breed is most interesting. Breed choice is a matter of personal taste.
3. The novice also enjoys the benefit of seeing how things work and being seen. Participating in cat shows reveals your serious intent to breeders who might be the source of your next kitten. The novice also has the advantage of studying which breeders' cats best meet the standard and win at the shows.

Searching for the right breeder from whom to purchase a show cat, either for Premiership or Championship competition, can be the same as searching for a pet-quality cat, but with many added considerations. If you are interested in breeding or showing cats, choose a breeder who will be a mentor and source of advice and information for years to come. The results of a person's selective breeding prac-tices are that breeder's "line"; some people seem to have the Midas touch for combining cats and their pedigrees and then producing winning cats. A visit to a cat show will reveal which cats are currently winning. Researching pedigrees and the Grand Champions, Regional, National, and Breed wins of a cattery as reported in the CFA *Almanac* will show which lines are producing consistently winning cats. Obviously, these cats will be in demand, and the breeder will likely have a waiting list for breeding and show-quality cats.

Here is a hard-and-fast-rule: If a "show kitten" is advertised in the newspaper or just happens to be sitting in the breeder's house "waiting" for a buyer, or if the bargain sounds too good to be true, it probably is and should be avoided.

SELECTING A CAT

There are three good reasons for getting a cat. The first is to live with a pet who will give you friendship and companionship. The second is to have a show-quality cat who can compete in CFA Championship cat shows. The third is to have a cat who will be an asset to a breeding program. Some aspects of the selection process apply to all cats and kittens, no matter what your purpose—mostly those pertaining to health and behavior—but there are different selection requirements for cats with show potential than for cats who will simply live as a member of the family. Of course, cats destined for a breeding program have a very specific set of selection aspects. Often, a kitten is selected for all three reasons. There are many show cats who are used in breeding programs and in addition are companion animals with the complete run of their house. The correct approach for selecting a kitten is not to consider which is best, but which is best for you, your home, and any aspirations you have that involve the cat fancy.

A HEALTHY KITTEN

When you are selecting a kitten, no matter what the purpose, it should be in obvious good health. This is essential for the happiness of all concerned. For this reason, you must be objective even when one or more kittens are tugging at your heart. All kittens are appealing and make it difficult to remain impartial, but you must closely examine the animal for any obvious medical problems. Get a written record of vaccines administered, the dates they were given, and their type. Save this record for your own veterinarian.

Here are several key points to check the kitten:

• **Start with the kitten's coat**, because it is the most apparent. It is also very useful to know about a specific breed's coat, for cat coats vary quite a bit. For that you can read Chapter 6, "Identifying Coat Colors and Patterns," or read any one of the 41 breed descriptions in Part II, "The Cat Fanciers' Association Breeds." Generally, the coat should be downy, lustrous, and void of clumps, mats, or bald patches. Run your fingers through the coat and feel the kitten's skin. It should be free of scaly areas or sores. Look for fleas or signs of fleas, which can be a serious health hazard. Small scabs may indicate fleabites. Sometimes fleas can be seen in the coat as they scurry to their hiding places, but often they cannot. Examine for bits of debris appearing as a salt-and-pepper mixture, which may indicate flea feces or flea eggs that are stuck onto the individual hairs of the coat. A healthy kitten's skin should be smooth without these signs. Bald or bare patches of skin are signs of ringworm or mange, caused by a lack of hygiene and an unhealthy living environment. (Some breeds,

however, such as the Cornish Rex and Devon Rex, have bald spots as kittens, but this is normal for them and not a sign of bad health.)

• **A kitten's eyes should be clear**, with no excessive tearing and with no ulcers on the surface, which start as small white spots and later appear as small indentations. Examine the kitten for anything that appears to be abnormal, such as large sores, redness, lumps, swelling, or physical injuries.

• **A blue-eyed kitten with a white coat may be deaf.** Jingle your keys or swat your hands behind the kitten for a reaction. If there is none, there is a strong possibility of deafness.

• **A kitten's nose should be cool and slightly damp.** A runny nose could indicate the presence of infection. The signs of upper respiratory infection are sneezing, coughing, and a constantly runny nose. Upper respiratory infections can be minor or life threatening with long-term consequences.

• **A kitten's ears should be clean** and uncluttered and have no unpleasant odor exuding from them. Ears that are dirty or show a dark, waxy material within indicate the presence of ear mites. Mites are microscopic parasites that cause an animal to shake its head and rub its ears with its paws. Ear mites, like many external parasites, can be eliminated with veterinary help and cause no permanent damage to the cat. However, it does create questions about the source of the kitten and its living environment.

• **A kitten should have white, clean teeth**, with the upper incisors meeting the bottom incisors evenly. The incisors are present by the fourth week of life. They consist of 12 small teeth in the front of the mouth. All 26 baby teeth are present by the sixth week. Adult cats ultimately have 30 teeth in all. A kitten's gums and inner mouth tissue should be pink; a pale color is a sign of anemia, which could be caused by internal parasites.

• **A kitten's stomach should not bulge abnormally**. If it does, this usually indicates the presence of internal parasites, a possible nutrition problem, or some other medical problem. A bump on or near the navel can be an umbilical hernia and may require medical attention. Important signs of parasitic infestation or many forms of disease in kittens can be of a behavioral nature, with lethargy being the dominant indication. A sick kitten is one with no energy, one with no curiosity, or one that continually sleeps. Other signs of medical problems are unusual secretions, irritated tissue, hair loss, or diarrhea. Chronic diarrhea is a common medical problem in young kittens. Coughing, sneezing, and a running nose or eyes are also common problems.

• **A sound and healthy kitten stands straight and tall**. Its legs will have a linear quality and its walk as well as its run will be bouncy, uninhibited, and effortless. Stilted movement warrants a closer examination.

• **An 8- to 12-week-old kitten should appear to be in good physical proportion**. This means that the individual components of their bodies create a total look that is pleasing and harmonious. You know it when you see it. Kittens this age should be between two and three pounds, with some slight variation depending upon the breed. A kitten that is obviously underweight and too thin or overweight and too fat may develop health problems. Such a kitten may also develop behavior problems. Also, most kittens should receive their first vaccination at 8 weeks of age and their second at 12 weeks.

OTHER ASPECTS OF KITTEN SELECTION

Beyond health considerations, one should take into account the kitten's behavior and personality. Some breeds are quite talkative and highly interactive, with a great desire to be with you most of the time. Other breeds are cool, casual, and laid back and just enjoy watching you. There are cat breeds that are highly energetic and extremely active and others that are quiet and demure. You can familiarize yourself with these aspects of specific breed behavior by reading any or all of the 41 breed descriptions in Part II, "The Cat Fanciers' Association Breeds." You should consider whether you want to live with a cat who likes to hop onto your lap, look you in the eyes, and meow at you or whether instead you want to live with one that prefers a greater degree of solitude and privacy. There are breeds that like to climb to high places and those that sleep much of the time. Is this a plus or a minus? It is a matter of personal taste and preference.

Male or female? The cat's sex is really of no importance if the cat is to be neutered or spayed. However, unneutered (whole) male cats must be mated on a frequent basis if they are to remain emotionally sound. Whole male cats past puberty spray powerfully odorous, sexually scented urine against walls, windows, and vertical objects when they are sexually aroused or in need of expressing their territorial rights. A whole male cat will roam if given the opportunity and may fight with other males (see Chapter 7, "Feline Behavior and Misbehavior").

Unspayed females experience estrus (heat) at least twice a year and perhaps more frequently. A female may experience heat cycles until bred. The behavior of a female in estrus is meant to attract a male cat and involves intense vocalization and sexually oriented body language. During estrus, the female cat secretes an odorous fluid intended to attract whole male cats for the purpose of mating.

It is best to have a female family cat spayed (ovariohysterectomy) or have a male neutered (castrated). This will prevent undesirable sexual behavior and unwanted pregnancies. Obviously, this does not apply to cats used for breeding. If registered, spayed females and neutered males can be shown at CFA shows.

Next to health matters, nothing is more important than selecting a kitten that has no abnormal behavior and appears to be emotionally stable. A playful yet calm and stable disposition is the ideal. Aloofness in a kitten is not the same as shyness and is more than likely a characteristic of its breed. On the other hand, a shy kitten is abnormally afraid of anything unfamiliar and avoids contact with humans, other animals, or changes of any kind. Constant attempts to escape, cringing, cowering, and defensive aggression are aspects of shy behavior. Kittens with no curiosity and who are not energetic, playful, and enthusiastic about greeting you may be physically sick or have a behavior problem. Of course, kittens can also be tired when being viewed and may simply need a nap.

Those that have been socialized early in life generally do not have an aversion to human handling. Knowledgeable breeders know that kittens are more adaptive to living in the human environment if they have been allowed to remain with their mother and littermates for a minimum of 10 weeks and have been lovingly held on a daily basis.

Characteristics inherited from a kitten's parents also have a decided effect on cat behavior. Pay attention to the kittens' mother, if she is available. If she is at ease with strangers, congenial, outgoing, and friendly, then her kittens are likely to behave in the same manner, providing external influences do not change them.

Kneel down and observe which kittens in the litter are curious and friendly and rub up against you. Lift them one by one. Are they at ease with you? A perfectly normal kitten will squirm about playfully or calm down and begin to purr. A friendly, outgoing kitten will respond energetically to anything dangled in front of it,

such as a peacock feather or to something round and rolling. A happy, self-assured kitten that delights in the company of humans is likely to enjoy good health and long life.

Selecting a show cat is a much more involved matter. Advice from someone with years of experience and a good eye for show-quality kittens is required. Before you do anything, it is best to go to CFA-sanctioned cat shows and see as many examples as you can of the breed in which you are interested. It will not be difficult at a cat show to make friends with a breeder who can serve as a mentor. Read as much as you can about your breed of interest and study its CFA show standard; the standard for each breed follows at the end of each of the 41 breed descriptions in Part II, "The Cat Fanciers' Association Breeds." From the standard and from an experienced mentor you will learn about your breed's characteristics as they pertain to coat color, pattern, physical proportion, and all the rest that is part of Championship competition at a CFA-sanctioned cat show. Experienced, highly knowledgeable exhibitors and breeders are capable of making educated guesses at which kittens have real show potential, which is to say which ones are good examples of their breed.

Looking for a cat to add to a breeding program is not for the inexperienced fancier. Established breeders will often bring in a new breeding cat to add a desired coat color, pattern, or physical type to a breeder's line of cats.

No matter whether you want a kitten or adult cat as a companion, for breeding, or for showing, the basics for selecting one as described above apply. Whether you decide to obtain a cat from a breeder or a shelter or whether you decide on pedigreed or nonpedigreed, doing careful screening and some homework on the subject will help ensure that you select a kitten that will give you joy for many years to come.

Chapter **5**

Cat Fanciers' Association Cat Shows

BY DAN PETTY AND TRACY PETTY

Attending a cat show is a wonderful way to see many breeds of cats up close. If you are thinking about buying a pedigreed cat, it is also a great way to meet people who breed the cat or cats you are considering. Often cat shows have nonpedigreed cats available for adoption from shelters or humane organizations, as well as vendors selling all types of cat supplies, toys, bedding, scratching posts, and cat trees.

WHAT IS A CAT SHOW?

A cat show is a competitive event offering exhibitors and breeders an opportunity to have their cats judged by trained professionals to determine how closely their cat meets the written standard established for that breed. Additionally, the cats are judged on their appearance, health, condition, and temperament. There are no obedience classes as at a dog show, nor do cats have to run or move about on a leash; however, they are inspected by each judge. The judge handles and examines every cat and compares each one to its own breed standard and decides which cats come closest to meeting that standard. The standard describes such things as the ear size and set, body length, and coat color and pattern for that particular breed. The official CFA breed standards are available at the end of each breed description in Part II, "The Cat Fanciers' Association Breeds."

Additionally, shows provide a social environment in which breeders and exhibitors have the chance to compare notes on things such as grooming and feeding or to discuss issues pertaining to the cat fancy. The cat show environment would not be complete without socializing and the opportunity to show off the results of one's dedicated breeding program.

Each cat in a show competes in one of five categories: Kittens, Championship, Premiership, Veteran, or Household Pet. Kitten Class is for pedigreed cats at least 4 months of age and younger than 8 months. There is no penalty if a kitten is neutered or spayed, but no kitten or cat in any category may be declawed. Championship Class is for intact (able to breed) pedi-

Within the Championship and Premiership Classes, cats compete at one of three levels. Each cat starts out as an Open. After receiving six Winner ribbons as an Open, whole cats become Champions and altered cats become Premiers. They are then eligible to earn Grand points. Champions and Premiers receive one Grand point for each Champion or Premier they defeat, either within their breed or by receiving an award in a final. A Champion must accumulate 200 points to reach the third level, Grand Champion, and a Premier needs 75 points to become a Grand Premier.

Cat shows happen every weekend of the year in many cities around the United States. To find a cat show, you can check your local newspaper for weekend activities. Several of the national cat magazines list upcoming cat shows. A list of CFA-licensed shows, along

greed cats 8 months of age and older. Altered (neutered or spayed) pedigreed cats compete in the Premiership Class. The newest class, the Veteran Class, is for pedigreed cats 7 years of age and older. Although cats over 7 years can compete in the other classes, this class is reserved especially for older cats. The competition is not as stringent as in the other pedigreed classes and is appreciated by owners whose cats have been "retired" from the show bench. Any cat may compete in the Household Pet Class if it is at least 4 months of age and is altered if it is 8 months or older. Household Pet Classes are usually for nonpedigreed cats, although occasionally a pedigreed cat with a feature that would disqualify the cat from championship competition (for example, a Scottish Fold with straight ears, a tailed Manx) will compete as a Household Pet. Pedigreed cats competing as Household Pets do not receive any special consideration or advantage because they are pedigreed.

CFA-licensed show judge evaluating a finalist.

with the phone number of a person involved with each show to contact for information, can be found on the CFA Web site at http://www.cfa.org/shows.html.

Many people arriving at their first cat show are overwhelmed by the size of the show hall and the hubbub of activity. Everyone is busy setting up cages, grooming the cats, or taking cats to and from the judging rings. No matter how big or small a show is, all show halls have at least two distinct areas: the benching cages, where the cats stay while waiting to be called to a judging ring; and the judging area, where the judge handles each cat in the show. Benching cages are usually arranged in aisles and are decorated with anything from simple sheets to extravagant lace, sequins, feathers, and beads. The judging rings have no decorations on the cages and are set up similar to a small stage, with seats in front of the judging table for people to sit and watch as the judge works.

Judging rings are divided into two types, Allbreed or Specialty. Allbreed rings, as the name suggests, means Kittens, Championship cats, and Premiership cats compete with all other breeds in the show. Specialty rings divide the breeds into longhair breeds and shorthair breeds, and the cats compete only with other breeds in their specialty.

Each cat in the show is assigned a number for the show (starting with Kitten Class and Number One), and each ring has a schedule of the order in which the cats will be judged. The ring clerk calls a group of cats to the ring by number and places a card with the cat's number on a cage. Usually the cards are either blue or pink, indicating the cat is male or female. In the Championship, Premiership, and Household Pet Classes, male cats are never placed in adjacent cages. The clerk will either assign females to the cages between the males or leave the cage empty. That is why sometimes the numbers are out of order in the judging ring,

and the judge will depend on the numbered cards to know which cat is which.

Each judge handles every cat in the show, checking for general health and condition, as well as comparing the cat to the written standard for its breed. The judge determines how the cat will be handled, but often the body style of the breed will dictate the handling. For instance, the long-bodied breeds, such as Siamese and Maine Coons, are often stretched to accentuate their length of body, while the more compact, round-bodied breeds, Persians and Burmese, for example, are usually placed on the table to show their roundness. The judge will feel the condition of the body and look at the head both from the front and in profile and usually will use a toy or sound to get the cat's attention and make it open its eyes and bring its ears to an attentive posture. The judge systematically goes through each cat in the class, awarding ribbons along the way, and finally hanging the best and second best of breed awards. This is called color class judging.

COLOR CLASSES

Watching color class judging can be confusing because often most or all of the cats seem to get the same ribbons. Actually, the judge is following a precise progression, beginning with cats of the same sex, color, and competitive level (Kitten, Championship, Premiership) and continuing through the class until the best of each breed is awarded.

Following color class judging is definitely a learned skill, so do not be discouraged if you do not catch on just from watching. One easy thing to remember is that the darker the color of the ribbon, the better the award. For instance, the first ribbons given are blue for first place, red for second place, and yellow for third place. These awards represent the very initial judging category, which is within sex, color class, and level. As many as six cats of the same color may get a first-place ribbon, and that is just the first step. Next, the judge will choose the best and second best of color class. Again, a color class is not necessarily all one color; each breed's standard prescribes how many color classes are in the breed. The judge will award a black ribbon for best of color class and a white ribbon for second best of color class. After judging all the color classes in the breed, the judge will then choose the best of breed and award a brown ribbon, and second best of breed will receive an orange ribbon. Even seasoned cat exhibitors sometimes get confused by color classes; just remember that the darker ribbons (blue, black, and brown) are the best.

There are two other ribbons that may be awarded in color class judging if eligible cats are present. A winners ribbon is a red-white-and-blue–striped ribbon awarded to the best male and female Open in the color class. A

purple ribbon may be awarded to the best Champion or Premier in the breed. Only cats that have received a blue ribbon are eligible for a Winners ribbon or best Champion or Premier ribbon.

After the judge has finished all the breeds within the group to be judged, 10 cats or kittens (or 15 kittens, if applicable on the basis of the number entered in the show) will be called back to the ring and the judge will present a Final, ranking the cats best through tenth best. At this point, the judge usually shows each cat to the audience and explains what is exceptionally good about the cat and how it meets its breed standard.

SHOW HALL ETIQUETTE

Want to fit right in at your first cat show? Here are a few tips on what you should do and what you should never do.

First and foremost, and probably the hardest rule to follow is do not touch the cats. Although many of the cats in the show would be happy to have an occasional stroke on the head or scratch under the chin, imagine having 500 people wanting to scratch your chin. You will notice in the rings that the judge squirts disinfectant on his or her hands and the table after each cat, and a steward wipes out each cage after a cat leaves. This is done because, as with people, cats are used to germs from their own environment, and what does not bother one cat may make the next one sick. It also helps prevent the cats from smelling previous cats, which can be very stressful, especially to male cats. These are the same reasons spectators cannot go from one cat to the next, petting each one or letting cat after cat touch the same toy. Some exhibitors may let you pet their cat if they are not getting ready to go to a ring, but they will almost certainly ask you to disinfect your hands first. Do not be offended; they are just looking out for their cat's health.

Second, give people carrying cats the right of way. Aisles in some show halls become very crowded and difficult to navigate, and the exhibitors are responsible for getting their cats to the rings on time so that they will not be marked absent. Spectators are welcome to sit in the chairs in front of the judging ring but should not walk behind the judging table into the ring. Youngsters must be kept calm when they are near the cats; running or wild movements can upset cats who are not used to the behavior of children.

While most exhibitors are happy to talk to you about their breed, they probably will not have time when their cat is due to be called for judging. Exhibitors also need to listen for the announcements that are being made in the show hall, so conversations may be frequently interrupted if they are listening for their cat's class to be called. Remember that exhibitors' first priority is to show their cats in the best condition they can, but if you will be patient, they usually will be happy to answer your questions.

Exhibitors are almost always willing to talk about their breed and their cats if they are not busy getting them ready for judging, but be sensitive in how you approach the subject. You probably will not get a very warm reception if you try to open a conversation with a Japanese Bobtail breeder by asking, "What did you do to its tail?" or if you tell an American Curl breeder that "That's the weirdest thing I've ever seen." All cat breeds are shown naturally with all the physical properties they were born with and without surgical alterations (such as ear trimming or tail bobbing) or special haircuts. And even if you think it's true, don't tell an exhibitor that you have a cat at home that looks just like their cat, or that their cat looks like one on TV.

Getting ready to show with some last-minute touch-ups.

Good subjects to ask about are the cat's personality or what is involved in getting it ready for a show. Some cats take only a few minutes of grooming; others need hours in the bath and with a hair dryer the day before the show. You can ask about size of litters or activity level of the breed, but it is unacceptable to ask breeders how many cats they have. While you may just be curious, they may view it as an invasion of privacy. You will probably not get an answer, and the conversation with the breeder may end right there.

Whether you can ask questions in the judging ring will depend on the judge. Some judges like to talk about the cats as they judge them, and they will probably be receptive to one or two questions about a breed. Other judges prefer to focus all their attention on the cat and would not appreciate being interrupted to answer a question while they are judging.

Most judges are happy to answer a question during a break or when they are waiting for cats to come to the ring, but remember that they are following a schedule and cannot spend a lot of time talking, as that might result in a schedule conflict with another ring.

Another thing to be aware of at a cat show is the "cat loose" call. Felines, of course, have a will of their own and sometimes they just feel like taking off at an inappropriate time. Cats in a show should never be on the floor, so if one does escape the control of its exhibitor or the judge, someone nearby will usually yell, "Cat loose." That is the signal for all doors to the room to be shut so that the cat cannot leave the show hall. If you are standing near a door, close it and stand nearby until the cat is caught to make sure no one opens the door from the other side. If you see the loose cat, do not try to catch it or run after it. Raise your hand to signal that the cat is in your area, and let the owner retrieve it. Even a very sweet cat may be confused or frightened by the commotion and unfamiliar surroundings and may bite or scratch a stranger, so it is best for the cat if the owners pick it up.

SHOWING YOUR CAT

Do you think your cat has the temperament and good looks to be in a cat show? You can find a show to enter the same way you find a show to visit; check magazines or the CFA Web site (www.cfa.org/shows.html). If your cat is not a CFA-registered pedigreed cat, you'll need to ask the contact person if there will be a Household Pet Class at the show, and which day or days it will take place. The contact person can also tell you how to get your cat entered in the show, because all cats must be entered in advance.

Before the show, you will need to get your cat as clean as you can. Clip the sharp points off all of the cat's claws; this is very important, and if you cannot do it yourself, ask someone at your veterinarian's office to help you. Unclipped nails can be as sharp as needles, and clipping the nails prior to a bath reduces the possibility of being badly scratched during the bathing process. Further, CFA Show Rules require that all of a cat's nails be clipped prior to competing in a cat show. Bathe the cat if it will let you, being sure to rinse all the shampoo out of the coat. Use a cotton swab and gently clean the inside parts of the ear that you can see.

You will need to bring your cat to the show in a cardboard, fabric, or plastic carrier. Bring along a litter pan, food, and a food and water bowl. You will also need some sheets or towels to put around the inside of the cage and something like binder clips or safety pins that you can use to attach them. Finally, a cat bed or rug to lie on and a favorite toy may make your kitty's cage almost as good as home.

When you arrive at the show, you will have to check in, and you will receive a catalog with your cat's number. You will also be assigned a benching cage. There will be a schedule either in the catalog or one available at the check-in table, so you will know when your cat will be judged in each ring. Set up your benching cage, and when the show starts, listen for your cat to be called to a ring. Before going to the ring, check again to make sure your cat is as clean and presentable as he can be. Longhaired cats should be combed, and all cats need to have their eyes checked and wiped with a clean tissue if any moisture has accumulated in the corners. If your cat wears a collar, it should be removed before you go to the judging ring. Now you are ready to compete.

When you arrive at the judging ring, one of the cages will have your cat's number on it. Place your cat in the cage with its number. You can sit or stand in front of the ring and watch the judging. When the clerk or judge lays the number card down on top of the cage, you may remove your cat and return it to its benching cage. Listen for the Final to be announced when the judge finishes judging all the cats in your class. If your cat's number is called for a Final, you should follow the same procedure as you did for the judging. You may be called to another ring for judging before the Final, depending on how many cats are present and the schedule, so listen to any announcement concerning your cat's group.

Keep in mind that the judges who will be handling your cat(s) are trained professionals who met stringent requirements prior to entering the judging program (that is, at least 10 years of experience in the cat fancy as an exhibitor and breeder of numerous titled cats). Once the individual is accepted into the program, other CFA-licensed judges train that person. It usually takes a minimum of 5 years of hands-on experience to advance through the various levels of the program to reach the ultimate goal of Approved Allbreed Judge. More than half of the CFA's judges have been judging for over 15 years, with many of these judges having 25 or more years of judging experience.

JUNIOR SHOWMANSHIP

To attract the younger individuals in a household, the CFA created the Junior Showmanship (JS) Program in 1999. JS provides the opportunity for young people between ages 8 and 15 to be involved in an educational and meaningful competition focusing on pedigreed cats. The program is designed to foster knowledge of CFA pedigreed cats and their written standard, general feline health considerations, and grooming and care of cats, as well as to develop self-confidence and sportsmanship in young people. Junior Showmanship Classes are judged on the ability of the exhibitor to handle his or her cat and the knowledge of his or her breed. The quality of the cat is not judged. Handlers will be asked to present their cat to the judge in a manner that emphasizes its best attributes, answer basic questions on the breed standard, answer questions on general care of cats, and answer questions on the CFA's rules and regulations. The program provides a competition in which they can learn, practice, and improve in all areas of handling skills and sportsmanship. It is intended that JS competitors will become further educated in the care of cats, including feeding, vaccinations, habitat. Junior Showmanship classes are available at many CFA shows.

The people you will meet at cat shows are from all walks of life, but they have one common bond: cats. Cat shows are a wonderful opportunity to see the variety of pedigreed breeds available, meet breeders of cats you might like as companions someday, and have fun.

Identifying Coat Colors and Patterns in the Domestic Cat

BY PAT JACOBBERGER

When people acquire a kitten or a cat, the first thing they do is decide on a name for their new pet. Beyond that, you may wish to identify and understand the color and pattern characteristics of your new friend. Many of the colors and patterns found in the domesticated cat, such as white spotting and tortoiseshell, can be traced back thousands of years. Learning the specifics about the color and pattern of your cat or kitten can be fun, interesting and, ultimately, important if you become separated from your pet. For these reasons, this chapter contains some basic information to help you discover the color and pattern of your special friend.

HISTORICAL BACKGROUND

The domesticated cat has associated with humankind for over 4,000 years. Many of the colors and patterns that are discussed here have developed over the intervening centuries. The progenitor of the domesticated cat is generally regarded by experts as *Felis libyca*, a small, short-haired, brown mackerel tabby cat that roams today in limited numbers in North Africa, the Middle East, Corsica, Sardinia, and Majorca. It is from the basic template—brown mackerel tabby—that the domesticated cat has derived the richness of the color and pattern palette available today. The earliest coat, color, and pattern mutations are referred to as "the seven ancient mutations." They form the basis of further coat patterns and color mutations that we now regard as commonplace.

- **Long hair:** Because early domesticated cats lived and evolved on high plateaus, their coats may have mutated to a longer length for warmth.
- **Blotched or classic tabby pattern:** The classic tabby pattern mutation was most likely the result of a change in the environment where cats roamed. The mackerel pattern is more suited to provide camouflage for an animal in the tall grasses of the tundra or the steppes. A blotched pattern seems more suited to camouflage cats who are living in forested or jungle surroundings.

- **Solid color or self color:** A solid or self-colored cat is one where there is one single solid color throughout the coat.
- **Dominant white:** The genetics of this color and pattern create a coat that is completely white. The dominant white gene "masks" or suppresses the expression of any other color or pattern. The cat may have blue, yellow, gold, or odd eyes (one blue and one yellow or gold).
- **White spotting:** The gene that causes white spotting or piebalding can produce as little white as a locket on the chest or belly, one white toe, or a smear of white down the nose all the way to white that nearly covers the entire cat.
- **Sex-linked orange or red:** Cats displaying the tortoiseshell, calico, patched tabby patterns, or any of these patterns occurring at the points and/or combined with white are nearly always female because two X chromosomes are required to carry both of the required red genes.
- **The dilution factor:** The dilution gene influences the intensity of color in the cat and affects a number of colors and patterns.

EYE COLOR

The variance in eye color in the domesticated cat is vast. Colors most often seen are yellow, gold, green, hazel, and blue. In pedigreed breeds, eye color is dependent primarily on selective breeding for stability. This is not the case in randomly mated cats, so there are a number of cats with eye color and patterns that are not considered correct or appropriate in some pedigreed cats.

Notable exceptions where eye color is directly affected by coat color and pattern genes include the blue eye color of the Siamese gene; the blue eye color associated with the dominant white gene; the yellow eye color related to the Burmese gene, and the blue-green (aqua) eye color that results from the combination of the Burmese and the Siamese genes.

PATTERNS AND COAT COLORS

Patterns and colors are not, in and of themselves, breeds. They are the decoration that a cat wears. In pedigreed cats, patterns and colors are used to identify, group, and classify cats within distinct breeds. For some breeds, a pattern is a defining characteristic that helps to distinguish the breed (e.g., Ocicat, Egyptian Mau, Turkish Van).

A pattern can become the backdrop for the addition of just about any color. While the colors may change from cat to cat, a pattern remains the same. For example, in the solid-color pattern, the expectation is that there are no markings or white of any kind. It does not matter, then, if the solid-colored cat is black, blue, white, or lilac. The same color covers the entire cat.

Consider the classic tabby pattern as another example. The markings are specific. It makes no difference, then, if the cat is a silver tabby or a brown tabby, a pedigreed cat or not. The swirls, barring . . . all the markings are the same. Many patterns can combine as well—there is no end of possible combinations. Each pattern described below can be seen in full color in the color insert following page 194.

SOLID COLOR
The coat is made up entirely of one color. There are no tabby markings, no white lockets, and no readily apparent changes between the tip of

the hair and where it exits the skin. Colors in the solid color spectrum include

- Black—also known as Ebony
- Blue—often referred to as gray
- Red—also termed orange, sometimes tangerine
- Cream—also known as beige, yellow or tan
- White
- Chocolate—sometimes called sable or brown
- Cinnamon
- Lavender
- Lilac
- Fawn—a beige-toned lilac

TABBY

There are five tabby patterns known to occur in the domestic cat. They are

- Mackerel tabby
- Classic tabby (called blotched tabby in Europe, Australia, and New Zealand)
- Spotted tabby
- Ticked tabby
- Patched tabby

A tabby pattern is actually a combination of two patterns—one superimposed on the other. The ground color (the lighter areas of the coat) is a universal camouflage pattern found in a number of mammals such as mice, rabbits, and squirrels. In this portion of the tabby pattern, each individual hair has alternating bands of yellow and black. The second pattern of the tabby is created by the replacement of the agouti-banded hairs with solid-colored hairs. This is made up of all the ornamental markings—the pencilings, swirls, and spots.

Mackerel Tabby Pattern

The mackerel tabby is referred to as the "wild type" tabby pattern. The markings are dense and clearly defined and are made up of narrow pencilings. The legs are barred with narrow bracelets, which come up to meet the body markings. The tail is barred with tail rings. The necklaces on the neck and chest look like multiple chains. There is an M on the forehead and lines run back from the eyes. The spine lines run together to form a narrow saddle, and narrow pencilings run around the body.

Classic (Blotched) Tabby Pattern

The name blotched is derived from the irregular spirals and whirls of tabby markings. The markings are dense, clearly defined, and broad. The legs are evenly barred with bracelets that come up to meet the body markings. The tail is ringed, and there are several necklaces on the neck and upper chest. On the forehead is an intricate letter M, and there are swirls on the cheeks and vertical lines that run over the back of the head and extend to the shoulder markings. The shoulder markings are in the shape of a butterfly, with both the upper and lower wings outlined and marked with dots inside the outline. The back markings include a vertical line that runs down the spine from the butterfly to the tail, with a vertical stripe paralleling it on each side. There is a large solid blotch on each side of the body that is encircled by one or more rings. There is a double vertical row of buttons on the chest and stomach.

Spotted Tabby Pattern

The markings on the body are spotted. The spots may vary in size and shape and sometimes seem to run together in a broken mackerel pattern. A spine line, usually composed of spots, runs the length of the body. The markings on the face and forehead are the typical tabby markings. The underside of the body has "vest buttons," and the legs and tail are barred.

Ticked Tabby Pattern

The body hairs are ticked with various shades of the main marking color and ground color. The body, when viewed from the top, is free from noticeable spots, stripes, or blotches, except for some darker shading along the spine. The lighter underside usually shows tabby markings. The face, legs, and tail show distinct tabby striping. Most cats with this pattern have at least one distinct necklace.

Patched Tabby Pattern

Patching can occur in any of the tabby patterns—classic, mackerel, spotted, or ticked. Patches or softly intermingled areas of red or cream on the body and extremities characterize the patched tabby pattern. There are several tabby colors:

- **Brown tabby:** The ground color runs the gamut from a brilliant coppery brown to a darker, more subdued brown. The markings are dense black.
- **Blue (gray) tabby:** The ground color is a pale, bluish ivory. The markings are a very deep blue.
- **Red Tabby:** The ground color is red. The markings are a deeper-colored rich red.
- **Cream tabby:** The ground color is a very pale cream. The markings are buff or cream.
- **Silver tabby:** The ground color is pale, clear silver. The markings are a dense black.
- **Cameo tabby:** The ground color is off-white. The markings are red, and the undercoat is white.
- **Brown patched tabby:** The ground color is the same as for the brown tabby, and the markings are dense black. There are patches or softly intermingled areas of red on the head, body, and extremities.
- **Blue patched tabby:** The ground

color is pale, bluish ivory. The markings are very deep blue or gray. There are patches or softly intermingled areas of cream on the head, body, and extremities.
- **Silver patched tabby:** The ground color is pale silver with markings of dense black. There are patches or softly intermingled areas of red and/or cream clearly defined on the head, body, and extremities.

SHADED

Cats with shaded patterns all share the common characteristic of having color only at the tips of the hair and a pure white undercoat. The three primary groupings are chinchilla, shaded, and smoke. The major difference between each is the extent of the tipping.

In the chinchilla pattern, all of the color is at the very tip of the guard hair. The color may be one of any of the solid colors or tortoiseshell. The coat on the back, flanks, head, and tail is tipped with enough color so that you can see that the cat is not pure white. The legs may be slightly shaded with tipping, but the chin, ear tufts, stomach, and chest are pure white.

In the shaded pattern, all of the color is on the last quarter of the guard hair and may be of any solid color or tortoiseshell. The general effect is much darker than the chinchilla pattern. There is a mantle of colored tipping shading down from the sides, face, and tail from dark on the spine to white on the chin, chest, stomach, and under the tail.

The smoke pattern is characterized by all of the color being on the last half of the guard hair. As before, any recognized solid-color or tortoiseshell-colored cat can have the smoke-pattern. When a smoke-patterned cat is resting, it appears to be a solid color. When the cat is in motion or when you pull the coat backward, the white undercoat is clearly and dramatically apparent.

PARTI-COLORS

The colors influenced by the sex-linked red gene are popular among pet owners. Among those colors are the tortoiseshell and the blue-cream (dilute tortoiseshell).

Generally speaking, a tortoiseshell is a black female cat with random patches of red. If you look carefully at the red areas, you will often see red tabby patterning. This has given

rise, over the years, to the popular belief that the tortoiseshell coat is comprised of three colors—black, red, and cream. In fact, what looks like cream is actually the ground color of the red tabby pattern.

The blue cream (dilute tortoiseshell) is a blue female cat with patches of solid cream. The tortoiseshell pattern can also be colored with chocolate and red or lilac and cream.

BICOLOR PATTERN—CATS WITH WHITE

White spotting or piebalding can occur with any of the colors and patterns discussed so far and with the pointed pattern.

There can be as little white spotting on a cat as a spot or two, or the cat can be nearly white. Referring to the bicolor pattern diagram below, you can see that examples 1 and 10 are cats on the opposite ends of the bicolor continuum.

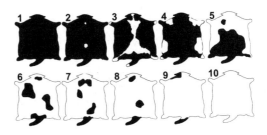

Solid color and white bicolor colors include black and white, blue and white, red and white, cream and white, chocolate and white, and lilac and white.

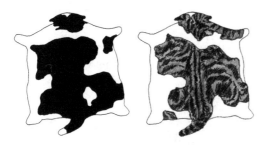

In tabby and white bicolors, the colored portions of the cat may be the classic, mackerel, spotted, ticked, or patched tabby pattern. And of course, bicolored cats may also be black smoke and white or blue smoke and white. The most commonly seen bicolored cats are solid and white (left) and tabby and white (right).

Calico is a color and pattern related to the sex-linked red gene, and calico-patterned cats are generally regarded as bicolors. The archetypical calico cat is a white female cat with large, solid areas of black and red patching, but the calico pattern can be colored in with a number of other colors as well, such as blue and cream—often referred to as a "dilute calico"—lilac and cream, or chocolate and red. As with the bicolor, calico-patterned cats may have just a little bit of white, a lot of white, or anything in between.

POINT RESTRICTED PATTERNS

The Siamese cat is one of the most easily recognized breeds of cat primarily because of its characteristic point-restricted pattern. However, when many people think they are looking at a

Siamese cat, they are in fact looking at a different breed or a cat with a mixed genetic background. The confusion arises because we use the term *Siamese* to identify a pattern, a gene, and a breed of pedigreed cat.

The Siamese pattern is also referred to as the point-restricted pattern, the Himalayan pattern, and the pointed pattern. It is a pattern that is created by the Siamese gene. The Siamese gene is an albino gene, and it influences where and to what degree pigment and/or pattern will be deposited in the animal's hair, skin, and the irises of the eyes. In the case of the Siamese gene, color and pattern are deposited at the coolest parts of the body—at the extremes. As a result, the face, ears, feet, and tail have color and/or pattern while the body of the cat is creamy-colored or white. As a cat with a pointed pattern grows older, the body color darkens because there is an overall decrease of blood flow to the skin.

All cats that have the pointed pattern have blue eyes as a result of the albinism created by the Siamese gene. But remember, all cats with blue eyes are not "Siamese cats."

Any number of colors and/or patterns may appear at "the points" of a pointed-patterned cat, including

- Brown (seal point)
- Blue (blue point)
- Chocolate (chocolate point)
- Lilac (lilac point)
- Red (red or flame point)
- Cream (cream point)
- Tabby (lynx or tabby point)
- Tortoiseshell (torti point)

The pointed pattern may be mixed with white. The amount of white may vary from

just a little (left) to a lot (right). In addition, the points may be any number of colors in any number of patterns.

NAMING CONVENTIONS FOR COLORS AND PATTERNS

So how do you figure out what color and pattern *your* cat is? And then, how do you verbally express that information? Well, there are a number of naming conventions for identifying the pattern and colors of cats.

One common approach is to start with the actual color of the cat. Next, add the basic pattern. After that, add "and white" if the cat is a bicolor. Then add the hair length. Last, add the name of the breed if you can reliably identify it. Now, if you and your cat are separated by accident or by the forces of nature, give this information to the rescue workers at your local humane society. For example, a short-haired cat that is a mackerel tabby in brown and white is termed a "brown mackerel tabby and white short-haired cat." A tabby longhair in silver with red patching is a "silver patched tabby long-haired cat." A long-haired cat with brown and white hair on the feet and head and brown hair on the tail is a "seal point and white long-haired cat."

Hopefully, you will never have to use this information to locate your missing companion cat. Even if you do not, perhaps you now know much more about your wonderful pet than before.

Part

IV

Knowing Cats

7

Feline Behavior and Misbehavior

BY KITTY ANGELL

*W*ith a better understanding and knowledge of feline behavior, you are more equipped to establish *a happy, healthy, and more successful relationship with the cat in your life. This chapter explains what is normal cat behavior, what is not, what is acceptable, what is not, what is correctable, and how to correct it.*

Cats are solitary creatures and have been since they lived in the wild. They are not pack or herd animals. They prefer to hunt alone. Probably the reason they accepted domestication is because they found it easier to get a free meal than hunt for one.

Understanding the behavior basics of the domestic cat will most certainly help you appreciate your new home companion and enjoy her on a deeper level. Knowing your cat—really knowing your cat—allows you to best appreciate one of nature's most fascinating creatures and to cope with what only appears to be mischief and misbehavior.

Through the many years of domestication, the cat has learned to live with humans as well as other domestic animals. The adaptation has not always been easy, and is not complete. As a result, cats in multianimal environments have established certain rules and pecking orders.

If you keep in mind that there is no such thing as a bad cat, both you and your cat will live happier lives. Cats exhibit normal behavior and what we consider misbehavior. Bear in mind that cats misbehave because of health problems, lack of handling, early negative environmental episodes, stress, or abuse.

Certain breeds of cat express different types of behavior. For instance, Persians, American Shorthairs, and Scottish Folds are easygoing, calm cats that are not extremely vocal. Conversely Siamese, Abyssinians, and Cornish Rex are very vocal, tremendously active, and interested in all that goes on around them. This statement holds true most of the time but not *all* the time. Cats are individual creatures just like human beings, so there will always be exceptions to the rule, such as the wired-for-action Persian or the lazy Abyssinian.

NATURAL BEHAVIOR
HUNTING INSTINCT

Cats are true carnivores. They have never lost their hunting instinct, even though few are required to go out and catch their meals. It is not unusual to see a cat in a crouched position, teeth chattering in anticipation, when it sees a bird. An unfortunate mouse in the house of a cat will not be allowed to live very long, although the cat may want to play with it a bit before putting it out of its misery.

SOCIAL HIERARCHY

Cats have evolved from living solitary lives into patterns of group living in which they sort themselves out into social hierarchies without human intervention. Tomcats are still wary of each other and will mark their territories by spraying urine if left unaltered. Female cats generally will interact with each other much more easily. In multicat households as well as in colonies of homeless cats found on or near farms or other unattended areas, they may even groom each other and share nursery duties. Many times a lactating female will nurse another female's kittens without incident.

Cats tend to develop a group hierarchy. Even in homes where all the cats are altered, there will be a contest to establish the top cat. Once this has been decided, subordinate cats will acquiesce to the top cat's demands. Unfortunately, there is also usually a "low cat" who just tries to stay out of everybody's way.

COMMUNICATION

Cats communicate in three primary ways: voice, body language, and the senses.

Voice

Purring is the most common voice message of a cat. This communicates contentment, whether with a human or another cat. A cat that sits on your lap, purrs, and kneads your body with its paws is displaying the same feeling of security and nurturing with you as with its mother. Newborn kittens knead the areas on each side of their mother's nipples to express milk. When your cat kneads you, it is simply making you its surrogate mother.

Vowel sounds are used by the cat to complain, express bewilderment, beg, or demand. These sounds are variations of the traditional *meow* and can express urgency.

High-pitched, high-intensity sounds are made when the cat is agitated, excited, or in some form of stress. The mating call of the female, for example, has a high-pitched cry and is similar to the shriek of a cat in pain. Other sounds in this category include growling, wailing, hissing, and the 'spit' sound used in fighting.

Body Language

Cats have five basic facial expressions that they combine with body language to communicate:

1. A relaxed and happy cat carries its ears in its normal position, and the pupils of the eyes are normal size for the prevailing light. The body is in a relaxed level position. The tail is held out at a 40-degree angle or lower.
2. An angry cat keeps its ears erect but rolled back, and its whiskers bristle forward. The pupils constrict to slits. Some angry cats walk very erect and on tiptoe while their body slants downward because of their longer back legs. Sometimes cats arch their bodies and the hairs on their tails stand on end. This "Halloween cat" position can happen with an angry or a frightened cat.
3. A frightened cat will lay its ears and whiskers flat. Its pupils of the eye will dilate. Fear will cause the cat to assume a crouched position, curling its paws close

together under its body. It will salivate and spit.

4. When hunting, a cat assumes an intense look, its pupils open and ears and whiskers thrust forward. It may assume a semi-crouched position, like a bird dog on point, as it prepares to spring.

5. An ecstatic cat when being loved and petted, has half-closed eyes. Its ears and whiskers are in their normal position.

The Senses

Smell, vision, and hearing are extremely important forms of feline communication. While cats are known as fastidious creatures, their most common form of communication with scent is through urine marking, anal secretions, and skin secretions.

Unaltered males are highly territorial, and marking the perimeters of their dominion is extremely important to them. Females that have not been altered spray sexually scented urine during their estrus cycle to alert nearby males to their presence and sexual receptivity.

Cats that circle each other are usually trying to get a whiff of anal secretions to investigate whether they have encountered a friend or foe.

When a cat winds between your legs and rubs or butts its head against your body, it is called *bunting behavior*. This action transfers the cat's scent onto the human by means of glandular secretions from its facial area, in the case of head-butting, or from the olfactory glands in the tail, when winding between the legs.

In both visual and auditory acuity, cats have the advantage over humans in most instances. They have a reflective layer (*tapetum*) inside the eye that allows them to see better with less light than humans. Because of their advanced range of hearing, they can detect the ultrasonic calls of rodents and are more responsive to the calls of their kittens.

FAST FACTS ABOUT FELINE BEHAVIOR

CATS SLEEP MOST OF THEIR LIVES. True. Cats spend 40% to 60% of their lives sleeping. Much of this depends on whether they are indoor cats with no need to hunt or outdoor cats who must catch their dinner. Their sleeping habits involve catnaps rather than long 8-hour snoozes. They are nocturnal by nature, which can cause problems for those who require a good night's sleep. For this reason, good social interaction and play during the daylight hours are important.

CATS ALWAYS LAND ON THEIR FEET. Almost true. Cats possess a remarkable trait called a *righting reflex*. Kittens use this reflex as newborns to orient themselves into an upright position even though they are born blind and unable to walk. In this process, data reaching the brain from the eyes and vestibular apparatus in the inner ear enables the neck muscles to turn the falling cat's head so that it is horizontal and upright. This repositions the body to line up with the head as a result of a reflex action involving nerves along the spinal column. Using this sequence of body movements, the cat nearly always lands on all four feet. It arches its back to help cushion the impact of landing from a fall. The balance of a cat is not supernatural. They can miscalculate, especially when carrying things in their mouths, and fall on their heads. A cat falling from a great distance will most likely land on its feet, but the impact will break its legs.

CATS CAN TRAVEL GREAT DISTANCES TO BE REUNITED WITH THEIR OWNERS. True. *Psi-trailing* is a documented phenomenon in cats. Dr. J. B. Rhine of Duke University, a pioneer of animal extrasensory perception studies, explains: "Psi-trailing is that in which an animal, separated from a person or mate to whom it has become attached, follows the departed companion into wholly unfamiliar territory and does so at a time and under conditions that would allow the use of no conceivable sensory trail. The distance being long enough, then the animal would have to be guided by a still unrecognized means of knowing." The psi-trailing ability of the cat is just one trait that has both astounded and fascinated humans. Totally aware of its environment, the cat responds to the slightest stimuli with utmost confidence and lack of hesitation. The cat also is a master of foreknowledge, and this special sense can be both amusing and lifesaving.

MISBEHAVIOR

Misbehavior in cats comes from learned experiences as well as from environmental influences. Rarely are they from inherited characteristics. If the cause of the improper behavior is not from a physical problem, then it is almost always from acquired bad habits. Cats are creatures of habit, and once they have learned a behavior, good or bad, it is very difficult to unlearn it.

The most common forms of misbehavior are improper elimination, aggression, antisocial behavior, late-night attention-seeking and vocalizing, and improper scratching and chewing.

People who excel at parenting children have been known to turn their pussycats into terrible little tigers! They create misfits who make everyone's life miserable with inappropriate behavior by giving their cats no boundaries or house rules and by never using the word *no*.

Cats who are taken from their mothers too soon or who are left alone for long periods of time with no socialization will have difficulty learning how to interact with others. Abandoned cats who have had to fend for themselves and have suffered from cruelty either from other animals or people will have a hard time adjusting to a normal life.

When attempting to retrain a cat whose behavior is unacceptable, try to understand the source of the cat's motivation. What is causing the cat to act this way? Forget about the spite theory. Your cat does not misbehave just to get back at you.

IMPROPER ELIMINATION

Mother cats are wonderful. They teach their kittens how to eat properly, clean themselves, and use the litter box. Then something happens. The well-brought-up kitten stops using the litter box and starts peeing in a corner of your dining room or on your favorite plant. Even worse, you might find unwanted droppings left in your bathtub or in your shoe. What do you do?

First, take the cat to the veterinarian to make sure there is no health problem. Lower urinary tract disease is one of the most common causes of cat's not using their litter boxes. Once health issues have been ruled out, explore the cat's motivation for the unwanted behavior and start a process of retraining.

The single worst mistake people make is imposing punishments such as spanking, rubbing the cat's nose in the urine, or hollering at the cat. This teaches the cat that the very action of urination is improper, which will cause a new set of problems, including possible medical ones.

Many stressful circumstances can cause improper elimination. Unclean litter boxes, changes in types of litter, repositioning of the litter box, moving to a new home, and adding a new cat, dog, or person to the household can create emotional stress and trigger this upsetting behavior.

If there is more than one cat in the house, more than one litter box should be used. Each litterbox should be cleaned frequently, with new litter added as needed. If a different type of litter is introduced, try gradually mixing it with the old type in an attempt to familiarize the cat with the new product. Bear in mind that cats hate change.

If your cat stops using the litter box, you will have to retrain it. Confine the cat to a small area, such as a wire cage, where it must use the litter box because of limited floor space. If it is not possible to obtain a wire cat cage for this purpose, a small bathroom or utility room with linoleum or ceramic tile floors will suffice. The cage is a better choice because its food, water, and bedding inside leave little room for the cat to eliminate outside the litter box.

As the cat begins to use the litter box with more frequency, it should be allowed gradual access to other parts of the house. Depending on the appropriateness of behavior, these periods out of the isolation area can become longer and longer. During the periods of free roaming around the house, the cat should be closely supervised.

It usually takes several weeks to complete this retraining process. During this period, the target spots for the improper elimination should be thoroughly cleaned. In severe cases, the carpet and pad may need to be replaced. It is very important that the cat smell no reminder of its old ways when it is once again allowed to roam the house.

For cats who use potted plants as their personal toilets, try rimming the edge of the pot with double-stick tape. Cats despise the feeling of double-stick tape on anything. Dump out the old soil and replenish the pot with new soil. Then add a layer of decorative rocks to the top of the soil, but make sure they are too large for the cat to swallow.

Unaltered cats will automatically spray urine to mark their territory. If an altered cat starts spraying, it is usually because it feels threatened by something or someone. There might be a new neighborhood cat peeking in the window; the house might have been redecorated, thus changing the cat's territory; or one of the other cats in the household might have decided it is time to terrorize him.

In such cases, it is wise to visit your veterinarian and discuss the advisability of antianxiety drug therapy. Another approach is using holistic medications such as the Bach Flower Remedies. Walnut is an excellent remedy choice when retraining a cat. It can be found in large health food stores. Animal behavioral experts can also be of great help in a traumatic situation.

AGGRESSION

Broadly speaking, there are two types of aggression: aggression toward humans and aggression toward other animals.

When cats are aggressive toward people, it is usually because of the way they have been handled. Some people allow their play with cats to overextend into the realm of rough handling. The result is that the cat strikes back. Remember that cats are predators by nature and therefore should never be teased or manhandled. Petting a cat roughly or petting for long periods of time can cause a sensitive cat to react with a swift bite or scratch. Avoid turning a cat on its back for rough petting. This elicits a defense mechanism. In the "hunting games" that cats play all their lives, Bird, Mouse, and Rabbit, they catch the hunted animal, pin it down, and then shake it vigorously. This is similar to turning the cat onto its back for petting.

Some behaviorists feel that using a water squirt gun for aggressive behavior is appropriate. Use this method as a last resort only. Instead, use a key word like *no* or *ouch* in a high-pitched voice. Then pick the cat up and isolate it in a cage or small bathroom for at least 30 minutes. It will soon learn that when it bites, it triggers the key word and isolation.

When a cat exhibits aggression toward another cat it can be a long, hard battle to retrain it. Keep the cat and the other animal separated at first. Give each cat a piece of cloth such as a rag or undershirt with the other cat's scent on it. Allow one cat to roam freely through the house, spreading its scent. Then do the same with the other animal so that each can pick up the scent of the other. Set up litter boxes and food areas for each that are in different places.

Before reintroduction, trim the cat's nails and make sure they've each eaten a good meal. Having a full stomach will act as a calming influence for both animals.

Bring one cat in a carrier into the room with the other animal. This way, both animals can see each other and sniff each other first. In the beginning, do not leave them in a room together without your presence. To be on the safe side, keep a squirt bottle handy in case a fight breaks out. Even a broom used to separate them in a fight is better than reaching in and trying to stop them. Stopping a catfight with your hands is dangerous. Allow your cats to have a means of escape such as a cat tree or an open door to another room, if things go badly.

This process may take several weeks or several months, depending on the personalities of the animals involved and the intensity of their aggression.

ANTISOCIAL BEHAVIOR

Noted vet Soraya V. Juarbe-Diaz, D.V.M., has said that kittens handled daily for the first month of their lives (up to 5 minutes per kitten) have accelerated eye opening, and approach humans more readily. Kittens raised in isolation will be reluctant to approach people, even if they are genetically of a friendly nature. Orphaned kittens who are raised by hand without contact with other cats will often fail to learn to play properly and will have a difficult time interacting with other animals.

It is important, especially for cat breeders, to give individual attention to shy or fearful kittens during their first 3 months of life. Early handling, however, doesn't ensure the development of a good temperament in a kitten. Genetic or other constitutional factors are the cause for approximately 15% of all kittens who resist socialization.

In treating a cat who doesn't like to be touched or petted, you must understand that it is not because the cat does not like you. Some cats just do not like physical contact with anyone. If your cat likes to sit by you, allow this to happen but do not try to pet it. Most owners find that when they stop trying to force physical affection on their cats, the cats become affectionate in other ways. Stop actively trying to make contact by chasing or reaching out to the cat. Find other ways of interacting, such as playing with a peacock feather or throwing a catnip mouse. When the cat does approach, respond with slow, calm movements and a soft voice.

If visitors make sudden or loud noises or

swiftly grab the cat, it will react by hissing and growling to fend off the supposed predator. Be sure to provide the cat with a way to escape should it decide to run. Do not attempt to grab the cat with your hands if it runs off, and let it be.

Using a *systematic desensitization* program is usually successful. Systematic desensitization is a therapy that involves gradually introducing the cat to the situation it fears or dislikes for very brief periods of exposure and rewarding its nonaggressive behavior with a food treat along with gently spoken compliments. At subsequent sessions, gradually increase the exposure time to the frightening situation along with increased rewards. Just give the cat time to establish boundaries of its own for your relationship.

LATE-NIGHT ATTENTION-SEEKING AND VOCALIZATION

Cats are creatures of the night. In the wild, they rest and conserve their energy during the day and stay out of sight of larger carnivores. At night, they gain a heightened sense of smell, hearing, and sight. Cats are also creatures of habit, and once they are accustomed to getting attention by howling and keeping their owners up at night, they will just continue to do it unless they are trained to do otherwise.

Purchase a large cat cage and place it as far away from your bedroom as possible. The cage should be large enough to allow the cat to walk around. Be sure to place water, food, and a litter box in the cage.

Every night, play with the cat just prior to putting it into the cage for the night. The play session will make the cat more inclined to sleep and less likely to howl and prowl all night. Save the evening meal until you put the cat up for the night, thus rewarding it with food when it goes into the cage. Place some favorite toys in the cage for it to play with

should it become restless. Also, keep a small radio in the room and play soft music throughout the night. This method is not cruel punishment; it just makes night roaming a thing of the past.

Try this nighttime caging for about a week. Eliminate the use of the cage for one night to see if the problem has been solved. In any event, the cat needs a night off from the cage whether it vocalizes or not. Your problem may be solved at this point. If not, place the cat back in the cage immediately, when the vocalizing happens. Do not wait for the morning. Repeat the nighttime caging for the next 2 or 3 nights, and then try leaving the cat out of the cage again for the night. If the cat stops the behavior once out of the cage and does not go back to the annoying behavior, there is no need to use the cage anymore. What is wanted is to create an association in the cat's mind of unwanted behavior with being placed in the cage. Eventually the cat will make the connection between its misbehavior and something happening that it does not like (loss of freedom) and will change.

IMPROPER SCRATCHING AND CHEWING
Scratching

Next to sleeping, cats love to groom themselves. One grooming mechanism, which is quite normal, is to scratch an object to remove layers of claw that are loosened and need to be shed. It is very easy to control scratching. First, clip the cat's claws every 10 days to 2 weeks. Second, provide a scratching post that will take the place of your grandmother's settee or other cherished furniture. Purchase a manufactured cat tree. Some of the best cat trees are those with carpeted bases and sisal rope wrapped around their trunks. Cats love to scratch sisal and will choose it over the family furniture.

Chewing

There are two different theories about wool chewing. Some feel it is a behavioral problem that occurs when a kitten is weaned from its mother too soon. In the wild, feral kittens are not weaned until they are 6 months old. Many people want to purchase a very young kitten (6–8 weeks old) because they are so cute. Unfortunately, this is far too soon for a kitten to leave its mother.

Drs. Katherine A. Houpt and T. Richard Houpt presented another theory in *Animal Newsletter*, published by Cornell University College of Veterinary Medicine. The Houpts offered the theory that wool chewing is related to feeding. Cats off their feed were stimulated to chew wool, whereas cats with access to plants and dry food were not as tempted to chew wool. The Houpts feel that wool chewing appears to signal a craving for fiber or indigestible roughage. Give the cat a constant source of fiber. Nontoxic plants such as oats (that are easy to sow and grow) provide both pleasurable nibbling as well as healthful roughage. This measure should be used for cats who like to gnaw on houseplants. If providing the little oat garden isn't enough to stop the chewing behavior, then houseplants and wool must be made unappealing. Give the offending cat an old wool sweater or sock that has been treated with a small amount of hot pepper sauce and sprayed or dabbed with strong perfume. Do the same with the houseplant, but only in a location that will not allow damage to the plant. The cat will come to relate the smell of the perfume on the wool objects and plants with the unpleasant taste of the hot pepper sauce. Once done, you should be able to deter the cat from chewing good wool items and houseplants simply by spraying them with the perfume.

New Kitten Basics

BY MARSHA ZAPP AMMONS

IT'S A NEW . . . CAT!

Bringing a new kitten or cat home can be as exciting as moving into a new home, an occasion remembered for years. In a move, household possessions are carefully wrapped and packed for a safe journey. Likewise, a new companion needs a carrier to ensure its safety en route to its new home, whether being carried there by walking human, by car or by air. The carrier should be large enough to permit the cat to move around comfortably, with enough ventilation holes to help keep it cool.

Department and pet supply stores offer a wide assortment of sizes, styles, and colors. Although cardboard pet carriers are available, plastic carriers will withstand many years of use and are easy to clean. A towel or disposable incontinence pad on the bottom becomes a bed as well as protection in case of litter box accidents; the plastic water cup provided with most carriers snaps on the grated door. A towel or small blanket draped over the carrier provides a windbreak and added warmth in cold weather.

There should be a variety of goodies and necessities awaiting the new arrival at home:

• **Litter box and litter:** These are available in a wide assortment of styles and materials: Hooded or open? Scoop-it-yourself or high-tech self-sifter? Clumping or not? (Remember to buy a scoop.) The breeder or previous owner can advise you about which type of litter box and litter box filler has been used; it's often best to begin with the same type of box and filler. Some cats object to hooded boxes; others will use them. If desired, the type or brand of filler can be changed later by mixing 25% new filler with 75% regular filler, then gradually increasing the new and decreasing the old. A quiet, private location, perhaps a utility room, is best for a litter box, which should be out of reach of toddlers or dogs. A daily scoop, frequent changes, and periodic scrubbing of the litter box with mild soap and a 1:32 bleach–water solution will keep the cat happy and its new home free of waste odors. Special litter-catching mats under the box are a plus in keeping litter particles from being tracked through the house.

• **Food, water, and containers:** The breeder or previous caregiver can offer suggestions on when, how much, and what to feed a cat and often furnishes samples. Keeping the cat on its regular food while it adjusts to a new lifestyle minimizes potential for stress-caused diarrhea. Fresh water must be available at all times and should be replaced daily. Bowls can be plastic, crockery, metal or glass; glass or crockery is easy to clean, has no reaction to flavors, and will not promote bacteria. The depth of the bowl should depend on the cat's head structure: Abyssinians, Siamese, Russian Blues, Maine Coons, and many other breeds can use a deeper dish, while shallower bowls are better for shorter-muzzled cats, such as Persians and Orientals. Food also can be served on small paper plates, which can be thrown out after each meal.

• **A cat bed:** The bed can be a cardboard or plastic box lined with a towel, a fuzzy or cozy manufactured cat bed purchased at a cat show or pet supply store, or your own bed. Because of allergies or special situations, some humans put their cat's bed in an unused guest room or utility room. Bedding should be machine-washed occasionally in hot water.

• **Toys:** Sometimes the best toys are the least obvious—empty spools of thread, an empty paper sack, long feathers, tennis balls. Vendors at cat shows sell a bounty of toys to keep the most discriminating feline entertained. *Warning:* Toys can disappear down a cat's throat, creating a medical emergency. A toy should be big enough, sturdy enough, and durable enough so that the cat or kitten will not eat it or break it.

• **Grooming tools and supplies:** A cat needs its nails trimmed periodically, perhaps a combing, and sometimes an occasional bath. Cat claw trimmers, a comb or brush appropri-ate for the hair length (ask the breeder or caregiver), feline shampoo, and antiseptic wipes for the ears make up a beauty kit for the new feline.

• **Veterinary examination:** Make an appointment with a veterinarian a day or two after your new cat's arrival. Most breeders or adoption contracts require a veterinary visit within a set time. Healthy cats allow a veterinarian to examine them while there are medical problems. Bring your cat's vaccination records, assuming it was given to you by your kitten's breeder, so that the information can be entered in the vet's records. This will enable him or her to provide additional shots or tests that may be needed. If your cat is not already surgically altered, the doctor can discuss a convenient time to do this. It should be done as soon as possible.

• **Flea prevention:** During the first veterinary visit, learn how to eliminate existing fleas and how to prevent them from infesting your pet. Always ask your veterinarian about flea products before using them; products marketed for dogs should not be used on cats, as they can be toxic for them.

GETTING TO KNOW YOU

A new home can be intimidating to a cat or kitten. After all, this might be the first time it has been separated from its mother, littermates, or previous home. The advice of experienced cat people is to allow a newcomer to get used to a new home gradually. An unused guest bathroom or bedroom gives the cat an opportunity to sniff the odors of its new home while in a small, secure place, which should contain the new cat's food, water, litter box, bedding, and a few toys.

If the newcomer is not an only pet but is the latest kitten on the block, it will have to blend in with the others, even if there is a dog on the premises. Most experienced cat people believe a period of quarantine is necessary to impose on the new kitten or cat to be sure it is not introducing a disease that could infect the others. It is also felt that young kittens are susceptible to the potential aggression of the established pets in addition to any ailments they might have. Many breeders believe that the newcomer should be quarantined for 30 days before being introduced to the others in the household. Others feel that 21 days are sufficient to determine if the newcomer will develop an upper respiratory condition. It is not uncommon for cats to have a disease for 14 days before showing signs of it. Unfortunately, most pet owners do not impose the quarantine because they are impatient and do not understand the potential medical risk. They take a chance and almost always end up seeing hissing, growling, and, on occasion, overt aggression.

Assuming that you take the precaution of quarantine, the cat's fur will have absorbed odors unique to its new home, giving it the smell of a longtime resident, which will help protect it from aggression. The newcomer will then begin to recognize the odors of the other feline residents. After the quarantine, preliminary introductions can begin.

A partially opened door will allow your cats to meet while offering the newcomer the ability to dart back into safe quarters if necessary. Several meetings later, review their progress, and if the time is right, move the newcomer into the mainstream of the household. Here is another way to introduce the new cat. After the quarantine, put the cat in its carrier in a room with the other cats for about 30 minutes. Either way, gradually increase the time together until it appears that the cats can be integrated safely. Separate their food and water containers to avoid needless competition among the cats, who might still consider one another strangers. Toys such as cat teases get them all playing at the same time and serve as an icebreaker.

Integration might be rapid or could take weeks, depending on the cats. Older cats already in the home will take longer to accept a new, younger cat or kitten. Often, people get so excited with a new cat or kitten that the older feline residents are often ignored and the adjustment becomes more difficult. However, giving the existing cats a little more TLC (extra attention, extra time, or special treats) can help to smooth the transition.

Introductions with an existing canine resident follow the same general methods. However, all sessions between the two must be monitored until it is certain that they get along. Obedience-trained dogs will respond to simple commands such as *sit* and *stay* during the sessions with the new resident. At first, keep the cat separated from the dog; then gradually bring them together, perhaps with the cat in a carrier. Because cats have higher protein requirements, they should be fed separately to ensure that the cat is not pilfering some of the dog's food, which is lower in protein.

If war erupts once in a while between your animals, the confrontation can be disrupted by banging a spoon on a skillet or making a similar loud, sudden noise or even by a squirt of water from a spray bottle. Bare hands should never be used to separate the combatants; a bath mat or thick towel thrown over participants will protect you from injury. While speaking in a soothing voice, calm the animals down and watch them carefully for a while.

Many cats and kittens are acquired as companions for children. Because toddlers and infants are still in the grabbing stage, an adult should supervise any play between pets and young children. Children should be shown how to pick up and hold cats. *Never pick up a cat by the neck; instead, place one hand under the front legs and across the chest and use the other hand to support the back end, in case the cat becomes frightened. A cat is held with its back toward your body, to keep its teeth and claws away from your face in case it becomes scared.* A cat with trimmed nails is less likely to hurt children; frequent nail trimmings are a must in any case. Cats often manage to get away when children go through doors leading to the outside. To avoid this, children should be taught to check when opening an outside door. An identification tag on a collar can help get a wayward cat home; in many areas, a cat must wear its rabies tag as well.

Using patience, observing body language (including hisses or growls), and understanding cat behavior help make your newcomer welcome in its home.

CALL OF THE WILD

A happy indoor cat? Sure. Indoor cats are healthier, do not dart across streets in front of moving cars, and do not need to find a place to sleep in a blizzard or rainstorm, drink antifreeze, get shot at, or get attacked by other animals. The list of outdoor dangers is a big one. Signs of illness in indoor cats are also more detectable, such as a food bowl ignored, watery stool in the litter box, repeated regurgitation. On the average, an indoor cat also lives many years longer—and so do the birds and other wildlife the cat is not preying on.

However, living indoors does not mean a cat needs to become a couch potato. Cat furniture, which can be purchased at cat shows or pet supply stores or can be built by do-it-yourselfers, allows them to exercise their muscles. Enterprising pet owners build walkways with lumber and shelf supports along walls near ceilings, approachable by a tall cat tree, and enjoy watching their cats scale the tree

and take to the walks. Owners can help keep their cats in shape by using a short cat fishing pole to which a piece of fabric is the lure at the end of the line. Versions of these are sold at cat shows and are advertised in cat magazines. People with video cameras can film birds, insects, the outdoors, skaters, skiers, and other interesting activities or scenery, and entertain their cats via the VCR.

Fresh air for cats can be achieved with the use of screened windows, but the screens must be reinforced to prevent escape. Some cats take to walking on a leash and a secure harness (not good with a quick-release collar). Some homeowners screen a large porch into a sunroom for their cats. Renters can transform hardware cloth and lumber into five modular panels (four walls and a roof) for a portable cage on the patio. Because a cat's paws and nose must be kept out of reach of wildlife or stray pets to avoid contagious disease, an additional barrier wall may be necessary and can be made of chicken wire or hardware cloth.

COFFEE, TEA, OR CATNIP?

Although cats are content to stay at home, sleeping, eating, and playing, they can travel and hit the road with their human companions. The time of the year is a factor in deciding whether to take your cat along or find a pet sitter. If the weather is extreme, it is best to leave your cat home rather than risk the consequences of intense hot weather or frigid temperatures. *Warning:* Do not leave your cat in a parked car in warm weather. Even cracking the window will not prevent an intense heat buildup. Because health codes prohibit taking a cat into a restaurant, plan to take sandwiches or pull up at a fast-food restaurant with a drive-through window for meals on long trips.

A carrier or kennel large enough to comfortably house the cat is a must for car trips; a ride of longer than a couple of hours warrants a carrier big enough for a small litter box at the back, a bed at the front and a divided water and food dish clipped onto the front door. The grate door and ventilation holes on the sides should provide enough air circulation to keep the cat cool; direct sun can be blocked with a suction-cup window shade.

In cold weather, wrap a blanket around the carrier, especially when going to and from the car. Additional items needed for travel include

- A vaccination record
- A rabies shot certificate
- Rabies shot and ID tags on cat collar
- An ID tag and name on the carrier or kennel (in case of an accident). Health records and medications can be kept in a plastic self-sealing bag and taped to the top of the carrier. In some states, a cat must travel with its rabies shot certificate and tag, and they are required when crossing from the United States into Canada or Mexico.
- Veterinary medications and veterinarian's name and phone number
- An extra litter pan and litter
- Bottled water and food
- Plastic garbage bags for used litter
- A car vacuum for spilled litter
- A favorite toy or two
- An old bedsheet

A cat roaming about in a moving vehicle can cause a collision or, in the case of a crash, can be thrown about or even attack other passengers. Restricting the cat to its carrier at all times when moving will keep everyone safe. On long trips, pause at a rest stop every 2–3 hours and check on the cat.

Before planning a trip, plan the itinerary.

If a stop will be at a private home, find out whether the residents like and welcome cats and have their own cats. If the residents do not like cats, stay at a hotel or motel or leave the cat at home with a sitter. If the residents will welcome a visiting cat, remember that courtesy means leaving a room free of cat litter or food. To avoid problems, restrict your cat to its carrier, a bathroom, or a bedroom during a stay in a home with a cat; take extra precautions to make sure your cat and the resident cats do not dart out of or into rooms when humans go through doors.

Not all hotels and motels accept pets. Travel guides usually indicate whether a facility accepts pets, but because policies can change after publication, it is wise to double-check when making a reservation. Many guides will note whether guest rooms have interior or exterior entrances. Interior entrances are better; because if a cat darts out of a room, it will do so into a corridor, not into a street, and can be more easily rescued.

On arriving at the room, inspect it before letting a cat out of its carrier. Check for possible safety hazards such as exposed electrical wires; pesticide or insecticide containers or trash left under beds; uncovered toilets; holes in walls enabling a curious cat to investigate the inner walls of the hotel, open windows, and openings around air-conditioning and heating units. A cat will be drawn to nooks and crannies around platform beds, but towels or extra pillows can be stuffed into these to avoid having to take the bed apart the next morning to retrieve the cat.

A bedsheet from home is ideal for a litter box set up in a corner of the room or bathroom; the sheet will catch stray litter particles and the location will provide some privacy. Food and water dishes can be placed in another area of the bathroom, taking care that litter cannot be flung into the dishes. The traveler can then be released from its kennel and allowed to inspect the room. A DO NOT DISTURB sign should be hung on the doorknob when you leave the room. Housekeeping staff should be notified that a cat is inside if the stay is more than one night, so that the cat will not be given chances to escape. Guests can decline to have beds and bathroom tidied and instead pick up clean towels themselves or have them left outside the door.

All used litter should be discarded in a garbage bag in the hotel trash bin, not left in plastic wastebasket liners in the hotel room. Pick up stray litter particles and leave the room free of pet traces so that the hotel will continue to allow pet guests in its rooms.

Air travel is stressful to a cat and also presents unique challenges to its human traveling companions. A nonstop flight with the cat inside the cabin is the least stressful. A reservation must be made for a pet in the cabin and a pet ticket must be purchased during check-in. Each airline has a limit on pets in the cabin. If the limit has already been met for a flight, the passenger will need to book another flight or have the cat ride in the cargo hold. Many airlines have cargo holds that accommodate animals in carriers, but most airlines will not accept animals during extreme temperatures—for example, under 40 degrees or over 80 degrees Fahrenheit. During summer months, airlines will not accept animals for shipment in the baggage compartment. A few airlines do not accept animals in baggage ever. Cat owners anticipating flying with a cat should verify and then reverify all details with the airline before arriving at the airport.

Whether a cat travels in the cabin or rides below with baggage, a rabies shot certificate and health certificate, dated within 10 days of the flight, are required. These can be placed in a self-sealing plastic bag. An animal traveling in baggage will need a sturdy hard-plastic kennel large enough in which to stand up and turn around, with a divided food and water cup attached. The carrier should be examined for loose bolts or latches. A cat flying in the cabin can travel in a small kennel or a specialty carrier made for air travel; the airline will provide dimensions of carriers that will fit under the seat for a specific aircraft. A cat should be fed and watered far ahead of departure time to ensure that it has time to visit a litter box at home or in a large carrier en route to the airport. Because a litter box is easily spilled or tossed about while in the air, line the bottom of the carrier going into the baggage compartment with disposable adult diapers or old bath mats in case of an accident. In addition, a fuzzy cat bed will provide warmth in cool weather. Refreezable ice packs can be placed under the diapers or bath mat in hot weather. The cat's favorite dry food should be packed in a self-sealing plastic bag and attached to the top with duct tape.

A cat riding in baggage is checked along with luggage at the ticket counter. A cat going into the cabin remains with its owner during check-in at the ticket counter. Some paperwork is involved when the pet ticket is purchased, which is usually an adhesive label with shipper and shippee noted for a checked carrier. An in-cabin cat passenger must be handcarried securely (airports are very dangerous for an escaped cat). When going through the X-ray area, the in-cabin carrier must go along the conveyor belt through the X-ray machine while you hold the cat in your arms. Once on the other side, the traveler must place the cat back into the empty carrier. Cats are generally well behaved in airline cabins. Your cat may mew a little before the plane begins taxiing from the gate, but by the time the aircraft reaches its cruising altitude, it will probably have gone to sleep. Some cats who must fly do not like traveling in general. For them, a veterinarian can prescribe medications to ease the problem.

Once you arrive at your destination, the first priority after claiming baggage and getting to lodging should be to make the cat comfortable with its litter box, bed, food, and water.

A MANICURE ON ALL FOURS

One of a cat's basic actions is extending its nails and scratching. Scratching helps a cat shed its nails as they grow out, is used as a marking device to communicate to other cats, and is a sign of happiness. Watch a cat wake up from a sleep: It usually yawns, stretches its front legs, and scratches with its nails several times.

Untrimmed, nails become sharp. They can be trimmed with human nail clippers or cat nail trimmers, which are short scissors with a curved blade. The easiest tactic is to wait until the cat is relaxed, pick it up, and then sit down with the cat in your lap, facing forward. Pick up one front paw and extend the nail. Look for the pink line (a vein) in the nail. Trim the nail, just missing the pink line. Continue until all its nails are done on that paw, and then move to the next paw. Occasionally, a cat may decide there are better things to do; release it and wait until it is in a relaxed mood again. A veterinarian or veterinary technician can also demonstrate nail trimming during a visit if needed. Nails should be trimmed frequently, about every 10 days.

Cats who scratch can be diverted with cardboard scratching strips, usually sold with a packet of catnip, or cat furniture. An inexpensive scratching post can be built from several pieces of wood: a sisal-covered post fastened to a plywood base covered with carpet scraps, or a sisal-covered 2" × 4" wood plank with a sisal loop hung from a doorknob. Cats enjoy exercising on the posts and shed their nails on the sisal.

Rough textures are especially appealing to cats. Have you ever noticed how a cat will walk up to a person wearing jeans and then proceed to try to climb or scratch the jeans? Avoid rough or nubby fabrics when shopping for new furniture or fabric for recovering a sofa or chair. Likewise, steer away from leather and vinyl, which puncture easily, especially if a cat due for a nail trim hops onto a leather chair. Cats tend to avoid tightly woven fabrics—chintz-type cottons or velvets. Samples of fabrics can be taken home to gauge a cat's response. Using clear plastic guards, sold through mail-order pet catalogs or cat magazine ads, can protect corners of furniture. Some cat breeders report success with wide, double-stick tape placed over furniture corners. (See also "Improper Scratching and Chewing" in Chapter 7, "Feline Behavior and Misbehavior.")

Another option some cat owners use are plastic claw caps, available from veterinarians and pet supply catalogs. These come in several colors and are applied with an adhesive after the claws are trimmed and can remain on for 30–45 days.

Cats can be successfully trained not to scratch furniture and instead be redirected to scratching posts. However, owners sometimes request declawing without investigating these alternatives. Declawing, or onychectomy, is amputation of the claw and the end toe bone. Afterward, the cat must relearn how to walk because it is walking on less toe bone. The cat can still go through the motions of scratching but cannot do any damage. An alternative procedure, a tendonectomy, involves severing the tendon attached to the end toe digit, preventing the cat from extending its claws. However, the claws must still be trimmed and claws can grow into the paw pads. Declawing and tendonectomy carry risk of infection, pain, and nail regrowth.

The Cat Fanciers' Association (CFA) opposes declawing and tendonectomy. At its October 1996 meeting, the board of directors approved a condemnation of the procedures:

> CFA perceives the declawing of cats (onychectomy) and the severing of digital tendons (tendonectomy) to be elective surgical procedures, which are without benefit to the cat. Because of discomfort associated with any surgery and potential future behavioral or physical effects, CFA disapproves of routine declawing or tendonectomy surgery in lieu of alternative solutions to prevent household damage.

CFA show rules prohibit the showing of any cats that have undergone declawing or tendonectomy; however, household pet cats wearing claw covers can be shown.

"I'M FIXED—HOW ABOUT YOU?"

True or false?

- Female cats have to be at least 6 months old or have a litter first before being spayed.
- Males do not have to be neutered; after all, they are not the ones who have kittens.

Both statements are false.

Pet cats make the best companions when they are free of the biological urge to reproduce. Female kittens can come into season—crying, crouching low to the floor, trying to find a mate, and even spraying an odorous fluid—as early as 4–5 months of age. They can go into season (also called heat) numerous times a year. Males can sire kittens as early as 6 months of age. Because of this, many breeders sell pet kit-

tens or cats only after they have been neutered. This can be done at 6 weeks of age, a common practice in animal shelters for a newly adopted pet. Breeders typically wait until approximately 12 weeks of age—after the third set of vaccinations—before having a pet kitten neutered or spayed. Information on early spaying and neutering can be found at the CFA Web site: http://www.cfa.org/health/early-spay-neuter.html.

A female who has undergone an ovariohysterectomy—spaying—will not produce kittens that may or may not find good homes. She will not have complications of labor or delivery or require an expensive emergency cesarean section. She will not develop pyometra, a serious uterine infection. She is much less likely to develop breast cancer. A neutered, or castrated, male is much less likely to spray vertical surfaces with a sexually odorous substance than is an intact one. He will not want or look for a female cat and impregnate her.

Females and males are much more loving to humans after surgical alteration because they are not being driven by powerful hormones. They do not have to produce kittens to be more lovable, contrary to a widespread misconception. Another fallacy is that altered cats become lazy and fat. With exercise and proper diet, an altered cat can stay trim, healthy, and energetic.

"IT WAS A DARK AND STORMY NIGHT . . ."

Fire. Tornado. Hurricane. Earthquake. Flood. Ice storm. Power failure. A human-made or natural disaster can upset the calm of a pet's home in a matter of seconds and often without warning. In extreme situations, a family may have to evacuate, and that means planning for emergency care of a cat and perhaps other pets.

The CFA's animal rescue and disaster relief workers suggest taking the following steps:

• Take several pictures of all pets in the household and keep these, with full descriptions of the animals, in a self-sealing plastic bag with important papers, copies of any registration certificates proving ownership, and immunization and health records. Additionally, an extra photo could be placed in the veterinarian's records for each pet to help identify a missing animal. Make sure all pets wear a collar with rabies shot tag and an ID tag with owner's name, address, and phone number. (A good option is to have a microchip surgically implanted on each pet and register it with the microchip manufacturer.)

• Have at least 1 week's supply of pet food, bottled water, and cat litter on hand. Dry food should be stored in watertight containers; buy flip-top cans of food to avoid the need for a can opener. Keep these items in a plastic crate or container so that they can be easily gotten in an emergency. Add food and water bowls, a litter scoop, trash bags, and a litter pan or two to the emergency pet kit. Rotate the use of food and water to keep them fresh.

• The emergency pet kit also should include supplies of any medications a pet regularly needs: prescription medications and any medical supplies for thyroid, diabetes, kidney, or heart patients; food supplements; heartworm preventive; flea-control preparations; and so on.

• Have a cat carrier for each animal, ideally large enough to accommodate a small shoe-size litter box at the back, a bed at the front and a partitioned water and food cup attached to the front door. An occupied carrier should always have plenty of ventilation and should never be left directly in the sun.

• Compile a list of names, addresses, and phone numbers of hotels, motels, friends and relatives willing to accept emergency guests with pets. Humans may be welcome at emergency shelters, but their pets will not, because of health and safety reasons. In case of a large-scale disaster, such as a hurricane, the evacuation site may be hundreds of miles from home.

• Compile a list of names and phone numbers of animal shelters and veterinarians in the area. After a disaster, many displaced animals find their way into shelters or are taken to veterinarians.

A household that prepares for emergencies is more likely to handle the emergency successfully. American Red Cross chapters have information on general disasters, and the CFA's Disaster Relief Committee has made available the article "Tips for Keeping Your Cat (or Dog) Safe During a Disaster" at http://www.cfa.org/articles/disaster-planning-tips.html.

CURIOSITY CAN BE DEADLY

Cats are curious creatures, but their nine lives will not pull them through encounters with many dangerous items found in every home, such as

• **Household cleaning agents:** All cleansers and supplies should be kept out of reach of inquisitive cats (and human toddlers). Read labels thoroughly before using any product to check for toxicity to animals or humans. Cleansers can burn or irritate the paws and the mouth. Consult a veterinarian for specific products that are safe and and those that are unsafe around cats and other animals.

• **Pesticides, insecticides, fertilizers, and other gardening chemicals:** These should be kept away from animals. Insect and rodent baits and traps must be kept out of the reach of pets (and toddlers).

• **Plants:** Plants commonly found in and around homes that could harm or kill cats include aloe veras, asparagus ferns, bluebonnets, caladiums, calla lilies, oleanders, pencil cacti, dracaena, rubber plants, poinsettias, and mistletoe. The entire list can be found on the CFA Web site: http://www.cfa.org/caring.html.

• **Holiday decorations:** Christmas tree trimmings (tinsel, glass ornaments, hangers, an so on) are not cat toys. Ingested tinsel and angel hair (fiberglass) can tear up an intestinal tract. Search for safe decorations that cannot break or be eaten. Ribbons should be added to packages at the last minute, to prevent cats from eating them.

• **Medications:** Never give any medication to a cat unless instructed by a veterinarian. Many preparations for humans are deadly to cats. One extra-strength acetominophen tablet (500-milligram Tylenol) can kill a 7-pound cat. Keep all prescription and over-the-counter medications out of reach and out of sight of pets.

• **Ordinary household items:** A cat can eat a sponge and choke or suffer a digestive obstruction. Cords to window blinds can become wrapped around a cat's (or toddler's) neck; check home-improvement supply stores for winding devices for the excess cord. Some cats eat bits of aluminum foil. Homemade modeling compound is extremely salty. Cigarettes, coffee grounds, alcoholic drinks, chocolate, and fatty foods (such as turkey or chicken with the skin attached) will send a cat to a veterinarian. Other dangerous items are fabric softener sheets, undiluted bleach, mothballs, dishwasher detergents, and batteries. Electrical cords attract teething kittens and bored cats; cords can be dabbed with bitter-tasting products sold at pet supply stores or through a veterinarian. Treat the household cat as if it were a toddler: Cap unused electrical outlets and install childproof latches on all cabinet doors.

Doors to appliances such as washers, dryers, microwaves, ovens, refrigerators, and freezers should be kept shut; if a cat noses around when an appliance is opened, double-check before closing.

• **Flea preparations:** Flea-fighting products made for dogs are not always safe for cats. Clear all flea products—foggers, carpet cleaners, sprays, shampoos, dips, powders, pills—with a veterinarian before use on a cat or kitten.

"OH, NO—NOT A BATH!"

One of the best things about cats is they are self-cleaning animals. Their tongues have tiny devices made to catch loose hair while they are bathing themselves. In the spring and early summer, cats shed some hair. Once ingested, the hair can produce hairballs. (A flavored petroleum-based product such as Petromalt, Laxatone, Femalt, or Cat Lax helps those hairballs make their way out cats and into their litter boxes.) Brushing your cat several times a week helps avoid this. Different types of coats require different types of brushes and brushing. Some cats only require a chamois because they are so sleek. Some cats require a wire/slicker brush, and others use something resembling a curry brush used for horses. The most common brush is a simple, natural Bristol brush similar to a human's hairbrush. However, there is no one-brush-fits-all type. In many of the "Grooming Requirements" portions of each breed description a brush type is recommended. (See Chapter 3, "Introduction to the Breeds: 41 Breed Descriptions and Their Cat Fanciers' Association Show Standards.") Most cats enjoy the attention and the massage-like effect of having their coats brushed.

Sometimes a cat needs a hand from a human to keep clean. Cat owners often fear giving a bath, which need not be a traumatic event. The first step is to trim the cat's nails on all four feet. Then the cat's ears must be cleaned with an antiseptic wipe; in the case of an extremely dirty ear, a veterinarian may need to check for ear mites or prescribe an ear-cleaning product. For a long-haired or semilong-haired cat, the next step is to comb or brush the coat to remove tangles and loose hair.

Next comes the bath. Required items include

- Several large towels
- A mild pet shampoo or even tearless baby shampoo and perhaps a conditioner
- A hair dryer

The cat can be bathed in a bathtub, using a plastic dishpan, or in a kitchen sink; the bathroom is a more secure area and a soapy cat can less easily escape the hands of a novice groomer.

First, fill the dishpan or sink with enough warm water to let the cat's hair float when immersed. Gently place the cat in the water. At this point, a few soothing words will calm a nervous cat. Work the water into the hair; some cats have thick hair, which resists water. Then take the cat out of the water and begin working a small amount of shampoo onto the tail, behind the ears, on the belly, around the rectal area, the back, and all four feet—everywhere except for the face. The face can be wiped clean later with a damp washcloth or a washcloth and some diluted baby shampoo and then rinsed free of soap traces.

When the cat has been shampooed and massaged all over, rinse the soap with a shower massager or sink sprayer, beginning along the spine and onto the sides. The sound of a massager or sprayer may frighten a cat; a few reassuring words help at this point. Rinse, rinse, and rinse again. If desired, use 2–4 ounces of vinegar in a sink of warm water to help cut remaining soap residue. Rinse thoroughly afterward. At this point, a long-haired cat may benefit from a conditioner, formulated for cats, mixed thoroughly in a sink of water. Place the cat in the water and let the conditioner work its way into the cat's coat. Remove the cat and once again rinse, rinse, rinse, and towel-dry the cat. A short-haired cat will finish the job itself. A long-haired cat will need its hair gently combed to eliminate tangles. Tough tangles can be eased out by gently raking them with the comb's end. Finally, dry the cat by placing it in a carrier or wire cage, working a dryer on a low setting around the cat. Some cats may tolerate a dryer at a closer distance. If the cat says, "No thank you" to the dryer, towel-dry the cat and then place it in a warm bathroom while the hair dries.

Although bringing home a new kitten may seem a bit overwhelming if it is your first one, the process is not really as difficult as it may seem. Most of the requirements rely on your common sense and are clear and obvious. In the unlikely event that the answers to your questions are not in these pages, help is just a phone call away to your breeder or your mentor, or you can visit the CFA Web site, at htpp://www.cfa.org. Despite the mountain of information dealing with the dos and don'ts of a new cat, you are in for the treat of your life. Enjoy it.

Chapter **9**

Breeding Cats

BY BETTY WHITE

There is an excitement and a challenge to becoming a breeder that is positively heady. Most people approach it with keen anticipation and joy. However, to enter the world of breeders of fine cats is to accept a weighty responsibility that ought to be examined thoroughly before you take the plunge. The Cat Fanciers' Association (CFA) is rightly concerned about ensuring that breeding is done ethically and that breeders always consider the well-being of the cats involved. With this in mind, responsible and ethical breeders should be proud of what they do because of their conviction that pedigreed cats need to be preserved.

Breeding cats is a costly undertaking in terms of money and time and should be approached only in a serious fashion, with the promotion and preservation of the breed at heart. It must not be forgotten that these are living, breathing creatures whose future is being arbitrarily shaped beyond the realm of natural selection. As caring human beings, breeders must always be mindful of their role in the health, nurturance, and future of these lovely animals. While this is certainly true of the cat with top show qualities, it is especially true of its siblings who will spend their lives as beloved pets. Ultimately, it is the perception of a breed as a pet, created in the minds of people all over the world, where breeders do the most to promote, preserve, and protect the pedigreed cat.

Thus, a breeder's responsibility to his or her cats extends also to his or her fellow human beings, a responsibility that is best served when cats not only with breeding potential but also cats eagerly sought as pets find loving homes.

GATHERING INFORMATION

Having come to the decision to produce fine cats, a novice breeder must first learn as much about the chosen breed as possible. This means researching the literature available about the breed, its history, its origin, development, and CFA breed standard. It is particularly valuable to have a thorough knowledge of the evolution of the breed standard, because it will help you to evaluate old photographs encountered during research of your chosen breed. These same photographs will then translate into an intelligent evaluation of pedigrees, which is a necessary skill that all breeders must hone if they are going to be successful. Armed with this knowledge, the new breeder then has the tools to use in learning when visiting experienced breeders, attending cat shows, and observing various types of any breed and to use in making informed decisions concerning foundation breeding cats.

STARTING A CATTERY

Anyone planning to become a breeder needs to give careful consideration to the housing and care of his or her cats. Important information is available on this subject in the pamphlet, "CFA Cattery Standards," which can be obtained from the CFA by writing to

Cat Fanciers' Association, Inc.
1805 Atlantic Avenue
P.O. Box 1005
Manasquan, NJ 08736-0805

Although the pamphlet details only minimum requirements, it is a place to start. There are any number of publications that may be studied to understand the optimum in care and environmental needs for breeding cats. An article entitled "Planning and Designing a Cattery" is offered on the CFA's Web site at http://www.cfa.org/articles/cattery-design.html. Learning about proper feline husbandry is as important as learning breed history and the acquisition of fine cats for breeding. The best cats in the world will not successfully reproduce if their care is less than adequate. It is an expense in both time and money that must be considered from the beginning.

Like everything else in life, a new breeder needs a plan. Should you begin with a male,

female, or both? Which is most important? The answers to these questions, while certainly basic to breeding, may be academic. The intelligent breeder will search for the best possible example of his chosen breed in whatever gender is available, all things being equal. When things are not equal, such as the inability to house a male, the answer is obvious. Cats of apparent good health, free from defects, and of pedigrees reflecting good health and condition are the essential ingredients for a successful breeding program. Once this requirement is met, a breeder will choose sires and dams that complement one another. Whether beginning with a single female, a pair, or another gender mix, the same principles apply. These principles should be followed throughout the ensuing generations.

SELECTING CATS FOR BREEDING

In selecting cats, a breeder needs to be most cautious and attentive to everything. Health, of course, is the most important consideration. What about type? What about coat color and pattern? A comprehensive knowledge of a breed's standard reveals the significant aspects of that standard to any breeder. If a balance is maintained, if no one important aspect of a breed's standard is sacrificed in favor of another, then a breeder will ultimately find the shortest route to the goal of consistently fine cats. Where coat color and pattern is important to a breed, it is folly to neglect it. Conversely, if a breed's standard gives scant importance to coat color and pattern, it makes no sense to stress it. All aspects of the breed are important in the final analysis, which is what improving a breed is all about. The cats a breeder selects show the breeder's talents and are proof of the level of commitment of a breeder to his or her chosen breed.

MAKING THE COMMITMENT

The question of commitment is raised because breeding is not easy. Quite apart from the selection decisions a breeder must make because of health, there is the perverseness of the process itself. *Perverseness* is a good word, for it mirrors the frustration breeding can cause. Contrary to logic, some cats—even those with excellent pedigrees—simply do not reproduce their excellent type. We human beings should understand this, because beautiful human parents do not necessarily produce beautiful children! A new breeder needs to be aware of this unhappy fact. Disappointments will happen, but they can be offset by the surprises. For example, there are times when the breeder-quality cat, kept because of necessity, may produce show cat after show cat. Frustrations in breeding abound, such as breeding seasons with too many male kittens. Special housing for males precludes any breeder from keeping more than a limited number. There are also females that come into season at home, but not anywhere else.

No doubt, the most universal fact of life for the breeder is the difficulty in realizing that the pick of the litter for a breeding program will be the best overall example of the breed rather than the kitten with the flashiest show potential. This is one form of commitment.

There is another form of commitment, briefly alluded to above: the commitment to maintain and improve the health of the breed and keep it free from defects. Keeping the most robust cats to produce the next generation seems straightforward enough, yet there is more to the picture than this: observing temperament, ascertaining proper structure, and determining general stamina. Unwise selections made because of lack of commitment to these criteria will be the hardest to rectify in the future. Finally, the primary commitment to the cats themselves is to find them good homes. The conscientious breeder willingly accepts all these responsibilities whenever he or she allows two cats to breed. It is a process that can be tedious, maddening, and utterly rewarding. A new breeder should accept the fact that it will be all of these things at one time or another.

Once you make the decision to become a breeder and have accepted all the related responsibilities, you must study feline reproduction. Just as intensive research is called for in choosing cats for breeding and in planning their matings, there can be no less attention paid to how kittens come into the world. A thorough knowledge of reproduction will enable you to identify potential problems early.

PRODUCING KITTENS

Breeding a male and a female cat usually produces kittens in approximately 65 days. This is a rule honored by the exception. It is only common sense not to be alarmed if everything else seems normal but the kittens appear a day or so later. Lengthier periods of pregnancy are not all that unusual and result in completely satisfactory results. The key is careful monitoring. It is important for a breeder to know exactly when to expect the miracle of birth. This means that sire and dam are observed until the initial mating occurs. Careful notation should be made so that the approximate date of delivery can be calculated. Despite the obvious estrus cycle (period of heat), ovulation (release of an egg from the ovary) does not occur in the feline until actual copulation takes place between a male and female cat. The prudent breeder therefore allows his or her cats to breed for only 2 or 3 days so that the development time of the litter in the uterus will be virtually the same as the time of copulation and a relatively precise due date is known.

Diet and exercise are important throughout the gestation period. Consultation with your veterinarian as well as your own research will dictate the addition of vitamin and mineral supplements to the female's diet. Some careful thought must also be given to what happens the last week or two before the kittens are born. Individual circumstances differ in the housing of cats, from elaborate catteries with individual quarters to quiet birthing areas in a breeder's home. Whatever the case, the new breeder needs to give careful consideration to the coming litter. Many feel it is wise to restrict the mother's movement during this time. This not only prepares her for a different lifestyle once her kittens are born but in the case of very active females, it also lessens the possibility of injuries or other unforeseen problems. While a *kittening box* in a quiet bedroom shared with a family member might sound just fine, it is possible that the new mother will disagree and move her babies to a place of her own liking. This may be not only troublesome but also tragic if kittens appear suddenly underfoot.

A roomy bed, either an open one or an enclosed one with an easily removable top, is ideal. An apple box from the grocery store is an excellent choice, with a hole cut for entrance and exit. Several layers of bedding are suggested. The top ones can be removed during and after the birthing process, allowing the lower ones to remain for a day or so to retain a familiar smell.

The birth of the kittens may be routine, which means that it may be uneventful. It could also mean that delivery takes place at any time of the day or night, may take any length of time from minutes to several hours, and may present any maternal behavior from matter-of-fact to "What is happening to me?". Here is where good records are important. Documenting what is usual for this particular

queen will assist you in preparing for her next birthing. Some females know instinctively what is going on, while others seem totally perplexed. The wise breeder will keep birthing cats company, complimenting the mother who is calm or reassuring the mother who is flummoxed.

Be prepared to assist the timid and unsure mother in welcoming her new kittens into the world, which may mean watching to be sure she tends to each kitten as it is born. Newborn kittens, newly licked and dried, may be placed on a heating pad nearby to give the new mother additional maneuvering room. Be sure to keep them in her view and be prepared to return them to her if she objects. Most new mothers will noticeably settle down to nurse their young after the last kitten is born. They usually know when there are no more to be born. Because the breeder does not have that information, it is wise to observe the new family for a while to make that determination. This is an excellent time to finish the paperwork on that litter's birth, check the clock for time elapsed, note the sex of the kittens, and make any other observations that may be helpful in the future.

PROVIDING POSTNATAL CARE

It is almost possible to watch new kittens grow, which is another way of saying that thriving kittens will noticeably gain weight. If a kitten is not gaining weight, it is in trouble. Learn ahead of time how to tube-feed a kitten, and have the equipment and formula on hand. This information is available from your veterinarian or from another breeder. If it is a matter of getting insufficient milk, as opposed to a physical impairment, the problem will correct itself in a few days. If this is not the case, you will need veterinary assistance. A healthy, growing litter is a readily visible thing.

Kittens, however, should be weighed at least once a day at the same time. Little to no weight gain is a sign of some kind of problem. This is where a good relationship with a veterinarian is an advantage; the breeder can call to discuss home care before rushing into a clinic.

Kitten food needs to be readily available sometime after the third week. Although it is unusual, kittens between 3 and 4 weeks of age have been known to get curious about their mother's food and begin eating it. This varies from breed to breed. There are breeders who start kittens on soft foods and formulas, gradually weaning them to dry food or other diets once the kittens become curious. Decide on your own weaning regimen. When evaluating a litter, the wise breeder will note when each kitten begins eating. Many breeders consider the early eating of solid food as another indication of a robust individual and/or perhaps a sign of a highly intelligent one.

Kittens should be handled from a very early age in order to be thoroughly socialized. This not only makes them better pets but it also makes them better show cats. It is also through the handling process that temperament can be measured. Cats are the same as people in this regard; there are those who are more outgoing than others. While some cats need very little attention to be friendly to strangers, others need a good deal more contact with human beings to overcome their timidity. It is best for breeders to choose an outgoing kitten from a litter for breeding purposes. Temperament is inherited, just as color and type are. Of course, there are exceptions that defy genetics.

A proper vaccination schedule should be determined after careful study and in consultation with a veterinarian. Suffice it to say that no kittens should leave your home until their inoculations are complete, which means no sooner than 12 weeks of age. Some breeders keep their first litters longer than this.

Not only do breeds develop differently, but lines within breeds do so as well. Some breeders find that they make fewer mistakes if they wait until the kittens are 4–5 months old. (By this age, most kittens have developed to the point where show potential is apparent.) It is a matter of personal judgment, one that involves weighing the possibility of an error against the easier task of finding homes for younger kittens.

Breeding—being part of the feline reproduction process—is a thrilling avocation. Approached with careful thought and practiced with excellent feline husbandry in pursuit of a worthwhile goal, breeding fine cats can be one of the most rewarding of undertakings. Apart from the joy of being with the cats themselves, breeding leads to a wider circle of friends and acquaintances and a deeper understanding of the relationships among living beings in the world.

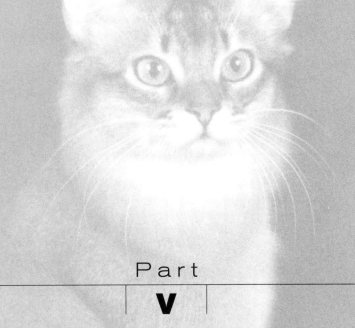

Part
V

Feline Nutrition

10

Feeding Cats and Aspects of Feline Nutrition

BY DANIEL P. CAREY, D.V.M.

Feeding your kitten or adult cat is possibly the first thing that comes to mind once you set those four paws to the ground in the new home. What's for dinner is a major concern for cats that have come to live with you because they are not in a natural setting where they can capture and then consume their own food. Once you assume the responsibility for the well-being of a feline friend, feeding your cat a proper diet on a regular basis is of paramount importance in terms of growth, sustained good health, long life, and your cat's sense of safety and contentment.

Because of the length of this chapter, it is divided into four sections: "Feeding Management," "Nutrients," "Major Organ Systems," and "Comparing Cat Foods." The information here is available in both uncomplicated form and in technically sophisticated form for those who may require more than simple label instructions on the can or bag of cat food. Feline nutrition is a science and an important aspect of cat care. With that in mind this chapter goes as far as you are willing to travel within the subject. Please bear in mind that it is misleading to offer specific amounts of food to feed a cat because there are many variables having to do with your cat's lifestyle, stage of life, size, breed, and other aspects. The most efficient way to determine feeding amounts is to consult the breeder of your kitten or a vet-

erinarian about your cat's individual needs. Nevertheless, the information offered here is sufficient to help you make sound judgments of your own if you desire.

FEEDING MANAGEMENT

The energy requirements of cats varies depending on size and weight, activity levels, environmental factors, the presence of disease, and stress levels. There are also special energy and nutrient requirements during different stages of life, such as growth, pregnancy, reproduction, and old age. Cats are obligate carnivores (that is, meat-eating is biologically necessary) and have specific nutritional requirements due to their dependence on meat-based diets.

A common way of looking at cat nutrition is by life stages: growth (kittens), adults, and seniors. However, the concept of lifestyle, or feeding for activity, is more comprehensive and better explains how the nutritional needs of adult cats can best be met. Compared with a healthy, normally active adult animal, energy needs are increased for growing, pregnant, lactating, and very active animals. In addition, there are specific nutritional considerations for cats with specific diseases.

ADULT CATS

Adult cats require sufficient nutrients to meet energy needs and to maintain and repair body tissues. Feeding amounts for maintenance of adult cats should be based on the animal's size and energy output. Activity levels vary dramatically between cats and play an important role in determining caloric intake. Demands for energy can vary as follows:

• House cats can have a wide variety of activity levels. An animal with a "normal" activity level should receive what we will call maintenance energy. A pampered lap cat may require 10% below maintenance, while an active cat that regularly exercises outdoors may require maintenance plus 20% to 40%.

• Show cats must be fed a balanced diet and the correct amount of energy because deficiencies may be quickly reflected in coat quality. While the cat is on the show circuit, its energy requirement may increase by more than 20%. However, the cat should be fed maintenance amounts when not on the show circuit.

• Environment influences energy needs. Extreme hot or cold weather can increase the cat's energy needs so that the cat can maintain body temperatures. Both keeping warm and keeping cool require extra energy expenditure.

• An animal recovering from surgery or suffering from a disease may have an increased nutritional requirement for repair and healing and to fight infection.

Energy Needs

The significance of determining energy requirements is that cats eat to acquire energy. Once the energy needs of the body are met, intake is supposed to stop. Although some animals go beyond this and overeat, the principle is important and determines how diets are balanced between the energy content of the food (calories) and all the other nutrients.

We will walk through the steps in determining the feeding amounts for cats, but you will not normally need to be able to figure this out for yourself. The feeding guidelines on packages are already set so that owners with cats fitting the food's purposes will have an excellent starting point. The amount may need to be adjusted up or down a little to meet individual variation, but the feeding guidelines do provide a sound, scientific starting point.

Methods of Feeding

Cats may be fed successfully in a number of ways that meet both the owners' and the animals' needs and circumstances:

• **Portion-control feeding:** The food for a meal is measured and offered as a meal, thereby controlling the amount of food that can be consumed. This method is used for weight-control programs and for animals who might overeat if free-choice feeding were used. Food can be provided in one or more meals daily. Veterinarians and other professionals often recommend feeding adult cats twice a day. This means that the package feeding guidelines are divided into two meals spaced 8–12 hours part. Kittens, lactating queens, and animals recovering from certain medical conditions often require more than two meals per day.

• **Free-choice feeding:** This is also known as ad-lib feeding or free feeding. Food is available at all times, as much as the cat wants, whenever the cat wants it. Most lactating queens are fed by the free-choice method, and it is generally the method of choice for feeding most cats. This method is most appropriate when feeding dry food, which will not spoil if left out. Some cats, however, will overeat with this method, so an associated disease must be considered: obesity. If the cat begins to put on too much weight, the owner will need to switch to portion-control feeding.

• **Timed feeding method:** This method involves making a portion of food available for the cat to eat for a specified period of time. For example, the food can be placed in the cat's bowl for 30 minutes. After that time, if the cat has not consumed the food, it is removed. This is the usual method by which canned foods are fed.

SPECIAL NUTRITIONAL CONSIDERATIONS
Kittens

Kittens receive total nutrition from mother's milk for about the first 4 weeks of life. After that, food is gradually added, and after a few more weeks, they are fully weaned. During the first weeks of life, body weight may double or triple, and this rapid growth will continue (although at a gradually decreasing rate) until maturity. Large amounts of energy and nutrients are required in balanced quantities to support this spectacular growth.

Kittens are best fed mother's milk; it is perfect for their needs. However, circumstances may require that the kittens be fed a commercial milk replacer: if the queen is ill,

has an extremely large litter, does not produce enough milk, wanders off, or dies. Research has shown that a properly formulated milk replacer can come very close to producing the growth of kittens nursed by the queen. The feeding instructions on the kitten milk replacer container should be followed explicitly, and nothing should be mixed with a premium-quality formula other than water. The balance for kittens is delicate and precise; additions can upset the nutrient relationships.

Generally, orphaned or hand-fed kittens will be offered moistened kitten food at about 3 weeks of age. The moistener should be their milk replacer and should be gradually reduced over time until the kittens are eating dry kitten food at about 5 or 6 weeks of age. Initially, the food will be more of a plaything than food, but the youngsters will soon catch on as they watch Mom eat her food. When the kittens are 5–6 weeks old, they should be nibbling on their dry food consistently. This process of gradually introducing kitten food is important in training the kittens to eat when they are weaned. It also helps the queen by providing a separate source of nutrition for the rapidly growing kittens.

After weaning, kittens are usually fed free-choice—dry or nutrient-dense canned food—with fresh water available at all times.

Most queens will suckle their kittens until 7–8 weeks of age. By this time, 80% to 90% of the kitten's total nutrient intake should be from kitten food. Kittens need large amounts of energy equaling about two to three times that of an adult cat, based on kilograms of body weight. Kittens also need about 30% of total energy from protein. Therefore, kitten food must meet all the nutritional needs, including high amounts of energy and protein, from weaning until maturity at about 1 year of age.

Females in the Reproductive Years

Nutritional needs of cats during reproduction are different for gestation (pregnancy) and lactation. The gestation period in cats is about 9 weeks—65 days. The important point to remember is that cats in any life stage or with any lifestyle should be fed to condition. Keep them looking healthy and avoid laying down excess fat.

Gestation

During the first 6 weeks of gestation, the fetuses do not grow significantly and the mother's nutritional needs can be met with her maintenance food, providing it is suitable for all life stages or specifically identified as a gestation diet.

Beginning with the seventh week of gestation, food intake should be increased gradually by up to 50% over her maintenance intake at the time of breeding. The mild increase is continued until delivery (which is called queening in cats). This will support the rapid growth of the fetuses during the last 3 weeks of gestation.

A queen with a large litter may need to be fed more frequently, especially in the final stages of pregnancy, because her stomach may not be able to expand sufficiently to accommodate normal-size meals. Also, it is not unusual for the appetite to drop near queening. At queening and the day immediately after, queens frequently lose their appetite. Keeping nutrient-dense, highly palatable foods available at this time is beneficial so that when they do eat, they get as much nutrition in each mouthful as possible.

PRACTICAL FEEDING TIPS FOR GESTATION

- Feed a diet that is highly digestible and energy and nutrient dense.
- Do not increase food intake until the seventh week of gestation.
- Provide several small meals per day during gestation.
- Increase food intake to approximately 1.5 times maintenance by the end of gestation (a 50% increase).
- Queens should gain about 15% to 25% of their body weight by the end of gestation.
- Queens should weigh 5% to 10% above their normal body weight after queening.

Lactation

Large amounts of nutrients are required for a lactating cat. During the first week of lactation, food intake will typically be about 50% to 75% greater than the maintenance level. During the second week, food intake may be increased to twice the maintenance level and to three times maintenance during the third week.

The third and fourth weeks of lactation are the most nutritionally demanding for the new moms. Their offspring are still consuming almost all of their nutrients from milk and have not begun substantial intake of either dry or canned food. Once the kittens start eating some of the mother's food or food placed out specifically for them, their consumption of milk will begin to level off and may even decrease until weaning. Because the large volume of food the queen needs to support this large milk production may be difficult to consume, it is important to feed a nutrient-dense diet to prevent the breakdown of body proteins and fats. Lactating queens can usually be fed free-choice during lactation.

At weaning time, the food amount for the queen should be tapered back to the amount she was receiving when she was bred. Continued feeding of the lactation amount will only put extra weight on her.

The quantity and quality of dietary protein influence milk production. If a queen is being fed a high quality, nutritionally balanced pet food, she will not require additional vitamin or mineral supplementation during her breeding cycle. The use of such supplements is unlikely to be beneficial and, in some cases, may actually do harm.

PRACTICAL FEEDING TIPS FOR LACTATION

- Feed a diet that is highly digestible and energy and nutrient dense.
- Provide adequate calories to prevent excess weight loss.
- Feed two to three times maintenance level during peak lactation.
- Provide free-choice feeding or several small meals per day during peak lactation.
- Slowly reduce the mother's intake for the week before weaning.
- Always provide clean, fresh water free-choice.

Geriatric Cats

Cats begin to show visible age-related changes when they are 7–12 years old. Before those changes become visible, though, there are metabolic, immunological, and body composition changes that slowly begin. Some of the changes are unavoidable. Others can be managed with diet. If, however, those dietary changes are not made until the overt signs are visible, the opportunity to prevent or slow those changes is past. Nutritional adjustment should begin early. Cats should start eating a senior diet at about 7 years of age. As a cat ages, changes in body tissues may result in health issues, including

- Deterioration of skin and coat
- Loss of muscle mass
- Decreased antibody response
- Decreased ability to fight off infection
- Obesity
- Dental problems
- More frequent intestinal problems

The main objectives in the feeding of geriatric cats should be to maintain health and optimum body weight, slow or prevent the development of chronic disease, and minimize or decrease clinical signs of diseases that may already be present.

Older cats have been shown to progressively put on body fat in spite of consuming fewer calories. This change in body composition is inevitable and may be aggravated by either reduced energy expenditure or a change in metabolic rate. Either way, it is important to feed a diet with a lower caloric density to avoid weight gain from fat and with a normal protein level to help maintain muscle mass.

Studies have shown that the protein requirement for older cats does not decrease with age and that protein levels do not contribute to the development or progression of renal failure. It is important to feed older cats diets that contain optimum levels of highly digestible protein to help maintain good muscle mass. Avoid senior diets that have reduced levels of protein.

Other special nutrients have been shown to be beneficial in older animals:

Vitamin E: Antibody response decreases as cats age. Increasing the intake of vitamin E in cats older than 7 years can increase their antibody levels to those seen in younger cats.

Antioxidants: As cats age, free radical particles accumulate and can damage body tissues and contribute to the signs of aging. Antioxidants such as vitamin E and beta–carotene help eliminate the free radical particles. Senior diets should contain higher levels of these antioxidants to help nutritionally manage the free radical particles at the cellular level. Antioxidants can also increase the effectiveness of the immune system in senior cats.

Geriatric care should involve a consistent daily routine, regular attention to normal health care procedures, and periodic veterinary examinations for assessment of the presence or progression of chronic disease. Stressful situations and abrupt changes in daily routines should be avoided. If a drastic change must be made in an older pet's routine, attempts should be made to minimize stress and to accomplish the change in a gradual manner.

Obese Cats

An obese cat is not a pretty sight. Cumbersome and clumsy, unable to reach all the places on his body that need grooming, he suffers a marked deterioration in athletic ability and appearance and is subject to skin problems. Obese cats also face increased risk of contracting diabetes and are poor candidates for surgery and anesthesia.

Obesity results when an animal consistently takes in more calories than needed. Some contributing factors include overfeeding, inactivity, reproductive status, environment, body type, age, and genetic predisposition. Assessing body condition is an important step in the overall evaluation of a cat's nutritional well-being and can especially help in determining feline obesity. Comparing a cat to the pictures and descriptions in the Body Condition Chart makes it easy to determine if a cat is overweight or not. If you suspect that your cat is either overweight or obese, a complete evaluation by a veterinarian is always recommended. You will want to rule out the few medical conditions that may contribute to obesity before you proceed with any weight-loss or weight-management program.

As a subjective assessment of body condition, you should be able to feel the backbone and the ribs in a cat of healthy weight. If the ribs cannot be felt or cannot be felt without pressing, there is too much fat. In addition, looking down on the cat from above, there should be a noticeable "waist" between the back of the rib cage and the hips. Viewed from the side, there should be a "tuck" in the tummy; the abdomen should go up from the bottom of the rib cage to inside the thighs. Cats who fail this simple evaluation may be overweight.

Obesity is easier to prevent than to cure. However, it is never too late to reverse obesity, though it requires long-term patience and commitment. Increased activity, behavior modification—for both you and your cat—and calorie restriction are your weapons against feline obesity. Increased activity burns extra calories and tones muscles. Well-conditioned muscles will burn extra calories during the day—even after the exercise has stopped.

Exercising a cat can be fun. Often, the owner ends up burning more calories than the cat, but there are activities that work for the cat:

• Find a toy that your cat particularly likes and play with her daily. Feathers on the end of short sticks, the light from laser pointers, table tennis balls, crumpled paper, and climbing towers can all encourage play. The activity needs to be sustained for 20 minutes or so each day to help tone muscles and burn a few calories, but any activity is better than none.

• Place your cat's food and water in a different part of the house from where she spends her free time. This should be away from the litter box too. Although it is not a lot of exercise to walk from one area of the house to another, it is exercise and it discourages eating out of boredom.

• Make your cat work for her food. There are small, round plastic balls that can be filled with food. To get the food, the cat must roll the ball around so the food spills out a small round hole, one kibble at a time. This forces your cat to exercise. You can go one step further and use several balls hidden around the house. Your cat must then hunt for her supper. Of course, you must still measure the food so she doesn't get too much each day, and you may have to go find the empty balls if she leaves them under the couch or dresser.

• Provide cat trees for climbing.

• Throw things for your cat to chase. One ingenious owner throws her cat's dry food ration, a piece at a time!

• Take your cat for walks. Many cats learn to enjoy walking on a leash.

Use your imagination, but be cautious. Don't let a fat cat become exhausted, overheated, or out of breath. Also keep in mind that an old cat may not be able to exercise vigorously.

BODY CONDITION CHART

THIN CAT

- Ribs, lumbar vertebrae, and pelvic bones easily visible
- Thin neck and narrow waist
- Obvious abdominal tuck
- No fat in flank folds; folds often absent

UNDERWEIGHT CAT

- Backbone and ribs easily palpable
- Minimal fat covering
- Minimal waist when viewed from above
- Slightly tucked abdomen

IDEAL CAT

- Ribs palpable but not visible
- Slight waist ovserved behind ribs when viewed from above
- Abdomen tucked up; flank folds present

OVERWEIGHT CAT

- Slight increase in fat over ribs, but ribs still easily palpable
- Abdomen slightly rounded; flanks concave
- Flank folds hang down with moderate amount of fat; jiggle noted when walking

OBESE CAT

- Ribs and backbone not easily palpable under a heavy fat covering
- Abdomen rounded; waist barely visible to absent
- Prominent flank folds that sway from side to side when walking

Replace food treats as expressions of love with play, grooming, stroking, or conversation. If you cannot resist the fat cat that begs for food at the dinner table, put her in another room when it's your dinner time. If yours is a multicat household, the consistent winner of the food competition sweepstakes is often obese. If this is the case, separate the cats at mealtimes if at all possible.

Cats use fat as their primary energy source. A cat who consumes more energy (calories) than its body uses stores that excess energy in the form of fat. An overweight or obese cat will store fat more easily if the calories consumed are in the form of fat rather than in the form of carbohydrates. A diet based on replacement of some fat with highly digestible carbohydrates is a good low-calorie alternative. Digestible carbohydrates contain less than half the calories of equal quantities of fat and do not have the disadvantages of indigestible fiber. Recent research has also shown that a blend of low-glycemic carbohydrates, such as corn or sorghum, can help cats lose weight and avoid regain. Advantages of these foods include low calories so the owner can still fill up the bowl, normal fiber levels for less stool volume, and easier cleanup. Portion control is still necessary but need not be as stringent as if you were feeding the regular diet.

It is important to feed an overweight cat a diet with a normal fiber level. In premium dry cat food, normal fiber is usually rated at approximately 3% of the guaranteed analysis of the contents. Avoid high-fiber diets that are often promoted for feline weight loss. High-fiber foods may reduce the digestibility and absorption of many nutrients and lead to frequent urges to defecate. In addition to providing what would be considered poor-quality nutrition, high-fiber diets may also result in large, frequent stools and poor skin and coat condition.

If a cat is started on a weight-loss program using a regular adult food, a good way to begin is to reduce caloric intake by 25% of his maintenance intake, then decrease the intake by 10% increments every 2–3 weeks until a 1% weight loss per week is achieved. This means that if the cat weighs 15 pounds, a 1% loss would be about 2.5 ounces. If the cat has been fed one large meal a day or free-choice, divide the daily ration into several small meals (at least two meals a day) and pick up what has not been eaten 30 minutes after each meal.

Proceed slowly when changing diets, mixing the new with the old in ever-increasing proportions over a period of 4 days. This method increases the likelihood of acceptance of the new diet and decreases the occurrence of gastrointestinal upsets. Be patient. Weight reduction in cats is necessarily a slow process. If food intake is too severely restricted, the cat risks developing a serious liver disorder called hepatic lipidosis. Expect a few setbacks and plateaus. It will take at least 4 months for an obese cat to realize a 15% weight loss. At this point, reassess your cat's body condition and proceed from there.

However, changing diets is not the only consideration for the owner of an obese cat. There is also owner behavior. A successful weight management program requires a permanent change in the behaviors that have allowed the pet to become overweight. Here are some tips for a successful weight loss program:

- Ensure that you are committed to the cat's weight loss.
- Place the cat in another room when the family eats.
- Feed the cat several small meals throughout the day.
- Place all food—meals and treats—only in the cat's bowl.

- Reduce the amount of snacks or treats.
- Provide non-food-related attention.

To summarize the approach to overweight cats:

- Check with a veterinarian before starting your cat on a weight-management program.
- Obtain a baby scale and weigh your cat every 2 weeks.
- Feed a low-fat, normal-protein, low-glycemic carbohydrate food to restrict the calories available from fat.
- Eliminate all food treats.
- Increase your cat's activity level.
- Try combining feeding time with playtime by tossing your cat dry food kibbles one piece at a time.
- Divide the daily food allotment into several smaller meals.
- Make sure that your cat does not lose more than 1% to 1.5% of its initial weight per week.
- Be patient and consistent.

NUTRITIONAL NEEDS UNIQUE TO CATS

The cat evolved as a carnivore—an obligate carnivore. That is, it requires certain nutrients that are available only from animal sources. The feline intestine is adapted for a high-fat, high-protein diet.

Some people tend to treat the cat like a small dog, but the cat has very specific nutritional requirements. This is because the cat is unable to synthesize certain essential nutrients from other food components and therefore requires these nutrients to be preformed in its diet:

- **Protein:** Cats have the highest requirement for protein of all domesticated species. When cats were evolving, a high-protein and high-fat diet was always available, so cats never found it necessary to conserve proteins. Cats always "waste" some of the dietary protein by breaking it down for energy.
- **Taurine:** Cats require taurine because they cannot convert other amino acids into taurine. Taurine is important to prevent visual, cardiac, and reproductive problems and is found only in meat and fish.
- **Fats:** Cats also require both linoleic and arachidonic acids to prevent skin and coat problems and poor reproduction. Arachidonic acid is found only in animal sources of fat.
- **Vitamins:** Preformed vitamin A must also be present in the cat's diet. Cats cannot break beta-carotene into two molecules of vitamin A. Preformed vitamin A is also found only in animal tissues.

Cats are also somewhat peculiar in their eating behavior. They tend to eat and drink limited quantities on numerous occasions, consuming up to 16 small meals during a 24-hour period when fed on an ad-lib basis.

NUTRIENTS

Water, proteins, fats, carbohydrates, vitamins, and minerals are the six major nutrient groups required by cats, and each is discussed separately in this section:

- **Water** is required for digestion, chemical reactions, transportation of nutrients and wastes, and temperature regulation and as a component of cells, blood, and lymph.
- **Proteins** supply amino acids that are needed for cell structure, maintenance, and repair; are needed for production of enzymes, hormones, and antibodies; and can be broken down to supply energy. It is essential that the food provides high-quality proteins to the cat.

Protein quality is determined by the presence and availability of the essential amino acids (EAAs).

• **Fats** supply fatty acids needed for cell structure, some hormones, and chemical reactions and as a major source of energy. Feline diets must provide essential fatty acids. A ratio of omega-6 to omega-3 fatty acids between 5:1 and 10:1 has been shown to be beneficial in cats.

• **Carbohydrates**, such as starches, are used for energy, and as fiber. Fiber is important for gut health, bacterial population stability, nutrient availability, and stool formation. Remember two important factors: fiber level and fiber source. A diet should contain optimal fiber levels and a source that is moderately fermentable.

• **Vitamins** are needed for chemical reactions and energy transfer. There are two main groups: fat-soluble vitamins and water-soluble vitamins. An excess of fat-soluble vitamins is potentially toxic because they are stored in the body fat reserves.

• **Minerals** are needed for bones, teeth, fluid balance, chemical reactions, and oxygen transport.

• **Energy** is required for movement and chemical reactions within the body. Energy can be derived from the breakdown of fats, carbohydrates, and protein. Metabolizable energy is the best measure of the energy content of a food. The most accurate way to measure metabolizable energy is from animal tests.

WATER

Water is the most important nutrient. It is essential for life; is present in blood and lymph, inside cells, and between cells; and accounts for approximately 60% to 70% of the body weight of an adult cat. A deficiency of water may have serious repercussions, while a 15% loss can result in death.

Functions

Water has many functions. It

- Acts as a liquid solvent for digestion and for chemical reactions
- Disperses heat produced by chemical reactions away from tissues and organs
- Regulates body temperature through evaporative cooling from the skin and respiratory tract
- Transports nutrients, by-products of metabolism, and wastes
- Is the principal component of cells, blood, and lymph

There are two basic sources of water: ingested and metabolic. *Ingested water* is taken into the body by drinking or eating. For example, a dry pet food may contain up to 10% moisture, while a canned pet food may contain up to 85% water. *Metabolic water* is produced when fats, carbohydrates, and proteins are broken down into energy.

Inadequate water intake may result from reduced availability, incorrect temperature (too hot or too cold), or poor quality. It will result in reduced food intake, which in turn will affect physical activity, reproduction, lactation, or growth.

Water is excreted in urine, feces, and expired air. In humans, water is also lost in sweating. Sweating is unimportant in cats, as they decrease their body heat through panting and loss of water from the respiratory tract. Vomiting, diarrhea, blood loss, and lactation are other forms of water loss.

PROTEINS

There has always been controversy over the type and amount of protein required in the diet. Proteins in food are the basic building materials for cells, tissues, organs, enzymes, hormones, and antibodies and are essential for growth, maintenance, reproduction, and repair.

Structure

Amino acids are the building blocks of proteins. Chains of amino acids link together to form proteins. There are 20 different amino acids commonly found in proteins. They can be joined together in different sequences, lengths, and shapes, much like the 26 letters of the alphabet that form many thousands of words. Two amino acids are joined together to form a *dipeptide*. Three amino acids form a *tripeptide*, and more than three makes up a *polypeptide*. Proteins have large numbers of amino acids.

When analyzed closely, amino acids are composed of carbon (C), hydrogen (H), oxygen (O), nitrogen (N), and sometimes sulfur (S). Proteins contain nitrogen, but fats and carbohydrates do not.

Classification

Amino acids are divided into two groups:

• **Essential amino acids:** These cannot be synthesized by the animal in sufficient quantities to meet the cat's needs and *must* be supplied in the diet.

• **Nonessential amino acids:** These can be synthesized by the animal, so they are not needed in the diet.

ESSENTIAL AMINO ACIDS

Arginine	Threonine
Methionine	Taurine
Histidine	Leucine
Valine	Tryptophan
Phenylalanine	Lysine
Isoleucine	

Taurine

Taurine is usually classed as an amino acid but is more accurately described as an amino sulphonic acid. Taurine is an essential nutrient for cats because cats cannot create within their own bodies enough taurine to meet their needs. In humans, taurine can be produced from the essential amino acid methionine and cysteine. Cats lack the enzyme for this reaction, so taurine must be obtained from the food. Taurine is found only in foods of animal origin, such as meat, eggs, and fish. Grains and vegetables do not contain taurine. Taurine is required for

- The prevention of eye disease (feline central retinal degeneration)
- The prevention of heart disease (feline dilated cardiomyopathy)
- Healthy reproduction, fetal growth, and survival

Functions

The role of protein in the diet is not to provide body proteins directly but to supply sufficient quantities of the amino acids so that the cat can make its own proteins. If the diet does not contain enough of any one of the EAAs, the cat cannot manufacture the proteins required for a healthy life.

During digestion, proteins are broken down to small sizes: individual amino acids, dipeptides, or tripeptides. These are then absorbed from the small intestine into the bloodstream and distributed throughout the body.

The individual amino acids are used for

- The synthesis of structural proteins such as muscle, hair, and skin
- The synthesis of functional proteins, such as enzymes, antibodies, and hormones
- Energy. However, its primary uses should be for structure and function.

Proteins for Energy?

If energy from carbohydrates and fats is insufficient for the body's needs, proteins may be used as an energy source. In these cases, the body will generally break down tissues, such as muscle, to use as energy, resulting in muscle wasting and tissue loss. However, even if carbohydrates and fats in the diet supply sufficient amounts of energy, a small part of the protein in the food will always be used for energy.

Cats use the protein in their food by breaking it down and using it for energy. For this reason, cats have a high minimum requirement for total protein in the diet: 26% to 30%, versus 18% to 22% for dogs.

Quality

Protein quality tests measure the ability of protein in food to provide EAAs, to be metabolized, and to support growth. Various tests that are used:

- **Amino acid profile** measures the types and levels of the EAAs contained in a protein. If all the EAAs are present in sufficient amount for the cat, the protein is called a *complete* protein. If an EAA is missing or present only in reduced amounts, the protein is called an *incomplete* protein. Meat, fish, and egg proteins have complete amino acid profiles. Vegetable proteins and cereal grains, such as soy flour and soybean meal, have incomplete amino acid profiles. Soy has insufficient levels of methionine, while other cereal proteins may have poor levels of lysine and tryptophan.
- **Digestibility** measures how well the protein can be broken down into its amino acids. In general, the greater the digestibility, the better the protein quality. A complete protein may not be a "quality" protein if it cannot be digested well in the body. An incomplete protein of high digestibility will

still not be a quality protein, because it is missing some amino acids.

• **Biological value** (BV) measures the percentage of protein that is actually absorbed and retained in the body and not excreted through the urine or feces. The higher the value, the better the protein source. In general, meat proteins have higher biological values than plant proteins. The quality of even the same type of meat proteins, however, can vary quite considerably. The challenge is to use only the high-quality animal-based proteins. Grain or cereal proteins have low biological value; they are not complete proteins.

• **Protein efficiency ratio** measures the rate of growth of an animal when fed different proteins. It is a measure of the efficiency of use and retention of the protein in the animal.

Sources

Proteins can be obtained from a number of sources:

• Meat can be high quality, but this will depend on the cut, source, and type of meat. Animal-based proteins such as chicken, lamb, turkey, beef, and egg have *complete* amino acid profiles.

• Fish is a very good protein source.

• Eggs are regarded as the quality standard for protein sources. They have a high BV, often given as 100, but the true value is about 98. (However, raw egg white contains avidin, an antivitamin, which ties up or binds biotin from egg yolk. Eggs should therefore be cooked before they are fed to cats.

• Vegetable/cereal protein quality will vary with the type, age, and conditions under which the plant was grown. Generally, vegetable and cereal proteins are deficient in some EAAs and have a low BV. Cereal grains also contain starch, and poorly processed starch can

depress the digestion of the proteins in the diet, decreasing the efficiency of the proteins.

• Soy is often used as a protein source. It is an incomplete protein. Improperly processed soy contains an enzyme inhibitor that prevents proper protein digestion. Soy also contains phytates that can bind calcium, phosphorous, and zinc and contains large amounts of nonabsorbable oligosaccharides that may be rapidly fermented by intestinal bacteria, leading to gas production and flatulence.

FATS

Fats include both oils and fats and may be called lipids. Oils are liquids at room temperature, while fats are solid. Adult cats should typically get no less than 21% of the contents of a premium cat food.

Functions

Fats perform several functions:

• As the most concentrated form of food energy, they provide more than twice the energy that proteins and carbohydrates do. Fats can also be stored, so they are an important form of stored energy.

• They are essential in the structure of cells and for the production of some hormones.

• They are required for absorption and use of fat-soluble vitamins.

• They provide insulation and protection under the skin and around internal organs.

• They are important in inflammation. Fat contains fatty acids, which are incorporated in the cell membranes of every cell in the body. When those cells are irritated or injured, the fatty acids break down and contribute to inflammation. Some inflammation is good; it is a protective process that helps deal with infections, irritants, and invaders of all sorts. Too much inflammation—for example, an allergy—is not helpful. With the right choice of fats and the composition of those fats, inflammation can be helped. Not too much, not too little—just right.

Classification

Saturated Fatty Acids

Saturated fats are common in red meats such as beef. These fats tend to be solid at room temperature.

Unsaturated Fatty Acids

There are two types of unsaturated fatty acids: monounsaturated and polyunsaturated. Olive oil is a monounsaturated fat. Margarine is a polyunsaturated fat. These fats tend to be softer or liquid at room temperature.

Essential Fatty Acids

Essential fatty acids must be provided in the diet because cats cannot produce them within their own bodies in sufficient amounts to meet their needs. A deficiency of essential fatty acids may result in reduced growth or increased skin problems. *Linoleic acid* and *arachidonic acid* are essential fatty acids for cats. Humans can convert linoleic acid into arachidonic acid. Cats do not have enough of the enzyme needed for this step. Therefore, cats require both linoleic *and* arachidonic acid in their diets. Arachidonic acid is important for the maintenance of the skin and coat, for kidney function, and for reproduction.

Fatty Acids and Inflammation

Omega-6 and omega-3 fatty acids play a vital role in inflammation. These fatty acids are found in the cell membranes of all cells in the body. When a cell is damaged, the fatty acids are released and broken down into smaller compounds (end products, or metabolites). These end products play a role in causing the redness, swelling, and itching of inflammation.

The end products from omega-6 fatty acids are highly inflammatory and can cause a high degree of redness, swelling, and itchiness. The end products from omega-3 fatty acids are far less inflammatory, so the reaction to the cell damage is far less.

The saying "You are what you eat" is true for cats when it comes to the amounts of each type of fatty acid found in the cell walls. As the omega-6 fatty acid content of the diet increases, more omega-6 fatty acids are built into the cell membranes, resulting in a greater inflammatory reaction when the cell is damaged. Replacing some omega-6 with omega-3 fatty acids can lessen the inflammatory reaction. This appears to be true regardless of whether the inflammation is in the skin (from allergies), the joints (from arthritis), the intestines (from inflammatory bowel disease), or even in the kidney (from progressive renal failure).

Adjusted Ratios of Omega-6 and Omega-3 Fatty Acids

Studies in cats have shown that the ratio of omega-6 to omega-3 fatty acids appears best when it is between 5:1 and 10:1. It is impossible to accurately determine the fatty acid ratio of a diet if the owner prepares home-cooked foods. Obtaining an accurate ratio by supplementing homemade or other commercial diets with omega-3 capsules is also unlikely; the ratio of fatty acids in the base diet is not known and may vary from batch to batch. If cats are to benefit from the effects of these fatty acid ratios, they must be fed a fixed-formula food that guarantees these ratios. Omega-3 fatty acids come from cold-water fishes either as fish oil or in fish meal. Omega-6 fatty acids come from grains and from fats of animals that were fed grains. Some animal fats, such as lamb, may contain omega-3s if the lambs were fed on grasses that contain omega-3s.

CARBOHYDRATES AND FIBER

The evolving carnivores derived most, if not all, of their carbohydrate intake as semidigested material from the gut of their prey. There is as yet no accepted minimum dietary carbohydrate requirement for cats, but carbohydrates and fiber play a vital role in the health of the intestine and are likely to be important for reproduction. Carbohydrates are made of carbon (C), hydrogen (H), and oxygen (O) and include sugars (such as glucose, fructose, and sucrose), starches, and fiber.

Functions

Dietary carbohydrates have several functions:

- Providing a source of quick energy
- Providing bulk (fiber) for peristalsis (muscular contractions of the gastrointestinal tract that result in the movement of food material through the intestines). The type and quantity of fiber may increase the absorption of nutrients.
- Providing short-chain fatty acids (SC-FAs, from bacterial fermentation of fiber) for use by intestinal cells for healthy gut formation
- Helping to maintain an optimal bacterial population in the small intestine, which serves to nutritionally manage chronic diarrheas
- Aiding in proper stool formation and consistency: fiber attracts and holds a certain amount of water, which helps prevent constipation.
- Helping to balance the intestinal bacteria within the small intestine. Fructooligosaccharides (FOS) can be used by "good" bacteria such as *Lactobacillus* and *Bifidobacterium* but not by the "bad" bacteria such as *Escherichia coli* (*E. coli*) and *Salmonella*.
- Cellulose can increase the movement of hair from a cat's intestine. If properly balanced with a moderately fermentable fiber, the

combination can promote both intestinal health and prevent hairballs.

Classification

The building blocks of carbohydrates are simple sugars, or *saccharides*. The number of sugars combined together and their structure classify carbohydrates.

Monosaccharides

Monosaccharides are single sugars, such as glucose, galactose, and fructose.

Disaccharides

Disaccharides are two monosaccharides joined together, such as lactose and sucrose (which is table sugar).

OLIGOSACCHARIDES

Oligosaccharides are 2–10 monosaccharides joined together.

FRUCTOOLIGOSACCHARIDES

Fructooligosaccharides (FOS) are oligosaccharides that have two or four fructose molecules attached to a glucose molecule. Fructooligosaccharides can be broken down by certain "good" or beneficial intestinal bacteria, hence their role in modifying the intestinal bacterial population by "feeding the good bugs."

POLYSACCHARIDES

Polysaccharides are chains of three or more saccharides (sometimes hundreds). Examples include starch, glycogen, and cellulose, which are all long chains of glucose molecules. However, because of their different chemical bonds between the glucose molecules, they have vastly different properties:

- **Starch** is the form in which plants store energy. (Animals store extra energy as fat.) Corn, sorghum, barley, rice, and wheat contain starch, which is soluble in water (soluble polysaccharide) and can be digested by cats if processed properly.

- **Fiber** is a polysaccharide present in plant cell walls that is resistant to digestion by the cat's intestinal enzymes. Cellulose is an insoluble polysaccharide (fiber) that is not broken down by animal digestive enzymes.
- **Glycogen** is a form of energy storage in animals and is a source of rapid energy. Compared with fat, there is not much energy stored in the body as glycogen.

Fiber is a carbohydrate that is resistant to digestion by mammalian enzymes; however, bacteria in the intestine of the cat may be able to break down these bonds in a process known as fermentation. Fermentation produces SCFAs, which are beneficial to the cells that line the intestine.

Disadvantages of Excess Fiber

While including the correct type and amount of fiber in the diets of cats is beneficial, there are numerous problems that may be encountered if the wrong levels or wrong types of fibers are used. Fiber levels of more than 3% may be excessive for cats. If the fiber is moderately fermentable and blended with a nonfermentable fiber, such as cellulose, it can help move hair through the intestinal tract and avoid hairballs. If a level greater than 3% is used and it is nonfermentable, it does nothing more than create extra stool volume, decreases nutrient digestibility, and dilute calories.

- High levels of fiber can hold water and prevent its absorption from the large intestine, increasing the amount of feces and also the frequency of defecation.
- High levels of fiber decrease the digestibility of protein, fat, and carbohydrates.

- High levels of fiber can trap some minerals and vitamins in the stool.
- Highly fermentable fiber sources can lead to gas production and flatulence. This also occurs commonly in cats fed foods containing underprocessed soybean meal or soy flour, which contain indigestible oligosaccharides.
- High levels of poorly fermentable fibers can result in very dry stools and may lead to constipation.

VITAMINS

Vitamins are catalysts for enzyme reactions. They facilitate reactions but are not part of the reaction themselves. Tiny amounts of vitamins are essential to cats for normal metabolic functioning. Vitamins neither are used as building blocks nor can be broken down for energy. Most vitamins cannot be synthesized in the body and are therefore essential in the diet. Vitamins are classified as fat-soluble or water-soluble.

Because of supplements hypervitaminosis (poisoning due to excess vitamins) is more common than hypovitaminosis (vitamin deficiencies). When feeding a complete and balanced diet, it is unnecessary to supplement unless a veterinarian diagnoses a specific vitamin deficiency. Excess water-soluble vitamins are excreted via the urine. Fat-soluble vitamins are stored and, therefore, are potentially toxic. Excess vitamin A may result in bone and joint pain, brittle bones, and dry skin. Excess vitamin D may result in very dense bones, soft-tissue calcification, or joint calcification.

Fat-Soluble Vitamins

The fat-soluble vitamins—A, D, E, and K—play important roles in developing structure and supporting the immune system, and they serve as antioxidants. Absorbed together with fat, they are stored wherever fat is deposited.

Hence, there is a risk of accumulating excess and possibly toxic levels if high levels are given. Though they are normally stored, they can be excreted via the feces.

Vitamin A

Vitamin A is essential for growth, vision, and the structure and function of skin and mucous membranes. It is also an important antioxidant. Vitamin A may be obtained directly (preformed) from liver, fish oils, egg yolks, or butter, or it may be converted from a precursor called *beta-carotene* (also written as β-carotene), which is present in carrots and other red, orange, or dark green vegetables. Cats cannot convert beta-carotene to vitamin A and must have preformed dietary vitamin A, which is present only in animal tissues.

Vitamin D

Vitamin D is essential for calcium metabolism. It is required for growth and for proper bone and tooth development. Vitamin D must be activated by metabolism in the liver and kidneys. It exists in several forms, depending on whether it is from plant or animal sources. Vitamin D is found in liver, kidney, fish oils, and eggs.

Vitamin E

Vitamin E is another important antioxidant and provides support for the immune system. Senior cats (those over 7 years of age) benefit from increased vitamin E intake compared with their younger counterparts. It is extracted from soybean oil and is also found in liver, egg, wheat germ oil, milk, and butter.

Vitamin K

Vitamin K promotes normal blood clotting. It is produced naturally in the intestines of cats by normal intestinal bacteria.

★ ★ ★

Good-quality foods contain all the vitamins a cat will need; no supplements should be necessary.

Water-Soluble Vitamins

The water-soluble vitamins—C and B—are involved in the use of food and transfer of energy in reactions. They are required in small, regular amounts. They are absorbed from the intestine along with water and are not stored. Water-soluble vitamins are excreted primarily in the urine but also in the feces. Because they are not stored, excesses of these vitamins are rare except when given in massive doses.

Vitamin C (Ascorbic Acid)

Vitamin C is essential for wound healing and tissue repair and also acts as an antioxidant. Cats can synthesize their own vitamin C from glucose; therefore, a dietary source is not important if sufficient glucose is present. Stressed animals have benefited from dietary vitamin C, which is why it is included in some premium foods. Deficiencies are rare. It occurs naturally in citrus fruits and green vegetables. Incidentally, humans and guinea pigs cannot synthesize vitamin C.

Vitamin B$_1$ (Thiamine)

Thiamine is important in carbohydrate metabolism and normal functioning of the nervous system. It occurs naturally in a variety of sources, including green peas, liver, and the seed coats of cereal grains.

Vitamin B$_2$ (Riboflavin)

Riboflavin is essential for cell growth. It is found naturally in milk, meat, eggs, and leafy vegetables or can be produced synthetically.

Vitamin B₆ (Pyridoxine)

Vitamin B$_6$ (Pyridoxine)

Pyridoxine is essential for the many steps in metabolism. It occurs naturally in meats, fish, and whole-grain cereals.

Vitamin B$_{12}$ (Cobalamin)

Cobalamin is essential in the development of red blood cells. It can be obtained from meat, liver, eggs, fish, oysters, and clams. Cobalamin contains the mineral cobalt.

Pantothenic Acid

Pantothenic acid is essential for cell growth and development. It is found naturally in animal tissues and plants.

Niacin

Niacin is essential for growth, carbohydrate metabolism, and functioning of the gastrointestinal tract and nervous system. Cats cannot produce niacin from the amino acid tryptophan, so niacin must be supplied in the diet. It is found in meat, cereals, and yeast.

Biotin

Biotin is essential in protein, fat, and carbohydrate metabolism. It is found in many plant and animal tissues and is synthesized by intestinal bacteria. Biotin deficiency can result from eating excess amounts of raw egg whites (which contain a protein called avidin that binds biotin) or from treatment with some antibiotics that kill intestinal bacteria. Deficiencies, however, are very rare.

Choline

Choline is essential for normal liver function, for fat metabolism, and as a structural component of fat and nerve tissue. It is one vitamin that does find its way into structure. It can be found in meats and vegetables.

Folic Acid

Folic acid is important in the synthesis of DNA, the genetic material of cells, and in red blood cell formation. Folic acid deficiency results in anemia. It is present in many plant and animal tissues.

MINERALS

Minerals are inorganic compounds that are not metabolized and yield no energy. These nutrients cannot be synthesized by animals and must be provided in the diet. In general, minerals are most important as structural constituents of bones and teeth, for maintaining fluid balance, and for their involvement in many metabolic reactions. Minerals required in relatively large amounts are called *macrominerals*. Those needed in small quantities are called *microminerals*, or trace minerals. With commercial foods, true deficiencies are extremely rare, but imbalances may occur if the food is supplemented.

Ash Content

You may have heard the term *ash content* in relation to cat food. The value for ash is derived by burning a certain amount of the food and measuring the ash left behind. This ash is a measure of all the minerals in the food but does not allow levels of individual minerals to be determined. Therefore, ash as a percentage of the diet is not useful information. A high ash content in a diet may indicate lesser quality, because poor-quality protein sources will often raise the ash level.

Classification
Macrominerals

Macrominerals are required in comparatively greater amounts and are usually expressed as a percentage. Calcium, phosphorus, potassium, sodium, chloride, and magnesium are the most significant macrominerals for cats.

CALCIUM AND PHOSPHORUS

Calcium (Ca) and phosphorus (P) are the major structural components of bones and teeth. Ninety-nine percent of body calcium is stored in bone and is moved from bone to blood plasma when required for other functions such as blood clotting, muscle function, and nerve transmission. Calcium from blood plasma will be stored in the bones in cases of excess calcium supply. Apart from its role in the skeleton, phosphorus also is involved in enzymatic reactions and is critical to the production of cellular energy.

In addition to the level of calcium that must be in the food, the ratio of calcium to phosphorous is important. Cat foods should have a ratio of between 1:1 and 1.3:1. However, because so few problems occur in cats related to these two minerals, it is seldom an issue. When there is a problem, it is generally one of two: bone growth problems associated with oversupplementation with calcium, and bone growth problems associated with homemade diets that *do not contain enough calcium.*

Too much calcium is unlikely with commercial foods because the efforts to minimize magnesium and control total mineral avoids excess calcium. Cats fed homemade diets or fed commercial diets with supplements of calcium-rich substances are at risk. There is seldom a need to add calcium to the diet of any cat. In rare instances, a veterinarian might prescribe calcium.

Calcium deficiency is virtually nonexistent when commercial foods are fed. This problem is generally seen only in kittens fed a homemade diet consisting mostly of meat. Meat contains very low levels of calcium and very high levels of phosphorus—a very unbalanced diet. There is too little calcium to support the growth of the bones. With this low intake of calcium, proper mineralization of the bones does not occur, leading to weakening of the skeleton and bowed or broken bones.

Vitamin D is also needed for a cat to be able to properly absorb calcium into bone. If there are low levels of vitamin D in the diet, the result may be a skeletal disease called rickets. Similar in appearance to an absolute calcium deficiency, the growing kitten will develop very weak bones that can break easily.

Although the phosphorus level in the food is of lesser importance than the calcium level, when the supply of phosphorus is very high and the calcium supply is low (as is the case when a home-cooked diet contains mostly meat), the result will be a severe demineralization and weakening of the bones.

POTASSIUM

Potassium (K) is essential for nerve transmission, muscle function, and body fluid balance. Potassium deficiencies induce muscle weakness, growth problems, and heart and kidney disorders. Deficiencies are uncommon but may be associated with drug therapy (some diuretics). Potassium deficiency may also occur in some diseases, such as chronic renal failure in cats or in cats fed diets that overacidify their urine, despite adequate amounts of potassium being present in the food.

SODIUM AND CHLORIDE

Sodium (Na) and chloride (Cl) are found together as salt (NaCl). Sodium is the major electrolyte in body water and is critical in maintaining the body's balance of water. Chloride is important in producing stomach acid. Deficiencies of these two minerals are uncommon.

MAGNESIUM

Magnesium (Mg) functions with calcium in bone development and in nerve impulse conduction. Magnesium deficiency can lead to loss of appetite, vomiting, nervousness, and convulsions. Very high levels of magnesium in cats had been linked with the development of struvite urinary stones (also called uroliths). Although magnesium is a component of struvite, research has shown that magnesium is only a secondary factor in this disease. The most important cause of struvite urinary stone formation is an alkaline urinary pH, often seen when cats are fed a diet that contains high levels of cereals.

Microminerals (or Trace Elements)

IRON

Iron (Fe) is a key component of hemoglobin, the oxygen-carrying protein in red blood cells. Deficiency results in anemia.

COPPER

Copper (Cu) is involved in many enzyme systems. It is important in hemoglobin synthesis and cell protection as well as hair pigmentation. Copper deficiency can result in anemia.

MANGANESE

Manganese (Mn) is involved in many enzyme reactions, but deficiencies or excesses are rare.

ZINC

Zinc (Zn) is important for skin health and immunity. A deficiency of zinc can result in skin lesions. Calcium supplementation and phytates (found in cereals) may result in reduced zinc availability.

IODINE

Iodine (I) is essential for the synthesis of thyroid hormones that control body metabolism. A deficiency results in thyroid enlargement (goiter) in humans but is uncommon in pets. If it occurs in animals, iodine deficiency causes drowsiness and skin, hair, and reproductive disorders.

ENERGY

Energy is the primary requirement of all living organisms. The metabolism (breakdown) or oxidation of carbohydrates, fats, and proteins will yield energy, which drives all the processes that occur within the cells of cats. It is the fuel the body needs for movement, growth, maintenance, repair, and reproduction and must be obtained from food.

A cat eats to fulfill its energy needs. The major determinant for controlling food intake is the energy content of the diet. Once the demand for energy is met, consumption normally ceases; therefore, the intake of all nutrients depends on the energy content of the food. (Yes, some cats will overeat, with the excess energy stored as fat.)

Classification

Energy can be converted to heat, which can then be measured. In laboratory tests, the *gross* amount of energy in a food is determined by burning the food and measuring the amount of heat produced. In the body, the energy from the food is released via chemical reactions. A cat cannot use all the gross energy in the food because some is lost in the feces and urine.

Energy is measured in calories (cal). One calorie is the amount of heat required to raise the temperature of 1 gram (g) of water by 1 degree centigrade (C), from 14.5° to 15.5°C. All foods in the United States are labeled in kilocalories; 1,000 calories = 1 kilocalorie (kcal).

Gross Energy

Gross Energy (GE) is the total energy contained within the food. Not all of the gross energy is available to the cat.

Digestible Energy

After eating, some food passes undigested through the intestinal tract and leaves the body via the feces. The energy "trapped" in this undigested food is lost. Digestible energy (DE) is the energy digested and absorbed from the intestinal tract and equals gross energy minus the energy lost in the feces.

Metabolizable Energy

Some of the DE that enters the body is lost in the urine. The energy that remains and is available for metabolism is metabolizable energy (ME).

Components in the Diet

Fats, carbohydrates, and protein are the only sources of energy in the diet. The amount of energy produced by a gram of each energy source varies:

1 gram fat = 8.5 kcal ME
1 gram carbohydrate = 3.5 kcal ME
1 gram protein = 3.5 kcal ME

Fat is the most efficient source, producing over twice as many calories as either protein or carbohydrate. Fat is used in many premium foods as the primary source of energy, producing a concentrated food of very high quality.

In some situations, carbohydrate is used in place of fat to reduce the number of calories in the food. This is important in weight-control diets or diets intended for cats with reduced activity (such as seniors). Other foods may rely heavily on carbohydrates for energy, because carbohydrates are less expensive than protein or fat. A greater volume has to be fed because of the lower energy density of the food.

Protein is an expensive and wasteful source of energy. Poorly balanced diets may rely too heavily on protein for energy and be inadequate for muscle and coat requirements. If a diet has too low an energy content, the protein will be used as an energy source instead of supplying amino acids for the production of muscle and a healthy coat.

MAJOR ORGAN SYSTEMS

Several physical systems are involved in helping your cat's diet to provide the necessary nutrition to sustain life. For those with a need or a desire to understand how the cat's body processes food, this section examines the organ systems involved.

Food is processed by your cat in different ways in the mouth, esophagus, small intestine, and large intestine. Saliva and mucus moisten food. Stomach acid, enzymes, and other digestive substances break food down from large complex compounds into the building blocks of proteins, fats, and carbohydrates. The pancreas and liver secrete enzymes and bile into the small intestine to facilitate digestion. After absorption into the circulatory system through the intestinal wall, nutrients are transported to all cells in the body. The circulatory system also removes cell wastes, which are filtered out by the kidneys and removed from the body as liquid wastes in the urine. Skin is important in nutrition as a regulator of body heat and a signal of nutritional deficiencies and other diseases.

GASTROINTESTINAL TRACT

The gastrointestinal tract of the cat is the path through which food and water travel from ingestion to defecation. It includes the mouth, esophagus, stomach, small and large intestines, rectum, and anus. Other organs important in the digestive process are the pancreas, gallbladder, and liver. Foods are processed in the tract to provide energy and materials for growth, maintenance, reproduction, and repair. Various parts of the tract have differing functions, including mastication, digestion, and absorption.

The gastrointestinal tracts of animals reflect their evolutionary development according to their needs. Carnivores (meat eaters, such as cats) and omnivores (meat and plant eaters, such as humans) are somewhat similar. However, there are some differences. The feline stomach is similar in shape and function to the human stomach but is larger in proportion of the entire gastrointestinal tract. This probably reflects the need for the stomach to accommodate eating relatively large amounts of food at a given time (after catching prey).

The small intestine in cats and that in humans are similar in structure and digestive functions. The large intestine of cats is more simplified, straighter, and shorter than in humans because most digestion in carnivores is completed before food reaches the large intestine. Food does not remain for very long in the large intestines of cats; therefore, intestinal bacteria do not have as much time to break down fiber.

Mouth/Oral Cavity

Food begins its journey through the gastrointestinal tract at the mouth. Because cats evolved as carnivores, their teeth are designed primarily for tearing apart prey. They may chew food very little or not at all. Saliva lubricates the food and facilitates swallowing. Enzymes in saliva may begin the breakdown of food, but this is limited in cats.

Esophagus

The esophagus is a tube connecting the oral cavity to the stomach. Swallowed food passes into the esophagus and is moved along by rhythmical muscular contractions called *peristalsis*.

Stomach

The valve at the opening to the stomach, the *cardiac sphincter*, is stimulated to open by the presence of food at the base of the esophagus and by peristaltic movement.

Food entering the stomach is mixed with mucus, acid, and enzymes. The acid begins to break up proteins, fats, and carbohydrates. More extensive protein breakdown is accomplished with the stomach enzyme *pepsin*.

Food leaving the stomach has a semiliquid consistency and is called *chyme*. Chyme enters the small intestine through the *pyloric sphincter*, the exit area of the stomach that controls the chyme leaving the stomach.

Small Intestine

The small intestine is a long tube with a relatively small diameter. Its length and the presence of small projections called *villi* provide a large surface area through which nutrients can be absorbed into the bloodstream. The cells lining the small intestine are called *enterocytes*.

Partially digested food from the stomach is further broken down in the small intestine. Secretions of the first part of the small intestine are alkaline and help to neutralize the stomach acid. Enzymes from both the pancreas and the lining of the small intestine, as well as secretions from the liver, help break down proteins, fats, and carbohydrates. Bile from the liver is stored in the gallbladder and released into the small intestine, where it breaks up large fat molecules so that they are small enough to be acted on by enzymes.

Digestion is the process whereby proteins, fats, and carbohydrates are broken down into short chains or individual amino acids, fatty acids, or sugars. These smaller particles, along with vitamins and minerals, can then be absorbed through the wall of the small intestine into the bloodstream and lymphatic system. From here, these nutrients are transported to tissues, where they are used for energy, growth, maintenance, or repair.

An important digestive concept to understand is that of the *glycemic response*. This is a measure of the absorption of glucose from the intestine into the bloodstream and the insulin response to the rise in blood sugar. As glucose is absorbed into the blood, the blood glucose level rises. To counter the rising blood glucose, the pancreas responds by secreting insulin. Insulin's role is to lower the blood glucose back to the fasting level. This intricate interaction occurs after every meal.

Helpful small intestinal gut bacteria, such as *Bifidobacterium* and *Lactobacillus*, can use special fiber sources, such as FOSs, for their own energy and growth. Potentially harmful bacteria such as *Salmonella* and *E. coli* cannot. FOSs can therefore play a vital role in restoring and maintaining a healthy and balanced bacterial population within the small intestine.

Compared with other animal species, cats have relatively short small intestines, which means that the transit time of food through the small intestine is less and there is less surface area available for digestion and absorption. Therefore, it is important to feed cats highly digestible ingredients, such as animal-based protein sources.

Large Intestine

Chyme leaving the small intestine enters the large intestine through a valvelike muscular area at the end of the small intestine. This valve prevents most movement of contents back into the small intestine. Unabsorbed material from the small intestine passes into the large intestine, which is shorter and has a much larger diameter. The contents are now known as feces, and the cells lining the large intestine are *colonocytes*.

Important functions of the large intestine are:

- Water absorption
- Fermentation of fiber by bacteria
- Further breakdown of proteins and carbohydrates
- Storage of feces until the next defecation

The absorption of water is a major function of the large intestine and helps to keep the cat from becoming dehydrated.

The volume and consistency of the feces will depend in part on the amount of indigestible matter contained in the original food eaten—as well as the transit time, amount of water absorbed, bacterial action, and the health status of the animal. Bacteria leading to gas production and flatulence or other digestive disturbances, including diarrhea, may ferment large amounts of poorly digestible matter reaching the large intestine.

If the transit time through the intestine is shorter than normal (increased motility), less water is absorbed and diarrhea results. Conversely, longer transit time (decreased motility) often results in more absorption than normal and can lead to constipation.

As discussed earlier in the section entitled "Nutrients," fermentation of moderately fermentable fiber sources within the large intestine is beneficial to the cells that line both the small and large intestine and that use the short-chain fatty acids which are produced for energy.

Rectum and Anus

The rectum is the final few inches of the large intestine, and the opening through which the feces exits is called the anus. Feces move through the large intestine by peristalsis and are periodically expelled through the anus. Feces contain undigested food, digestive wastes, bacteria, and some water. Ideally, feces should contain between 25% and 45% moisture. Drier feces are harder to pass.

PANCREAS

The pancreas is a large gland that secretes enzymes directly into the intestines for digestion (an *exocrine* function) and secretes hormones, such as insulin, internally into the bloodstream (an *endocrine* function). The pancreas is located near the liver on the right side of the body and is attached to the small intestine and stomach.

Pancreatic juices enter the small intestine through a duct not far from the pyloric sphincter of the stomach. These juices help neutralize the acidic chyme and contain enzymes (*protease*, *lipase*, and *amylase*) that break down food into smaller components.

- **Proteases** split proteins into polypeptides, tripeptides, dipeptides, and amino acids.
- **Lipases** split fats into fatty acids.
- **Amylases** split starches into polysaccharides, disaccharides, and monosaccharides.

Insulin is produced by specialized cells (beta cells) of the pancreas and is secreted directly into the bloodstream. Insulin is essential in the metabolism of glucose by body cells. When insulin is absent, is ineffective, or its levels are very low, glucose and abnormal products of glucose metabolism accumulate in the body. This disease is known as *diabetes mellitus*.

LIVER

The liver is the largest internal organ in the body and one of the most important. It is involved in many body functions and is located in front of the stomach.

The liver produces *bile*, which is stored in the gallbladder and secreted through a duct that enters the small intestine at the same place as the pancreatic duct. Bile and pancreatic juices enter the intestine as a mixture. Bile is a combination of bile salts, pigments, and waste products of the liver. The detergent-like action (emulsification) of bile salts begins to break up fats. This allows pancreatic lipases to split the fats further into fatty acids that can be absorbed into the bloodstream. Bile pigments are the waste products of the breakdown of *hemoglobin* in red blood cells. Bile also includes other by-products of metabolism and taurine derivatives.

When nutrients are absorbed from the small intestine, they are carried to the liver by the blood. Amino acids can be rebuilt in the liver to various proteins required for the body. Some of the glucose from the breakdown of carbohydrates is converted into glycogen and stored in the liver as a short-term energy reserve. Sometimes, bacteria enter the body through the intestinal wall and are removed from the circulation by the liver.

KIDNEYS

Although not part of the digestive process, the kidneys figure prominently as excreters of metabolic wastes. The kidneys are important organs located on the right and left sides of the body behind the stomach and liver and up against the inside of the back muscles. Kidneys make urine. They have two broad functions: filtering blood and modifying the filtered material. The steps that go into these two functions are complex but are essential for the filtration of waste products from the blood and in the control of body water content, electrolytes (ions that affect metabolic processes), and the acid–base balance of the body. They produce urine through the filtration of the blood and selective resorption of substances required by the body.

Blood enters each kidney through the renal artery. Inside the kidney are increasingly smaller arteries that end in tiny bundles of blood vessels called glomeruli. The glomeruli act as small filters. Small molecules and water (but not large molecules or blood cells) pass through the glomeruli. The large molecules and blood cells remain in the blood and are taken away from the kidney in blood vessels.

The small molecules and water that pass through each "filter" (or glomerulus) are known as the filtrate. The filtrate moves through a series of tubules. From these tubules, most of the water and many small molecules needed by the body are resorbed and returned to the bloodstream. The remaining filtrate (which is then called urine) collects in the kidney and moves via the ureters to be stored in the urinary bladder. Urine is eliminated from the body through the urethra.

The rate at which urine is filtered through the glomerulus is known as the glomerular filtration rate (GFR) and is used to evaluate kidney function. The GFR decreases when the kidneys are damaged.

The kidneys also have some roles that are unrelated to urine: vitamin D activation and production of the hormone that stimulates red blood cell creation.

The final step in the synthesis of vitamin D in the body occurs in the kidney. The process begins in the skin, proceeds to the liver, and is completed in the kidney. In kidney disease, this final, necessary step may be impaired.

Red blood cells are produced in the bone marrow, but *erythropoietin*, the hormone that stimulates the production of red blood cells, is made in the kidneys. Without erythropoietin, anemia results. In chronic renal failure, anemia due to decreased production of erythropoietin often complicates the case.

SKIN AND COAT

The skin is not involved in the digestion or absorption of food but can be a very good indication of a cat's nutritional status. The skin is the largest organ in the body. Its primary function is protection, but it also helps prevent water loss, regulates body temperature, and provides sensory input to the nervous system.

Skin helps protect the body from injury caused by trauma, chemicals, or pathogens such as bacteria and viruses. Skin also helps to regulate body heat by dispersing heat in hot weather and conserving it in cold weather. In humans, sweating releases large amounts of heat. Cats do not have sweat glands except in very limited areas around their foot pads or nose leather. Their excess heat is released primarily by panting, allowing body water to evaporate from the respiratory tract.

The skin is important in the synthesis of vitamin D. Chemicals in the skin called sterols form a precursor of vitamin D in the presence of ultraviolet light. The precursor is synthesized to vitamin D in the liver.

As nutrients are distributed in the body according to relative need, the nutrient will first be allocated to the most critical areas of the body such as the brain. Organs that are of less vital importance, such as the skin, will show signs of nutritional deficiencies earlier than other areas and will often signal nutritional problems. For example, insufficient protein, low fat, or poor amino acid profiles in the diet can produce dry, scaly skin beneath the hair coat.

Hair is 95% protein, and at times, up to 30% of a cat's protein intake is used for coat maintenance. Protein deficiency can result in thickening of the epidermis, pigment changes, and hair loss. Fatty acids are important for hair structure and provide energy and a medium for fat-soluble vitamins. Deficiencies of fatty acids can lead to dry, scaly skin, thickening of the epidermis, hair loss, itchiness, greasy skin, and secondary skin infections.

COMPARING CAT FOODS

There are many different commercial foods available for owners to feed their cats. Similarly, extensive ingredient choices are available to pet food manufacturers when preparing a commercial cat food. Combinations of ingredients or the quality of ingredients used in any given food are quite variable and will determine the overall quality of the food. Given the advances in feline nutrition and the important role that diet plays in a cat's life, it is important to understand the factors that make foods different and be able to make on-the-spot comparisons between cat foods.

Many different ingredients are available for use in preparing diets for cats. Different ingredients provide different nutrients, such as protein, fat, or carbohydrates, and some ingredients have advantages and disadvantages when used in pet foods. Cat foods can also vary in the form in which they are presented: dry, canned, and semimoist. By using the information provided on the label, examining the food, and conducting feeding studies, you can evaluate the nutritional adequacy of a cat food.

THE CAT FOOD LABEL—A LEGAL DOCUMENT

Pet food labels are reasonably useful for both consumers and veterinarians in evaluating feline diets. Labels can provide important information about the diet, including the purpose, ingredients, and nutrient composition. The information included on a label is regulated by both federal and state laws. The required information is

- Statement of identity (the brand name)
- Declaration of net quantity
- Guaranteed analysis
- Nutritional adequacy statement
- Feeding guidelines
- Ingredient list

- Manufacturer's or distributor's identity and address

Standards

Label requirements vary from country to country, with some countries using essentially the same standards as the United States. Other countries have their own regulations regarding packaging.

In the United States, state and federal laws govern labeling information. At the federal level, the U.S. Food and Drug Administration (FDA) oversees many labeling aspects but mainly health claims. It has become increasingly involved in pet food labeling with the evolution of veterinarian-exclusive products.

The Association of American Feed Control Officials (AAFCO) is a North American organization composed of state and federal regulatory officials. AAFCO defines ingredient names and requirements and prescribes label text content. Because AAFCO is not a government agency, its purpose is to establish standards. Each state decides whether to institute or enforce these standards. Many do, but some do not. Nevertheless, if a manufacturer conforms to AAFCO guidelines, its products will generally meet the requirements of all 50 states. Because of the experience and work that has gone into developing the AAFCO guidelines, many countries outside the United States also use parts of these standards.

The Pet Food Institute (PFI) is a pet food industry association formed to provide a uniform industry voice. The PFI deals with regulations and issues affecting the industry at large. PFI is not a regulatory agency.

Label Contents

Pet food product labels are divided into two sections: the principal display panel on the front and the information panel, usually on the back of the bag/box.

The following is usually contained on the principal display panel:

• The statement of identity consists of the product's name—the brand name. The designator is part of the identity statement and refers to the species for which the product is intended.

• The declaration of net quantity is the net weight of the product's contents and is shown in both English and metric units. For example, a net weight of 2 pounds 2 ounces is the same as 936 grams.

Nutritional information is contained on the information panel. The guaranteed analysis provides information regarding major components of the product expressed as percentages:

• Crude protein—minimum level
• Crude fat—minimum level
• Crude fiber—maximum level
• Moisture—maximum level

Additional guarantees may be stated. For cat products, optional guarantees include ash and magnesium maximums and taurine minimums. If a guaranteed nutrient is not recognized as essential by AAFCO, it will be noted as such. Further, for guarantees, which require a minimum, a maximum amount can be listed at the manufacturer's discretion. For maximum guarantees; minimums are optional.

Unfortunately, the guaranteed analysis is mainly so that regulatory agencies can check to see if the food meets basic minimum requirements. It is not very useful for the pet owner. In some cases, it does not closely reflect what is actually in the food, as it is only maximums and minimums, not actual levels.

The nutritional adequacy and nutritional validation statements are included if the food is nutritionally complete and balanced and contains all of the required nutrients. The product label states that the product is "complete and balanced." The regulations require that the nutrition claim identify the life stage to which it pertains:

• Growth
• Maintenance
• Gestation/lactation
• All life stages, which include all of the above

The method by which the claim is substantiated must be stated in one of two ways:

• ". . . Animal feeding tests using Association of American Feed Control Officials' procedures substantiate that this product provides complete and balanced nutrition for all life stages." This means that the food was actually fed to cats during the life stage claimed and that the claim was found to be appropriate.

• ". . . is formulated to meet the nutritional levels established by the AAFCO Cat Food Nutrient Profiles for all life stages," which means that the food was chemically analyzed and compared to a recognized industry standard.

The first statement reflects a more accurate measure of nutritional adequacy and is preferred.

Always look for a claim of nutritional adequacy. Generally, if the food does not carry a claim of being complete and balanced, then it is not and should be used only as a treat or not at all. In some countries outside the United States, locally produced pet foods may be able to carry a "complete and balanced" claim without reference to any authority. This can make it difficult to rely on the claim or to check whether it is true.

Feeding guidelines are required by law.

They are defined as guidelines because animals differ and each may require more or less than the feeding amount suggests. Feeding guidelines are usually displayed as charts; however, this may not be feasible on smaller packages such as 3-ounce cans. Feeding guidelines must be closely examined because they can be expressed by weight ("Feed X ounces") or by volume ("Feed X cups"). Product bulk densities vary and must be considered when evaluating feeding recommendations.

The feeding guidelines give you an indication of the energy density and, in some cases, quality of the product. If the feeding amounts seem high for a particular weight of cat, then the food is low in energy density, is recommending a higher caloric intake, perhaps contains high water content, or is poorly digestible.

In the ingredients list, all of the ingredients must be listed in descending order according to preprocessing weight. Ingredients of equal amounts may be listed interchangeably. The ingredient list can be very helpful when comparing pet foods. However, the requirement to list ingredients differs from country to country. In the United States, the manufacturers have to list every ingredient, according to a specific definition, in descending order of quantity by weight. Other countries use different terminology to describe ingredients, and some countries may allow grouping such as "meat and meat by-products" or "cereals and cereal by-products." This can make it quite difficult to accurately compare pet foods that originate from different countries.

The ingredient list does not provide information regarding the absolute amount of each ingredient. Not only would this divulge formulas, which are trade secrets, but it also would deprive some manufacturers of least-cost products a way to adjust their formulas when ingredient cost or availability changes.

Manufacturers who produce their foods using the least expensive ingredients adjust the formula for each batch on the basis of the cost of ingredients that day. If the price on meat meal goes up, for example, they will decrease the amount of meat meal and increase the amount of soybean meal in the batch. They will have developed the ingredient list so that these changes will not alter the sequence of the list. This is called an open formula. There is nothing on the package, however, that alerts you to foods that are based on open formulas.

You may not be able to look at an ingredient list and know if the manufacturer has an open formula unless they group ingredients. (This is not allowed in the United States except for vitamins or minerals.) The grouping of ingredients also allows manufacturers to vary the ingredients they use from one batch to another. If the ingredient listed is "meat and meat by-products," one batch may contain lamb by-products, while the next batch may contain beef by-products. On other pet food labels, open formulas are clearly evident, because the ingredient list will state, for example, "beef and/or mutton" (which is also not allowed in the United States). Other open-formula ingredients you will see are vegetable protein concentrate, cereals, and meats without the actual source stated.

The opposite of the open formula is the fixed formula. Ingredients of a fixed-formula product remain the same from bag to bag, with no surprise changes. Only top-quality premium brands commit to this; it provides consistent nutrition and helps to avoid those mysterious bouts of diarrhea that cats get when, unknown to the owner, their diets have been altered. Fixed-formula foods cost more than open-formula foods.

Most ingredient names are set by AAFCO, with common names, such as chicken, being understood without a specific definition. The actual ingredients in the food must conform to the label. A major weakness in the ingredient list is that it is allowed to make no reference to ingredient quality. Two ingredient lists may appear very similar even though the quality of the food may be very different.

The manufacturer's or distributor's identity and address must be included on the label. In addition, a toll-free number may be provided, although it is not required by regulation.

Ingredients

Ingredients are the foundation of a good food and can make or break the nutrition of the final mix. Whether the owner is preparing a diet at home or the pet food manufacturer is preparing a diet at the plant, both have various choices as to what to include. The owner at home does not have the latest scientific findings, the testing facilities, or the knowledge to prepare an optimal diet to meet the specific nutritional requirements of cats.

The naming of ingredients is subject to regulations set up by AAFCO. Each name comes with a definition that prescribes minimum or maximum characteristics and sometimes both. Nevertheless, because the names are regulated, all manufacturers have to use similar words for similar ingredients even though the ultimate quality may differ.

In looking at the ingredients used in pet foods, it is easiest to separate them into the nutrient group they contribute to the diet. Because vitamins and minerals are generally added as part of the vitamin or mineral "premix," the key ingredients all provide one or more nutrients in the groups of protein, fat, or carbohydrate.

To be considered a source of one of the nutrient groups, the ingredient must contain at least as much of the nutrient as will be in the finished food. That makes it a primary contributor. Just because an ingredient contains protein, for example, does not mean that it is a protein source for the food. Cornmeal contains 6% to 8% protein but is not a protein source because it cannot be used to supply protein in a practical diet.

Protein Sources

Pet foods that use meat-based proteins tend to be of higher quality than pet foods containing mostly cereals or vegetable proteins. By studying the labels, it is possible to identify whether the food relies on animal-based or cereal/vegetable sources of protein. Remember, cats evolved as carnivores, so they will perform best when fed diets containing animal sources of protein.

A meal is a meat ingredient that has been cooked (rendered) and dried into a powdery form. Many meat protein sources can be found both as the "wet" ingredient containing the natural moisture and as a meal; lamb and lamb meal are good examples.

Grains are slightly different. A grain that is termed a meal is simply ground into a granular or powdery form. In some situations, a grain meal is not a protein source: Cornmeal is a carbohydrate source. Other grain meals are protein sources and are used by some companies to supply the protein in cat foods. Examples include soybean meal and corn gluten meal.

By-products are the secondary products from the production of human foods. These are the parts that are not necessarily economical for use in human foods. This does not make them poor quality or unsuitable. Some protein by-products contain exceptional amino acid profiles and add to the quality of a food.

An ingredient common to many cat foods is chicken (poultry) by-product meal. This ingredient is termed chicken meal in many countries outside of the United States. According to AAFCO definition, this ingredient may include necks, feet, undeveloped eggs, and intestines; however, poultry feet would drive the protein quality down and would not be included in the high-quality, refined chicken by-product meal.

MEAT

Meat includes muscle tissue as well as the associated fat, connective tissue, and blood vessels. The quality and nutrient content of meat will depend in part on the amounts of connective tissue and fat present in the cuts of meat as well as the amount of foreign material and bone chips.

Meat should not be fed as the sole diet because it is deficient in many nutrients. Meat is very low in calcium and has an extremely adverse calcium to phosphorus ratio of 1:15 or higher; the ideal ratio is between 1:1 and 1.3:1 for cats. As would be expected, this unsatisfactory calcium to phosphorus ratio and low calcium level will result in extreme bone growth malformation if meat is fed as the sole diet.

FISH

Fish is a very good source of protein, but many different types of fish are available. Ocean fishes also contain oils that carry the omega-3 fatty acids. The vitamin and mineral content may vary significantly from one variety to another. Sometimes "fish" includes the skeleton, so the mineral level could be high; at other times, "fish" contains only the fish fillet, or meat, so the mineral content is low. Some raw fishes contain the enzyme thiaminase that destroys thiamine (vitamin B_1). This enzyme is inactivated by heat.

Cat owners will often feed canned tuna, thinking they are doing their cats a palatability favor. This is ill-advised. Canned tuna is very high in polyunsaturated fatty acids that deplete the cats' antioxidant reserves leading to a serious body fat inflammation called yellow fat disease, or steatitis. Tuna also tends to be high in magnesium.

EGGS

Eggs are one of the best-quality protein sources available. They also contain large quantities of vitamins A, B_{12}, and D and of iron. Eggs are highly digestible and are used as the reference on which other protein sources are graded. Eggs are assigned a biological value of 100.

Eggs should be cooked before being fed to cats, because raw egg white contains an antivitamin, avidin. Avidin binds the vitamin biotin, making it unavailable to cats. Cooking the eggs will destroy this biotin-binding effect. Raw eggs may also cause diarrhea in some cats.

Some cat foods use dried eggs that are called dried egg product in the pet food industry. This gives a real boost to the protein quality of most cat foods.

DAIRY PRODUCTS

Dairy products include milk and milk products such as casein, cheese, cottage cheese, butter, and yogurt. Dairy products generally contain high levels of fat and protein as well as vitamins A and B, calcium, and other minerals.

Not all cats can tolerate milk and milk products. Cow's milk contains milk sugar, or lactose, in substantial quantities. Queen's milk does not contain much lactose, and many kittens lose the ability to digest it after weaning. Without this enzyme, eating or drinking milk can result in diarrhea. Also, some dairy products are felt to be responsible for food allergies in many cats.

PLANT PROTEINS

Plant products also contain proteins, which can be concentrated and used in animal foods. These sources are the primary protein sources in livestock feeds. Soybean meal is also used in many lower-cost pet foods. Although soybean meal is a consistent source, it is not complete and does not provide all the amino acids needed by cats. Some manufacturers also use gluten meals. Gluten is the name of the protein portion of plants and can be separated and concentrated apart from the starch in grain. Corn gluten meal is concentrated corn protein. Similar ingredients exist for wheat and rice.

Cats perform better on animal-based diets than on diets containing plant protein. Cat diets should be from highly digestible meat sources such as chicken, lamb, fish, beef, turkey, or egg and not from vegetable proteins such as soybean meal or wheat. There is one exception: renal diets. These very special diets cannot include animal proteins without increasing the level of phosphorus in the finished diet; that would be harmful to the patient. In kidney diets or sick cats, a very refined, high-quality soy protein can be used, but specific amino acids will still have to be added to make the finished diet complete for the patient.

Fat Sources

Primary fat sources are rather obvious in the ingredient list: chicken fat, animal fat, beef tallow, fish oil, and so on. Many of the protein sources also bring a source of fat to the formula. Protein ingredients such as chicken, chicken by-product meal, and fishmeal are also good sources of fat.

Fat quality can vary but usually is not as variable as protein quality. The main concerns with fats are

- Contribution of essential fatty acids (linoleic and arachidonic acids)
- Contribution of omega-3 fatty acids
- Absence of rancidity

Chicken fat provides the essential fatty acids. Flax meal, fish oil, and fish meal are used as sources of the omega-3s. Because these fats are sensitive to going bad—rancid—they are carefully protected with antioxidants, which may be natural or synthetic. Canned foods do not need specific antioxidant protection because the canning process provides the protection.

Carbohydrate Sources

Carbohydrate sources are included in the diets as a source of quick energy (starch) and as a source of fiber. Some ingredients contain both starch and fiber, while others are primarily one or the other.

Cereals, grains, and vegetables sometimes used as part of an animal's diet include wheat, barley, grain sorghum (milo), oats, rice, corn, soybeans, potatoes, carrots, and other vegetables. These ingredients are generally used as an energy source for cats, but they can also provide a significant proportion of the protein in many pet diets.

It can be difficult to get cats to eat diets with a high cereal or vegetable content, as the palatability of these ingredients is not great. Pet food manufacturers that make cereal-based foods may add artificial flavors or ingredients to try to improve the palatability of the foods and artificial colors to improve the appearance.

Cornmeal is ground whole corn and is an excellent, highly digestible carbohydrate source. You may hear some individuals claim that corn is not digestible, but when finely ground and cooked, it is as digestible as any other carbohydrate, including rice.

Ground wheat, wheat flour, and whole wheat are all forms of the same ingredient simply ground to different textures. This is worth mentioning because using these three forms of the same ingredient is known as splitting ingredients. By using three forms, the amount of any one of the three will be much less than if only one form was used. The result is that the position of each of the three will be lower in the ingredient list, allowing other ingredients to become higher in the list. Some manufacturers use this label game to push a protein ingredient to the top of the list. While multiple carbohydrate ingredients are commonly used and can provide unique qualities, splitting one ingredient into several is playing a game with the consumer and the label.

Specific carbohydrate blends have qualities that do not exist in some of the carbohydrates alone. The blend of corn and grain sorghum (milo) results in a lower glycemic response than for other carbohydrates alone or other blends. The benefit of these innovative combinations is that less insulin is required by the cat, which can help with obesity and, in prescribed diets, help control diabetes mellitus.

FIBER

Fiber is the portion of food that is not broken down by mammalian enzymes. However, the bacteria that live in the cat's intestinal tract can digest certain fibers. It is important to note that not all fibers are the same. Some are totally resistant to digestion by bacteria and are called nonfermentable. To varying degrees, bacteria ferment other fibers. Some fibers are moderately fermentable, while others are highly fermentable. The degree of fermentability is not related to the solubility of a fiber. There are incorrect assumptions in some publications and by some pet food manufacturers that a soluble fiber is also fermentable. That is not always the case. There are many soluble fibers that are nonfermentable and vice versa.

Fiber is included in a cat's diet to be broken down by intestinal bacteria and provide SCFAs (short-chain fatty acids). The SCFAs are an important energy source for the cells lining the intestinal tract. A second reason for including fiber is that the portion of fiber that is not fermented contributes some form and bulk to the stool. Too much bulk, and the fecal volume gets excessive. Too little, and the stimulation that intestinal contents provide to the intestinal lining is lost.

Beet pulp is a moderately fermentable fiber that has been shown to provide both the right amount of SCFAs and the necessary "scratch factor" for keeping the contents moving properly. It results in a formed stool with a typical dry matter content of between 30% and 40%. If dry matter increases much beyond 40%, the feces becomes drier and are harder to pass.

Fibers such as cellulose, peanut hulls, and soy hulls are nonfermentable. They do not supply the needed SCFAs to the intestinal lining and they typically result in stools with higher dry matter (hard stools) if included as the sole fiber source.

Recent research has shown that cellulose can help move ingested hair out of a cat's intestinal tract—80% more! This can be beneficial for those cats prone to hairballs. Nevertheless, by itself, cellulose does not supply the SCFAs necessary for intestinal lining cells. By combining moderately fermentable beet pulp with the cellulose, both intestinal health and hair removal can be achieved.

FOSs (fructooligosaccharides) are a unique fiber. Like all fibers, mammalian intestinal enzymes do not digest it. Certain bacteria can break it down, though. The type of bacteria that can use FOSs contributes to their importance in foods. Beneficial bacteria such as *Lactobacillus* and *Bifidobacterium* can use FOSs as an energy source and release those important SCFAs. Undesirable or potentially harmful bacteria such as *Salmonella* cannot use FOSs. By feeding the "good bugs," they can grow and crowd out the bad bugs. In senior cats, this can help maintain a healthy intestinal environment. In prescribed diets, it can help nutritionally manage bacterial overgrowth. Some companies have added chicory as a source of FOSs.

MOSs (mannanoligosaccharides) are used in some prescription feline diets to help nutritionally manage bacteria in the intestine. They trick the bacteria into grabbing MOSs instead of cells lining the intestine. The result? The bacteria are lost in the fecal stream.

FORMS OF COMMERCIAL CAT FOODS

There are many forms of commercial foods available for cats that differ mainly in their method of processing and preservation. The quality of a food is not necessarily related to its form.

Dry Foods

The caloric density of dry foods varies widely, from between 2,500 and 3,300 kcal ME/kg in the basic brands to between 3,500 and more than 4,500 kcal ME/kg in the premium brands. The moisture content of dry foods is usually between 8% and 12%.

There are three main processes by which dry foods are manufactured:

• **Extruded/expanded:** The food is cooked in a continuous-flow device at high temperature and pressure and then forced through a die that results in the food's shape and the carbohydrate's expansion (cooking).
• **Baked biscuit:** The food is baked on a sheet and then broken into pieces or left as biscuits/shapes.
• **Pelleted:** The food is cooked and formed but with less pressure than is used in extrusion.

• **Advantages:** Dry foods are less expensive, and the abrasive effect of dry foods helps decrease dental tartar accumulation. No refrigeration is required, and dried foods often may be fed free-choice.
• **Disadvantages:** There are very few disadvantages. Most of the poorer-quality dry foods have a high carbohydrate and fiber content because of the use of grains and vegetables for protein. These tend to have a lower digestibility and therefore produce a greater fecal volume.

Canned Foods

Canned foods vary widely in their form. Some canned foods contain textured vegetable protein (TVP). TVP is extruded soy flour mixed with red or brown food coloring to look like chunks of beef, lamb, or chicken. Basic canned foods contain approximately 650 to 1,100 kcal ME/kg, while premium canned foods contain around 1,000 to 1,500 kcal ME/kg. Canned foods will contain anywhere from 64% to 84% moisture.

• **Advantages:** Palatability is generally very good for canned food and often higher than for dry foods.
• **Disadvantages:** Canned foods cannot be fed free-choice because they spoil easily and can attract insects. Canned food offers no abrasive texture to the teeth, so tartar may build up more quickly. Because of the water content, it is a more expensive way of feeding. A basic canned product can actually be more expensive than a premium-quality dry food.

Soft, Moist Foods

Soft, moist foods contain more water than dry foods but less water than canned foods. Antibacterial, antifungal, and moisture-retention agents are usually included. An approximate caloric density is 1,500 kcal ME/kg with a moisture content of around 30%.

- **Advantages:** They may be fed free-choice because they require no refrigeration.
- **Disadvantages:** Stabilizing the moisture content of semimoist foods to protect the nutrients is always a challenge. Sugar and a water stabilizer called propylene glycol are often used. The propylene glycol preservative was found to cause anemia in cats and cannot be used in cat foods.

Treats

Treats come in a variety of forms produced by a wide variety of methods. Some treats use the same basic ingredients found in dry foods. Many treats are designed to be given only in small quantities and are not complete and balanced. Some have very low protein levels, some are very low or very high in fat, and others (especially fish varieties) can contain very high levels of minerals (such as magnesium). The semimoist types often have high levels of sugars to preserve the pieces; this method replaces the propylene glycol that had been used in semimoist cat foods and treats until it was found to cause feline anemia.

Treats, if not formulated as complete and balanced, should not constitute more than approximately 5% of the cat's diet because of the dangers of unbalancing the diet.

High-Quality Ingredients

Considerable skill is necessary to put together a satisfactory diet from raw materials. It is not enough simply to buy meat on the assumption that this is the natural diet of a cat. As a hunter, the cat did not restrict itself to the muscle meat of its prey but ate the whole body—obtaining minerals, vitamins, and even roughage from the bones, brains, skin, gut, and gut contents.

In homemade diets, although there are some foods that can be fed raw, cooking is advisable, particularly for meats. Cooking will kill bacteria, viruses, and parasites and will improve digestibility of some foods. On the other hand, overcooking should be avoided because this will reduce the food value of proteins and destroy vitamins. Minerals and vitamins will be lost if the cooking water is discarded.

In some countries of the world, sulfur dioxide is used to preserve pet meat. Sulfur dioxide destroys the natural thiamine (vitamin B_1) in the meat and has led to many cases of thiamine deficiency in cats. This deficiency has also been seen when cats have been fed some varieties of pet "meat rolls." This has not been a problem in North America or Europe.

EVALUATING CAT FOODS

The assessment and comparison of different cat foods is somewhat involved. This is due to the limited information written on the packaging or in the literature of some pet foods. Simplistically, the first step is to study the pet food label, which does give a variety of information. Next, examine the food itself. Finally, feed the product to cats and observe the results over a period of time. There is still a lot of information that can be gained from the label.

Evaluate the Label

Here are the four steps to follow in using a pet food label to evaluate and compare foods:

1. Determine the food's purpose.
2. Check the nutritional claim.
3. Group and compare ingredients.
4. Note the unique benefits.

COMMON PET FOOD INGREDIENTS

Animal-Based Proteins
Animal digest
Beef
Casein
Catfish
Chicken by-products
Chicken by-product meal
Chicken liver meal
Chicken digest
Chicken meal
Dried egg product
Fish
Fish meal—n3
Glandular meal
Lamb
Lamb meal
Liver
Meat and bone meal
Meat by-products
Meat meal
Poultry by-product meal
Turkey

Vegetable-Based Proteins
Alfalfa meal
Brewer's dried yeast
Corn gluten meal
Soy flour
Soybean meal
Soy protein concentrate
Soy protein isolate
Wheat germ meal

Minerals
Calcium carbonate
Cobalt carbonate
Dicalcium phosphate
Ferrous sulfate

Copper sulfate
Copper oxide
Manganous oxide
Manganese sulfate
Magnesium oxide
Magnesium sulfate
Monosodium phosphate
Potassium chloride
Potassium iodide
Salt
Sodium selenite
Zinc oxide
Zinc sulfate

Carbohydrates (Starch and Fiber)
Apple pomace—MFF
Barley
Brown rice
Carrageenan—HFF
Carrots
Cellulose—PFF
Citrus pulp—MFF
Corn
Corn bran—PFF
Cornmeal
Dried beet pulp
Dried whey
Grain sorghum meal
Ground corn
Ground yellow corn
Guar gum—HFF
Lactose
Molasses
Oat bran—PFF
Oat groats
Oatmeal
Pea fiber—MFF
Peanut hulls—PFF

Pearled barley
Peas
Potato flour
Rice bran—MFF
Rice, ground rice, rice flour
Soybean hulls—PFF
Sugar
Tomato pomace—MFF
Vegetable gums—HFF
Wheat bran
Wheat, wheat flour, ground wheat
Whole corn
Whole-grain sorghum
Xantham gum—HFF

Vitamins
Ascorbic acid
Calcium pantothenate
Folic acid
Niacin
Pyridoxine hydrochloride
Riboflavin
Thiamine mononitrate
Vitamin A acetate
Vitamin B_{12} supplement
Vitamin D_3 supplement
Vitamin E supplement

Fats
Animal fat—n6
Beef tallow—n6
Borage oil—n6
Chicken fat—n6
Corn oil—n6
Ground flax seed

Poultry fat—n6
Fish oil—n3
Flax seed—n3
Safflower oil—n6
Sunflower oil—n6
Vegetable oil—n6
Whole flax seed

Other
Animal digest—E
Caramel color—C
Citric acid—P
Choline chloride
DL-methionine—AA
Ethoxyguin—P
Garlic powder—E
Iron oxide—C
L-lysine—AA
Mixed tocopherols—P
Natural flavors—E
Onion powder—E
Potassium sorbate—F
Propyl gallate—P
Taicome—AA
Titanium dioxide—C
Water

Key
MFF = modified fermented fiber
PFF = poor fermented fiber
HFF = high fermented fiber
E = flavor enhancer
C = color
P = preservative
AA = amino acid

It is easier to understand a label than you think. Here are some questions to ask as you go through the four steps:

1. Determine the food's purpose. Make sure it is a cat food. Is it for growth, performance, weight reduction, or maintenance? Are the guaranteed analyses similar? Do not compare foods intended for differing purposes (such as growth versus senior).

2. Check the nutritional claim. Is the food "complete and balanced"? If it is, does the life stage match the purpose? Performance, adult maintenance, and weight-reduction foods are listed as "adult maintenance" or "all life stages." Growth foods are listed either as "growth" or "all life stages." Gestation/lactation foods indicate "gestation/lactation" or "all life stages." Compare the nutritional claims statement. Does it meet the nutrient profiles of AAFCO, or do feeding studies established by AAFCO substantiate it? AAFCO feeding protocols provide the highest level of nutritional assurance because they test the product's formulation by measuring its performance in real-life cats. If a food is complete and balanced on the basis of AAFCO nutrient profiles, it has simply been analyzed and compared to a recommended content. It may not have been test-fed to cats. Beware of claims for a pet's primary diet that are analytical calculations of nutritional adequacy.

3. Group and compare ingredients. Identify the ingredients that contribute to protein, fat, and carbohydrate nutrient groups. For evaluation purposes, assume that a "complete and balanced" diet has a good source of vitamins and minerals.

- Most of the major ingredients contain more than one nutrient or nutrient group, but often in widely varying amounts. For example, corn contains a substantial amount of carbohydrates and a small amount of protein. Thus, corn is considered mainly a carbohydrate source. Chicken, on the other hand, is a good source of both protein and fat.

After grouping the ingredients, observe the contribution each ingredient might make to the food:

- Look for high-quality, animal-based protein sources. A food that contains no plant sources of protein will have more protein from animal sources than a food with any plant protein sources.
- One caution, though: Animal protein sources such as chicken, chicken by-product meal, chicken liver meal, egg, poultry by-product meal, fish, fish meal, or other muscle meats can range in quality from excellent to poor. They affect the nutritional quality of the food, but quality cannot be determined without conducting a feeding study.

Quality is an unknown factor in your evaluation.

- Pick foods that use high-quality animal protein sources. High-quality animal proteins are highly digestible and contain complete balance of EAAs (essential amino acids) that cats need for optimal growth and development. Contact the manufacturer for EAA profiles. If profiles are available, it is a good indication that the manufacturer is paying close attention to protein quality.
- Grain or plant protein sources such as soybean meal, corn gluten meal, wheat gluten meal, wheat flour/ground wheat

and barley flour/pearled barley are usually very consistent but are not as balanced in their amino acid profiles as quality animal sources of protein. Remember, cats are obligate carnivores.

- Animal and vegetable fat sources vary in quality, but both are typically good. A grain- or plant-based diet that relies totally on vegetable fat (oil) as a fat source may have higher-than-desirable levels of linoleic acid and no arachidonic acid. Animal-based foods generally contribute high-quality fats with both feline essential fatty acids.

- The more carbohydrate sources listed, the lower each is placed in the ingredient list. A company that separately lists similar carbohydrates, such as several forms of wheat, in the ingredient panel artificially elevates its protein sources to a higher place in the ingredient list, in an attempt to show animal protein as a greater contributor than it actually is. That is because animal protein is more expensive than grain ingredients. An example of split carbohydrate ingredients is the use of whole wheat, wheat flour, and ground wheat in the same product.

  Multiple protein sources are often used to improve the amino acid profile and overall protein quality of a food. This is true of chicken, chicken by-product meal, and chicken meal.

  Corn and grain sorghum are examples of two different carbohydrate sources often used in combination to improve glycemic response and to contribute to improved processing and texture or mouth feel. This is not an example of split carbohydrates.

- Look for high-quality animal protein sources and be wary of the split-ingredient trick.
- Look for a toll-free number and a customer satisfaction guarantee. The fact that a manufacturer is willing to back its products and invites customers to call is a good indication of a company's commitment to quality.

4. Note the unique benefits. The advances made since the early 1990s go far beyond the high-quality ingredients used. Benefits such as intestinal health, immune system enhancement, and antioxidant support are unique and should be considered in any label review.

Going through these four steps, you can make reasonable evaluation of a pet food from the package label. Further assessment requires feeding the food to cats.

Look for More In-Depth Evaluation
Although labels provide us with quite a bit of information, they are not complete. Trying to compare two different foods, for example, on the basis of the guaranteed analysis can be inaccurate or misleading. For example, if a particular pet food has a very low energy content, the animal will need to eat a far greater volume of food when compared to an energy-dense product. They therefore may consume greater quantities (in grams or ounces) of a particular nutrient, even though the "percentage" may be lower than the energy-dense product. The "cheaper" product may actually work out to be more expensive to feed when considered on a cost-per-day or cost-per-week basis.

For an accurate determination of nutrient intake or comparison of nutrient levels for two diets, the amount of each nutrient must be indexed to a common factor: dietary ME (metabolizing energy). The relationship that results is called nutrient density. Because animals eat to meet a need for ME, nutrient density is an accurate method for describing the nutritional composition of a food. It relates the amount of each nutrient to the food's ME content. The standard is to express the amount of each nutrient per 1,000 kcal of ME. This allows comparisons between dry and canned foods, foods of differing caloric content, and foods with different weights or volumes.

Examine Nutrient Density

Nutrient density is a measurement of the nutritional value, or nutrient content, of a pet food. Examining nutrient densities can provide meaningful comparisons of different foods, even if they vary by weight, moisture, or energy content. Understanding nutrient density can help you choose the better food for a cat.

Like all animals, cats eat because they are hungry. The hunger trigger is a need for energy. Once the proper amount of energy (measured as calories) has been consumed, the body signals the brain to stop eating. Once the cat has stopped eating, all of the other nutrients must have been already eaten that are needed to both process the food as well as to maintain the body. This means that the nutrients are balanced to the energy because the intake of those nutrients is determined by the food's energy content.

Unfortunately, the guaranteed analysis on the package contains limited information about the true nutritional value of the food and can be misleading. For example, a cat owner interested in the magnesium content of a food might see foods A and B shown below. On the basis of the package guaranteed analysis, the two foods appear the same.

GUARANTEED ANALYSIS NUTRIENT DENSITY

	Crude Magnesium (% As Is)	Grams Magnesium/ 1,000 kcal Metabolizable Energy
Cat food A	0.085	219
Cat food B	0.085	190

Food B has less magnesium than food A. The difference is due to food B containing much fewer calories per ounce of food. For every calorie that a cat eats, it gets 10% more magnesium from A than from B.

To determine the nutrient density of a product, it is still necessary to contact the manufacturer and get either the actual nutrient densities or ask for the measured ME and the average analysis.

Dry matter is a common way to try to compare foods. However, dry-matter comparisons do not take into consideration the calories in the food. The amount of food needed to satisfy the pet's energy requirement is therefore not included in the equation. Because caloric intake is the primary determinant of food intake, dry matter is not as accurate a comparison as nutrient density.

The feeding guidelines can help you determine approximately how much it will cost per day to feed the cat. Determine how many days of feeding the bag of food will provide, and then divide the bag cost by the number of days. If the package does not list the cups per bag, contact the manufacturer. In many cases, the cheaper bag of food will indicate that more volume per feeding is required, resulting in a comparable or even higher cost per day when compared with premium food.

Examine the Food

By actual visual examination of different cat foods, it is possible to evaluate other aspects of pet food quality. Specific points to observe include the following.

Dry Foods

• **Uniformity of size and color of kibble:** Lesser-quality products may contain kibbles that vary in size and color. This may indicate poor manufacturing processes.

• **Fines:** The presence of broken or finely crumbled product implies a poor manufacturing process whereby the product is inclined to crumble and break.

• **Foreign matter:** The presence of material other than that intended for feline consumption is indicative of poor-quality control.

• **Gimmicks:** Many gimmicks are used to sell products. For example, manufacturers add food coloring to make some dry food appear like meat or peas and carrots. This may appeal to the owner but does nothing to improve the nutrition of the food.

Canned Foods

• **Food coloring:** This is added to many canned foods to give the red-brown appearance of meat to the cereal contents. Depending on the country of origin, some manufacturers of pet foods, unlike human-food manufacturers, do not have to indicate which specific coloring agents are used. Food colorings do nothing to improve the nutritional quality of the pet food.

• **TVP (textural vegetable protein):** In some canned foods, soy flour is mixed with food coloring to form TVP, giving the appearance of "meaty chunks" in the food.

• **Swollen cans:** These are indicative of bacterial fermentation. Do not use them.

Soft, Moist Foods

• **Moisture protection:** Make sure the package is intact so that there is no moisture leakage.

• **Fillers:** Examine particles for cereal by-products, such as hulls or cereal waste, which are indicative of an inferior product.

Test by Giving the Food to Cats

Of course, the best method to determine nutritional adequacy of a pet food is to feed it to cats and observe the results. Some authorities such as AAFCO have set out particular feeding study protocols to help manufacturers assess their pet foods. Foods meeting these standards have at least passed the minimum criteria.

At home, you can get a good idea about how a cat food performs by observing the results in areas such as skin and coat, activity levels, stool characteristics, and palatability responses to the food. Remember, however, that some foods are also helping on the inside, where the results cannot easily be seen—for example, special fiber sources and fatty acid balances that can help with the health of the intestine, skin, and coat.

Though obviously, evaluating the nutritional adequacy of a cat food is not an easy task, the steps listed above should help.

Part
VI

The Healthy Cat

11

A Home Veterinary Guide

BY SUSAN LITTLE, D.V.M.
DIPLOMATE ABVP (FELINE PRACTICE)

A *lthough cats have shared our lives for countless centuries, the relationship between them and their own-ers has changed dramatically in the last 100 years. At the turn of the last century, cats were valued mainly for their skill at catching mice, and interest in breeds of cats was just starting. Now, cats are the most popular companion animals. More than 70 million of them live as companions in the United States alone, compared with approximately 60 million dogs, according to the American Veterinary Medical Association.*

Along with their rise in popularity as friends and companions have come tremendous strides in the development of our understanding and ability to meet their physical and emotional needs. Although the first feline vaccine was developed in the 1930s and the first medical book on cat care was printed in 1925, most of the great advances in feline medicine have occurred since the 1960s—and what great advances they have been.

Cat owners now enjoy the benefits of so much progress in medical science, which allows their cats to live longer, healthier lives. They are also benefiting from commercially formulated diets designed to fill the needs of cats of every life stage as well as for a number of medical conditions. Specialists understand more than ever about the unique behaviors, both normal and abnormal, of the cat. Since

the 1970s, veterinary practices restricted to cats have flourished, offering medical care tailored to the needs of these remarkable animals. Many textbooks devoted to cats currently fill the shelves of libraries everywhere, written for both owners and veterinarians.

In the twenty-first century, cat owners expect and their cats receive state-of-the art medical care when it is necessary. Owners assume that their cats will benefit from the many technological advances made in veterinary medicine, and with increasing frequency, they do. No longer are cats viewed as small dogs—they are now a major veterinary specialty.

Maintaining the health of a pet and getting excellent medical care when it is needed are ways of expressing the strong bond that exists between feline and human friends. Our

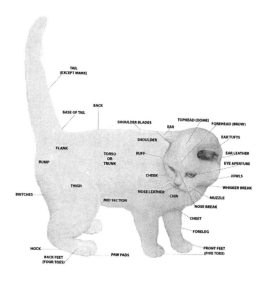

Labels on the diagram: TAIL (EXCEPT MANX), BACK, BASE OF TAIL, SHOULDER BLADES, TOPHEAD (DOME), FOREHEAD (BROW), EAR, EAR TUFTS, SHOULDER, FLANK, RUFF, EAR LEATHER, TORSO OR TRUNK, RUMP, EYE APERTURE, CHEEK, JOWLS, THIGH, NOSE LEATHER, WHISKER BREAK, BRITCHES, CHIN, MUZZLE, MID SECTION, NOSE BREAK, CHEST, FORELEG, HOCK, FRONT FEET (FIVE TOES), BACK FEET (FOUR TOES), PAW PADS

tions is also invaluable, for an informed owner is more likely to recognize a medical condition early, when veterinary intervention stands the best chance of successfully diagnosing and treating illnesses. Because cats cannot convey their medical problems to us in words, the obligation is ours as responsible and caring owners to be sure we are well informed and observant.

ABBREVIATION KEY

AIDS: Acquired immunodeficiency syndrome. A clinical syndrome of diseases associated with human immunodeficiency virus infection (HIV).

ASD: Atrial septal defect. A hole in the septum or wall that separates the left and right atria in the heart.

AZT: Azidothymidine, also called zidovudine. A drug sold under various brand names used in the treatment of some viral diseases of humans and animals.

CRF: Chronic renal failure. The progressive deterioration of kidney function in cats over time, most often associated with old age but occasionally seen with specific kidney diseases.

CPR: Cardiopulmonary resuscitation. Lifesaving procedure that combines heart massage and assisted breathing (artificial respiration).

CRT: Capillary refill time. A method of assessing the cardiovascular system in an injured or ill animal.

ELISA: Enzyme-linked immunosorbent assay. A test methodology commonly employed for the detection of many diseases in human and

cats now share a significant place in our lives, and we give them all the respect and devotion such a position deserves. What other companion offers unconditional and uncritical love? They give us just as much affection whether we are paupers or kings and queens. Such loyal and nonjudgmental companionship is now recognized as especially important in the lives of seniors, the chronically ill or disabled, and others in our society. The cat has truly taken its rightful place in all of our lives, equally happy sleeping peacefully beside the fireplace or on top of the computer.

Cat owners are now more informed about their pets than ever. Whether a new cat is acquired from a shelter or a friend or is a well-researched purchase from a breeder of pedigreed cats, owners are likely to seek out information on cat health and care from the beginning. A wealth of information is readily available in libraries and bookstores, from veterinarians, and on the Internet. Learning about the normal behaviors and habits of cats is essential for owners to understand their own pet. Awareness of common medical condi-

veterinary medicine, such as detection of certain viruses.

FCV: Feline coronavirus. The general name for a common virus of all cat species that has both benign (FECV) and disease-causing forms (FIPV).

FECV: Feline enteric coronavirus. The benign form of feline coronavirus that infects the intestinal tract of cats and is especially common in multicat homes or shelters.

FeLV: Feline leukemia virus. A retrovirus that is the leading cause of contagious disease and death in cats worldwide.

FIP: Feline infectious peritonitis. A fatal disease of cats caused by a feline coronavirus (FIPV) that has no effective treatment and no definitive test for detection.

FIPV: Feline infectious peritonitis virus. The mutated form of feline coronavirus that is capable of causing feline infectious peritonitis.

FIV: Feline immunodeficiency virus. A lentivirus of cats found throughout the world that can cause depression of the immune system and is mainly spread through bite wounds.

FLUTD: Feline lower urinary tract disease. A general name for the various causes of symptoms associated with diseases of the bladder and urethra of cats.

FPV: Feline panleukopenia virus. The feline parvovirus, also called feline distemper, which infects the nervous system, intestinal tract, and bone marrow of cats, especially kittens.

FUS: Feline urological syndrome. An older name for FLUTD.

FVR: Feline viral rhinotracheitis. The disease caused by the respiratory virus, feline herpesvirus type 1.

HCM: Hypertrophic cardiomyopathy. The most common disease of the heart muscle found in cats; known to be inherited in some breeds.

HIV: Human immunodeficiency virus. A human virus related to FIV that is the cause of acquired immunodeficiency syndrome in people.

IBD: Inflammatory bowel disease. A common disease that may affect any part of the digestive tract in cats and cause vomiting or diarrhea.

IFA: Immunofluorescence assay. A type of test methodology employed to detect some infectious diseases in cats and other species.

IN/IO: Intranasal/intraocular. A method of vaccination in which drops are applied to the nose and eyes.

KV: Killed virus. A type of vaccine in which the virus is killed or inactivated so that it cannot cause disease.

MLV: Modified live virus. A type of vaccine in which the virus is weakened or attenuated so that it cannot cause serious disease.

PDA: Patent ductus arteriosus. A birth defect of the heart sometimes seen in kittens that can be surgically repaired.

PKD: Polycystic kidney disease. An inherited disease that causes fluid-filled cysts to form in the kidneys and may be associated with kidney failure.

PRAA: Persistent right aortic arch. A type of heart defect occasionally seen in kittens that can be surgically repaired.

VSD: Ventricular septal defect. A hole in the septum or wall that divides the right and left ventricles of the heart.

THE VETERINARIAN
CHOOSING A VETERINARIAN

Choosing a veterinarian and a clinic that meets the needs of both you and your cat may not be an easy task, but making the right choice is essential for your cat's health care. Because cats can live 15 years or more, the veterinarian you choose may be looking after your cat for many years. In many urban areas, there may be a bewildering array of clinics from which to choose. In cities, factors such as accessibility to public transit or on-site parking can be very important in choosing a clinic.

Veterinary clinics may be small one- or two-person practices or large multidoctor facilities. In rural areas, they may be mixed practices that serve both large- and small-animal clients. Veterinarians who are in general practice may staff them, or specialists in various disciplines may staff them. They may or may not offer intensive care, 24-hour care, or after-hours emergency care. They also vary in how much advanced equipment they have and what types of laboratory facilities are on the premises. While most work on an appointment system, some are walk-in-style clinics. Deciding which of these factors is important to you can help guide your choice.

One criterion to use when evaluating a new hospital is to check its accreditation status. The American Animal Hospital Association (AAHA; http://www.healthypet.com) has a voluntary veterinary hospital accreditation program in the United States and Canada. The AAHA established certain standards for hospital facilities and services covering 12 specific areas. To be accredited, a hospital must meet the standards and be evaluated periodically by trained practice consultants to ensure ongoing compliance.

Regardless of the size of clinic, some factors are common to all well-run clinics. The waiting room should be clean, tidy, and comfortable and reception staff members should be professional, well-mannered, and informative. If it is a general practice, separate waiting areas for cats and dogs is a desirable feature. Whether you are being served in person or on the telephone, your needs should be attended to promptly and courteously. When you meet the veterinarian, you should have adequate time and not feel rushed. Even if the occasion is a routine annual examination, you will have important information to impart about your cat, and the veterinarian should ask questions and listen carefully to your answers. The results of the visit should be noted in a permanent medical record for each pet.

Veterinarians vary in their ability to relate to and handle cats. It is important to find one who is comfortable with cats and seems to understand their body language. During the physical examination, it may be necessary for the veterinarian to be patient and not handle the cat roughly. A safe and acceptable way should be offered to examine and treat irritable or fearful cats. Many veterinarians either work with an assistant in the examination room or will ask an assistant for help with difficult patients to avoid any potential for injury to the cat's owner.

Good communication skills are essential for a veterinarian to treat your cat effectively. This means you should fully understand any tests that are being suggested or any treatments that are being recommended. A good veterinarian does not mind questions and encourages clients to do further reading and research. Most will provide informational material. He or she will be able to use terms you can understand when explaining medical issues. Ideally, you should be asked to consent to any tests or procedures in writing with a form that explains exactly what will happen and what are the estimated fees. If your cat is hospitalized, you should receive regular updates and be encouraged to visit your cat as long as the pet's condition is stable. Once your pet returns home, your veterinarian should be willing to make follow-up telephone calls and schedule visits for reevaluation.

Veterinary fees vary not only by geographical area but also with the type of practice. Clinics that have extensive equipment and services such as intensive care and overnight monitoring will often set their fees higher than smaller clinics that do not provide such things. Do not be tempted to pick a veterinarian on the basis of inexpensive fees alone; a clinic that charges more than others may provide services worth the extra costs. Many veterinary clinics will give you a schedule of fees for routine procedures, such as examinations and elective surgeries.

One way to locate a good veterinarian for your cat is to ask for recommendations from other cat owners—friends, breeders, cat clubs, and animal organizations. Telephone directories usually list local clinics. There are also Web sites that can direct you to a veterinarian in your area. Once you have located a few possibilities, assemble a list of questions and factors to take into consideration. Call and ask the clinic for a get-acquainted visit and a tour of the clinic, if possible. Veterinary clinics are busy places and the courtesy of making an appointment for your visit will be much appreciated.

WHAT TO EXPECT FROM A VETERINARIAN

When trying to select a veterinarian, it is a good idea to have a checklist of questions with which to work. Here are some suggested questions you could ask when interviewing a veterinarian:

- What are the clinic's hours of operation, and is an appointment system used?
- If overnight care is needed, is there an arrangement for this?
- How are emergencies handled after hours? Does the clinic have a veterinarian on call, or does it refer to a local emergency clinic?
- Is the clinic a full-service or satellite location? Would your cat have to go to another location if testing (such as X-rays) or surgery is needed?
- Are there board-certified specialists on staff, or can your cat be referred to a local specialist if a second opinion is needed? Are services such as ultrasound or endoscopy offered or available locally?
- What is the veterinarian's approach to vaccinations and preventive health care? Are special programs of health monitoring available for different age groups?
- Are house-call services offered?
- What type of monitoring during anesthesia is used? Ensure that the clinic has a policy to provide pain management for surgical patients and other pets in need.
- What laboratory facilities are available on-site?
- If this is a general practice, is there a hospital ward set aside only for cats?
- What type of feline continuing education is planned for the veterinarians and technicians in the practice?
- Are boarding or grooming facilities available (if these are services you use)?
- What is the clinic's policy on payment of accounts? Does it offer a payment plan or

credit service for large bills? Does it honor pet health insurance?

• Is the veterinarian a member of the American Association of Feline Practitioners (AAFP)?

Ask for a tour of the clinic's facilities (usually by appointment only) to ascertain the following:

• Is the clinic clean and free of bad odors?
• Are the animals in the hospital cages clean and well tended?
• Is the atmosphere calm and nonstressful?
• Are the working areas well ordered and tidy?
• Are there separate areas for sterile surgeries and nonsterile surgeries (such as dental cleanings)?
• Is the staff well groomed and pleasant?
• Is the clinic secure with no way for pets to escape?

FELINE-ONLY VETERINARY PRACTICES

In many areas of North America, cat owners are now able to choose feline-only veterinary practices. Dr. Louis Camuti established the first feline house-calls-only practice in the 1940s in New York. Now there are literally hundreds of feline-only clinics available. Their number has increased most dramatically since first appearing in the early 1970s. Feline-only practices offer several advantages over general practices. Typically, veterinarians at feline practices have more experience with feline problems and they may or may not have specialty certification. Feline clinics also tend to be quieter and allow cats to be calmer because no dogs are on the premises. They often have more specialized equipment because they have to buy only for one species of animal.

As the interest in feline medicine has grown, so have organizations and continuing-education opportunities for feline veterinarians. The AAFP is an organization that has promoted feline health care since 1971 and sponsors conferences and publications intended to keep veterinarians informed of advances in feline medicine and surgery. The AAFP also maintains a searchable directory of feline veterinarians in North America on their Web site at: http://www.aafponline.org.

Other organizations and institutions now offer veterinary medical conferences and publications solely on feline medical topics. The Cornell Feline Health Center (FHC; http://web.vet.cornell.edu/public/FHC/felinehealth.html), first conceived in 1973 by the College of Veterinary Medicine at Cornell University (Ithaca, New York), is a specialty center devoted to improving the health and welfare of cats everywhere. FHC staff members focus their attention on educating both veterinarians and owners about feline health issues, providing consultation services to veterinarians, and directing research efforts to prevent and cure feline diseases. The Louis J. Camuti Diagnostic and Consultation Service was founded in the 1980s to provide aid to feline veterinarians around North America. To date, the FHC has been involved in many important research projects, including those investigating several infectious diseases, establishing vaccination recommendations, developing temperament tests for kittens, and examining the role of blood pressure in cats with heart disease. The FHC has also supported the Vaccine-Associated Feline Sarcoma Task Force. Finally, the FHC has sponsored a feline medicine conference for veterinarians every year since the late 1980s where the most up-to-date information and research are presented.

BOARD-CERTIFIED FELINE SPECIALISTS

Since 1995, it has been possible for veterinarians around the world to achieve board certification in feline medicine and surgery through the American Board of Veterinary Practitioners (ABVP; http://www.abvp.com). ABVP is a specialty organization under the American Veterinary Medical Association (AVMA; http://www.avma.org) that certifies veterinarians in several different specialty areas. Veterinarians who are certified by ABVP in their specialty area are called diplomates. Typically, such a veterinarian will have the letters *Dipl. ABVP* or *DABVP* after his or her name, often with the specialty area noted as well. For example: *Susan Little, D.V.M., DABVP* (Feline Practice). Diplomates must recertify every 10 years to ensure that they have current knowledge in their field. Achieving board certification is a process that often takes 2–3 years.

Requirements for ABVP Board Certification in Feline Practice

The candidate veterinarian must

- Be a graduate of an AVMA-approved college of veterinary medicine
- Have finished 1 year of practice or internship, plus have finished 5 years of excellent work in feline medicine and surgery or an approved residency program
- Have three letters of recommendation from professional colleagues, one of which must be from a board-certified veterinarian
- Submit two articles or case reports suitable for publication
- Be able to demonstrate a commitment to continuing education over the previous 6 years
- Successfully pass a three-part examination conducted over several days

FELINE RESEARCH

The popularity of pet cats has grown since the 1970s, and investigations into their behavior, nutrition, and health have kept pace. Feline medical research is now carried out at all major veterinary institutions in the world. Because the cat is also an important medical model for many human diseases, research has benefited both species.

Money for feline research is made available through several funding organizations, but the Winn Feline Foundation (http://www.winnfelinehealth.org) is one of the oldest. Established as a nonprofit organization by the Cat Fanciers' Association (CFA) in 1968, Winn provides funding for studies designed to improve feline health and welfare. In the years since its founding, Winn has awarded over $2 million in grants. A unique feature of Winn is that 100% of every dollar donated to the organization goes to fund research because the CFA covers all operational costs. Money for Winn-funded projects comes directly from pet owners and the general public, many of whom give money in memory of a cherished pet. Donations also come through the hard work of many CFA-affiliated cat clubs.

The Winn Feline Foundation has funded many important studies over the years. In addition, Winn has sponsored annual symposia and has cosponsored several unique feline conferences.

PET HEALTH INSURANCE

While pet health insurance sounds like a new idea, it was first offered in the 1950s in the United Kingdom. In the United States, pet health insurance appeared in 1982, and several companies have since come and gone. The AVMA endorses pet health insurance as long as the companies have clearly written policies and there is freedom for the pet owner to choose a veterinarian and freedom for the veterinarian to direct the medical care of the patient without interference.

Considering that U.S. pet owners spend over $11 billion every year on pet health care, insurance can range from being a helpful tool to a vital necessity. Costs for some procedures, such as orthopedic surgery, chemotherapy and other cancer therapies, and newer procedures, such as kidney transplants, can be very high. Many pets are euthanized because an owner cannot afford necessary treatment. While most veterinarians will offer payment plans or credit services to help with large bills, this may still not be enough in some cases. Pet health insurance can make the difference.

Companies offer various policies covering different things, and evaluating which policy is best for your cat can be time-consuming and difficult. Some policies cover routine care such as vaccinations, elective surgery, and dental cleaning, while others cover only illnesses or injuries. In addition, reimbursement for covered items may be complete or partial. In general, policies are bought on an annual basis, with prices ranging from $100 to $200 per year. Insuring kittens is less costly than insuring adult cats, and some companies have an age limit. Insurance coverage may end at a certain age, or pets over a given age may not be accepted for new policies. Often, the company will ask for a transcript of the cat's medical record at the time of enrollment, and preexisting medical conditions may be excluded.

Knowing what questions to ask can help guide the decision-making process. It is also helpful to speak to your veterinarian and ask about the clinic's experience with any company you are considering. Here are some important points to think about:

- What does each type of policy cover and, most important, not cover? There may be some hereditary conditions, for instance, that are not covered.
- Is there an option for coverage of routine treatments and elective surgery costs, such as vaccinations, flea control, dental cleanings, and spaying or neutering?
- Are there multiple pet discounts if you enroll more than one pet?
- Are additional services offered, such as lost-and-found?
- What is the deductible, and how is it applied (that is, on a per-illness basis or annually)?
- What, if any, situations require a copayment on your part?
- Does the policy have a yearly maximum amount that is covered?
- Are there age limitations? Or does the cost of the policy increase as your cat ages?
- If you move to a different part of the country, will the amount of your premium change?
- Are alternative medicine treatments covered?
- How does a policyholder contact the company (phone, fax, e-mail)? Is there a toll-free number?
- What is the company's track record and how long has it been in business? Can you contact existing policyholders for references?

ALTERNATIVE VETERINARY MEDICINE

As veterinary medicine evolves and changes, new ideas and approaches appear, are tried, and incorporated into the health care of our pets if they prove themselves. In recent years, increasing interest in alternative medicine for human health care has resulted in a similar interest for pets.

Alternative medicine is a term that describes

treatments that are unlike conventional medical techniques. The term also embraces a wide range of therapies and belief systems that are very diverse. The therapies included in alternative medicine come from various historical backgrounds and from different geographical places. Another common term is *holistic medicine*, which refers to systems that diagnose and treat the whole patient, not the disease by itself. Holistic care can incorporate the principles of acupuncture, chiropractic, homeopathy, and other therapies.

Several veterinary organizations are involved in the investigation and promotion of alternative medicine, such as the International Veterinary Acupuncture Society (http://www.ivas.org), the American Veterinary Chiropractic Association (http://www.animalchiropractic.org) and the American Holistic Veterinary Medical Association (http://www.ahvma.org). As well, the AVMA has established guidelines for alternative and complementary veterinary medicine that cover many treatments.

Increasingly, veterinarians can get advanced training in alternative medicine. Courses in acupuncture, homeopathy, and veterinary chiropractic are becoming more widely available. Publications dealing with various aspects of alternative medicine are available, and veterinarians now can take alternative medicine courses in several veterinary colleges. At least one veterinary college now offers an advanced degree in complementary medicine for veterinarians.

The most important point to remember when considering alternative medicine for your cat is to consult a professional. Many communities now have veterinarians who practice holistic or alternative medicine. Any type of therapy, conventional or alternative, can have the potential to cause harm to a patient if it is wrongly used or applied to the wrong patient. While many alternative therapies, such as homeopathy and herbal medicine, seem more accessible to laypeople, they should still be viewed with the same respect as conventional medicine and the guidance of a professional should be sought.

THE VETERINARY EXAMINATION

Perhaps the most important thing you can do for your cat is to seek regular veterinary examinations. In the past, the attention for annual visits to the veterinarian has been focused on vaccinations, but we now know that regular physical exams may be more important, just as for people.

Veterinarians do a systematic examination of all major body systems during these visits. After weighing the patient, most vets start at the head of the cat and examine eyes, ears, mouth, and nose. Special attention is paid to the teeth. The skin and coat are checked for evidence of external parasites, hair loss, skin lesions, redness, or lumps and bumps. The heart and lungs are checked with the stethoscope. Many cats have had heart diseases detected in a physical examination and thus were able to live longer and healthier lives because of early intervention. The veterinarian also examines the abdomen carefully, checking the internal organs, especially the kidneys, liver, bowel, and bladder.

Another important part of the examination involves taking the patient's history. Veterinarians usually ask questions about the cat's diet, eating habits, bowel and bladder habits, behavioral issues, and lifestyle changes (for example, is a previously indoors-only cat now going outside?). This is an opportunity to identify irregularities and investigate them. Finally, risk factors are evaluated so that any appropriate vaccinations can be given.

Depending on the age of the cat, other issues may be emphasized at the visit.

Examining Kittens

Attention is paid to the type of food best suited for the kitten, the schedule of visits necessary for vaccinations, as well as testing for feline leukemia virus (FeLV) and feline immunodeficiency virus (FIV). Fecal analysis and deworming are essential, as are discussions of kitten behaviors (interacting with older cats in the home, play and biting, and so on), plans for neuter or spay surgery, and grooming needs. It is also a good time for the veterinarian to demonstrate nail trimming and home dental care.

Examining Young to Middle-Aged Adults

For young and middle-aged cats, particular attention is paid to diet and obesity prevention, behavior issues (especially house soiling, and aggression), success of home dental care routines, and routine blood, urine, and fecal testing.

Examining Senior Cats

For senior cats, a physical examination may be recommended every 6 months because significant changes in health can occur rapidly. Other important issues are weight loss, signs of disease (such as increased appetite, thirst, or urination), dental care, and blood pressure measurement. Behavior changes common in older cats such as the inability to maintain awareness of surrounding conditions (cognitive dysfunction) are considered, as well as routine blood, urine, and fecal testing and diets best suited for senior cats or those with special health problems. The AAFP Academy of Feline Medicine (AFM) has published information on health issues of older cats in its Panel Report on Feline Senior Care (1999), available on its Web site (http://www.aafponline.org).

VACCINATING YOUR CAT

One of the most significant advances in veterinary medicine has been the development of vaccines for the prevention of many feline diseases. While vaccines have been responsible for the wellness of many hundreds of thousands of cats, their usage is also under scrutiny as concerns about adverse effects and the frequency of vaccination are investigated. The release of the Feline Vaccination Guidelines by the AAFP/AFM in 1998 and 2000 provided cat owners, breeders, and veterinarians with new information about vaccinating cats. The guidelines are available on the AAFP Web site (http://www.aafponline.org).

CORE VACCINES

Veterinarians no longer think in terms of a standard vaccination program for all cats. It is important to assess the relative risks for each cat, taking into account both individual and environmental factors to make appropriate decisions. The AAFP/AFM guidelines designated four feline vaccines as core, or essential, vaccines because of the serious nature of the diseases and their widespread distribution in the feline population:

• **Feline panleukopenia (FPV, formerly known as feline distemper or feline infectious enteritis):** FPV is caused by the feline parvovirus, which is capable of surviving long periods of time in the environment. Until recently, FPV was one of the most feared feline diseases. Vaccines have dramatically reduced the number of cats that die from FPV every year. FPV is most common in cats under 1 year of age and can also cause prenatal infections. The brain, gastrointestinal tract, and the bone marrow are the sites targeted by this virus. When properly administered, available FPV vaccines confer excellent protection.

• **Feline viral rhinotracheitis (FVR) and feline calicivirus (FCV):** These two viruses account for approximately 80% of all feline upper respiratory tract infections. They are highly contagious, are widespread in the cat population, and can become endemic in multicat households. Kittens are most susceptible. While most cats survive infection, chronic respiratory disease and the carrier state are common consequences. Currently available vaccines, both injectable and topical, shield against serious disease but cannot fully protect against infection.

• **Rabies:** A serious fatal disease of mammals, rabies is transmitted by direct contact with an infected animal, most often through a bite wound (see "Rabies," pages 440–441). In North America, more cats than dogs are diagnosed with rabies but both species remain a potential source of infection for humans. In cats, rabies is always fatal and treatment is never attempted. Local or municipal regulations govern rabies control issues, including vaccination. A 3-year rabies vaccine is available and should be used wherever local laws allow.

NONCORE VACCINES

Several other feline vaccines are available, and even more may be available in the future, such as new vaccines for bartonellosis (cat scratch disease), see "Cat Scratch Disease (Bartonellosis)," pages 443–444, and toxoplasmosis (see "Toxoplasmosis," pages 441–443). These noncore vaccines are not appropriate for all feline patients and should be administered only to those at realistic risk of contracting the disease. Currently, the following noncore feline vaccines are available:

• *Chlamydophila felis:* Formerly called *Chlamydia psittaci*, this is a bacteria-like organism that primarily causes respiratory disease in cats. It is transmitted directly from cat to cat and does not persist in the environment. Its prevalence varies geographically; it is considered a more important respiratory pathogen in the United Kingdom than in North America. As for vaccines against feline viral rhinotracheitis (FVR) and feline calicivirus (FCV) *Chlamydia* vaccines protect only against severe disease, not against infection. Many veterinarians feel that *Chlamydia* vaccines are associated with higher adverse reactions than other common vaccines.

• **Feline leukemia virus (FeLV):** An important retrovirus that infects domestic cats worldwide and causes a variety of disease syndromes. In areas with large feline populations, such as urban centers, the infection rate is highest and FeLV is the leading viral killer of cats. The virus is transmitted through prolonged cat-to-cat contact, bite wounds, or from queen to kitten. The youngest kittens are the most susceptible; partial resistance to infection appears to develop with age. The most important weapon against FeLV is testing and identifying positive cats. Cats at highest risk include feral and stray cats, cats in open multicat households, and cats with access to outdoors. Available vaccines against FeLV vary in their effectiveness, but most are considered to offer fair to good protection.

• **Feline infectious peritonitis (FIP):** Caused by a coronavirus that infects both domestic and nondomestic cats, FIP is the disease that develops when the benign feline enteric coronavirus (FECV) mutates into a disease-causing form within susceptible individuals. While infection with FECV is common, especially in multicat households, FIP is much less common. Young cats are at greatest risk, and susceptibility appears to be at least partly inherited. The different forms of the disease are invariably fatal. Considerable controversy surrounds both the effectiveness and safety of the only available vaccine (Primucell FIP, manufactured by Pfizer), which is administered intranasally.

• ***Bordetella bronchiseptica (FeBb):*** Long considered to be primarily a canine disease, this bacterial infection is now known to be a cause of respiratory disease in cats as well. Prevalence of the infection seems to vary geographically, and cats at highest risk are those in shelters or catteries. The infection can cause significant mortality in young kittens because of bronchopneumonia. An intranasal vaccine (Protex-Bb, manufactured by Intervet) is now available for cats.

• ***Giardia felis:*** This protozoan parasite of the intestinal tract affects both humans and companion animals. It is found worldwide, and the incidence of the infection in the general cat population is estimated to be about 5%. It may be much higher in multicat situations, such as shelters or catteries, and in some geographical areas. The infection is treated with certain medications and disinfection of the environment. A vaccine (GiardiaVax, manufactured by Fort Dodge Animal Health) is available.

• **Feline immunodeficiency virus (FIV):** Another important retrovirus, FIV affects 1% to 8% of cats in the United States. In other countries, the incidence of this virus may be as high as 25%. FIV eventually suppresses the immune system of infected cats, leaving them predisposed to a variety of illnesses. The virus is transmitted primarily through bite wounds, although it can be passed from an infected queen to her kittens. Cats at highest risk are stray cats and those owned cats with access to outdoors. Unneutered male cats are especially at risk because they are more likely to fight. FIV is diagnosed by screening a cat's blood for antibodies. In 2002, a vaccine developed against FIV was released (Fel-O-Vax FIV, manufactured by Fort Dodge Animal Health). This vaccine has made accurate diagnosis of FIV infection more difficult because vaccinated cats will also test positive on routine antibody screening tests commonly used by veterinarians. Other test methods that detect the virus itself instead of antibodies, such as polymerase chain reaction (PCR) techniques, have not been sufficiently validated to be recommended.

RISK ASSESSMENT

Vaccination protocols should take into account several factors. The most important areas of risk assessment are the patient, the environment, and the infectious disease:

• **The patient:** Most important of the patient factors is age. Kittens, especially those 6 months and younger, are at highest risk for infectious diseases. It is therefore important that kittens receive an adequate initial series of vaccinations to provide a basis for future health and vaccination decisions. A common cause of vaccination failure in kittens is failure to vaccinate after interfering maternal immunity has waned (usually by about 12 weeks of age but sometimes earlier). Maternal immunity consists of antibodies provided to the kitten in colostrum, the milk produced by the queen for the first days of the kitten's life. The health status of the patient, including any history of previous adverse reactions, will also affect vaccination decisions. Patients with any serious illness or who are debilitated or suffering from a high fever may have their vaccinations postponed. It is probably safe to vaccinate cats with minor or mild illnesses, such as mild upper respiratory disease or diarrhea.

- **The environment:** Of critical importance is the risk of exposure to disease. Cats that are free-roaming or that have some outdoor access are at the highest risk. Totally indoor cats who live in small (one- or two-cat), stable households are at the lowest risk. Cats that live in multicat households or in shelters or catteries are also at high risk because of population density and turnover. Some infectious diseases vary in geographical distribution, so that risk of exposure also varies.

- **Infectious disease:** Factors that affect the infectious agent itself, while hard to measure, are also important. They include virulence, dose, and stability of the organism in different environments.

VACCINE TYPES

Veterinarians also have different types of vaccinations to choose from. In general, vaccines are either live-virus or noninfectious. Live-virus vaccines are usually modified to increase their safety. Common examples of modified live virus (MLV) vaccines are those for FVR, FCV, FPV, and *Chlamydia*. Noninfectious vaccines are most commonly killed virus (KV) or purified subunit vaccines. While these vaccines may be safer than modified live vaccines, they may not induce immunity as easily, so they may contain a larger dose of viral antigen and may also contain substances called adjuvants to enhance the immune response. Vaccines for FVR, FCV, and FPV are also available in killed virus formulations. FeLV vaccines are available as purified subunit vaccines, where only certain viral proteins are selected for inclusion in the vaccine, rather than the whole virus.

The field of vaccine technology is rapidly producing new ways of making vaccines, especially using recombinant DNA techniques. Many of these vaccines will be available in the future without adjuvants. For instance, a nonadjuvant recombinant feline rabies vaccine has recently been introduced (PureVax Feline Rabies, manufactured by Merial).

Vaccines may also be administered through different routes. KV vaccines are given only by injection, either subcutaneously (beneath the skin) or intramuscularly. MLV vaccines may be given by the topical route, IN/IO (intranasally/intraocularly), or injected subcutaneously or intramuscularly. If droplets of an injectable modified-live respiratory virus vaccine inadvertently contact the mucous membranes of the cat (eyes, nose, mouth) or are licked from the coat, a mild form of the disease may be produced. MLV (IN/IO) vaccines produce a good generalized immunity as well as a strong local immune response. They also provide a more rapid onset of protection. This rapid local immune response is especially valuable in the case of FVR and FCV where the site of vaccination (eyes, nose) is also the target site of the disease. An additional benefit is that IN/IO vaccines have no risk of producing injection-site reactions or tumors. A summary of the advantages and disadvantages of the various vaccine types is presented in the following table.

	LIVE VIRUS VACCINES	NONINFECTIOUS VACCINES
Formulations	Modified live (attenuated)	Killed, subunit
How given	Topical, injectable	Injectable only
Immunity	Longer and more complete	Shorter
Doses needed	Fewer for initial series, fewer for revaccination	Multiple doses for initial series and revaccination
Safety	Small potential for vaccine-induced disease, shedding	Cannot cause disease
Side effects	Occasional, usually mild	Occasional to frequent
Adjuvant needed	No	Yes (newer technologies may eliminate this need)
Cost	Generally low	Moderate
Antigen per dose	Low	Moderate to high

VACCINE-SITE RECOMMENDATIONS

In the past, veterinarians commonly used only a few sites on the body to inject vaccines. For subcutaneous injections, this was typically between the shoulder blades. For intramuscular (IM) injections, either the muscles of the lower back or the large muscles of the thigh were used. In recent years, concern over the ability of vaccines to induce tumor formation in rare cases has led the AAFP/AFM to produce vaccination-site guidelines. The guidelines were designed to help identify the vaccines most associated with tumor formation and to make treatment (usually surgical resection) easier to perform. It is also recommended that products intended for subcutaneous or IN/IO use be considered over those for IM use where possible. The use of multiantigen vaccine products versus single-antigen vaccines is controversial, and the risks and benefits of each type are unclear. However, it is clear that the use of multidose vials should be discouraged because the risks of uneven distribution of antigens and adjuvant and of contamination are significant.

Veterinarians are encouraged to standardize their vaccination protocols and ensure that they record the location of the injection, the type of vaccine, and the manufacturer and serial number of the vaccine in the patient's record. A summary of the vaccine site recommendations is presented in the following table.

SITE	VACCINE
Right shoulder	FPV, FVR, FCV with or without *Chlamydophila*
Left rear leg	FeLV with or without any other antigen except rabies
Right rear leg	Rabies with or without any other antigen except FeLV
Left shoulder	Any other injectable drug (such as antibiotics, flea-control products)

FCV = feline calicivirus, FeLV = feline leukemia virus; FPV = feline panleukopenia; FVR = feline viral rhinotracheitis.

VACCINATION PROTOCOLS: SPECIAL SITUATIONS

Once the patient's risk factors are examined and the types of vaccines are chosen, a vaccination protocol can be developed. Ideally, kittens should receive their first vaccination at about 8 weeks of age, as the immunity from colostrum (mother's milk produced shortly after birth) begins to dissipate. However, there are circumstances where vaccinations are not started until kittens are older. As well, there may be circumstances where vaccination before 8 weeks of age is desirable. Orphan kittens present special situations because they may not have acquired adequate immunity from their mothers. It can be appropriate to vaccinate orphans or kittens in catteries and shelters earlier, although vaccines generally have not been tested in animals younger than 6 weeks, and their use in this manner is considered off-label.

The earliest kittens should be vaccinated is 2 weeks of age, because the lower body temperature of the neonatal kitten compromises its ability to mount an immune response before this time. Vaccination before 2 weeks of age will provide little or no protection and could possibly cause serious disease in some situations. The ability of neonatal kittens to respond to vaccinations varies greatly because of genetic and environmental factors that affect their immune system.

When kittens younger than 8 weeks of age are vaccinated, a few rules must be observed. MLV vaccines containing FPV (whether injectable or IN/IO) must not be used in kittens under 4 weeks of age to avoid damage to the part of the brain called the cerebellum. When young kittens receive an injectable vaccine, each kitten should get a full dose. Getting less than the full dose could result in inadequate production of immunity.

When kittens 2–4 weeks old get IN/IO vaccines, one drop of vaccine is administered in each eye and in each nostril. It is also important to ensure that each kitten receives a final vaccination at 12 weeks of age or older to avoid maternal antibody interference and the subsequent risk of vaccine failure.

Other special situations will affect vaccination protocols as well. Often in catteries it is desirable to vaccinate pregnant queens to ensure that the kittens will receive maximal protection. Stray queens that are pregnant may receive vaccines for the same reason. MLV vaccines containing FPV (whether injectable or IN/IO) must not be given to pregnant queens, so that potential brain damage in the kittens can be avoided. Pregnant queens can be vaccinated with a KV vaccine containing FVR/FCV/FPV in the last 2–3 weeks of pregnancy. An IN/IO vaccine containing only FVR and FCV can also be used. In general, KV vaccines and IN/IO vaccines without FPV are safe in pregnant queens, but there is always some risk in using them, mainly connected to the possible occurrence of a vaccine reaction. While the vaccine itself is unlikely to be dangerous, the fever, lethargy, or loss of appetite that could accompany vaccination might affect the unborn kittens detrimentally. This is a situation in which it is especially important to assess the risks and benefits of vaccinating a given patient, and the routine vaccination of pregnant queens should generally be avoided.

Cats who are suffering from immune system suppression may require vaccination. A common situation is when cats who are receiving corticosteroid therapy for any one of many common illnesses require a vaccination. Ideally, it is best to avoid giving vaccines to patients receiving these drugs because they may not respond adequately to the vaccination. To avoid the risk of vaccine-induced disease, Patients on high doses of corticosteroids should not be given MLV vaccines. However, studies have shown that patients on short courses of low or moderate doses of these drugs can probably be safely and adequately immunized.

Another common instance of immune system suppression occurs when cats are FeLV or FIV positive. Many of these cats remain healthy for considerable periods of time, so the question of vaccinations may need to be addressed. The AAFP/AFM (American Association of Feline Practitioners/Academy of Feline Medicine) guidelines suggest that only core vaccines be given to these patients unless there is a critical need for one of the noncore vaccines. KV vaccines are probably also safer, because there could be risk of vaccine-induced disease if MLV vaccines are used.

VACCINATION PROTOCOLS: CORE VACCINES

Common vaccination protocols for FVR, FCV, and FPV vaccines in high- and low-risk patients have been developed in part by the AAFP/AFM and are presented below. Rabies vaccination is given as a single dose at 12 weeks of age, followed by a booster vaccination 1 year later.

It must be noted that giving vaccines at intervals less than 3–4 weeks apart is not recommended. If vaccines are given less than 14 days apart, the immune response may be inadequate. The question of what to do if booster vaccinations are delayed for more than 4 weeks is not as easy to answer. There is little research available for guidance. Factors such as the length of the delay, the age of the patient, and the type of vaccine must be considered. Many experts recommend that if KV vaccines are being used and the booster has been delayed for more than 2 months, it is best to start a two-dose series of vaccinations again.

RISK LEVEL	PROTOCOL
Low: Pet cat in home with few cats	MLV or KV at first visit; then every 4 weeks until over 12 weeks old
If first vaccination <12 weeks of age	
If first vaccination >12 weeks of age	MLV: One dose KV: 2 doses, 4 weeks apart
High: Catteries/shelters	MLV at 4, 8, 12 weeks
High: Catteries/shelters with endemic respiratory disease	IN/IO (FVR/FCV only) at 2–4 weeks, then MLV (FVR/FCV/FPV) every 4 weeks until over 12 weeks old

FCV = feline calicivirus; FPV = feline panleukopenia; FVR = feline viral rhinotracheitis; IN = intranasal; IO = intraocular; KV = killed virus; MLV = modified live virus.

VACCINATION PROTOCOLS: NONCORE VACCINES

Feline leukemia virus vaccination is associated with unique factors influencing risks and benefits. Research has shown that the most susceptible patients are those under 16 weeks of age and that susceptibility seems to decline with age. Ideally, only those cats at risk of contracting the disease should be vaccinated for FeLV. Risk is strongly associated with lifestyle; outdoor cats, those in open multicat households, and those in multicat households where the FeLV status of all cats is not known or known FeLV-positive cats are present are at risk. Assessing the risk for newly acquired kittens can be difficult because lifestyle changes can and do occur over time. In many cases, a kitten's environment will change in the first few years of its life. A kitten initially kept indoors may start venturing outside, or a single-cat household may become a multicat household. For these reasons, and because the most susceptible period in a cat's life for FeLV infection is when it is young, many kittens will be vaccinated for FeLV by the veterinarian. As time goes by, the risk of FeLV infection can be reassessed and the vaccine may or may not be given again in the future.

Another vaccination with controversial and unique features is the FIP vaccine. The natural history of this virus is very complex, and in many ways, the mode of transmission and development of disease are quite different from other common feline viruses. Most kittens are infected with the parent virus, the benign FECV, before 16 weeks of age, which is the age recommended by the manufacturer for first vaccination. Once a kitten is infected with FECV, the vaccine has no benefit. There continues to be controversy surrounding the efficacy of this vaccine, with published studies showing conflicting results.

Assessing risk factors for FIP is also difficult, because research has implicated individual genetic susceptibility in the very small number of cats who develop FIP after infection with FECV (about 5%). An age-associated immunity also seems to develop, with peak susceptibility at about 10 months of age. It seems likely that the best use of the vaccine is in shelters or catteries experiencing significant losses due to FIP. Dr. Johnny Hoskins (Louisiana State University) has recommended a protocol for early vaccination for use in catteries and shelters where losses due to FIP are occurring in kittens under 16 weeks of age. In this protocol, kittens are vaccinated at 9, 13, and 17 weeks of age. This protocol must be used with the knowledge that no controlled studies have been done on kittens under 16 weeks of age and that this constitutes off-label use of the vaccine.

Vaccination recommendations for non-core vaccines have been developed in part by the AAFP/AFM and are summarized in the table that follows. Controversies exist surrounding efficacy and potential adverse effects for all vaccines. Noncore vaccines are not appropriate for all feline patients and should be administered only to those at realistic risk of contracting the disease, after consultation with a veterinarian.

VACCINE	RECOMMENDATIONS
Bordetella	1 dose at least 72 hours before potential exposure; kittens 4 weeks of age or older
Chlamydia	
KV	2 doses, 4 weeks apart, annual revaccination
MLV	Single dose, annual revaccination
FeLV	2 doses, 4 weeks apart; first dose given at 8 weeks or older; annual revaccination
FIP	2 doses, 4 weeks apart; first dose given at 16 weeks or older; annual revaccination
FIV	3 doses, 2–3 weeks apart; first dose given at 8 weeks or older; annual revaccination
Giardia	2 doses, 4 weeks apart; first dose given at 8 weeks or older; annual revaccination

FeLV = feline leukemia virus; FIP = Feline infectious peritonitis; FIV = feline immunodeficiency virus; KV = killed virus; MLV = modified live virus.

DURATION OF IMMUNITY AND REVACCINATION

In the past, manufacturers of vaccines other than rabies vaccines have not been required to show how long the immunity from their products will last. Rabies vaccines have been under stricter guidelines, and manufacturers are required to show that immunity from their vaccine lasts either 1 or 3 years. Manufacturers have recommended annual revaccination in the absence of this information for the other feline vaccines, and veterinarians have followed this recommendation. On the basis of vaccine protocols in human medicine and knowledge of the immune system, it seems reasonable that annual revaccination may not be necessary for all cats. However, very few studies have been performed to evaluate this.

Research in recent years on immunity to FVR, FCV, and FPV has suggested that many cats will have protective titers (a measure of the concentration of antibodies in the blood) against these diseases for at least 3 years, and sometimes longer, after proper initial immunizations. This information has prompted the AAFP/AFM to suggest that many cats, especially those in low-risk situations, may not need annual revaccination for FVR, FCV, and FPV. Their guidelines recommend that all cats receive the initial series of vaccinations, and a booster 1 year later. Cats in low-risk situations may maintain adequate immunity to FVR, FCV, and FPV if they are then revaccinated every 3 years. Risk assessment is critical to the determination of future revaccination intervals for individual cats. Cats in catteries or shelters, outdoor cats, or those who may enter boarding facilities may well benefit from more frequent revaccination for FVR, FCV, and FPV.

ASSESSING ANTIBODY TITERS

It is possible to test the level of antibodies to FVR, FCV, and FPV in the blood of cats using various antibody titer methods, and there is interest in using titers to determine revaccination intervals. Titration is a method used to estimate the amount of antibody present in a blood sample. Serum is separated from the blood sample and is diluted in a series of decreasing concentrations. The highest dilution of serum in which the antibody is detected is reported as the antibody titer. Titers may be expressed as fractions or ratios. Higher amounts of antibody will be reported as smaller fractions or ratios. For instance, a blood sample with an antibody titer of 1:16 contains more antibody than a sample with a titer of 1:2.

However, it is not necessarily easy to interpret titers in light of protection against disease. For FPV, an antibody titer of 1:8 or greater will prevent infection and provide protection against disease. For FVR and FCV, however, the situation is not so clear. A cat with a negative antibody titer to FVR or FCV may still be protected against disease because of the memory function of the immune system that allows for a rapid response to be mounted when needed. It is always important to remember that vaccines for FVR and FCV cannot protect against infection but do protect against serious disease. It is thought that an FVR titer of 1:2 or higher and an FCV titer of 1:4 or higher will provide substantial protection against serious disease.

Further complicating the issue of using antibody titers to determine revaccination intervals is the fact that quality control in laboratories performing these tests is of critical importance. Private laboratories are not under any specific requirements to maintain quality control, and it is disturbing that disagreement on antibody titer results commonly exists between labs when a single sample is tested. It is therefore very important to ensure that a reliable laboratory with experience in antibody titers is used if this information is going to help determine revaccination intervals.

ADVERSE REACTIONS

Every vaccine has produced adverse reactions, ranging from minor events to serious ones. Any type of vaccine reaction, no matter how mild, should be reported to the veterinarian. Adverse reactions generally fall into three categories:

• **Systemic reactions:** A fairly large number of cats experience mild systemic responses after vaccination, including fever and lethargy. The majority of these cases will resolve on their own in a day or two; occasionally, supportive care and medications may be needed. More severe allergic reactions occur rarely in cats but are very important. This type of reaction, called anaphylaxis, includes hives, wheezing, facial swelling, swelling in the mouth or throat, difficulty breathing, and even shock. Milder forms of anaphylaxis are somewhat more common and include vomiting and diarrhea. The adverse effects may be seen as quickly as 30 minutes after vaccination, or they may be delayed for hours or a few days. Severe allergic reactions do require veterinary care because in rare cases, they can cause death.

A particular type of systemic reaction is seen with modified live *Chlamydia* vaccines. About 3% of vaccinated cats will suffer mild to severe responses that include lethargy, fever, lameness, and loss of appetite. Typically, it is not realized that these symptoms are associated with the vaccination, because they tend to occur 7–21 days later. Anti-inflammatory medications are usually able to resolve the reaction in a few days.

• **Injection site reactions:** Local reactions at the site of vaccine injection are not uncommon in cats. Some cats will experience stinging or pain at the injection site. Swelling, caused by tissue inflammation, can also form at the injection site, but it may not appear for several days after vaccination. These swellings should always be reported to the veterinarian. Fortunately, the majority of them will resolve in less than 4–8 weeks with no treatment. Vaccines given topically (IN/IO) may also cause reactions in some cats, typically mild sneezing, coughing, or conjunctivitis. This vaccine virus can be shed into the environment and transmitted to other cats.

• **Vaccine-associated sarcomas:** In recent years, an association has been established between vaccines and the development of aggressive tumors at the injection site. The tumors typically appear months to years after vaccination. Tumors have been associated with adjuvanted as well as non-adjuvanted vaccines. There is no evidence to show that there is any difference in risk among various brands of vaccine. A few cases have even been reported in association with injection of other substances, such as some medications. The mechanism of tumor formation at these injection sites is poorly understood, but it is suspected that inflammation, as well as genetic susceptibility, plays a role. The true rate of tumor formation is not known but has been estimated to be between 1 and 3 cases per 10,000 cats vaccinated.

The vaccine-site recommendations developed by the AAFP/AFM are designed to help in treatment should a tumor form and to help understand which vaccines are implicated. The site guidelines do not reduce the risk of tumor formation, however. It is very clear that despite the various adverse effects that vaccines can cause, for the majority of cats, the benefits of vaccination outweigh the risks.

VACCINE-ASSOCIATED SARCOMAS

The most common type of tumor associated with vaccines is the fibrosarcoma. This is a type of aggressively invasive connective tissue cancer. While this tumor type rarely spreads to distant sites of the body, it invades deeply and extensively into local tissues. Any soft-tissue swelling that appears at a vaccination site should be reported to the veterinarian and monitored closely. Fortunately, most of these lumps are benign reactions and will disappear on their own.

If, however, a lump persists for more than several weeks, the veterinarian may decide to biopsy the lump to determine its nature. Initially, attempts to remove the lump are not recommended; instead, a biopsy method that removes only a tissue sample is advised. Unfortunately, there is no single treatment type that has a good success rate for treatment of fibrosarcomas. Some studies show that the median survival time with treatment is less than 2 years, because of aggressive recurrence of the tumor. Survival time for cats who receive no treatment may only be a few months.

There are three possible treatments for fibrosarcomas, and many experts recommend that they be used in conjunction with one another. Surgical removal is the mainstay of therapy. The surgery must be very extensive and remove a wide margin of normal tissue around the lump. These tumors have been likened to an octopus, where the lump is only the creature's head. Simply removing the lump is like removing only the head of the octopus. The arms remaining behind quickly increase in size, so that the disease reappears.

Radiation therapy is also commonly used to treat fibrosarcomas in areas where it is available. It is often used together with surgery in a carefully planned protocol. Chemotherapy alone is rarely successful for this type of tumor, but some experts recommend using it as part of a surgical or surgical-radiation protocol.

Some sites on the body present great difficulties should removal of a tumor become necessary. Two common vaccination sites, between the shoulder blades and on the lower back, are not good areas for wide excision of tissues. Tumors in these sites can invade deeply into local tissues and may be impossible to remove totally. Accordingly, cats should never receive injections in these areas. Using the limbs for injections increases the chances that a tumor can be totally removed if needed, because

amputation of the affected limb becomes a treatment option that could save the patient's life. Because cats cope very well with loss of a limb from any cause, many owners will opt to have the limb amputated. If the injection was not given in a limb and the tumor arises in a more inaccessible site, this option to save the cat's life is no longer available.

DIAGNOSTIC TESTING

There are many situations in which veterinarians wish to use diagnostic testing. It may be part of a preventive health care plan or it may be required to help diagnose the cause of illness. Often testing might be repeated to monitor the course of a disease. Laboratory testing can be the starting point and might suggest the need for more involved testing strategies. In some cases, testing is required for other purposes, such as to comply with regulations for travel to another country (such as obtaining a rabies antibody titer) or for pedigreed cats before breeding or sale (such as feline blood typing or viral testing).

BLOOD TESTS

There are many situations in which testing blood samples can be helpful. A common use would be as part of a preventive health care program. For instance, a veterinarian might recommend that a newly adopted cat have blood tests for certain viral diseases. Or a veterinarian might advise preanesthesia blood screening, even for young healthy patients, before any elective surgery. Results of such screening tests help identify hidden problems and also serve as a baseline for future monitoring of the cat's health. Blood testing is also used to diagnose medical conditions and then to monitor the progress of treatment.

A variety of very specialized blood tests are available, and the list is growing each year. Different commercial labs and university labs have developed specialized tests for certain diseases and situations. For instance, special tests are available to evaluate cats for pancreatic disease (feline TLI [trypsinogine-like immunoreactivity]), for long-term monitoring of diabetes (serum fructosamine and glycosylated hemoglobin), and to detect immune-mediated diseases (Coombs test). Many infectious diseases have specialized blood tests. In some cases, there are various types of tests available to detect one disease and the veterinarian will have to choose the test most applicable to the patient.

Here are some tests commonly employed in daily veterinary practice:

Complete Blood Count

The complete blood count (CBC) is one of the most commonly employed blood tests in veterinary medicine. This test is designed to evaluate the red and white blood cells. A total white blood cell count is determined, and then the individual types of white blood cells are examined and counted as a percentage of the total count (called the differential). Typically, some parts of the CBC are done manually in the clinic laboratory and other parts must be done by machine. The total red blood cell count, hemoglobin determination, and evaluation of the red blood cell size and volume are usually done by machine, sometimes in a referral laboratory. A separate red blood cell test, the hematocrit or packed cell volume (PCV), can be done using a centrifuge in the veterinary office. Additionally, the CBC also evaluates the blood platelets, the cells responsible for blood clotting.

Typically, the CBC is used to evaluate the patient for evidence of infection or inflammation. Evidence for blood parasites such as *Hemobartonella felis* may be found. Information from the CBC can be used to determine how long the problem has been present and whether the cause of an infection is likely to be viral, bacterial, or fungal. The red blood cell tests can help assess anemia and characterize its nature. Altogether, the CBC can also be used to help evaluate a wide variety of problems, including bone marrow disease, some endocrine diseases, and some toxicities.

Blood Chemistries

One of the most useful diagnostic aids in veterinary medicine is the blood chemistry panel. This is a collection of blood tests used to assess the function of major organs and body systems. Chemistry panels vary in size by the number of tests ordered and the focus of the tests. For example, a chemistry panel may be general in scope, or it may focus on the kidneys or on the liver. Typically, the tests are performed on serum, which is the clear liquid formed after blood has clotted. Serum contains many different substances used to evaluate health. Some important parts of the chemistry panel are the total protein, electrolytes, glucose, urea nitrogen, creatinine, and enzymes.

The *serum total protein* is made up primarily of albumin and globulin. Albumin is a protein produced in the liver, and the globulins are components of the immune system used to fight diseases. Low levels of protein in the blood (hypoproteinemia) are associated with diseases that interfere with protein production (such as liver and intestinal diseases) or loss of protein through intestinal or kidney disease. Increased levels of protein in the blood (hyperproteinemia) can occur through dehydration, shock, infection, and some immune system disorders.

Electrolytes are chemicals necessary for life. The main ones evaluated in veterinary medicine are sodium, potassium, calcium, chloride, and bicarbonate. Electrolyte imbalances can be due to several disorders, including excessive vomiting or diarrhea and kidney or endocrine diseases.

Blood glucose is the simple sugar that is the major energy source for the body's cells. Increases in blood glucose levels (hyperglycemia) are associated with stress or anxiety but also with diseases such as diabetes mellitus. Low blood glucose levels (hypoglycemia) can be a complication of insulin therapy, of inadequate nutritional intake in a young kitten, or of less common problems, such as tumors.

Blood urea nitrogen (BUN) and *creatinine* are waste products of metabolism normally found in low levels in the blood. They are cleared from the body via the kidney; so increased levels may point to kidney disease. The BUN may also be increased in cases of dehydration or decreased in severe liver disease.

Serum enzymes are a type of protein associated with cellular function. Certain enzymes found in the blood are associated with certain organs. Most typically, enzymes associated with the liver are evaluated. Because the liver can also react to diseases in other parts of the body, an increase in liver enzymes might be associated with intestinal disease or hyperthyroidism, for example, in addition to liver disease. Veterinarians can gain clues to the cause of a cat's illness by evaluating the pattern of liver enzyme elevations.

Viral Tests

Veterinarians now routinely use blood samples to screen for specific viral infections. The most commonly used and reliable tests are for FeLV and FIV. In-clinic screening tests employing ELISA (enzyme-linked immunosorbent assay) technology are used as a rapid, low-cost method of assessing cats for these two viruses. All viral test methods come with attendant risks of false positive and false negative results. ELISA tests for FeLV detect viral antigens, and ELISA tests for FIV detect antibodies to the virus. Any positive result from an ELISA test should be followed up by a second test done with a different methodology. DNA-based tests (usually called PCR tests) directly assay viral antigens and can detect the presence of a very small amount of virus. Many labs now offer DNA-based blood tests for FeLV and FIV. However, the reliability and accuracy of this new test methodology is largely unknown and requires further investigation.

Another common feline virus is FIP, a type of coronavirus. While no accurate and reliable blood test exists to detect FIP, several antibody and viral antigen tests for feline coronavirus are available commercially. These tests are very difficult to use and interpret. Currently, no reliable tests are available that are suitable for screening purposes in healthy cats, although some labs offer them as such. Results of coronavirus testing can be used as part of an overall diagnostic effort to help verify or rule out FIP as the cause of illness in a sick cat, however.

Thyroid Hormone

In feline medicine, routine evaluation of thyroid hormone levels is common, especially for older cats. While dogs might commonly suffer from an underactive thyroid gland and low levels of thyroid hormone in the blood (hypothyroidism), cats typically suffer from an overactive thyroid and high levels of thyroid hormone in the blood (hyperthyroidism). While certain findings on other routine blood tests can aid in the diagnosis of feline hyperthyroidism, veterinarians can also measure the thyroid hormone level itself. Because thyroid hormone comes in different forms, the most common hormone tested for is thyroxine (also called T4).

BLOOD GROUPS AND NEONATAL ISOERYTHROLYSIS

Animals and humans have blood groups that are determined by the antigens present on the surface of their red blood cells. The different blood groups are identified by letters, such as *A* and *B*. In humans, it has long been known that an A–B–O blood group system exists and that people can have blood transfusion reactions. For example, people with type B blood can have a reaction if they receive a transfusion with type A blood. People with type O blood can have a reaction if transfused with any other blood type. This is because humans carry natural antibodies against other blood types; for example, a person with type B blood carries antibodies against type A blood. This is why blood is typed before being given to a recipient, and why it is important to know one's own blood type. In domestic animals, natural antibodies against blood types are uncommon, so that transfusions using different blood types do not usually cause problems.

The existence of feline blood groups was first suspected as early as 1912. Research done over the years discovered that cats have an A–B blood group system. However, this system is unrelated to the human A–B–O system, despite the similarity in names. The gene for type A blood is completely dominant to the gene for type B blood. There is also a rare type AB that is inherited separately. Further research established that cats have naturally occurring antibodies against blood types, unlike most other domestic animals. These antibodies are present in the blood and also in colostrum or milk produced by nursing queens. This accounts for the two types of incompatibility reactions seen in cats.

About 95% of cats with type B blood carry strong antibodies against type A blood. This means that most type B cats will have a transfusion reaction if they are given type A blood. The anti-A antibodies destroy the transfused red blood cells, causing a variety of severe effects, such as low blood pressure, difficulty breathing, slow heart rate and irregular heart rhythm, seizures, and even shock and death. Even a small amount of mismatched transfused blood can cause a severe reaction. However, type A cats carry only weak anti-B antibodies, so they do not have severe, life-threatening reactions if transfused with type B blood.

The second important incompatibility reaction associated with feline blood types is neonatal isoerythrolysis (NI). This occurs in type A kittens born to type B queens. The kittens are born normal and healthy, but problems begin to develop in the first few days of life. As they nurse from the queen, they ingest anti-A antibodies present in the queen's colostrum. These antibodies bind to and destroy the kittens' red blood cells. This produces anemia as well as failure of the kidneys and other major organs. The symptoms of NI include failure to thrive, brownish red urine, jaundice, pale mucous membranes, and sometimes sudden death with no signs of illness. Sick kittens must be removed from the queen immediately and hand-raised or foster-nursed by a type A queen. If anemia is present, a blood transfusion may be required. Unfortunately, the mortality rate of affected kittens can be high.

Prevention of the problem is obviously the best approach to incompatibility reactions. Cats who belong to breeds with a high percentage of blood type B should ideally be blood typed so that their own status is known. All blood donor cats should also be blood typed to avoid mismatched transfusions. Feline blood typing is a simple procedure that can be done with test kits in the veterinarian's office or at a referral laboratory. Breeders working with breeds having a high percentage of type B cats should find out the blood types of the individual cats they are breeding. Many breeders are now listing each cat's blood type on pedigrees. Then breeding a type B queen to a type A male can be avoided, or if the breeding is desirable, plans can be made to prevent NI in the kittens.

In those situations in which a type B

queen may give birth to type A kittens, certain steps will help avoid NI. If possible, the kittens should be blood typed at birth using a commercial blood typing kit and blood from their umbilical cord or placenta. Any type B kittens can remain with the queen. Type A kittens, or any kittens whose blood type is not known, should be removed from the queen for the first 12–18 hours of life. The digestive tract of newborn kittens is able to absorb antibodies from the queen's colostrum or milk for only about 12–18 hours. Once this time is past, no incompatibility reaction will occur. The kittens are hand-fed for the period of time they are away from the queen with kitten milk replacer and then can be returned to her.

Surveys of cats in the United States have shown that most domestic, nonpedigreed cats (98%) are type A. Less than 2% are type B and only about 0.1% are the rare type AB. Interestingly, there are more type B cats on the West Coast (about 4% to 6%). The least number of type B cats were found in the Northeast (under 0.5%). Worldwide, the frequency of blood types also varies. France and Italy have the highest number of type B cats (11% to 15%), with Finland and Switzerland having the lowest number (under 0.5%).

FREQUENCY OF BLOOD TYPE B IN PEDIGREED CATS

Breeds	Percentage
British Shorthair, Devon Rex	Up to 50
Cornish Rex, Exotic Shorthair	20–30
Abyssinian, Japanese Bobtail, Persian/Himalayan, Somali, Sphynx, Birman, Scottish Fold	10–20
American Shorthair, Burmese, Ocicat, Oriental Shorthair, Maine Coon, Norwegian Forest Cat, Siamese, Russian Blue, Tonkinese	Under 5

URINALYSIS

Urine tests are useful in the diagnosis of many diseases in the cat, including lower urinary tract disease, kidney disease, diabetes, and others. A urinalysis is divided into two parts: chemical analysis and examination of urine sediment. Chemical reagent test strips are used to check urine samples for the presence of several substances, such as blood (present because of infection or inflammation), glucose (present in diabetes), bilirubin (present in liver disease) and others. The concentration of the urine is also evaluated and is called the specific gravity. A specific gravity that is too high (a concentrated urine sample) can be associated with conditions such as dehydration. A specific gravity that is too low (a dilute urine sample) can be associated with many diseases, such as kidney disease, diabetes mellitus, hyperthyroidism, and others.

Examination of the urine sediment involves centrifuging the sample to concentrate the cells present. When a urine sample is centrifuged, a small layer of sediment forms at the bottom of the test tube. This sediment is stained with a special dye and examined under the microscope. The number of red and white blood cells is counted. The sample is examined for bacteria. Any abnormal or unusual cells are noted. Mineral crystals, associated with lower urinary tract disease, are also noted.

Finally, the sample may be submitted for culture. Urine samples destined for culture must be obtained in a sterile manner to avoid contamination. Cystocentesis is a rapid and relatively painless procedure commonly employed to collect urine samples in a sterile manner. In this method, a thin needle is placed through the abdominal wall into the bladder and a urine sample is withdrawn into a syringe. The sample can then be sent to a commercial laboratory, where an attempt will be made to culture any bacteria present. The veterinarian can also ask the laboratory to test any bacteria found against a panel of antibiotics to find the appropriate drug for treatment.

FECAL ANALYSIS

A very common test in veterinary medicine is examination of a cat's stools or feces. There are a variety of tests that can be performed, and while most are aimed at identifying intestinal parasites, diagnosis of a few other disorders may include a fecal examination. This is especially important because some parasites of cats and dogs are also human health threats. When the purpose of the examination is to look for parasites, it is very important that the sample be as fresh as possible. As the feces sit in the litter pan and dry out, many parasites and their eggs become unrecognizable and may produce false negative results.

Fecal examinations are routinely done on young kittens to identify parasites such as coccidia, roundworms, hookworms, and *Giardia*. These parasites can cause young kittens to have diarrhea and poor growth. Hookworms can cause a significant and sometimes life-threatening anemia. When new cats are brought into a breeding cattery, it is recommended that a fecal examination be performed. The frequency at which catteries need to perform fecal examinations depends on several factors, such as the deworming program in use, the number of new cats added to the cattery, whether any dogs live in the home, and whether any cats have access to outdoors.

The three most common fecal examination techniques are

• **Direct smear (wet mount):** This method is quick and simple and involves a small sample of feces directly from the animal (often the small amount adhering to a rectal thermometer after the cat's temperature is taken). The sample is examined directly under the microscope with a small amount of saline solution added. This technique is often chosen to examine for *Giardia*.

• **Fecal flotation:** This technique involves larger amounts of voided feces and will concentrate any parasites present for more accurate results. Feces are mixed with water to suspend the material, then with a flotation solution (such as zinc sulfate). The solution sits in a special container, which allows parasite eggs to float to the top and adhere to a glass slide. The slide can then be examined under a microscope. This technique is best for roundworm and other nematode eggs, coccidia, *Giardia*, and tapeworm eggs. It can be necessary to examine up to five samples from an animal in some cases to find a suspected parasite.

• **Baermann technique:** This technique is used to identify nematode larvae and is often used to check for lungworms. A sample of feces is wrapped in cheesecloth or put in a strainer, then suspended in warm water in a funnel. This will encourage any larvae present to move into the water and collect at the bottom of the funnel, which is held closed. After a set amount of time has elapsed, a sample of water is taken from the bottom of the funnel and examined under the microscope.

A variety of other tests can be done on fecal samples. Fecal cultures are used to identify bacterial infections, especially of the large bowel. Bacteria commonly cultured from fecal samples include *Salmonella*, *Clostridia*, and *Yersinia*. Interpretation of results can be difficult, because many bacterial species are normal inhabitants of the bowel. Increasingly, DNA-based tests are being developed to detect some pathogens in feces, such as *Giardia* and *Cryptosporidia*. Chemical tests can also be employed to look for the presence of fat or starch in fecal samples. This might be done in cases in which small intestinal diseases causing malabsorption or maldigestion are suspected.

Fecal cytology is a nonspecific test often done in cases of diarrhea. A thin smear of feces is stained with dye and examined under the microscope to evaluate the number and type of bacteria and cells present. Finally, a chemical test can be performed to check for occult blood in feces (that is, blood that cannot be seen with the naked eye), but these tests are fairly inaccurate, and false positive results are common.

DIAGNOSTIC IMAGING

There are a great many situations in which a veterinarian will find it useful to be able to see inside a patient using an imaging technique to visualize major organs as well as skeletal elements. While the oldest and most common imaging technique is radiography, newer techniques such as ultrasonography, endoscopy, computed tomography (CT), and magnetic resonance imaging (MRI) are becoming more commonplace.

Radiography (X-rays)

For many reasons, mainly ease of use and low cost, radiography is usually the imaging method of first choice in veterinary practice. Most veterinary clinics have X-ray machines. Taking an X-ray is a relatively simple procedure in which the unexposed and undeveloped X-ray film is placed inside a special metal cassette. The patient is required to lie on top of the flat cassette while the X-ray exposure is performed. This typically takes $1/10$–$1/20$ of a second, and the cat is typically held in place by an assistant or with the use of soft sandbags. In most circumstances, cats can be x-rayed while awake, but there can be some situations in which sedation is desirable, especially with patients in pain or fractious patients.

The main use of radiography is to assess the size, shape, and position of major organs, especially the cardiovascular, respiratory, digestive, and urinary systems. It is most useful to evaluate the skeleton and can be used to detect fractures, dislocations, and tumors. Some foreign bodies, such as swallowed objects or gun pellets, are visible on X-rays. There are also many different special radiographic procedures used to increase the information that can be obtained. They usually involve administering a contrast agent, or dye, which is used to accentuate the spinal cord, gastrointestinal tract, urinary tract, or heart. These procedures are almost always done with sedation or general anesthesia because they are more invasive.

Ultrasonography

This imaging technique is rapidly gaining in popularity among veterinarians, as more are trained and equipped to perform ultrasound procedures. Previously only available in referral institutions, ultrasound is now available in many private clinics. Ultrasonography uses reflected sound waves to form a detailed image of internal organs. This imaging method is free of risk to the patient and can usually be performed on cats while awake. Only touchy patients need sedation for the procedure. Ultrasonography gives better detail to soft tissues than radiography does and so is often used to visualize abdominal organs and the heart. Ultrasounds of the heart, called echocardiograms, are becoming indispensable for the diagnosis and management of feline heart disease. Blood flow within the heart can also be assessed by most ultrasonographers using Doppler techniques.

Other than echocardiograms, some common uses of ultrasound include evaluation of the pancreas, kidneys, liver, and urinary bladder. Ultrasound can visualize stones present in the kidneys or bladder and can also detect masses or tumors. In many cases, ultrasound guidance can be used to perform needle biopsies in place of exploratory surgery. Patients undergoing guided biopsies are almost always given a short-acting general anesthetic. As well, ultrasound can be used to assess reproductive problems (cystic ovaries, uterine diseases) and to detect pregnancy and estimate fetal ages.

Computed Tomography and Magnetic Resonance Imaging

The computerized techniques of CT and MRI, borrowed from human medicine, are now often available at institutions or large specialty referral practices. CT uses X-rays to make two-dimensional images of a patient's body that are visualized in slices or sections. Computers can then reconstruct the information into a three-dimensional image. MRI uses magnetic fields to create a similar kind of two-dimensional image. Both of these modalities are very expensive and require general anesthesia. The most common usage of these techniques in veterinary medicine today is for brain and nasal cavity lesions such as tumors.

ENDOSCOPY

Unlike the other techniques discussed, endoscopy allows for direct visualization of structures. An endoscope is a flexible, fiberoptic instrument that comes in various sizes. The most common sizes are used to visualize the gastrointestinal tract and the respiratory tract. The instrument has a long, narrow tube that can be inserted into a body orifice to gain access to the organ being examined. Very narrow endoscopes (called cystoscopes) can be used to visualize the bladder and urethra. Rigid endoscopes (called laparoscopes) can be used to enter the abdominal cavity through a very small incision and visualize the major organs. With all types of endoscopes, the opera-

tor is able to view images through an eyepiece. All endoscopic procedures are done under general anesthesia.

The most useful function of an endoscope is the ability of the operator to use various instruments that can be inserted through a channel in the equipment. This allows for the retrieval of foreign bodies that were swallowed or inhaled and can also allow for the acquisition of small biopsy samples. A very common use for endoscopy is the examination and biopsy of the gastrointestinal tract. Cats undergoing endoscopy and biopsy of their stomach and small intestine are often home from the clinic on the same day and have minimal discomfort. In many cases, endoscopy can be used to avoid traditional exploratory surgeries, thereby greatly minimizing discomfort to the patient and markedly reducing the risks normally associated with surgery.

SIGNS OF ILLNESS IN CATS

A cat owner's best tool for evaluating signs of illness in a cat is his or her own intimate knowledge of the pet and powers of observation. Because there is normal variation in feline behavior, knowing when your own cat is not behaving as it usually does is the most valuable information. For instance, vomiting is a common event for cats in general. Some cats have occasional vomiting, especially of hair, which is not indicative of disease. For such a cat, an increase in the frequency of the vomiting or a change in its nature could be a sign that something is wrong. Other cats never vomit at all, so that even one event of vomiting could be significant.

It is therefore a good idea to be sure you are familiar with your cat's normal habits in order to help assess signs of illness. When you take an ill cat to the veterinarian, you may be asked several routine questions, such as:

- Are there any changes in your cat's appetite? That is, is your pet eating more or less than you would normally expect?
- Are there any changes in the amount of water your cat is drinking?
- Is there any change in the amount of urine being produced?
- Is there any change in the volume, frequency, or characteristics of the feces being produced?

Many signs of illness in cats are nonspecific; that is, they can be associated with a number of disease conditions. This can make diagnosis of illness more difficult and often necessitates the use of diagnostic tests.

YOUR CAT'S SYMPTOMS AND WHAT MAY BE BEHIND THEM

Symptom	Possible Causes
Bad breath	Oral infection/abscess, dental disease, oral tumor, kidney failure, oral foreign body
Behavior changes (erratic, unusual, or aggressive behavior)	Encephalitis, FIP, head trauma, hyperthyroidism, hypertension, kidney failure, tumor, portosystemic shunt (an abnormal blood supply to the liver that impairs its function), poisons/toxins, rabies
Blindness	Cataracts, retinal disease, head trauma, taurine deficiency, eye injury, FIP, FeLV, glaucoma
Coughing	Asthma, heartworm, fluid in chest/lungs, respiratory parasites, tracheal disease, cancer
Decreased urination	Dehydration, urinary obstruction
Decreased appetite	Almost any feline disease
Diarrhea	Enteritis (infectious, noninfectious), food intolerance/allergy, poisons/toxins, intestinal parasites, inflammatory bowel disease, cancer, hyperthyroidism, pancreatic insufficiency, liver disease, FeLV/FIV, drug reaction
Difficulty breathing	Asthma, heart disease, fluid in chest/lungs, pneumonia, heartworm, anemia, poisons/toxins, nasal congestion, tracheal disease, trauma, cancer, diaphragmatic hernia, upper respiratory virus infection
Discharge from eyes	Upper respiratory virus infection, corneal disease, foreign body, blocked tear ducts, allergies
Discharge from ears	Ear mites, yeast infection, polyps, tumors, bacterial infection, foreign body, abscess
Drooling	Trauma, oral ulcers, foreign body, dental disease, cancer, poisons/toxins, rabies, nausea from any cause
Fever	Infectious/inflammatory/immune-mediated diseases, drug or vaccine reaction
Hair loss and/or itchiness	Abscess, eosinophilic granuloma complex (a group of inflammatory skin diseases seen in cats that cause various types of skin lesions), external parasites, atopy, food allergy, psychogenic alopecia, ringworm, endocrine disease

Symptom	Possible Causes
House soiling (urine/feces)	Urinary tract disease, gastrointestinal disease, behavioral problem
Increased urination	Kidney failure, diabetes, hyperthyroidism
Increased thirst	Kidney failure, diabetes, hyperthyroidism, pyometra (an infection of the uterus that causes an accumulation of pus)
Jaundice	Anemia, liver disease, gallbladder disease
Lameness	Trauma (sprain/strain/fracture), joint disease, hypokalemia, diabetic neuropathy, abscess
Low body temperature	Shock, heart failure, exposure, kidney failure
Pale gums	Shock, anemia from any cause
Paralysis	Brain/spinal cord disease or trauma, aortic thromboembolism, poisons/toxins, snakebite
Raised third eyelids	Gastrointestinal tract disease, nonspecific finding with many illnesses
Seizures	Heatstroke, kidney failure, epilepsy, hydrocephalus, cerebellar hypoplasia, low blood glucose or calcium, portosystemic (liver) shunt, encephalitis, cancer, poisons/toxins, trauma, stroke, infectious diseases (rabies, FeLV/FIV, fungal, bacterial, toxoplasmosis)
Skin swellings	Abscess, cyst/mass/tumor, insect bite
Sneezing/nasal discharge	Nasal foreign body, upper respiratory virus infection, polyps, allergies, fungal/bacterial infection, tumor, sinusitis
Straining in litter box	Constipation, urinary tract obstruction, bowel obstruction
Sudden death	Poisons/toxins, heart disease
Swollen abdomen	Fluid accumulation, tumor, bladder distension, pregnancy, constipation
Vomiting	Panleukopenia, gastroenteritis, hairballs, food intolerance/allergies, inflammatory bowel disease, kidney disease, liver disease, urinary tract obstruction, intestinal blockage/foreign body, constipation, hyperthyroidism, diabetes, heartworm, internal parasites, poisons/toxins, cancer, *Helicobacter* infection (ulcer causing), drug reaction, diet change, motion sickness
Weight loss with normal or increased appetite	Diabetes, hyperthyroidism, intestinal parasites, inflammatory bowel disease
Weight loss with poor appetite	Kidney failure, cancer, liver disease, severe dental disease, inflammatory bowel disease, heart disease, FIP

FeLV = feline leukemia virus; FIP = feline infectious peritonitis; FIV = feline immunodeficiency virus

CARING FOR THE SICK CAT

There are many situations in which a cat owner might have to provide nursing care, such as convalescence after surgery or recovery from trauma or illness. Cats do not always make the most cooperative patients, because their nature is independent and instinct compels them to hide when they feel ill. They do not always take easily to the administration of medications, both internal and external, or to wound care.

Patience, calmness, and a confident manner go a long way to persuading cats to accept treatment. Some basic home nursing techniques can be learned and used with most cats. In general, owners should consult their veterinarians for specific instructions when cats are ill.

RESTRAINT AND GIVING MEDICATIONS

Many oral medications for cats come in both liquid and pill forms, so that the easiest method can be employed. Some medications taste quite bitter, and veterinarians are often able to package these pills inside tasteless gelatin capsules. As well, there are pharmacies that specialize in compounding special orders for pet owners. They can make many medications up in various forms, such as a flavored chewable pill or a flavored liquid suspension. Some medications are even available now in transdermal creams, designed to be absorbed across the skin. However, there is little information available to know which veterinary drugs may be safely and effectively administered in this fashion, so caution is advised. If you are having difficulty administering a medication to your cat, be sure to ask your veterinarian about an alternate delivery form.

There are many methods of restraint for administering medications to cats. In general, the less restraint, the better. Cats are often increasingly uncooperative when increasing restraint is applied. Above all, be gentle, calm, and confident. Forceful movements or loud, angry voices will make the situation much worse. Whenever possible, an assistant is a valuable aid. Have the assistant restrain the cat's body on a flat, comfortable surface so that the cat is facing toward you. The floor is a good place to work or on a table that is sturdy. For owners working alone, the cat can be wrapped in a large towel with its head left uncovered. Alternately, you can kneel on the floor with the cat between your knees, head pointing away from you. Both positions make the cat feel more secure.

Once the cat is restrained, grip its head with one hand (use your left hand if you are right-handed) so that your thumb is on one side of the head near the angle of the jaw and your forefinger is on the other side. Tilt the cat's head backward until its nose is pointing upward toward the ceiling. In this position, the cat's jaw is easiest to open. With your other hand, press down on the front part of the lower jaw and then drop the pill as far back on the cat's tongue as possible. You can even place the pill at the back of the tongue and give it a gentle nudge. Then close the patient's mouth and hold it closed until the cat swallows. A gulp and the tongue appearing to lick the cat's lips usually indicate swallowing.

In some cases, it can help to coat the pill with a substance the cat enjoys, such as butter or cream cheese. There are also small tools that hold pills and release them via a plunger (called pillers or pill guns) that can be very useful, because they avoid the need to get your fingers into the cat's mouth. Regardless of how a pill or capsule is administered, it should be followed by a drink of about 5 milliliters of water that can be administered using a syringe. This prevents the pill or capsule from lodging in the cat's esophagus, where some medications, such as the antibiotic doxycycline, can cause significant damage. Liquid medications are given in essentially the same manner, except that the tip of the dropper or syringe containing the medication is placed between the teeth, at the side of the jaw, and the contents are administered. Droppers used for oral medications should be made only of plastic, never glass, to avoid a frightened cat biting and breaking glass in its mouth.

Some liquid or pill medications can be mixed in the cat's regular food or given in a treat. You must consult your veterinarian to be sure that it is possible to do this with the medication you are using. Also, consult your veterinarian before crushing any tablets or opening any capsules. Many cats are highly suspicious of additives to their food and may not eat food with medication in it. It can help to be sure the cat is not overfed, so that she is hungry at mealtime. Use a very palatable food and the minimum amount of food necessary to hide the medication (usually a tablespoon or so). Once this is eaten, you can be sure the medication has been ingested as well. Then the rest of the meal can be given.

The same restraint positions used for oral medications can be used to administer eye or ear medications. It is best to approach from behind the cat's head, rather than straight on. For eye medications, hold the cat's eyelid open firmly but gently with the thumb and forefinger of one hand (use your left hand if you are right-handed). With your other hand, squeeze the eyedrops or the ointment directly on to the surface of the eye without touching the bottle or tube of medication to the eye. This prevents it from getting contaminated. Typically, one to two drops of a liquid eye or $\frac{1}{4}$–$\frac{1}{2}$ inch of ointment medication is used. You may have to clean the eyes of any discharges first. This can be done using a cotton ball and warm water.

Eardrops are given while the cat is firmly restrained. Turn the cat's head to one side and hold the earflap in one hand, gently pulling slightly upward (use your left hand if you are right-handed). Then, using your other hand, squeeze the eardrops into the ear canal without allowing the tip of the bottle to touch the ear. Gently massage the area behind and below the ear to help disperse the drops throughout the ear canal.

A general rule for any kind of medication, whether external or internal, is to give the whole course of treatment as prescribed by your veterinarian. Treatment may not be successful if it is stopped prematurely, even if the cat appears to have recovered from the illness. As well, be sure to clean out old medications in your home regularly and take them to your veterinary clinic or pharmacy for disposal. Just as for human medications, veterinary products have expiration dates (which should be clearly marked on them), and they will deteriorate after that date and should be discarded. While most expired drugs simply lose their effectiveness, it can even be dangerous to use an expired product.

Elizabethan Collars

Elizabethan collars are circular collars made of plastic or cardboard with a hole cut in the center for the cat's head. They have a slit or opening down one side to allow the collar to be put on and taken off. Elizabethan collars have many uses. For wounds on the face or head, the collar can prevent the cat from scratching the affected area with the front or hind paws. For wounds or incisions elsewhere on the body, the collar can prevent the cat from licking or chewing at the site. And the collar can also be used as a means of restraint, allowing the cat to be given medication or have a wound treated without the owner getting scratched or bitten. Most veterinarians will sell or loan these collars to their clients. However, one can also be made at home using a large circle of cardboard. Make the circle at least 12 inches across and cut a 4-inch diameter hole in the middle. Remove a section of the circle about 3 inches wide so that the collar pulls into a cone shape when the edges are aligned. Pad the inner edge of the circle where it will contact the cat's neck. Lacing the edges together or taping them can secure the collar. It should be comfortable for the cat to wear, yet be large enough to accomplish its purpose.

Force-Feeding

Restraining the cat in the same manner as for giving medications can be used to force-feed a cat that will not eat because of illness. Veterinarians carry special diets for recuperation from illness that are designed to be fed through a syringe. Your veterinarian should be able to supply you with a large (10- to 20-milliliter) syringe for this purpose. Follow the guidelines your veterinarian has established for your cat with regard to how much to feed and how often.

Sometimes, ill cats will eat on their own with some coaxing. Because the sense of smell is very important to cats, be sure the nostrils are clear of any discharges. Studies have found that cats prefer foods that are heated to just below their body temperature; so warming foods can encourage eating. In some circumstances, such as recovery from an upper respiratory tract infection, offering a food with a strong smell is helpful. Consult your veterinarian to see if you can offer a strong smelling fish such as tuna or sardines. Veterinarians carry special diets designed to help with recuperation that are highly palatable. As well, many cats will eat a meat-based baby food when they will not eat other foods. Finally, one of the varieties of high-calorie nutritional supplements sold as a paste in a tube will be acceptable to some cats.

In cases where prolonged anorexia is anticipated, veterinarians can place various types of feeding tubes to assist. Often, a feeding tube is the least stressful way to feed an ill cat over a period of several weeks and enables the owner to provide the nutrition necessary for recovery. For example, cats recovering from hepatic lipidosis (fatty liver disease) often have a feeding tube placed in their esophagus (esophagostomy tube) or stomach (gastrostomy tube). These feeding tubes are quickly and easily placed by the veterinarian, are well tolerated by the cat, and can be a lifesaver.

When the need to provide tube feeding is very short term, a nasogastric tube can be placed. Because these tubes go in through a nostril and enter the stomach through the esophagus, they must be of a very small size. This limits the type of diet that can be fed to a liquid one, and in general, cats do not tolerate this type of tube for more than a few days.

SPECIALIZED HOME CARE

Most cats recover better at home than in the hospital, so as soon as possible, most veterinarians will discharge ill cats, provided they can be given the necessary care at home. There are some circumstances in which an owner might have to give special convalescent care at home. In general, it is important to keep the ill cat as comfortable as possible. In a multicat home, this might mean segregating the ill cat in a room by itself. The temperature should be kept comfortable, neither too hot in summer nor too cold in winter. Many ill cats feel better if they have a source of heat, and a hot water bottle is the safest way to provide this. Heating pads are associated with thermal burns in some patients and should be avoided, as should heat lamps. Another safe method is to place some thick towels in the dryer until they are warm and use them for bedding.

An ill cat may not feel strong enough to travel far to reach food and water dishes or the litter box. These things should be brought near enough for the cat to use. Be especially careful if a cat has to negotiate stairs to get to food and water or the litter; in this case, it might be better to temporarily relocate them. Try not to put the food and water bowls too close to the litter box, for most cats dislike this arrangement. Wash and replace any soiled bedding promptly.

Remember that adequate disinfection is an important part of convalescent care, especially if a contagious disease is present in a multicat household. The safest and most effective home disinfectant is household bleach. It can be used at the dilution of 1 part bleach to 32 parts water (1 cup of bleach in 2 gallons of water). Bleach can be used to disinfect floors, cages, litter boxes, food and water bowls, and bedding. Proper cleaning technique involves three steps: (1) removal of any organic debris, first using a detergent and water; (2) disinfection; and (3) thorough drying of the surfaces. *Note:* Be sure never to mix bleach and ammonia, another common disinfectant, because a toxic gas is formed by a chemical reaction between the two compounds.

There are some situations in which a veterinarian might wish a cat owner to administer subcutaneous fluid therapy at home. This is a method of fluid therapy used to correct mild dehydration and provide for ongoing fluid needs during convalescence. In some situations, such as chronic kidney failure, a cat might need long-term subcutaneous fluid therapy at home.

Subcutaneous fluids are administered using a bottle or bag of fluids, an administration set (called an IV, or intravenous, line), and a large-gauge hypodermic needle. Your veterinarian will provide the correct type of fluids and put the set together, ready for use at home, as well as teach you how to administer the fluids. In general, a comfortable place at home is selected, such as a bed or chair, where the fluid set can be hung above the cat. This is because the fluid flows via gravity from the bag, through the IV line, into the cat. Once the bag is ready and the cat is in place, the hypodermic needle on the end of the IV line is inserted under the cat's skin, usually between the shoulder blades, and the valve controlling the flow of fluids is opened.

Fluids are best administered at the cat's own body temperature for comfort and to prevent chilling. At the very least, they should be at room temperature. Fluids can be warmed in a warm-water bath to the right temperature. The veterinarian determines the amount and frequency of fluid administration. A 1-liter bag of fluids will allow for several fluid administrations to a sick cat. Once the required amount of fluids has been given, the valve is closed and the hypodermic needle is withdrawn. A new hypodermic needle is used for each administration. There is often a bit of fluid leakage from the injection site for 5 or 10 minutes, and occasionally the fluid may be slightly blood-tinged. Neither situation is cause for alarm. The small mass of fluids will appear as a lump between the cat's shoulder blades, and it will be absorbed over the following 12–18 hours.

DENTAL CARE

The cat has 26 deciduous teeth (12 incisors, 4 canines, 10 premolars) and 30 permanent teeth (12 incisors, 4 canines, 10 premolars, 4 molars). The deciduous teeth start appearing between the ages of 2 and 3 weeks in kittens, and all are present by about 6 weeks of age. The permanent teeth start erupting by about 5 months of age and are usually all present by 6 months of age.

The field of veterinary dentistry has made enormous strides since the 1990s, so often, the level of dental care available to our cats is comparable to human dental care. Veterinarians who are board-certified in dentistry can now be found in many larger cities and are available for referral patients and consultations. Part of every cat's annual examination should be inspection of the mouth, teeth, and gums. Dental cleanings are recommended to preserve the cat's teeth and prevent disease. Check for cleaning at yearly examination.

Dental home care is frequently overlooked for cats. Owners often assume that cats will not accept dental care at home, when in reality many cats can become accustomed to daily dental care. With a new kitten, home care can be started immediately. Kittens will easily learn to accept gentle dental care and will grow into adult cats that are amenable to this necessary procedure. If oral hygiene is not improved, plaque will start to accumulate again immediately after a dental prophylaxis. Even for cats that accept home care, a professional prophylaxis will be needed from time to time.

Dental prophylaxis is the term used to describe the procedures involved when your cat is admitted to the hospital for a dental cleaning. A general anesthetic, which lasts about 20–30 minutes, is given to permit manipulation of the patient's mouth and alleviate any anxiety or discomfort. For cats with conditions causing dental pain, additional medication is given for analgesia. Modern, quick-recovery anesthesia provides a maximum degree of safety for the dental cleaning. In older cats, a preanesthetic blood screening is recommended to uncover any unidentified health problems, such as kidney or liver disease, that could affect the anesthesia, and intravenous fluid administration may be advised to provide added safety.

Scaling is performed to remove the hard calculus (tartar) from the tooth surfaces above and below the gum line. Scaling is usually done with a combination of hand tools and ultrasonic cleaning equipment. After this, tooth surfaces are polished with a special compound to remove any tiny calculus deposits and stains, and also to smooth and protect the enamel surface. Then the gingival space around each tooth is flushed with an antimicrobial solution to remove any debris and decrease the amount of bacteria present. A long-lasting varnish or coating is applied to strengthen and protect the enamel.

Not only are the teeth cleaned, but each tooth and its surrounding structures are thoroughly examined for problems that would not be apparent during the office visit. The area around each tooth is checked for periodontal pockets. Teeth are examined for discoloration, which may be due to staining of the enamel or damage to the pulp of the tooth. Each tooth is checked for lesions, and many veterinarians have special X-ray units to take dental radiographs. These radiographs can help to identify teeth with lesions, areas of bone loss, and tooth root problems.

Here are some of the most common dental problems seen in cats.

- **Plaque:** A thin film covering the teeth, consisting of bacteria, saliva, food particles and sloughed cells. Plaque is the underlying cause of many dental problems, so controlling it is the essential ingredient of home dental care for cats.
- **Tartar:** Also called calculus, this is the hard, yellow-brown mineralized plaque on the surface of the teeth. These deposits thicken with time and cause significant irritation and gum recession.
- **Gingivitis:** Inflammation of the gingiva, or gums, characterized by redness, swelling, and a tendency to bleed.
- **Periodontal disease:** Disease of the supporting structures of the teeth, such as the gingiva, periodontal ligament and bone.
- **Resorptive lesions:** Also called neck lesions, cervical line lesions, and odontoclastic lesions, these are erosive lesions that start at the cervical line or neck of the tooth and destroy and demineralize the tooth.

Periodontal disease is a significant and painful disease in cats. It is graded by its severity in order to determine the best treatment options:

- **Stage 1:** Characterized by gingivitis and a mild amount of plaque; no significant disease yet present
- **Stage 2:** Earliest stage of disease where increasing plaque accumulating around the tooth starts the inflammatory process
- **Stage 3:** Well-established disease with loosened tooth attachments and accumulation of plaque, tartar, food, and bacteria around the teeth; gum recession is also occurring
- **Stage 4:** Very advanced disease with severe inflammation, marked gum recession, loose teeth, bleeding gums, infection, and bad breath

Cats with stage 1 disease need a professional dental cleaning and regular home care. Cats with stage 2 or stage 3 disease need a thorough professional cleaning above and below the gum line, an enamel coating, and good home care. Cats with stage 4 disease may need extractions, antibiotic treatment, and advanced periodontal treatment techniques, as well as a plan for ongoing home care.

In people, dental caries (decay of the teeth) causes cavities. Cats do not develop dental caries, but they do develop a similar problem called resorptive lesions. These represent a uniquely feline phenomenon whose cause is not fully understood. These lesions are common in cats, with veterinarians reporting that up to 67% of cats that they have examined are affected. As cats get older, resorptive lesions are also more common. Most often, the molars and premolars are affected on their buccal (cheek) surfaces. Tartar may cover the lesions, making them hard to detect. Once a resorptive lesion begins, it will progress to destroy the crown and root structure of the tooth. As these lesions erode through the

enamel surface of the tooth, they are very painful. Some cats will show signs of this pain by a change in behavior, decreased appetite, a change in food preference, or by difficulty chewing and by dropping food from the mouth. However, many owners do not realize that cats can be suffering significant dental pain and still appear to eat normally.

The treatment of resorptive lesions in cats is controversial. Because they are painful and progressive, the long-term goals of treatment must be to minimize pain and promote good dental health. Scaling and polishing the teeth, followed by an enamel varnish, may treat early and mild lesions. Moderately advanced lesions require a decision to either attempt restoration or extract the tooth. The long-term prognosis for saving restored teeth is poor in most studies that have been done. For this reason, and because restoration may not stop progression of the lesion, these teeth are often extracted.

Resorptive lesions that have eroded into the pulp of the tooth are poorly amenable to therapy. While root canal therapy and restoration might save a small number of these teeth, the majority of them are too extensively damaged and must be extracted. While it is regrettable, this is often the best treatment option. Effective and safe pain medication is available for cats when extractions must be performed. Once a damaged tooth is extracted, healing occurs rapidly, and many owners notice an increase in activity level, playfulness, and appetite soon afterward.

There are a wide variety of devices and cleaning products for feline home dental care. There are small, soft toothbrushes designed for cats and also toothbrushes that fit over the owner's finger. Even gauze sponges or pads can be used. Cleaning pastes for cats and dogs do not foam and do not have to be rinsed. They are usually flavored with malt, chicken, beef, or seafood. There are also oral rinses and gels, which are antimicrobial or contain fluoride. No one product or method has been proven to be 100% effective, so it is best to try different approaches and products to find which one is best for both cat and owner.

Finally, several companies make dental treats designed to decrease the amount of plaque and tartar on teeth. While not effective on their own, they can add to an overall dental home care plan. Pet food manufacturers are now producing diets designed to help keep teeth healthy (for example, Hill's Feline Prescription Diet t/d and Friskies Dental Diet). These diets are designed to encourage cats to chew their food longer and to minimize plaque and tartar through a scrubbing effect as the cat chews.

ELECTIVE SURGERY AND ANESTHESIA

One of the most common reasons for cats to go to a veterinary clinic is for elective surgery.

SPAY SURGERY (FOR FEMALE CATS)

In North America, spay surgery (called ovariohysterectomy) is the primary means of birth control for female cats. Its affordability, low rate of complications, safety, and effectiveness are the reasons why this is the method of choice. While birth control is a very important goal, there are other clear benefits to spaying female cats. Disorders of the ovaries and uterus, including tumors and infections, cannot occur in a spayed female cat. Spayed cats have a lower risk of mammary cancer than unspayed cats. Because unspayed females cannot control the instinctive drive to mate, they will make strong attempts to get outside and roam. This exposes them to many hazards, from automobile accidents to infectious diseases spread by other roaming cats. Spaying re-

moves this instinctive and risky behavior. Additionally, spayed female cats make better companions because their behavior is usually friendlier toward humans and objectionable behaviors, such as calling and spraying urine, are absent.

Spay surgery is an abdominal surgery, so general anesthesia and postoperative pain management are needed. An incision is typically made on the abdomen, although a few vets use a flank approach that is popular in Europe. Once the abdomen is opened, the uterus and ovaries are removed. The abdomen is closed by suturing the incision in three layers. Skin sutures may be used or a type of surgical adhesive may be used in place of sutures. If skin sutures are used, the veterinarian typically must remove them 10–14 days after surgery. In most cases, cats who have undergone spay surgery will be hospitalized overnight.

There are few complications associated with spay surgeries, provided the patient is in good health. Veterinarians ensure wherever possible that patients have been examined, vaccinated, and dewormed before they are spayed. Ideally, only those cats in good health should undergo the stress of anesthesia and surgery. The most common complication is probably hemorrhage. This is more likely to occur in cats who are in heat or who are pregnant at the time of surgery. Rarely, damage to the ureters (the tubes that carry urine from the kidneys to the bladder) may occur, which can require corrective surgery. Also rarely, some ovarian tissue may not be identified and removed during the surgery, causing the cat to eventually exhibit signs of being in heat again. A second surgery, done while the cat is in full heat, will usually identify the stray tissue and make its removal possible.

Postoperative care after spay surgery is generally simple and easy. Cats, especially those under 8–10 months of age, recover quite quickly from this surgery. They may be quieter and eat less for a few days. Owners should report any symptoms that are not mild or short term. In addition, the surgical incision should be checked daily for swelling, redness, or discharge. Occasionally, a lump will appear at the surgical site that represents reaction of the subcutaneous tissues. These lumps almost always resolve without treatment. Sometimes, the lump represents an accumulation of fluid in the space between tissue layers, called a seroma. Veterinarians will want to check any lumps noticed by owners and may elect to drain fluid from a seroma.

Owners should also watch for cats who lick or chew at the incision or at the sutures. While uncommon, it is possible for a cat to open the incision if excessive licking or chewing occurs within the first few postoperative days. If the cat removes some sutures after several days, it is usually not of major concern but should still be reported to the veterinarian. In some cases, a bitter-tasting product can be applied to the sutures to discourage this behavior, or a plastic cone-type collar (an Elizabethan collar) can be used to make it difficult for the cat to reach the incision.

NEUTER SURGERY (FOR MALE CATS)

Just as for spaying, the main reason for neutering cats is population control. However, other good reasons to have male cats neutered are well known. While the risk of testicular diseases, such as infections and tumors, is generally low in male cats, it can be completely avoided by neutering. Just as for unspayed females, unneutered male cats cannot control the urge to mate and they will make repeated attempts to get outdoors in search of a female. This also exposes them to the hazards of outdoor life and especially increases the chances of wounds and infections (such as the life-threatening FeLV and FIV) associated with

fighting. Unneutered male cats are more aggressive to other cats and can make less desirable pets than neutered males. In addition, hormones give a strong and unpleasant odor to the urine of male cats.

The neuter (or castration) surgery is a simple one. Under general anesthesia, an incision is made in the scrotum over each testicle. The blood vessels and spermatic cord are ligated (tied off) and the testicles are fully removed. The skin of the scrotum is thin and easily irritated. Sutures have a potential to cause irritation and discomfort and so are not used. The edges of the incision seal quite quickly, and the rate of infection is surprisingly low.

Complications of this surgery are rare. Hemorrhage is uncommonly seen and would require intervention only if significant amounts of blood were being lost. Occasionally, infection will cause an abscess to form in the scrotum, which requires drainage and antibiotic treatment. Postoperative care is minimal and mainly involves checking the surgery site for any swelling, redness, or discharge.

EARLY AGE SPAY AND NEUTER

Early-age altering (surgeries done between 6 and 14 weeks of age) has been performed in the United States for over 25 years. Altering cats between the ages of 5 and 7 months was established by tradition, rather than for any specific medical or scientific reason. Concerns that early-age altering could increase the incidence of feline lower urinary tract disease or affect skeletal development or behavior have been laid to rest by good scientific studies.

Specific anesthetic and surgical techniques have been established for spay and neuter surgeries on these young patients. Simple precautions, such as reducing stress levels, ensuring body temperature is regulated, shorter periods of fasting, and early return to eating after surgery make early-age surgeries safe.

Most pet cats will not have a particular need to be spayed or neutered any earlier than the traditional age of 5–7 months. However, in some situations, early-age surgery is very desirable. Shelters and agencies can alter cats before they are adopted, thus eliminating the need to depend on the adopting owner to have the surgery performed. Studies have shown that compliance with spay and neuter requirements by adopting owners is a dismal 50%. Also, many cat breeders will want to alter kittens destined for pet homes for the same reason. Early altering is a safe and effective way for breeders to ensure that they do not unwittingly add to the burden of unwanted pets.

THE POSITION OF CAT FANCIERS' ASSOCIATION ON DECLAWING

The Cat Fanciers' Association (CFA) recognizes that scratching is a natural behavior of cats and that cats may be defenseless without full use of their claws if they, either intentionally or unintentionally, go outdoors. Scratching damage to household furnishings can be minimized or avoided by routine clipping of the claws, by the use of claw covers, and by redirecting the cat's activity to acceptable surfaces.

CFA perceives the declawing of cats (onychectomy) and the severing of digital tendons (tendonectomy) to be elective surgical procedures, which are without benefit to the cat. Because of postoperative discomfort or pain, and potential future behavioral or physical effects, CFA disapproves of routine declawing or tendonectomy surgery in lieu of alternative solutions to prevent household damage. In certain situations, including high risk of injury or disease transmission to owners with bleeding disorders or compromised immune systems, declawing may be justified in order to maintain the cat–human bond.

DECLAWING AND ALTERNATIVES

Scratching is a normal feline behavior. It serves many different functions, such as territorial marking and claw conditioning. Usually, solid vertical objects are the objects of choice for cats to scratch. Outdoors, this might be a tree trunk, whereas indoors, it might be a piece of furniture. Scratching behavior begins in kittens by about 1 month of age, for it is a strongly instinctive behavior. The amount of scratching performed by cats does vary and probably depends on both inherited and environmental factors.

Declawing (onychectomy) is both a common surgery and a controversial one. The surgery should be undertaken only after a thorough discussion of the alternatives with a veterinarian, including appropriate attempts at using scratching posts and modifying the unwanted behavior.

The main purpose of declawing is to prevent indoor cats from causing damage to furniture through normal scratching instincts. However, declawing is also performed to allow people with compromised immune systems to enjoy the company of cats. For people with some illnesses, a cat scratch could present significant health problems, so declawing is a viable option to allow those in this special situation to keep their cats.

Typically, only the front claws are removed, but in some cases, such as in homes with immunocompromised people, the rear claws may also be removed. It is recommended that declawed cats remain as indoor pets.

While the surgery can be performed at any age, it is best done on young cats, usually at the time of spay or neuter surgery. Young cats recover from this surgery much quicker and easier than mature cats or obese cats. The main consideration with this surgery is adequate pain control, because it is a musculoskeletal surgery. There are several options for providing pain control immediately after surgery. For mature or obese cats, using a method such as a patch that delivers pain medication via absorption through the skin for a period of several days is an excellent option.

While variations in protocols and surgical approaches exist for declawing, some features are standard. When preoperative preparation of the feet is done correctly, there is no need to administer antibiotics as a routine measure. The surgery is performed under general anesthesia and a tourniquet is used to control bleeding. The only way to ensure that there is no claw regrowth is to remove the entire last bone (phalanx) in the toe. The surgical incisions are closed in various ways, such as with sutures or with surgical adhesive. In some cases, bandages may be applied for a short period of time. Length of hospitalization varies but is typically 2 days.

Most cats experience temporary discomfort after declawing surgery, which can be minimized with adequate pain-control measures. Occasionally, limping or favoring of one foot is a persistent problem. Veterinarians will check such patients for any inflammation or infection at the surgical sites, but often the area is normal and the limping eventually resolves on its own. The most common complication is regrowth of claws after surgery, but with modern, well-known surgical techniques, this should be a very rare occurrence. Infection of the surgical sites is also sometimes seen, even if excellent precautions are taken, and is treated with antibiotics and sometimes with wound cleaning and repair. Finally, if the tourniquet is applied incorrectly during surgery, some nerve damage may occur, which usually resolves after several weeks.

Postoperative care after declawing surgery primarily involves using a softer material in the litter box for a period of a few days.

Shredded paper or recycled newspaper litter are common choices. Some cats will not accept these alternative litters, and in this case, some regular clay litter can be added to the new litter material in order to tempt the cat to use the box. Owners need to monitor the incision sites for discharge, pain, or swelling and report any symptoms to the veterinarian.

An alternative surgery to traditional declawing is deep digital flexor tendonectomy. In this procedure, the claw is not amputated, but a portion of the flexor tendon is removed to prevent the cat from extending its claws. The result is that the claws are always held in a retracted position, making it difficult, but not impossible, for a cat to scratch destructively.

The main complication associated with tendonectomy is that the claws not only continue to grow, but tend to become roughened and grow excessively. Owners must be able to perform regular claw trimming to avoid overgrowth of the claw into the pad. Owners who have difficulty in trimming their cat's claws before surgery should not opt for tendonectomy but should consider traditional declawing or an alternative.

A nonsurgical alternative preferred by some cat owners is the use of vinyl nail covers. Soft Paws is one brand of nail cover that has been on the market for several years. The nail covers are glued to the cat's claws with a special adhesive. They will last approximately 1 month before they have to be replaced. For cats who tolerate having their feet and claws handled, owners may be able to replace the nail covers at home using one of the kits sold by the manufacturer. One potential drawback is the difficulty in applying the nail covers every month on cats who do not tolerate handling or nail trimming. Another potential drawback is the considerable cost of buying the product over the lifetime of the cat.

Ideally, a scratching post should be pro-vided for all kittens. Scratching posts should be made of durable material and should be taller than the cat or kitten when it is stretched out on its hind legs. This means that a scratching post the right size for a kitten might be too small when the kitten reaches maturity. Posts should be covered with a loosely woven material, which cats prefer over more tightly woven materials like carpeting. Large scratching posts or cat trees that also have platforms for sleeping and playing are excellent choices.

It is best to begin training a kitten to a scratching post after it has awakened from a nap, because this is a time that cats feel compelled to stretch and scratch. A food treat or a toy can be used to lure the kitten to the post and then dangled to encourage the kitten to jump at it and make contact with the post. Gently rubbing the kitten's front paws on the post transfers scents to the post material and may aid in attracting the kitten back in the future. Catnip, toys, and food treats can be left on the platforms of the large cat trees as encouragement.

ANESTHESIA

Anesthesia is the process of using various drugs and anesthetic agents to induce unconsciousness and freedom from pain for various procedures. While most commonly used for surgical procedures, anesthesia in one form or another is also used for other medical procedures, such as taking X-rays, placing urinary catheters, performing biopsies, and in many other circumstances. Veterinarians have a wide variety of drugs to choose from and so can tailor the anesthesia to the needs of each individual patient. Use of anesthesia always involves some small risk, even in healthy patients. It has been said that there are no safe anesthetic drugs, only safe anesthetists. This points out that the greatest factor in delivering safe and effective anesthesia is the skill and experience of the veterinarian. Anesthesia is truly part art and part science.

Anesthetic drugs come in many forms but typically are given via injection (IV, IM, or subcutaneous) or are inhaled. The patient and the procedure being performed dictate the type of anesthesia needed. A simple short-term procedure might require only sedation or tranquilization. Longer or more painful procedures will require general anesthesia. Overall, the goal is always to eliminate patient anxiety and produce freedom from pain in as safe a manner as possible.

Drugs are not only given individually, but are also often given in combinations. Combinations allow the veterinarian to tailor the anesthetic regimen, allowing each drug to produce its best effect. Some drugs are best at inducing tranquilization, others at protecting the heart rate and reducing secretions, and still others at analgesia (freedom from pain). Some drugs have a short duration of action, and others may last for hours. Some drugs have reversal agents so that the majority of their effect can be reversed when they are no longer needed. Veterinarians can take advantage of newer and safer anesthetic drugs, often the same medications and protocols that are used in human anesthesia.

General anesthesia typically involves three stages: premedication, induction, and maintenance. Cats are often given premedication drugs to protect their heart rate and reduce secretions, provide analgesia, and induce tranquilization. Once this is achieved, a second drug or drug combination is given to induce unconsciousness rapidly and safely. This can also be achieved by mask induction, where a face mask is used to deliver inhalant anesthesia and induce unconsciousness. For most procedures, the cat is then intubated. Intubation involves placing a breathing tube (endotracheal tube) into the airway to keep it open and pre-

vent any stomach contents or secretions from entering the lungs. After intubation, anesthesia is maintained by an inhalant anesthetic in combination with oxygen delivered by an anesthetic machine.

To increase the safety of anesthesia, several things can be done. Veterinarians may advise the placement of an intravenous drip during anesthesia. This has several purposes: It delivers fluids to the body to stabilize blood pressure and protect the heart, brain, and kidneys, and it provides rapid access should an emergency drug need to be given intravenously. A variety of anesthetic monitoring devices are used in veterinary medicine to monitor heart rate, breathing rate, oxygenation of the blood, body temperature, and blood pressure. Use of these devices greatly increases the safety of the procedure, and some type of monitoring should always be used. Anesthetic machines also allow for assisted breathing, if this should prove necessary.

ANALGESIA

Pain medication deserves special mention. Unfortunately, in the past, veterinarians were reluctant to give analgesics routinely to their patients for several reasons. This largely revolved around the inability to measure pain responses objectively in cats and dogs and lack of knowledge of how analgesic drugs work. In modern veterinary medicine, however, much attention has been focused on how to assess animals for pain and how to provide pain relief safely and effectively.

Because cats and dogs have different ways of dealing with pain from human patients, it can be difficult to interpret their behavior accurately. Veterinarians have long been looking for less subjective ways to measure pain, such as a blood test. However, attempts to find such an objective measure have not been clearly fruitful, so veterinarians must use subjective guidelines. More precise criteria need to be developed to aid in this goal. For instance, there are differences between breeds of dogs and cats as to how they respond to pain. Some animals are far more stoic than others. It is now possible, however, to use pain managment scoring systems, which help grade an animal's pain from mild to severe, and then select the best analgesic.

One of the most important rules to observe is to expect pain to occur from a surgical procedure and give an analgesic in advance rather than waiting to see if the animal appears to be in pain after surgery. Pain is better controlled if the drug is given before the pain is felt. Many different drugs can be used for pain management. They vary from narcotic drugs to nonsteroidal anti-inflammatory drugs.

For chronic pain (such as cancer pain) or orthopedic pain, skin patches containing a pain medication called fentanyl have come into widespread use for dogs and cats. These patches are designed to deliver pain medication across the skin over a period of several days. Although no veterinary versions currently exist, the lowest-strength human patch can be applied to an area of shaved skin in adult cats. It can deliver pain relief for 3–5 days. Safety issues are important if the patch is being used on a cat at home—the patch is often not used on cats in homes where young children are present who might apply it to themselves. Patients also must return to the hospital to have the patch removed and safely disposed of. Other types of pain management can involve using local anesthetics for some procedures in conjunction with analgesic drugs.

EMERGENCIES

It is important for all pet owners to understand what situations constitute an emergency.

Most veterinarians either provide after-hours emergency service themselves or refer their patients to a local after-hours emergency clinic. As well, some clinics have extended evening hours, often as late as 10 or 11 PM. You should familiarize yourself ahead of time with how your veterinarian handles after-hours emergencies. Many urban areas now have large emergency clinics where veterinarians board-certified in emergency medicine and critical care practice. Their assistance is most valuable, especially in cases of major trauma, such as motor vehicle accidents.

There are several situations that should be considered true emergencies:

- Any trauma, such as a motor vehicle accident or a fall from a height (even if the cat appears to be uninjured at first)
- Any injury to the eyes
- Any burn
- Straining in the litter pan (often interpreted as constipation, when it might actually be a urinary tract obstruction)
- Frequent bouts of vomiting or diarrhea within a few hours
- Difficulty breathing
- Seizures
- Paralysis
- Suspected poisonings, and poisonous insect or snake bites
- Any hemorrhage or wounds that are bleeding
- Loss of consciousness
- Frostbite or cold exposure
- Heat exhaustion or stroke
- Electrical shock (such as from biting an electrical cord)
- Prolonged labor or difficult delivery
- Smoke inhalation
- Any situation that *you* think requires emergency care

FIRST AID

First aid is exactly what the name implies, the first assistance given to an injured pet. This can be a very critical factor influencing the recovery of the animal. In many cases, first aid can save a cat's life. The main goal is to stabilize the injured cat until veterinary attention is available. There are some inherent difficulties encountered when attempting to assist a sick or injured cat that it is wise to think about beforehand. The instinctive reaction of an injured cat is often to flee and hide. A rescuer must be prepared to approach injured and frightened cats slowly and carefully, equipped with a blanket or towel to help restrain the cat without injury to the handler. Such cats must be handled firmly but gently, with no sudden movements or loud noises on the part of the rescuer. It is also possible to handle a frightened cat by grasping the skin at the back of the neck firmly and lifting her with your other hand, giving support under the chest or abdomen. Remember that frightened or injured cats may not behave normally toward their owners: A normally docile cat may bite or strike out in fear or pain. Cat bite wounds can be very serious, and precautions should be taken to avoid this. Having an assistant to help you restrain and assess the cat is a very good idea. Injured or frightened cats can be transported in various ways to the veterinarian, including a secure box or carrier, or inside a pillowcase or other fabric bag that permits airflow.

Once a sick or injured cat is restrained, attempt to ascertain certain important facts as quickly as possible. Assess the cat's breathing, heartbeat, pulse rate, and temperature. Check for bleeding or obvious trauma. While vital signs vary individually, most cats should fall within the following ranges for normal:

VITAL SIGN	NORMAL RANGE
Temperature (rectal or ear)	100.5°–102.5° F (38.0°–39.2° C)
Pulse rate	140–200 beats per minute (a nervous or excited cat may have a pulse rate as high as 240 beats per minute)
Respiration rate	20–40 breaths per minute (a nervous or excited cat may have a respiratory rate up to 60 breaths per minute for very short periods)

It is a good idea to practice evaluating vital signs in your healthy cat so that you will be able to assess your cat quickly and accurately should she become ill. It will also help you establish what is normal for your cat. The temperature can be taken with an ear thermometer, but unless you are practiced in using these on a regular basis in cats, the readings are not reliable. It is better to use a rectal thermometer lubricated with petroleum jelly and inserted up to 1 inch in the rectum. Most cats dislike this procedure, so you may require an assistant. The thermometer should be left in place for at least 1 minute and then read.

The respiration rate can be obtained by watching the movements of the chest or by feeling the airflow from the nostrils. Count the number of breaths in 15 seconds and multiply by 4 to get the rate per minute. The character and quality of respiration should also be noted, such as labored breathing, panting, or shifting of position to ease breathing.

A cat's heart rate can usually be felt by placing your fingers and thumb on either side of the chest above the sternum (the breastbone, to which the ribs are attached). With a little practice, you will find that this is the best way to take the heart rate. Again, count the beats in 15 seconds and multiply by 4 to get the rate per minute. The heart rate can also be taken using a stethoscope at home; many pharmacies or medical supply stores sell inexpensive stethoscopes for this purpose. The pulse can also be felt at the femoral artery inside the hind leg, although it takes some practice to find this spot.

Capillary refill time (CRT) is the time it takes the small blood vessels (capillaries) in the gums to refill with blood after pressure is put on them. This is a valuable indication of how well the heart and lungs are working. Press firmly on the gum, usually above a canine tooth, for a few seconds and then release to determine CRT. Count the number of seconds until the normal pink color returns to the gum tissue. A normal CRT is 1–2 seconds. The CRT is increased to more than 2 seconds in shock, heart failure, and dehydration.

Cats who have suffered major trauma, such as from a car accident or falling from a height, may be badly injured. The same principles of first aid that apply to humans also apply to cats. All owners should be familiar with the principles of cardiopulmonary resuscitation (CPR), both for humans and for their pets. Artificial respiration and heart massage (together called CPR) can be given to pets in need. Many organizations, such as the American Animal Hospital Association (AAHA), offer pet first aid charts and guides that are valuable references. The AAHA can be reached as follows:

American Animal Hospital Association
12575 W. Bayaud Avenue
Lakewood, CO 80228
Phone: 303-986-2800
Web site: http://www.healthypet.com

When assessing a critically injured cat, first determine if the cat is breathing and if there is a heartbeat. Inspect the cat's mouth and nose and be sure the airway is clear. Pull the cat's tongue forward. You may have to clear away blood, fluids, or debris. Faint breathing may be hard to detect. Look for the rise and fall of the chest or try to feel air movement from the cat's nose. Quickly pluck a few hairs from the cat's coat and hold them to the nose. If there is even faint breathing, you will be able to see the hairs move. If you cannot detect breathing, artificial respiration should be started. This can be accomplished by laying the cat gently on a flat surface with its right side down. Hold the cat's mouth closed and place your mouth over the cat's nose. Blow gently into the cat's nostrils. If you do not see the chest rise and fall, blow more forcefully or try to seal the cat's lips closed with your hand. Blow into the nostrils every 4–5 seconds (about 12–15 times per minute). You will continue artificial respiration until the cat is breathing on its own, until veterinary help is available, or as long as you can feel a heartbeat.

If you do not detect a pulse or heartbeat, heart massage should be attempted. When both artificial respiration and heart massage are needed together, it is much easier to do with two people but not impossible for one person. The cat should be positioned as described for artificial respiration. Place your fingers and thumb on either side of the sternum, just behind the cat's elbows. Compress the chest firmly six times, then apply a breath through the nostrils. This pattern is repeated over and over. Try to accomplish a heart massage rate of about 100 per minute. Pause every few minutes to check for a spontaneous pulse or breathing. Continue CPR until the cat responds, until veterinary help is available, or until there has been no heartbeat for 20 minutes.

It is also important to check for bleeding wounds and to apply pressure to control bleeding. A pressure dressing can be made from sterile nonstick dressing pads or from any clean material at hand. Place the material directly over the wound and use a gauze roll to secure the bandage snugly. If the limb swells below the dressing, it must be loosened to restore circulation. If there is no bandage material immediately at hand, place a piece of the cleanest material available on the wound and hold it firmly until help arrives. Once a wound has stopped bleeding, resist the temptation to wipe or clean it, because that may cause bleeding to start again.

Tourniquets can be very effective for major hemorrhaging, but they must remain in place no longer than 20 minutes, and you should use them only if bleeding cannot be controlled any other way. Never place a tourniquet over an obvious fracture or over a joint, as more damage will be caused. Use a piece of cloth, gauze roll, or any long material available. Loop it around the bleeding limb and tighten it by hand or with the assistance of a stick inserted in the loop and twisted. Tighten it only enough to stop the hemorrhage. If veterinary assistance is not available for more than 20 minutes, loosen the tourniquet for about 1 minute to restore blood flow and then reapply it. Any major wounds can be covered with a clean towel or cloth to prevent further contamination.

Seizures or fits are sudden and uncontrolled bursts of activity that can take many forms in cats. Along with an altered level of consciousness, seizing cats may make chewing motions, foam at the mouth, collapse, jerk or paddle their legs, or lose control of bowel or bladder. In some cases, the seizure may be atypical and consist of strange or inappropriate behaviors. The seizure itself generally lasts only a minute or two, but it may take an hour or more for the pet to completely return to normal behavior. In most cases, seizures occur as single events, but they can occur in rapid succession with no time in between for the cat to recover. This is called status epilepticus and requires emergency veterinary attention.

Seizing pets can be very traumatic for owners to see. However, it is important to know that the pet is unaware of the event and is not in any pain. Resist the temptation to restrain the cat or manipulate the mouth or tongue. This could lead to injuries to the cat or to you. Simply be sure the cat is not lying in a dangerous position; use a blanket or towel to move the cat to a safe place, if needed. If a cat suffers one seizure and recovers within several minutes, there may not be an emergency, but a phone call to your veterinarian is definitely required. However, a cat that seizes for more than a few minutes without recovery or who has several seizure events in a short period of time does require emergency attention.

Cats who have been injured may lose the ability to regulate their body temperature, and hypothermia (abnormally low body temperature) can occur quickly, especially if the environmental temperature is low. Be sure to cover the injured cat with blankets or thick towels for warmth, and move the cat to a warm place, such as a car or home, if possible. When you do try to move an injured cat, disturb the cat's body position as little as possible to prevent further injury. Using something like a heavy piece of cardboard, a wooden board, or a blanket as a stretcher is helpful.

It is best not to give any medications or even water by mouth to an injured cat, most especially if it is weak or unconscious. If you suspect a fractured limb, it is best not to try to splint or bandage it. This can cause more pain and trauma. Once you have stabilized the cat as well as possible, arrange to transport the animal to a veterinary hospital. Have someone call ahead to the facility to warn the staff that an injured animal is on the way.

Many situations are not critical, and it can be very useful for the cat owner to have a first aid kit at home. When you make up such a kit, be sure the products in it remain fresh and do not go out of date. After you use an item in the kit, be sure to clean and replace it or replenish it. Here are some suggestions for items that could be in a standard first aid kit:

Equipment:

- Your veterinarian's phone number and the number of an animal emergency clinic with directions on how to get there
- Phone number of a local poison control hotline or the National Animal Poison Control Center (888-426-4435; http://www.aspca.org). Note that a consultation fee is charged.
- A pet first aid manual or chart for quick reference
- Sterile bandaging material, such as gauze bandages (1-inch roll) and non-stick dressing pads (2 inches square)
- Adhesive tape (1-inch roll)
- Roll of cotton wool
- Pencil or stick for a tourniquet
- Cotton balls
- Material for a muzzle (can be a discarded nylon stocking or an old thin necktie, for example)
- Thermometer (rectal or ear), generally, rectal temperatures are more reliable unless you are very experienced at using one of the infrared ear thermometers
- Syringes (without needles attached) for administering medications (3-milliliter and 10-milliliter)
- Eyedropper (plastic) for administering small amounts of medications
- Readily available towels, blankets, and material for a stretcher

Medications:

- Hydrogen peroxide (3%) for wound care and to induce vomiting (use only when directly advised by a veterinarian); syrup of ipecac can also be used to induce vomiting, if recommended by a veterinarian
- Milk of magnesia or activated charcoal for poisonings (use only when directly advised by a veterinarian)
- Kaolin liquid for diarrhea
- Broad-spectrum antibacterial eye and skin ointments (ask your veterinarian for advice on selection)
- Antiseptic such as Betadine to clean wounds

TRAVELING WITH YOUR CAT— MEDICAL ASPECTS

North Americans increasingly expect to be able to travel with family pets, both domestically and abroad. Many owners are reluctant to leave pets at home or in a boarding facility while they vacation and look for ways the family and pet can travel together. A 1996 survey by the AAHA showed that more than 50% of pet owners have vacationed or traveled with their pets. More hotels and motels are now "pet friendly," and some resorts are even tailoring vacation packages for owners and their pets. A guide put out by the American Automobile Association (AAA; http://www.aaa.com) *Traveling with Your Pet—The AAA Pet Book* (ISBN: 1-56-251453-9) lists pet-friendly hotels and motels across Canada and the United States. (The book can be obtained from major booksellers.) Before you make any travel plans that include your cat, several things should be done. Whether you are traveling by air or car, be sure that travel is the right thing for your cat. Some cats are very good travelers; others are best left either at home under the care of a pet-sitter or in a boarding facility. Elderly cats or those with some chronic health problems may be best left at home. Schedule an appointment with your veterinarian to discuss these issues and have a full health exam performed. In many cases, you will be required to carry certification that your pet has had a recent examination and that all vaccinations, including rabies, are up-to-date. This is especially true for international travel or domestic travel across state lines.

TRAVEL BY CAR

Whether your trip is a long one or a short one, you will benefit from good planning. If you will be staying in a hotel or motel along the way, check ahead to ensure that your cat will be accepted. Many facilities will levy a surcharge for pets, and they usually have certain rules and regulations by which you must abide. If you plan to stay in a campground, you should also call ahead to see what regulations govern pets, if pets are allowed. Be sure to get a list of veterinary hospitals along your travel route in case of emergency. The AAHA maintains a list of hospitals on their Web site (http://www.healthypet.org).

If your cat is unaccustomed to car travel, it will help to acclimatize her by making many short trips in the weeks before your vacation or travel. Be sure you have a comfortable cat carrier; it is not safe for people or cats to allow cats to travel loose in the car. The carrier should be big enough for the cat to stand up in, but not too large. Line the bottom with something absorbent, such as towels or newspaper. Take along a portable litter tray and scoop, with a supply of litter.

Most cats will have little motion sickness if they travel on an empty stomach. However, if motion sickness is a problem, ask your veterinarian about administering an over-the-counter product made for humans such as diphenhydramine or dimenhydrinate. These products not only help prevent motion sickness but also often provide a small amount of sedation, which might be valuable. Tranquilization of cats for car travel is somewhat controversial and problematic; it is best to consult your veterinarian for advice if you think this may be required for your cat.

Don't feed your cat for about 4 hours before setting out on your travels, but do allow access to water. If you will be traveling for more than 1 day, stop to offer water frequently. You may want to offer food only twice daily initially to help avoid travel sickness. Once your cat is accustomed to travel, you could offer more frequent small meals. It is best to take along a supply of your cat's regular diet, especially if it is a prescription or therapeutic diet. Bottled water from home can also help limit digestive upsets due to unfamiliar water.

You must never leave your cat in the car unattended. In the summer, heatstroke (hyperthermia) can happen very quickly inside a car, even if the windows are left partly open. It can even happen when a cat is left in a carrier in the sun. Short-nosed cats, such as Persians, and cats with asthma or who are overweight are especially susceptible to heatstroke. If you suspect your cat has heatstroke, move her to the shade and cool her down with a wet towel and small drinks of water. Seek veterinary attention immediately, because other treatments such as oxygen and intravenous fluid therapy may be necessary.

TRAVEL BY AIR

Most airlines accept pets for travel, either in the baggage compartment or in the cabin of the aircraft. You should ask the airlines for their current regulations at the time you book your tickets. Confirm your pet on the flight again 24–48 hours before travel. It is best to try to use direct flights where possible and to travel during nonpeak times (midweek is best). In the summer, try to schedule early-morning or late-evening travel to avoid hot temperatures. On the day of travel, check in early. If your cat is traveling in baggage, be sure to pick her up promptly once you arrive.

Certain pets are not acceptable for air travel. In general, elderly cats, kittens younger than 8 weeks, ill or injured cats, and pregnant cats should not travel by air. Airlines usually require a health certificate dated within 10 days of your trip and proof that vaccinations, including rabies, are up-to-date.

Cat carriers for air travel must meet certain requirements. Carriers that are acceptable for travel in the aircraft cabin will be restricted to a certain size and type, so you should check out these requirements in advance. Carriers for air travel must

- Be large enough for the cat to stand up, turn around, lie down
- Be made of strong material, have no protrusions on the inside, and have handles for carrying
- Be leakproof, and have absorptive materials in the bottom
- Have ventilation on opposite sides and external rims to prevent blockage of airflow
- Have a live animal label as well as a label with the owner's contact information

Just as for car travel, it is best to avoid feeding your cat for about 4 hours before air travel. Access to water should be unrestricted until you leave for the airport. In case of any delays, or for long trips, put a label on the carrier with food and watering instructions for airline staff.

In general, it is usually best to avoid sedation or tranquilization of cats (or any pets) for air travel. The leading cause of illness and death for pets traveling by air is complications associated with tranquilization. There is significant potential for cardiac and respiratory problems under travel conditions with these drugs, especially with changes in altitude. If you feel your cat will be unable to travel without some help, ask your veterinarian about prescribing an antianxiety medication (such as amitriptyline) well before your departure date. Currently, most major veterinary organizations, including the American Humane Association, (http://www.americanhumane.org), the American Society for Prevention of Cruelty to Animals (ASPCA; (http://www.aspca.org), and the AVMA (http://www.avma.org) advise against tranquilization for air travel.

Checklist for Travel with Your Cat

- Supply of familiar food, bottled water from home
- Food and water dishes (can opener if needed)
- An ample supply of any medications your cat is taking
- A first aid kit
- Portable litter box and scoop
- Copy of your cat's medical records and health and vaccination certificate
- Your cat's microchip or tattoo number
- A recent photo of your cat in case of loss
- A collar with temporary tags listing contact information while you travel; a microchip is also an excellent idea
- Familiar toys, cat bed

INTERSTATE AND INTERNATIONAL TRAVEL

If you are going to be crossing state lines in the United States or are considering travel abroad with your cat, you must check out regulations beforehand. Information on interstate movement of animals is available from the

U.S. Department of Agriculture, Animal and Plant Health Inspection Service and Veterinary Services (USDA-APHIS-VS). Check their Web site for up-to-date information on traveling with your pet (http://www.aphis.usda.gov/travel/pets.html).

For international travel, you should check with the embassy of the country in question at least 9 months in advance. Regulations vary greatly from country to country. In some cases, lengthy quarantines are required. Some countries require specific vaccinations or testing for certain infectious diseases before entry. Some countries are now requiring that pets have microchip identification implanted.

If the country you are traveling to has a different native language, it is wise to translate all necessary information fixed to the carrier into the appropriate language. An envelope containing copies of the pet's medical record, as well as feeding and watering instructions, should be attached to the carrier. Medical record information should contain:

- Owner's name, address, telephone and fax numbers, e-mail address
- The pet's name, age, sex, breed, color, and distinguishing markings
- The microchip number, implantation site, and type of scanner needed
- Any tattoo and its location
- The name and address of the exporter as well as the name and address of the consignee
- The flight numbers and other means of transport
- Vaccination information
- Health records, including any current disease conditions and medications required

Carry a copy of this information yourself, as well as a current photo of your pet, which will be helpful, should your pet become lost. It is a good idea for the photo to include both you and your cat, in case the pet is stolen or accidentally released to the wrong person. Also, carry both contact information for your cat's veterinarian and your pet's medications with you.

When returning to the United States from abroad, your cat should have a complete physical examination before travel. If there are any parasites or diseases easily contracted in your travel area, testing should be done before departure. A fecal analysis should be performed to ensure that no intestinal parasites have been acquired, and the cat should be checked thoroughly for external parasites, such as fleas and mites.

There are specific restrictions for reentry to the United States through certain ports, especially in Hawaii, Puerto Rico, and Guam. Contact the port's health inspector if you are planning to return via one of these ports. On reentry, the United States Public Health Service visually inspects all dogs and cats. Animals free of gross evidence of infectious disease will be admitted. Cats are not required to have a rabies vaccination to reenter the United States.

EXTERNAL PARASITES
FLEAS

Around the world, the most common external parasite of cats is the flea. There are several species of fleas that can parasitize cats and dogs, but in North America the most common species is *Ctenocephalides felis* (cat flea). The flea is a highly specialized parasite, well adapted for survival in a variety of conditions. Its entire life cycle can be completed in as little as 12 days or as long as 174 days, as needed. Fortunately, there have been major developments in flea control in recent years as well as improved understanding of the life cycle of the flea.

The adult flea is a small, dark brown, wingless insect with a remarkable ability to jump. It can jump so quickly and so far that it can be hard to spot on an infested pet. Instead, the flea "dirt" (incompletely digested pellets of blood defecated by adult fleas) found in the cat's hair is often the only sign that this parasite is present. The flea has a four-stage life cycle: egg, larva, pupa, and adult.

The adult flea lives only a short time and depends on blood from its host to survive. Adult fleas therefore spend all of their time on the cat. The female flea starts to produce eggs within 2 days of finding a host cat. She can produce up to 50 eggs per day, and these eggs fall off the cat into the environment. They will be present in high numbers in areas where the cat spends a lot of time, such as sleeping areas. The eggs are insecticide-resistant.

The larvae then hatch from the eggs in a matter of days. They are free-living and will move deep into the environment, hiding in carpet pile, cracks in the floor, upholstery, or deep in organic debris outdoors. Because they are susceptible to high heat and dryness, they survive best in moist, shaded areas outdoors where the flea-infested pet spends a lot of time or in carpeting or cracks in wood flooring indoors.

Eventually, the larva will produce a cocoon in which the next stage of the life cycle occurs—the pupa. The flea is capable of remaining at the pupa stage for up to 140 days, depending on the environmental conditions. While in the pupa stage, the flea is resistant to insecticides. After about 8 days, an adult flea is formed in the cocoon, but it waits inside until conditions to emerge are ideal. This is called a preemergent adult, and it is resistant to insecticides. This adult waits for a signal that there is a suitable host nearby, such as heat, the presence of carbon dioxide, or vibrations. Under some conditions, the preemergent adult flea can wait in the cocoon for as long as 2 years.

There are many reasons to eliminate fleas from cats and their environment: Fleabite hypersensitivity or allergy occurs when the adult flea bites the cat to obtain a blood meal. Some cats do not have a hypersensitivity to fleabites and can harbor huge numbers of fleas without any apparent discomfort. Other cats who are quite sensitive to fleabites may have obvious clinical signs of allergy from only a few fleas. The flea can also transmit various infectious diseases (such as tapeworms and bartonellosis) to the host cat. In addition, flea infestations can remove so much blood from young kittens that they may become seriously ill and even die. Some people are sensitive to fleabites and may be affected if pets in the home are flea-infested.

There are several ways to check a cat for fleas. One method is to use a flea comb, which has fine teeth designed to trap fleas. Thoroughly comb the entire body and check for adult fleas in the teeth of the comb. In many cases, the adult fleas are hard to find but the flea dirt is visible. Part the hair to examine the skin, especially over the back. Flea dirt resembles specks of pepper and sometimes assumes a coiled or question-mark shape. Another method to find flea dirt involves standing the cat on a light-colored surface, such as a white sheet. Rub the hair vigorously in all directions to loosen flea dirt. Examine the sheet for the characteristic shapes. If in doubt, blot any black specks with a moistened white tissue. Flea dirt will dissolve, leaving behind a rust or brown-colored stain, because it contains partially digested blood.

A flea eradication program must be well planned to cover all stages of the flea life cycle and must be thoroughly carried out with appropriate products in order to ensure success. The goals of a flea control program are

- To eliminate immature flea stages in the environment
- To eliminate adult fleas on the cat

- To prevent reinfestation of the cat and environment

The first step in environmental control involves mechanical measures. In warm climates, the outdoor environment should be altered. Dense areas of vegetation near the home or cattery should be clipped or mown. Leaf litter and other piles of organic matter should be removed to allow the soil to dry. These measures help remove areas of refuge for immature stages of the flea life cycle. It is also important to note that many species of wildlife, such as squirrels, raccoons, and possums, will also harbor fleas and can be a source of infestation for domestic pets, especially through contaminating the environment. Measures to remove wildlife from the area around and in the home, such as woodpiles, attics, and outbuildings, should be undertaken.

Inside the home or cattery, areas where cats spend much time should be carefully treated. This involves washing any pet bedding and thoroughly vacuuming any sleeping areas to remove eggs and larvae. Carpets and upholstered furniture should be vacuumed regularly. This stimulates preemergent adult fleas still inside cocoons to emerge so they can be treated with insecticide. Vacuum cleaner bags should be removed and disposed of promptly.

Insect growth regulators (IGRs) are a new class of substances that interfere with the development of flea larvae into adults. They are a safe and effective group of products. When used properly, IGRs will help prevent reinfestation of the indoor environment. The most common IGR is methoprene (sold under the brand name Precor, manufactured by Wellmark International). Many indoor sprays combine an IGR with an adulticide (such as a pyrethrin) to provide up to 7 months of activity. IGRs are also available in flea collars, which are effective for up to 12 months.

Traditional flea control products for topical use typically contain organophosphates such as carbamate, or pyrethroids/pyrethrins. These agents are potentially toxic to animals, and cats are particularly susceptible to their effects. In the past, a wide variety of formulations have been available, such as powders, sprays, mousses, shampoos, and flea collars. These have largely been replaced with a new generation of safer and more effective products. It is extremely important that products designed for use on dogs are never used on cats. Because of cats' increased susceptibility to toxicities, flea products designed for dogs are not appropriate for use on cats and can cause serious harm if misused in this way.

Fipronil (Frontline, manufactured by Rhone Merieux) is an agent that kills adult fleas and ticks and is available either as a pump spray or a spot-on formulation. Fipronil diffuses over the body of the cat by affinity with the sebum layer of the skin and thus can provide complete coverage. After application, fipronil acts rapidly, and all fleas are usually killed within 24 hours. The residual action is very good, and fipronil is generally reapplied monthly as a preventive. Adult fleas are killed before they have time to lay eggs, so the product also indirectly helps with environmental control. All animals in the home should be treated at the same time. Fipronil is considered safe and can be used on young kittens. Uncommon adverse reactions have been reported and are likely associated with the alcohol base of the formulation.

Imidacloprid (Advantage, manufactured by Bayer) is another product designed to kill adult fleas (but not ticks). It comes in a spot-on formulation that is applied to the back of the cat's neck. Its characteristics are very similar to fipronil, in that there is rapid onset of activity after application and good residual action. It is also reapplied once monthly for prevention. The product specifications state it should not be used on kittens under 8 weeks of age. This is because control in this age group is achieved by treating the nursing queen.

Lufenuron (Program, manufactured by Novartis Animal Health) is a product that interrupts the flea life cycle but does not kill adult fleas. It is a type of insect development inhibitor that works by inhibiting the formation of chitin. Chitin is a structural protein found in insects but not in mammals. When administered to the cat either orally or by injection, lufenuron is absorbed and stored in the cat's own body fat. When the adult flea bites the cat, it ingests some lufenuron. The eggs laid by these adult fleas are unable to develop properly, so the life cycle is interrupted. Provided all animals in the home are treated at the same time, the flea infestation will eventually be eliminated. Ideally, a product that kills adult fleas should also be used at the start of treatment. In cases of significant sources of reinfestation, lufenuron may not be sufficient by itself to control fleas.

In the oral formulation, lufenuron is administered monthly as either a tablet or a suspension. It must be given with food to be properly absorbed. Inadequate dosing can result if the cat vomits after ingesting the product or if the cat is reluctant to eat food mixed with lufenuron. There is also an injectable form of lufenuron that is given every 6 months and can remove the problems associated with oral dosing.

One new flea control product on the market is selamectin (Revolution, manufactured by Pfizer Animal Health). Produced in a spot-on formulation designed to be applied just in front of the cat's shoulder blades, selamectin has the broadest spectrum of activity of the newer parasite control products. It is labeled as effective against heartworm, adult fleas (as well as preventing the development of larvae), ear mites (*Otodectes cynotis*), hookworms (*Ancylostoma tubaeforme*) and roundworms (*Toxocara cati*). It is applied once monthly for parasite control and is safe in kittens (after 6 weeks of age) as well as pregnant and nursing queens. Selamectin is absorbed from the skin into the cat's bloodstream and concentrates in the sebaceous glands of the skin. It is also effective in the gastrointestinal tract.

Another very new flea control product is nitenpyram (Capstar, manufactured by Novartis). It is supplied in tablet form and may be dosed daily if needed. Nitenpyram provides a very rapid kill of adult fleas but does not have any residual effect. It begins working within 30 minutes of administration and kills more than 90% of the fleas on a cat within 6 hours. It may be given to kittens over 4 weeks of age and weighing more than 2 pounds. The manufacturer says the drug is also safe for nursing or pregnant queens. It may also be combined with other flea control products as part of a comprehensive flea control plan.

TICKS

While ticks are not commonly found on cats, they can be picked up by cats that have access to outdoors and roam in areas with long grass or low bushes. They are most common in warm, humid climates. Ticks are eight-legged parasitic insects whose larvae have six legs. Typically, ticks attach to the cat's ears and neck, or between the toes. They will appear as blue or brown lumps or growths of various sizes. As the tick feeds on blood, it increases greatly in size.

Ticks seem to cause little irritation to cats, but a sore can develop at the site of attachment if the tick is improperly removed, leaving the head behind. Ticks will fall off of their own accord when they are finished feeding. Manual removal can be accomplished by using forceps or large tweezers and grasping the tick as close to the cat's skin as possible. The tick is then pulled straight out using firm, steady pressure.

Most cats have only a few ticks, but large infestations can be treated with a topical product designed to kill fleas and ticks.

EAR MITES

The ear mite, *Otodectes cynotis*, causes inflammation of the external ear canal (otitis externa) and sometimes an accompanying skin disease in cats called otodectic mange or otoacariasis. Ear mites cause at least 50% of the cases of otitis externa in cats. The mites live on the surface of the skin inside the ear canal, and occasionally on the head, neck, or paws. Inside the ear canal, the mites irritate the wax glands, causing them to produce excess wax. The discharge produced in the ear is composed of this wax, plus blood and exudate from the mites.

Cats with ear mites have a dark brown-black discharge in the ear canal, and they may scratch or rub at their ears and shake their heads excessively. Occasionally, untreated cases of ear mites lead to so much head shaking and trauma from scratching that a hematoma, or blood blister, forms near the tip of the ear. Some cats may have no symptoms of ear mite infestation at all, whereas others are very sensitive and react to only a few mites. Ear mites are highly contagious and commonly will spread from an infected queen to her kittens. Mature cats tend to be less commonly affected.

Any cat with a brown-black ear discharge and scratching at the ears should be suspected of having ear mites. While the mites are fairly large compared with other parasites, they usually require magnification to be visible. They may be seen when the veterinarian uses an otoscope to examine the ear. Typically, the ears are cleaned using mineral oil and some of the debris is examined under a microscope to identify the mites.

Treatment for ear mites usually involves gentle cleaning of the ear canal to remove much of the debris. This allows topical medications to penetrate more effectively. Ongoing ear cleaning is seldom necessary and cat owners should never attempt to clean ears at home using cotton swabs. There are many topical medications available for ear mites, both prescription and nonprescription. They are often combination products, containing drugs to kill mites (miticides) along with antibiotics, antifungals, and corticosteroids. There is some evidence that administration of products containing oils and waxes with no miticide is also effective.

Two topical parasiticides are effective against ear mites. Selamectin (Revolution, manufactured by Pfizer Animal Health) is a broad-spectrum product that is also effective against fleas, heartworm, hookworm, and roundworm. It comes in a spot-on formulation, which is designed to be applied to the back of the cat's neck once monthly. A suspension containing 0.01% ivermectin (Acarexx, manufactured by Blue Ridge Pharmaceuticals) recently became available in the United States for use in the ears. It may be used in cats and kittens 4 weeks of age and older. It is currently not labeled for use during pregnancy or lactation, although ivermectin is known to be safe in such circumstances. One treatment with Acarexx was shown to be 94% effective in clearing ear mites within 7–10 days. Finally, the newest ear mite treatment is milbemycin (MilbeMite, manufactured by Novartis Animal Health). This product comes as a liquid in a small tube and can be administered to kittens as young as 2 weeks of age. The manufacturer states that one dose is 99% effective within 7 days of treatment.

OTHER SKIN PARASITES

After fleas, the two most common external parasitic skin diseases of cats are cheyletiellosis and notoedric mange. Less common diseases are caused by the cat fur mite (*Lynxacarus radovskyi*), the *Demodex* mite, and lice (*Felicola subrostratus*).

Cheyletiellosis, also called walking dandruff, is caused by the mite *Cheyletiella blakei*. These mites are highly contagious and may also infect humans, dogs, and rabbits. The mites do not burrow into the skin but live on the skin surface. They do bite and suck body fluids from the host cat. These mites live their entire lives on their host, and their life cycle is thought to take about 35 days. However, adult female mites can live for up to 10 days off the host.

The most common patient with cheyletiellosis is a young cat, but any age, any breed, and either sex can be affected. The most common physical sign is scaling or dandruff that may or may not be itchy. Some cats also have a scabby rash (miliary dermatitis) on their back. Other cats have no clinical signs at all and are considered asymptomatic carriers.

Cheyletiella mites can be challenging to find and diagnose. They are identified in only about 50% of cases where they are suspected to be the cause of skin disease. Various methods are used to identify them, such as skin scrapings, flea combing, and acetate tape impressions. A response to treatment is often the only way the diagnosis is made.

All animals in a home where cheyletiellosis has been diagnosed should be considered infected and should be treated. The mites are susceptible to most external parasite products, such as lime sulfur, pyrethrins, and carbamates. Cats are most often given a weekly dip with lime sulfur for a minimum of 6–8 weeks. Ivermectin is very successful in eliminating *Cheyletiella* mites in cats, although it is an off-label use of the drug. Cats may be given injections of ivermectin every 2 weeks for two or three treatments. Selamectin (Revolution, manufactured by Pfizer Animal Health) also seems to be effective for *Cheyletiella* mites, although this is an off-label use of the product. Environ-

mental treatment should also be carried out with products designed for flea control.

It has been estimated that for up to 80% of animals with cheyletiellosis, there are also humans involved. People may have a red and itchy rash, most commonly on their arms, legs, and trunk. If cheyletiellosis is suspected, a physician should be consulted. If the source of the infestation is treated and eliminated, most human lesions will resolve on their own in a few weeks.

Notoedric mange is less common in cats than fleas or cheyletiellosis. It is caused by the sarcoptic mange mite, *Notoedres cati*. It is spread by direct contact between cats and is highly contagious. This mite can also infect humans, dogs, and rabbits. Notoedric mange appears to have a few pockets in North America where it is endemic.

This mite burrows into the upper layers of the skin and feeds on epidermal cells and lymph fluid. In cats, the mite causes intense itchiness, especially of the head and neck. The affected cat will scratch excessively and shake its head. Skin lesions involve crusting, scaling, redness, and hair loss. The itching may be so intense that self-trauma lesions also appear. Occasionally, whole litters of kittens can be affected with widespread lesions. Rarely, death can occur in kittens as a result of secondary bacterial infections, fluid loss, and emaciation.

Notoedric mange mites are usually easily seen on skin scrapings. Once they have been identified in a cat, all other animals in the home should be considered infected as well. Treatment involves dips as for cheyletiellosis. Ivermectin is also effective against notoedric mange. Some patients will require antibiotics to control secondary bacterial infections or corticosteroids to control severe itching. This mite does not live very long once off the host, so a simple cleaning and vacuuming of the environment is sufficient.

As for cheyletiellosis, notoedric mange can also affect humans. It causes red bumps, hives, or crusting skin lesions, most often on the arms, legs, chest, and abdomen. A physician should be consulted if this infection is suspected. Most lesions in humans will resolve in a few weeks if the animal source of the mite is identified and treated.

The mite *Lynxacarus radovskyi* is known as the **cat fur mite**. An uncommon disease in cats, this mite spends its entire life on the cat attached to the base of the hair shaft. It is a large mite that can be mistaken for lice. Affected cats have a dull coat with hairs that are easily pulled out at the roots. Diagnosis is by skin scrapings or acetate tape impressions, and treatment is the same as for notoedric mange.

The chewing **louse** of the cat, *Felicola subrostratus*, is a host-specific parasite that feeds on sloughed off skin cells. It spends its entire life cycle on the cat. The adult lice can be seen with the naked eye, and their eggs (nits) are cemented to hair shafts. Infestations of lice are most often associated with poor health, overcrowding, and unsanitary conditions. Infected cats may have dandruff, a scabby rash, or no lesions at all. They may or may not be itchy. Treatment is the same as for notoedric mange.

Demodectic mange is a rare skin disease in cats, caused by two species of *Demodex* mites. These mites are normal residents of cat skin, and their life cycle is not fully understood. They are not considered to be contagious. In general, cats with demodectic mange are very likely to have an underlying immunosuppressive disease, such as FeLV, FIV, or diabetes.

Lesions of demodectic mange may be localized areas of redness, hair loss, and crusting, or they may be generalized. The head and neck are most commonly affected. *Demodex* mites can also cause a form of otitis externa in cats. The mites are diagnosed on skin scrapings and ear swabs. Localized lesions may respond to a topical miticide product, and otitis externa is treated with an ear preparation containing a miticide. Generalized disease is treated with dips or shampoos. Interestingly, spontaneous remission of some cases without treatment has been reported.

INTERNAL PARASITES
GASTROINTESTINAL PARASITES

The most common intestinal parasite of the cat is the **roundworm**, *Toxocara cati* (see "Toxocariasis," page 449). A less common feline roundworm is *Toxascaris leonina*. Roundworms are acquired when cats eat infected hosts, such as mice, birds, or insects. Kittens may acquire roundworms during nursing through infected queen's milk. An infected queen may harbor the larvae of the parasite in her body tissues for years. These larvae can undergo reactivation during pregnancy and lactation and infect the nursing kittens. Typically, kittens are more likely to be clinically affected and may have diarrhea, vomiting (sometimes with worms in the vomitus), and a swollen abdomen and may not grow. Since *T. cati* also migrates throughout the liver and lungs of the cat, kittens can also cough because of pneumonia.

These white worms live in the small intestine of the cat and grow to be up to 6 inches long. The eggs produced by the female worms are shed in the cat's feces and can persist in contaminated soil for years. Roundworm infections are diagnosed by finding the adult worms in vomitus or by finding the eggs during a fecal examination. Treatment is simple and involves a deworming program using multiple doses of a drug such as pyrantel pamoate. Catteries and shelters may be advised to use a routine deworming program for roundworm control. All kittens being adopted into a new home should receive deworming for roundworms if it has not already been done.

Roundworms have considerable public health significance. In humans, they can cause a disease called larva migrans. This disease occurs when larvae of one of various parasites migrate into the deep tissues of the human body. In most cases, the larvae are from the dog roundworm, *Toxocara canis*, but cases associated with *T. cati* have been documented. Children can become infected by accidental ingestion of eggs from contaminated environments. If a heavy infestation occurs, severe disease in the eye, lung, or liver requiring treatment can occur.

Tapeworms are parasites of the small intestine that typically cause no signs of illness in the host cat. The most common tapeworm in the cat is *Dipylidium caninum*, but infections are also seen with *Taenia taeniaeformis*. Adult tapeworms are ribbonlike worms and can grow to be a few feet long. They are composed of hundreds or thousands of individual segments and can live for 2–3 years. A heavily infected cat can contain dozens of tapeworms and can suffer malnutrition and inflammation of the intestinal wall.

Unlike other intestinal worms, tapeworms rarely shed eggs in the cat's feces but rather shed motile units called proglottid segments. The proglottid segments, about the size of a grain of rice, are passed with the feces and are often found clinging to fur under the cat's tail or dried up in the cat's sleeping areas. These segments crawl around, releasing tapeworm eggs into the environment.

The eggs of *D. caninum* are ingested by flea larvae, which eventually develop into adult fleas infected with tapeworm larvae. Cats become infected when they ingest these adult fleas during grooming. Between 2 and 3 weeks later, the infected cat starts to shed proglottid segments and the cycle is repeated. Control of *D. caninum* therefore also involves control of fleas, which act as a reservoir for reinfection. Cats become infected with *T. taeniaeformis* by eating infected rodents.

There are common prescription dewormers that are effective against tapeworms, such as praziquantel and epsiprantel. These medications may be available alone or in combination with pyrantel pamoate to make a broad-spectrum dewormer. Only one dose of dewormer is necessary to treat tapeworm infections. Unlike roundworms, tapeworms rarely cause human disease.

The cat is host to three types of **hookworms**: *Ancylostoma tubaeforme*, *Ancylostoma braziliense*, and *Uncinaria stenocephala*. The most commonly found is *A. tubaeforme*. These small intestinal parasites are usually acquired by ingestion of feces, which contain infective larvae, although they can also be acquired through skin penetration. Cats may also be infected by eating rodents carrying hookworm larvae. This parasite is not known to spread to kittens from an infected queen through the placenta or through milk.

Most larvae develop to adult hookworms in the small intestine and live for 6 months to 1 year. However, some larvae become dormant and hide in body tissues. It is possible for them to reactivate at some later date and reestablish adult hookworms in the small intestine. The adult hookworms shed eggs into the feces of the cat, and infective larvae later develop to repeat the cycle.

Kittens are most severely affected by this blood-sucking worm and may suffer diarrhea with dark or bloody stools, vomiting, weight loss, weakness, and anemia. In some cases, especially in adults, the infection can be asymptomatic. Cats with chronic hookworm can develop significant anemia. The infection is diagnosed by finding the parasite eggs in feces under a microscope. Treatment of hookworm infection is the same as for roundworms.

Hookworms are transmissible to humans and are one cause of the skin disease called cutaneous larva migrans. The infective larvae can penetrate human skin and cause a red, itchy rash. When large numbers of larvae infect a human, they may migrate to the lungs and cause significant disease.

Cats are also host to a very small **stomach worm**. *Ollulanus tricuspis* is spread when an infected cat vomits the contagious larval form of the worm. This parasite is found worldwide and can also infect dogs, although not commonly. This is another parasite, like the tapeworm, that is not often diagnosed on a fecal examination, because the larvae are not usually passed in the feces. Diagnosis can be challenging, because the only sure way to detect the parasite is by finding it in vomitus. It is probable that many cats have *O. tricuspis* and are asymptomatic, because the worm does not often cause illness. In some cats, however, the worm causes inflammation of the lining of the stomach (gastritis) that can lead to chronic vomiting and loss of appetite. The parasite may be more common in multicat households, catteries, and shelters. No one treatment has been identified as the treatment of choice, but several dewormers, such as levamisole and fenbendazole, have been used successfully in some cases.

The cat is home to several **protozoal parasites**. The most important of these are *Toxoplasma gondii, Isospora* species. *Cryptosporidium* species, and *Giardia* species. Toxoplasmosis is discussed with other zoonotic diseases (see "Toxoplasmosis," pages 441–443).

Although *Toxoplasma* and *Cryptosporidium* are classed as coccidian parasites, when the term **coccidia** is used, it is usually assumed to mean *Isospora* species. It is thought that almost all cats will become infected with *Isospora felis* in their lifetime. *I. felis* and *I. rivolta* are the most common coccidian parasites found in cats. These protozoan parasites primarily inhabit the small intestine of cats and most infections cause no clinical signs of illness. Kittens are most likely to show symptoms of diarrhea (sometimes with blood or mucus) and, in rare cases, may die. Symptoms are most common at the time of weaning and are often seen in crowded conditions. Kittens suffering from other ailments, such as malnutrition, and concurrent bacterial or viral infections, are most likely to become ill.

Isospora infects cats through the ingestion of either infective oocysts from the environment or prey animals infected with the parasite. The parasite completes its life cycle in the intestinal tract of the cat, and new oocysts are then shed in the cat's feces. These oocysts require several days in the environment before they are infective, although under the right conditions, this can occur in as little as 6 hours. This fact means that good litter box hygiene and prompt removal of feces can help break the fecal–oral route of transmission in a cattery or shelter.

Diagnosis of *Isospora* infection is through identification of the oocysts during fecal examination under the microscope. Sulfonamide antibiotics are the drugs of choice for cats, although many infections clear spontaneously. However, these drugs can only curtail some stages of parasite reproduction and cannot eliminate the parasite from an infected cat.

Another coccidian parasite, **Cryptosporidium**, is too small to be seen on routine fecal examinations. *Cryptosporidium* is found in many types of animals, and *C. parvum* is probably the species most commonly associated with illness. This parasite's life cycle occurs in the intestinal tract of its host, and it sheds infective oocysts in the host's feces. These oocysts can contaminate water, leading to infections in animals and people. It is also thought that transmission can occur between cats and people and vice versa. A cat with diarrhea due to *C. parvum* infection can be the source of infection for humans and other animals in the home. This is a significant health risk for immunocompromised people.

As for other coccidia, infection with *C. parvum* is thought to be common, while clinical disease is rare. Signs of illness include severe diarrhea, weight loss, weakness, and dehydration. Kittens are more susceptible than adult cats. Affected cats and humans often have a predisposing underlying disease causing immunosuppression. Disease caused by *C. parvum* is seen in human patients with AIDS and in cats with FeLV. Other predisposing conditions seen in cats include inflammatory bowel disease, intestinal lymphoma, and FIV.

The diagnosis of *C. parvum* can be difficult because of the extremely small size of the parasite. It may be identified on tissue biopsies. A special fecal test for *Cryptosporidium* species is also available and is undergoing assessment for reliability in veterinary medicine. Unfortunately, there are as yet no drugs known to be effective in the treatment of this parasite. One drug currently receiving attention as a possible treatment is paromomycin, although adverse effects have been reported in cats receiving this drug.

Giardia is the most commonly diagnosed intestinal parasite found in humans, and its distribution is worldwide. While the infection rate in cats is lower, it also often goes undiagnosed. *Giardia* species can be found in the small intestine of many types of animals. The question of whether dogs and cats can function as a reservoir for human infections is unclear, but precautions should be taken. This protozoan parasite is most common in cats under 1 year of age and in catteries and other multicat situations, such as shelters. Most infected dogs and cats have no signs of illness.

The parasite lives primarily in the small intestine of the cat, although it can sometimes be found in the large intestine. It is spread by fecal–oral transmission when infective cysts are passed in the stools and then contaminate the environment, including food and water. These cysts can survive for months in the right conditions. When a cat ingests cysts from its environment, signs of illness can occur in less than 2 weeks. The most common clinical sign is diarrhea, often containing mucus. The diarrhea can be mild or severe, and it may be constant or intermittent. Some cats also suffer from weight loss. Young cats and kittens are most severely affected, and they may be dehydrated and lethargic and may lose their appetite.

The parasite is diagnosed by examination of fresh fecal smears using various techniques. Some commercial laboratories are now offering more accurate fecal ELISA tests for *Giardia*. It is currently recommended that all cats found to have *Giardia* receive treatment, whether they are ill or not. The most common drug used to treat this parasite is metronidazole, but resistance to this drug can cause treatment failures. Other drugs, such as albendazole or fenbendazole, may be more effective. Environmental control is also very important, especially in catteries, where bleach is the disinfectant of choice.

Trichomoniasis is an infection of the large intestine of humans, cats, dogs, and other animals. Originally it was thought that *Pentatrichomonas hominis* was the form found in cats, but recent research points to a different trichomonad, *Tritrichomonas foetus-suis*, which is also found in swine. While it is debatable how much disease this parasite causes in cats, some cases of refractory diarrhea in kittens have been reported associated with *T. foetus-suis*. The parasite may be mistaken for *Giardia* under the microscope because its appearance is similar. Infection with *T. foetus-suis* is difficult to treat, and no single drug therapy is considered effective. The zoonotic potential of this parasite is also not known.

HEART AND LUNG PARASITES

Feline **heartworm disease** is caused by the parasite *Dirofilaria immitis*, the same heartworm that infects dogs. It is spread by the mosquito. Heartworm disease in cats was first documented in 1921 in Brazil, but since that time, it has been found in any area where canine heartworm occurs. Increasing awareness of feline heartworm has led to earlier detection. In the past, it was most commonly diagnosed after death. Differences between feline and canine heartworm make detection of the disease and its treatment more difficult in the cat.

We now know that while cats can get heartworm, they are more resistant to infection than dogs are. The cats at greatest risk live in areas of high canine heartworm infection and where they are at risk for bites from infected mosquitoes. However, the infection rates for indoor and outdoor cats are the same. While a dog can be infected with dozens of adult heartworms, cats typically harbor only one to nine adult worms, and their development from larvae to adults is slower. As well, adult heartworms will live for about 5 years in dogs but live less than 2 years in cats. For reasons not fully understood, male cats are more susceptible to infection than female cats.

The heartworm has a complex life cycle. An infected mosquito can transmit infective heartworm larvae to cats, and these larvae must then go through several developmental stages before they mature into adults. In dogs, the adult heartworms produce microfilaria, which circulate in the dog's bloodstream and are transmitted back to the mosquito when the insect bites an infected dog. Thus, the disease is transferred back and forth between mosquitoes and dogs. However, cats produce very few microfilaria and so rarely transfer the infection back to mosquitoes. This fact means that a common blood test for heartworm used in the dog to detect microfilaria is of little use in the cat.

Despite its name, heartworm disease in the cat is primarily a disease of the lung. The lung experiences acute inflammation, especially as the adult heartworms die. Many of the symptoms of feline heartworm infection mimic feline asthma: wheezing, coughing, difficulty breathing. Other symptoms include vomiting, lethargy, loss of appetite, and weight loss. However, cats infected with heartworm may have no signs at all, may have chronic signs of illness, or may die acutely. In acute cases, death may occur rapidly, with no warning, because of heart and lung failure.

Diagnostic testing for feline heartworm is an area of constant research. Currently, there are at least three blood-testing methodologies available. Tests are used both for screening purposes and to rule out heartworm as a cause of illness in cats showing appropriate clinical signs. In addition to blood tests, veterinarians may also use chest X-rays, heart ultrasound, and other tests in their examination.

Unfortunately, treating heartworm disease in cats is quite difficult. Treating these patients has been described as a lose-lose proposition. The chronic intermittent nature of the clinical symptoms some cats have can mislead owners into thinking the disease is not serious. However, sudden death occurs in a small percentage of cats. In general, there are two approaches to managing feline heartworm patients. One is to use drugs to kill the adult heartworms (adulticide therapy). This treatment is sometimes chosen for cats who are seriously ill at the time of diagnosis. Serious complications can follow this type of therapy, mainly associated with the death of the adult worms all at once. A more conservative approach is to use corticosteroids as anti-inflammatory treatment and allow the adult heartworms to die naturally over the course of several months or more. This type of treatment is often chosen for cats with either no signs of illness or only mild symptoms. Cats undergoing corticosteroid therapy can develop acute disease, however, that might necessitate emergency treatment, or they may collapse and die suddenly.

Given the problematic nature of treating heartworm-infected cats, attention should be focused on prevention. In areas with endemic canine heartworm, cats should be taking a monthly preventive medication. The first medication approved for use in cats as a heartworm preventive was ivermectin (Heartgard for Cats, manufactured by Merial), which is given orally once monthly. Other products are now available, such as selamectin (Revolution, manufactured by Pfizer Animal Health). It is administered topically once monthly and also controls fleas, ear mites, hookworms, and roundworms. Milbemycin (Interceptor, manufactured by Novartis Animal Health) is a monthly oral medication effective against heartworm as well as roundworms and hookworms.

In areas with a high incidence of canine heartworm, cats should be first given preventive medication as kittens and then continue receiving it for life. Because the incidence of heartworm is equal in indoor and outdoor cats, even cats that live totally indoors but in endemic areas should be given preventive medication.

Two types of **lungworm** are found in cats: *Capillaria aerophila* and *Aelurostrongylus abstrusus*. Their incidence varies geographically, with certain lungworms being more common in some areas than others. These worms live in the airways of cats. When they shed their eggs, they are coughed up and swallowed by the cat. Many cats infected with lungworm have no clinical symptoms, whereas others will have a chronic dry cough. Lungworms are primarily transmitted when cats eat an infected host animal, such as earthworms, rodents, birds, snails, slugs, amphibians, and reptiles.

Lungworm infection is diagnosed by examining feces for lungworm larvae (using the Baermann technique), taking X-rays of the lungs, and by performing an airway wash (such as a transtracheal wash or bronchoalveolar lavage). Treatment is relatively simple, using drugs such as fenbendazole or ivermectin, and the prognosis for recovery is good.

BLOOD PARASITES

The most common blood parasite in cats, *Hemobartonella felis*, is also called feline infectious anemia. Recent research has shown that this organism is actually a *Mycoplasma*, and renaming has been proposed. It was first described as a parasite of cats in 1942. The mode of transmission is not fully understood but might include vectors such as mosquitoes and fleas. It is also possible that the parasite can be transmitted from an infected queen to her unborn kittens in the womb. This parasite attaches itself to the surface of the feline red blood cell and damages it. The cat's immune system then identifies these red blood cells as being abnormal and destroys them. In this way, some cats with *Hemobartonella* develop anemia.

Cats ill with *Hemobartonella* usually are lethargic and suffer from loss of appetite. They may have pale gums because of anemia and enlarged spleens. The disease is diagnosed using blood tests, such as a complete blood count and examination of stained blood smears for the parasite. It may take examination of several blood smears over a period of days to find the parasite. It is also possible to find small numbers of *Hemobartonella* in the blood of cats who have no signs of illness at all. These cats act as carriers for the parasite.

Some cats with *Hemobartonella* infections are very anemic, whereas others have only mild disease. Of the cats that are acutely ill, about one third will die if they are not treated. Treatment involves both specific and supportive therapies. Cats with severe anemia might require a blood transfusion and corticosteroids to counteract the immune-mediated aspect of the disease. A tetracycline antibiotic, such as doxycycline, can be used to treat the disease. A new drug, imidocarb dipropionate, is being investigated for its efficacy in treating *Hemobartonella* in cats. However, no drug has yet been found that can completely clear an infected cat of the parasite, and recovered cats probably remain carriers for the rest of their lives.

A few other blood parasites occur in the cat, such as *Ehrlichia* species and *Cytauzxoon*. However, they are uncommon in cats in North America. Only a few cases of each disease have been reported in the veterinary medical literature.

POISONS AND TOXINS

Both inside and outside our homes, there are many potential toxic and poisonous hazards to cats. Some of these are hazards cats might encounter accidentally, and others might be medications we give to our cats without knowing the danger. When you acquire a new kitten, it helps to think about making your home safe in the same way you would to protect children. Childproofing a home can also make it kitten-safe.

Just as parents are advised to keep the number of the local poison control hotline handy, owners should also know about access to such services for their pets. The ASPCA runs the National Animal Poison Control Center (NAPCC). This 24-hour emergency service is the first and only animal-oriented poison information service in the United States that operates nationwide. In existence since 1978, veterinarians and specialists in veterinary toxicology staff the NAPCC.

While human poison control centers can often make generalized poison information available for animals, the NAPCC has information specific to animal poisonings, which can be invaluable to veterinarians and pet owners. Callers must be prepared to pay a fee for the service.

When calling the NAPCC, be prepared to give your name, address, and telephone number. You will then be asked for information about the substance that your cat has ingested, such as the amount taken and the time of the ingestion. You will also be asked for information about your pet, such as age, breed, sex, and body weight. Finally, you will be asked to describe the particular symptoms your pet is experiencing. Be sure to have accurate information ready. The specialists will then give you specific information to help treat your pet. With the flat-rate service, the NAPCC will also follow up the case with the owner or veterinarian via telephone to monitor the progress of the patient. Here is contact information for the NAPCC:

ASPCA National Animal Poison Control
Center
1717 South Philo Rd., suite #36
Urbana, IL 61802
1-888-426-4435 (flat-rate billing)
Web site: http://www.aspca.org (click on
the Animal Poison Control Center link)

The three common groups of hazards to cats are poisonous plants, prescription and nonprescription drugs, and toxic household chemicals and other products.

PLANTS

Indoor gardening is a widespread hobby in the United States. Unfortunately, many beautiful indoor plants are also toxic to humans and animals in some way. Ideally, indoor gardeners should strive to be aware of the botanical names of their plants and their potential toxicities. Plants that could be dangerous should be kept out of reach of children and pets, or avoided altogether. Many excellent indoor gardening reference works have descriptions and photos of plants to aid in identification and also provide information about any potential toxicity. Nurseries are another good source for plant identification and information, as are county extension offices throughout the United States.

Many cats will readily chew on houseplants for a variety of reasons. Cats are natural foragers and often chew on vegetation in the wild. Indoor cats may also chew on houseplants because of boredom, because of a need for more fiber in their diet, or to relieve teething irritation. They may nibble on a plant simply because it is new in the home.

Depending on the plant and its toxic components, a variety of signs of illness can occur when cats ingest it. Common symptoms include vomiting, diarrhea, and salivation. Very many plants are gastrointestinal irritants, producing unpleasant but not lethal effects. However, other plants can produce kidney damage, serious effects in the cardiovascular system, blindness, neurological problems, and even coma or death. Symptoms may occur immediately, such as oral pain and swelling, or they may be delayed for many hours.

Ideally, a veterinarian should carry out treatment for poisonings. However, there are some circumstances when a pet owner can give simple treatments at home. For instance, many plants simply cause irritation of the mouth, and treatment at home can consist of rinsing the mouth with water or milk. Where inducing vomiting is recommended as treatment, it should be done only under the direct supervision or specific advice of a veterinarian to avoid serious complications in some patients. Other veterinary treatments include activated charcoal and cathartics. Activated charcoal is available in a thin, watery mixture for treatment of poisonings. It is given orally, sometimes by stomach tube, and helps absorb the toxin so that its effects on the animal are reduced. Cathartics are substances given to induce diarrhea and elimination of a toxin. Additionally, supportive care such as intravenous fluids and drugs to counteract cardiac and neurologic effects may be needed. Analgesics may be given for pain and antihistamines to counteract allergic reactions and reduce swelling. In some cases, severe difficulties in breathing might require assisted ventilation.

INDOOR PLANTS TOXIC TO CATS

Plant Name	Toxic Part	Type of Toxicity
Aloe vera (burn plant)	Latex or juice of plant	GI
Araceae family: arum, calla lily, peace lily, philodendron	Every part: contains oxalates which can form calcium oxalate crystals in organs if eaten in sufficient quantity; also causes acute allergic reaction	GI, R, K, O. The oral pain and swelling usually stop cats from eating large quantities.
Bird of paradise (Barbados pride, dwarf poinciana)	Seeds	GI
Caladium species	Leaf, stem, stalk	GI

Plant Name	Toxic Part	Type of Toxicity
Chinese evergreen (*Aglaonema* species)	Leaves	GI
Croton (*Codiaeum, Croton* species)	Every part, especially seeds, sap, and stems	GI, N, dermatitis
Cyclamen	Rhizomes and sap	GI, N, dermatitis
Dieffenbachia (dumb cane)	Every part	GI, R—can cause severe mouth/throat swelling
English ivy (*Hedera helix*)	Every part	GI
Euphorbia (pencil cactus)	Every part	GI, dermatitis
Glory lily (*Gloriosa* species)	Every part	GI
Golden pothos (*Scindapsus*)	Every part	GI
Holly	Leaves and berries	GI
Jerusalem cherry, Christmas cherry (*Solanum* species)	Berries	GI
Kaffir lily (*Clivia*)	Bulbs	GI
Kalanchoe	Every part	C—can be fatal
Lily (Easter lily, tiger lily, Madonna lily, Turk's cap lily, Asiatic lily)	Every part of plant, even the water that plants have been standing in	K—many patients die, especially if treatment is not begun early
Mistletoe	Every part, especially berries	GI, N, C: collapse and death in severe cases
Poinsettia (Christmas flower)	Leaves, stems, sap	GI—research has been unable to confirm that this plant is highly toxic; poison control centers report problems are rare after ingestion
Rhododendron species (azalea, various rhododendron hybrids)	Every part, even nectar from flowers; contains a cardiac glycoside that mimics the effects of digitalis	C, GI, N

C = cardiovascular toxicity (direct effects on the heart causing cardiac abnormalities such as irregular rhythm and collapse; GI = gastrointestinal toxicity (oral pain and swelling, difficulty breathing due to throat swelling, nausea, vomiting, diarrhea); R = respiratory toxicity (difficulty breathing, respiratory failure); N = neurological toxicity (excitation, depression, coma, seizures); K = kidney toxicity (kidney failure); O = organ failure (toxic to multiple organs, especially kidney and liver).

OUTDOOR PLANTS TOXIC TO CATS

Plant Name	Toxic Part	Medical Problems
Baptisia species (false/wild indigo)	Every part; contains alkaloids	GI, R
Bleeding heart (*Dicentra*)	Every part	C
Buttercup (*Ranunculus*)	All top growth	GI, N
Cardinal flower (*Lobelia* species)	Every part	GI, R, N
Christmas rose (*Helleborus*)	Leaves, stems	C, G, N
Chrysanthemum	Every part—source of natural pyrethrins	GI, N
Clematis	Every part	GI
Crocus (*Crocus* species, *Colchicum*)	Every part, primarily bulbs	G, K, C
Daffodil, narcissus	Every part, especially bulbs	GI
Daylily (*Hemerocallis*)	Every part	K
Delphinium (also larkspur)	Flowers, seeds	GI, C, N—can cause death
Elder	Every part, especially berries, roots, sap	GI, R—contains cyanide
Euonymus	Leaves, berries, stem, sap	C
Flowering tobacco (*Nicotiana* species)	Every part; contains alkaloids	GI, N, R, C, dermatitis
Foxglove (*Digitalis*)	Every part, especially seeds—even water in flower vases	C—contains digitalis; can cause death
Garlic, onion	Especially bulbs	GI, hemolytic anemia
Hyacinth	Bulbs	GI
Hydrangea	Every part	GI, C
Jack-in-the-pulpit (*Arisaema* species)	Every part; contains calcium oxalate	GI, K, O
Jimson weed (*Datura*, thornapple)	Every part, especially seeds	N, R
Lily (*Lilium* species: Easter lily, tiger lily, etc.)	All parts, including water in flower vases	K
Lily of the valley (*Convallaria*)	Every part, especially bulbs	C, K—can cause death
Lupine	Every part	N
Monkshood (*Aconitum*)	Every part, especially seeds; contains alkaloids	GI, N, C—can cause death
Morning glory (*Ipomoea* species)	Every part, especially seeds; contains hallucinogenic compounds	N
Nightshade (*Solanum, Atropa*)	Every part	GI

Plant Name	Toxic Part	Medical Problems
Oleander	Every part	C—can cause death
Poppy (*Papaver* species)	Berries, stems, sap	N, R
Potato	Leaves, stem	GI, N, C
Purple flag iris, yellow iris	Bulbs	GI, N
Rhubarb	Leaves	GI, K
Sweetpea (*Lathyrusodoratus*)	Leaves and stems	N
Tulip	Bulbs	GI, N
Virginia creeper (American ivy)	Leaves, stems	GI
Yew	Foliage, bark, seeds	C, N—can be fatal.

C = cardiovascular toxicity (direct effects on the heart causing cardiac abnormalities such as irregular rhythm and collapse; GI = gastrointestinal toxicity (oral pain and swelling, difficulty breathing due to throat swelling, nausea, vomiting, diarrhea); R = respiratory toxicity (difficulty breathing, respiratory failure); N = neurological toxicity (excitation, depression, coma, seizures); K = kidney toxicity (kidney failure); O = organ failure (toxic to multiple organs, especially kidney and liver).

Many common indoor and outdoor plants are nonpoisonous and so are safe around children and pets, including the following:

African violet (*Saintpaulia*)
Asparagus fern
Carnation (*Dianthus*)
Christmas cactus (*Zygocactus*)
Coleus
Corn plant (*Dracaena*)
Dandelion
Dracena
Ferns
Fig tree (*Ficus*)
Fuchsia

Gardenia
Geranium
Hens and chicks (*Sempervivum*)
Hibiscus
Honeysuckle
Impatiens
Jade plant (*Crassula*)
Lilac
Marigold
Norfolk Island pine tree (*Araucaria*)
Palm

Pansy
Peperomia
Petunia
Prayer plant (*Maranta*)
Prickly pear cactus (*Opuntia*)
Purple velvet plant (*Gynura*)
Rose
Rubber plant (*Ficus*)
Snake plant (*Sansevieria*)

Snapdragon
Spider plant
Swedish ivy (*Plectranthus*)
Umbrella tree (*Schefflera*)
Wandering Jew (*Tradescantia*)
Wax begonia
Yucca
Zebra plant (*Calathea*)
Zinnia

Refer to the ASPCA Animal Poison Contol Center Web site for further information: http://www.aspca.org.

PRESCRIPTION AND NONPRESCRIPTION DRUGS

Luckily, cats are not subject to poisonings as frequently as dogs are, probably because of many behavioral factors. However, cats are certainly inquisitive, and this can easily expose them to many toxic hazards. As a species, cats are noteworthy, for they cannot metabolize certain compounds. Many drugs and chemicals are poorly metabolized and excreted by cats. Of all companion animal species, cats are the most susceptible to adverse drug reactions. They have deficient levels of a key liver enzyme that helps break down many drugs. In addition, the red blood cells of cats are particularly prone to damage from many compounds, leading to problems such as Heinz body anemia and methemoglobinemia. Heinz body anemia is a type of hemolytic anemia associated with damage to the hemoglobin in the red blood cells. Methemoglobinemia occurs when normal hemoglobin is replaced with a related form that is useless for carrying oxygen.

There are several classes of drugs important in toxic and adverse reactions in cats:

- **Analgesics (painkillers):** Many of the opiate analgesics, such as **codeine**, cause serious adverse effects and should not be given to cats. This type of medication can cause extreme excitement, muscle spasms, and death. Other common pain relievers, such as aspirin and acetaminophen, are also problematic for cats. **Aspirin** (acetylsalicylic acid) is used for some purposes in cats, mainly as an anti-inflammatory. The dosage and dosing interval must be established carefully by a veterinarian. In general, cats are given aspirin only twice weekly, instead of more than once daily, as for humans. Cats with aspirin toxicity will initially have depression, vomiting, loss of appetite, and rapid breathing. This can progress to bloody diarrhea, loss of balance, seizures, and death. Toxic hepatitis can develop, as can bone marrow suppression.

Acetaminophen is the most common drug toxicity seen in cats. Cats are unable to metabolize acetaminophen properly and can become seriously ill from a single dose. Symptoms include pale or blue mucous membranes, salivation, loss of appetite, vomiting, facial swelling, and difficulty breathing. Occasionally, liver damage results. Deaths from acetaminophen are usually due to methemoglobinemia, a condition in which the blood can no longer carry necessary amounts of oxygen. Many other nonsteroidal anti-inflammatory drugs have also produced toxic reactions in cats, such as ibuprofen, naproxen, and others. Typically, vomiting, depression, and sometimes gastritis and kidney damage are seen.

- **Antimicrobial agents:** Certain commonly used drugs can cause adverse reactions in cats. There are three common examples: griseofulvin, chloramphenicol, and ototoxic antibiotics.

Griseofulvin is a drug used to treat fungal infections, especially ringworm (see "Oral Medications," pages 445–446). Adverse reactions can occur in cats because they metabolize the drug more slowly than dogs or humans do. Kittens are especially susceptible. Symptoms may include anemia, loss of appetite, depression, vomiting, diarrhea, and neurological signs. Most of the more serious adverse effects are seen at higher doses of the drug. Cats who are FIV-positive are at great risk for bone marrow suppression when given this drug. In addition, pregnant queens given this drug during the first trimester have decreased survival rates for their kittens and increased numbers of kittens with cleft palates.

Chloramphenicol is a broad-spectrum antibiotic that has many potential uses in veterinary medicine. Cats have a high adverse reaction rate to this drug, which includes loss of appetite, vomiting, depression, diarrhea, and even death. Rare cases of severe aplastic anemia have been noted in humans exposed to chloramphenicol. Because there are newer, safer broad-spectrum antibiotics available, use of this drug should be restricted to situations in which no other antibiotic is suitable. Several antibiotics in the **aminoglycoside** family can cause deafness (ototoxicity) in cats. These antibiotics include streptomycin, gentamycin, neomycin, and related drugs. They may be used safely only under the direct supervision of a veterinarian. Affected cats may have not only impaired hearing but also loss of balance. Sometimes the effects are reversible after the drug is withdrawn.

HOUSEHOLD AND OTHER PRODUCTS

Because cats are often confined indoors, they have significant possible exposure to toxic chemicals and products within the home. Many **cleaning agents** contain strong acids or alkalis. Cats can suffer from serious damage to the skin, especially on the feet, by contacting these chemicals or walking on surfaces cleaned with them. The mouth and tongue can also be affected when cats try to clean the chemicals off their body. Washing the affected areas with copious amounts of water and applying bicarbonate to neutralize any strong acids can treat exposures. If some of the chemical has been swallowed, veterinary attention must certainly be sought, and vomiting should never be induced.

Many **detergents** contain strong alkalis that are directly irritating to tissues. If they are ingested, they produce vomiting, diarrhea, and pain. Common **disinfectants** used in veterinary medicine and in shelters and catteries often contain cationic detergents, such as quaternary ammonium compounds. Exposure to these chemicals causes salivation, eye and nose discharges, depression, and difficulty breathing. Contact with them can produce hair loss and ulcers on the skin. If they are ingested, significant damage can be done to the esophagus and stomach, and expert medical attention is required. Vomiting should not be induced.

Other common household cleaners contain pine oils or phenols. **Pine oils** can be toxic on ingestion or inhalation, and cats are particularly sensitive to these products. They can produce symptoms in many body systems, including neurological problems. Some products can cause methemoglobinemia (similar to the toxic effect of acetaminophen). **Phenols** can be present alone or combined with pine oils in cleaning products. Direct contact with phenols can cause corrosive lesions of the skin—or of the digestive tract, if they are ingested. Cats often ingest these compounds while trying to clean them off their fur. Phenols can also damage the liver and kidney and can also cause methemoglobinemia. Various other cleaning products found in the home are toxic. It is safest to assume that any cleaning product is toxic and treat it as such, keeping it safely locked away from children or pets.

Many other chemicals and products commonly found in homes are potentially toxic. Even shampoos can be toxic to cats if ingested, especially the antidandruff products. Methemoglobinemia can also occur in cats from ingestion of such common products as mothballs and matches. Antifreeze deserves special attention because it is a common poisoning in cats. It contains ethylene glycol, which is odorless but sweet-tasting, which makes it attractive to cats. Cats who ingest antifreeze will first suffer from vomiting and depression. This can be followed by neurological problems, such as loss of balance and seizures. After 12–24 hours, effects on the heart and lungs will be seen. Cats who survive for over 24 hours will eventually suffer from kidney failure and can die. Successful treatment of antifreeze toxicity depends on very early diagnosis and treatment. It is now possible in some areas of North America to buy antifreeze that does not contain ethylene glycol.

MAJOR FELINE ILLNESSES BY AGE GROUP

Many diseases and illnesses in cats are more prevalent in certain age groups than others. With that in mind, we can categorize cats into three age groups or life stages:

- Birth to 1 year (kittenhood)
- 1–8 years (young adult to middle age)
- 8 years and over (geriatric)

The following is a discussion of the most important illnesses or diseases seen in each age group. This list is not exhaustive but highlights the most commonly seen problems.

BIRTH TO 1 YEAR (KITTENHOOD)
Infectious Upper Respiratory Disease
Perhaps the most common problem seen in kittens under 1 year of age is upper respiratory disease. While there are several agents responsible for upper respiratory disease in cats, the symptoms of all tend to overlap. General symptoms include sneezing, discharge from the eyes or nose, fever, lethargy, and loss of appetite. The two most common agents of upper respiratory disease in cats are the viruses, feline viral rhinotracheitis (FVR) and feline calicivirus (FCV). FVR and FCV are each found in about 40% of cats with upper respiratory disease. Other nonviral agents may also be involved, and it is not uncommon for a cat to be infected by more than one agent at the same time.

Feline viral rhinotracheitis (FVR) was first isolated in 1957 and has long been known as one of the major causes of infectious upper respiratory disease in cats. FVR is caused by feline herpesvirus-1 (FHV-1). This virus is related to other herpesviruses, such as those that cause cold sores and chicken pox in humans. However, FHV-1 infects only cats—never humans.

FVR tends to produce more severe symptoms than any other cause of upper respiratory disease. After an incubation period of from 2–6 days, affected cats will become depressed, have a poor appetite, and suffer from fever and sneezing. Drooling may be seen if ulcers develop on the tongue. Severely affected kittens with inadequate immunity may die. In the acute stages of the disease, the virus may damage the turbinate bones in the nasal cavity, leading to chronic sinusitis later in life. Cats with chronic sinusitis suffer from bouts of sneezing and purulent nasal discharge.

SYMPTOMS ASSOCIATED WITH FELINE VIRAL RHINOTRACHEITIS

Most Common	Less Common
Depression	Drooling
Loss of appetite	Tongue ulceration
Fever	Coughing, breathing difficulty
Sneezing	Pneumonia
Conjunctivitis	Abortion
Nasal discharge	Skin ulcers
Corneal ulcers	Neurological problems

Feline calicivirus (FCV) was also first isolated in the 1950s. Along with FVR, it is a leading cause of infectious upper respiratory disease in cats. FCV is related to other caliciviruses that cause disease in humans and other animals, such as Norwalk virus. Like FVR, FCV does not infect humans.

FCV is associated with milder disease than FVR is although it can be associated with a wide spectrum of symptoms. These can range from inapparent infections, in which cats have no symptoms at all, to fatal pneumonia, especially in kittens. In addition, some strains of FCV found in modified live vaccines seem to cause an illness characterized by acute lameness and fever with no respiratory symptoms. FCV may also be one agent or factor associated with chronic stomatitis in cats.

In recent years, a new strain of virulent calicivirus has caused serious illnesses and deaths in several outbreaks in the United States. This strain appears to cause a very severe hemorrhagic disease with a high mortality rate. It is highly infectious and spreads readily in multicat facilities, such as shelters. Current calicivirus vaccines cannot protect cats against this new hemorrhagic strain.

SYMPTOMS ASSOCIATED WITH FELINE CALICIVIRUS

Most Common	Less Common
Nasal and ocular discharge	Lameness
Sneezing	Skin ulceration
Tongue ulceration	Abortion
Fever	Pneumonia, sometimes fatal
Conjunctivitis	Chronic stomatitis
Loss of appetite	

Bordetella bronchiseptica (FeBb) is a bacterium more commonly associated with kennel cough in dogs, although it has been known for over 30 years that it infects cats. However, in the last several years, it has become obvious that FeBb can cause primary respiratory disease in cats. The symptoms associated with FeBb are usually milder than for the viral respiratory diseases. The most severe cases of FeBb are reported in weaned kittens, when bronchopneumonia that may be life-threatening can

develop. FeBb is most common in multicat situations, especially shelters and catteries, where a high percentage of the population may carry the bacterium.

SYMPTOMS ASSOCIATED WITH *BORDETELLA BRONCHISEPTICA*

Fever

Sneezing

Nasal discharge

Swollen lymph nodes

Coughing

Chlamydia psittaci is a highly specialized organism, often called an intracellular bacterium. It has recently been renamed *Chlamydophila felis*. After it was isolated in 1942, it was considered to be the major cause of feline respiratory disease, at that time called feline pneumonitis. Now, *C. felis* is thought to cause primarily conjunctivitis. There are some very rare reports of it being associated with conjunctivitis in humans. Disease caused by *C. felis* is thought to be less common in North America than in the United Kingdom.

SYMPTOMS ASSOCIATED WITH FELINE CHLAMYDIA

Most Common	Less Common
Conjunctivitis	Mild sneezing
Clear ocular discharge	Nasal discharge
	Depression
	Lameness

Transmission:

Each agent of respiratory disease has different aspects of transmission and behavior in the cat. *C. felis* is shed primarily in ocular discharges and, to a lesser degree, in nasal discharges. Affected cats may shed the organism for many months after infection. Although *C. psittaci* is also shed from the vagina and rectum, the significance of this for transmission of the disease is unknown. Cats between 5 weeks and 9 months old seem to be the most susceptible. Maternal antibodies probably protect younger kittens.

Cats infected with FeBb will shed bacteria in secretions from the mouth and nose for many weeks after infection. However, many cats with FeBb have no clinical symptoms at all and may act as carrier cats. Very young kittens seem to be protected by maternal antibodies, but once they are a bit older, they may become susceptible to infection. Stressful situations such as travel, weaning, overcrowding, having kittens, and poor ventilation can promote disease caused by FeBb. It seems possible that dogs infected with *B. bronchiseptica* can transmit the infection to cats, although this has yet to be proven.

FCV and FVR are very successful viruses. A large proportion of the cat population has been exposed to one or both of these viruses at some time. The viruses are spread directly from cat to cat via secretions from the eyes, nose, and mouth. FCV is also sometimes shed in the urine and feces of infected cats. Indirect spread of the viruses also occurs via contact with contaminated bowls, cages, feeding and cleaning utensils, and hands of people who touch or care for infected cats. Aerosol spread is not the most important means of transmission, although the viruses are occasionally spread in large droplets during sneezing. As well, neither FVR nor FCV will persist long in the environment. FVR is the most susceptible and can live for only about 18 hours outside the cat. FCV is more resistant and may persist in the environment for up to 7 days.

The most important factor in the persistence and spread of FVR and FCV is the existence of carrier cats. Almost all cats infected with FVR become carriers. The virus can enter latency, or become dormant, and hide in nervous tissue in the cat. During latency, no virus is shed and the cat cannot infect others. However, the virus can be reactivated, often after a stressful event, such as having kittens or treatment with drugs such as corticosteroids. In the reactivated state, the cat will again shed virus, starting about 1 week later and usually lasting for about 2 weeks. The affected cat often has a recurrence of mild respiratory symptoms at the same time.

In contrast, FCV does not enter a latent phase. Rather, infected cats shed the virus almost continuously. Surveys have found that as much as 20% to 25% of cats are shedding FCV at any given time. The rate of shedding is lowest in households with few cats and highest in multicat situations. It is not known how long an infected cat remains a shedder of virus, but it is lifelong in some cats. Most cats will eventually eliminate the virus spontaneously and stop shedding. In addition, different cats will shed different amounts of virus. High-level shedders are very infectious to other cats, while low-level shedders are much less infectious.

A cat who has antibodies to FVR and FCV from vaccination will be protected against developing severe disease in most cases but may not be protected against infection by these viruses. Some of these vaccinated cats will become infected and shed virus without ever having displayed any symptoms of respiratory disease. These cats are sources of infection for other cats and are one reason why these viruses can spread so successfully, especially in multicat situations.

CAUSES OF FELINE UPPER RESPIRATORY DISEASE

Agent	Comments
Feline viral rhinotracheitis	• Found in about 40% of cases
	• Can cause severe disease
	• Has a latent stage in carrier cats
	• Injectable, IN/IO vaccines available
Feline calicivirus	• Found in about 40% of cases
	• High rate of carriers that shed virus continuously
	• Causes milder disease than FVR
	• Injectable, IN/IO vaccines available
Chlamydophila felis	• Found in about 30% of cases of chronic conjunctivitis
	• Injectable vaccines available
Bordetella bronchiseptica	• Can be present in high levels in some groups of cats
	• Causes mild disease in adults
	• Can be associated with severe pneumonia in kittens
	• IN vaccine available

FVR = feline viral rhinotracheitis; IN = intranasal; IO = intraocular

Diagnosis

Diagnosis of the cause of respiratory disease can be difficult since there is considerable overlap of symptoms. In some cases, cats may be infected with more than one of these agents. The traditional method of diagnosis for FVR and FCV has been isolation of the virus in cell cultures. Swabs of the throat are taken by the veterinarian and sent to a laboratory that performs this type of virus isolation. Testing blood for antibodies to these viruses is not very helpful, because a great many cats will have antibodies from being vaccinated. It is likely that newer DNA-based tests will be used for these viruses in the near future. Such techniques are currently in place for FVR in selected laboratories. FeBb is also diagnosed by swabs taken from the throat or nose and submitted to a laboratory where an attempt is made to grow the bacterium in culture. *C. felis* is diagnosed by taking swabs of the conjunctiva and submitting them to a laboratory that may use one of several methods, including newer DNA-based techniques, to identify the organism. In most cases, if an organism is found in a cat with respiratory disease, it is likely the cause of the illness. However, for FeBb and FCV, many cats are infected but still healthy, so that finding the organism in an ill cat might be coincidental.

Treatment

As with viruses in human medicine, veterinarians have very few antiviral drugs to treat illnesses such as respiratory disease caused by FVR and FCV. Antivirals such as acyclovir are not very effective and are associated with adverse effects in cats. However, topical solutions of antivirals, such as trifluridine, can be administered as eyedrops for treatment of eye lesions caused by FVR. Most cats with viral respiratory disease will benefit from taking a broad-spectrum antibiotic to control secondary bacterial infections, which are common.

Most important is good nursing care, which may involve tempting the patient to eat with baby food or a specialized commercial cat food designed for recuperation. Many cats with moderate to severe respiratory disease are very reluctant to eat, sometimes because of congestion, which impairs their sense of smell, and sometimes because of pain from tongue ulcers. Veterinarians may prescribe an appetite stimulant, such as cyproheptadine, if needed. Some severe cases also require supplemental fluid therapy, which might be administered at home. Relief of nasal congestion can be accomplished by using a nasal decongestant such as phenylephrine. However, a conventional steam humidifier or saline nebulizer is effective too. If a nebulizer or humidifier is not available, simply placing the patient in a steamy bathroom will help.

C. felis will respond to several antibiotics, but the tetracyclines such as doxycycline are most effective. Treatment for 2–3 weeks with oral doxycycline has been shown to be very effective. Most cases should also be treated with a topical tetracycline eye drop or ointment. A newer oral antibiotic, azithromycin, shows promise for treatment of C. felis but has not yet been extensively studied in cats. FeBb is also sensitive to several antibiotics, such as doxycycline and enrofloxacin. Ideally, the choice of antibiotic should be based on culture of the organism and antibiotic sensitivity testing.

Prevention

Vaccines against FVR and FCV have been available for many years. It has been a relatively effective means of controlling disease. Viral respiratory disease can still be a problem, especially in multicat households and in kittens, the latter because maternal immunity may disappear before vaccinations have begun. Protocols for vaccinations against FVR, FCV, and C. felis

appear elsewhere in this book. Recently, an intranasal vaccine against FeBb has become available for cats (Protex-Bb, manufactured by Intervet). It may be advisable for cats in high-risk situations, such as in shelters and catteries, to be vaccinated against FeBb. As well, it may also be considered prior to lodging a cat in a boarding kennel and, in some cases, might be required by the kennel operator. The duration of immunity provided by vaccines against FeBb and C. felis are not known.

Feline Infectious Peritonitis

One of the most poorly understood and enigmatic feline diseases is FIP. It is no exaggeration to say that this is one of the most feared diseases in catteries. The virus responsible for the disease is the feline coronavirus. While the first description of FIP was reported in 1963, there are reports going back to 1914 of clinical cases that closely resemble FIP. Even though we have known about the feline coronavirus for a long time, we know frustratingly little about it. However, research from recent years is slowly shedding more light on this virus and the disease it causes. Hopefully, the pace of discovery of new information will continue in the future as researchers worldwide work on this feline health problem.

Feline coronavirus operates differently from any other feline virus. Antibodies produced by the cat in response to infection by the virus are not protective and may even play a role in development of FIP. Antibody titers are virtually useless to diagnose FIP. Finally, while a vaccine is available, it has been surrounded by controversy concerning its safety and efficacy.

Even the terminology surrounding this disease is confusing. *FIP* is the term for the clinical disease associated with feline coronavirus infection. The most common form of feline coronavirus is FECV (feline enteric coronavirus). Disease-causing forms of feline coronavirus are called feline infectious peritonitis virus (FIPV).

FECV is a very common, highly infectious feline virus. It belongs to the genus *Coronavirus*, which has members that infect other species (humans, swine, dogs, and so on). However, feline coronaviruses infect only domestic cats and wildcats, never humans. The majority of cats with FECV (about 95%) will remain perfectly healthy. But in a small number of cases, FECV infection is the first step in a chain of events that leads to FIP. This happens because coronaviruses are very large viruses, made up of many nucleotides (the basic unit of genetic material). As they reproduce, errors are made in copying these nucleotides so that mutations are produced. While most of the copying errors result in harmless changes, some will have the effect of giving FECV the ability to cause disease. These mutant strains of FECV are then called FIPV.

Recent research has shown that mutant FECV strains arise within individual cats. We now know that the vast majority of cats do not "catch" FIP in the usual sense. They have developed the disease themselves from their own mutant FECV. There are some uncommon instances where FIP has behaved more like a conventional infectious disease and many cats have been affected in a short period of time, but these outbreaks often occur in catteries where many cats are related and so may share a genetic susceptibility to the disease. Therefore, in most cases, cats that are ill with FIP are unlikely to be a risk to other cats, because they are rarely shedding FIPV and thus may not need to be isolated unnecessarily.

It has been estimated that in multicat households where FECV has been introduced, 80% to 90% of cats will be infected. Catteries and shelters are especially likely to be FECV-positive because traffic of cats and kittens in and out of these establishments is common. However, the incidence of cases of FIP is quite low by comparison. Generally, most catteries experience losses far less than 10% to FIP over the years. Uncommon instances have been seen where an apparent epidemic of FIP is associated with mortality rates of over 10% in a short period of time. One possible factor in these epidemics is the shedding of a particularly virulent virus, an uncommon situation. Usually, losses are sporadic and unpredictable. The peak age range for losses to FIP is between 6 months and 2 years old (with the highest incidence at 10 months of age). Age-associated immunity to FIP appears to be possible, so that adult cats over the age of 2 years are least likely to be affected. However, cases of FIP are sometimes seen in elderly cats, probably associated with decreased immune system function. Transmission of FIP from a queen to her unborn kittens has not been known to occur.

FIP is a systemic disease; that is, it attacks many organ systems in an affected cat. Unfortunately, it is a progressive disease that is almost always fatal within a few weeks. There are two classic forms of the disease recognized: wet (or effusive) and dry (or noneffusive). In wet FIP, fluid accumulates within the chest and abdominal cavities. These patients may have a swollen abdomen or difficulty breathing. In dry FIP, no fluid is produced, but the virus can damage most major organs, including the kidneys, liver, central nervous system, and eyes. These patients may be jaundiced, may be suffering from seizures or other neurological problems, or may have kidney failure. General symptoms associated with FIP, such as weight loss, persistent fever, and poor appetite, are also found in other feline diseases. This can make the definitive diagnosis of FIP quite difficult, especially for the dry form.

SYMPTOMS ASSOCIATED WITH FELINE INFECTIOUS PERITONITIS

Wet (effusive) form

- Potbellied appearance if fluid accumulates in abdomen
- Difficulty breathing if fluid accumulates in chest

Dry (Noneffusive) Form

- Jaundice
- Seizures, abnormal gait
- Uveitis (inflammation in the eye) and other eye changes
- Kidney failure (increased thirst, increased urination)
- Abdominal masses

Common to both forms

- Gradual weight loss
- Poor growth rate in kittens
- Loss of appetite
- Persistent fever
- Dull, rough coat
- Depression

There is no single reliable blood test for FIP. Antibody titers have been shown to be highly unreliable for diagnosing the disease. Newer DNA-based technologies for detecting FIPV in the blood of cats are beginning to appear in commercial laboratories, but they remain unproven and unvalidated. Therefore, veterinarians have to rely on a combination of physical findings, clinical symptoms, and the results of various diagnostic tests to reach a diagnosis of FIP in a sick cat. Certainly, the diagnosis should never be made based solely on a blood test for feline coronavirus.

If the wet form of FIP is present, fluid samples from the patient's chest or abdomen can be analyzed. The typical fluid is clear or straw-colored and somewhat thick. It contains high levels of protein and no evidence of bacterial infection. The dry form of FIP can be very challenging to diagnose. Veterinarians may use a combination of test results, such as a very high coronavirus antibody titer (over 1:1,600), a high globulin level (a reflection of the activity of the immune system), and a low lymphocyte count (a particular type of white blood cell). If all three of these factors are present, a cat is about 90% likely to be suffering from FIP. The only way to confirm FIP with certainty is by examination of biopsy samples from affected organs. For example, a liver or kidney biopsy may be able to confirm the diagnosis. In many cases, a definitive diagnosis of FIP is not reached until after death, when tissues are submitted for examination during necropsy.

There is no proven successful treatment for FIP. No antiviral drug has been shown to be effective. The majority of patients will be euthanized during their illness. In some cases, palliative therapies may improve quality of life for a short period of time. These include medications such as prednisone to suppress the immune system (because the reaction of the immune system helps cause organ damage in FIP) and supportive care, such as fluid and nutritional support.

Researchers are currently trying to find what factors predispose a small percentage of cats with FECV to the development of FIP. It has been observed that some families of cats seem to be more susceptible to the development of FIP. Interestingly, among other cat species, the cheetah is particularly susceptible to FIP. Three key risk factors seem to be involved: genetic susceptibility, the presence of cats who shed FECV chronically, and cat-dense environments that favor the spread of FECV.

A genetic predisposition to the development of FIP was identified in 1996. The trait is likely polygenetic in nature; that is, it is controlled by more than one gene. Cats who are susceptible to FIP are also likely susceptible to other infections as well, especially fungal and viral infections. This finding gives breeders the ability to achieve success in reducing the risk of FIP by using pedigree analysis to select breeding cats from family backgrounds that have strong resistance to FIP and other infectious diseases.

Research has shown that a small number of cats that become infected with FECV will become persistent shedders of the virus into the environment. They are a source of infection for other cats. Therefore, the key to eliminating FECV (and thus the risk of FIP) in a household or cattery would be the identification and removal or isolation of chronic shedders. Currently there is no easy way to accomplish this. The traditional antibody test for feline coronavirus cannot predict which cats are shedding virus. Newer DNA-based techniques may soon make this type of testing more feasible.

In addition to selecting disease-resistant breeding stock, breeders can initiate husbandry practices that discourage the spread of FECV and the development of FIP. Cat-dense environments favor the transmission of the highly contagious FECV. Ideally, cats in catteries or shelters would be housed singly. However, this is not always possible or desirable, so that the next best choice is to house them in stable groups of three or four cats. Kittens should remain in groups of similar ages and not be mixed with adults in the facility. Any measure that reduces environmental and social stress in the population will also have a beneficial effect.

FECV is a highly contagious virus, spread primarily by the fecal–oral route and, to a lesser degree, through saliva or respiratory droplets. The virus can persist in the environment in dried feces on cat litter for 3–7 weeks, so scrupulous cleaning of cages and litter pans is important to reduce the amount of the virus in the environment. It is also important to have adequate numbers of litter pans available, and they should be scooped at least daily and dumped and disinfected at least weekly. Litter pans should be kept away from food bowls, and spilled litter should be regularly cleaned up from the floor.

Until they are about 6 weeks old, kittens are protected from infection with FECV by antibodies acquired from their mothers. A method of early weaning and isolation of kittens born to FECV-positive queens has been developed. It involves rigorous barrier nursing techniques to prevent the spread of FECV, and so it is not feasible for every breeder or shelter. Kittens are weaned at about 4 or 5 weeks of age and raised in strict isolation until they leave the facility. When properly carried out, breeders can produce FECV-negative kittens for sale as pets. However, the difficulties of controlling FECV spread and issues concerning proper socialization of kittens raised in strict isolation can be considerable barriers.

In 1991, a vaccine against FIP was introduced (Primucell FIP, manufactured by Pfizer Animal Health). The vaccine is an MLV temperature-sensitive mutant that is licensed for IN use in cats 16 weeks of age or older. The vaccine aims to stimulate local immunity and so block the entrance of the virus into the cat's body through antibody production. Evaluation of the risks and benefits associated with this vaccine has been difficult and is the cause of much controversy.

Because FIP is a severe and fatal disease, the safety of any vaccine is of paramount consideration. Recent assessments have concluded that the risks associated with Primucell FIP are minimal in most situations. The vaccine has been in use for several years without any increase in the incidence of FIP. However, troubling reports of a phenomenon called antibody-dependent enhancement (ADE) of infection arose from several researchers. Cats vaccinated against FIP and then experimentally exposed to FIPV developed the disease instead of being protected by the vaccine. It is not known whether the phenomenon of ADE occurs in the real world, and there is no easy way to find out. If it does occur, it is likely an uncommon event.

On the other side of the issue, the protective effects of Primucell FIP appear to be small. Its efficacy is estimated to be between 70% and 75%. Most kittens infected with FECV become infected before 16 weeks of age, the age at which the vaccine is licensed for use. Once a cat is infected with feline coronavirus, the vaccine has no benefit. Some experts have suggested off-label use of the vaccine at ages younger than 16 weeks in catteries or shelters experiencing significant losses to FIP. Certainly, vaccination alone cannot be used to control FIP. In the general cat population, where the overall incidence of FIP is very low, widespread use of the vaccine would not seem to be appropriate.

Congenital Heart Diseases

Congenital heart disease refers to a defect in the heart that is present at birth. This is in contrast to acquired heart disease, where the origins of the disease occur later in life. However, as new technologies allow for more complete investigation, it may be that some common heart diseases, such as hypertrophic cardiomyopathy, are indeed present at birth, although they are not detected until later in life. Congenital heart diseases may be inherited or may be a spontaneous occurrence, so that their presence does not necessarily mean the patient has an inherited disease. Detailed studies are still needed in cats to help determine the cause, genetic or otherwise, of almost all congenital heart diseases. In general, however, it is recommended that cats with an identified congenital heart disease not be used in a breeding program.

While congenital heart diseases account for less than 10% of the heart diseases seen in cats, they are the most common heart diseases seen in cats younger than 1 year. No studies have been carried out to determine the overall occurrence of congenital heart disease in cats, but it is likely that these diseases affect less than 3% of all cats.

SOME CONGENITAL HEART DISEASES IN THE CAT

Valve defects
  Mitral valve dysplasia*
  Tricuspid valve dysplasia*
  Aortic stenosis*
  Pulmonic stenosis
Septal defects
  Ventricular septal defect (VSD)*
  Atrial septal defect (ASD)*
Vascular anomalies
  Patent ductus arteriosus (PDA)
  Persistent right aortic arch (PRAA)
Miscellaneous defects
  Tetralogy of Fallot
  Endocardial fibroelastosis
  Peritoneopericardial diaphragmatic hernia

*Most commonly found diseases

Congenital heart disease may be suspected when a kitten is found to have a heart murmur (short, periodic abnormal sound) during a visit for the initial series of vaccinations. The presence of a murmur does not necessarily mean the kitten has heart disease. Innocent or functional murmurs may be temporarily found in the hearts of young growing kittens. They are not associated with any heart disease and generally disappear by 4 months of age. If the kitten is otherwise healthy, it may be appropriate to wait and see if the murmur disappears.

Murmurs that persist after 4 months of age or that are accompanied by signs of illness are very likely associated with congenital heart disease. Affected kittens may be stunted in growth, lack energy and tire easily, have a fast respiration rate, or suffer from fainting spells (syncope). However, many kittens with congenital heart disease have no symptoms other than a heart murmur.

Diagnosis of congenital heart diseases usually involves generating images of the heart with X-rays or ultrasound (also called echocardiography). In some cases, referral to a facility that can provide ultrasound or that has a veterinary cardiologist on staff may be necessary. Prognosis and treatment very much depend on the diagnosis, with some diseases having a graver prognosis than others.

The anatomy of the feline heart and the pattern of blood flow are the same as for most mammals. The feline heart has four chambers: the left and right atria (singular: *atrium*) and the left and right ventricles. Two atrioventricular valves (the mitral and tricuspid valves) ensure one-way flow of blood between each atrium and its corresponding ventricle. The right atrium is the chamber that receives blood from the large veins of the body (the venae cavae). This oxygen-depleted blood flows through the tricuspid valve into the right ventricle. From there, it is pumped out into the pulmonary artery through the pulmonic valve. The blood then becomes reoxygenated in the lungs (and cleansed of carbon dioxide) and leaves via the pulmonary veins to reenter the heart via the left atrium. It then flows through the mitral valve into the left ventricle. The left ventricle is the main pumping chamber of the heart. As it contracts, blood leaves through the aortic valve into the aorta. Traveling via the aorta and an ever-branching set of arteries, oxygenated blood reaches all body tissues. The process is repeated continuously as blood is collected in the venous system, eventually entering the venae cavae and returning to the heart.

Malformations of the **mitral and tricuspid valves** (also called valvular dysplasias) are one of the most common congenital heart defects seen in cats. The valves may be misshapen or positioned abnormally or may have a variety of other problems. These valvular dysplasias can be present alone or they may be associated with other defects (such as ventricular septal defects). The affected valves cannot function normally and may be associated with a number of changes. A murmur is usually detected and other problems, such as an enlarged heart (cardiomegaly) or, in severe cases, congestive heart failure, may occur. Many mild cases of mitral or tricuspid valve dysplasia are not life-threatening and are not associated with congestive heart failure. More advanced cases may eventually cause heart failure. If this occurs, it is often manageable with medications. At this time, surgical correction of valvular defects is not possible in cats.

The atrioventricular septum is the wall that separates the right and left atria, and the right and left ventricles. A defect, or hole, in the septum between the atria is called an **atrial septal defect** (ASD). A defect in the septum between the ventricles is called a **ventricular septal defect** (VSD). Defects can be small and insignificant, or they may be large and severe. Both ASDs and VSDs are commonly associated with heart murmurs. Small, uncomplicated ASDs or VSDs seem to be well tolerated, and many cats with them lead a normal life. A septal defect can lead to cardiomegaly and, in the worst cases, to congestive heart failure. A cat with a VSD that survives to 6 months of age generally has a good prognosis, because most cats with significant VSDs will experience symptoms of congestive heart failure before this age.

Patent ductus arteriosus (PDA) is not as common in the cat as in the dog. However, it is important because it is one of the few congenital heart diseases that can be surgically corrected. The name of the defect refers to the ductus arteriosus, a structure present in fetal life that permits blood to bypass the lungs, because the fetal lungs are nonfunctional. After birth, the ductus arteriosus closes so that blood is able to flow into the lungs to be oxygenated. However, if the ductus arteriosus fails to close fully, some blood continues to bypass the lungs. Most cats with a PDA will experience cardiomegaly and eventually congestive heart failure. PDA may be an isolated defect or it may be associated with other heart defects in some patients.

The aortic arches are six paired arteries present near the heart during fetal development. Remnants of them persist and help form major arteries in the adult circulatory system. If an aortic arch fails to fully regress, it may cause problems in the chest by forming a ringlike structure that can enclose the trachea and the esophagus. The most common type is a **persistent right aortic arch** (PRAA). When present, it forms a constriction around the esophagus that causes it to dilate. Problems such as regurgitation occur at weaning when kittens begin to eat solid food. The problem is most often diagnosed within the first 6 months of life. PRAA can be successfully corrected surgically in most patients.

Aortic stenosis refers to a narrowing of the pathway whereby blood leaves the left ventricle and enters the aorta. It may involve lesions of the aortic valve or of the aorta itself. It is an uncommon congenital defect in the cat but is sometimes seen in conjunction with other heart anomalies, such as mitral valve dysplasia. Aortic stenosis causes a heart murmur in affected cats and, in severe cases, enlargement of the left side of the heart, which can lead to congestive heart failure. **Pulmonic stenosis** refers to any obstruction of the pathway whereby blood leaves the right ventricle and enters the pulmonary artery. It is also an uncommon defect in the cat. Cats with pulmonic stenosis may live normal lives, or they may develop right-sided congestive heart failure. Diagnosis of both aortic and pulmonic stenosis requires echocardiography. There is no specific surgical or medical treatment for either condition. The prognosis is generally good for patients with mild disease. Patients with more severe disease may require therapy for congestive heart failure.

Tetralogy of Fallot is an uncommon congenital heart disease in the cat that involves multiple defects. It was first identified by, and named for, a French physician (Etienne Fallot, 1850–1911). This defect is composed of four problems: pulmonic stenosis, enlarged right ventricle, a VSD, and an abnormally positioned aorta (so that it receives blood from both the right and left ventricles). Diagnosis is achieved with echocardiography. Some patients with this defect live normally for years, while others suffer from heart failure or sudden death. Surgical correction of the defect is possible and may allow patients to live longer lives. Where surgery is not an option, supportive therapy can be used to improve quality of life.

Peritoneopericardial diaphragmatic hernia is a defect of the diaphragm that allows for communication between the abdomen (peritoneal space) and the pericardial space surrounding the heart. The heart is normally surrounded by a saclike membrane called the pericardium, which covers it loosely. The defect allows some organs from the abdomen to enter the pericardial space, most commonly lobes of the liver. Some cats with this defect have no symptoms of illness at all, while others may have vomiting or difficulty breathing. The diagnosis is reached using X-rays and ultrasound.

Many cats will benefit from surgical correction of the hernia.

Feline Leukemia Virus

FeLV is caused by a retrovirus, the feline leukemia virus. Since its discovery in 1964, FeLV has become known as perhaps the most important infectious disease of cats. Retroviruses are a family of viruses that infect cats and cause disease and death in cats around the world. Another well-known feline retrovirus is FIV. Less well-known retroviruses include feline syncytium-forming virus. Cats can be infected by more than one retrovirus at the same time—for instance, FeLV and FIV together. There is no known human health risk associated with any feline retrovirus.

The prevalence of FeLV varies geographically and also according to population densities. In single-cat households, the prevalence is estimated to be about 3%, but it can be as high as 11% in stray cat populations. In large multicat households and in households where cats roam freely outdoors, the prevalence can be as high as 70%. Cats roaming in urban areas are more likely to be exposed to FeLV (40%) than cats roaming in rural areas (6%).

KEY CHARACTERISTICS OF FELINE LEUKEMIA VIRUS

- It is contagious but does not survive in the environment
- It directly causes both fatal cancerous and noncancerous diseases
- It can lie dormant in the bone marrow for a long time
- It can be protected against by vaccination

Since its discovery, FeLV has been studied extensively, both for its relevance to the cat population and because it serves as an animal model for some human diseases. It is a fragile virus that does not survive in the environment. Ordinary household disinfectants, including bleach, can effectively kill the virus. There is therefore no danger that cats can be exposed to FeLV in veterinary clinic waiting or exam rooms, in hospital cages, at cat shows, or in boarding facilities unless direct contact is made with a positive cat who is shedding virus. Transmission of FeLV requires intimate, moist contact. The most common route is contact with infected saliva through grooming, licking, biting, and sharing dishes. FeLV can also be transmitted through a blood transfusion, so all cats who are blood donors must be screened for FeLV. Kittens can be infected by their mother before birth or during nursing after birth.

OUTCOMES OF FELINE LEUKEMIA VIRUS (FELV) EXPOSURE

- Effective immune response: infection is resisted
- Healthy carrier with persistent infection
- Latent virus in bone marrow: eventually eliminate virus or become persistently infected
- Latent virus in bone marrow: remains as sequestered infection

When a cat is exposed to FeLV, there are four possible outcomes. In about 30% of cats, an effective immune response is produced and the infection is resisted. These cats then become naturally immune to FeLV infection for an unknown period of time. In about 40% of cats, the virus is successful and the cat eventually becomes persistently infected and excretes virus in its saliva. Another 30% of cats do not produce immunity but also do not become persistently infected immediately. In these cats, the virus hides in the bone marrow for up to 30 months. Eventually, these cats either overcome the virus or become persistently infected. Finally, a very small number of cats develop a latent or sequestered infection. In these cats, the virus is hiding in sites such as the bone marrow, and they are rarely contagious. They are unlikely to develop illness and will test negative on routine testing. In general, young cats, especially those under 4 months of age, have the least ability to mount an effective immune response and so are most susceptible to FeLV.

FeLV is capable of producing a wide variety of associated diseases and symptoms. Degenerative diseases, such as anemia, liver disease, intestinal disease, and reproductive problems, can be seen. In other cases, the virus produces cancerous diseases, such as lymphosarcoma and leukemia. Many cats suffer from suppression of the immune system and other illnesses, depending on which organ is involved. Cats whose immune systems are suppressed by FeLV are susceptible to a wide variety of infectious diseases and other problems, such as chronic respiratory infections, chronic gingivitis and stomatitis, FIP, poor healing of wounds and abscesses, and chronic generalized infections.

Testing is the basis for diagnosing and managing FeLV infections in groups of cats. The most common screening test for FeLV is the ELISA (see "Viral Tests," page 352), while the IFA (immunofluorescent antibody) is the most common confirmatory test. Newer DNA-based tests are becoming available, although their reliability and accuracy are yet unknown. Vaccination for FeLV does not affect test results, because the tests look for viral antigens, not antibodies. Kittens can be tested at any age because maternal immunity does not interfere with testing.

The ELISA is the preferred screening test because it is quick and readily available in veterinary clinics. It should be performed on a blood sample, because ELISAs done on tears or saliva have been shown to be unreliable. Any positive or equivocal ELISA test result should be confirmed using the IFA test, which is usually done at a commercial laboratory. It is possible to have results on ELISA and IFA that do not agree for a variety of reasons, including errors in the testing procedures. Veterinarians will follow retesting guidelines to determine the true viral status of any such cats.

The AAFP has published recommendations for FeLV testing. The guidelines state that the FeLV status of all cats should be known because FeLV is responsible for the illness and death of more cats than any other single disease condition. Testing and identifying positive cats is the mainstay of FeLV control in groups of cats and cannot be replaced with vaccination alone. Cats who have had a recent exposure to a cat known to be FeLV-positive should be tested before being added to a household with resident cats. Even if the household does not already have resident cats, new pets should be tested, because the emotional bond that forms between owners and pets justifies knowing any future threats to the pet's health.

Cats who test positive for FeLV may live for months to years. Euthanasia of these cats must be addressed on an individual basis in consultation with a veterinarian. In many cases, it is both possible and feasible to keep an FeLV-positive cat and ensure good quality of life through the combined efforts of the owner and the veterinarian. Positive cats are capable of transmitting their infection to other cats, so they should neither live with other cats nor be allowed to roam outside. This not only protects other cats from FeLV, but also protects the infected cats from the many diseases and illnesses they may contract because of their increased susceptibility.

There is no specific treatment for FeLV and no known cure. A large number of therapies have been investigated for FeLV-positive cats, but most have not shown encouraging results. Antiviral drugs, such as azidothymidine (AZT) show some promise, but are associated with many side effects in cats. A drug that stimulates the immune system, interferon-alpha, can be given orally to cats without side effects and may be helpful in many cases. Experimental protocols have been developed that combine interferon with AZT or another immunostimulant, *Propionibacterium acnes*. Specific cancers associated with FeLV have their own chemotherapy protocols. However, cats with cancer associated with FeLV have an average survival time of 6 months even with aggressive chemotherapy. Drugs that are being developed to treat AIDS in humans are often tested in cats first, so that studies on new drugs against AIDS may produce drugs that we can also use to treat cats with FeLV.

GENERAL CARE RECOMMENDATIONS FOR FELV-POSITIVE CATS

- Protect from exposure to other diseases (keep indoors)
- Ensure good nutrition
- Give regular vaccinations with killed virus vaccines (but not FeLV vaccines)
- Reduce stress
- Control internal and external parasites
- Treat any symptoms of illness early and aggressively

FeLV = feline leukemia virus

The best protection against infectious disease is to eliminate possible exposure. The FeLV test and removal program was developed to remove infected cats from multicat households. Using this program, no new cats are added to the household and all resident cats are tested by IFA (immunofluorescence assay) every 3 months. Any cats with positive results are removed from the household. When every cat tests negative by IFA for two tests in a row, the household is declared free of FeLV. New cats are not admitted to the household without a 3-month waiting period in which they must have negative results for two IFA tests. This program has proven to be very effective for multicat households and catteries affected by FeLV.

There are presently a number of companies that make and sell vaccines against FeLV. Vaccines may be against FeLV only, or they may combine FeLV with other antigens. Many trials have been conducted to compare the effectiveness of the various vaccines, but unfortunately, the study results are hard to interpret, largely because of inconsistencies in study design. On average, FeLV vaccines can prevent infection in about 80% to 90% of cats. The manufacturers recommend that all the vaccines be given as a two-dose regimen spaced 2–4 weeks apart, starting with kittens 8–9 weeks old. Thereafter, annual boosters are recommended because we do not know the duration of immunity from FeLV vaccines.

The AAFP has designated FeLV vaccines as noncore vaccines. Vaccination is recommended only for those cats whose lifestyle places them at risk for FeLV. This includes outdoor cats or those that are indoor-outdoor, feral cats, cats in open multicat households, cats in FeLV-positive households, and cats in households where the FeLV status of all resident cats is not known. Because young cats are at the greatest risk and their lifestyle is most likely to change in the future, it may well be appropriate to suggest initial FeLV vaccination for all kittens, with subsequent annual vaccinations only for those who continue to be at risk. Cat owners should discuss these issues of testing and vaccinating with their veterinarian so that the best decision can be reached for each cat.

Feline Immunodeficiency Virus

FIV was first discovered in 1986 in a cattery in California where some cats appeared to have an illness similar to AIDS in people. Since that time, FIV has been discovered in every country that has tested cats for its presence. It appears likely that FIV has been present in cats for a great many years. The rate of infection in North America varies from about 1% (in healthy cats) to as high as 14% (in sick cats). FIV is sometimes also found in cats who are positive for FeLV.

FIV belongs to the same family of viruses as human immunodeficiency virus (HIV) and immunodeficiency viruses in other species. This family of viruses (Lentivirus) is known for being species-specific, for lifelong infection, and for slowly progressive diseases. FIV is not transmissible from cats to people, and HIV is not transmissible from people to cats.

FIV is known to be present in the blood, saliva, and cerebrospinal fluid of infected cats. However, the virus is extremely fragile and does not survive outside the cat's body. Therefore, the main method of transmission of FIV from one cat to another is through a bite wound during a cat fight. The virus is only rarely spread through casual cat-to-cat contact. However, female cats infected with FIV during their pregnancy can pass the virus to their unborn kittens.

Male cats are twice as likely as female cats to be infected with FIV. This reflects the greater tendency of male cats (especially those not neutered) to roam and fight with other cats. Outdoor, free-roaming cats are more likely to contract FIV than indoor cats. The virus is least common where cats are kept indoors or in rural areas where the cat population density is low. In Japan, for example, where there are a large number of free-roaming cats, the virus is three times more common than in the United States. The average age of infected cats is 3–5 years.

When a cat becomes infected with FIV, there may be no clinical symptoms for many years. However, it is known that 4–6 weeks after infection, the white blood cell count decreases and some cats will have swollen lymph nodes. Also, some cats have a fever, anemia, or diarrhea at this early stage. FIV is toxic to a type of white blood cell, the T-helper cell, which is critical for a healthy immune system. The virus slowly depresses the function of the cat's immune system, leading to chronic health problems and opportunistic infections. Many FIV-positive cats have chronic inflammatory conditions of the teeth and mouth (stomatitis and gingivitis). Other chronic problems, such as diarrhea, pneumonia, skin disease, sinus infections, and some eye diseases as well as neurological problems have been seen in FIV-positive cats.

FIV is diagnosed by testing blood for antibodies. The most common test is an ELISA test, which can be done at a veterinary clinic. Commercial diagnostic laboratories also offer other types of FIV testing. Owners whose cats test positive for FIV using an in-hospital ELISA test should have the results confirmed by another test, such as the Western blot. Veterinarians may want to test a cat for FIV if there are unexplained chronic symptoms of disease. As well, the AAFP recommends testing any cat being introduced to a household with resident cats. Kittens under 6 months of age may carry antibodies to FIV acquired from their mothers without having the virus itself. Therefore, any young kitten who tests positive should be retested when older than 6 months.

There is currently no treatment that has proven effective for FIV. Experimental treatment with some antivirals such as AZT has been promising, but adverse side effects can be a significant problem. FIV-positive cats may also benefit from treatment with interferon-alpha. Therapy primarily revolves around managing the complications of FIV infection. FIV-positive cats may live for many years. With good health care aimed at recognizing and treating FIV-associated problems early, these patients can enjoy good quality of life. All efforts should be taken to preserve their health by protecting them from other diseases and injuries. This is best accomplished by requiring FIV-positive cats to live indoors; this also helps prevent spread of the disease. FIV-positive cats should also receive regular vaccinations with KV vaccines against the diseases they have a significant risk of contracting.

In 2002, a vaccine developed against FIV was released (Fel-O-Vax FIV, manufactured by Fort Dodge Animal Health). The release of this vaccine may cause confusion when cats are tested for FIV because it is unlikely that currently available antibody tests can distinguish a naturally infected cat from a vaccinated cat. DNA-based tests for FIV have yet to be validated as reliable.

1 TO 8 YEARS (YOUNG ADULT TO MIDDLE AGE)

Inflammatory Bowel Disease

Gastrointestinal disorders are among the most commonly encountered problems in feline medicine. Many vomiting and/or diarrhea episodes occur suddenly but resolve quickly. The causes are most often benign, such as eating an unfamiliar food. However, some patients may have vomiting and/or diarrhea over a period of weeks to months. The symptoms may be present every day or they may be intermittent. In the diagnosis of chronic disease, veterinarians first rule out other possible causes of the symptoms using blood tests, fecal examinations, X-rays, and possibly other tests. It is important to ensure that the patient is not suffering from an illness such as chronic kid-

ney failure, pancreatitis, or hyperthyroidism that can also cause vomiting and diarrhea.

SOME CAUSES OF CHRONIC VOMITING AND/OR DIARRHEA IN CATS

Gastrointestinal Causes	Nongastrointestinal Causes
• Food intolerance	• Hyperthyroidism
• Food allergy	• Kidney failure
• Intestinal parasites	• Pancreatic disease
• Inflammatory bowel disease	• Liver disease
• Intestinal cancer	• Diseases related to feline leukemia virus/ feline immuno-deficiency virus
• *Helicobacter* gastritis	• Cancer (other than intestinal)
• Infectious diseases, such as Salmonella	• Diabetes mellitus

Inflammatory bowel disease (IBD) is one of the most common causes of chronic gastrointestinal disease. It is actually a group of gastrointestinal disorders that are characterized by an increase in the number of inflammatory cells found in the lining (mucosa) of the stomach or intestinal tract. The type of inflammatory cells present determines the type of IBD. The most common type is lymphocytic-plasmacytic gastroenteritis or colitis. Gastroenteritis indicates inflammation of the stomach and small intestine. Colitis indicates inflammation of the colon. Patients with colitis often have blood or mucus in the stools and have pain or difficulty with bowel movements. The causes of IBD are variable and not fully understood. Often no single cause can be identified in a given patient. Some suggested causes include immune-mediated disease and genetic influences.

The most common patient with IBD is middle-aged or older. The average age of affected cats is 8 years, but it has been diagnosed in kittens as young as 5 months. The symptoms include chronic vomiting, diarrhea, or both, and in some cases, weight loss and changes in appetite. Some patients may defecate outside the litter box, especially if diarrhea is present. On examination, most cats with IBD appear normal, although some will have weight loss. The symptoms may be intermittent, with the cat appearing to be normal at times. It is not unusual for these patients' condition to be misdiagnosed as the presence of hairballs.

SYMPTOMS OF INFLAMMATORY BOWEL DISEASE

- Vomiting (most common)
- Diarrhea
- Weight loss
- Poor appetite
- Increased appetite (uncommon)

Before arriving at a diagnosis of IBD, it is important to rule out other gastrointestinal causes of vomiting and diarrhea. A hypoallergenic diet should be tried for 8–10 weeks. Attempts should be made to rule out intestinal infections and parasites. This may involve special fecal examinations and cultures and deworming with broad-spectrum dewormers.

A definitive diagnosis of IBD is only possible by intestinal biopsy. This is best accomplished using fiberoptic endoscopy, which is less invasive than exploratory surgery. This technology allows veterinarians to diagnose and treat many gastrointestinal disorders more easily than in the past. The endoscope is an instrument that allows visualization of the stomach and intestinal tract through a flexible tube that is passed into either the patient's stomach or colon. The tube contains fiberoptic bundles that deliver bright light to its tip and transmit images back into an eyepiece. Small but adequate biopsies (about the size of this capital letter O) can be taken using this instrument. The procedure is performed under a short-acting general anesthetic, with most patients able to return home the same day. Because endoscopic procedures are minimally invasive and short in duration, they are less traumatic to the patient and recovery time is quicker than after surgical biopsies.

IBD is considered a controllable but not necessarily curable disease. Goals of therapy are to decrease the inflammation and prevent pain and discomfort for the cat. Treatment is also aimed at preventing possible complications of the disease, such as liver disease, malnutrition, and possibly the future development of lymphoma. Many medications can be used to control IBD. Corticosteroids (such as prednisone) are the drugs of choice and are combined with dietary therapy. All cats with IBD should be fed a digestible hypoallergenic diet. In addition to corticosteroids and dietary therapy, some cats may require other drugs, such as metronidazole or stronger immunosuppressants. Cats who suffer from colitis alone may benefit from a high-fiber diet and sulfasalazine, a drug that reduces inflammation in the colon. Once drug therapy is started for IBD, it is usually continued for 2–3 months before attempts are made to decrease the dosages. In some patients, the disease is eventually manageable with dietary therapy alone, but relapses can and do occur.

Feline Asthma

Feline asthma has been called by many other names, including chronic bronchitis, bronchial asthma, and allergic bronchitis. Regardless of the name, it is a common feline ailment. Inhaled allergens cause sudden contraction of the smooth muscles around airways, leading to typical clinical symptoms. It is usually impossible to determine which allergens cause asthma in individual cats, but common ones include grass and tree pollens, cigarette or fireplace smoke, various sprays (hair sprays, deodorants, flea sprays, deodorizers), and dust from cat litter. It is also possible that food allergies are involved in a few cases.

Feline asthma is found in all areas of the world and in cats of all ages. The prevalence in the general adult cat population is about 1%. The most common symptoms in cats with asthma are wheezing and coughing. The cough has been described as dry hacking that could be confused with gagging or retching. Paroxysms of coughing occur frequently. Severely affected cats will be lethargic, which can lead to obesity. In mildly affected cats, coughing and wheezing may occur only occasionally. A few cats with asthma are asymptomatic in between acute and severe bouts of airway constriction. The most severely affected cats have daily coughing and wheezing and many bouts of airway constriction, leading to open-mouth breathing and panting that can be life-threatening.

The symptoms of asthma can mimic other diseases, such as pneumonia, heartworm infection, and congestive heart failure. A diagnosis is reached by using chest X-rays, a CBC, a heartworm test, and one of several techniques to sample cells from the lower airways (transtracheal wash, bronchial wash, or bronchoalveolar lavage). Chest X-ray findings may be normal in some cats with asthma, while others will have signs of bronchial inflammation, collapse of the right middle lung lobe, and hyperinflation of the lungs.

Unfortunately, feline asthma is a chronic progressive disease that cannot be fully cured. Medications can reduce the symptoms of asthma a great deal but may not fully eliminate cough-

ing. Some severely affected cats will eventually develop fibrosis and emphysema, which have a poor prognosis. The drug of choice for feline asthma is a corticosteroid, such as prednisone or injectable methylprednisolone acetate. These drugs are potent anti-inflammatories, and many cats can eventually go to low, alternate-day oral doses or occasional injectable doses. Chronic use of corticosteroids, especially at high doses, is associated with a number of adverse effects in cats. Predisposed cats may suffer from diabetes mellitus or chronic infections, among other problems.

A bronchodilator, such as theophylline or terbutaline, may be given as well to help prevent constriction of the airways. Some cats require treatment with a third drug, cyproheptadine, to help control inflammation if a corticosteroid and a bronchodilator together are not sufficient. Inflammation in the feline lung is mediated by serotonin, and cyproheptadine has antiserotonin effects. About 25% of cats with asthma also have a bacterial or mycoplasmal infection of the lungs, and so antibiotics may be prescribed for these patients. Newer human asthma drugs that counteract inflammation in a different manner, such as zafirlukast (Accolate, manufactured by AstraZeneca) and montelukast (Singulair, manufactured by Merck), are being explored as possible treatments for feline asthma. It is important to note that certain drugs, especially the beta-blocker drugs (such as propranolol and atenolol) used to treat some heart diseases, cannot be given to asthmatic cats.

An exciting development in the treatment of feline asthma is the discovery that cats can benefit from inhaler-based medications. A mask and chamber system has been designed and marketed for cats (AeroKat; http://www.aerokat.com). It is based on the mask and chamber systems used for human children. This system allows cats to inhale corticosteroid medications such as Flovent (GlaxoSmithKline) and bronchodilators as well. Inhaled medications may prove to be more effective in treating feline asthma and will likely avoid the side effects that can be associated with oral or injectable corticosteroid use.

Some actions can be taken in the home to reduce the symptoms of feline asthma. Avoiding smoke from fireplaces and cigarettes is very important. This type of smoke tends to settle near the floor in a room at the cat's breathing level. Reducing the use of air fresheners and other household sprays can also be effective. Use human grooming products that are in spray form, such as hair sprays or deodorants, well away from the affected cat. Change to a low-dust clay cat litter or one that is made of an alternate material. Any activity that is associated with symptoms of asthma in the individual cat, such as going outside in cold weather, should be avoided. Finally, obese cats will benefit from weight reduction.

Cardiomyopathy

The most common heart diseases in cats are the cardiomyopathies—literally, heart (*cardio*) muscle (*myo*) disease (*pathy*). Several forms of cardiomyopathy are known to exist in the cat, but only hypertrophic cardiomyopathy is seen with any frequency.

TYPES OF CARDIOMYOPATHY IN THE CAT

Type	Characteristics
Dilated (uncommon since 1987, when commercial diets had taurine levels increased)	• Severe enlargement of both ventricles with thin ventricular walls • Pulmonary edema, pleural effusion can develop • Risk of blood clot formation • Associated with taurine deficiency • Poor prognosis
Hypertrophic (most common feline heart disease)	• Thickened ventricular walls with or without left atrial enlargement • Pulmonary edema, pleural effusion can develop • Risk of blood clot formation • Irregular heartbeats (arrhythmias) • More common in males than females • Prognosis for most patients is good
Restrictive (or intermediate—uncommon)	• Poorly understood • Right atrium and ventricle enlarged; left ventricular wall thickened; left atrium enlarged • Pulmonary edema, pleural effusion can develop • Risk of blood clot formation • Prognosis is guarded

Hypertrophic cardiomyopathy (HCM) is the most common heart disease in the cat. It is found not only in pedigreed cats but commonly in nonpedigreed cats of all backgrounds as well. This disease is not fully understood in the cat, but recent research is helping to provide some answers as to possible genetic causes and the different subtypes of HCM seen in cats. Similar types of heart disease also occur in cats with hyperthyroidism and hypertension (high blood pressure), but HCM specifically refers to the presence of the characteristic changes with no immediately identifiable cause.

HCM means the heart muscle is increased in size, or hypertrophied. The left ventricle is the main pumping chamber of the heart and it is most significantly affected by HCM. The thickened chamber is then unable to pump efficiently and becomes stiff, somewhat like an inflexible, muscle-bound body builder might be. As the disease progresses, secondary changes set in, such as enlargement of the left atrium. Heart murmurs are often, but not always, detectable. Further progression can lead to heart failure, characterized by fluid accumulation in the lungs (pulmonary edema) or within the chest itself (pleural effusion). When the left atrium enlarges in size, the heart is predisposed to irregular rhythms, which can be fatal. Blood clots easily form within the enlarged left atrium where they can break free and enter the main circulation, eventually causing a blockage of blood flow in a smaller blood vessel. This is called a thromboembolism and typically affects blood flow to the hind legs (where it is called a saddle thrombus), causing an acute and painful paralysis.

The typical patient with HCM is a middle-aged male cat. About 75% of patients are males, for reasons that are not fully understood. Ages can range from 8 months to over 13 years, but the mean age is about 6 years. After being found to have HCM, many cats live years with good management and monitoring. The disease is progressive, but it progresses at different rates in different patients. The symptoms of HCM vary widely. Many times, the disease is diagnosed because a veterinarian found an unexpected heart murmur or an arrhythmia during a routine checkup. It may not be diagnosed in other cats until they are in heart failure and present with collapse and difficulty breathing. Unfortunately, many cats with HCM have no warning symptoms at all and may simply die suddenly and unexpectedly, usually from a fatal arrhythmia.

Diagnosis of HCM is accomplished by using various tests, including X-rays, electrocardiography (ECG), and most important, echocardiography (ultrasound of the heart). There are typical changes seen on an echocardiogram that confirm the diagnosis and indicate the degree of severity. The characteristics of each cat's own changes will help determine which medications will be most beneficial. In addition, blood testing is done to rule out other causes of similar heart diseases, such as hyperthyroidism, and blood pressure measurements are done to rule out hypertension.

Treatment measures depend on the stage of the disease. Seriously ill cats in heart failure may require hospitalization and critical care. Fluid can be drained from the chest to help ease breathing. Oxygen can be administered if necessary. All efforts are made to avoid stressing these patients, whose condition can be fragile. Cats with thromboembolism are the most seriously ill and require drug therapy to relieve pain and restore blood flow. There are many different cardiac drugs available to treat feline heart disease: calcium channel blockers such as diltiazem, beta-blockers such as atenolol, and angiotensin-converting enzyme inhibitors such as enalapril. Other drugs used to treat HCM include aspirin, to decrease the formation of blood clots, and furosemide, to reduce fluid accumulation in the lungs and chest. It is entirely possible that a cat and its owner may be taking the same heart medication.

In recent years, it has been recognized that certain breeds have a high familial incidence of HCM. Those most prominently affected are the Maine Coon, Persian, and American Shorthair. However, it is very important to understand that any pedigreed or nonpedigreed cat can have HCM. The Maine Coon breed has been most extensively researched, and the disease is inherited in a dominant fashion in that breed (that is, only one parent need carry the defective gene to produce an affected kitten). The disease becomes apparent in affected cats as early as 6 months of age, although it may be delayed until 2 or 3 years of age. Male cats are more seriously affected and tend to get symptoms of disease earlier. Most affected cats will develop heart failure by 4 years of age, and sudden death does occur. Currently, breeders are using ultrasound screening to try to identify breeding stock clear of HCM. It is recommended that male cats be screened at 2 years of age and female cats be screened later, perhaps at 3 or 4 years of age.

Feline Hip Dysplasia

Until very recently, veterinarians and breeders felt that cats were free of the hip dysplasia problems so common in many large dog breeds. New information and research, however, has shown that this disease does exist in the cat and is likely an inherited disorder. As in the dog, no one gene in the cat seems responsible for the problem. Rather, a complex interplay of several genetic factors is probably involved.

Dysplasia is a term that means abnormal development of a tissue. The hip is a ball-and-socket type of joint, where the ball is at the top of the thighbone (head of the femur) and the socket is a depression in the pelvis called the acetabulum. Normally, the head of the femur fits very snugly into the acetabulum, allowing for efficient and smooth joint function. In hip dysplasia, parts of the hip joint are abnormally shaped, so that the fit of the ball into the socket is poor. This means the head of the femur can move out of place to some variable degree (called subluxation). Over time, chronic changes develop due to the subluxation, and degenerative joint disease can result.

In many cats with hip dysplasia, the condition goes undetected. Cats are naturally agile, have a relatively small body size, and are not exercised as much or as vigorously as dogs. These factors make detection of hip dysplasia more difficult for the owner. The more severely affected cats will have obvious symptoms and experience joint pain. They may appear to be stiff when they walk and they may become reluctant to jump or climb objects. Occasionally, they may appear to be lame. In many cases, the symptoms of hip dysplasia do not appear until the cat has suffered some traumatic event, such as a fall.

Veterinarians who suspect hip dysplasia in a cat will diagnose the disease using X-rays. Many cats with mild cases will not require any treatment at all. If an affected cat is obese, weight reduction will be recommended. Several different treatments are available for cats who have pain and discomfort from moderate to severe hip dysplasia. Veterinarians prescribe anti-inflammatory medications and pain-relief medications, as well as dietary supplements designed to improve joint health for these patients. Restricting exercise in outdoor cats and limiting the ability of indoor cats to climb or use stairs is also helpful. For severely affected cats, veterinarians may recommend a surgical procedure called a femoral head and neck excision arthroplasty. This surgery removes the damaged and painful tissue and allows the cat to return to normal function, free of pain and discomfort.

It is predictable that the largest, heaviest breeds of cats are likely to be more at risk for hip dysplasia. Hip dysplasia has been noted in some pedigreed breeds of cat but is also found in nonpedigreed cats as well. It is not confined to any one breed or type of cat. A condition in which the kneecap moves out of place easily (patellar luxation) is often associated with hip dysplasia in cats.

Just as dog breeders can use screening tests for their breeding stock, cat breeders now can screen breeding cats. The most common screening test is an X-ray taken according to strict specifications that is then submitted to the Hip Dysplasia Registry of the Orthopedic Foundation for Animals (OFA) at the University of Missouri (http://www.offa.org). OFA veterinarians who are orthopedic specialists examine the X-rays and assign a grade to the cat's hips. Preliminary examinations can be done on cats younger than 2 years, but a final certification is not issued until a cat is over 2 years old. Breeders can use the certification to determine which cats are best selected for breeding.

Another method of screening hips for cats and dogs, called PennHip, was developed at the University of Pennsylvania (http://www.vet.upenn.edu/research/centers/pennhip//). This method uses a different X-ray procedure designed to measure the degree of laxity, or looseness, in the hip joint. Researchers at the University of Pennsylvania have used this system to evaluate cats for hip dysplasia. One of the first tasks in this type of research is to establish a database of what constitutes normal hips in a cat. Only then can veterinarians use screening systems to determine if an individual hip is normal or abnormal.

Polycystic Kidney Disease

Feline polycystic kidney disease (PKD) is a disorder in which normal kidney tissue is displaced by the growth of fluid-filled cysts. Cysts start as very small structures, just a few millimeters or less in size, and grow progressively larger. As they grow, they begin to impair kidney function and can lead eventually to kidney failure. The rate at which cysts grow appears to be quite variable; in mild cases, cysts may stay small for the life of the cat and cause little kidney dysfunction, but in severe cases kidney failure will develop at a young age.

While reports of PKD appeared in the literature in the late 1960s, the disease was not studied extensively until 1990. Work with a research colony of related Persian and Persian-type cats demonstrated that feline PKD is a disease inherited in a dominant fashion (that is, only one parent need carry the defective gene to produce an affected kitten). This research also characterized the disease more accurately, showing that the cysts are actually present from birth in affected cats. Older cats will have larger and more numerous cysts than younger cats. Typically, signs of kidney failure will occur between the ages of 3 and 7 years, although some very mildly affected cats may never experience kidney failure. Symptoms of kidney failure include weight loss, poor appetite, increased thirst, increased urination, and depression.

Blood and urine tests are used to establish the diagnosis of kidney failure in affected cats. Because kidney failure can have several different causes, definitive tests must be performed to confirm PKD. Palpation of the kidneys in affected cats usually shows the kidneys are enlarged, and X-rays will confirm this. Other diseases can also cause enlargement of the kidneys, especially lymphoma, so ultrasound is used to demonstrate the presence of the cysts typical of PKD. Ultrasound is a noninvasive diagnostic tool that can detect the presence of even very small cysts in apparently healthy cats who may be at risk of developing PKD. For this reason, ultrasound can be used as a screening tool, in conjunction with pedigree analysis, for breeders to examine their breeding cats.

As for most causes of kidney failure, there is no cure for PKD. Treatment is the same as for any other cause of chronic kidney failure and is aimed at stabilizing the patient's condition and reducing the effects of the disease. Diets low in protein and phosphorus are a mainstay of treatment for kidney failure. Secondary changes, such as increased blood phosphorus levels, anemia, or low potassium levels, can occur with kidney failure and these complications are treated specifically if they occur. Kidney failure patients may remain stable for considerable periods of time, or they may be in fragile health. Regular monitoring, both with physical examinations and periodic blood and urine testing, is essential for effective treatment of these patients.

In theory, it should be possible to eliminate PKD from breeding cats by neutering and spaying affected cats. However, widespread ultrasound screening of cats in the United States in recent years has shown that ultrasound results may be hard to interpret when the cysts are solitary or very small in size. Variations in the quality of ultrasound equipment and in the expertise of the ultrasonographer account for some of the problems. As well, the best age to screen breeding stock has yet to be definitively established. Mildly affected cats may pass ultrasound screening at a young age but be found positive for PKD as they get older. As more data is accumulated and more research is carried out, it may be possible to resolve these questions.

Amyloidosis

Amyloidosis is actually a diverse group of diseases seen in many species of animals. In all of these diseases, a type of protein is deposited in major body organs that eventually leads to impairment of organ function and illness or death. In cats, amyloidosis usually occurs infrequently. However, veterinarians have known since the early 1980s that the Abyssinian breed has an unusually high rate of amyloidosis. In recent years, some oriental-type breeds have also been identified as susceptible. Research on the disease has demonstrated that amyloidosis is an inherited disease, but the mode of inheritance has been very difficult to determine. As well, it is suspected that environmental stresses and the response of the immune system also play some role in the development of amyloidosis.

Amyloidosis in Abyssinians primarily attacks the kidneys, but deposits of amyloid protein have also been found in other organs, such as the adrenal and thyroid glands, the stomach and intestines, the liver, and the heart. In oriental-type breeds, amyloidosis primarily attacks the liver. DNA sequencing of the amyloid proteins found in different breeds has confirmed that these proteins are different from one another, suggesting that there are different genes responsible.

In Abyssinians, the disease has a variable presentation in affected cats. Only those cats with moderate to severe disease usually become ill, which is when the disease is detected. Symptoms are the same as those of chronic kidney failure: weight loss, poor appetite, increased thirst and urination, and depression. The disease is typically diagnosed when the patient is between the ages of 3 and 5 years. However, amyloid deposits have been found in the kidneys of older cats who died of other causes and never showed signs of kidney disease. Yet some of these cats produced offspring confirmed with amyloidosis.

Blood and urine testing is used to confirm kidney failure as the cause of illness in affected Abyssinians. However, amyloidosis can be confirmed as the cause only by kidney biopsy. There is no foolproof way to detect mildly affected cats who may not show signs of kidney failure. Work on a blood test that can be used for screening has not proven fruitful. However, new research proposes to use DNA technology to find the gene or genes responsible for the disease and thus provide a genetic test to identify affected individuals. This will give breeders a screening tool for breeding cats so that kittens can be checked and predisposed cats can be eliminated from breeding.

In susceptible oriental-type breeds, amyloidosis primarily affects the liver, leading to sudden episodes of hemorrhage from the swollen liver. Sudden death is frequently seen, and there may be no warning signs. The few cats who survive an episode of hemorrhage from the liver may go on to develop kidney failure later in life, as is seen in Abyssinians.

The typical patient with the oriental form of amyloidosis is younger than 5 years. Both males and females are equally affected. The only test available to confirm the disease in suspected cases is liver biopsy or by examination of tissues at necropsy. Unfortunately, there is no definitive treatment for cats presenting with this form of amyloidosis. Cats suffering from sudden liver hemorrhage may survive with aggressive supportive care, which can include blood transfusions, intravenous fluid therapy, and vitamin K supplementation.

Lower Urinary Tract Disease

It has been estimated that up to 1% of all cats in the United States suffer from lower urinary tract disease. One survey showed that up to 9% of cats taken to veterinarians in Japan also suffer from this problem. Feline lower urinary tract disease (FLUTD) is actually a group of problems found in the bladder and urethra of the cat. Various terms have been used in the past to try to describe this group of conditions. Two common terms are FUS (feline urologic syndrome) and FLUTD (feline lower urinary tract disease). The confusion over what name to use reflects the confusing and changing nature of the problem in the cat. As far back as the 1930s, veterinarians commonly saw signs of lower urinary tract disease in cats. Today, this disease remains one of the most challenging and frustrating problems in feline medicine.

Regardless of the cause, there are common signs seen in cats with FLUTD. They can include hematuria, dysuria, pollakiuria, and urinating outside the litter box. Some conditions can also lead to partial or total urethral obstruction, which can be an emergency situation. Obstruction (or blockage) is more commonly found in male cats because of their narrower urethra. However, most cats with FLUTD do not have an obstruction and are brought to the veterinarian for one of the other signs. The typical FLUTD patient is young to middle-aged and can be of either gender.

Veterinarians will perform a thorough physical examination on cats who have symptoms of FLUTD and take a detailed medical history from the owner, including the type of diet the cat is fed. The bladder is palpated for thickenings, fullness, and possible bladder stones. Because many cats urinate in inappropriate places in response to both behavioral and medical problems, one of the first tasks is to determine what type of problem exists. At the least, a urinalysis is usually performed. In other cases, more diagnostic testing must be done, such as blood work, urine cultures, X-rays, or ultrasound of the urinary tract.

A urinalysis is performed to check for the presence of crystals, bacteria, blood, and glucose (as in diabetes) and the concentration (or specific gravity) and pH (measure of acidity or alkalinity) of the urine. Recent studies have found that the stress of taking a cat outside its home for a trip to the veterinarian can lead to rapid changes in the urine pH. In some cases, a veterinarian may recommend ways to collect a urine sample at home using products such as a synthetic litter that will not absorb urine but allow it to be collected. Once urine is collected, whether at home or in the clinic, it should be analyzed within 60 minutes for the results to be accurate.

Determining the significance of crystals in the urine of a cat can be problematic. It is known that many normal cats have small numbers of crystals in their urine. On the other hand, up to 50% of cats who have bladder stones may have no evidence of crystals at all in their urine test results. Generally, only moderate to severe crystalluria is considered significant and is treated. These cases are usually dietary in origin and identifying the type of crystal present is necessary to pick the right therapeutic diet.

While there are many types of crystals in feline urine, the most common are struvite (magnesium ammonium phosphate) and calcium oxalate. These crystal types each require different dietary therapy. Struvite crystals typically form in urine that is too alkaline (pH too high) and are more common in younger cats. Calcium oxalate crystals form in urine that is too acid (pH too low).

If the cause of the cat's symptoms is not readily identified with a urinalysis, other testing may be necessary. A urine culture is used to check for bacterial infection, although this is present in less than 5% of FLUTD cases. Blood work is done to check for other diseases that can also influence the urinary tract, such as diabetes, hyperthyroidism, and kidney failure. Radiographs (X-rays) or ultrasound are used to identify bladder uroliths (stones), anatomical defects, or tumors.

Therapy for FLUTD is directed against the underlying factors discovered during testing. Prescribing the appropriate therapeutic diet treats significant crystalluria. If a positive bacterial culture has been found, antibiotics are prescribed. Anatomical defects may require surgical repair. Bladder tumors are rare in cats and may require surgery or chemotherapy. Various other medications can be used to decrease the pain and irritation associated with FLUTD.

A urolith is a stonelike object that can be found in the bladder or, less commonly, in the kidney of cats (where it is often called a nephrolith). Some studies have shown that up to 13% of cats with FLUTD have uroliths. They can be present without causing any symptoms in the cat, but they are very often associated with hematuria, pollakiuria, and dysuria. In some cases, uroliths can be responsible for partial or total obstruction of the urethra, especially in male cats.

Uroliths are formed of minerals plus some organic, mucuslike material. Cats can have several different types of uroliths, but the two most common types are struvite and calcium oxalate. In the past, the most common type was struvite. However, since the 1990s, the number of calcium oxalate uroliths has increased so that now the two types occur with almost equal frequency. Changes in formulation of commercial feline diets are suspected to be the cause of this increase, for the acidic diets that discourage formation of struvite uroliths and crystals can actually encourage formation of calcium oxalate uroliths in some cats.

Struvite uroliths can be found in both male and female cats, but female cats seem to be at higher risk. The highest risk cat is the female between the ages of 1 and 2 years. The mean age for all affected cats is 5 years, but kittens as young as 1 month and cats as old as 20 years have been found to have struvite uroliths. When struvite uroliths are found in very young kittens, the cause is usually a bacterial infection. In older cats, bacterial infections usually do not play a role.

Calcium oxalate uroliths affect males a bit more frequently than females. The risk for this type of urolith increases with age. The patient with the greatest risk is the 10- to 15-year-old neutered male cat. Researchers are attempting to determine if high blood calcium levels are associated with calcium oxalate uroliths, especially in those predisposed breeds. Bacterial infections are usually not associated with calcium oxalate uroliths.

Management and prevention of uroliths depends on the type of urolith and the current state of the patient. If a cat is experiencing a partial or total obstruction, emergency treatment to relieve the obstruction is required. Urethral obstructions can also be caused by an accumulation of crystals and mucus, forming a urethral plug. Cats with urinary obstructions are often dehydrated, have electrolyte and acid–base imbalances, and have increased levels of waste products in their bloodstream from compromise of kidney function. If left untreated, these cats can experience heart or kidney damage as well as bladder damage, and even death. A cat with a total urethral obstruction will die in 2–4 days if not treated.

Typical treatment for a urethral obstruction revolves around stabilizing the patient's condition, correcting any metabolic imbalances, and restoring the flow of urine from the bladder. The urethra is catheterized and intravenous fluid therapy is started. Blood and urine tests are done to determine the patient's status and guide further treatment. Any uroliths or crystals recovered from the urethra are analyzed. Most cats require several days of

hospitalization for recovery. After the patient is stabilized, testing might be done to determine if uroliths are present in the bladder.

X-rays can detect many uroliths. Single or multiple uroliths can be present. However, some uroliths do not show up well on X-rays, or they may be too small to be detected. Feline uroliths are often flattened, much like the shape and size of a dime, although they can be pebblelike as well. In some cases, a bladder ultrasound is the best method of detection. In other cases, or where ultrasound is not available, special X-rays may be done that involve injecting a contrast agent (such as a dye) into the bladder.

It can be almost impossible to determine what type of urolith is present from only an X-ray or ultrasound. It takes surgical removal of the urolith through an incision in the bladder (called a cystotomy) and analysis of the urolith by a laboratory to determine the type for sure. Struvite uroliths can often be dissolved with a therapeutic diet called Feline Prescription Diet s/d (Hill's Pet Nutrition). It can take up to 4 months of feeding this diet exclusively to dissolve the urolith. During this time, the original symptoms of the problem may still occur. Calcium oxalate uroliths cannot be medically dissolved. For these reasons, many cat owners opt for surgical removal and analysis of the uroliths instead of dietary dissolution. This has the advantage of correct identification of the urolith type (which is important to prevent recurrences) and a quicker resolution of the problem for the cat.

Just as for crystalluria, cats who have had a urolith are always at risk for future occurrences. However, dietary management can prevent both struvite and calcium oxalate uroliths. Struvite prevention diets typically aim to produce mildly acidic urine, while calcium oxalate prevention diets produce slightly alkaline urine. There are several commercially prepared diets on the market for each type of urolith or crystal. Before acidified diets were commercially available, cats were usually given an acidifier in pill or gel form. Dietary therapy is a safer way to accomplish this. Occasionally, cats with calcium oxalate uroliths may need other measures in addition to dietary therapy (such as some medications) to prevent recurrences. In general, canned diets do a better job of preventing future problems than dry diets because they encourage more water consumption.

Increasingly, many cats are found to have moderate to severe signs of FLUTD without having a readily identifiable cause. They typically have hematuria but no bacterial infection. They do not have tumors, anatomical defects, or bladder stones. The term *interstitial* or *idiopathic cystitis* (IC), borrowed from human medicine where a similar condition afflicts women, has been used to describe these cats. The only way to confirm the diagnosis is by examination of the bladder using a procedure called cystoscopy or a biopsy. Many cases are tentatively diagnosed after all other possible conditions have been ruled out.

Therapy for IC is still evolving as more is learned about the disease. No one therapy has been found that helps all cats. One approach is to use a drug such as amitriptyline, which has many valuable qualities. It decreases the pain associated with the condition and also can decrease inflammation in the bladder. However, it may also be associated with adverse effects in some cats. Corticosteroids such as prednisone, or nonsteroidal anti-inflammatories such as ketoprofen, are also sometimes used to decrease inflammation. Other types of drugs, such as pentosan polysulfate or glucosamine and chondroitin sulfate (Cosequin, manufactured by Nutramax), are used to help repair the lining of the bladder. Feeding canned diets rather than dry diets may also be helpful.

No matter what type of therapy is used, it is important to decrease any stress factors as much as possible because stress seems to exacerbate the disease. Feeding stations and litter boxes should be located away from sources of stress, such as noisy appliances, heating and cooling ducts, and other pets. Any changes in diet or litter type should be made slowly and cautiously, with the old food or litter still available until the new choice is accepted. Providing a place for these cats to feel safe and secure, such as a bed in a quiet location, is also helpful. A promising new therapy involves the use of a synthetic cat pheromone spray (Feliway, manufactured by Veterinary Products Laboratories). This product may have a calming and stress-reducing effect for some cats. To some degree, the episodes of IC seem to be self-limiting and most resolve after 3–7 days, only to return again in the future.

Chin Acne and Stud Tail

Chin acne and stud tail are two related skin conditions seen in cats. On the top surface of the tail near its base and on the chin are glands in the skin called sebaceous glands. These glands produce an oily secretion called sebum. The function of sebum is to keep the skin and coat in good condition. In addition, cats probably use the secretion from these sebaceous glands to mark territory. Many cat owners have noticed their cats rubbing the chin or base of the tail on convenient objects for this purpose. When the sebaceous glands become overactive, they produce an excessive amount of sebum, potentially leading to chin acne or stud tail.

Chin acne is probably quite common, and many mild cases go unnoticed. Most commonly, pet owners notice the formation of blackheads, or comedones, on the chin. Secondary bacterial infections can occur, leading to folliculitis and formation of pustules. The chin itself may become quite swollen. A few cases of chin acne are caused by dermatophytosis (ringworm), yeast infection (*Malassezia*), or a parasite called *Demodex*. The veterinarian will want to rule out these potential underlying causes by performing some diagnostic tests, such as skin scrapings and cultures.

Treatment of chin acne may involve gentle daily cleansing of the skin using a product containing 2.5% benzoyl peroxide. A topical treatment consisting of either an antibiotic or an antibiotic and steroid combination may be prescribed by the veterinarian. Common topical antibiotics include clindamycin and mupirocin. While it has been traditional to advise removal of plastic food dishes to control chin acne in cats, there is no proof that this is an effective strategy.

Stud tail is most common in intact mature male cats, but it is also sometimes seen in female cats and in neutered male cats. It is characterized by greasiness, crusting of the skin, and matting of the fur on the top of the tail. Mild cases of both chin acne and stud tail may cause the cat no discomfort, but moderate to severe cases are accompanied by inflammation and irritation.

Control of stud tail can be accomplished by several methods to reduce the accumulation of sebum. A shampoo containing sulfur and salicylic acid may be recommended by the veterinarian for this purpose. Other products designed for this purpose include D'Grease by PurePet and MalAcetic Wet Wipes/Dry Bath by DermaPet. Some success may be achieved by using topical products that are not intentionally designed for this purpose, such as dishwashing detergent or GOOP hand cleaner. A veterinarian should be consulted before any topical product is used, especially those not originally intended for use on cats. Severe cases of stud tail may also be associated with bacterial infection, and treatment involves the same antibiotics used for chin acne.

8 YEARS AND OLDER (GERIATRIC CATS)

The proportion of the feline population over 6 years of age almost doubled between 1983 and 1996. The average life span for most cats is now about 15 years, although many cats live to be 20 or even older. Advances in the control and treatment of infectious diseases and a better understanding of nutritional needs for cats have been major contributors to this phenomenon. The development of screening tests for diseases common in this age group have enabled veterinarians to detect diseases earlier and treat them better. Most cat owners are committed to quality care in the remaining years of their elderly cat's life. These years can sometimes be the most rewarding years of companionship because the increased needs of the older cat often seem to strengthen the bond between pet and owner.

While the World Health Organization considers people over the age of 60 to be elderly, and those over the age of 75 to be aged, there are no such established guidelines for cats. In general, cats are considered geriatric when they reach 8–10 years of age. Many changes associated with old age are easily recognized in cats, such as graying of fur on the face and muzzle, stiffness due to arthritis, and dulling of the senses (especially sight, hearing, and smell). Older cats are more affected by changes and stressors in their environment. They are less tolerant of cold, and they tend to sleep more. They may even be less socially interactive with other cats or humans and more irritable. Changes that are not so easy to appreciate can take place in the internal organs, especially the kidneys. Certain diseases, such as hyperthyroidism and chronic kidney failure, occur more commonly in geriatric cats.

CHANGES ASSOCIATED WITH AGING

Organ or Body System	Changes
Gastrointestinal system	Possible decreased ability to digest and absorb nutrients, constipation
Heart and lungs	Heart function not impaired significantly, but hypertension can cause problems; lung function not impaired significantly, but cough reflex is weaker
Immune system	Decrease in immune system function, especially if chronic disease present
Kidneys	Kidney size and function decline; potassium loss through urine increases
Mouth	Dental disease is common and can cause pain and difficulty eating
Nervous system	Cognitive dysfunction seen in some cats: wandering, vocalizing inappropriately, disorientation, withdrawal from social contact
Musculoskeletal system	Wear and tear of cartilage occurs; degenerative joint disease common; muscles atrophy
Skin and coat	Skin is thinner and more prone to infection; decreased grooming by cat leads to hair matting and dermatitis; claws may be overgrown, thick, brittle
Special senses	Most aging changes in eyes do not affect vision, but hypertension can cause blindness; hearing loss is common in very old cats; sense of smell can dull and contribute to loss of appetite
Thyroid gland	Thyroid nodules common in aging cat, some associated with hyperthyroidism

The American Association of Feline Practitioners and the AFM (http://www.aafp online.org/about/guidelines.htm) have published a booklet, *Panel Report on Feline Senior Care*, to help veterinarians provide specialized care for geriatric cats. These guidelines outline the factors that are important for preventive health care. A thorough physical examination, preferably every 6 months but at least yearly, is essential for early detection of problems. In addition, senior cats should have routine yearly blood screening and blood pressure measurement for the common problems associated with this age group. Dietary changes may be necessary because of disease (especially for chronic kidney failure). Many geriatric diets are now available that provide tailored nutrition for the aging cat.

Diabetes Mellitus

Diabetes mellitus is a common endocrine disease of cats and other animals, including dogs and humans. Another disease with a similar name, diabetes insipidus, is very rare in cats, so that the short form *diabetes* is understood to mean diabetes mellitus. It was first recognized in cats in 1927. Most commonly found in middle-aged to older cats, it is estimated to occur in 1 in every 400 cats. It is actually best to describe diabetes as a group of disorders in which insulin secretion by the pancreas is impaired or where the body's cells are resistant to the action of insulin. The end result is impairment of the body's ability to regulate blood glucose (also called blood sugar) levels. Insulin is the main factor that controls the storage and metabolism of fuels found in food. Glucose is a type of monosaccharide and is found in certain foods and in the blood of all animals. It is the end result of carbohydrate metabolism and is the chief source of energy for living organisms. The brain is especially dependent on adequate levels of glucose for normal function.

Diabetes is usually seen in cats over 6 years of age, but it can develop in cats of any breed or age, and in both sexes. The typical patient is an older, obese, neutered male cat. Many cats who develop diabetes are overweight. However, if the disease is not recognized and treated, an overweight cat with diabetes will lose weight and can become emaciated. Most owners will notice that the cat has become increasingly thirsty (polydipsic) and hungry (polyphagic) while losing weight over a period of weeks to months. In addition, there is an increase in the amount of urine produced (polyuria). Many cats with diabetes are also lethargic. In most cases, the cause of diabetes is not known, but some predisposing factors include pancreatitis or treatment with certain medications (such as corticosteroids and megestrol acetate).

Most cats with diabetes are bright and alert when a veterinarian examines them. However, if the signs of diabetes were not recognized early enough, the cat might be very ill by the time veterinary attention is sought. These very ill cats may be depressed, weak, and dehydrated; some may even be in a diabetic coma. The coat of most cats with diabetes is dull with flakes of dandruff. Fortunately, cats rarely develop cataracts from diabetes as dogs and humans do. The liver will be enlarged and some cats with diabetes are jaundiced. Some cats with diabetes may walk flat-footed on their hind feet (called a plantigrade stance) rather than up on their toes. This condition is called tibial neuropathy and is the effect of chronically high blood glucose on the peripheral nerves.

SYMPTOMS OF DIABETES MELLITUS IN CATS

Early in the Disease	Later in the Disease
• Increased appetite	• Loss of appetite
• Increased thirst	• Lethargy, depression, weakness
• Increased urination	• Vomiting
• Weight loss	• Tibial neuropathy
• Flaky, dry coat	• Coma

The alterations in body functions that result from diabetes are complex. They result in the metabolism of carbohydrates, proteins, and fats being profoundly disturbed. The cells in the body need glucose to sustain life. In the normal cat, insulin helps glucose enter into body cells, where it provides fuel. In cats with diabetes, the glucose in the bloodstream cannot enter cells properly. The result is that glucose accumulates in the bloodstream (hyperglycemia) and the body's cells appear to starve in the face of plenty. The fuel they need is available, but they cannot use it. Consequently, the body behaves as if it is starving and breaks down fat tissue and the protein of muscle tissue to provide the needed energy for cells.

Diabetes is diagnosed using a combination of laboratory testing and the patient's symptoms and physical condition. Cats with diabetes will have high blood glucose levels (hyperglycemia) and also glucose in the urine (glucosuria). A normal concentration of glucose in the blood would be about 100 milligrams per deciliter. The level in cats with diabetes is consistently over 300 milligrams per deciliter. However, normal cats that are frightened or stressed may also have fairly high blood glucose levels and even glucose in the urine. This can make the diagnosis of diabetes difficult in some cases. Newer blood tests, such as serum fructosamine and glycosylated hemoglobin, may be very valuable to help separate true diabetes from stress-induced hyperglycemia. Some cats with diabetes will also have increases in their liver enzymes.

Treatment of diabetes depends on the degree of illness. Complicated cases of diabetes occur when the patient has the presence of organic chemicals called ketones in the urine and a condition called metabolic acidosis; together called ketoacidosis. This is a more serious and urgent situation. These cats are often the sickest, sometimes with vomiting and diarrhea, severe weight loss and dehydration, loss of appetite, and difficult breathing. Some people can detect the odor of acetone associated with ketoacidosis on an affected cat's breath. Without treatment, ketoacidosis is a major cause of death in cats with diabetes. They require intensive care, which might include intravenous fluids and other treatments, along with insulin therapy.

Cats with uncomplicated diabetes have no ketoacidosis or diabetic coma. However, some can be quite ill and may need stabilization in the hospital with intensive care for a few days. They may require intravenous fluids and therapy to correct electrolyte imbalances as well as insulin. Other cats with diabetes are reasonably well and stable at the time of diagnosis and may not require any hospitalization. Any concurrent illnesses must be identified and treated. Many cats with diabetes have a bacterial infection at the time of diagnosis. Dental and urinary tract infections are the most common. Many veterinarians therefore treat all cats with newly diagnosed diabetes with a course of antibiotics.

Insulin is the mainstay of therapy for diabetes. Insulin preparations vary in their action, with some being short-acting and others long-acting. In general, cats metabolize insulin more quickly than other species, so medium- or long-acting insulins are usually chosen for therapy. The cat's own insulin is closest to bovine insulin, so a long-acting bovine preparation has been one traditional choice. Another long-acting insulin used in cats is PZI (protamine zinc insulin). However, these insulins are either discontinued or very hard to find, and so most cats are now treated with a human recombinant product (such as Humulin U, Humulin N, or Humulin L, manufactured by Lilly). In some countries, a veterinary insulin is available (Caninsulin, manufactured by Intervet). It is important to understand that because individual cats have different responses to insulin, the insulin treatment regimen will need to be custom-tailored to the individual cat's needs. As well, variations in diet and exercise plus any concurrent disease conditions will markedly affect the need for insulin. Intact female cats will undergo dramatic changes in insulin requirements related to their heat cycles, so they should be spayed.

Insulin is a relatively fragile molecule and must be kept refrigerated. The bottle must be mixed by gentle rolling rather than shaking so that the insulin is not damaged. Special insulin syringes are used to measure and administer the dose. Most cats require insulin twice daily, and it is best absorbed if injected on the cat's side, over the ribcage. Most veterinarians are skilled at teaching owners to give insulin injections, and the majority of cats find no discomfort from the small, thin insulin needles. In addition, most veterinarians will supply owners with information about the disease and treatment to keep on hand at home for reference.

The most serious complication of insulin therapy is low blood glucose (hypoglycemia). When this happens, usually at the time of peak insulin activity several hours after the injection is given, the cat may become weak, lethargic, and disoriented and may have difficulty walking. Left untreated, this situation has the potential to progress to seizures and, in rare cases, death. If mild symptoms are observed, the cat should be fed immediately, or corn syrup (a good source of glucose) can be smeared on the cat's gums. This will allow you time to call your veterinarian. Food or fluids should never be given to a weak or unconscious cat, as some may enter the airway accidentally.

Drugs in the class called sulfonylureas are often used as oral medications to regulate blood glucose in humans with diabetes. When used in conjunction with dietary therapy, these drugs can be somewhat effective in controlling uncomplicated diabetes in a few cats. In only about 10% to 40% of cats with diabetes can the disease be controlled with these drugs instead of insulin. The most commonly used drug is glipizide, which is given in pill form twice daily. It may take several weeks to determine if it will work for a particular cat, however. During this period, if the patient becomes ill, develops ketoacidosis, or has any adverse side effects from the drug, oral medication must be stopped and insulin therapy started. The ease of administration and expense of medication must also be taken into account. Glipizide treatment is more costly than insulin. As well, many owners find it much easier to give insulin injections than to give pills twice daily.

There is much controversy surrounding the right diet for cats with diabetes. Many studies show that diets high in soluble fiber will help lower insulin requirements. More recent studies show that high-protein, low-carbohydrate diets (such as Purina DM) may be successful in managing feline diabetes, even allowing some cats to stop insulin therapy. Obese cats should be fed a diet that encourages safe weight loss. Rapid weight loss or fasting in obese cats can result in a liver disease called hepatic lipidosis (fatty liver disease). Experts are divided about the right amount of protein and carbohydrate for cats with diabetes and whether dry or canned food is best. Your veterinarian will help you decide which is the right food for your cat.

Once a suitable insulin dose has been determined for a cat with diabetes, regular monitoring is essential. Cats can experience changes in their insulin needs, so that the dose of insulin might need to be changed from time to time. There are various ways to monitor diabetes, such as determining serial blood glucose levels in the clinic over a 10- to-12 hour period (called a blood glucose curve), using urine glucose measurements taken at home, or using serum fructosamine levels. Many owners can monitor blood glucose levels in their cats at home, using a glucose monitor designed for humans with diabetes. If home monitoring is chosen, the blood or urine glucose test results should always be relayed to the veterinarian and no changes in the cat's therapy should be undertaken without veterinary supervision. Different veterinarians may have different ways of monitoring diabetes, but the most important thing is that some type of monitoring is done and that the cat's owner regularly communicates with the veterinarian. It is also important for owners to monitor the cat's weight, food and water consumption, and urine output.

Beyond the monetary cost of diagnosing, stabilizing, treating, and maintaining the health of a cat with diabetes, there is a time commitment required of owners. Such a commitment may seem daunting at first, but it can be very rewarding for both cat and owner. It adds to the quality of the cat's life and can be paid back in years of healthy companionship. Cats with diabetes now live longer than ever with good care. And on a hopeful note, not all cats with diabetes remain insulin-dependent. Occasionally, a cat may have an ever-decreasing need for insulin over time and eventually stop taking the medication. These cats may never need insulin again, or they may have months to years before they require it to regulate their diabetes once more.

Hypertension

Hypertension is a term that means high blood pressure. While many people are familiar with hypertension in humans, it is increasingly recognized as an important problem in veterinary medicine, especially in cats. Hypertension in cats is more common than previously thought and is probably underdiagnosed because of limitations of equipment and test methods. Stress and excitement can cause temporary increases in blood pressure in cats, and it can be difficult in some cases to differentiate this from true hypertension.

The most common type of hypertension in humans is primary, or essential, hypertension. In cats, however, hypertension is almost always secondary to another disease. Several common diseases, such as chronic kidney failure, hyperthyroidism, and cardiomyopathy, can cause elevated blood pressure in cats. It has been estimated that up to 65% of cats with chronic kidney failure and 87% of cats with hyperthyroidism have hypertension too. Therefore, it is very important that cats with any of these diseases have their blood pressure evaluated. A few very uncommon diseases can also cause hypertension, such as hyperadrenocorticism (Cushing's disease).

The average feline patient with hypertension is 12–18 years old and can be of either gender. However, cats as young as 7 years old have been found to have hypertension. Symptoms tend to reflect the underlying disease and can include lack of energy, increased thirst and urination, sudden blindness, seizures or stroke, changes in behavior (such as howling at night), and congestive heart failure. Chronically high blood pressure can cause bleeding inside the eye and detachment of the retina. Acute blindness is the result, and the cat may have pupils that are constantly dilated. If the blindness is diagnosed and treated within the first 24 hours, it may be possible to restore vision.

SYMPTOMS ASSOCIATED WITH HYPERTENSION

- Lethargy
- Increased thirst and urination
- Sudden blindness
- Stroke
- Seizures
- Behavior changes, especially inappropriate vocalization
- Congestive heart failure

Blood pressure can be measured in cats by using a Doppler monitor and a blood pressure cuff. The technique is very similar to that used for humans. The Doppler equipment uses sound waves to detect the blood flow and amplify it so it can be heard more easily. The measurement can be taken using the radial artery of the front leg, the tarsal artery of the hind leg, or even a tail artery. Usually five to seven measurements are taken with the cat as calm as possible. For cats, a systolic blood pressure of 170–180 mm Hg is usually the upper limit of normal.

Treatment of hypertension first involves diagnosis and treatment of the underlying disorder. If the main problem is hyperthyroidism, control or cure of the disease may normalize the blood pressure. If the underlying problem is not curable, such as in chronic kidney failure, most cats will require daily medication to control their blood pressure for the rest of their lives. Some of the same medications used to control hypertension in people can be used in cats as well. Probably the most effective and widely used drug is amlodipine (Norvasc, manufactured by Pfizer).

The prognosis for cats with hypertension largely depends on the underlying reason. In most cats, the disease can be controlled using medical therapy. However, diligent monitoring is required because medication may need to be changed or adjusted occasionally. Because most cats with hypertension are older cats with other health problems, attention to overall wellness is also important.

Hyperthyroidism

The thyroid is a small gland consisting of two lobes on either side of the trachea just below the larynx. The name of the gland comes from the Greek word *thyreos*, or shield. One of the most common diseases of the middle-aged and older cat is hyperthyroidism (also called thyrotoxicosis). It is also the most common disease of the endocrine system in cats. This disease affects multiple organ systems and is caused by an increase in the amount of thyroid hormones (called T3 and T4) produced by an enlarged thyroid gland. It was first documented in cats in the 1970s, but the underlying cause of the disease remains elusive. Although the enlargement of the thyroid gland is caused by a tumor, 99% of these tumors are of a noncancerous type called an adenoma.

The average age of cats affected by hyperthyroidism is 13 years, although it has been found in cats under 5 years of age and as old as 20 years. About 95% of affected cats are over 10 years of age. It occurs equally in both sexes and in any breed of cat. Most hyperthyroid cats have very typical clinical signs as outlined in the table below, but about 10% have what is called apathetic hyperthyroids. In these cats,

the predominant symptoms are poor appetite, depression, and weakness.

COMMON SIGNS ASSOCIATED WITH HYPERTHYROIDISM

- Weight loss
- Increased appetite
- Vomiting
- Diarrhea
- Increased thirst
- Unkempt appearance, thickened nails
- Increased urination
- Increased respiration rate
- Difficulty breathing
- Hyperactivity
- Behavior changes, including irritability and aggression

Many of the signs of hyperthyroidism are similar to other diseases seen in older cats. Veterinarians use blood chemistry panels, urinalysis, and a serum thyroid hormone (T4) level to aid in the diagnosis. In addition to the physical signs of weight loss and an unkempt appearance, the thyroid gland will generally be enlarged. It can be palpated in the neck just under the larynx. In about 70% of cats, both lobes of the thyroid gland are enlarged. Hypertension is very often associated with hyperthyroidism, so a blood pressure measurement should also be performed.

It is important to evaluate the health of other major organs in the hyperthyroid cat, especially the kidneys, liver, and heart. Many cats with hyperthyroidism have elevations in their liver enzymes. Chest X-rays and ultrasound may reveal secondary hypertrophic cardiomyopathy. These patients may have a heart murmur, difficulty breathing, a high heart rate, and arrhythmias. Generally the cardiac changes will reverse once the hyperthyroidism is treated. In some cases, specific heart medications may be needed to stabilize heart function. If left untreated, hyperthyroidism can lead to congestive heart failure, kidney damage, severe diarrhea, and blindness associated with retinal detachment (due to hypertension), as well as severe physical debilitation from weight loss.

Most hyperthyroid cats will have elevated levels of the thyroid hormone T4 in their bloodstream on a routine screening test. However, a small percentage of hyperthyroid cats will have normal T4 levels. If hyperthyroidism is still strongly suspected in these patients, sensitive tests such as the T3 suppression test or the thyrotropin-releasing hormone (TRH) stimulation test can be performed to confirm the diagnosis.

Once hyperthyroidism has been confirmed, there are several treatment options, including treatment with radioiodine (I-131), surgical removal of the abnormal thyroid gland (thyroidectomy), and treatment with antithyroid medications. The initial choice of treatment is often guided by concern about the patient's kidney function status. In recent years, it has been recognized that many hyperthyroid cats have concurrent chronic kidney failure that is being masked by the effects of hyperthyroidism. It has also been found that treatments directed at curing hyperthyroidism in these patients could lead to a worsening of their kidney function.

Some cats will have detectable impairment of kidney function at the time of their diagnosis with hyperthyroidism, but many do not. It is difficult to assess kidney function accurately from routine blood and urine testing in cats because blood levels of creatinine and urea, the waste products used to assess kidney function, can be normal in the early stages of kidney insufficiency. A newer and more sensitive type of test called the iohexol clearance test is able to measure kidney function and de-

tect insufficiency even when routine blood test results are normal. However, this test is more involved and expensive, as it requires several blood samples and an intravenous injection of a radiographic contrast agent. Processing is done at only one laboratory at this time (Michigan State University).

Because hyperthyroidism induces an increase in blood supply to the kidneys, treating the disease will result in a reversal of this situation. In a cat with occult kidney failure, this can cause a worsening of kidney function in the few months after treatment for hyperthyroidism (with either thyroidectomy or radioiodine). For this reason, patients with known kidney insufficiency (either detected on routine blood work or with the iohexol clearance test) are often treated with antithyroid medications rather than surgery or radioiodine in an effort to preserve their remaining kidney function. Using medication allows veterinarians better control over the concurrent kidney disease, because the dose can be adjusted if needed. A few cats with kidney failure and hyperthyroidism are better off with no specific treatment for the thyroid disease because their kidneys may be healthier with hyperthyroidism than without.

Antithyroid medications in current use in North America include propylthiouracil (PTU) and methimazole. Although they are both effective in decreasing thyroid hormone levels, PTU is associated with more adverse side effects than methimazole. Methimazole is better tolerated and safer for long-term use in cats. Approximately 15% of cats will have adverse side effects when taking methimazole, which can range from poor appetite, vomiting, lethargy, and a skin rash to more serious problems such as bone marrow suppression and liver toxicity. Fortunately, in most cats, the adverse effects are mild and transient and do not interfere with continued treatment. A small percentage of cats cannot tolerate the medication at all. Many pharmacists can now formulate methimazole in a transdermal gel that allows the drug to be absorbed through the skin. This method of administering the drug can be very helpful for owners whose cats dislike oral medications.

More recently, a drug called ipodate has been used to treat hyperthyroidism in cats. Cats with severe hyperthyroidism do not respond to treatment with ipodate as well as cats with milder disease do. While most cats have no side effects from ipodate, the effect of the drug may be, unfortunately, only transient, lasting from several weeks to a few months. This drug is therefore most useful for short-term disease management in cats who cannot tolerate methimazole in preparation for surgery or radioiodine treatment. Unfortunately, ipodate is expensive and increasingly hard to find. Other antithyroid compounds, such as potassium iodate, are being investigated to determine their usefulness in the treatment of feline hyperthyroidism.

For hyperthyroid cats with adequate kidney function, surgery or radioiodine is often recommended. Both these options provide a cure for the disease and avoid the need for lifelong administration of medications. Cats do not require thyroid replacement therapy after either type of treatment. In areas where radioiodine is available, often in a specially constructed facility, it is the treatment of choice because it avoids the risks of anesthesia and surgery. It does require a stay of several days to a few weeks in the facility, depending on local regulations governing radiotherapy.

Thyroidectomy is an excellent option for treatment of hyperthyroidism where radioiodine treatment is not available or where a long hospital stay is not desirable. There are various techniques for this surgery, involving either removal of both lobes of the gland at the same time or a staged procedure where only one lobe is removed at a time. The main consideration during thyroidectomy is adequate preservation of the closely associated parathyroid gland. The parathyroid gland is responsible for maintaining calcium balance in the body, and disruption of the parathyroid glands can lead to hypocalcemia (low blood calcium levels). This occurs in up to 15% of patients but is usually only short term after thyroidectomy and is rarely permanent. Regrowth of hyperthyroid tissue is possible after surgery or radioiodine, but it occurs in less than 10% of patients.

Chronic Kidney Failure

The kidneys are very important organs with complex functions. Their main job is to filter the bloodstream and remove waste products produced during metabolism of nutrients. These waste products must be continually removed so that toxic levels do not accumulate. The kidneys also help regulate the volume and composition of the blood. They are located high in the abdomen, lying just behind the rib cage, one on either side of the cat's spine. They are connected to the bladder via the ureters, so that urine produced by the kidneys can accumulate in the bladder before being voided from the body via the urethra.

One of the most common disorders of geriatric cats is chronic kidney insufficiency, or chronic renal failure (CRF). While CRF can occur in cats of any age and may have various causes, such as infections, trauma, or congenital defects, the most common form is seen in geriatric cats. Our cats now live much longer lives due to advances in nutrition and feline medicine. After a lifetime of wear and tear, kidney function declines as the cat ages. This has meant that more cats are seen now with CRF than decades ago and that CRF accounts for a significant amount of illness and death in elderly cats. Fortunately, our understanding of kidney function and CRF has also increased dramatically in recent decades, so that effective treatment options are available.

Each kidney is composed of thousands of nephrons, the individual functional unit of the kidney. There is such an abundance of nephrons that cats can continue to live should damage or disease compromise one kidney or part of both kidneys. Throughout the cat's life, individual nephrons sustain damage from wear and tear, but enough functioning nephrons remain to provide adequate kidney function. Indeed, two thirds or more of total kidney function must be lost before most cats will show signs of illness. CRF is a chronic, irreversible disease process that progresses over months to years.

Many of the signs of CRF are also seen in other geriatric cat diseases. These include weight loss, poor appetite, lethargy, vomiting, increased thirst, and increased urination. Diseases such as diabetes mellitus and hyperthyroidism can have similar symptoms so that diagnostic tests are required to differentiate them. As CRF advances, other signs become apparent, such as ulcers in the mouth and bad breath produced by toxic levels of waste products. Severe weight loss, dehydration, and low blood potassium levels can contribute to debilitation and weakness. As well, the kidneys produce a hormone called erythropoietin that stimulates the bone marrow to make new red blood cells to replace older damaged ones. In CRF, erythropoietin levels may drop, the bone marrow may decrease its production of red blood cells, and anemia may result. The anemia further contributes to weakness and general debilitation.

SIGNS ASSOCIATED WITH CHRONIC KIDNEY FAILURE

Most Common	Other Signs
• Weight loss	• Constipation or diarrhea
• Poor appetite	• Dry, unkempt coat
• Lethargy	• Sudden blindness (hypertension)
• Vomiting	• Oral ulcers, dental disease
• Increased thirst	• Dehydration
• Increased urination	• Seizures (late in the disease)

Veterinarians will want to perform a complete physical examination as well as a blood pressure measurement on any geriatric cat with symptoms of CRF. When the abdomen is palpated, the kidneys are usually found to be small in size and their surfaces may be lumpy instead of smooth. Painful ulcers may be found in the mouth, which contribute to a poor appetite. Dental disease may be present, with loose teeth and bleeding gums. The cat's coat is often dry and unkempt. Many CRF patients are dehydrated and may also suffer from constipation. Hypertension (high blood pressure) is commonly associated with CRF in cats. Cats with hypertension may be lethargic, have behavior changes (especially vocalizing at inappropriate times), and suffer damage to the retinas that can result in sudden blindness.

Laboratory testing for CRF includes blood chemistries, a urinalysis, and a CBC. Problems such as anemia, low potassium levels, high phosphorus levels, and increased amounts of BUN (blood urea nitrogen) and creatinine are associated with CRF. Urine samples are dilute and a urinary tract infection may be present. Because hyperthyroidism is also a common disease in elderly cats, a blood thyroxine level (T4) should be checked. It is not uncommon to find elderly cats with more than one age-associated illness.

Once the cat's health status is fully known, a treatment plan can be devised. Wherever possible, geriatric cats are best treated on an outpatient basis. However, some cats with CRF are in need of hospitalization for rehydration with intravenous fluids, correction of metabolic imbalances, and sometimes tube feeding. Many cats improve markedly when their dehydration is corrected and nutrition is supplied. In some cases, several days of treatment with intravenous fluids can help lower the levels of waste products in the bloodstream (this is termed diuresis). While dialysis is commonly available for human patients with CRF, it is not commonly available for cats.

Dietary therapy plays an important role in the treatment of CRF patients. Many companies make special diets for kidney disease, in both canned and dry versions that are low in protein (to reduce the kidney's workload), low in phosphorus, higher in potassium, and higher in calories. Some patients with CRF with low potassium levels will benefit from daily potassium supplementation. This can be done in pill form or in a powder that can be mixed into canned food (Tumil-K, manufactured by Daniels Pharmaceuticals). Other medications that might be prescribed include phosphate-binders to reduce phosphorus intake, appetite stimulants such as cyproheptadine, acid-blockers (to reduce nausea and improve appetite) such as famotidine, and medications to control hypertension. If anemia is severe, synthetic forms of human erythropoietin can be given by injection. Correction of severe anemia often results in the patient's having more energy and feeling better overall.

While most cats with CRF drink increased amounts of water, they may not drink enough to supply their requirements. Improving fluid intake helps prevent dehydration and improves kidney function. For this reason, canned food is preferred over dry foods. An-

other method of increasing fluid intake at home is the use of subcutaneous fluid therapy. The method is described elsewhere in this book and is relatively easy for an owner to learn. It can have a profound impact on the cat's health status and improve quality of life.

Cats with CRF will need frequent monitoring by their veterinarian. Those with uncomplicated, mild to moderate disease may need to be reevaluated only every 1–3 months. Those with more advanced disease with complications may require very frequent monitoring. Some medications, such as synthetic erythropoietin, initially require weekly monitoring. Cats taking medications for hypertension may also require more frequent monitoring. Repeat blood testing at intervals will help to judge the success of any treatments and allow for any adjustments that might be needed. Owners are also encouraged to monitor thirst and urination, appetite, weight, and the patient's overall quality of life. Many cats with CRF will eventually be euthanized when their disease becomes intractable and their quality of life poor. Good communication between veterinarian and owner can help determine when this time has come.

Obviously, the amount of care a patient with CRF needs depends on the severity of the disease and whether complications such as anemia and hypertension are present. In many cats, CRF progresses slowly, allowing time to improve quality of life without too much intervention. In other cats, the disease may not be recognized until it is quite severe, in which case more intensive treatment will be needed. The earlier in the course of the disease it is diagnosed and treated, the better the prognosis. One way to detect kidney disease early is to use routine blood screening and blood pressure measurements for cats over the age of 8 years. Many veterinarians offer these services for older cats as part of their annual wellness examination and before any procedures that require anesthesia (such as dental cleanings).

Cancer

Cancer is one of the most important causes of illness and death in cats in the United States, although cats develop cancer only half as often as dogs. Unfortunately, a cat's chances of developing cancer (also called neoplasia) increase with age. Why cancer develops at all, and why it is seen more commonly in older animals, is not well understood. Many factors, including genetic and environmental ones, have been identified as potential causes. However, *cancer* is a general term used to encompass many different diseases, and each disease may well have its own causative factors. Some of these factors are known, but in most cases, the cause of an individual cat's cancer is not. That can make it very hard to answer the question "Why does my cat have cancer?" Fortunately, cancers in cats and dogs often have counterparts in humans, so that cancer research tends to benefit both our pets and us.

Some feline cancers are associated with viral infections, particularly FeLV and FIV. The risk of developing lymphoma is increased more than 60 times for cats infected with FeLV. FIV has been associated with some lymphoid malignancies. One way to decrease the risk of cancer in cats, therefore, is to protect against infection with these two viruses. Other specific ways to decrease the risk of some cancers also exist. For instance, avoiding exposure to strong sunlight reduces the risk of squamous cell carcinoma of the skin in white cats, and early spaying reduces the risk of mammary cancer for all female cats.

Regardless of the type of cancer a cat may have, the disease usually leads to disturbances that cause common signs. These may include lethargy, poor appetite, depression, and weight loss. Sometimes the presence of a possible cancer is obvious (such as a skin mass), but in many cases, it is not. Veterinarians must rely on a good physical examination plus diagnostic testing to pinpoint the cause of a cat's illness. Screening tests for specific types of cancer are yet to be developed for veterinary medicine. When evaluating a cat that may have cancer, it is important not only to get a definitive diagnosis of the type of cancer but also to evaluate the cat's overall health status. Many elderly cats have more than one disease process present.

COMMON SIGNS OF CANCER

- Abnormal swellings that persist or continue to grow
- Sores that do not heal
- Weight loss
- Loss of appetite
- Bleeding or discharge from any body opening
- Offensive odor
- Difficulty eating or swallowing
- Hesitation to exercise or loss of stamina
- Persistent lameness or stiffness
- Difficulty breathing, urinating, or defecating

Adapted from the American Veterinary Medical Association, http://www.avma.org/careforanimals/animatedjourneys/pethealth/pethealth.asp#2

A process called staging is also used in the evaluation of cancers. Staging determines the degree of cancer involvement in the patient. It can help determine the prognosis and suggest treatment options. There are various systems devised to stage a cancer, but they primarily rely on answering three questions:

- How large is the primary tumor?
- Are local lymph nodes involved (local metastasis)?
- Are tissues distant from the primary tumor involved (distant metastasis)?

In addition to the usual blood and urine tests employed by veterinarians, some sophisticated techniques are often available to aid in the diagnosis and staging of cancer patients. Imaging techniques such as radiology (X-rays), ultrasonography, and CT scans are very useful. For instance, CT scans are the tool of choice to image tumors of the brain and ultrasonography is the tool of choice for imaging tumors in the abdomen. Conventional X-rays are best for tumors in the chest. A veterinarian's choice of imaging technique will also be influenced by what services are available locally.

One of the most important tools for evaluating cancer is the biopsy. This can be performed by several different methods, such as fine-needle aspiration or a surgical biopsy. The type of cancer suspected and its location often dictate the type of biopsy that is performed. Biopsies of internal masses can often be accomplished by using ultrasound guidance. Biopsies can help determine not only the type of cancer present but also whether it is aggressive in its behavior. Such information is often necessary to help owners and veterinarians decide which course of action is in the cat's best interests.

The decision to treat a given cancer can be a difficult one. In some cases, where the prognosis is poor or the owner is not in an emotional or financial position to attempt treatment, the best option might be euthanasia. Some cancers are potentially curable; others have a poorer prognosis and may provide short- or long-term survival possibilities. In every situation, the quality of life for the cat must be considered. The treatment itself may not be appropriate for some patients, even if it could provide long-term remission or a cure.

Just as for humans with cancer, various treatment options are available for cats, depending on the type of cancer and what is available locally. It is true that in a great many cases, cancer is still a surgically treated disease. But some cancers are most amenable to chemotherapy, or radiation, or a combination of therapies. As newer modalities such as photodynamic therapy and immunotherapy are established for cats, they will become more widely available. Treatment of cancer may also involve other issues, such as nutritional support and pain management.

SELECTED FELINE CANCERS

Cancer	Treatment Options	Comments
Ceruminous gland tumor: external ear	Surgery with or without radiation	Prognosis is fair with extensive surgery
Lymphoma/lymphosarcoma: lymph nodes, kidneys, intestines, other sites	Depends on organ affected: chemotherapy, surgery	Prognosis depends on many factors including whether feline leukemia virus is present
Mammary adenocarcinoma: mammary glands	Surgery	Prognosis depends on the size of the tumor at diagnosis; early spaying reduces risk
Mast cell tumor: skin	Surgery	Good prognosis if tumor is solitary

Cancer	Treatment Options	Comments
Mast cell tumor: spleen, lymph nodes, intestine	Surgery with or without radiation and with or without corticosteroids	Best prognosis is for tumors that involve the spleen
Meningioma: brain	Surgery	Prognosis is good; tumor is slow-growing
Squamous cell carcinoma: ears, nose, eyelids	Surgery, radiation, photodynamic therapy, intralesional chemotherapy	White cats should avoid strong sun exposure
Squamous cell carcinoma: oral	Radiation with or without surgery and with or without chemotherapy	Aggressive tumor that responds poorly to treatment
Vaccine-associated sarcoma: at any vaccination site	Surgery with or without radiation and with or without chemotherapy	Prognosis is often poor, as tumor regrowth is common

INHERITED DEFECTS AND ANOMALIES

The word *genetics* was not coined until 1906, soon after the principles of heredity worked out by Gregor Mendel were rediscovered by the world of science. Breeders, scientists, and veterinarians have long been aware of the common genetic defects seen in the cats and various lists of them have been drawn up over the years. As more is learned about feline genetics and diseases, especially in this age of DNA technology, the list will undoubtedly grow as each year passes. Because the cat also serves as a model for the study of many diseases in humans, both species have reaped benefits from this type of collaborative study.

The spectrum of genetic abnormalities found in cats encompasses different types of defects. Some defects cause affected fetuses to die in utero. Other defects are capable of causing some degree of health impairment and perhaps even an early death (such as heart defects). Finally, many defects are primarily cosmetic and do not impair health in any significant way (such as a kinked tail).

It is important to understand the difference between the terms *congenital* and *inherited*. Congenital defects are those seen in newborns or the very young; they may or may not be inherited. An example of a noninherited congenital defect is the occurrence of cleft palates in kittens born to queens given the drug griseofulvin during pregnancy. Inherited defects may or may not be present at birth. In many cases, they do not become evident until later in life.

In general, inherited diseases and problems can affect any cat, whether pedigreed or not. Some pedigreed breeds are associated with certain inherited diseases. These cats have most often been used as medical models to study similar human diseases, thereby adding a new dimension to their service to humans as companion animals. The development of screening tests to detect affected and carrier animals benefits both cats and humans.

Some defects are more common than others in the cat population, although geographical variation plays a role.

Cataracts are sometimes present as an inherited defect in cats. They can also have other causes (such as trauma to the eye). In comparison to the dog, cataracts in the cat are rare. Inherited cataracts are usually present at birth and become visible by 8–12 weeks of age. If the cataract is in only one eye or is affecting only a small portion of the lens in both eyes, no treatment is indicated. If there is significant impairment of vision, a veterinary ophthalmologist can surgically remove the abnormal lens to help restore some vision.

A more common congenital defect is the **cleft palate**. A defect can exist in the hard palate or the soft palate, or both. Cleft palates can also occur after trauma, such as a fall from a height or as a consequence of some medications if given to a pregnant queen. Kittens born with a cleft palate are usually detected in the first few days of life because they are unable to nurse effectively. A common symptom is milk seen at the nostrils after nursing. They can also develop aspiration pneumonia or be found suddenly dead. In milder cases, the defect may not be detected for several weeks. This defect is seen in both pedigreed and nonpedigreed kittens. Kittens with a cleft palate require special care and feeding until they are large enough for surgical correction of the defect.

Cryptorchidism refers to the failure of one or both testicles to descend into the scrotum and remain there. The testicles are present in the abdomen during fetal life and descend into the scrotum by birth or shortly afterward. While unilateral cryptorchidism is most common, bilateral cases are occasionally seen. This is the most common congenital defect of the urinary and genital systems in the cat and is found in all breeds and in nonpedigreed cats.

Cryptorchidism is called a sex-limited trait because only the male cat can be physically affected. The trait is likely a recessive defect, and for this reason, both the sire and dam of an affected cat should be considered carriers. Some full siblings of affected cats will also be carriers. There is no treatment that will cause a retained testicle to descend into the scrotum. Surgical removal of the retained testicle is routinely recommended.

It is fairly well known that many blue-eyed white cats are deaf. **Deafness** can also occasionally occur in odd-eyed cats, with the ear on the same side as the blue eye being deaf. This form of deafness is associated with the dominant gene that is responsible for white coat color. Not all white cats are deaf; studies show that up to 15% of blue-eyed white cats have normal hearing. While there is no effective treatment for congenital deafness, cats can live very well with this defect. They are best kept as indoor pets to safeguard them from outdoor hazards. Owners of deaf cats often report that they tend to use a louder voice than other cats, perhaps because they can't hear themselves.

Pectus excavatum is a defect in which the sternum is displaced upward into the chest to varying degrees. While the mode of inheritance is not known, it has been seen in various cat breeds as well as nonpedigreed cats. The defect tends to become obvious in affected kittens by about 12 weeks of age. If the degree of displacement of the sternum is mild, no particular treatment is required. In severe cases, the displacement of the sternum begins to compress the heart and lungs as the kitten grows. These kittens will require surgical repair of the defect to lead a normal life. Luckily, the defect is not usually this severe.

It has long been known that cats may have blindness associated with retinal disease. **Progressive retinal atrophy** (PRA) is an inherited disease found in some breeds of cats and in nonpedigreed cats as well. Depending on the form of the disease, blindness due to deterioration of the retina may occur early in life or as a young adult. There is no treatment or cure for PRA, although blind cats can live a quite normal life in an indoor, controlled environment.

One of the more common congenital defects seen in cats is the **umbilical hernia**. This defect results from a weakness in the abdominal wall at the site of the umbilicus so that abdominal contents bulge outward. The defect can range from very small to quite large. In many cases, umbilical hernias are an inherited defect, although the mode of inheritance is not well understood. Any trauma to the umbilicus in the first days of life can also cause a hernia. It is sometimes seen with frequency in some breeds or family lines of cats, but it is also reasonably common in nonpedigreed cats as well. Very small defects require no treatment; larger ones require surgical repair.

Cats with extra toes are called **polydactyl**. Reports of these cats have abounded for at least 150 years. The presence of the anomaly appears to vary geographically. For instance, the east coast of the United States seems to have more polydactyl cats than other areas. There is wide variation in expression of this defect, ranging from simple extra toes on the front feet only to multiple extra toes on all four feet. The hind feet are hardly ever affected unless the front feet are too. This variability likely means more than one gene is responsible for polydactyl cats. In most cases, polydactyl cats have no particular health problems, although in some cases, the formation of the extra toes may make it very difficult to keep the cat's nails trimmed. In these cases, the nail sometimes overgrows and penetrates into the pad, causing an infection. For this reason, veterinarians occasionally recommend removal of particularly problematic extra toes.

ZOONOSES—ILLNESSES THAT CAN MOVE FROM CATS TO HUMANS

Zoonoses are diseases that can be transmitted between humans and animals. Most human infectious diseases are acquired from other humans, but a small number are associated with pets. People at special risk of contracting zoonotic diseases are those who are immunocompromised, such as patients with acquired immunodeficiency syndrome (AIDS), transplant recipients, patients with cancer and patients with diabetes. The cat is associated with a number of human diseases, many of which are rare or unknown in North America. Some diseases have only limited zoonotic potential (such as giardiasis), while others are quite serious (such as rabies). A few of the most important zoonoses are discussed below.

RABIES

Rabies is a serious, always fatal, viral disease of all warm-blooded animals, including cats and humans. In the United States, 7,437 cases of rabies in wild and domestic animals were reported in 2001. Cats represented 270 cases. The rabies virus is in the genus *Lyssavirus* and family *Rhabdoviridae*. The virus gains entry to the body through a wound or across mucous membranes. Transmission is usually through the bite of a rabid animal. The virus then travels to the central nervous system and causes a lethal form of encephalitis. While rabies is found worldwide, with the exception of a few areas, the incidence of the disease can vary by geographical region and over time. In the United States, four strains of rabies are endemic within the wild populations of skunks, foxes, raccoons, and bats. All of these strains can be transmitted to cats and to humans.

Common symptoms of rabies in cats include changes in attitude and behavior, especially nervousness, shyness, and aggression or erratic and unusual behavior. Other signs include muscular incoordination, disorientation, seizures, and paralysis, as the virus affects the brain and nervous system. Some animals show excessive drooling or frothing due to a paralyzed jaw and inability to swallow.

Cats who roam outside and who may come in contact with wildlife are at the greatest risk. As well, bite or scratch wounds from unvaccinated cats or dogs can also transmit the disease. Statistically, more cats become infected with rabies virus each year in the United States than dogs. Fortunately, rabies vaccines offer excellent protection against this dreaded disease. All cats should be vaccinated according to local regulations, because some jurisdictions mandate that even totally indoor cats be vaccinated. Cats are given their first vaccine after 12 weeks of age and receive their first booster vaccination 1 year later. Subsequent revaccinations depend on the type of vaccine used (vaccines that provide 3 years of protection are available) and local regulations (some mandate yearly revaccination regardless of the type of vaccine used).

Rabies is a fatal disease with no treatment. Most infected cats die within 10 days. Once the diagnosis is made, euthanasia is the only outcome. Any cat showing unusual behavioral changes or neurological disease that cannot be accounted for in any other way, especially if unvaccinated, must be suspected of having rabies. There is considerable risk to any human handlers because the disease can be transmitted during care of the sick cat. Local laws govern the circumstances surrounding the handling and quarantine of cats suspected of having rabies, because rabies is a reportable disease of considerable importance to animals and humans. In most jurisdictions, an apparently healthy rabies-vaccinated cat who has bitten a human will also be monitored for rabies. A 10-day monitoring period is usually considered sufficient; if the cat has no signs of illness within that time, it is unlikely that the person bitten is at risk for rabies infection. An unvaccinated cat who is exposed to or bitten by a known rabid animal usually must be quarantined for up 6 months, depending on local regulations.

TOXOPLASMOSIS

Toxoplasmosis is a disease caused by the microscopic parasite *Toxoplasma gondii*. This parasite infects almost all mammals, including humans, but domestic cats and their wild relatives are the definitive hosts (that is, the parasite requires a cat to complete its life cycle). There are different infectious stages in the complex life cycle of this parasite. There are three main ways the parasite is transmitted to people and animals:

- Congenital infection (before birth)
- Ingestion of an infected tissue source (raw or undercooked meat)
- Ingestion of oocyst-contaminated food or water

Only domestic cats and wildcats shed the oocysts of the parasite in their feces. These oocysts can contaminate the environment because they are resistant to freezing and drying and most disinfectants. Once shed, they require 24 hours to a few days to become infectious. When another mammal, such as a mouse, ingests the infectious oocysts, it then becomes infected with *Toxoplasma*. If it survives the infection, it may function as the source of infection for any animal that eats it. Cats usually become infected by ingesting the infectious oocysts or by eating prey or raw meat containing the *Toxoplasma* organism. There are also cases in which kittens have been infected before birth.

The parasite initially infects the cells of

the intestinal tract and the associated lymph tissue in the cat. It can then spread to other organs via the blood or lymph system. Once infected, cats begin to shed oocysts in their feces a few days to a few weeks later. However, oocysts are shed for only 1–2 weeks after the initial exposure, so most cats are not shedding at the time they have signs of illness. Shedding is heaviest when kittens 6–14 weeks old are infected.

Disease is most severe in those kittens infected before birth. These kittens can be stillborn or may fail to thrive and die before weaning. Affected kittens may have inflammation of the lungs, liver, and central nervous system. Fluid can accumulate in the abdomen. Cats infected after birth may have clinical signs of disease that include loss of appetite, lethargy, and trouble breathing due to pneumonia. Other clinical signs can include fever, weight loss, jaundice, vomiting, diarrhea, stiff gait, shifting leg lameness, and neurological problems. The eye can be involved, especially inflammation of the retina. The symptoms of illness may occur suddenly, or they may have a slow onset. If the respiratory or neurological signs are severe, death can occur rapidly.

The type of illness and its severity depend on what tissues of the body are infected. The majority of animals and people infected with this parasite do not develop disease. Why this is so is not fully understood, but factors such as stress, concurrent illness, and immunosuppression play a role. In cats, clinical toxoplasmosis has been seen in association with hemobartonellosis, FeLV, FIV and FIP. Long-term immunity is not 100%, so cats can be reinfected with *Toxoplasma* in the future and shed oocysts again, but the amount of shedding in future episodes is relatively insignificant.

Diagnosis of toxoplasmosis is challenging and may involve X-rays, fecal examinations, blood tests, and other diagnostic methods. Very often, the diagnosis is made after death at necropsy. Antibody titer tests for the IgG (immunoglobulin G) class of antibodies are available, but interpretation can be difficult. A cat who has had toxoplasmosis in the past and has recovered from the infection and is now immune will have a positive titer. A cat with an active infection will also have a positive titer. As well, false positive titers for *Toxoplasma* antibodies can occur after any routine vaccination and this effect can persist for up to 10 months after the vaccine was given.

Using paired blood samples to monitor antibody titers can be more helpful. Active toxoplasmosis can be documented if the antibody titer increases fourfold over a 2- 3-week period. A newer antibody test, which assays the IgM (immunoglobulin M) class of antibody, shows promise as a more reliable indicator of active infection, but it is not widely available. Fecal examinations for oocysts are usually unrewarding. Despite the wide distribution of this parasite throughout the world, it has been estimated that on any given day, less than 1% of the cats in the United States are shedding oocysts.

Treatment of cats ill with toxoplasmosis can be difficult. Little is known about the efficacy of most drugs against this parasite. The most effective drug is clindamycin, and it must be given for 2–3 weeks. Good hygiene must be practiced by any people handling and treating a cat ill with toxoplasmosis to avoid human infection.

The importance of toxoplasmosis lies mainly in the seriousness of human infections. People are infected in the same way as cats and infection is probably more widespread than we know. Healthy adults rarely become ill with toxoplasmosis. Signs of a new infection may be transient swollen lymph glands and flulike symptoms. However, adults who are immunosuppressed, because of either AIDS, cancer, or taking certain medications, may become quite ill with toxoplasmosis. In patients with AIDS, toxoplasmosis can be life threatening.

In the United States, it is estimated that about 60 million people carry *Toxoplasma* antibodies in their bloodstream. However, very few people have symptoms. But up to 1 of every 1,000 babies born in the United States is born infected with *Toxoplasma*. This is where the parasite exerts its most devastating effects. When a pregnant woman acquires a toxoplasmosis infection for the first time, the infection can be severely damaging to her fetus. The effects depend on when during pregnancy the infection occurs. The most severe effects occur during the second or third trimesters of pregnancy. Some of these infants are afflicted with fatal central nervous system lesions. In some cases, infants appear normal at birth, but evidence of disease appears years later. Children infected with *Toxoplasma* after birth can also suffer serious effects, especially in the eyes and brain.

Here are some simple steps that can be taken to minimize the risk of infection for both cats and owners:

• Scoop the litter box daily, because a 24-hour period is necessary after the oocysts have been shed in the feces for them to become infective.

• Make sure that someone other than a pregnant woman cleans litter boxes, and if you are pregnant, avoid contact with soil and raw meat.

• Prevent cats from defecating in play areas, especially sandboxes.

• Do not put used cat litter or fecal material in compost piles or on gardens.

• Do not feed raw or undercooked meat to cats or consume it yourself; cook meat (especially pork, lamb, and venison) to an internal temperature of 160°F (70°C). Also avoid other possible sources of infection, such as raw goat's milk and raw eggs.

• Prevent cats from hunting.

• Wash hands, surfaces, and utensils well with soap and water after handling raw meat.

• Wear gloves when gardening to avoid contacting oocysts in the soil, and wash any fruits and vegetables well before eating them.

• Women planning a pregnancy should consult a physician about prenatal blood testing to see if they have already contracted the infection.

CAT SCRATCH DISEASE (BARTONELLOSIS)

Cat scratch disease (CSD) is also called cat scratch fever or benign lymphoreticulosis. While CSD is found all over the world, it is an uncommon disease. The Centers for Disease Control estimate that there are about 2.5 cases of CSD per 100,000 people per year in the United States. While multiple cases of CSD in one household have occurred, this situation is rare. The majority of individuals who contract CSD are under the age of 17 and are usually under the age of 12.

Typically, a small skin lesion (resembling an insect bite) develops at the site of a cat scratch or (less commonly) a bite, followed within 2 weeks by swollen lymph nodes and sometimes a fever. The illness is mild and self-limiting in the majority of patients, although it may take some months for the swollen lymph nodes to return to normal. Treatment is usually not required. Reports over the last few years, however, have extended the spectrum of problems associated with CSD to include such things as tonsillitis, encephalitis, hepatitis, pneumonia, and other serious illnesses in a very small number of cases. People with compromised immune systems, such as those with acquired immunodeficiency syndrome (AIDS) or cancer, are most at risk of becoming seriously ill.

Diagnosis of CSD may not be easy. There is no one simple diagnostic test. Most physicians rely on history of exposure to a cat, the presence of typical clinical signs, failure to find another cause, and examination of tissues, such as a biopsy of an abnormal lymph node. Other diseases, such as tuberculosis, brucellosis, and lymphoma, can cause similar symptoms.

Over the years, the cause of CSD had remained elusive, although bacteria were commonly suspected to be the culprit. In recent years, studies have implicated the bacterium *Bartonella henselae* as the primary (but probably not the sole) cause of CSD. *B. henselae* is related to the agent of trench fever, *B. quintana*, a disease common in the trenches of World War I. Other *Bartonella* species may also be involved in CSD.

Cats are the main reservoir for *B. henselae*. Surveys for *B. henselae* antibodies in cats in the United States have found average infection rates to be from 25% to 41% in clinically healthy cats. The lowest rates were in the Midwest and Great Plains regions, and the highest were in the Southeast. Warmer, more humid climates are most supportive of fleas, which have been shown to transmit *B. henselae* from cat to cat. It appears that the majority of cats do not become ill when they are infected and that kittens are more commonly infected than adults. Once infected, cats carry bacteria in their blood for many months. It is important to note, however, that despite widespread presence of *B. henselae* in cats, CSD itself is uncommon. It appears that CSD is not easily acquired.

While most patients with CSD have a history of a cat scratch or bite, not all do. Some patients have had no contact with cats at all. This makes the exact modes of transmission unclear. It is likely that CSD can also be contracted from environmental sources of the bacteria or from other animals. For this reason, the term *bartonellosis* is a better way to describe the variety of illnesses that are caused by *B. henselae*. Recently, it has been found that dogs can become ill with a related *Bartonella* species, so the role of dogs as a possible reservoir for human infection is undergoing study.

CSD is primarily a concern in homes with immunocompromised people. Because kittens are more likely to carry *B. henselae* than adult cats, it is recommended that people with compromised immune systems adopt cats older than 1 year of age. Any cat suspected of carrying *B. henselae* should be isolated from sick or immunocompromised people. While diagnostic tests based for *bartonella* are available for cats, interpretation of the test results is difficult. Because carrier cats are always healthy and multiple cases of CSD within a household are rare, euthanasia of a suspected carrier is not warranted. Declawing is also not recommended, because infection can occur without a cat scratch. As is always the case, any cut or scratch should be promptly washed with soap and water. In addition, children should be taught not to tease or annoy cats, and rough play should be discouraged. A commonsense approach is the best way to safeguard against CSD.

RINGWORM (DERMATOPHYTOSIS)

Contrary to its name, ringworm is caused not by a worm but by a fungal infection of the skin. The fungus *Microsporum canis* causes almost 95% of cases in cats. Cats are exposed either directly through contact with an infected animal or through a contaminated environment. Fungal spores can remain viable in the environment for up to 2 years. It is interesting to note that exposure to this common fungus does not necessarily mean a cat will become infected, and also that infected cats do not necessarily show any signs of skin disease. Long-haired breeds do seem to be more susceptible to infection with *M. canis*, and they also may become inapparent carriers of the fungus.

Skin lesions associated with *M. canis* typically appear within 4 weeks of exposure. The most common appearance is a circular lesion with hair loss, but this disease can mimic almost any other type of skin lesion. Therefore, any cat with skin disease should be tested for ringworm. Some cats are very pruritic (itchy) with a ringworm infection, while others are not. Young kittens most typically have lesions on their face and legs. Occasionally *M. canis* infection is confined to the nail beds, a condition called paronychia. Certain factors can increase a cat's susceptibility to infection with *M. canis*, such as a suppressed immune system, overcrowding, poor nutrition, poor sanitation, genetic predisposition, excessive bathing and grooming, and concurrent diseases (especially FeLV and FIV).

Ringworm is diagnosed using two types of tests. Wood's lamp examination is quick and accessible. However, the test must be done with care. The lamp should be turned on for at least 5 minutes before use and then the hairs should be exposed for another 5 minutes. Infection with *M. canis* gives a typical apple-green fluorescence under these circumstances. However, even when performed properly, the test is subject to many false positive and false negative results and should never be relied on as the sole test for the infection.

The definitive test is a fungal culture. Several brands of fungal culture kits are available commercially for veterinarians. Hairs are collected from the entire body of the cat using a sterile toothbrush as a comb. The hairs are then carefully deposited in the culture receptacle. This test is also useful to detect inappar-

ent carriers of the fungus. The fungal culture medium will change color at the same time that the growth of the fungal colony appears, usually within 7–14 days after inoculation.

Once ringworm infection is diagnosed, treatment options depend on the circumstances. In almost all cats, the infection will resolve spontaneously without treatment in a few months. However, during this time, an infected cat can pass the infection to other animals and to humans, so it is not usually acceptable to wait for a natural cure. Treatment of ringworm may involve several strategies.

Oral Medications

The traditional drug used to treat ringworm is the antifungal griseofulvin. Before starting therapy with this drug, the patient must have blood test results that are negative for FIV. Cats with FIV have been known to have severe reactions to this drug, but FIV-negative cats may have adverse reactions to griseofulvin as well. The most common are vomiting and diarrhea, but reducing or dividing the dose usually manages these reactions. Some cats can experience bone marrow depression, so regular blood counts are used to monitor for this complication. Griseofulvin cannot be given to pregnant queens, as it is associated with birth defects such as cleft palate. Drug therapy must be maintained until two follow-up fungal cultures are negative; this typically takes 6–8 weeks.

Newer antifungal drugs such as itraconazole and fluconazole are drugs made for humans that may be chosen instead of griseofulvin. One advantage is that these drugs may be associated with fewer adverse reactions. However, blood monitoring of liver enzymes may still be recommended. They cannot be given to a cat with preexisting liver disease or in pregnancy. There are some disadvantages to these drugs, primarily the higher cost and the need to reformulate the medication to a size appropriate for cats, because veterinary formulations are not currently available. These newer drugs are useful for cats who are unable to tolerate griseofulvin or have failed a course of treatment. Cats are treated for several weeks, until two follow-up fungal cultures are negative.

Another drug for humans called terbinafine has received some attention for the treatment of ringworm in cats because it may provide a cure quicker than other drugs and it appears to have a low rate of adverse effects. However, it has not yet been widely used or evaluated for cats. Recent information indicates that a product designed for flea control, lufenuron (Program, manufactured by Novartis Animal Health), may also be an effective treatment for ringworm when used in conjunction with other treatments. Lufenuron inhibits the formation of a structural protein called chitin, an important component of the fungal cell wall.

Topical Treatments

In the past, various topical treatments (shampoos, dips, ointments/creams) were often used as the sole therapy for ringworm. Recent studies have shown that these therapies are rarely effective and do not provide a cure any faster than if the disease was allowed to resolve on its own. It has actually been found that shampooing might worsen the disease and cause it to spread. Most topical creams and ointments contain active ingredients that are not effective against *M. canis*. Current recommendations limit the use of topical therapy to lime sulfur dips used in conjunction with drug therapy. These dips are applied once or twice weekly and allowed to dry on the coat. Cats must wear an Elizabethan collar until the coat is dry, because the lime sulfur is irritating to the mouth.

Another traditional recommendation was to clip or shave the hair of all infected cats. It was thought that clipping would remove infected hairs and make recovery occur faster. However, recent studies have shown that clipping the hair often leads to worsening of the skin lesions, possibly because the clipping itself helps spread the fungal spores throughout the cat's coat. Current recommendations are to clip the hair in most long-haired cats or in any cat with severe and widespread disease. For solitary skin lesions, the hair may simply be clipped short around them using blunt scissors. It is important to dispose of clipped hairs properly so as to not contaminate the environment.

Fungal Vaccine

Since early 1994, a killed *M. canis* vaccine has been available (Fel-O-Vax MC-K, manufactured by Fort Dodge Animal Health). While it is called a vaccine, it is actually intended to aid in the treatment of ringworm and is not generally thought to be able to protect cats against new infections. There is limited data available to evaluate the vaccine properly, so it should be considered only as an adjunctive therapy. Its most appropriate use might be in multicat homes or catteries, especially when the owner is unable to use lime sulfur dips. It is hoped the vaccine will hasten recovery and lessen the amount of fungal spores being shed into the environment.

Environmental Treatment

Fungal spores will readily contaminate the environment and are very long-lived. In multicat households and catteries with more than one infected cat, the contamination of the environment can be extensive and hard to manage. Unfortunately, most available disinfectants are not effective against these spores. The most effective common product is household bleach used at a dilution of 1:10. Standard recommendations for environmental cleanup include vacuuming all surfaces in the home on a daily basis as well as cleaning all nonporous surfaces with bleach. Heating and cooling air ducts and vents should be cleaned. Ideally, all bedding, grooming tools, collars, and toys should be discarded. Cat carriers should also be cleaned with bleach. It can be very helpful to confine the infected cat or cats to one room in the home for 1–2 weeks to allow the rest of the home to be decontaminated.

Catteries present special problems for prevention and control of ringworm. Breeders should be careful not to share grooming tools or cage furnishings with other exhibitors at cat shows. Equipment used at cat shows should be stored separately away from the cattery and cleaned regularly. Nonporous surfaces (such as show tables, cages and carriers) should be cleaned with bleach after each use. Cats who are being shown regularly should be confined to an isolation area in the home or cattery. Periodic fungal cultures on long-haired cats being shown heavily should be considered. Many breeders of long-haired cats keep the hair of noncompeting cats clipped. The practice of shampooing cats frequently, especially after a show in an attempt to avoid ringworm, is dubious because studies have shown this actually might worsen the situation by spreading fungal spores. In general, only the minimal amount of bathing necessary for long-haired cats should be performed.

Infected catteries present a special challenge. It is possible to clear them of ringworm, but it requires exceptional work and dedication and may involve considerable expense. The cattery must be isolated (no cats leave or enter, which means breeding and showing plans must be put on hold) until all cats are culture-negative at least two times. For long-haired breeds, the hair coats of all cats, whether showing skin lesions or not, should be clipped. All nonpregnant cats are treated with oral medication, and all pregnant queens are treated twice weekly with lime sulfur dips. After the litters are born, the queens can start on oral drug therapy. The environment must be aggressively treated to decontaminate it. In extreme situations, it may be necessary to discard carpeting and draperies. Surfaces in the cattery can be periodically cultured to help monitor the success of the program.

PLAGUE

Many old diseases seem to be undergoing a modern reemergence, and plague is one of them. This disease exists in the wild rodent population, especially in the western United States. It is most common between the months of May and October. Cats can acquire plague through contact with an infected wild rodent and its fleas, and it is possible for the cat to transmit the disease to humans. Humans can also acquire plague through direct contact with infected rabbits, rodents, and fleas, as well as from cats.

Plague is caused by the bacterium *Yersinia pestis*. Fleas bite an infected host animal and ingest the bacterium. When the flea bites its next victim, it transmits the infection. Direct contact with an infected animal can also spread the infection. Cats are highly susceptible to this disease and it is often fatal. The incubation period is from 2–7 days after being bitten by an infected flea or eating an infected animal.

Plague can manifest in different forms, but cats most often exhibit the bubonic form. Swellings (called buboes) occur on the head and neck from enlarged lymph nodes. These nodes may abscess and then rupture and drain. Other symptoms include fever, depression, vomiting and diarrhea, loss of appetite, weight loss, and ocular discharges. Diagnosis is by special cultures and blood tests designed to identify the causative agent.

Survival depends on early diagnosis and

treatment with antibiotics and requires hospitalization and good supportive care. This disease has high potential for transmission to people, so handling of the patient requires the caregiver to wear a protective mask, gloves, and gown. Keeping cats indoors prevents the disease by curtailing hunting. Control of flea infestations is important. Strict rodent control, including elimination of their habitats in and around the home, is also essential.

INTESTINAL INFECTIONS

There are several types of intestinal infections that can be transmitted between cats and people. Two intestinal parasites, *Giardia* and *Cryptosporidia*, are discussed elsewhere in this book (see "Gastrointestinal Parasites," pages 385–389). Two bacterial diseases, salmonellosis and campylobacteriosis, are also important zoonoses.

Salmonellosis is a bacterial disease caused by various *Salmonella* species, the most common of which is *S. typhimurium*. *Salmonella* can infect many types of mammals, birds, reptiles, and even insects. The bacteria can cause various disease syndromes, or it may be present as an asymptomatic infection. Some studies have shown that up to 18% of normal, healthy cats have *Salmonella* bacteria in their gastrointestinal tract. In general, cats contract salmonellosis by coming into contact with infected feces, eating infected prey animals, or ingesting contaminated food or water. The bacteria can live in the environment for long periods of time and remain infective. *Salmonella* is also often resistant to common disinfectants.

In general, cats are relatively resistant to *Salmonella* infection. Illness due to salmonellosis is most common in young cats or adults subjected to stressful conditions (overcrowding, diet changes, transportation, immunosuppressive and other drug therapy). In cats, signs of illness associated with salmonellosis include gastroenteritis (vomiting, diarrhea, abdominal pain, loss of appetite, weight loss), sepsis (bacterial infection of the bloodstream leading to fevers, dehydration, depression), and chronic fevers with vague signs of illness but without gastroenteritis. In addition, many infected cats have no symptoms of illness at all.

Salmonellosis can be difficult to diagnose. Most often, the diagnosis is confirmed using special fecal cultures combined with the results of blood tests. In very mild cases, the disease may be self-limiting and antibiotic treatment may not be necessary. There is some evidence that treatment with antibiotics should be reserved for seriously ill patients because it may actually prolong the carrier state. Cats with salmonellosis can be shedding large amounts of bacteria in their feces, so strict isolation of the patient is very important. Owners and others handling these patients must observe strict hygiene guidelines, including frequent hand washing, disinfection of the environment, and proper handling of feces for disposal. A minimum number of people should have access to the ill cat, and certainly immunocompromised individuals should have no contact at all.

Campylobacteriosis is also a bacterial disease. It is caused by *Campylobacter jejuni*, which is commonly found in the gastrointestinal tract of many mammals, including dogs and cats. Some studies have shown that a very large number of healthy cats (up to 45%) can carry and shed *C. jejuni* in their feces. Those most frequently infected are kittens up to 6 months of age; especially those kept in crowded or confined conditions (shelters, kennels, catteries) with poor hygiene. The infection is acquired from contaminated food or water or from an environment contaminated via infected feces.

Infected cats with signs of illness due to campylobacteriosis are usually under 6 months of age. Older cats typically harbor the infection without signs of illness unless they have a suppressed immune system. Kittens may have watery diarrhea with blood and mucus present. They may also have fever, loss of appetite, vomiting, and weight loss. The symptoms tend to last 3–15 days. However, *C. jejuni* can be shed in the feces for many weeks or months.

The disease is diagnosed using fecal cultures combined with the results of other routine tests. Mild cases may be self-limiting and require only supportive care. Seriously ill patients may require hospitalization for supportive care and antibiotics. Because this illness has a high potential to infect people, good hygiene while caring for infected cats is essential. In addition, shelters and other multicat environments must have strict disinfection procedures for the cages, runs, litter boxes, and food/water dishes to prevent the disease.

TOXOCARIASIS

Toxocariasis is a syndrome caused by infection of people with the larval stages of the *Toxocara* roundworms found in dogs and cats (*T. canis* in dogs and *T. cati* in cats). The larval stages of the parasite migrate through organs and tissues in humans, causing damage. The syndromes caused by the parasite are called larva migrans. The combination of growing pet populations in North America and the high frequency of roundworm infections in dogs and cats leads to many opportunities for transmission of this infection to people. Surveys carried out in North America and Britain show that 3% or more of people have antibody titers to *Toxocara*. The number of infections is probably much higher than the number of reported cases. People become infected when they ingest *Toxocara* eggs in contaminated soil or on contaminated hands or other surfaces. Those most at risk are children under the age of 12. Direct contact with infected cats and dogs plays only a minor role in human infections.

Ingested *Toxocara* eggs hatch in the human small intestine and the larvae migrate through body tissues. They have been found in virtually every organ and tissue in the body. The mechanical movement of the larvae and the resulting inflammatory response causes damage. The most common form of toxocariasis seen in people is ocular larva migrans, which causes a variety of eye diseases. The infected person is often an adult, but the disease is also seen in children, typically 7 or 8 years old. Visceral larva migrans is the form of the disease seen when the larva migrate through nonocular tissues. The lungs, heart, and brain are commonly affected organs and deaths have been reported. The typical patient with this form of the disease is between 1 and 4 years old and there is often a history of eating non-food objects (pica) such as dirt.

Prevention of toxocariasis in people revolves around three factors: preventing the contamination of public and play areas with the feces of dogs and cats, education of pet owners about the hazards of roundworm infections, and treatment of dogs and cats with drugs to eliminate roundworms. The Centers for Disease Control in the United States recommends that all puppies and kittens be treated for roundworms as a matter of routine. It is not necessary, and may actually be misleading, to treat only on the basis of identifying the parasite on a fecal examination. The most common and effective medication is pyrantel pamoate, sold under a variety of brand names. Typically, kittens are given two to three doses of this medication with the doses spaced 2–3 weeks apart. Nursing queens should also be treated to prevent transmission of the parasite to her kittens. When an older cat or kitten is first acquired, it should be given two treatments and existing adult cats can be treated once or twice yearly or on the basis of fecal examination result, depending on their risk factors.

CAT OWNERSHIP FOR IMMUNOCOMPROMISED PEOPLE

There are many situations in which people must protect a compromised immune system: diabetes, kidney failure, some types of cancer, HIV, AIDS. Also, some people who are being given medications for cancer treatment, organ transplantation, and treatment of autoimmune diseases may experience suppression of their immune system. Physicians often counsel such patients not to have pets to avoid zoonotic diseases. However, many studies have proven the value of companion animals for immunocompromised people. Such patients have especially been shown to experience less depression than nonpet owners with similar illnesses. It is important for immunocompromised people to observe some guidelines for pet ownership to protect their health.

The most common diseases transmissible from animals to humans are the intestinal infections caused by *Salmonella* and *Campylobacter* (see "Intestinal Infections," pages 448–449) bacteria. The intestinal parasites *Giardia* and *Cryptosporidia* (see "Gastrointestinal Parasites," pages 385–389) are causes of diarrhea and are also zoonotic. Two fungal diseases, ringworm (dermatophytosis, [see "Ringworm (Dermatophytosis)," pages 444–447] and sporotrichosis, can cause skin infections and can be transmitted directly from pets to humans. Cat scratch disease [bartonellosis; see "Cat Scratch Disease (Bartonellosis)," pages 443–444] is associated with scratches or bites, or simply exposure to a cat.

GENERAL GUIDELINES FOR SAFE PET CARE

- Keep your pet healthy and clean throughout his or her life.
- Keep your pet's vaccinations up-to-date and ensure that your pet receives an annual health examination.
- Never let your pet drink from the toilet.
- Keep your pet indoors or outside only on a leash under supervision.
- Never feed your pet raw or undercooked meat, raw eggs, or unpasteurized milk.
- Have a plan each year for good flea and tick control.
- Keep your pet's feeding and sleeping areas clean at all times.
- Ensure that your pet is spayed or neutered at the appropriate age.
- Wash your hands after handling any pet.
- Have someone else do the litter box cleaning chores; if you must do it yourself, wear gloves and a face mask available from any drugstore or pharmacy.
- Always use a disinfectant when cleaning up urine, stools, or vomit.
- Be careful when handling any pet under 6 months of age, especially ones who appear to be ill or have diarrhea.

Cats in particular should be kept indoors and not allowed to hunt. They can acquire the parasite *Toxoplasma* (see "Toxoplasmosis," pages 441–443) by eating wild animals or undercooked meat. Being outside also increases their exposure to other cats and their risk of disease. When cleaning cat litter boxes, be sure the soiled litter is sealed in a plastic bag for disposal. The risk of cat scratch disease is less if a cat over 1 year of age is adopted. In general, a healthy mature adult cat who is already spayed or neutered and is free of fleas is best for an immunocompromised person to adopt. Any cat being considered for adoption should have blood tests to ensure that its FeLV and FIV status is negative. While these two viruses are not transmissible to people, they can make a cat more susceptible to other diseases.

The cat's claws should be kept trimmed short and any scratches or bites should be cleaned immediately with soap and water and treated with an antiseptic. A doctor should be consulted if any redness or swelling develops. Routine health care for cats is important to protect the people they live with. Yearly physical examinations, fecal tests for parasites, and appropriate vaccinations should all be attended to with care. Be prepared to seek the advice of a veterinarian quickly in the event of any signs of illness in the pet cat, especially if diarrhea or vomiting is involved.

Finally, it is wise to consider designating someone to care for your pet should you become ill or hospitalized. Advance arrangements can be very valuable in the case of a sudden illness, either on the part of the owner or the pet. Let your veterinarian know if someone in your home is immunocompromised and if any arrangements have been made to designate a person to act as agent for the pet. It may also be necessary to arrange in advance for a permanent home for the pet should the owner be unable to care for it at some point. Having these arrangements in place can decrease the stress associated with an unexpected or difficult situation by removing the worries about who will care for a beloved pet.

EUTHANASIA

When a cat enters our life, we are acquiring a friend who often sees us through many life stages and changes, such as marriage, divorce, and the birth of our children. Regardless of what happens, our cats are steady and nonjudgmental companions. In return, we lavish constant love and attention on them. However, in every cat's life, the natural cycle runs its course and a time will come when we must say good-bye.

In many cases, our cats die natural deaths in happy old age. Sometimes, however, we must make the decision to euthanize a sick or injured cat. While such decisions are difficult to make, the ability to do so is actually one of the greatest gifts we can give to a treasured companion. When our cat is so sick or injured that a return to a good quality of life is not possible, humane euthanasia must be considered.

Many cat owners find it difficult to determine when it is time to make such a decision. Invariably, however, we know our pets best and truly are capable of making that personal and individual decision. There are several factors that can be taken into consideration, and they should be discussed with other family members and your veterinarian when possible.

The most important criteria to use when making a decision about the timing of euthanasia revolve around quality of life. If your cat is no longer able to do the things she enjoyed most and no longer responds to family members in the same way, it may be right to consider euthanasia. Another consideration is the amount of pain a cat is experiencing. In cases of chronic illness or terminal diseases, the day will come when there is more pain and discomfort in your cat's life than good times, and this is the point at which to consider euthanasia. Finally, in some circumstances, the emotional or financial burden of a cat's illness may be beyond an owner's means or abilities and this, too, can be a valid reason to consider euthanasia.

In most cases, there is time to consider all the factors and discuss all the options with your family and with your veterinarian. We are rarely forced to make hasty decisions, and this should be avoided wherever possible. When you are discussing euthanasia, you should also explore the options for care of your cat's remains. Depending on where you live, several options may be available. Most commonly, owners can choose between burial and cremation. Burial might be on family-owned property (providing local laws allow this) or in a pet cemetery or memorial park. Cremation might be a simple affair or an arrangement where the cat's ashes can be returned to the owner, usually in a tasteful urn or container. Many owners choose to keep their beloved cat's ashes nearby or will bury them in a garden setting later on.

Try to plan the actual euthanasia appointment in advance. You will need to discuss with your veterinarian what options are appropriate for your family and your pet. Some veterinarians offer a home visit for this purpose, or will set aside time in the clinic for the family to attend. Some veterinarians do not wish to have owners in attendance for the actual administration of the drugs that induce euthanasia but will set aside time for visiting afterward. Each cat owner must make a personal decision about whether to attend the actual event; your own emotional makeup is a considerable factor. It is generally not desirable for young children to be involved in such events, and for older children, the decision to include them should be made only after careful consideration.

Much has been written about how to discuss euthanasia with children and how to handle the death of a beloved pet. It is wise to consult some of the excellent books and publications on the topic, especially when a pet has been with the family for a long time. In many cases, children cannot remember a time when the family pet was not there and their sense of loss and confusion can be significant. In general, it is best to be truthful and straightforward with children, giving them simple answers to their questions to help them understand at a level appropriate to their age.

Veterinarians are skilled at making euthanasia a smooth and pain-free event for pets.

Most veterinarians will administer a tranquilizer to the cat first to ensure that the pet is calm and free of fear. Euthanasia itself is induced by the intravenous administration of a drug, often through a catheter that might be placed in advance.

PET LOSS AND GRIEF

Once euthanasia has been performed on a beloved pet, the next phase begins. It is very natural and normal to feel grief and sorrow after the loss of a pet. People go through grieving in their own way and at their own pace, but some features of the process are common to all of us.

The first feelings are often those of shock or denial. These feelings may start even before the pet has died, when a serious illness or injury is diagnosed. Anger follows denial in many people, and it may be directed toward other people around you. You may be angry with yourself or others for not recognizing a serious situation earlier, or you may be angry with others for things they have unintentionally said that hurt you. Some people then go through a phase in which they bargain with a supreme being to bring their beloved pet back. Guilt and depression are also common symptoms after the death of a pet. This is the stage when your loss is acutely and deeply felt. You may find yourself thinking of your absent pet often, or you may be surprised when something simply triggers a memory. Some people experience significant signs of depression, having trouble with day-to-day tasks and wondering if they can go on. In these cases, it is possible to seek the assistance of a professional counselor for help. Good sources for help are clergy, social workers, grief counselors, your physician, or a therapist or psychologist. Many such professionals are specifically trained for pet loss and grief.

Finally, a degree of acceptance of your

loss will set in. This happens to each of us in our own time, and well-meaning comments from friends and family that you should "get over it" will not help. Many people do not recognize the true importance of pets in the lives of others and so may not understand the depth of grief at a loss. It is best to be honest with yourself and others about your feelings and not be ashamed of them.

It is comforting for some owners to memorialize their cat in some way. There are many good ideas on how to do this, ranging from a memorial donation to feline medical research to planting a special tree or plant that will always remind you of your cat. Photographs and mementos can also be used to make pictures or displays that recall the good times of companionship.

Many people have found it helpful to talk to others who have been through the loss of a pet as well. Depending on where you live, there may be a local pet loss support group that meets regularly. Your veterinarian will know if such a group exists and how to contact it. There are also several good pet loss hotlines available for telephone support, which are often run by veterinary colleges.

BOOKS ABOUT PET LOSS

Books for Adults

The Loss of a Pet (revised and expanded), by Wallace Sife, published by Howell Book House (1998), ISBN 0876051972

Angel Whiskers: Reflections on Loving and Losing a Feline Companion, by Laurel E. Hunt, published by Disney Press (2001), ISBN 0786865784

Saying Goodbye to Your Pet: Children Can Learn to Cope With Pet Loss, by Marge Heegaard, published by Fairview Press (2001), ISBN 1577491068

Three Cats, Two Dogs: One Journey Through Multiple Pet Loss, by David Congalton, published by Plutonium Press (2000), ISBN 0939165376

Books for Children

For Every Cat an Angel, by Christine Davis, published by Lighthearted Press (2000), ISBN 0965922510

Barn Kitty, by June Kirkpatrick, published by Azro Press (1999), ISBN 0966023951

My Pet Died, by Rachel Biale, published by Tricycle Press (1997), ISBN 1883672511

The Legend of Rainbow Bridge, by William Britton, published by Savannah Publishing (1994), ISBN 0964501805

Cat Heaven, by Cynthia Rylant, published by Scholastic (1997), ISBN 0590100548

DELTA SOCIETY

The Delta Society (http://www.deltasociety.org) is an international nonprofit organization devoted to the human–animal bond, and service and therapy animals in particular. On their Web site, they maintain a directory of pet loss resources that contains information about pet loss, recommended books, and pet loss support hotlines and Web sites.

GLOSSARY

acupuncture, acutherapy: Therapies, used to diagnose and treat many conditions, that involve the stimulation of specific points on the cat's body using any one of several methods, including acupuncture needles, moxibustion, injections, lasers, and magnets.

allergen: Something that can induce an allergic reaction or hypersensitivity.

alter: To surgically render a cat unable to reproduce. *Also:* A castrated male cat or a female cat that has had its reproductive organs removed.

amylase: Enzyme that breaks down carbohydrates in the small intestine; secreted from the pancreas and cells lining the small intestine.

antioxidant: A substance that either prevents the formation of potentially harmful free radicals or one that helps to remove free radicals once they have formed.

AOV: Any Other Variety. Any registered cat or registered kitten, the ancestry of which entitles it to Championship or Premiership competition, but which does not (colorwise; coatwise; sexwise; tailwise, as in the case of naturally tailless or naturally partially tailless breeds; or earwise) conform to the accepted show standard.

arachidonic acid: Essential fatty acid for cats.

artery: Blood vessel in which blood moves away from the heart.

as-fed: Term used to describe diet composition as it is in the package or as it is fed to the pet; contrast with **dry matter**.

bacterial cystitis: Inflammation of the bladder associated with a bacterial infection.

Beta-carotene: Also spelled β-carotene. Precursor of vitamin A that stimulates the immune system. Cannot be converted to vitamin A by cats.

bile: Produced by the liver and stored in the gallbladder; secreted into the small intestine, it breaks up fat into smaller sizes for absorption.

biological value: Measure of protein quality—the ratio of nitrogen retained to nitrogen absorbed. Higher is better, with 100% being perfect (for example, an egg).

blockage: Obstruction of the urethra so that no urine can be passed; potentially life-threatening.

bloodline: A group of cats related by ancestry or pedigreed.

blue slip: An application required for individual registration of a cat from a registered litter. Issued to the breeder by the Cat Fanciers' Association at the time the litter is registered. It is usually given to the new owner of a cat/kitten by the breeder at the time of sale.

borage oil: A liquid fat source derived from the borage plant and a rich source of gamma-linoleic acid (GLA).

BW: Breed Winner. Similar to the title of National Winner, but for adult cats that have achieved a Best of Breed win.

calling: The noise made by a female cat when in season.

calorie: Measure of energy; amount of heat required to raise the temperature of 1 gram of water 1°C at 15°C. Cat food labels actually use kilocalories; 1 kilocalorie is 1,000 calories.

capillary: Small blood vessel that connects small veins and arteries.

carbohydrate: Includes starches and fiber; substance composed of carbon, hydrogen, and oxygen.

cardiac sphincter: Valve between the stomach and esophagus.

carnivores: Animals that feed on other animals.

carotene: Actually *beta-carotene*, a precursor of vitamin A; cannot be converted to vitamin A by cats.

cat fancy: Refers to the overall group of people, clubs, and registration associations involved with breeding and showing, all having an interest in the betterment of the cat.

cattery name: A name registered by a breeder to identify the line of breeding. A registered cattery name always appears as a prefix to the name of a cat bred by that cattery/breeder. A registered cattery name is not required in order to register a litter with the Cat Fanciers' Association, but a cattery name must be registered if it is to be used in cat names bred by a particular breeder.

cell: Basic building block in the body; contains a nucleus and cytoplasm surrounded by a cell membrane.

cellulose: Carbohydrate chains of glucose found in plant cells. It is indigestible and non-fermentable.

certified pedigreed: A document showing a cat's background for three to six generations. A pedigree is the cat plus the appropriate number of generations back, and gives names, colors, and registration numbers of each cat in the pedigree. Show titles, if any, are also provided.

CH: Champion, the title given to an adult cat who competed at Cat Fanciers' Association cat shows and received six winner ribbons. This is the first title a cat can achieve.

chiropractic: A system of diagnosis and treatment through manipulation and adjustment of certain joints in the cat's body.

chyme: Semiliquid food that leaves the stomach for the intestinal tract.

colonocytes: Cells lining the large intestine.

complete protein: Contains all the essential amino acids.

cross-breed: The allowable mating of two pedigreed varieties. The resulting offspring would be considered a hybrid. *See* **hybrid**.

cryptorchid: A male cat whose testicles have not descended.

crystalluria: Presence of crystals in urine.

dam: The mother of a cat.

diabetes mellitus: Disease caused by absence of or abnormally low insulin levels.

digestible energy: Gross energy minus energy lost in the feces.

digestion: Process in which food is taken in, broken down, and absorbed in the gastrointestinal tract.

dilute: A recessive color. *See* **recessive**.

dipeptide: Two linked amino acids.

disaccharide: Two sugar molecules joined together.

DM: Distinguished Merit, the title given to a cat who has produced the required number of Grand Champions, Grand Premiers, or Distinguished Merit cats (5 for females and 15 for males).

dominant: A characteristic that expresses itself wholly or largely to the exclusion of the alternate recessive characteristic. *See* **recessive**.

dry matter: Term used to describe diet composition in which the water has been mathematically removed; appropriate for comparing livestock diets but not for cat diets.

DW: Divisional Winner, similar to the title of Regional Winner but reserved for cats competing only in the Cat Fanciers' Association International Division.

dysuria: Painful or difficult urination.

electrolyte: Mineral (such as sodium or potassium) that dissociates into ions and helps with numerous functions within the body.

endocrine gland: Secretes hormones into the bloodstream for regulation of activities of other tissues.

energy: Ability to do work, produce motion, or cause changes; measured in kilocalories in cat foods.

enterocytes: Cells lining the small intestine.

enzyme: Protein that facilitates chemical reactions including the digestion of food.

erythropoietin: Hormone produced in the kidneys that stimulates red blood cell production in the bone marrow.

essential amino acid: Amino acid that cannot be produced in the body; must be obtained from food.

essential fatty acid: Fatty acid that cannot be produced in the body; must be obtained from food.

exocrine gland: Secretes substances through a duct, such as the saliva glands in the mouth.

fat: Substance composed of carbon, hydrogen, and oxygen in the form of combinations of fatty acids.

fatty acid: Building block of fats.

feline: Of the cat family.

feline lower tract urinary disease: *See* **FLUTD**.

fetus: Animal developing in the uterus.

fiber: Indigestible carbohydrate from plants; may be digested (fermented) by intestinal bacteria to provide energy for the lining of the small intestine; adds bulk to food and aids in movement of food through the gastrointestinal tract.

FLUTD: Feline lower urinary tract disease; sometimes caused by struvite or calcium oxalate uroliths in the bladder.

foreign registration: Any application and subsequent registration of a cat from non-CFA registered parentage when the cat is currently registered in any other cat association recognized by the Cat Fanciers' Association, either inside or outside the United States.

free radicals: Potentially harmful by-products of oxidation.

fructooligosaccharide: Abbreviated as FOS. It is a short chain of sugars composed of one sucrose molecule with two to four fructose molecules attached.

genotype: The genetic composition of a cat. All individuals of the same genotype breed alike. *See* **phenotype**.

gestation: Pregnancy, the period during which animals are growing in the uterus—typically, 63 days in cats.

glomerulus: The filtration unit of the kidney.

glycogen: Carbohydrate with long chains of glucose molecules. It is the storage form of carbohydrate in liver and muscles.

gluten: A vegetable protein; a tough, thick, protein-containing substance remaining when grain is washed to remove the starch, as in corn gluten.

glycemic response: The increase in blood glucose following a meal; the amount of the increase and the timing of the increase are characteristic of the carbohydrate source being digested.

GC: Grand Champion, the title awarded to an adult cat who continued to compete at Cat shows and received 200 points in its competition category.

GP: Grand Premier; equivalent title to Grand Champion for an altered cat.

gross energy: Total energy available from food; determined in the laboratory by burning of food.

hematuria: Presence of blood in the urine.

hemoglobin: Iron-containing substance in red blood cells that transports oxygen.

herbal (botanical) medicine: A branch of veterinary medicine that uses plants and includes the disciplines of Western herbal medicine, Ayurvedic (Hindu) medicine, and Chinese herbal medicine.

homeopathy: A system of treatment in which the veterinarian administers substances that can produce clinical signs in healthy cats that are similar to the symptoms of the ill cat under treatment. The substances are used in very minute doses.

hormones: Substances produced by endocrine glands that regulate activities of many body tissues.

household pet: A nonregistered altered cat, usually from unregistered stock and of no particular breed.

hybrid: The result of the breeding of two different breeds. Can also refer to those kittens produced from such a mating that do not conform to the accepted standard for the resulting breed.

idiopathic (interstitial) cystitis: Poorly understood, painful, inflammatory condition of the bladder not associated with bacterial or viral infection.

inbreeding: The mating of two closely related cats, such as mother and son or brother and sister. There are no rules in the Cat Fanciers' Association against the registration of kittens produced from such a breeding.

incomplete protein: Does not contain all the essential amino acids.

inflammatory bowel disease:. Abbreviated as IBD. A group of disorders of unknown cause that result in inflammation of the intestinal lining. Diet can be important in management.

inorganic: Nonliving (not plant or animal); mineral.

insulin: Hormone produced by the pancreas that regulates glucose metabolism in the body.

intense: A dominant color. *See* **dominant**.

kilocalorie: 1,000 calories; a measure of energy.

kitten: A cat up to the age of 8 calendar months.

lactation: Secretion of milk for nourishment of newborn animals.

linoleic acid: Essential fatty acid; required in cat diets.

lipase: Enzyme that breaks down fats.

lipid: Fat.

lipoprotein: Substance made of lipid and protein; important part of cell membrane structure.

litter: The name given to the product of any one breeding. A litter can consist of one or more kittens.

litter registration: The recording by the Cat Fanciers' Association of the birth of a litter, giving the date of birth, number of kittens, and the sire and dam. Litter applications are submitted by the breeder of the litter.

lymph: Tissue fluid that circulates in the lymph system.

metabolic water: Water formed when nutrients are metabolized to form energy in the body.

metabolism: All the chemical reactions in the body that produce energy or provide for growth, maintenance, and repair.

metabolizable energy: Digestible energy minus energy lost in the urine; energy available to the animal to perform activities and bodily functions.

mineral: Inorganic material required in small amounts for fluid balance and chemical reactions; important for teeth and bones.

monorchid: A male cat with only one descended testicle. Does not affect breeding capability or the quality of the cat; however, a male cat with only one descended testicle is subject to disqualification in Cat Fanciers' Association shows.

monosaccharide: Single-sugar molecule, the basic building block of carbohydrates.

NW: National Winner, the highest and most prestigious title a cat (adult cat, kitten, or altered cat) can achieve by competing at Cat Fanciers' Association shows.

neuter: An altered male. *See* **alter**.

nitrogen balance: Measure of nitrogen metabolism—the ratio of retained nitrogen to consumed nitrogen; used to measure protein nutrition.

not for breeding: A cat who has been registered as a nonbreeding cat at the request of the breeder and agreement of the new owner of the cat at the time of sale. No litters will be registered by Cat Fanciers' Association from a cat so registered.

nutrient: Substance that provides energy or material for body reactions.

nutritional therapy: A therapy using nutrition to prevent disease in healthy cats and to treat some illnesses. This category of therapy encompasses glandular therapy, cell therapy, and orthomolecular (vitamin and mineral) medicine.

obesity: Overweight caused by energy intake being greater than output; excess energy stored as fat.

omega-6 or omega-3 fatty acids: Fatty acids that promote formation of natural inflammatory (omega-6 fatty acids) or anti-inflammatory (omega-3 fatty acids) substances.

organic: Living or derived from living things—plant or animal.

outcross: To breed one registered breed to another, resulting in a registerable hybrid breed. Also those breeds allowable in the background of a registered hybrid breed. *See also* **hybrid**.

oxalate: A type of urinary tract crystal or stone, often expressed as calcium oxalate.

oxidation: Burning; combining with oxygen.

papers: Usually refers to a cat's certificate of registration and pedigreed form.

pedigreed: A form on which a cat and its background is recorded for three generations back.

pedigreed cat: Usually refers to a cat whose heritage is known, documented, and registered.

pepsin: Stomach enzyme that helps break down proteins.

peristalsis: Rhythmic contractions that cause food to move through the gastrointestinal tract.

pH: A measure of acidity or alkalinity on a scale of 1–14; a pH of 7 is neutral.

phenotype: The outward appearance of a cat. Two individuals with the same phenotype may not necessarily have the same genotype. *See* **genotype**.

physical therapy: A therapy for enhancing rehabilitation of injured cats, using such noninvasive techniques as chiropractic, massage, stretching, hydrotherapy, heat and cold therapy, and stimulation with lasers, electricity, magnets, or ultrasound.

plasma: Liquid portion of blood.

pollakiuria: Increased frequency of urination.

polypeptide: Chains of more than three amino acids.

polysaccharide: Chains of more than three sugars.

preformed: Already formed; substances required in a diet because they cannot be formed in the body from other nutrients.

PR: Premier, an altered (neutered or spayed) adult cat who received six winner ribbons at Cat Fanciers' Association cat shows. Equivalent to the title of Champion.

protease: Pancreatic enzyme; breaks down proteins.

protein: Composed of carbon, hydrogen, oxygen, and nitrogen; chains of amino acids; basic building materials for body cells, enzymes, antibodies, and some hormones.

protein efficiency ratio: Abbreviated as PER. A measure of protein quality—the ratio of weight gain to protein intake; higher is better.

pyloric sphincter: Valve between the stomach and the small intestine.

queen: A breeding female cat or the process of delivering kittens.

recessive: A characteristic that is unable to express itself in the presence of the alternate dominant characteristic. *See* **dominant**.

RW: Regional Winner, similar to the title of National Winner but at a regional level.

renal: Referring to the kidney.

respiration: Exchange of gases between an animal and its environment.

saccharide: Sugar; basic building block of carbohydrates.

saliva: Liquid secreted by glands into the mouth; moistens food and contains some enzymes that begin food breakdown.

sire: The father of a cat.

skeletal muscle: Striated muscle attached to bone; produces voluntary movement.

small intestinal bacteria overgrowth: Abbreviated as SIBO. The growth of excessive numbers of bacteria in the intestine that oftentimes results in diarrhea and weight loss.

smooth muscle: Nonstriated muscle in internal organs; produces involuntary movement.

spay: An altered female. *See* **alter**.

spraying: A male cat's habit of micturating (urinating) anywhere, probably to establish his territory.

standard: The ideal characteristics for each breed.

starch: Chains of glucose molecules present in plants; soluble polysaccharide.

stranguria: Straining to urinate; often confused with constipation.

struvite: Magnesium ammonium phosphate crystals that are associated with one form of FLUTD.

stud book: A book, last published in 1967, listing those cats that became registered parents for the first time during the publishing year.

stud cat: A breeding male cat.

stud tail: A medical condition in some male cats involving excess oil production along the tail.

suffix: The registered cattery name of the current owner of a cat, located at the end of a cat's name and preceded by the word *of*.

taurine: Essential amino acid required in cats' diets; important in vision and heart function.

tissue: Groups of similar cells combined to perform various functions within the body such as covering surfaces, lining tubes, connecting body structures, or forming specialized components of the anatomy such as muscle and nerves.

tripeptide: Three amino acids linked together.

urethritis: Inflammation of the urethra.

urolith: Stone in the urinary bladder associated with FLUTD.

vein: Blood vessel through which blood is returned to the heart.

villi: Small projections in the lining of the small intestine that increase the surface area for the absorption of nutrients.

vitamin: Catalyst for enzyme reactions required in small amounts. Does not provide energy.

wean: Discontinuation of nursing; when a young animal has adapted from mother's milk to other food.

NOTES AND REFERENCES

CHAPTER 2

1. Merritt Clifton, "Woods and Barn Cats," *Animal People,* July/August 1997.

2. Stephen Budiansky, *The Covenant of the Wild: Why Animals Chose Domestication.* New York: William Morrow, 1992.

3. American Pet Product Manufacturers Association (APPMA), *1998 National Pet Owners Survey.* Greenwich, CT: APPMA.

4. M. Salman et al, National Council for Pet Population Study & Policy, "Human and Animal Factors Related to the Relinquishment of Dogs and Cats in 12 U.S. Animal Shelters," *Journal of Applied Animal Welfare Science* 1(3): 207–226, 1998.

5. Leslie Larson Cooper, D.V.M., "Starting Out Right—Nurturing the Perfect Kitten," *Cats Magazine,* August 1999.

6. Niels Pedersen, D.V.M., and Joan (Wastlhuber) Miller, "Cattery Design and Management." In *Feline Husbandry: Diseases and Management in the Multiple-Cat Environment* (Niels C. Pedersen, ed.). Goleta, CA: American Veterinary Publications, 1991.

7. Niels Pedersen, D.V.M., "Common Infectious Diseases of Multiple-Cat Environments." In *Feline Husbandary: Diseases and Management in the Multiple-Cat Environment.* Goleta, CA: American Veterinary Publications, 1991.

CHAPTER 7

Chapter Resources

1. "Ask the Experts," Kitty Angell, *CATS* magazine, March 1998, August 1997, July 1997.

2. Edward Bach, M.D., *The Bach Flower Remedies*, revised edition. Saffron Walden, Essex, England: C. W. Daniel, 1997.

3. Cornell Feline Health Center, Cornell University, *The Cornell Book of Cats,* edited by Mordecai Siegal. New York: Villard Books, 1989.

4. "Dear Kitty," Kitty Angell, *CATS* magazine, June 1999, May 1999, August 1995.

5. Pam Johnson, *Twisted Whiskers*. Freedom, CA: Crossing Press, 1994.

6. Soraya V. Juarbe-Diaz, D.V.M., Diplomate, American College of Veterinary Behav-

ior Adjunct Faculty, College of Veterinary Medicine, Royal Palm Beach, FL.

7. Niels C. Pedersen, D.V.M., Ph.D., *Feline Husbandry, Diseases and Management in the Multiple-Cat Environment*. Goleta, CA: American Veterinary Publications, 1991.

8. *The Book of the Cat*, edited by Michael Wright and Sally Walters. New York: Summit Books, 1980.

9. Joseph Wylder, *Psychic Pets: The Secret Life of Animals*. Avenel, NJ: Gramercy Books, 1978.

INDEX

Page numbers in *italics* refer to illustrations.

allergies, in cats:
    to fleabites, 380
    food, 317
    to vaccinations, 349
allergies, in humans, 268, 301
    Devon Rex and, 94
    Siberian and, 198–99
    Sphynx and, 211
allowable breeding outcrosses.
    See specific breeds
alternative veterinary
    medicine, 338–39
alters, 22, 455
American Animal Hospital
    Association (AAHA),
    334, 374, 376, 377
American Association of
    Feline Practitioners
    (AAFP), 336, 426
    Academy of Feline
    Medicine of, 340, 344,
    346, 347, 348, 349, 410,
    412, 426
    Web site of, 340
American Automobile
    Association (AAA), 376
American Board of Veterinary
    Practitioners (ABVP),
    337
American bobcat, 136
American Bobtail, 12, 27,
    36–41
    CFA show standard for, 39–41
    description of, 37
    grooming of, 38
    Longhair, *36,* 37, 40
    origin and history of, 38
    personality of, 37–38
    Shorthair, *36,* 37, 40
    tail of, 37, 40
American Cat Association, 4
American Cat Fanciers'
    Association, 6

American Curl, 11, 27, 41–45,
    245
    CFA show standard for,
    44–45
    description of, 41–42
    ears of, 41–42, 45
    grooming of, 42
    Longhair, *41,* 44, 45
    origin and history of, 42–44
    personality of, 42
    Shorthair, *41,* 44, 45
American Holistic Veterinary
    Medical Association,
    339
American Humane
    Association, 234, 378
American Shorthair, 4, 7, 20,
    27, 46–50, *46*
    in American Wirehair
    breeding, 53, 54
    in Bombay breeding, 65–66,
    68
    in breeding Exotic, 105,
    106–7
    British Shorthairs and, 70
    CFA show standard for,
    49–50
    in Devon Rex breeding,
    96
    grooming of, 47
    in Havana Brown breeding,
    112, 115
    HCM in, 418
    name change of, 48
    in Ocicat breeding, 152–53
    origin and history of, 47–48
    personality of, 46–47, 259
    in Scottish Fold breeding,
    181, 185
    in Sphynx breeding, 212,
    213, 215
American Siamese Cat Club of
    Japan, 10

American Society for the
    Prevention of Cruelty
    to Animals (ASPCA),
    378
    National Animal Poison
    Control Center of, 376,
    391
American Veterinary Medical
    Association (AVMA),
    337, 339, 378
American Wirehair, 27, 51–54,
    51, 60
    American Shorthairs in
    breeding of, 53, 54
    CFA show standards for,
    53–54
    coat of, 51, 52, 53–54
    description of, 51
    grooming of, 52
    origin and history of, 52
    personality of, 51–52
amino acid profile, 299, 300,
    325
amino acids, 208, 296, 298,
    299, 305, 309, 311, 312,
    318
    essential, 297, 298, 299, 324,
    458
    nonessential, 298
aminoglycosides, 397
amino sulphonic acid, 299
amitryptyline, 424
amylase, 311, 455
amyloidosis, 420–21
analgesia, 371–72
analgesics (painkillers), toxicity
    of, 396
anal secretions, 261
anaphylaxis, 349
anemia, 307, 321, 353, 410,
    434, 435
    feline infectious, 351,
    390–91

breathing tube, 371

breed clubs, xxiii, 138, 148, 234

breeders, 22, 240
    and kitten development, 22–23, 235
    and kitten health, 23–24, 235–36
    lines of, 237
    neonatal care and, 24
    neutering or spaying by, 274
    pet shops not favored by, 233–34
    responsible, 234–36

breeding, 21, 279–83
    commitment to, 281
    genetics in, 19–20
    health in, 280, 281
    perverseness of, 381
    postnatal care in, 282–83
    producing kittens in, 281–82
    research for, 279–80
    selecting cats for, 236–37, 280

breed rescue organizations, 234

breeds, 3
    in animal shelters, 21
    behavior of, 259
    CFA, 27–230
    characteristics of, 19
    "creating" of, 7
    development of, 17–18
    of dogs, 19
    preservation of, 21
    rare, 17–18, 234
    See also specific breeds

breed standards, xix–xx, xxiv, xxix, 6–7, 19, 20, 27, 43, 75, 80, 115, 236, 241, 244, 247, 279–80, 462

Breed Winner (BW), 28, 237, 456

British Blue:
    Chartreux crossed with, 80
    See also British Shorthair

British Burmese, 93

British Shorthair, 9, 27, 68–73, *68*, 89, 93
    as ancestor of Manx, 142
    CFA show standards for, 72–73
    description of, 68–69
    in Devon Rex breeding, 93, 96
    grooming for, 69
    history of, 69–71
    Persians in breeding of, 70
    personality of, 69
    random-bred cats in breeding of, 70
    registered as Domestic or American Shorthairs, 70
    in Scottish Fold breeding, 181, 183, 185
    in Selkirk Rex breeding, 191

bronchial asthma. *See* feline asthma

bronchial wash, 415

bronchoalveolar lavage, 390, 415

bronchodilators, 415

bronchopneumonia, 399

Bronze Age, 228

brown, 251

Brown, Mrs. Fred, 3, 137

brown mackerel tabby, 249

brown patched tabby, 252

brown point, 9

brown tabby, 252

brucellosis, human, 444

brushing, 268, 276, 277

Bubastis, 98

buboes, 447

buccal (cheek) surfaces, 365

Buckfastleigh, 93

Buddhist temples, cats in, 17

Buffon, George-Louis Leclerc, Comte de, 18, 80

bunting behavior, 261

burial, 452

Burma, 60–61

Burmese, 6, 18, 27, 73–77, 89, 109
    in breeding Bombays, 65–66, 68
    CFA show standards for, 76–77
    description of, 73–74
    dilute division, *73, 74*
    European Burmese distinct from, 101, 102, 103
    grooming of, 74
    history of, 74–75
    judging of, 243
    personality of, 74
    sable division, *73, 74*
    in Scottish Fold breeding, 181
    Siamese and, 75, 101, 102, 194
    Tonkinese and, 215, 216, 217

burns, 372

butter, 304, 317

by-products, 316

calcium, 305, 306, 307, 317, 351

calcium channel blockers, 417

calcium oxalate, 422–24

calculus (tartar), 364

calico, 9, 17, 250, 254

California, 10, 101, 123, 164

calling, 366, 456

complete blood count (CBC), 351, 393, 414, 415, 434

complete protein, 299, 457

computerized tomography (CT), 356, 357

Concerning Cats (Winslow), 198

condition, 29–30

congenital defects, 438–40

congenital heart diseases, 406–9, *406*

congestive heart failure, 407, 415, 430, 432

conjunctivitis, 399

consciousness:
altered levels of, 375
loss of, 372

constipation, 302, 303, 310, 372, 434

containers, 268

Coombs test, 351

copper, 307

Copper cats. *See* Burmese

copulation, feline, 281

core vaccines, 340–41
protocols for, 346

corn, 295, 303, 318, 319

Cornell Feline Health Center (FHC), 336

Cornish Rex, 8, 18–19, 27, 87–91, *87,* 93, 189
bald spots in, 238
behavior of, 259
CFA show standards for, 90–91
coat of, 88, 89, 90, 91–92, 188
description of, 88
grooming of, 89
history of, 89
personality, 88

cornmeal, 318

corn syrup, 429

Cornwall, 89

Coronavirus, 403

Corsica, 249

corticosteroids, 345–46, 383, 384, 389–90, 391, 400, 414, 415, 424, 427

Cosequin (chondroitin sulfate), 424

cottage cheese, 317

coughing, 239, *358,* 385, 389, 415

Council Rock Farm, 52

Coupar Angus, 182

Cox, Beryl, 93

CPR (cardiopulmonary resuscitation), 332, 374

cream, 251

cream and white coat, 254

cream point, 254

cream tabby, 252

creatinine, 434

cremation, 452

cross-breeding, 60, 70, 107, 148, 457

Crusades, 163

cryptorchidism, 439, 457

Cryptosporidia, 355, 387–88, 448, 450

Cryptosporidium parvum, 387–88

crystalluria, 422–23, 457

Crystal Palace, cat shows at, 18, 69, 177, 193

curiosity, danger and, 275–76

Curlniques Cattery, 42

Cushing's disease (hyperadrenocorticism), 430

cutaneous larva migrans, 387

Cymric. *See* Manx, Longhair

Cymric Breed Council, 142

cyproheptadine, 402, 415, 435

Cyprus, 79

cysteine, 299

cystic ovaries, 357

cystocentesis, 354–55

cystoscopy, 357, 424

cysts, 419–20
infective, 388

dairy products, 317
See also specific dairy products

Dalai She, 152

dams, 280, 281, 457

dander, 65, 199

dandruff, 383, 384, 385

Daniels Pharmaceuticals, 435

deafness, 223, 238, 397, 439

death:
grief and, 452–53
natural, 451
sudden, *359*
See also euthanasia

deciduous teeth, 363

declawing, 28, 273–74, 368, 369–70, 444
and immunocompromised owners, 368, 369

degenerative diseases, 410

dehydration, 352, 354, 363, 388, 434, 435

delivery, difficult, 372

Delta Society, 453

demodectic mange, 385

Dent, Thomas H., x–xi, xxi–xxvi, 9

dental care, 340, 363–66
home cleanings, 363–64, 365–66
veterinary cleanings, 363, 364

dental cleaning pastes, 365–66

dental disease, 428, 434

dental prophylaxis, 364

gluten, 318, 458

glycemic response, 310, 458

glycogen, 302, 303, 458

glycosylated hemoglobin, 351, 428

goiter, 307

gold eyes, 250

GOOP, 42, 425

Governing Council of the Cat Fancy (GCCF), 70, 157

grains, 304, 305, 318
  as protein sources, 299, 300, 316, 320, 324–25

grain sorghum (milo), 318, 319

Grand Champions (GC), 6, 8, 28, 237, 242, 458

Grand Premiers (GP), 6, 28, 242, 458

gray, 251

gray tabby, 252

Great Britain, 16, 70, 449
  See also England; Scotland; United Kingdom

green eyes, 250

green peas, 304

grief, pet loss and, 452–53

griseofulvin, 396, 438, 445–46

grooming, 30, 237, 245
  tools and supplies for, 268
  See also specific breeds

gross energy (GE), 307, 458

ground wheat, 318–19

group hierarchy, 260

growling, 260, 269

growth, 355, 385
  protein efficiency ratio and, 300

Guam, 379

guard hairs, 51, 88, 91–92, 252

guardians, owners vs., 21

gums, pale, *359,* 390

habitat, 247

hairballs, 276, 302, 319

hairlessness, 20

hair loss, 239, *358*

Halloween cat, 260

handling, 370
  of Abyssinians, 34
  of kittens, 264

Hartz Mountain Corporation, xxv

Havana Brown, 8, 27, 52, 109–15, *109*
  American Shorthair in breeding, 112, 115
  CFA show standards for, 114–15
  description of, 109–10
  grooming of, 111–12
  Oriental Shorthair in breeding of, 112, 115
  personality of, 110–11
  Russian Blue in breeding of, 112
  Siamese in breeding of, 109, 112, 113, 115, 194

Hawaii, 379

hazel eyes, 250

head:
  standards for, 29
  types of, 19

health, 23–24, 331–453
  in breeding, 280, 281

health certificates, 378

health insurance, pet, 337

health research, feline, xxv, 337

hearing, 261

heart, 306, 431
  enlarged, 407

heart diseases, 299
  congenital, *404,* 406–9

Heartguard for Cats (ivermectin), 390

heart massage, 374

heart murmurs, 407, 408, 417, 431

heart parasites, 389–90

heart rate, 373–74, 431

heartworm, 382, 383, 389–90, 415

heat. *See* estrus

heat exhaustion, 372

heating pads, 362

heat lamps, 362

heatstroke, 372, 377

hematocrit, 351

hematomas, 383

hematuria, 421, 422, 424, 459

hemobartonellosis, 442

hemoglobin, 307, 311, 351, 458

hemorrhage, 366, 367, 372, 375, 420

hepatic lipidosis, 295, 362, 429

hepatitis, human, 443

HI-FI Cattery, 52

high blood pressure, 417, 430–31, *430,* 434, 435

high-fiber diets, 295

Highland Fold. *See* Scottish Fold; Longhair

Hill's Pet Nutrition, 366, 423

Himalayan, 6, 59, *160,* 161, 198
  CFA reclassification of, 8
  creation of, 7–8, 20, 194
  See also Persian

Himalayan pattern, 105, 171, 254

hip, as ball-and-socket joint, 418

hip dysplasia, feline, 418–19

hissing, 269

histidine, 298

Histoire naturelle (Buffon), 18

Hittites, 228

HIV (human immunodeficiency virus), 333, 412, 450

Hokkaido, 118
holiday decorations, 276
holistic medicine, 263, 339
Holland, 33, 228
Holland, Sylvia, 56
home care, environment for, 362–63
homeless cats, 15, 21, 234
    decline in numbers of, 22
    social hierarchy among, 260
hookworms, 355, 382, 383, 386–87, 389
hormones, 296, 297, 299, 300, 312, 367, 459
Horner, Nikki, 65–66
Hoskins, Johnny, 347
hotels, pets in, 271, 376, 377
hot pepper sauce, 266
hot water bottles, 362
Houpt, Katherine A., 266
Houpt, T. Richard, 266
household cleaning agents, 275
Household Pet Class, 28, 242, 243, 246, 459
house soiling, *359*
howling, 260
humane societies, 255
human immunodeficiency virus. *See* HIV
humans:
    campylobacteriosis in, 448–49, 450
    cat scratch disease in, 443–44, 450
    Cheyletiella blakei mites and, 384
    conjunctivitis in, 399
    Cryptosporidium in, 387–88, 450
    diabetes in, 426, 427
    Giardia in, 388, 450
    hookworms in, 387

notoedric mange and, 384–85
plague in, 447–48
rabies in, 440–41
ringworm in, 444–47
roundworms in, 386
salmonellosis in, 448, 450
sporotrichosis in, 450
tapeworms and, 386
toxocariasis in, 449
toxoplasmosis in, 441–43, 450
trichomoniasis in, 388
See also
        immunocompromised people
humor, 47, 66, 81, 216
hunger, 427
hunting, 17, 22, 38, 46, 47, 80, 92, 131, 260, 264, 321
    body language for, 261
    disease prevention and banning, 443, 448, 450
Hurricane Andrew, xxv
hybrids, 7, 75, 140, 213, 459
    American Shorthair, 107–8
    Bombay, 60, 65–66
    in breed development, 19
    Exotic, 107–8
    Ocicat, 19, 60
Hydon-Goodwin Awards, 8
hydrogen, 298, 302
hydrogen peroxide, 376
hyperadrenocorticism (Cushing's disease), 430
hyperglycemia, 352, 427
    stress-induced, 428
hyperproteinemia, 351
hypertension, 417, 430–31, *430*, 434, 435
hyperthermia, 377
hyperthyroidism, 352, 354,

417, 422, 425, 430, 431–33, 434
    apathetic, 431
hypertrophic cardiomyopathy (HCM), 333, 406, 416–18, *416*
hypervitaminosis, 303
hypocalcemia, 433
hypodermic needles, 363, 428
hypoglycemia, 352, 428–29
hypoproteinemia, 351
hypothermia, 375
hypothyroidism, 352
hypovitaminosis, 303

ibuprofen, 396
idiopathic (interstitial) cystitis (IC), 424, 459
illness:
    care during, 359–63
    in geriatric cats, 425–38
    home environment for care in, 362–63
    in kittens, 398–413
    signs of, 357–58, *358–59*
    in young adult to middle aged cats, 413–25
imidocarb dipropionate, 391
immune system suppression, 345–46
    demodectic mange and, 385
    in FeLV, 410
immunocompromised people, 440, 442–43, 450–51
    Cryptosporidium as risk for, 388
    CSD and, 443–44
    declawing and, 368, 369
immunoflourescence assay (IFA), 333, 410, 411
immunoglobulin G (IgG) antibodies, 442

neomycin, 397
neonatal care, 24
neonatal isoerythrolysis (NI), 353
neoplasia. *See* cancer
nephroliths, 422
nephrons, 434
nervous system, 305, 306
Netherlands, 11, 70, 212
neutering, 7, 21, 22, 28, 235, 239, 274, 340, 367, 369, 420, 450
  early age, 367–68
neuters, 460
  in cat shows, 6, 34, 237, 240, 242
Neva Masquerade, 198
New York, N.Y., xxv, 3, 18, 137
New Zealand, 70, 103, 251
niacin, 305
nighttime caging, 265
nitrogen, 298
nits, 385
noise, 269
noncore vaccines, 341–42, 411
  protocols for, 346–47
nonessential amino acids, 298
nonpedigreed cats, 240
  HCM in, 417, 418
  hip dysplasia in, 419
nonsteroidal anti-inflammatory drugs, 372, 396, 424
Norsk Skogkattring, 148
North Africa, 249
North America, 38, 212, 341, 391, 399, 412, 432, 449
  Chartreux breed standards in, 80
  Egyptian Mau in, 98
  zoonoses in, 440
Norvasc (amlodipine), 431

Norwalk virus, 398
Norway, 11, 147–48
Norwegian Forest Cat, 11, 27, 145–50, *145*
  CFA show standards for, 149–50
  description of, 145–46
  grooming of, 146–47
  history of, 147–48
  personality of, 146
nose, of healthy kitten, 238
notoedric mange, 383, 384–85
Novartis Animal Health, 382, 383, 390, 446
Novices, 8
nucleotides, 403
Nutramax, 424
nutrient density, 326
nutrients, 287, 296–308
nutrition, 287–327
  in breeding, 24
  cats' unique needs in, 296

oats, 318
obese cats, declawing of, 369
obesity, 292–96, *294,* 319, 340, 460
  diabetes and, 427, 429
  free-choice feeding and, 289
  hip dysplasia and, 418
  See also overweight
Ocicat, 9, 27, 43, 150–55, *150*
  Abyssinian in breeding of, 19, 152–53, 155
  American Shorthair in breeding of, 152–53
  CFA show standards for, 153–55
  description of, 151
  grooming of, 152
  history of, 152–53

pattern in, 54–55, 150, 151, 152, 153, 250
  personality of, 151–52
  Siamese in breeding of, 19, 152–53, 194
ocular larva migrans, 449
odontoclastic lesions, 364
oils, 300
oligosaccharides, 302, 303
omega-3 fatty acids, 297, 301, 317, 318, 460
omega-6 fatty acids, 297, 301, 460
onychectomy. *See* declawing
oocysts, 387, 441–42, 443
open-formula foods, 315
Opens, 8, 242, 244
opiates, 396
oral rinses, 366
orange, 251
  sex-linked, 250
ordinary household items, dangers of, 276
Oregon, 132
organophosphates, 381
organs, 300
Oriental, 27, 110, 152, 155–60, 190
  Balinese in breeding of, 160
  CFA show standards for, 158–59
  Colorpoint Shorthair in breeding of, 160
  description of, 156
  grooming for, 157
  in Havana Brown breeding, 112, 115
  head of, 268
  history of, 157
  Javanese in breeding of, 160
  Longhair, *155,* 156, 157, 158, 159–60
  personality of, 156

urinary tract:

   disease of, 333, 354, 421–24, 458

   infections of, 428

   obstruction of, 372

urine, 297, 300, 303, 312, 358, *358, 359,* 366, 450

   alkaline, 307

   crystals in, 421–22

   increased, 427

   ketones in, 428

   marking with, 261; *See also* spraying

   overacidified, 306

urine glucose test, 429

urine tests, 321, 340, 419, 422, 423, 437

uroliths, 307, 422–24, 462

uterine diseases, 357

uterus, 366

vaccinations, 24, 28, 235, 239, 247, 274, 283, 335, 340–50, 366, 400, 402, 410, 411, 413, 450

   adverse reactions to, 348–50

   protocols for core vaccines, 346

   protocols for noncore vaccines, 346–47

   protocols for special situations, 345–46

   records of, 271

   revaccination and, 347–48

   risk assessments for, 342–43

   sites for, 344, *344*

   for travel, 271, 377, 378, 379

Vaccine-Assisted Feline Sarcoma Task Force, 336

vaccine-associated sarcomas, 349–50

vaccines, MLV, 333, 343, *344, 345,* 346, *347,* 405, 446

   core, 340–41

   KV, 333, 343, *344,* 345, 346, 347, *347,* 413

   noncore, 341–42, 411

   for rabies, 271, 272, 377, 378, 379, 441

   types of, 343–44

valine, 298

valvular dysplasias, 407

Vancat. *See* Turkish Van

van pattern, 172, 225–26

vegetables, 299, 300, 304, 305, 317–18, 320, 324–25

   toxoplasmosis and, 443

Velcro cats:

   Abyssinian as, 33

   Burmese as, 74

   Cornish Rex as, 88

   Korat as, 126

venae cavae, 407

venison, 443

ventricles, 407, 417

ventricular septal defect (VSD), 334, 407, 408

vertebrae, 29

Veteran Class, 242

veterinarians, 271, 272–73, 275, 282, 283, 288, 296, 303

   choosing of, 334–36

   emergencies and, 375, 376

   euthanasia decisions and, 451–52

   examinations by, 268, 339–40

   feline medicine and, 331–32

   feline specialists, 336–37

   random-bred cats as primary patients of, 16

   routine questions of, 357–58

veterinary guide, 331–453

Veterinary Products Laboratories, 424

villi, 309, 462

viral infections, 436

viral tests, 352

viruses, 312, 321, 387

visceral larva migrans, 449

vitamin A, 296, 303, 304, 317

vitamin B, 304, 317

vitamin B_1 (thiamine), 304, 317, 321

vitamin B_2 (riboflavin), 304

vitamin B_6 (pyroxidine), 305

vitamin B_{12} (cobalamin), 305, 317

vitamin C (ascorbic acid), 304

vitamin D, 303, 304, 306, 312, 317

vitamin E, 292, 303, 304

vitamin K, 303, 304, 420

vitamins, 282, 291, 296, 297, 303–5, 321, *323,* 462

   fat-soluble, 297, 300, 303–4

   water-soluble, 297, 303, 304–5

vocalization, late-night, 262, 265

voice, 260

vomiting, 297, 357, *359,* 372, 376, 385, 386, 387, 389, 450, 451

   chronic, 413–14, *413*

vowel sounds, 260

wailing, 260

walk, of healthy kitten, 239

water, 268, 289, 293, 296, 297, 306, 358, 362

   ingested, 297

   metabolic, 297

   travel and, 377, 378

water squirt guns, 264
weaning, 387
weighing:
    of kittens, 282–83
    of overweight cats, 296
weight:
    ideal cat, *294*
    water in, 297
weight control, portion-
        control feeding in,
        288
weight loss, 340, *359,* 386, 389,
        429, 431, 434
Wellmark International,
        381
Western blot, 412
wheat, 303, 318–19
wheat flour, 318–19
wheat germ oil, 304
white, 9, 88, 164, 251
    in bicolor pattern, 253–54

deafness in, 223, 238, 439
dominant, 250
squamous cell carcinoma in,
        436
white blood cells, 351, 404,
        412
white spotting factor, 17, 250
whole wheat, 318–19
wildcats, 163
window screens, 270
Winn Feline Foundation, xxii,
        xxiii, xxv, 21, 337
    Web site of, xxv
working cats, 18, 20, 48–49,
        131, 138, 148
World Health Organization,
        425
World War I, 70, 222, 444
World War II, 6, 21, 61, 83,
        112, 177, 193
wounds, 376, 410

X-rays, 356, 357, 364, 389,
        390, 407, 408, 413, 415,
        417, 418, 419, 422, 423,
        431, 433, 437, 442

yeast, 305
yeast infection (*Malassezia*),
        425
yellow, 251
yellow eyes, 250
yellow fat disease, 317
Yersinia, 355
Yersinia pestis, 447
yogurt, 317

zinc, 307
zinc sulfate, 355
zoonotic diseases, 387, 440–49,
        450